KISETSU 2: Ginga

Kazuo Tsuda

United Nations International School
New York, NY

Masatoshi Shimano

St. Paul's School
Concord, NH

KISETSU EDUCATIONAL GROUP
New York

Additional Contributors

Timothy Vance	Peter Hendricks	Shino Takagi	Mami Masuya
Mark Weintraub	Kanae Sakakibara	Yoko Sakurai	Tomomi Iwamoto
Hiromi Yamashita	Yukiko Tamba	Ritsuko Yokota	Kanoko Yoshimoto
Aiko Miyakawa	Alejandoro Dale	Masayo Ohyama	Ayako Takeda
Mary Ellen Jebbia	Masahiro Tanaka	Joy Tsutsui	

Editors

Lynda Crawford   Ichiro Sata   Carol Lui

Illustrator

Kozumi Shinozawa   Mari Iwahara

Designer

Hitomi Obata-Ratthe

Cover

Katsuhiro Saiki

Donors

Fuji Xerox Co., Ltd.	Daisuke Hotta
Mitsubishi Corporation	Shinobu Takada
Sumitomo Kinzoku	Matsushita Electronics Industries Co. Ltd.
The Japan Forum	The Japan Foundation
Kajima Corporation	Kamei Corporation
Kawasaki Microelectronics, Inc.	Kikkoman Corporation
Kirin Brewery Co., Ltd.	Mitsui Fudosan Co., Ltd.
NEC Corporation	Nippon Paper Sales Co., Ltd.
Oji Paper Co., Ltd.	Pioneer Corporation
Sendai Coca-Cola Bottling	Sharp Corporation
Suntory Ltd.	Suzuyo & Co., Ltd.
Toshiba Corporation	Toyota Motor Corporation
Tyco Electronics Corporation	UMG ABS, Ltd.
Mr. Kato, Sumitomo Kinzoku Co.	

Supporters

NEASTJ/NECTJ   St. Paul's School

United Nations International School

Movement for Language and Culture

Kisetsu 2: Ginga

ISBN1-978-09678606-3-3

Published by Kisetsu Educational Group
c/o Movement for Language and Culture
111 West 11th Street. New York, NY 10011 USA #2FW

Contents

Unit 3: Reflection

Unit 4: Environment

Chapter 1: Let's Speak About Your Summer!
Conceptual Theme: Reflection

Chapter 2: Let's Teach Your Lesson Plan!
Conceptual Theme: Reflection

Chapter 3: Let's Write About Your Town!
Conceptual Theme: Environment

Chapter 4: Let's Present Your School!
Conceptual Theme: Environment

Welcome to Kisetsu 2, Welcome to Ginga

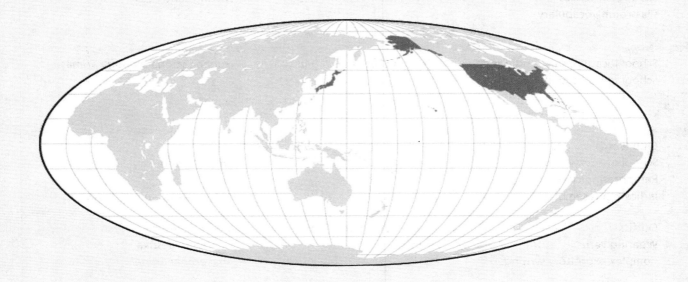

Welcome, everyone! Opening this textbook is a small but significant step on the road to a profitable relationship that may last a lifetime: a relationship with the Japanese language, culture, and people. Picking and choosing school courses are not always easy with all the options available, and with scheduling conflicts to consider, as well as the possible implications that your selection may have on your future. So it is only natural that you may still be wondering whether you made the right choice when you decided to begin studying Japanese. We think looking at this introduction to the course may clear this up for you.

The Kisetsu series is based on the recent adoption of the National Standards, a set of benchmarks for education in foreign language and other subjects — and it represents a drastic change in Japanese language education. These benchmarks are called the 5Cs: Communication, Culture, Connections, Comparisons, and Communities. The 5Cs are not merely about building grammar or learning the parts of speech. They focus instead on real world use. The 5Cs claim that it is necessary to bring Japanese language activities from the real world into the classroom.

Our aim is for authentic communication using the language skills of speaking, listening, writing, and reading, and promoting integrated and useful communication that reflects real life.

Your instruction will be project-based and employ various strategies that repeat at advancing levels throughout, ensuring that you always know what you need to do throughout the project. Kisetsu is a social process of learning with peer interaction and cooperative learning, where you hone your ability to maintain the flow of conversation, to paraphrase and make analogies, to use prior knowledge, to strengthen your vocabulary and reading, to solve problems, to clarify, analyze and compare, and to self-evaluate and reflect.

We have taken advantage of available technology to acquire authentic materials for the course and we have digitalized the Kisetsu textbooks. We are also in the process of building a website that will allow students to experience and interact with the Kisetsu instruction online.

Whether you are entering this study at beginner or intermediate levels, or as a heritage learner, we see our task as being facilitators for your autonomy and originality at acquiring the Japanese language, and we hope this experience will be a blueprint for living your whole lives as learners.

Organization of the Textbook

Kisetsu is a series of Japanese-language textbooks for junior high and high school students. *Kisetsu* means "season," and the first volume is called Haru Ichiban (literally, First Spring Wind). *Haruichiban* contains two preliminary sections (Getting Started I and Getting Started II) and two conceptual units. *Ginga* (literally, Galaxy), the second volume, also contains two conceptual units. The units are broken down into eight thematically organized chapters.

Haruichiban
Getting Started

Unit 1: Encounter

Unit 2: Awareness

Ginga
Unit 3: Reflection

Unit 4: Environment

Organization of the Chapters

1. Introduction

The goal of this section is to provide you with opportunities to hear, speak, and recognize everyday Japanese.

1. ***Objectives:*** This section is presented in terms of declarative and procedural benchmarks
2. ***Kisetsu Theater:*** The chapter theme is introduced through photographs, comics, pictures, and a visual overview of the unit
3. ***Warm-Up:*** A group of exercises emphasizing useful learning and communication strategies
4. ***Basic Vocabulary:*** A visual introduction to basic words and expressions
5. ***Mechanics:*** Drills employing basic vocabulary

2. Mechanics

This section offers practice with new vocabulary words. You also learn communication skills through varied activities and drills with many strategies and functions.

1. ***Culture Note:*** To help you understand the theme of the chapter
2. ***Language Note:*** To give you insight into important linguistic concepts
3. ***Pronunciation:*** To teach you how to pronounce the Japanese language
4. ***Kana and Kanji:*** To review and practice basic Japanese orthography
5. ***Listening:*** To confirm your realization of unit objectives
6. ***Reading:*** To teach you to become an effective reader using a process approach
7. ***Form:*** To check grammatical and functional concepts and sentence structures learned so far

3. Virtual Reality/Application

This section provides more meaningful interaction and activities and enables you to use the communicative skills you learned in the Mechanics section. In this section, you participate in real, comprehensive projects in which you use the new material creatively.

1. ***Kanji (Kana and Kanji):*** To review and practice basic and advanced Japanese orthography
2. ***Vocabulary:*** To give you a comprehensive list of useful words with their English equivalents
3. ***Reading:*** To teach you to become an effective reader using a process approach
4. ***Writing:*** To teach you to write effectively using a process approach
5. ***Assessments:*** A self-assessment or peer-assessment to check your performance, knowledge and skills
6. ***Checklist:*** A set of questions asking you to evaluate your own progress and reflect upon your learning experience
7. ***Additional Vocabulary:*** An advanced list of words useful for the Virtual Reality projects
8. ***Additional Information:*** Pictures of real Japanese life by several young Japanese photographers

Acknowledgments

We would like to thank many individuals and organizations whose unfailing support and contributions have been vitally important to us over the five years that this book was in the making. Our first and foremost debt of gratitude is to Fuji-Xerox Corporation (Miyahara, Kawabe, Hattori, Shimizu, Kato, Ichinose) for their generous grant and the Japan Forum (Nakano, Harashima, Jibiki, Ushijima, Takasaki, Takashima, Ito, Fujimaki, Mizuguchi, Muronaka, Fujikake) for making available their valuable resources including many photos in this book. We are also very grateful to St. Paul's School (Matthews, Hornor, Hirschfeld) and the United Nations International School (Blaney, Fuhrman, Wrye, Dymond) for letting us use their facilities and equipment; to the Northeast Association of the Secondary Teachers of Japanese and its members for allowing us to establish our group.

We also would like to thank the following corporations and organizations for their generous support.

Mitsubishi Corporation (Makihara, Masubuchi, Iizuka), Fuji Xerox Co., Ltd., Daisuke Hotta, Shinobu Takada, Matsushita Electronics Industries Co. Ltd., The Japan Foundation, Kajima Corporation, Kamei Corporation, Kawasaki Microelectronics, Inc., Kikkoman Corporation, Kirin Brewery Co., Ltd., Mitsui Fudosan Co., Ltd., NEC Corporation, Nippon Paper Sales Co., Ltd, Oji Paper Co., Ltd., Pioneer Corporation, Sendai Coca-Cola Bottling, Sharp Corporation, Suntory Ltd., Suzuyo & Co., Ltd., Toshiba Corporation, Toyota Motor Corporation, Tyco Electronics Corporation, UMG ABS, Ltd., Sumitomo Kinzoku Co. (Kato).

Japan Foundation Language Center (Yokoyama, Furuyama, Kabutomori, Kaneda, Tsujimoto), University of Colorado, Boulder (Lodd, Saegusa), Yamagata University (Takagi), US-Japan Foundation, University of Massachusetts (Austin, Horiba), MIT (Miyagawa, Lavin, Torii), Kodansha America (Asakawa, Kimata, Noma), Kanoya US-Japan Committee (Yamazaki, Ino, Yotsumoto), Yamaguchi University (Hayashi, Minomiya, Hayashi), Showa Woman's University (Hitomi, Takamizawa), Boston Showa (Kazakamaki, Ikuma, Provost), John Manjiro Center (Takahashi), Middletown High School (Magwire), Joba Group (Ogasawara, Mizuno, Deguchi, Shibuya, Nakano, Fujikake), Yokohama City Board of Education (Ueno, Ota, Takegoshi, Nagai, Isobe, Kishi, Kurisu, Takahashi, Futakami, Yagisawa, Matsui), Shizuoka prefecture Board of Education (Takagi, Watanabe, Fukami), Movement for Language and Culture group (Mr. and Mrs. Ohyama, Masuya, Tanaka) and Students in Japanese classes of Middletown High School (RI), St. Paul's School (NH), and United Nations International School (NY).

A great number of individuals have given us much-needed advice, feedback and encouragement. We would like to express our appreciation to Geraldine Carter, Core of Kisetsu group, for her contribution for basic works; to Hiromi Yamashita, Core of Kisetsu for her devotions to teaching ideas; Timothy Vance for his contribution to language, pronunciation section; Brain Kahn for his contribution to Samurai melodrama; Sahe Kawahara, Alejandro Dale, and Mary Ellen Jebbia for their contribution of culture; and Chihiro Kinoshita Thomson, Kyoko Saegusa, Shinichi Hayashi, Tazuko Ueno, TJF's committee members for feedback; to Cyrus Rolbin, Laura Kriska, Caryn Stedman, Jeffrey Johnson and Marcia Johnson for their invaluable comments on earlier drafts of our manuscript; to Chiaki Kataoka, Shoji Sato, Chiaki Murakami, Jun Ono, Kyoko Iwasaki, Hiroko Nagai, Peter Hendricks, Fumiko Bacon, and Kayoko Tazawa for workbook draft; and Shiho Hagi, Fuhito Shimoyama, Atsuko Isahaya, Kanae Sakakibara, Kuniko Yokohata, Ritsuko Yokota, Yukiko Tamba, Kanoko Yoshimoto, Tomomi Iwamoto, Yoko Sakurai, Kanae Sakakibara, Mark Weintaub, Shino Takagi for their contribution for Ginga textbook. Our special thanks also go to Kazuko Tsurumi, Sadako Ogata, Osamu Kamada, Carl Falsgraf, Hiroko Kataoka, Yasuhiko Tosaku, Mimi Reed, Mari Noda, Hiroshi Miyaji, Seichi Makino, Senko Maynard, Yasuko Watt, Ichiro Shirato, Norman Masuda, Lesliy Okada, Hitomi Tamura, and Carol Gluck who helped to develop our ideas and facility.

And finally, but not least importantly, we would like to acknowledge the contribution of the following technical staff: Lynda Crawford (chief editor), Masahiro Tanaka (editor for web) , Ayako Takeda, (editor in Japanese), Joy Tsutsui (bi-lingual editor), Carol Lui (editor), Mutsumi Kiyohara (editor in Japanese), Ichiro Sata (bi-lingual editor), Lisa Carter (editor for draft), Hitomi Obata-Ratthe (illustrator and main layout designer), Dawn Lawson (layout designer), Kozumi Shinozawa (main illustrator), Mari Iwahara (illustrator), Hiromi Yamashita (illustrator), Aka Chikazawa (illustrator), Yusuke Nakanishi, (photographer), Joan Greenfield (original layout designer), David Ascue (layout designer for draft), Mary Reed (proof reader), Kiyoshi Kanai (adviser for design), Minato Asakawa, and Chikako Noma (adviser for textbook), Fuji-Xerox Staff (Shimizu and Kato), and Katsuhiro Saeki (book cover designer). Their top-notch talent and creativity, as well as their patience, have been greatly appreciated.

This book could not have happened without the tremendous support we have received from those mentioned above. However, any errors or shortcomings in the manuscript are solely our responsibility.

Finally, this "Ginga" (Galaxy) text book is dedicated to the memory of Daisuke Hotta in token of his contribution to Japanese education.

Kazuo Tsuda
Masatoshi Shimano

Chapter 1: Let's Speak About Your Summer!
Conceptual Theme: Reflection

awareness of speech structure *awareness of audience*

VOCABULARY	STRATEGY HIGHLIGHTS	COMMUNICATIONS PERFORMANCE	CULTURES
Notional **Functional**	Affective **Cognitive** **Language**	Interpersonal **Interpretive** **Presentational**	Practice **Product** **Perspective**
Greetings • New school year greetings Profile Study of Japanese language Descriptive adjectives Connectors	Appreciate the Mindset/feeling Associated with a new School year meeting Group coordination Organization of a draft	**Oral Production highlights** Oral presentation Self introduction Greeting Wishes Evaluation Questions and answers	Summer vacation Summer experience in Japan or other places
Simple greeting Simple Greeting with wishing preference Hosting words Asking how something was Asking for descriptive information New Kanji: 書、話、読、聞、見、 来、言、行 飲、食、休、作、使、 帰、立、会 春、夏、秋、冬、次、 始、今、住 父、母、兄、姉、弟、 妹、私、友	Writing a draft for summer vacation part	**Reading & Writing** Reading a draft Listening to the other person's speech Listening to the question Writing a draft for speech Structure of writing	Show and tell your cultural experience and/or a product that you made or bought during summer Comparing summer vacation between Japan and your country

CONNECTIONS	COMPARISONS	FORM	COMMUNITY & ASSESSMENTS
Connection	**Language** **Pronunciation** **Kanji and kana**	**Grammar/Function**	**Assessments** **Community**
Summer vacation	Short and long syllables	Past verb sentences	Self-assessment
		i-Adjective negative	Sum-up
	The Japanese language in the modern world topics	*na*-Adjective negative	Video portfolio assessment
Mathematics (fire works in the summer night)		"be" verb past verb – *desu.*	
	Kana Long vowels in katakana	*tai*-form	Summer vacation in other place
	Recognition Kanji: 夏休み、オ、名前、学校、好き、中学、高校、年生、一日、二日、三日		
	四日、五日、六日、七日、八日、九日、十日、二十日、〜曜日	Asking questions	
	何人、何人、何年、何年、何語、何分、何時、父、母、兄、姉、妹、弟、私	• Asking how something was	
		• Asking for descriptive information	
		• Asking for support	
	正しい、答える、今週、先週、来週、来月、今月、先月	• Asking for cooperation	
		Indicating an order	
	Additional Kanji: 冬休み、野球、折り紙、出身、趣味、最高、若者、刀、紹介		
	売る、買う、誕生日、例えば、計画、環境、考える、発表、成果		
	全部、旅行、英語、勉強、東京、泳ぐ、終わり、仕事、週末、		

Chapter 2: Let's Teach Your Lesson Plan!
Conceptual Theme: Reflection

awareness of teaching by themselves   *awareness of assessment*

VOCABULARY	STRATEGY HIGHLIGHTS	COMMUNICATIONS PERFORMANCE	CULTURES
Notional **Functional**	Affective **Cognitive** **Language**	Interpersonal **Interpretive** **Presentational**	Practice **Product** **Perspective**
Class teaching • body parts • Physical exercises • questions • relative time • review sessions • teaching materials • class management Demonstrative words Direction Evaluation Forms Order Class teaching • Indicating a topic • Asking someone if x is done • Asking someone to do something New Kanji: 間、上、下、左、右、 前、後、回 体、手、足、目、耳、 口、頭、名 何、出、入、元、気、 音、電、国 大、小、男、女、子、 文、車、中	Cooperating Appreciate the mindset/feeling associated with classmates teaching his/her lesson Organizing a lesson plan Conducting a class Managing a class	**Oral Production highlights** Teaching a review session in Japanese **Reading & Writing** Making reading materials • Reading materials • Quiz • Teaching materials Reading materials • Writing on the board as a teacher **Design & Creation** Reading/hearing teaching Materials Writing/instructing Teaching materials	Japanese school in the morning Japanese school in the afternoon Time table at the Japanese school in the morning Schedule of Japanese school in the afternoon Comparing school life between Japan and your country

CONNECTION	COMPARISON	FORM	OTHER INFORMATION
	Language Pronunciation Kanji and kana		Assessments Community
Connection		**Grammar/Function**	
	Japanese dialect topics	*kosoado* words	Peer assessment
Japanese school	Word accent	Asking someone to do something - *te kudasai.*	Poster evaluation
			Sum-up
Reviewing other subjects materials	Kana Innovative katakana combinations	Asking someone not to do something - *naide kudasai.*	Video portfolio assessment
	Recognition Kanji:	Asking someone not to do something - *naide kudasai.*	Building a learning community with life-long leaning perspective
	復習、去年、今年、来年、回、昨日、今日、明日		
	毎日、毎週、毎年、毎月、午前、午後、早い、説明、漢字	Action in progress - *te imasu.*	
	会話、季節、一番、問題、名詞、動詞、形容詞、助詞	Making suggestions - *wa doo desuka.*	
	決める、記号、言葉、例、絵単語、選ぶ、質問、番号	Giving the order of action - *hajimeni, tsugini, owarini*	
	Additional Kanji:	Indicating repetition	
	深まる、新入生、増える、交流、講堂、始まる、全員、参加、健康		
	色々、次、写真部、面白い、国際、教育、別に、特に、撮る		
		Procedures for a meeting Procedures for teaching	

Chapter 3: Let's Write About Your Town!
Conceptual Theme: Environment

awareness of expository writing awareness of vocabulary building skills

VOCABULARY	STRATEGY HIGHLIGHTS	COMMUNICATIONS PERFORMANCE	CULTURE
Notional **Functional**	**Affective** **Cognitive** **Language**	**Interpersonal** **Interpretive** **Presentational**	**Practice** **Product** **Perspective**
Describing town • restaurants • directions • events • facilities • geography • Japanese cities • nature • stores • weather	Awareness of writer to audience Organization of writing styles	**Production Highlights** Writing essay • writing style • audience • Examination of the draft • Reading the draft	Town in Japan Town in Japan
Academic subjects Counters Descriptive adjectives Verbs Indicating existence expressions Comparative sentences Potential statements	Writing strategies • Attribution tactic • Analogy tactic	**Reading & Writing** Expository simple paragraph writing • topic sentences • supporting sentences Expository paragraph writing tactics 　* attribution tactic 　* analogy tactic Expository paragraph writing development • topic sentences • supporting sentences • example sentences 　* Sum-up sentences	Comparing a town between Japan and your country Comparing summer vacation between Japan and your country
New Kanji: 森、川、山、町、林、海、店、田 雨、天、度、雪、晴、暑、寒、化 島、平、野、校、石、道、市、村 花、魚、屋、肉、東、西、北、南 公、交、場、所、通、州、週、寺 社、夜、買、家、京、駅、園、地		Discussing the draft Reading composition **Design & Creation** Town description	

CONNECTION	COMPARISON	FORM	OTHER INFORMATION
	Language Pronunciation Kanji and Kana		
Connection	**Kanji and Kana**	**Grammar/Function**	**Assessments** **Community**
Social Studies (Japan)	Standard languages	Indicating existence	Self-assessment
Mathematics (One stroke order)	Syllable-final consonants	Y ni Xga Iru/aru X wa Y ni Iru/aru Y niwa Xga Iru/aru Y no PW ni X ga Iru/aru X wa Y no PW ni Iru/aru	Peer-assessment
			Web-evaluation
	Kanji		Sum-up
	Recognition Kanji: 自然、人口、交通、東京、家、会社、工場、店、東西南北	Comparative sentences	Video portfolio assessment
		X wa Y yori adj desu. X no hoo ga Y yori adj desu.	Comparison between a town in Japan and your country.
	池、空、湖、海岸、砂漠、空港、駅、公園、京都		
		X wa Y to hobo onaji desu.	Re-examine your town.
	電気、電話、厳しい、遠い、静か、便利、不便、重い、軽い、弱い、強い	X wa Y to onaji kurai desu.	
		X wa Y hodo + negative form of adjective	
	時間、場所、昼休み、食べ物、飲み物、入る、起きる、寝る、大阪	Counters	
	八百屋、市役所、案内所、火山、交番、銀行、寺、神社、勉強、復習、表現	-mai,hon, ken, dai, hiki, too, satu, ko, do, shuukann	
	平野、土地、都市、教会、港、橋、住宅、サッカー場	Potential statements ~ kotoga dekimasu	
	Additional Kanji:	Expressing uncertainty ~ deshoo	
	出会い、風景、日本的、観光客、音読型、道路、劇場、見学、遊ぶ	Adverb for indicating degree or existence of a state	
	野外、動物園、有名、習う、盆踊り、未来、地区、辺り、時代	Non-past negative	
	明治、昭和、建物、現代的、国連、関係、博物館、中華街		

Chapter 4: Let's Present Your School!
Conceptual Theme: Environment
awareness of essay writing and presenting skill, awareness of reading strategies

VOCABULARY	STRATEGY HIGHLIGHTS	COMMUNICATIONS PERFORMANCE	CULTURE
Notional **Functional**	**Affective** **Cognitive** **Language**	**Interpersonal** **Interpretive** **Presentational**	**Practice** **Product** **Perspective**
School words • location, surroundings •School types, students •campus, clubs, events Outfits Descriptive personal/ characteristic adjectives Wearing verbs Expressing permissions Expressing several actions Designating information expressions Paraphrasing expressions Descriptive expressions Comment expressions New Kanji:楽、新、古、 多、少、広、安、高 数、科、外、英、親、 朝、昼、半 育、教、門、物、理、 歴、史、問 正、低、明、暗、近、 長、短、早 青、赤、白、黒、速、 美、遠、静 心、知、好、思、同、 毎、意、味	**Awareness** • awareness of audience • awareness of culture on comment sentence • awareness of own observation skills when you want to describe something • awareness of audience and writing style • awareness of culture in comment sentence and writing style • awareness of own observation skills when you want to describe something and writing style Writing strategies to make something easy to understand • paraphrasing • classifying • indicating resemblance • describing content • attribution • analogy	**Oral Production Highlights** Editorial meeting Editorial meeting Editorial meeting **Reading & Writing** Expository complex paragraph writing • Two topic sentences • Two block arguments Kansoubun style writing • Describing parts * observation * explanation * comparison • Comment parts * direct comment sentence * indirect comment sentence Reading strategies • describing sentences • comment sentences **Design & Creation** Booklet on my town for Japanese sister school audience	Town in Japan Town in Japan Comparing a town between Japan and your country

CONNECTION	COMPARISON	FORM	OTHER INFORMATION
Connection	Language **Pronunciation** **Kanji and kana**	**Grammar/Function**	**Assessments** **Community**
Social Studies (Japan) Mathematics (One stroke order on map)	Related languages topics Vowel quality Recognition Kanji: 教室、宿題、行事、卒業生、生徒数、活動、科目、教員数 目的、地図、図、写真、教材、品詞、部屋、部長、生徒会、的、生徒 紹介、練習、3回、最初、最後、家族、曲げる 卒業式、試験期間、運動会、文化祭、文科系、運動系、新学期、制服、規則 洋服、和服、上着、下着、着る、付ける、着物、脱ぐ、靴、靴下 風が強い、雷雨、台風、気温、涼しい、暖かい、方角、気持ちがいい Additional Kanji: 料理店、中心、感じ、地下鉄、郵便局、果物、授業、忙しい 磨く、起きる、歯、洗う、頭、自転車、他に、主食、室内 変わる、活動、興味、持つ、覚える、機械、専攻、交通、事故	Expressing opinions Reported speech Language strategies • paraphrasing • classifying • indicating resemblance • describing content • attribution • analogy Reading Strategies • descriptive sentences • comment sentences Verbs past form Potential Verbs Expressing permission Expressing prohibition Indicating how easy or difficult something is to do Indicating excess Linking connectors • and connectors • but connectors • cause and effective connectors • rhetorical connectors Conjunctional directional words Structure of the Japanese paragraph • expository writing • essay style writing Basic particles	Self-assessment Peer-assessment Sum-up Portfolio assessment a booklet describing my town

Unit 3: Reflection

Do you often reflect upon your learning? Do you keep a journal, evaluate your past success and failures, observe how our peers may be learning, or share your learning experience with others? Activities, like these will help you become a purposeful and self-directed learner and enable you to obtain maximum benefits from this textbook that features six project-based chapters. This unit consists of two chapters and they are designed to facilitate reflective thinking and activities.

In Chapter 1 you will write and deliver a "back-to-school" speech. During the course you will monitor your progress, be engaged in peer reading and practice, and have a reflective session after your speech.

In Chapter 2 you will design and conduct group review sessions on your prior studies of Japanese in Japanese. Working in groups you will check if the activities and exercises you have made will work well in your session and you will make adjustments as you see fit.

By the end of the unit we hope reflection will become an integral part of your learning.

Photo: Tsukasa Yokozawa "Spilt Milk #2" 2001

Chapter 1
Let's Speak About Your Summer!

Photo: Tsukasa Yokozawa "Parallel Lives #C2" 2009

Chapter 1: Let's Speak About Your Summer!
夏休_{なつやす}みについて話_{はな}しましょう

1.1 Introduction 序論
じょろん

CHAPTER OBJECTIVES

AT THE END OF THIS SECTION, YOU WILL BE ABLE TO:

- draft and deliver a speech appropriate for the beginning of a new school year
- give instructions and lead simple review exercises
- describe actions that have taken place in the past
- describe the past state and contrast the past with the present
- ask someone to characterize or summarize his or her past actions or experience
- give a compact description of one's summer vacation
- express your wishes and desires
- make a speech notes based on the draft
- have a cooperative session for speech practice
- use connectors and hesitation sounds effectively in your speech
- give brief comments after listening to someone's practice speech
- introduce and thank speakers as a host
- conduct a reflective evaluation of your speech
- recognize about 32 kanji and their basic compounds
- read and write 24 kanji and their basic compounds

YOU WILL ALSO LEARN:

- how to organize a speech
- how to make the past tense of *-desu* and *-masu*
- basic instructional words and expressions
- how to ask someone how something was
- how to indicate what you want to do
- how to write your speech on a 400-character composition sheet

KISETSU THEATER 季節劇

Let's Speak About Your Summer!
夏休みについて話しましょう

Why Speech?

Those of you who have used *Haruichiban* may remember writing and giving a self-introductory speech. Lots of practice and experience are necessary in becoming a skillful public speaker, and *Ginga* will certainly facilitate such opportunities. Look at the script of a speech on the right. It's a sample product of this chapter in which you will prepare, practice and deliver a "back-to-school" speech. In fact, the beginning of the school year is an ideal time for delivering another speech. It's time to re-acquaint yourself with old friends and get to know new ones. It's also a time to reflect upon your summer vacation and set some goals for the new school year. In your speech you will first introduce yourself briefly and then assess and describe your summer vacation. Finally you will express your wishes including those related to your learning of Japanese. The flow chart on the following pages illustrates the production process step by step. Several new grammatical items will be introduced along the way and this speech will certainly be a bit more challenging than the one in *Haruichiban*. Try your best and start a new school year on a positive note!

Importance of Cooperation

You may assume giving a speech is an individual act. Although you will be standing alone in front of an audience when delivering your speech, you will be getting plenty of help from your classmates in getting there. *Ginga* fosters an active student involvement in the learning process and facilitates many opportunities for cooperation and mutual assistance. This is reflected in the procedure for practicing speech in which students will monitor each other's progress and offer comments and suggestions in Japanese. Remember, you and your classmates share the same goal and are valuable resources to one another. The process to get to the podium will be as much a learning experience as your performance on the podium.

Product 新学期<ruby>新学期<rt>しんがっき</rt></ruby>のスピーチ

Back-to-School Speech

はじめ	**GREETING**	こんにちは。はじめまして。レイチェル・リードです。
	SCHOOL	<ruby>去年<rt>きょねん</rt></ruby>の<ruby>学校<rt>がっこう</rt></ruby>はローズ<ruby>中学<rt>ちゅうがく</rt></ruby>でした。<ruby>今年<rt>ことし</rt></ruby>の<ruby>学校<rt>がっこう</rt></ruby>はセントラル<ruby>高校<rt>こうこう</rt></ruby>です。<ruby>高校<rt>こうこう</rt></ruby>1年生です。16<ruby>才<rt>さい</rt></ruby>です。いつも<ruby>姉<rt>あね</rt></ruby>と<ruby>車<rt>くるま</rt></ruby>で<ruby>学校<rt>がっこう</rt></ruby>に<ruby>来<rt>き</rt></ruby>ます。うちはポートランドです。ポートランドはきれいです。それから、あまり<ruby>暑<rt>あつ</rt></ruby>くありません。

<ruby>去年<rt>きょねん</rt></ruby>の<ruby>学校<rt>がっこう</rt></ruby>はローズ<ruby>中学<rt>ちゅうがく</rt></ruby>でした。<ruby>今年<rt>ことし</rt></ruby>の<ruby>学校<rt>がっこう</rt></ruby>はセントラル<ruby>高校<rt>こうこう</rt></ruby>です。<ruby>高校<rt>こうこう</rt></ruby>1年生です。16<ruby>才<rt>さい</rt></ruby>です。いつも<ruby>姉<rt>あね</rt></ruby>と<ruby>車<rt>くるま</rt></ruby>で<ruby>学校<rt>がっこう</rt></ruby>に<ruby>来<rt>き</rt></ruby>ます。うちはポートランドです。ポートランドはきれいです。それから、あまり<ruby>暑<rt>あつ</rt></ruby>くありません。

PROFILE

<ruby>出身<rt>しゅっしん</rt></ruby>はモントリオールです。<ruby>国籍<rt>こくせき</rt></ruby>はアメリカとカナダです。<ruby>英語<rt>えいご</rt></ruby>とフランス<ruby>語<rt>ご</rt></ruby>を<ruby>話<rt>はな</rt></ruby>します。<ruby>趣味<rt>しゅみ</rt></ruby>はアニメと<ruby>柔道<rt>じゅうどう</rt></ruby>です。それから、<ruby>好<rt>す</rt></ruby>きな<ruby>音楽<rt>おんがく</rt></ruby>はジャズです。

SUMMER VACATION

<ruby>私<rt>わたし</rt></ruby>の<ruby>夏休<rt>なつやす</rt></ruby>みは<ruby>最高<rt>さいこう</rt></ruby>でした。ハワイとメキシコに<ruby>行<rt>い</rt></ruby>きました。<ruby>毎日<rt>まいにち</rt></ruby><ruby>海<rt>うみ</rt></ruby>で<ruby>泳<rt>およ</rt></ruby>ぎました。よく<ruby>友達<rt>ともだち</rt></ruby>と<ruby>映画<rt>えいが</rt></ruby>を<ruby>見<rt>み</rt></ruby>ました。とても<ruby>面白<rt>おもしろ</rt></ruby>かったです。それから、たくさん<ruby>日本<rt>にほん</rt></ruby>の<ruby>食<rt>た</rt></ruby>べ<ruby>物<rt>もの</rt></ruby>を<ruby>食<rt>た</rt></ruby>べました。<ruby>私<rt>わたし</rt></ruby>は<ruby>日本<rt>にほん</rt></ruby>の<ruby>食<rt>た</rt></ruby>べ<ruby>物<rt>もの</rt></ruby>が<ruby>好<rt>す</rt></ruby>きです。<ruby>問題<rt>もんだい</rt></ruby>はありませんでした。だから、<ruby>最高<rt>さいこう</rt></ruby>の<ruby>夏休<rt>なつやす</rt></ruby>みでした。

WISHES

<ruby>新学期<rt>しんがっき</rt></ruby>です。これからは、もっとたくさん<ruby>本<rt>ほん</rt></ruby>を<ruby>読<rt>よ</rt></ruby>みたいです。それから、<ruby>毎朝<rt>まいあさ</rt></ruby>五時に<ruby>起<rt>お</rt></ruby>きたいです。そして、日本語のスピーチがもっと<ruby>上手<rt>じょうず</rt></ruby>になりたいです。

GREETING

<ruby>皆<rt>みな</rt></ruby>さん<ruby>応援<rt>おうえん</rt></ruby>してください。よろしくお<ruby>願<rt>ねが</rt></ruby>いします。

なか

おわり

7

Process フローチャート

はじめ
なか
おわり

しゅっしん
こくせき
しゅみ

ねがいごと
wishes

Mechanics

1.2 Review

1	**Practice giving directions** 指示の練習をします
2	**Direct simple review activities** 簡単な復習をします

1.3 Speech Preparation I - III

3	**Check organization of speech** 組み立てのチェックをします
4	**Beginning** 「始め」
5	**School** 「学校」
6	**Profile** 「プロフィール」

1.4

7	**Summer Vacation** 「夏休み」
8	**End** 「終わり」

1.5

9	**Revise and edit speech** 推敲と編集をします

Mechanics

1.6 Speech Practice

Virtual Reality

1.7

そして‥

こんにちは。

BASIC VOCABULARY 基礎語彙

3番の答えを
お願いします。

Answer Question No.3, please

答えは
Aです。

はい、
そうです。

CORRECT!

答えは
Bです。

いいえ、
ちがいます。

WRONG!

去年の学校はキング
中学でした。今年の
学校はケント・アカ
デミーです。

Last Year	This Year	Next Year
去年	今年	来年
King Junior HS	Kent Academy	Kent Academy
-でした	-です	
PAST	NON-PAST	

国籍^{こくせき}はカナダです。
英語^{えいご}とフランス語
を話^{はな}します。

プロフィール

国籍^{こくせき} nationality	→	カナダ
言葉^{ことば} language(s)		英語^{えいご}、 フランス語

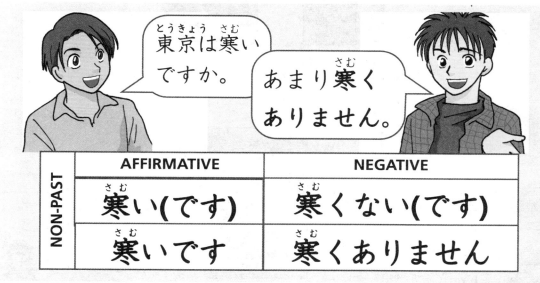

東京^{とうきょう}は寒^{さむ}い
ですか。

あまり寒^{さむ}く
ありません。

	AFFIRMATIVE	NEGATIVE
NON-PAST	寒^{さむ}い(です)	寒^{さむ}くない(です)
	寒^{さむ}いです	寒^{さむ}くありません

ダンスは
楽^{たの}しかったですか。

いいえ、楽^{たの}しく
ありませんでした。

	AFFIRMATIVE	NEGATIVE
PAST	楽^{たの}しかった(です)	楽^{たの}しくなかった(です)
	楽^{たの}しかったです	楽^{たの}しくありませんでした

11

テストはどうでしたか。　　やさしかったです。

Xはどうでしたか。　How was X?

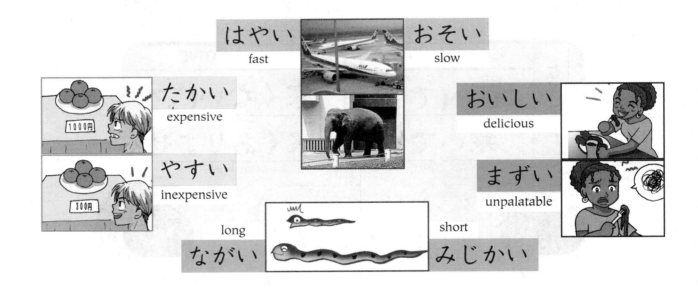

はやい
fast

おそい
slow

たかい
expensive

やすい
inexpensive

おいしい
delicious

まずい
unpalatable

long
ながい

short
みじかい

なつやす
夏休み

六月–八月

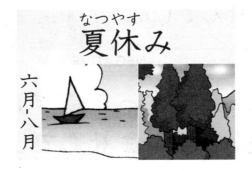

しゅうまつ
週末

	S	M	T	W	T	F	S
					1	2	3	4
	5	6	7	8	9	10	11
	12	13	14	15	16	17	18
	19	20	21	22	23	24	25
	26	27	28	29	30		

weekend　　weekend

| さいこう
最高 | SUPERB | まあまあ | SO-SO | さいてい
最低 | WORST |

僕の夏休みは最高でした。

私の夏休みは最低でした。

海

山

	AFFIRMATIVE	NEGATIVE
PAST	-ました	-ませんでした
NON-PAST	-ます	-ません

夏休みに海へ行きました。でも、山へ行きませんでした。

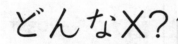

どんなX?

Asking for
a brief description of X

どんな映画
です か。

面白い映画
です。でも、
ちょっと長
いですよ。

Vたい(です)

Indicating what one wants to do

ラーメンが
食べたい

本が
読みたい

日本へ
行きたい

水泳が
したい

**Introducing
Speakers**

最初のスピーカーはAさんです。
[Our first speaker is A *san*.]

次のスピーカーはBさんです。
[Our next speaker is B *san*.]

最後のスピーカーはCさんです。
[Our last speaker is C *san*.]

かいわ
会話

はつおん
発音

日本語の
べんきょう
勉強

はっぴょう
発表

スピーチ

Want to become more skillful/proficient in X

Ｘがもっとじょうずになりたいです

わたし
私はスピーチが
じょうず
もっと上手に
なりたいです。

わたし　はつおん
私は発音が
じょうず
もっと上手に
なりたいです。

Asking for Support/Boost

おうえん
応援してください

Asking for Cooperation

きょうりょく
協力してください

1.2 Mechanics 組立て
Directing Simple Review Activities
簡単な復習

Objectives

Review some basic materials such as useful daily expressions in kana.
Conduct such a review in Japanese under student leadership.

Overview

As noted before, *Ginga* stresses student involvement in every aspect of learning. You'll be asked to take on some leadership roles that have been carried out by your teacher so far. In this section you will take turns and conduct simple review exercises in Japanese. This may sound overwhelming but don't worry. Knowing several simple directions and procedures will make you sound like an experienced teacher! The section begins with the learning of such directions and procedures and moves onto various review exercises as shown in the chart below.

| 1 | Practice giving directions | 指示の練習をします |

| 2 | Direct simple review activities | 簡単な復習をします |

| 1 | Greetings etc. | あいさつ表現 |

| 2 | Simple questions | 簡単な質問 |

| 3 | Kana | 仮名 |

| 4 | Kanji | 漢字 |

1 Practice giving directions

指示の練習をします

You will be practicing how to conduct simple review activities in Japanese. Two sample activities will facilitate your practice and each activity will consist of a review exercise and a model conversation that will show how a leader may typically interact with the rest of the class in conducting the exercise. Practicing with the sample activities will enable you to lead similar activities throughout *Ginga*.

A. Go over the following sample exercise. It is a very easy exercise, but the focus here is how to conduct it entirely in Japanese among yourselves.

問題の例を見ましょう。

Exercise A

An expression will be read to you. Match the following pictures with each expression and fill in the blanks with a letter representing an appropriate picture.

1. (　)　　2. (　)　　3. (　)

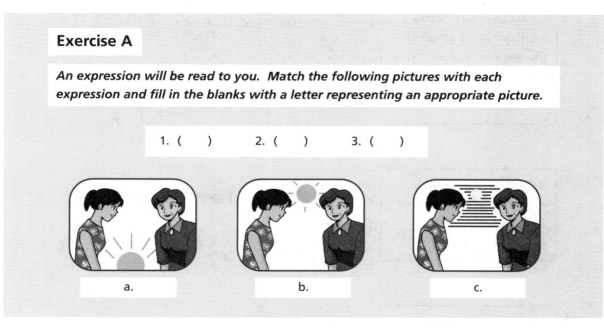

a.　　　　　　　b.　　　　　　　c.

答えは
aです。

はい、
そうです。

答えは
bです。

いいえ、
ちがいます。

B. Study the following conversation and practice conducting "Exercise A."

フローチャートに従って練習しましょう。

指示と会話の例1 (Sample Instructions and Conversation 1)

1. Indicate the page number and section and ask participants to read the instructions.

L: じゃ、17ページのAをしましょう。
指示を読んでください。

2. Signal the start of the activity. Read aloud all the answer choices. Make sure to pause several seconds after each one.

L: じゃ、始めましょう。聞いてください。
1番「こんにちは。」
2番「こんばんは。」
3番「おはようございます。」

3. Ask someone for an answer and check his or her answer (which happens to be correct).

L: スミスさん、1番の答えをお願いします。
S: cです。
L: はい、そうです。

4. Move onto the next question and ask someone else for an answer. Check his or her answer (which happens to be incorrect). Continue until all the questions are covered.

L: キングさん、2番の答えをお願いします。
S: ええと、bです。
L: いいえ、ちがいます。aです。

5. Announce the end.

L: これで、終わります。

C. Go over the following sample exercise. Although it requires two answers per question, it is still a choice question in which students are expected to indicate their choice by a letter.

問題の例を見ましょう。

Exercise B

Fill in the parentheses in Column A with a letter representing its hiragana reading and those in Column B with a letter representing its English equivalent.

Kanji	A.	B.	Hiragana	えいご
1. 一日	( )	( )	a. いつか	k. 3rd day
2. 二日	( )	( )	b. なのか	l. 4th day
3. 三日	( )	( )	c. ふつか	m. 5th day
4. 四日	( )	( )	d. ここのか	n. 6th day
5. 五日	( )	( )	e. みっか	o. 7th day
6. 六日	( )	( )	f. よっか	p. 10th day
7. 七日	( )	( )	g. ようか	q. 9th day
8. 八日	( )	( )	h. ついたち	r. 1st day
9. 九日	( )	( )	i. とおか	s. 2nd day
10. 十日	( )	( )	j. むいか	t. 8th day

D. Study the following conversation and practice conducting "Exercise B." It shows a slightly different way of checking answers from the previous example. This time the leader will first ask the rest of the class if the answer is correct. This will enable you to keep everyone focused and attentive.

指示と会話を練習しましょう。

指示と会話の例2 (Sample Instructions and Conversation 2)

1.	Indicate the page number and section and ask participants to read the instructions.	L: じゃ、20ページのBをしましょう。問題を読んでください。

2. Signal the start of the activity and ask someone for an answer for Question #1.

L: じゃ、始めましょう。<u>スミス</u>さん、1番の答えをお願いします。

3. Ask the class if the answer just given by one of the classmates is correct by saying いいですか. Make a final confirmation depending upon the response has heard. Continue until all the questions are covered.

S: <u>h</u>と<u>r</u>です。

L: いいですか。

C: はい、いいです。

L: じゃあ、<u>キング</u>さん、<u>2</u>番の答えをお願いします。

K: ええと、<u>d</u>と<u>s</u>です。

L: いいですか。

C: いいえ、ちがいます。<u>c</u>と<u>s</u>です。

L: はい、そうです。<u>c</u>と<u>s</u>です。
じゃあ、<u>ジョーンズ</u>さん、<u>3</u>番の答えをお願いします。

J: <u>f</u>と<u>l</u>です。

L: いいですか。

C: いいえ、ちがいます。<u>f</u>と<u>k</u>です。

L: そうですか。

C: いいえ、ちがいます。<u>e</u>と<u>k</u>です。

L: はい、そうです。<u>e</u>と<u>k</u>です。 continued.

4. Announce the end.

L: これで、終わります。

2 Direct simple review activities　簡単な復習をします
<ruby>簡<rt>かんたん</rt></ruby>

1 Greetings, etc.　あいさつ表現

A. Expressions will be read to you. Match the following pictures with each expression and fill in the parentheses with a letter representing the appropriate picture.

（　　）に記号を入れてください。

1. (　　)　　　2. (　　)　　　3. (　　)　　　4. (　　)　　　5. (　　)
6. (　　)　　　7. (　　)　　　8. (　　)　　　9. (　　)　　　10. (　　)

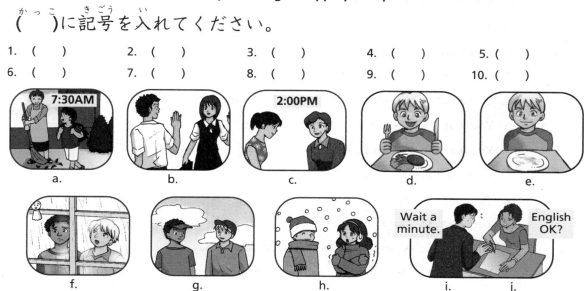

B. Expressions will be read to you. Match the following pictures with each expression and fill in the parentheses with a letter representing the appropriate picture.

（　　）に記号を入れてください。

1. (　　)　　　2. (　　)　　　3. (　　)　　　4. (　　)
5. (　　)　　　6. (　　)　　　7. (　　)　　　8. (　　)
9. (　　)　　　10. (　　)　　　11. (　　)　　　12. (　　)

C. What do you say when in the following situations? 次の時、何といいますか。
<ruby>次<rt>つぎ</rt></ruby>の<ruby>時<rt>とき</rt></ruby>、<ruby>何<rt>なん</rt></ruby>といいますか。

1. You want to greet someone in the morning.

2. You want to introduce yourself.

3. You are about to eat a meal.

4. You want to draw someone's attention.

5. You are leaving home for an errand.

6. You want to say goodnight.

7. You want to greet someone on a beautiful day.

8. You want to indicate that you will take attendance.

9. You want to greet someone in the afternoon.

10. You want to ask someone if it's okay to use English.

11. You just finished a meal.

12. You want to greet someone in the evening.

13. You want to apologize to a stranger.

14. You want to ask someone to pass something out.

15. You want to apologize to your teacher for being late.

16. You want to tell your classmate to be more careful next time.

17. You want to ask someone if she is well.

18. You want to tell your group member that her work is very well done.

19. You want to tell someone to wait a moment.

2 **Simple questions**

かんたん　しつもん
簡単な質問

*A. Short dialogues consisting of a question and a response will be read to you. Match the
following pictures with each dialogue and fill in the parentheses with the letter
representing the appropriate picture.*

かっこ　きごう　い
（　　）に記号を入れてください。

1. （　　）　　　　2. （　　）　　　　3. （　　）　　　　4. （　　）　　　　5. （　　）
6. （　　）　　　　7. （　　）　　　　8. （　　）　　　　9. （　　）　　　10. （　　）

A. *Choose a katakana character that matches the sound you hear, and fill in the parentheses with a letter representing the character.*

（かっこ）に記号（きごう）を入（い）れてください。

1. ( )	2. ( )	3. ( )	4. ( )	5. ( )
6. ( )	7. ( )	8. ( )	9. ( )	10. ( )
11. ( )	12. ( )	13. ( )	14. ( )	15. ( )

a. ニ	b. ブ	c. コ	d. モ	e. イ	f. サ
g. ツ	h. ネ	i. ド	j. ウ	k. ピ	l. メ
m. エ	n. ゼ	o. キ	p. ヘ	q. チ	r. レ
s. ソ	t. ア	u. テ	v. リ	w. ヨ	x. ヌ

B. *Choose a hiragana character that matches the sound you hear, and fill in the parentheses with the letter representing the character.*

（かっこ）に記号（きごう）を入（い）れてください。

1. ( )	2. ( )	3. ( )	4. ( )	5. ( )
6. ( )	7. ( )	8. ( )	9. ( )	10. ( )
11. ( )	12. ( )	13. ( )	14. ( )	15. ( )

a. の	b. ま	c. ろ	d. や	e. ゆ	f. い
g. す	h. ぼ	i. せ	j. ぎ	k. め	l. た
m. て	n. ぞ	o. ご	p. は	q. ぺ	r. あ
s. る	t. わ	u. う	v. つ	w. か	x. し

C. *Conduct katakana and hiragana writing exercises in which a student leader will read individual characters and/or words, and the rest of the class will write them on the board or a piece of paper.*

みんなでカタカナとひらがなの練習（れんしゅう）をしましょう。

4 Kanji　　　　　漢字

A. Arrange the kanji in numerical order and fill in the parentheses with the letter representing the appropriate kanji.

（　　）に記号を入れてください。

1. (　　)　　2. (　　)　　3. (　　)　　4. (　　)　　5. (　　)
6. (　　)　　7. (　　)　　8. (　　)　　9. (　　)　　10. (　　)

a. 八	b. 六	c. 一	d. 四	e. 七
h. 三	i. 九	j. 五	k. 十	l. 二

B. Fill in the parentheses in Column A with a letter representing its hiragana reading and those in Column B with a letter representing its English equivalent.

（　　）に記号を入れてください。

	Kanji	A.	B.	Hiragana		えいご	
1.	水曜日	(　)	(　)	a.	もくようび	h.	Sunday
2.	月曜日	(　)	(　)	b.	にちようび	i.	Monday
3.	土曜日	(　)	(　)	c.	かようび	j.	Tuesday
4.	木曜日	(　)	(　)	d.	すいようび	k.	Wednesday
5.	日曜日	(　)	(　)	e.	どようび	l.	Thursday
6.	金曜日	(　)	(　)	f.	きんようび	m.	Friday
7.	火曜日	(　)	(　)	g.	げつようび	n.	Saturday

C. Read the following kanji.　次の漢字を読んでください。

1. 八時　　　　2. 十六年　　　　3. 四時五分
4. 日本語　　　5. 学年　　　　　6. 先生
7. 三百円　　　8. 九千　　　　　9. 七万
10. 一万二千　　11. 九月八日　　12. 十二月十五日

Recognition Kanji 1: 認識漢字 1

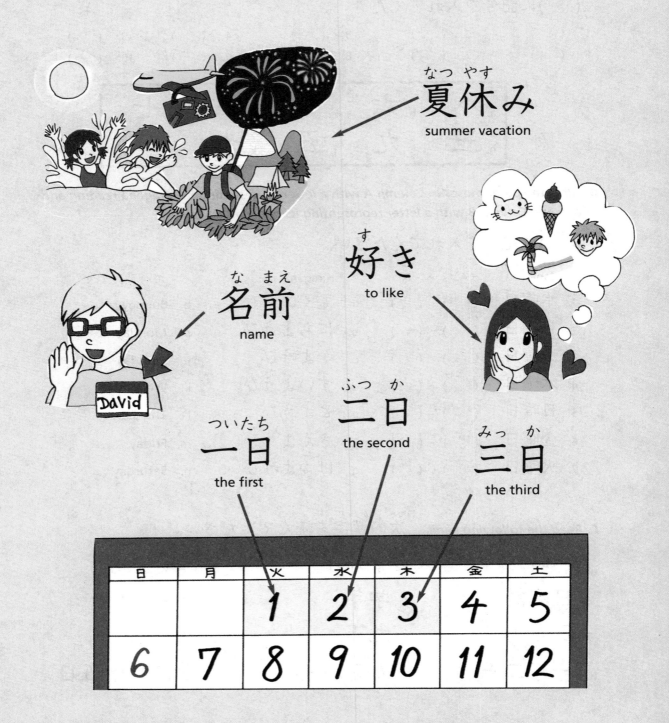

夏休み
summer vacation

好き
to like

名前
name

一日
the first

二日
the second

三日
the third

日	月	火	水	木	金	土
		1	2	3	4	5
6	7	8	9	10	11	12

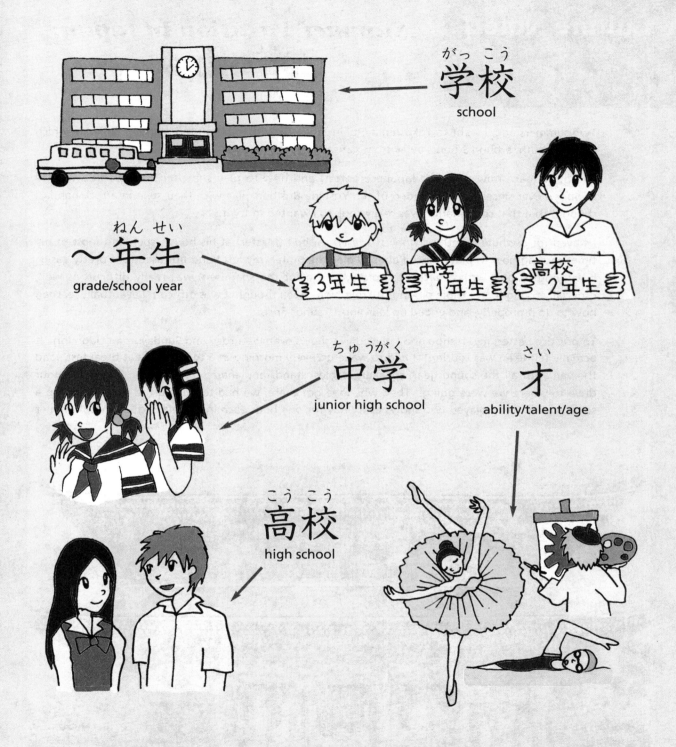

がっ こう
学校
school

～年生
ねん せい
grade/school year

中学
ちゅうがく
junior high school

才
さい
ability/talent/age

高校
こう こう
high school

Culture Note 1

Summer Vacation in Japan:
日本の夏休み

Two summers ago, I went to Tokushima City in Japan. Tokushima is on the island of Shikoku, which is down south, around 3 hours away from Kansai Airport in Osaka.

I went to learn how to speak Japanese better, and how to play *shamisen*. I'd wanted to play *shamisen* ever since I'd seen a video of the Yoshida Brothers play with their style in a rock band. I thought that that combination was really cool, so I wanted to try it.

I stayed for a whole month with my *shamisen* shishou (Master) at his house, spending most of my time learning how to play. Since I already play the guitar, my left hand got used to it pretty easily, but trying to play with a bachi (the pick you use for the *shamisen*) was really difficult as well, especially trying to get triple picking (sukui) down. Even though it was difficult, I eventually learned how to do it properly, and ended up learning 15 songs or so.

To practice better, my shishou and I played live shows every Saturday and Sunday at an Udon Inn. It actually felt like I was touring! I had to wake up every morning at 6 to shower, eat breakfast, load the van with all the sound gear, speakers, cables, stands and *shamisen*, and then it was a 2 hour drive to where we were going. Then when we got there, we had to unload the van, set up, do a sound check, and I played two shows every day for one hour each in the blazing Japanese summer

sun. When the day was done, we packed it up, ate, went back home to practice more *shamisen*, and repeating the whole thing again the next day.

Needless to say, it was exhausting. Nevertheless, it was very rewarding.

When I wasn't practicing *shamisen*, I was doing a lot of community service activities and sightseeing. I went to a nursing home to chat with them, and play for them a little *shamisen*. It was really difficult to try and understand their Japanese! Not only had I still not fully gotten the hang of the language, but also they were speaking in a dialect I wasn't familiar with, and it was several decades old. A language can change a lot in a small period of time. But I did understand some people, and a lot of them were very nice and fascinated that I was trying to learn Japanese. It was funny when I found out a lot of them knew Mexican songs and that Mambo had had a big fad in the 60's and 70's. On the last day, I taught them a little Spanish, and some of the things they were asking were not the things you would expect from old people!

Apart from the nursing home, I also did some *aisome* dyeing with Futaai-sensei. *Aisome* is a special indigo colored dye that comes from Shikoku, and is usually very expensive. I got to dye some scarves, and Futaai-sensei was a really kind man. He gave me his Bob Dylan CD live at the Royal Albert Hall!

All in all, Tokushima was a blast. Everybody should go at least once.

1.3 Mechanics 組立て
Preparation for Speech I
スピーチの準備 I

Objectives

Make a draft of the beginning, the school and the profile part of the speech.
Describe the past state and contrast the past with the present.
Give instructions and lead simple review exercises.

Overview

Now you will start preparing for your speech. After checking the organization of the speech, learning, and reviewing some useful materials, you will write a draft of the school and the profile segment of your speech. You will learn among other things how to describe the past state and make use of it in comparing last year and this year.

3	**Check organization of speech**	スピーチの組み立てチェック
4	**Beginning**	始め
5	**School**	学校

1	**Last year and this year**	去年と今年
2	**Grade levels and ages**	学年と年齢
3	**Commuting partners and transportation**	一緒に来る人と交通
4	**Hometown**	うち
5	**Preparing a draft**	ドラフト作り

| 6 | **Profile** | プロフィール |

3 **Check organization of speech** スピーチの組み立てチェック

A. Study the chart on the right and familiarize yourself with the organization of your speech.

スピーチの組み立てを
確認しましょう。

You may recall that the concepts of はじめ (beginning= introduction), なか (middle= main body) and おわり (ending=conclusion) were introduced in *Haruichiban* and your speech at this time will also be built based on this three-part model.

はじめ
あいさつ **GREETING**
名前 **NAME**

なか
学校 **SCHOOL**
去年の学校 last year's school
今年の学校 this year's school
学年と年 grade level and age
一緒に来る人 commuting partner(s)
交通 transportation
うち home
プロフィール **PROFILE**
出身 birthplace
国籍 nationality/ citizenship
言葉 language(s) you speak
趣味 hobbies
CREATE YOUR OWN
夏休み **SUMMER VACATION**

おわり
願いごと **WISHES**
あいさつ **GREETING**

B. Confirm your understanding of the organization of your speech by putting a letter in each parentheses to indicate the correct order.

（　）に記号を入れてください。

スピーチの組み立て

1. (**k**) → 2. (　) → 3. (　) → 4. (　) → 5. (　) → 6. (　) →
7. (　) → 8. (　) → 9. (　) → 10. (　) → 11. (　) → 12. (　) →
13. (　) → 14. (　) → 15. (　) → 16. (**k**)

a. 交通（こうつう）

b. 言葉（ことば）(language)

c. 今年の学校（ことし　がっこう）(this year's school)

d. 出身（しゅっしん）

e. 去年の学校（きょねん　がっこう）(last year's school)

f. 趣味（しゅみ）

g. 願いごと（ねが）(wish)

h. 一緒に来る人（いっしょ　く　ひと）(commuting partners)

i. 名前（なまえ）

j. 夏休み（なつやす）(summer vacation)

k. 挨拶（あいさつ）

l. 学年（がくねん）

m. うち

n. 国籍（こくせき）(nationality, citizenship)

o. 年（とし）

C. Fill in each parenthesis with an appropriate letter.

（　）に記号を入れてください。

1. きょねん　　（　）　2. あいさつ　　（　）　3. しゅみ　（　）

4. こくせき　　（　）　5. なつやすみ　（　）　6. うち　　（　）

7. ことし　　（　）　8. ねがいごと　（　）　9. ことば　（　）

10. しゅっしん　（　）　11. がくねん　　（　）　12. とし　　（　）

13. こうつう　　（　）　14. プロフィール（　）　15. なまえ　（　）

a. nationality	b. this year	c. age	d. language
e. summer vacation	f. greeting	g. hobby	h. transportation
i. profile	j. name	k. last year	l. grade level
m. birthplace	n. home	o. wish	

4　Beginning　始め

Start creating your speech. You will make the beginning part first and then the middle part, which will be divided into three segments - "school," "profile," and "summer vacation."

A. The beginning part consists of greeting and your name. Create it by choosing an appropriate greeting depending upon the time of the day you may be giving your speech.

「始め」の部分を作ってください。

はじめ	あいさつ　GREETING	こんにちは。(はじめまして。)
	名前　NAME	わたしは<u>レイチェル・リード</u>です。

5　School　学校

1　Last year and this year　去年と今年

Many items in the school segment are the same as those in the self-introductory speech in *Haruichiban* but it does include reference to last year. This means that you will learn how to write sentences in the past tense. See the note below.

ノート: Describing past states [affirmative]

$$\text{Noun/な adj.+です} \Rightarrow$$
$$\text{Noun/な adj.+でした}$$

The past tense of Noun +です and な adj. +です is obtained by replacing です with でした. い adj. + です takes a different form and will be introduced later.

母はカウンセラーです。
My mother is a counselor.

母はカウンセラーでした。
My mother was a counselor.

サラさんは元気ですか。
Is Sara fine?

サラさんは元気でしたか。
Was Sara fine?

A **Match the Japanese words on the left with their English equivalent on the right.**

（　　）に記号を入れてください。

1. らいねん　（　）

2. ことし　　（　）

3. きょねん　（　）

a. last year

b. this year

c. next year

B. **Circle the correct one.**　正しいものを○で囲みましょう。

1. トムさんは（きょねん、らいねん）18さいです。

2. 私は（きょねん、らいねん）ピザがきらいでした。

3. ジェニーさんは（きょねん、らいねん）中学三年生でした。

4. ジョンさんは（きょねん、らいねん）日本へ行きます。

5. （きょねん、らいねん）のクラブは科学クラブでした。

6. ジェニーさんは（きょねん、らいねん）キャプテンでした。

7. （きょねん、ことし）の日本語の先生は中野先生です。

8. ジョンさんは（きょねん、らいねん）毎日六時におきます。

C. **Make a sequence of sentences in which you will contrast a situation this (school) year with last year.**

文を作ってください。

	たんにんの先生	日本語の先生	学校	秋のスポーツ
きょねん			Kisetsu Jr High	
ことし			Ginga Academy	
	EX1.	EX2.	1.	2.

	アドバイザー	クラブ	りょう	make your own
きょねん		Dance	Midori Hall	?
ことし			Midori Hall	?
	3.	4.	5.	6.

例 (Examples)

EX1. 去年(きょねん)の担任(たんにん)の先生はスミス先生でした。でも、今年(ことし)の担任(たんにん)の先生はゴードン先生です。

EX2. 去年(きょねん)の日本語の先生は石田(いしだ)先生でした。今年(ことし)の日本語の先生も石田(いしだ)先生です。

2 Grade levels and ages　学年(がくねん)と年齢(ねんれい)

A. Group Work - Break up into groups of three.

グループワークです。三人(さんにん)のグループになってください。

Objective:
Review the terms for indicating grade levels.

Activities:
1. Meet with your group and help each other recall the terms for grade levels. Check *Haruichiban* and/or other resources if necessary.
2. Take turns and make a simple exercise in which one person gives a grade level based on the U.S. system and others in the group quickly say it based on the Japanese system.
3. Confirm your understanding with the class.

B. Practice the following conversation by substituting the underlined parts.

かいわ れんしゅう
会話を練習しましょう。

会話の例 (Sample Dialogue)

なんねんせい
A: 何年生ですか。

B: <u>11年生</u>です。

こうこう
A: じゃ、<u>高校2年生</u>ですね。

B: はい、そうです。

さい
A: <u>17</u>才ですか。

さい
B: いいえ、<u>16</u>才です。

A. Fill in the parentheses in Column A with a letter representing an appropriate Japanese word and those in Column B with a letter representing the English equivalent.

かっこ きごう い
( )に記号を入れてください。

one's own family (humble)	A.	B.		someone's family		えいご
1. 父 (ちち)	( )	( )	a.	おかあさん	j.	family
2. 姉 (あね)	( )	( )	b.	ごかぞく	k.	younger sister
3. 妹 (いもうと)	( )	( )	c.	おばあさん	l.	younger brother
4. 祖父 (そふ)	( )	( )	d.	いもうとさん	m.	mother
5. 弟 (おとうと)	( )	( )	e.	おじいさん	n.	older sister
6. 母 (はは)	( )	( )	f.	おとうとさん	o.	older brother
7. 祖母 (そぼ)	( )	( )	g.	おにいさん	p.	grandmother
8. 兄 (あに)	( )	( )	h.	おとうさん	q.	father
9. 家族 (かぞく)	( )	( )	i.	おねえさん	r.	grandfather

ノート: "Go" and "Come"

「行きます」 vs 「来ます」

We assume that you will be making your speech at your school. This means that you will be using きます (come) rather than いきます(go) when you describe how you commute to your school. Keep this in mind when you practice and make an adjustment depending upon the location of your speech.

毎日バスで学校に来ます。
I come to school by bus everyday.

YOU ARE AT SCHOOL.

毎日バスで学校に行きます。
I go to school by bus everyday.

YOU ARE NOT AT SCHOOL.

B. Practice asking and answering whom one will go (or come) to the following places with.

会話を練習しましょう。

会話の例 (Sample Dialogue)
A: だれと山に行きますか。
B: 姉と行きます。

EX1.

1.　　2.　　3.　　4.

会話の例 (Sample Dialogue)
A: だれと学校に来ますか。
B: 母と来ます。

EX2.

1. GRANDMOTHER
2. GRANDFATHER
3. FRIEND
4. OLDER SISTER

C. Match the words on the right with the pictures on the left, filling each parentheses with the appropriate letter.

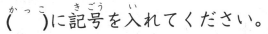（かっこ）に記号（きごう）を入（い）れてください。

a. くるま
b. バス
c. タクシー
d. ボート
e. でんしゃ
f. ひこうき
g. ふね
h. ちかてつ

 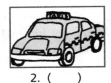 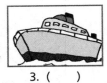 

1. (　　)   2. (　　)   3. (　　)   4. (　　)

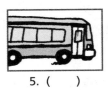 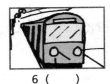 

5. (　　)   6 (　　)   7. (　　)   8. (　　)

D. Practice asking and answering by what means one will go to the following places.

会話（かいわ）を練習（れんしゅう）しましょう。

会話の例 (Sample Dialogue)
A: 何（なん）でデパートに行（い）きますか。
B: バスで行（い）きます。

EX1.

で で で で

1. MOVIE   2. オーストラリア   3. Hawaii   4. レストラン

で

会話の例 (Sample Dialogue)
A: 何（なん）で学校（がっこう）に来（き）ますか。
B: タクシーで来（き）ます。

EX2.

1.	CAR	
2.	BIKE AND SUBWAY	で
3.	TRAIN AND BUS	
4.	あるいて (on foot)	

4 **Hometown**　　　　　　　　　　うち

In addition to just identifying the location of your home, you may comment briefly about it by using both the affirmative form and the negative form of adjectives.

ノート: Negative Form of いAdjective

いadj. くありません
いadj. くないです

For polite style replace 〜いです with either 〜くありません or 〜くないです. The latter sounds a bit stronger than 〜くありません. For plain style just replace 〜い with 〜くない. Note that the negative form of いい(good) is よくない. いくない does not occur.

おもしろいです。⇒おもしろくありません／おもしろくないです。

いいです。⇒よくありません／よくないです。

A. *What do you think that you respond to someone's question or statement when your response has to be a negative one? Does it sound too harsh, too soft, or do you tend to use certain expressions to adjust the tone of your negation? In Japan someone who always contradicts the other is called an* あまのじゃく. *I know most of you will not fall into this category but let's play both non-amanojaku who uses* 〜くありません *for negation and amanojaku who uses stronger* 〜くないです *in this exercise. Respond negatively to the following statements as shown in the example.* よ *at the end is a particle which adds an emphatical tone to the statement.*

サッカーは
おもしろいです。
EX.
statement maker

そうですか。
サッカーはおもしろ
くありませんよ。

non-*amanojaku*

1. コーチはきびしいです。
2. ダンスは楽（たの）しいです。
3. リンダさんはやさしいです。
4. トムさんはうるさいです。
5. 明日（あした）の天気（てんき）はいいです。
6. ジェニーさんの犬（いぬ）はかわいいです。

いいえ、サッカーは
おもしろくないですよ。

amanojaku

ノート: Negative Form of な Adjective

な adj. じゃありません
な adj. じゃないです

For polite style replace 〜です with either 〜じゃありません or 〜じゃないです. The latter sounds a bit stronger than 〜じゃありません. For plain style just add じゃない.

好きです。⇒好きじゃありません／好きじゃないです。
便利です。⇒便利じゃありません／便利じゃないです。

B. Let's continue with the same exercise but using な-adjectives.

statement maker

amanojaku

EX. 教室は静かです。

いいえ、教室は静かじゃないですよ。

1. 図書館はきれいです。

2. サラさんは元気です。

3. 科学は重要です。

non-amanojaku

4. 掃除は大変です。

5. アンディさんはまじめです。

そうですか。教室は静かじゃありませんよ。

6. 日本語の勉強は必要です。

C. Were you an amanojaku type of child? Or were you a すなおなこども **(a docile and agreeable child)? Let's practice negative (and affirmative) forms of adjectives more through a short plain style conversation between a child and her mom. You will notice that mom's statements end with** 〜わねえ. **This ending is used by female speakers for soliciting listeners' agreement. Male speakers use** 〜ねえ **instead.** うん **is the plain/casual equivalent of** はい **and** ええ.

うん、とても寒い(わ)。

今日は寒い(わ)ねえ。

EX.

えっ？ ぜんぜん寒くない(わ)よ。

1.　今日は暑いねえ。

2.　トムさんは優しいねえ。

3.　日本語の先生は忙しいねえ。

4.　日本語の勉強はおもしろいねえ。

5.　歴史の宿題は難しいねえ。

6.　ハワイの冬はいいねえ。

5 Preparing a draft　　　　　　　ドラフト作り

A. Prepare a draft of the "school" part of your speech by replacing the underlined parts with your own words.

学校の部分のスピーチを作りましょう。

なか

学校 SCHOOL

去年の学校
last year's school

今年の学校
this year's school

学年
grade level

年
age

一緒に来る人
commuting partner(s)

交通
transportation

うち
home

去年の学校はローズ中学でした。

今年の学校はセントラル高校です。

> The particle here will be も instead of は if your last year's school and this year's school are the same.

高校1年生です。

十六才です。

いつも姉と車で学校に来ます。

うちはポートランドです。

ポートランドはきれいです。

それから、あまり暑くありません。

41

A. Circle the correct one. 正しいものを〇で囲みましょう。

1. （しゅっしん、しゅみ、こくせき）はボストンです。

2. 英語と中国語を（たべます、はなします、します）

3. 日本語やフランス語は（こくせき、ことば）です。

4. （しゅっしん、しゅみ、こくせき）はテニスです。

5. （くに、しゅみ、ことば）はアメリカです。アメリカ人です。

6. Q: ご（くに、しゅみ、しゅっしん）は。　A: カナダです。

7. Q: お（くに、しゅみ、しゅっしん）は。　A: カナダです。

ノート: Indicating your nationality or country of citizenship

こくせき
国籍

こくせき is used to mean "nationality" or "country of citizenship." Quite a few countries recognize dual citizenship today and some of you may be a citizen of more than one country. Note the difference between しゅっしん (birthplace) and こくせき.

出身はアメリカです。
My birthplace is America.

国籍はアメリカとカナダです
My countries of citizenship are America and Canada.

B. Prepare a draft of the "profile" part of your speech by replacing the underlined parts with your own situations and creating another category.

学校の部分までのスピーチを作りましょう。

プロフィール

な
か

出身 birthplace

国籍 nationality

言葉 language(s)

趣味 hobbies

出身はモントリオールです。

国籍はアメリカとカナダです。

英語とフランス語を話します。

趣味はアニメと柔道です。

CREATE YOUR OWN

Recognition Kanji 2: 認識漢字 2

曜日
days of the week

四日
the fourth

五日
the fifth

六日
the sixth

七日
the seventh

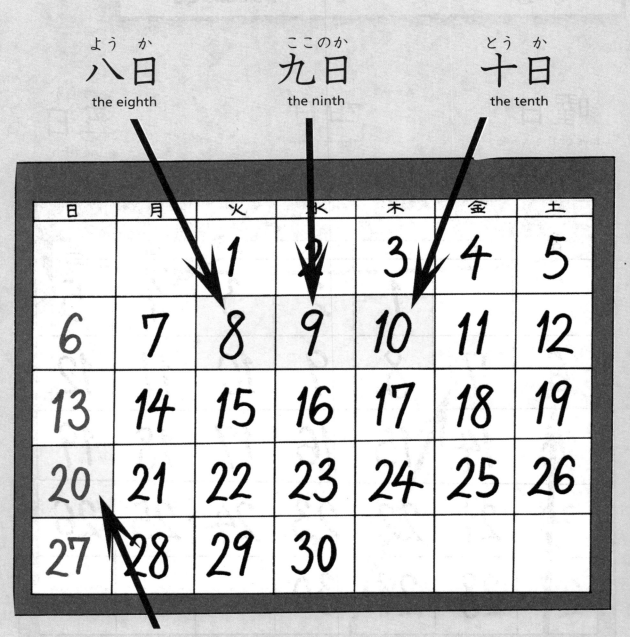

ようか
八日
the eighth

ここのか
九日
the ninth

とうか
十日
the tenth

はつか
二十日
the twentieth

New Kanji 1: 新出漢字 1
(しんしゅつかんじ)

行
ON: コウ、ギョウ　KUN: い(く)

行く/行きます:いく/いきます go

来
ON: ライ　KUN: く(る)

来る/来ます:くる/きます come　来月:らいげつ next month　来年:らいねん next year

見
ON:ケン　KUN: み(る)、み（える)、み（せる)

見る/見ます:みる/みます watch, see

聞
ON: ブン　KUN: き(く)、き(こえる)

聞く/聞きます:きく/ききます listen, ask

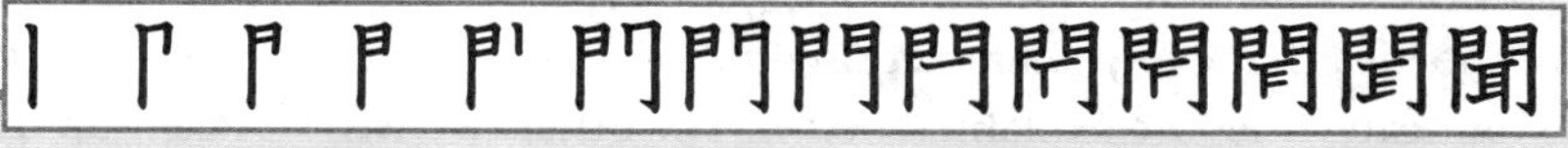

言
ON: ゲン、ゴン　KUN: い(う)

言う/言います:いう/いいます say

話
ON: ワ　KUN: はな(す)

話す/話します:はなす/はなします speak, talk

読
ON:ドク　KUN: よ(む)

読む/読みます:よむ/よみます read

書
ON: ショ　KUN: か(く)

書く/書きます:かく/かきます write　読書:どくしょ reading

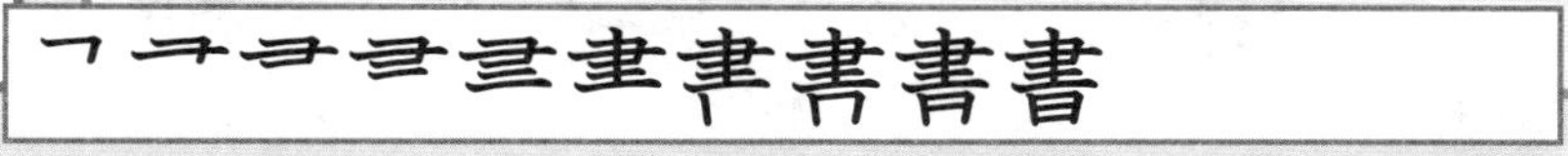

Language Note 1

The Origin of Chinese Characters

Fortune-telling

The oldest Chinese characters (kanji) that archeologists have discovered so far date from about 1200 B.C., but the Chinese writing system was already well developed by that time, so it must have been invented quite a bit earlier. These earliest examples of Chinese writing were scratched onto animal bones and tortoise shells that were used to predict the future. A fortune-teller would write a question about the future and then heat the bone or shell until cracks appeared. The fortune-teller would interpret the pattern of cracks as the answer and write that answer down next to the question.

Classification

The traditional Chinese classification of characters dates from around 100 A.D., more than a thousand years after the characters were first invented. There are some problems with this classification, but Japanese children still learn about it in school. It is based on the idea that every character originated in one of four basic ways, and two of these four categories are explained below. The other two will be taken up in the next chapter.

Pictographic characters

The pictographic category is the easiest of the four to understand. Each pictographic character originated from a picture of a concrete object. Those given below are some of the better known examples of this category. An ancient form of each character is given below the modern form, and some of these ancient forms are a little easier to recognize as pictures. One reason the modern forms look so different is that the shift to writing with brush and ink had a big impact on character shapes.

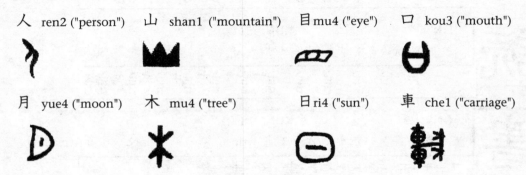

人 ren2 ("person")   山 shan1 ("mountain")   目 mu4 ("eye")   口 kou3 ("mouth")

月 yue4 ("moon")   木 mu4 ("tree")   日 ri4 ("sun")   車 che1 ("carriage")

馬 ma3 ("horse")　　土 tu3 ("earth")　　女 nu3("woman")　　刀 dao1 ("sword")

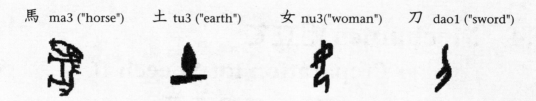

The romanization next to each character indicates the pronunciation of the modern Mandarin Chinese word that the character is used to write (with the superscript number indicating the tone). If you don't know any Mandarin, rough approximations are all you need to understand the explanations given here. Besides, the Chinese language has changed a lot in the more than three thousand years since the characters were invented, so these modern Mandarin pronunciations are very different from the ancient pronunciations anyway.

Diagrammatic characters

The diagrammatic category is also easy to understand. The characters in this group originated as diagrams of simple concepts. They aren't pictographic characters, because the words they represent don't refer to objects.

一　yi1 ("one")　　　　二　er4 ("two")　　　　三　san1 ("three")

上　Shang4 ("above")　　下　xia4 ("below")　　中　zhong1 ("middle")

The relationship between each of these characters and the meaning of the word it represents is still pretty obvious even from the modern character shapes.

Some of the characters that are included in the traditional diagrammatic category really belong in a separate group. The two below are well-known examples of this type.

本 ben3 ("root")　　　　刃 ren4 ("blade")

If you look back at the examples of pictographic characters, you will see that 本 is almost the same as 木, which represents mu4 ("tree"), and that 刃 is almost the same as 刀, which represents dao1 ("sword"). The extra stroke near the bottom of 本 suggests the idea of a root, since the roots of a tree are at the bottom. The extra stroke on the left side of 刃 marks the cutting edge. This method of adding an extra stroke to an existing character clearly isn't the same thing as just drawing a diagram.

The two categories discussed above together account for less than 10% of all characters, and it's not hard to understand why. Most of the words in any language don't refer to objects that you can draw pictures of or to simple concepts that are easy to diagram. Think about ordinary English words like "probably," or "should, " or "the." It's pretty hard to imagine how you'd draw a picture or a diagram that would suggest one of these words.

1.4　Mechanics 組立て
<ruby>組<rt>く</rt></ruby><ruby>立<rt>み た</rt></ruby>て

Preparation for Speech II
スピーチの準備 II
<ruby>準備<rt>じゅん び</rt></ruby>

Objectives

Draft the summer vacation part of the speech.
Describe actions that have taken place in the past.
Ask someone to summarize his or her past actions or experience.
Give a concise description of one's summer vacation.

Overview

This section focuses on writing a draft of the summer vacation segment of your speech. You will begin by learning the past tense of verbs and practicing to describe actions in the past. Then you will look back on your summer vacation and conduct a simple evaluation of it according to a three-scale model. Finally you will finish your draft.

7	**Summer vacation**	夏休み（なつやす）
1	**Describing past actions**	過去の活動の表現（かこ かつどう ひょうげん）
2	**Describing how something was**	感想とコメント（かんそう）
3	**Asking how something was**	感想とコメントの質問（かんそう しつもん）
4	**Evaluating and describing your summer vacation**	夏休みの評価と描写（なつやす ひょうか びょうしゃ）
5	**Preparing a draft**	ドラフト作り（づく）

| **7** Summer vacation | 夏休み
<small>なつやす</small> |

| **1** Describing past actions | 過去の活動の表現
<small>か こ　かつどう　ひょうげん</small> |

ノート: Describing past actions [Affirmative & Negative]

-ます
-ました

The past tense of ～ます is ～ました.

学校に行きます。　　I <u>go/will go</u> to school.
<small>がっこう</small>

学校に行きました。I <u>went</u> to school.

-ません
-ませんでした

The past tense of ～ません is ～ませんでした.

学校に行きません。I <u>don't go</u> to school.

学校に行きませんでした。

I <u>didn't go</u> to school.

A. To which of the four "zones" below do each of the following sentences belong? The zones are designated based on the vertical line serving as the "Time" axis and the horizontal line serving as the "Affirmative/negative" axis.

（　）にゾーンのイニシャルを入れてください。

	Past zone	Non-past zone
Affirmative zone	**PA**ゾーン	**NA**ゾーン
Negative zone	**PN**ゾーン	**NN**ゾーン

1. 六時にうちへ帰ります。　　　　　（　　　）ゾーン
   <small>かえ</small>
2. 数学の宿題がありませんでした。　（　　　）ゾーン
   <small>すうがく　しゅくだい</small>
3. 図書館で漢字を練習しました。　　（　　　）ゾーン
   <small>と しょかん　かんじ　れんしゅう</small>
4. 水曜日に友達とサッカーをします。（　　　）ゾーン
   <small>すいようび　ともだち</small>
5. 今日は朝ごはんを食べませんでした。（　　　）ゾーン
   <small>きょう　あさ　た</small>
6. 兄はガールフレンドがいません。　（　　　）ゾーン
   <small>あに</small>

B. Match the Japanese terms on the left with the appropriate English words on the right.

（　　）に記号を入れてください。

1.	明後日	（　　）	a.	last year
2.	去年	（　　）	b.	yesterday
3.	今日	（　　）	c.	the day after tomorrow
4.	昨日	（　　）	d.	next year
5.	一昨日	（　　）	e.	this year
6.	来年	（　　）	f.	the day before yesterday
7.	明日	（　　）	g.	tomorrow
8.	今年	（　　）	h.	today

C. Put a number in each parenthesis to indicate the order of occurrence with "1" being the most distant past and "8" being the most recent.

（　　）に番号を入れてください。

1. （　　）マークさんは今日日本語を勉強しました。

2. （　　）ピーターさんは去年日本へ行きました。

3. （　　）コートニーさんは明日六時に起きます。

4. （　　）プリヤさんは今日映画を見ます。

5. （　　）ジョッシュさんは一昨日すしを食べました。

6. （　　）ユーンさんは来年ハワイへ行きます。

7. （　　）リサさんは昨日七時に起きました。

8. （　　）ペドロさんは明後日うちへ帰ります。

Suggested additional work

Procedure:

1. Break up into small groups and make another set of exercises just like those above on a piece of paper. You can be creative and even a bit tricky though the instructions should remain the same as the model.
2. Prepare additional copies of your exercise for distribution.
3. Give a copy of your exercise to each group and ask them to begin.
4. Select the winning group based on accuracy, speed and teamwork.

D. Sentence expansion: How much information can you add? Extend the following original sentence according to the pictures.

文を作りましょう。

Original A：映画を見ました。

1. きのう映画を見ました。

2. きのうの9時に映画を見ました。

3. きのうの9時に弟と映画を見ました。

4. きのうの9時に弟とピッツバーグで映画を見ました。

1.

2. 3. 4.

Original B：ひるごはんを食べました。

the day before yesterday

1. the day before yesterday

2.

3. the day before yesterday

4. the day before yesterday

Suggested additional work

Procedure:

1. Break up into small groups and make another set of exercises just like the one above.

2. Lead an exercise session as a group in which you provide your original sentence first and cues for each piece of additional information. Your cues may be oral, written or pictorial.

E. Practice ～ませんでした as in the example. 練習しましょう。

会話の例 (Sample Dialogue)

A: 昼ごはんを食べましたか。

B: いいえ、食べませんでした。

F. Find out about your classmates' weekend. 週末の話をしましょう。

Preparation

1. Brainstorming and vocabulary building

Think about how your classmates may usually spend their weekends and list some probable activities. If you don't know how to say them in Japanese, ask others or check a dictionary. This can be done as a whole class, individually, or in small groups.

2. List initial questions

List simple and specific questions asking about activities your classmates might have done during the past weekend by completing the following.

EX1. 週末に買い物に行きましたか。　　　買い物 shopping

EX2. 週末に映画を見ましたか。

1. 週末に＿＿＿＿＿＿＿＿＿＿＿＿＿＿＿＿＿＿＿＿＿か。

2. 週末に＿＿＿＿＿＿＿＿＿＿＿＿＿＿＿＿＿＿＿＿＿か。

3. 週末に＿＿＿＿＿＿＿＿＿＿＿＿＿＿＿＿＿＿＿＿＿か。

4. 週末に＿＿＿＿＿＿＿＿＿＿＿＿＿＿＿＿＿＿＿＿＿か。

3 Think about follow-up questions

You will initially get an affirmative or a negative response to your questions from your partner. If his or her response is the former, ask him or her for some details about the activity. See the examples below and be prepared to ask a few follow-up questions.

EX1. Possible follow-up questions for Preparation 2-EX1.

どこの店ですか。	Where (Which store?) - Open ended
ショッピングモールですか。	Is it ~? - Yes/No
いつ行きましたか。	When?
だれと行きましたか。	With whom?
何で行きましたか。	By what transportation?
何を買いましたか。	What did you buy?

EX2. Possible follow-up questions for Preparation 2-EX2.

何を見ましたか。	What? - Open ended
「七人の侍」ですか。	Is it ~? - Yes/No
いつ見ましたか。	When?
どこで見ましたか。	Where? (Location of a viewing site)
だれと見ましたか。	With whom?

4. Practice developing conversation with じゃ

As you have learned in *Haruichiban*, じゃ is useful in developing conversation. You may use じゃ when you want to say something that would logically follow what your conversation partner has just said or when you want to indicate a shift of topic or focus in conversation. With this in mind, practice the following dialogues by paying attention to the use of じゃ.

会話の例 A (Sample Dialogue A)

A: 買い物に行きましたか。

B: はい、行きました。

A: ショッピングモールですか。

B: はい、そうです。

A: じゃ、だれと行きましたか。

B: 弟と行きました。continued.

会話の例 B (Sample Dialogue B)

A: 買い物に行きましたか。

B: いいえ、行きませんでした。

A: あ、そうですか。
じゃ、映画を見ましたか。

A: はい、見ました。

B: 何を見ましたか。continued.

Activities

1. Interview

Pair up and ask your partner questions you have prepared. Make sure to ask follow-up questions and use じゃ effectively.

2. Report

Report the results of your interview to the class.

例 (Example)

アニーさんは土曜日に弟と買い物に行きました。ショッピングモールで、ポスターを買いました。それから、友達と学校でテニスをしました。晩ごはんは家族とシーフードのレストランへ行きました。ロブスターを食べました。でも、日曜日はうちで日本語の宿題をしました。

2 **Describing how something was** 感想とコメント
かんそう

ノート：Describing how things were using い adjectives

さむい(です)→ さむかった(です)

The past tense of い adjective is obtained by replacing い with かった.

たのしい→たのしかった （informal/plain）

たのしいです→たのしかったです （formal/polite）

Q: ダンスは楽しかったですか。 Was the dance fun?
たの

A: とても楽しかったです。 It was a lot of fun.
たの

Note that the past tense is indicated by the presence of かった. When です is added to make the formal style, it should remain unchanged. おもしろかったでした does not occur. Compare the following.

サラさんのスピーチはすばらしいスピーチでした。
Sara's speech was a wonderful speech.

サラさんのスピーチはすばらしかったです。
Sara's speech was wonderful.

Note also the following irregularity concerning いい. いかった does not occur.

いい→よかった　　　いいです→よかったです

A. Change the following into ～かった. 過去形に変えましょう。
か こけい か

EX. 大きい→大きかった 6. かわいい→
おお おお

1. 難しい→ 7. 面白い→
むずか おしろ

2. うるさい→ 8. 楽しい→
たの

3. 小さい→ 9. つまらない→
ちい

4. やさしい→ 10. 暑い→
あつ

5. 厳しい→ 11. いい→
きび

B. Practice 〜かったです **according to the given cues.** 練習しましょう。

EX. delicious (おいしい)   1. cold   2. noisy   3. interesting

4. hot and humid   5. fun   6. good   7. difficult

会話の例 A (Sample Dialogue A: formal)	会話の例 B (Sample Dialogue B: Informal)
EX. A: <u>おいしかった</u>ですか。 B: はい、<u>おいしかった</u>です。	EX. A: <u>おいしかった</u>。 B: うん、<u>おいしかった</u>。

ノート: Describing how things were using な adjectives

しずかでした   (formal/polite)

しずかだった   (informal/plain)

As you know, the past tense form of な adjectives can be obtained by simply replacing です (as in しずか<u>です</u>) with でした. -でした marks a formal/polite ending and its informal/plain equivalent is obtained by ending with -だった instead.

図書館は静かでした。   The library was quiet. (Formal/polite)

図書館は静かだった。   The library was quiet. (Informal/plain)

C. Practice でした **according to the given cues.** 練習しましょう。

EX. clean, beautiful

1. healthy, spirited (げんき)   2. quiet (しずか)   3. attractive (すてき)

4. skillful (じょうず)   5. be poor at (にがて)

会話の例 A (Sample Dialogue A: formal)	会話の例 B (Sample Dialogue B: Informal)
EX. A: <u>きれい</u>でしたか。 B: はい、<u>きれい</u>でした。	EX. A: <u>きれい</u>だった。 B: うん、<u>きれい</u>だった。

3 **Asking how something was**　　　　　かんそう
感想とコメント

ノート: Asking how something was

どうでしたか
どうだった

どうでしたか and its plain/informal equivalent, どうだった are used to ask someone how something was. パーティーはどうでしたか means "How was the party?"

A: 歴史のテストはどうでしたか。　　　How was the history test?

B: 少し、難しかったです。　　　　　It was a bit difficult.

A: 先週のパーティー、どうだった？　How was the party last week?

B: よかったよ。　　　　　　　　　　It was good.

A. Asking and telling how something was.

Preparation

First, complete the following sentences by filling in the blanks according to your own experience. For example, in the third blank, write the name of a food you ate recently. さいきん means "recently" in Japanese.

1. 最近、＿＿＿＿＿＿＿のテストがありました。　(name of a subject)

2. 最近、＿＿＿＿＿＿＿＿＿を読みました。　(title of a book)

3. 最近、＿＿＿＿＿＿＿＿＿を食べました。　(name of a dish)

4. 最近、＿＿＿＿＿＿＿＿＿へ行きました。　(name of a place)

Next, look back on the four experiences and find a few adjectives suitable for describing each of them. Here are a few additional adjectives that may be useful in this exercise.

高い expensive

安い inexpensive

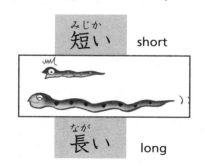

短い short

長い long

おいしい delicious

まずい unpalatable

57

Conversation

Go around the class and practice asking and telling how something was based on the information you have prepared.

会話の例 (Sample Dialogue)

A: 最近、科学のテストがありました。

B: どうでしたか。

A: ちょっと難しかったです。

B: そうですか。私は最近、数学のテストがありました。

A: どうでしたか。

B: あのう、とても難しかったです。 **Continued.**

4 | **Evaluating and describing summer vacation**   夏休みの評価と描写

A. Asking about and describing one's summer vacation.

夏休みの話をしましょう。

Assessing your vacation 1

How was your summer vacation? Choose your response based on your experience by circling an appropriate letter.

1. 夏休みに楽しいことがありましたか。

    A. はい、たくさんありました。

    B. はい、少しありました。

    C. いいえ、ぜんぜんありませんでした。

2. 問題がありましたか。

    D. はい、たくさんありました。

    E. はい、少しありました。

    F. いいえ、ぜんぜんありませんでした。

Assessing your vacation 2

Next, see the following chart. Which of the three statements (superb, so-so, or worst)
summarizes your summer vacation based your response to the 2 questions?

Choices of Response	Statement	
AとF	私の夏休みは 最高でした。	SUPERB
AとD　AとE　BとD BとE　BとF　CとF	私の夏休みは まあまあでした。	SO-SO
CとE　　CとD	私の夏休みは 最低でした。	WORST

Preparing to say sample activities

Now think about all the fun things you did this past summer and choose a few examples. If you are among the unlucky ones who did not do anything exciting this summer, create a few negative sentences. Make use of frequency words such as よく, ときどき, and あまり.

例 (Examples for "Superb" and "So-so" Vacation)

ハワイの海へ行きました。
よく友達と映画を見ました。
ときどきコンサートへ行きました。
日本の食べ物を食べました。

例 (Examples for "Worst" and "So-so" Vacation)

海へ行きませんでした。
山へ行きませんでした。
ぜんぜんコンサートへ行きませんでした。
あまり映画を見ませんでした。

Conversation Exercise

Have a conversation with your classmates in which you talk about each other's summer vacation.

会話の例 A (Sample Dialogue A)

A: 夏休みはどうでしたか。
B: 最高の夏休みでした。楽しいことがたくさんありました。
A: そうですか。
B: ハワイの海へ行きました。よく友達と映画を見ました。
それから、日本の食べ物をたくさん食べました。おいしかったです。
A: よかったですね。
B: Aさんの夏休みはどんな夏休みでしたか。
A: まあまあの夏休みでした。ときどきコンサートへ行きました。
それから、サッカーのキャンプに行きました。

5 **Preparing a draft**　　　　　　　　ドラフト作^{づく}り

A. Prepare a draft for the "summer vacation" part of your speech.

スピーチの夏休^{なつやす}みの部分^{ぶ ぶん}を作^{つく}りましょう。

Go over the sample descriptions for a "superb" vacation (left), a "so-so" vacation (center), and "the worst" vacation (right). Then create an account of your own summer vacation by replacing the middle part of one of the three samples below.

SUPERB

私^{わたし}の夏休^{なつやす}みは最高^{さいこう}でした。

ハワイとメキシコへ行きました。毎^{まい}日海^{にちうみ}で泳^{およ}ぎました。よく友達^{ともだち}と映画^{えい が}を見ました。とても面白^{おもしろ}かったです。それから、たくさん日本の食べ物^{もの}を食べました。私は日本の食べ物が好^すきです。

問題^{もんだい}はありませんでした。だから、最高^{さいこう}の夏休みでした。

SO-SO

私^{わたし}の夏休^{なつやす}みはまあまあでした。

小学生^{しょうがくせい}のキャンプのカウンセラーをしました。楽^{たの}しかったです。でも、忙^{いそが}しかったです。よく友達^{ともだち}とテニスをしました。それから、カメラを買^かいました。とてもいいカメラです。

でも、問題^{もんだい}もありました。だから、まあまあの夏休みでした。

WORST

私^{わたし}の夏休^{なつやす}みは最低^{さいてい}でした。

海^{うみ}に行きませんでした。山^{やま}にも行きませんでした。よく、うちでテレビを見ました。つまらなかったです。それから、毎日^{まいにち}レストランでアルバイトをしました。とても忙^{いそが}しかったです。

ほかにも、問題^{もんだい}がありました。だから、最低^{さいてい}の夏休みでした。

にんしきかんじ

なに じん
何人
what nationality?

なん ねん
何年
what year

1965?
1969?
1976?

MAN ON THE MOON

なん じ
何時
what time/hour?

なん ぷん
何分
how many minutes?

12
9   3
6

?? : ?? AM

なに ど し
何年
what year?
(Chinese zodiac)

なに ご
何語
what language?

ちち
父
father

はは
母
mother

わたし
私
me

あね
姉
old sister

あに
兄
old brother

いもうと
妹
younger sister

おとうと
弟
younger brother

なんにん
何人
how many people?

1 ... 2 ... 3 ... 4 ... 5 ... 6 ...

New Kanji 2: 新出漢字 2

食
ON: ショク　　　　**KUN**: た(べる)、く(う)
食べる/食べます:たべる/たべます eat
ノ 人 𠆢 今 今 今 食 食 食

飲
ON: イン　　　　**KUN**: の(む)
飲む/飲みます:のむ/のみます drink
ノ 人 𠆢 今 今 今 食 食 食 飲 飲 飲

休
ON: キュウ　　　　**KUN**: やす(む)、やす(み)
休日:きゅうじつ holiday　　休む/休みます:やすむ/やすみます rest　　夏休み
summer vacation
ノ イ イ イ 休 休

作
ON: サク　　　　**KUN**: つく(る)
作る/作ります:つくる/つくります make
ノ イ イ 作 作 作 作

使
ON: シ　　　　**KUN**: つか(う)
使う/使います:つかう/つかいます use
ノ イ イ 仁 仨 仴 伊 使

立
ON: リツ　　　　**KUN**: た(つ)
立つ/立ちます:たつ/たちます stand
丶 ㇒ 十 立 立

会
ON: カイ　　　　**KUN**: あ(う)
会う/会います:あう/あいます meet　　会話:かいわ conversation
ノ 人 𠆢 会 会 会

帰
ON: キ　　　　**KUN**:かえ(る)
帰る/帰ります:かえる/かえります return, go home
丨 刂 刂 刋 刋 帰 帰 帰 帰 帰

Reading 1: 読^よみ物^{もの} 1

Reading Dojo 1: Scanning
読解道場^{どっかいどうじょう} 1: スキャニング

Scan It Part I: Finding the Key Word

A. Find the different spelled word in each row.

	a.	b.	c.	d.
1.	グループ	グレープ	グレープ	グレープ
2.	かきます	かきます	さきます	かきます
3.	えいが	えいご	えいが	えいが
4.	ここのか	ここのつ	ここのつ	ここのか
5.	ディスク	ディスク	デッスク	デッスコ

B. In which column is the key word repeated?

KEY	A	B	C	D	E
1. ふたつ	ふたり	ふつか	ひとつ	ぶつり	ふたつ
2. コーチ	トーチ	コート	コーラ	コーチ	アーラ
3. すうがく	がくねん	だいがく	すうがく	おんがく	すうじ
4. なります	なきます	なります	ぬります	のります	ねます
5. 十円	十日	十時	十円	十年	十月

Scan It Part II: Finding the Mistakes

C. Rearrange the list below according to the Japanese practice of placing the (last) names in "a, i, u, e, o, ka, ki, ku, ke, ko..." order. Indicate the revised order by letters accompanying each name below.

A さえぐさ みか	B なかやま けんじ	C. つのだ ひさお
D いしかわ みなこ	E やすだ のりお	F きのした とおる
G ばんどう のぼる	H しもむら ゆうぞう	I もり さとみ
J こうの よしき	K. おかむら はるな	L わたなべ としや
M. あさの ひかる	N. ほった じゅんこ	O うの しろう
P よしかわ あいこ	Q. すだ かずお	R. みずたに せいじ
S かわべ じゅんじ	T にしむら まき	

D. Find the followings as quickly as you can.

1. Ruth Santiago's birthday ( )
2. A person who is born on October 1 ( )
3. Patricia Vargas' age ( )
4. Names of those who come from Costa Rica ( )
5. Names of those who are sixteen years of age ( )
6. Name of the youngest person ( )
7. Name of the oldest person ( )
8. Names of those who are born in February, March, or April ( )

なまえ	くに	誕生日	とし
アントニオ　ドミンゲス	メキシコ	12月8日	16
テレサ　ロドリゲス	エクアドル	3月20日	14
カルロス　バルデス	チリ	8月15日	17
パトリシアン　バーガス	ベネズエラ	10月1日	15
マリア　ラミレス	コスタリカ	4月11日	16
サンドラ　ゴンザレス	メキシコ	6月29日	18
ホゼ　オルテガ	ベネズエラ	10月7日	18
アドルフォ　バスケス	エクアドル	9月10日	14
ルーズ　サンチアゴ	コスタリカ	2月4日	17
エレナ　グーズマン	チリ	5月27日	16

Scan It Part III: Checking the References

E. Do the following descriptions include the reference to information listed below? Scan them and find out as quickly as possible.

1. Reference to an event

今日ジムでベークセールをします。時間は4時から6時までです。目的はユニセフのチャリティーのためです。みなさん、来てください。

2. Reference to means of transportation

わたしはあさ6時におきます。6時半に朝ご飯を食べます。トーストとコーヒーです。ときどき、フルーツを食べます。7時15分に学校へ行きます。妹とバスで学校に行きます。8時からクラスがあります。

3. Reference to weather

わたしの出身はテキサスです。テキサスはとても大きいです。私のうちはヒューストンです。ヒューストンにはナサ（NASA）があります。趣味はスポーツです。サッカーとバレーボールが好きです。ときどき、ゴルフをします。テキサスは暑いから、スキーはできません。

Scan It Part IV: Within Limited Time

F. Scan the following school club article within 30 seconds and describe what kind of club "The Lincoln Club" is.

私たちの学校にはユニークなクラブがたくさんあります。例えば、ハロウィーンクラブはパーティーのコスチュームをデザインするクラブで、秋と冬と春にコスチュームコンテストやファッションショーを計画します。エコアクションは環境について考えるクラブで、毎年「エコフェスト」という大きい行事を計画します。それから、リンカーンクラブは政治について考えるクラブで、政治がテーマのスピーチコンテストやディベートを計画します。

例えば：for example　計画：plan　環境：environment　行事：events　政治：politics　考える：think

G. Scan the following summer vacation story within 30 seconds and find what kind of summer vacation she had?

私の夏休みは最高の夏休みでした。ユニークな夏をすごしました。ニューヨークフィルハモニックと一緒にアジアのいろいろなところに行きました。まず、最初に日本に行きました。そこで、コンサートを五つしました。コンサートの後、日本のおいしい料理もたべました。それから、中国に行きました。そこでも、コンサートをしました。また、中国では万里の長城にも行きました。その後、タイに行きました。タイでもコンサートをして、面白かったです。辛いタイ料理もたくさん食べました。

万里の長城：the Great Wall　　辛い：hot

Scan It Part V: Finding the Mistakes

H. Scan the followings and find the mistakes.

私の冬休みは最高でした。よくスキーに行きました。12月26日から28日までニューハンプシャーでスキーをしました。すきー場は雪がたくさんありましたが、あまり寒くありませんでした。だから、すべりやすかったです。29日から31日までスケートのキャンプに行きました。このきゃんぷはバーモントでありました。そして、1月2日から4日まで家族とコロラドでスキーをしました。私はすきーが大好きです。だから、最高の冬休みでした。

私はインド人です。私の出身はシアトルです。シアトルはとても住みやすい町です。私のうちのそばにセーフコフィールドがあいます。それは、シアトルの野球とフットボールの球場です。
いちろはシアトルの野球選手です。でも、シアトルは冬はあめがよくふります。だから、すこし、さみです。シカゴよりあたいです。それから、夏はインドとほど暑くありません。

野球：baseball　球場：baseball stadium　選手：player

1.5 Mechanics 組立て

Preparation for Speech III
スピーチの準備 III

Objectives

Draft the ending part of the speech.
Indicate one's wishes and desires.
Revise and edit the draft.

Overview

This section focuses on writing a draft for the ending part of your speech, which consists of expression of your wishes and a final greeting. First you will learn how to indicate what you want or wish to do. Then you will create the ending part.

8	**End**	終わり
1	Indicating what one wants to do	願望の表現
2	Wishes and greeting	学年始めの抱負と終わりの挨拶
3	Preparing a draft	ドラフト作り
9	**Revise and edit speech**	スピーチの推敲と編集をします
1	Revising	推敲
2	Editing	編集

8 **End** 終わり

1 **Indicating what we want to do** 願望の表現

ノート: Indicating what we want to do

〜たいです

Verb Stem (Pre-ます form) + たい

By simply replacing 〜ます with 〜たい, you can obtain the form corresponding to "want to do" in English. For example, たべたい means "want to eat" and いきたい means "want to go." 〜たい represents the plain style by itself and です must be attached to make it polite.

来年日本へ行きたいです。   I want to go to Japan next year.

おいしいてんぷらが食べたいです。   I want to eat delicious *tempura*.

The particle が is often used in place of を to mark the direct object of 〜たい. Both てんぷらがたべたい and てんぷらをたべたい are possible but the former is more effective in conveying the speaker's urge than the latter.

As you can see from the examples below, 〜たい changes forms in the same manner as い-adjectives. It should be noted that the particle は is often used in place of を and が in the negative construction.

コーヒーを飲みたくありません。   I don't want to drink coffee.

コーヒーは飲みたくないです。   I don't want to drink coffee.

コーヒーを飲みたかったです。   I wanted to drink coffee.

A. Circle the correct one. 正しいものを○で囲みましょう。

1. コーヒーが (a. 飲みいたいです   b. 飲みたいです   c. 飲みたいます)。

2. 中国語を (a. 話たいです   b. 話したいです   c. 話しましたいです)。

3. どこに (a. 行きたい   b. 行きます   c. 行きいたい) ですか。

4. 何時に (a. 寝たいます   b. 寝たい   c. 寝またい) ですか。

5. 日本の映画が (a. 見たいい   b. 見いたい   c. 見たい) ですね。

6. 五時に (a. 起きたいじゃ   b. 起きたく   c. 起きたいく) ありません。

B. Express the following both in ～たいです and in ～たくありません.

<ruby>文<rt>ぶん</rt></ruby>を<ruby>作<rt>つく</rt></ruby>ってください。

 EX.
 1.
 2.
 3.
 4.

<ruby>例<rt></rt></ruby> (Example)

コーラが<ruby>飲<rt>の</rt></ruby>みたいです。

コーラを<ruby>飲<rt>の</rt></ruby>みたくありません。

 5.
 6.

C. Group Work - Break up into groups of three.

グループワークです。<ruby>三人<rt>さんにん</rt></ruby>のグループになってください。

Objective:

Practice converting ～ます to ～たいです and ～ません to ～たくありません.

Activities:

Repeat the following sequence six times by using six different verbs. Practice until you can do this group task smoothly and without any mistakes. Share your fruits of labor with the rest of the class. Your teacher may select the winning group and may even give you a prize!

1.	One person says a verb in the ます form.	<ruby>見<rt>み</rt></ruby>ます
2.	The person sitting to her right converts it to ～たいです.	<ruby>見<rt>み</rt></ruby>たいです
3.	The person sitting to his right says ～ません.	<ruby>見<rt>み</rt></ruby>ません
4.	The first person converts it to ～たくありません.	<ruby>見<rt>み</rt></ruby>たくありません

Variation:

Each group may prepare a list of six verbs written in English for another group to make the task more challenging.

ノート: Asking "what kind of-?" question

どんな〜

どんな is used to make questions equivalent to "what kind of-?" or "what type of-?" in English. It may also be used to ask for further description of something.

A: 科学の先生はだれですか。 Who is your science teacher?

B: キム先生です。 Ms. Kim.

A: どんな先生ですか。 What kind of teacher is she?

B 厳しい先生です。 She is a strict teacher.

でも、とてもいい先生です。 But she is also a very good teacher.

D. Practice asking someone about the following person or movie by using どんな **and responding to the questions by using a few of the adjectives on the list.**

会話の練習をしましょう。

EX.
おんがくのせんせい/せんせい

1.
にほんごのせんせい/せんせい

2.
テニスのコーチ/コーチ

3.
七人のさむらい/えいが

Descriptive Words
げんき（な）
やさしい
きびしい
すてき（な）
まじめ（な）
おもしろい
つまらない
たのしい

会話の例 (Sample Dialogue)

A: 音楽の先生はどんな先生ですか。

B: あのう、元気な先生です。それから、まじめな先生です。

E. Group Work - Break up into groups of three.

グループワークです。三人のグループになってください。

Objective:

Practice asking for descriptions of someone or something.

Activities:

Take turns and ask each other questions using どんな. You should be asking about someone or something you know little about. For example, you may ask about a teacher you have never had, if you think others in your group are taking her class or have taken it before. Take notes as you hear their descriptions and report your findings to the class.

会話の例 (Sample Dialogue)

A: スミス先生はどんな先生ですか。

B: あのう、元気な先生です。それから、厳しい先生です。

報告の例 (Sample Report)

リンダさんによると、スミス先生は元気な先生です。それから、厳しい先生です。

~によると means "according to -" and it is used to identify the source of information that is about to be given.

F. Find out your classmates' tastes and preferences.

好みのアンケートです。クラスメートに聞きましょう。

Preparation

Go over the following list. Each column should have a category word and its five subcategory words. Complete the columns for おんがく and りょうり. Avoid using words that refer to a specific product, such as the title of a song. You may draw relevant pictures as well.

音楽	映画	料理	デザート
クラシック	ホラー	イタリア料理	ケーキ
	コメディー	メキシコ料理	クッキー
	ロマンス	にほん料理	くだもの
	アクション		アイスクリーム
	ＳＦ（エスエフ）		パイ

Practice

Practice asking questions such as those below. Use 聞きます (to listen) for 音楽.

質問の例 (Sample Questions)

1. 今、どんな音楽が聞きたいですか。

What sort of music do you want to listen to now?

2. 今、どんな料理が食べたいですか。

What sort of dish do you want to eat now?

73

Interview

Go ask your classmates and find out their preferences in each of the five categories. Make sure to show your list to them during the interview so that they may respond by using one of the subcategory words you have prepared. アンケート in the sample dialogue below means "survey" or "questionnaire." このみ means "preference" or "inclinations."

会話の例 (Sample Dialogue)

A: あのう、ちょっと聞いてもいいですか。好みのアンケートです。

B: ええ、いいですよ。

A: ええと、今、どんな音楽が聞きたいですか。

B: そうですねえ。ジャズが聞きたいです。

A: ジャズですね。じゃ、今、どんな映画が見たいですか。

B: 映画ですか。ええと、アクション映画が見たいです。

A: ああ、そうですか。それから、今、どんな料理が食べたいですか。

B: イタリア料理です。　　A: イタリア料理ですね。じゃ、

continued.

Report:

List the three most popular answers in each category and report the results to the class.

おんがく	えいが	りょうり	デザート

報告の例 (Sample Report)

音楽はジャズが一番です。クラシックが二番です。

そして、ロックが三番です。

2 **Wishes and a greeting**　　<ruby>学年始<rt>がくねんはじ</rt></ruby>めの<ruby>抱負<rt>ほうふ</rt></ruby>と<ruby>終<rt>お</rt></ruby>わりの<ruby>挨拶<rt>あいさつ</rt></ruby>

A. Check the contents of the "end" part of your speech.

「<ruby>終<rt>お</rt></ruby>わり」の<ruby>部分<rt>ぶぶん</rt></ruby>の<ruby>内容<rt>ないよう</rt></ruby>を<ruby>確認<rt>かくにん</rt></ruby>しましょう。

As you know, the "end" part of your speech consists of "wishes" and a "greeting." More specific information is given below. Keep this in mind before you proceed.

| おわり | <ruby>願<rt>ねが</rt></ruby>いごと　WISHES | General wishes
Wishes specific to learning Japanese

Asking for support to realize the wishes
specific to learning Japanese |
| | あいさつ　GREETING | Closing words |

B. Think about what you want to do or may strive to do during this school year and make a wish list. Then choose one or two of the most important ones from the list. If you have wishes specific to your learning of Japanese, set them aside at this time.

<ruby>願<rt>ねが</rt></ruby>いごとのリストを<ruby>作<rt>つく</rt></ruby>りましょう。

たくさん<ruby>映画<rt>えいが</rt></ruby>が<ruby>見<rt>み</rt></ruby>たい
たくさん<ruby>本<rt>ほん</rt></ruby>が<ruby>読<rt>よ</rt></ruby>みたい
たくさん<ruby>友達<rt>ともだち</rt></ruby>を<ruby>作<rt>つく</rt></ruby>りたい
<ruby>毎朝<rt>まいあさ</rt></ruby><ruby>五時<rt>ごじ</rt></ruby>に<ruby>起<rt>お</rt></ruby>きたい・・・

たくさん＝
many, a lot

たくさん<ruby>本<rt>ほん</rt></ruby>が<ruby>読<rt>よ</rt></ruby>みたい
<ruby>毎朝<rt>まいあさ</rt></ruby><ruby>五時<rt>ごじ</rt></ruby>に<ruby>起<rt>お</rt></ruby>きたい

ノート：Expressing desire for improvement

Ｘが もっとじょうずになりたい

じょうず is a な adjective meaning "skillful' or "proficient" and なりたい means "want to become." もっと means "more" and the entire construction means "want to become more skillful/proficient in X."

サッカーがもっとじょうずになりたいです。
I want to become more skillful in soccer.

テニスがもっとじょうずになりたいですか。
Do you want to become more skillful in tennis?

C. Practice the following conversation, substituting the underlined part with another sport.

会話を練習しましょう。
かいわ　れんしゅう

会話の例 (Sample Dialogue)

B lost a game and came across A who did not see the game.	A: テニスの試合はどうでしたか。
	B: また、負けました。　　　まける to lose
	A: そうですか、残念でしたね。
	B: ええ、もっとじょうずになりたいです。

D. The construction Ｘがもっとじょうずになりたいです is useful in stating your desire to make an improvement with respect to the study of Japanese. Do the following substitution exercise and then think about what you want to say in your speech in this respect.

文を作りましょう。
ぶん　つく

例 (Example)

日本語の会話がもっとじょうずになりたいです。
かいわ

EX. 日本語の会話 (conversation)
かいわ

1. 日本語の発音 (pronunciation)
はつおん

2. 日本語のスピーチ

3. 日本語の発表 (presentation)
はっぴょう

4. 漢字
かんじ

5. 日本語

3 Preparing a draft　　　　　　　ドラフト作^{づく}り

ノート: Useful expressions to ask for support and cooperation

おうえん　　きょうりょく
応援・協力

Realization of one's wishes often requires other people's support and cooperation. It is appropriate to ask your classmates for support and cooperation in connection with your wishes regarding learning Japanese. The following expressions will be useful in this respect.

おうえん
応援してください。
Please support/root for me.

きょうりょく
協力してください。
Please help me and cooperate with me.

A. Prepare a draft of the ending part of your speech by replacing the underlined parts with your own words. しんがっき **means "new academic term."**

スピーチの終^おわりの部分^{ぶぶん}を作^{つく}りましょう。

おわり	願^{ねが}いごと WISHES	General wishes	新学期^{しんがっき}です。これからは、もっと たくさん本^{ほん}が読^よみたいです。 それから、毎朝五時^{まいあさ}に起^おきたいです。
		Wishes specific to learning Japanese	そして、日本語のスピーチが もっと上手^{じょうず}になりたいです。
	あいさつ GREETING	Asking for support	皆^{みな}さん、応援^{おうえん}してください。
		Closing words	よろしくお願^{ねが}いします。

77

9 Revise and edit speech　　　スピーチの推敲と編集をします

1 Revising　　　推敲

Put together all the drafts you have written for your speech and read it from beginning to end. Check if "connectors" such as それから and でも are effectively used and make any adjustments to make your speech flow better. Read the following note for information about some useful connectors. Finally, make sure that your speech is in good order and reorganize sentences or paragraphs as necessary.

ノート: "Connectors"

"Connectors" such as those below are useful in making your speech flow. They should sound familiar to you since they were introduced in *Haruichiban*.

それから	"and then" "after that" それから is useful when stating something in sequence or making some additional statements.
そして	"and then" "after that" "having done all that" そして is similar to それから but it carries the implication of "having done all that." Because of this そして is often used before the final statement in the sequence that may serve as a wrap-up and conclusion.
でも	" but" "however" でも is used to mean "but" or "however," but it should be placed in the beginning of a sentence.

---

2 Editing　　　編集

Self-editing

Peer-editing

Teacher-editing

Final Check

Check the following: Spelling, punctuation, grammar, sentence structure, consistent verb tense, and sentence endings. Do this by yourself first and then exchange your written speech with your classmates. Go over their speech and make note of any corrections you want to suggest to them. Your teacher will also read your speech and make any suggestions he or she may have. Take another look at your speech for a final check at the end.

Recognition Kanji 4: 認識漢字 4

答える
to answer

先月
last month

今月
this month

来月
next month

ただ
正しい
correct

せんしゅう
先週
last week

こんしゅう
今週
this week

らいしゅう
来週
next week

日　月　火　水　木　金　土

New Kanji 3: 新出漢字 3
しんしゅつかんじ

次
ON: シ、ジ　　　　　　　　**KUN:** つ(ぎ)
次:つぎ next　　　　　次回:じかい next time
丶 冫 ソ 沪 次 次

始
ON: シ　　　　　　　　　**KUN:** はじ(める)、はじ(まる)
始める:はじめる start　　開始:かいし start
く 女 女 如 始 始 始 始

春
ON: シュン　　　　　　　**KUN:** はる
春:はる spring　　　　　春休み:はるやすみ spring vacation
一 二 三 丰 夫 表 春 春 春

夏
ON: カ　　　　　　　　　**KUN:** なつ
夏:なつ summer　　　　夏休み:なつやすみ summer vacation
一 一 ア 百 百 百 百 戸 夏 夏

秋
ON: シュウ　　　　　　　**KUN:** あき
秋:あき fall
一 二 千 千 禾 禾 秒 秋 秋

冬
ON: トウ　　　　　　　　**KUN:** ふゆ
冬:ふゆ winter　　　　　冬休み:ふゆやすみ winter vacation
ノ ク タ 冬 冬

今
ON: コン、キョ　　　　　　**KUN:** いま
今:いま now　　　　　　今月:こんげつ this month　今日:きょう today
ノ 人 今 今

住
ON: ジュウ　　　　　　　**KUN:** す(む)
住む:すむ live, reside
ノ イ イ 仁 住 住 住 住

Reading 2:
読み物 2

Summer Vacation Diary:
夏休みの日記

1. こんにちは、海野恵です。これは私の今年の夏休みの7月20日からの日記です。私はこの夏次の場所に行きました。その場所を紹介します。

紹介 : introduce

2. 7月20日は海の日でした。だから、友達と江ノ島のある湘南海岸に行きました。たくさんの若者が来ていました。みんなビーチバレーやサーフィンをしていました。私達も少し泳ぎました。その後、ビーチバレーをしました。とても楽しい一日でした。

湘南海岸: place name　若者: young man

3. 7月22日にアメリカからマイク君が来ました。「浅草に行って日本の刀を買いたい。」と言っていました。浅草にはたくさんの小さい店があります。そこでは、日本の刀やきれいな折り紙や面白いゲームが売っています。マイク君は刀やゲームが大好きだと思います。

浅草: place name　刀 ; sward　思う; think

A. Scan the following words. 次の文をスキャンして、以下の言葉を探しなさい。

1. Scan the first and second descriptions, quickly find the following words and circle them.

    a. 今年　　b. 場所　　c. 海　　d. 夏　　e. 若者　　f. サーフィン

2. Scan the third description, quickly find the following words and circle them.

    a. 浅草　　b. 折り紙　　c. ゲーム　　d. 刀　　e. 店

B. Does the previous diary include the reference to information listed below? Scan them and find out as quickly as possible. スキャンして適切な言葉を選んでください。

1. Go over the first section and quickly find out where the subsequent story came from.
   Kei's letter, Kei's diary, Kei's speech, Kei's presentation

2. Go over the first section and quickly find out what Kei will be talking primarily about in her subsequent story.
   her profile, her friends, food, Japanese summer, places

3. Go over the second section and quickly list the activities that Kei did at the place where she went with her friends on that day.
   swimming and beach volleyball,   swimming and surfing,   surfing and beach volleyball

4. Go over the third section and quickly find out what Kei says about Asakusa has.
   arcade, movie theater, small shops, sword factory

C. After scanning the whole diary, choose which section fits to the most appropriate sum-up sentence given below?

前のページの文章をスキャンしてから、下の要点の文章に合うのはどれか1, 2, 3, NAから選んでください。

1. 恵さんの休みは友だちと買い物に行きました。　　(1, 2, 3, NA)
2. 恵さんの学校は海をきれいにしました。　　(1, 2, 3, NA)
3. 恵さんは夏休みに海に行ってあそびました。　　(1, 2, 3, NA)
4. 恵さんは7月20日から日記を書きました。　　(1, 2, 3, NA)
5. 恵さんは学校でマイク君とべんきょうしました。　(1, 2, 3, NA)

D. Link three items in the vocabulary list below.
線を結んで、漢字／語彙のリストを完成させてください。

単語	読み	意味
Ex. 学校 ⟷	がっこう ⟷	school
1. 今年	たのしい	sell
2. 夏休み	ばしょ	buy
3. 場所	かう	place
4. 店	ことし	summer vacation
5. 買う	なつやすみ	shop
6. 楽しい	うる	fun
7. 売る	みせ	this year

E. Check whether the following statements are true or false.
内容の正しいものを選びなさい。

1. 私は海で泳ぎました。　　　　　　　　　　　　（本当、嘘）

83

2. 若者が海に少しいました。　　　　　　　　　　　　　　　　　　　（本当、嘘）

3. マイク君はアニメが大好きだ。　　　　　　　　　　　　　　　　　（本当、嘘）

4. 浅草にたくさん電気屋がある。　　　　　　　　　　　　　　　　　（本当、嘘）

5. マイク君は日本的な所へ行きたい。　　　　　　　　　　　　　　　（本当、嘘）

6. マイク君は日本の刀を買った。　　　　　　　　　　　　　　　　　（本当、嘘）

F. Form a group and answer the guided questions in Japanese.

グループで日本語で答えてください。

1. 海野さんは7月20日にどこに行きましたか。

2. 7月20日は何の日ですか。

3. 湘南海岸はどんな所だと思いますか。

4. 浅草では何を買いましたか。

5. 湘南海岸と浅草を比べてみて、どう思いますか。

---

1. こんにちは、海野　恵です。これは私の今年の夏休みの7月20日からの日記です。私はこの夏次の場所に行きました。その場所を紹介します。

今年：this year　　日記：diary　　次：next　　場所：place　　紹介：introduce

2. 7月20日は海の日でした。だから、友達と海がきれいな湘南海岸に行きました。たくさんの若者が来ていました。みんなビーチバレーやサーフィンをしていました。私達も少し泳ぎました。その後、ビーチバレーをしました。とても楽しい一日でした。

海の日：Marine Day (National holiday)　　湘南海岸：name of sea shore in Japan
若者：young man　　　　　ビーチバレー：beach volleyball　　サーフィン：surfing
その後：afterward

3. 7月22日にアメリカからマイク君が来ました。「浅草に行って日本の刀を買いたい。」と言っていました。浅草にはたくさんの小さい店があります。そこでは、日本の刀やきれいな折り紙や面白いが売っています。マイク君は刀やゲームが大好きだと思います。

浅草：name of place　　刀：sword　　と言う：someone says that...　　アニメ：animation
売る：sell　　思います：I think that...

Additional Kanji 1: 追加漢字 1

冬休み	ふゆやすみ、winter vacation 冬：**ON:**トウ　　**KUN:**ふゆ 　　　　　　　　　　　　　　休：**ON:**キュウ　**KUN:**やす(み) 冬休みはどうでしたか。　How was your winter vacation?
折り紙	おりがみ、 origami　　折：**ON:**セツ　　**KUN:**お(る) 　　　　　　　　　　　紙：**ON:**シ　　　**KUN:**かみ 折り紙はどうでしたか。　How was your origami?
紹介	しょうかい、introduce　紹：**ON:**ショウ　**KUN:**まね(く) 　　　　　　　　　　　介：**ON:**カイ　　**KUN:**ー 家族を紹介します。　I introduce my family.
刀	かたな、sword　　　　刀：**ON:**トウ　　**KUN:**かたな その刀を買いたい。　I want to buy a sword.
野球	やきゅう、 baseball　　野：**ON:**ヤ　　　**KUN:**の 　　　　　　　　　　　球：**ON:**キュウ　**KUN:**たま 野球場はどこですか。　Where is the baseball studium?
出身	しゅっしん、birthplace 出：**ON:**シュツ　**KUN:**で(る)、だ(す) 　　　　　　　　　　　身：**ON:**シン　　**KUN:**み ご出身はどこですか。　Where is your birthplace?
最高	さいこう、 best/super　最：**ON:**サイ　　**KUN:**もっと(も) 　　　　　　　　　　　高：**ON:**コウ　　**KUN:**たか(い) 夏休みは最高でした。　My summer vacation was supper.
趣味	しゅみ、hobby　　　　趣：**ON:**シュ　　**KUN:**おもむ(き) 　　　　　　　　　　　味：**ON:**ミ　　　**KUN:**あじ 趣味はなんですか。　What is your hobby?
若者	わかもの、 young man　若：**ON:**ジャク　**KUN:**わか(い) 　　　　　　　　　　　者：**ON:**シャ　　**KUN:**もの この若者は何をしてますか。　What is this young man doing?

1.6 Mechanics 組立て
Speech Practice
スピーチの練習

Objectives

Make a speech note based on your drafts.
Practice your speech individually as well as with your classmates.
Practice giving comments and suggestions after listening to other people's speeches.
Practice hosting speeches.

Overview

You will have plenty of opportunities to practice your speech and improve your public speaking skills. During the course you will be practicing with your classmates and exchanging comments and suggestions with respect to each other's speeches. In fact, this is a great opportunity for cooperation and collaboration. You will not be relying much on your drafts throughout the practice, but you will be using a speech note, a sort of outline with keywords and cues, that you will make beforehand. When you give your speech in Virtual Reality, you will follow a format similar to a speech-contest in which you will be introduced by a host. You will do some preparatory work in this regard as well.

| **10** Make a speech note | スピーチ構成メモを作ります |

| **11** Review connectors | 接続語の復習をします |

| **12** Practice speech | スピーチの練習をします |

| **1** Giving and soliciting feedback | フィードバック |

| **2** Cooperative speech practice | スピーチの共同練習 |

| **13** Practice hosting speeches | 司会の練習をします |

10 **Make a speech note**　　　スピーチ構成メモを作ります

Although you may go over your speech script beforehand, you will not be using it during your speech. Instead you will use the speech note that you are about to make based on your script. This will prevent you from overly relying on the written text and will enable you to successfully "deliver" your speech to the audience.

A. Make a speech note by filling in the keywords and expressions in your speech.

スピーチ構成メモを作りましょう。

はじめ	あいさつと名前

なか

学校
去年の学校
今年の学校
学年と年
一緒に来る人
交通
うち

プロフィール
出身
国籍
言葉
趣味

夏休み　(最高, まあまあ, 最低)

おわり	願いごと **WISH**
	あいさつ

<small>せつぞくご　ふくしゅう</small>

ノート: "Hesitation sounds" and additional connectors

In the previous section you reviewed some useful connectors such as それから, そして and でも. They can be equally useful in speaking and writing. The ones that will be reviewed at this time are more colloquial and will be helpful during your speech.

ええと	"Let's see..." "Well.." ええと is used to avoid an awkward pause or silence while the speaker is recalling or thinking what should be said next. It is also used when you start speaking in order to soften the tone of your speech.
あのう	"Let's see..." "Well.." あのう is used interchangeably with ええと, although it sounds more formal than ええと. あのう is also used to draw someone's attention. Often called "hesitation sounds" or "hesitation noises," both ええと and あのう are used only in speaking.
じゃ	"Well then" "If that's the case" じゃ is used to develop a conversation based on what has been said and relates the current topic to what follows. It is also used to wrap up a conversation or a monologue. じゃ is used only in speaking.
だから	"That is why" "Therefore" だから is the Japanese equivalent of "that is why," "so," and "therefore." It is usually used at the beginning of a sentence.
ええと、あのう	ええと and あのう may be used consecutively depending upon the length of hesitation.
あのう、それから	あのう or ええと may be used with それから, でも, etc.

A. Choose and circle an appropriate connector word for each parenthesis. Choose an X if you cannot find any applicable connector.

<small>てきとう　せつぞくご　えら</small>
適当な接続語を選んでください。

1.
> こんにちは。ジェニー・キムです。どうぞよろしく。去年
> の学校はユニオン中学でした。今年の学校はワシントン高校
> です。**(でも、ええと、じゃ)** 高校1年生です。

2.
私は16才です。いつも弟と歩いて学校に来ます。
(あのう、じゃ、X) うちはマンチェスターです。

3.
趣味は映画です。**(でも、だから、それから)** よく映画館へ
行きます。**(じゃ、だから、それから)** スポーツも好きです。

4.
私の夏休みは最高でした。**(でも、それから、X)** ハワイと
メキシコに行きました。**(でも、そして、じゃ)** おいしい食べ
物をたくさん食べました。

5.
今年はたくさん科学の本が読みたいです。**(でも、だから、
それから)** 日本語の発表がもっと上手になりたいです。皆さ
ん、応援してください。

6.
おはようございます。ケビン・フェリスです。どうぞよろ
しく。去年の学校はシーサイドアカデミーでした。**(そして、
じゃ)** 今年の学校もシーサイドアカデミーです。

7.
日本語の会話がもっと上手になりたいです。皆さん、協力
してください。よろしくお願いします。**(でも、それから、
じゃ)** これでスピーチを終わります。

1 **Exchanging feedback**　　　　　　フィードバック

You will be practicing your speech individually, in pairs or in groups of three. When working with others, you will help each other by exchanging feedback in Japanese. To facilitate such an exchange, we will begin by learning the negative construction of い adjectives.

ノート: Negative past form of い adjectives

> ## さむくありませんでした
> ## さむくなかった(です)

The negative past form of い adjectives is obtained by either just adding でした to ～くありません or replacing ～くない (です) with ～くなかった (です).

寒^{さむ}くありません→寒^{さむ}くありませんでした

寒^{さむ}くない(です)→寒^{さむ}くなかった(です)　　　　(formal/polite)

Q: ダンスは楽^{たの}しかったですか。　　　　Was the dance fun?

A: あまり、楽^{たの}しくありませんでした。　　It wasn't so much fun.

Q: 映画^{えいが}はよかったですか?　　　　　Was the movie good?

A: ぜんぜん、よくありませんでした。　No, it wasn't good at all.

Note that the negative past form of いいです is よくありませんでした or よくなかったです. いくありませんでした and いくなかったです do not occur.

ぜんぜん、難^{むずか}しくなかった。

テスト、難^{むずか}しかった?

A. Practice the negative past form of い adjectives by doing the following substitution exercise.

れんしゅう
練習しましょう。

EX. 映画、面白い

1. カメラ、高い
2. テスト、やさしい
3. コンサート、いい
4. 先生、厳しい
5. スピーチ、長い
6. 昨日、蒸し暑い
7. 宿題、やさしい

会話の例 A (Sample Dialogue A: formal)

EX. A: 映画はどうでしたか。

B: とても、面白かったです。

C: そうですか。あまり、面白くありませんでしたよ。

D: ええ。ぜんぜん、面白くなかったです。

会話の例 B (Sample Dialogue B: informal)

EX. A: 映画、どうだった。

B: とても、面白かった。

C: え、あまり、面白くなかったよ。

D: うん。ぜんぜん、面白くなかった。

ノート: Negative past form of な-adjectives

しずかじゃありませんでした
しずかじゃなかった(です)

The negative past form of な adjectives is obtained by either just adding でした to 〜じゃあります せん or replacing 〜じゃない (です) with 〜じゃなかった (です).

きれいじゃありません → きれいじゃありませんでした

きれいじゃない (です) → きれいじゃなかった (です)

Q: プールの水はきれいでしたか。   Was the water in the pool clean?

A: あまり、きれいじゃありませんでした。   It wasn't very clean.

It should be noted that these formulas are applicable to nouns as well.

数学_{すうがく}のテストは火曜日_{かようび}じゃありませんでした。

Our math test wasn't on Tuesday (after all).

B. Complete the following and share it with the class.   クラスで発表_{はっぴょう}しましょう。

私は小学生の時_{わたし しょうがくせい とき}、(1)＿＿＿＿＿＿＿が好_すきでした。でも、

(2)＿＿＿＿＿＿＿は好きじゃありませんでした。科目_{かもく}は

(3)＿＿＿＿＿＿が得意_{とくい}でした。でも、(4)＿＿＿＿＿＿は得意じゃありませんでした。性格_{せいかく}は(5)＿＿＿＿＿＿でした。でも、あまり、(6)＿＿＿＿＿＿じゃありませんでした。

小学生の時_{しょうがくせい とき}：my elementary school student days

性格_{せいかく}：personality

(1) something you liked

(2) something you didn't like

(3) your strong subject

(4) your weak subject

(5) characteristic describing yourself (な adj.)

(6) characteristic that does not describe you (な adj.)

C. Pair Work - Find a partner.

ペアワークです。相手を見つけてください。

Objective:

Become accustomed to making various forms of adjectives.

Procedure:

1. One of the pair will say an adjective in the nonpast affirmative form plus です. Use both
   い and な adjectives.
2. His or her partner will give its nonpast negative, past affirmative and past negative in
   that order.
3. Take turns until both members of the pair can say all forms smoothly and accurately for
   three consecutive times.
4. Time permitting, change your partner and continue to practice.

Variation:

One of the pair (A) will say an
adjective in English and point
to one of the four zones. His or
her partner (B) will quickly give
the adjective in the appropriate
form. A points to another zone
and B responds accordingly.
Take turns and practice.

PAゾーン	**NA**ゾーン
(Past Affirmative)	(Non-past Affirmative)
PNゾーン	**NN**ゾーン
(Past Negative)	(Non-past Negative)

D. Suggested additional work: "Can you recall?" 思い出せますか。

Procedure:

1. Bring a picture that contains objects you can describe with adjectives. You may get
   your picture from a print or create it by yourself.
2. Prepare five "yes-no" questions by using the past affirmative form of adjectives. They
   will be used to test the memory of someone who has seen your picture very briefly.
3. Go around the class and show your picture to a classmate for several seconds.

E. Go over the following and get ready to exchange feedback.

<ruby>質問<rt>しつもん</rt></ruby>と<ruby>答<rt>こた</rt></ruby>えの<ruby>練習<rt>れんしゅう</rt></ruby>をしましょう。

<ruby>質問<rt>しつもん</rt></ruby>と<ruby>答<rt>こた</rt></ruby>えの<ruby>例<rt>れい</rt></ruby>1	Question and its possible response 1

<ruby>内容<rt>ないよう</rt></ruby>はよくわかりましたか。

Did you understand the content well?

とてもよくわかりました。 (very well)

だいたいわかりました。 (for the most part)

あまりよくわかりませんでした。
(not so well)

ぜんぜんわかりませんでした。
(not at all)

<ruby>質問<rt>しつもん</rt></ruby>と<ruby>答<rt>こた</rt></ruby>えの<ruby>例<rt>れい</rt></ruby>2	Question and its possible response 2

<ruby>速<rt>はや</rt></ruby>かったですか。

Was my speech (too) fast?

とても<ruby>速<rt>はや</rt></ruby>かったです。 (very fast)

<ruby>少<rt>すこ</rt></ruby>し<ruby>速<rt>はや</rt></ruby>かったです。 (a bit fast)

<ruby>時々<rt>ときどき</rt></ruby><ruby>速<rt>はや</rt></ruby>かったです。 (sometimes)

ちょうどよかったです。 (just about right)

あまり<ruby>速<rt>はや</rt></ruby>くありませんでした。
(wasn't very fast)

ぜんぜん<ruby>速<rt>はや</rt></ruby>くありませんでした。
(wasn't fast at all)

<ruby>質問<rt>しつもん</rt></ruby>と<ruby>答<rt>こた</rt></ruby>えの<ruby>例<rt>れい</rt></ruby>3	Question and its possible response 3

スムーズでしたか。

Was my speech smooth?

とてもスムーズでした。 (very smooth)

だいたいスムーズでした。 (mostly smooth)

あまりスムーズじゃありませんでした。
(not very smooth)

ぜんぜんスムーズじゃありませんでした。
(wasn't smooth at all)

質問と答えの例4

Question and its possible response 4

声は大きかったですか。

Did I speak loud enough?

とても大きかったです。 (very loud)

だいたい大きかったです。
(for the most part)

ちょうどよかったです。 (just about right)

あまり大きくありませんでした。
(wasn't too loud)

ぜんぜん大きくありませんでした。
(wasn't loud at all)

質問と答えの例5

Question and its possible response 5

間違えましたか。

Did I make mistakes?

よく間違えました。 (often)

時々間違えました。 (sometimes)

あまり間違えませんでした。
(didn't make many mistakes)

ぜんぜん間違えませんでした。
(didn't make any mistakes)

質問と答えの例6

Question and its possible response 6

姿勢はよかったですか。

Did I have good posture?

とてもよかったです。 (very good)

だいたいよかったです。
(for the most part)

あまりよくありませんでした。
(wasn't too good)

ぜんぜんよくありませんでした。
(wasn't good at all)

Here are some more useful expressions that will be helpful when exchanging feedback. For example, you may elaborate your responses to the questions you just practiced by using one of the expressions under "SPECIFIC SUGGESTIONS" below.

ノート: Useful comments and suggestions upon hearing someone's speech

A. GENERAL COMMENTS

1. よくできました。   Well done.
2. たいへんよくできました。   Very well done.
3. すばらしかったです。   Wonderful.
4. まあまあでした。   So-so.

B. SPECIFIC SUGGESTIONS

1. もっとはっきり話してください。   Speak more clearly, please.
2. もう少しはっきり話してください。   Speak a bit more clearly, please.
3. もう少し速く話してください。   Speak a bit faster, please.
4. もっとゆっくり話してください。   Speak slower, please.
5. もう少しスムーズに話してください。   Speak a bit more smoothly, please.
6. もっと大きい声で話してください。   Speak louder, please.
7. もう少し顔を上げてください。   Face the audience, please.
                                        (Lit. Lift your face a bit more, please.)
8. もう少し接続語を使ってください。   Use a few more connectors, please.

As you can see, もっと means "more" and もうすこし means "a little bit more." You may decide which one to use depending on the severity of the problem.

F. **What brief comment or suggestion will you give in the following situations?**

コメントや提案をしてください。

EX. The speaker's head was down most of the time.
もっと(or もう少し)顔を上げてください。

1. The speaker's voice was weak and you could not hear the speech well.
2. The speaker appeared to mumble and you could not hear the speech well as a result.

3. The speaker spoke too fast.
4. The speech was very well done.
5. It was a so-so speech.
6. The speech was a bit choppy.
7. The speech was well done.
8. The speaker could use more connectors.
9. The speaker spoke too slowly.
10. It was a wonderful speech.

G. Pretending that you have just finished listening to a speech, practice giving short comments and suggestions by replacing (1) below with a general comment, and (2) and (3) with other specific suggestions.

コメントと提案の練習をしましょう。

例 **(Example)**

(1) よくできました。でも、もう少し (2) はっきり話してください。
それから、(3) もう少し顔を上げてください。

H. Practice giving comments and suggestions through role play.

ロールプレイをしましょう。

Role A (Speaker)

Think about a few comments and suggestions you may want to draw from your partner. Stand up in front of him/her and give a 30-second speech about yourself or anything else you like. Deliver your speech in such a manner that you will successfully draw from your partner the comments and suggestions you thought about in the beginning. After hearing from him/her, tell him/her what comments and suggestions you were expecting.

Role B (Listener) & feedback giver

Your partner will deliver a 30-second speech. Listen carefully and give a few appropriate comments and suggestions at the conclusion of his/her speech in a format similar to the examples in the previous exercises. He or she will also tell you what comments and suggestions he or she was trying to draw from you.

97

2 Cooperative speech practice スピーチの共同 練習

It's time to practice your speech. It is important that you pay attention not only to the linguistic aspect of the speech, but also to its delivery.

A. Your practice will proceed according to the five stages. Read the explanation below and start your practice.

スピーチの練習を始めましょう。

Stage 1 (Individual Work)

Individually practice your speech. You may look at your speech note (and your draft if necessary), but reduce your dependency on it as you become more familiar with your speech.

Stage 2 (Pair Work)

Pair up with one of your classmates and exchange each other's notes. One will become a speaker and the other a monitor. As a speaker, you will deliver your speech right in front of your partner and then solicit your partner's feedback by asking him or her a few questions such as はやかったですか *(Was it fast?) and* しせいはよかったですか *(Did I have good posture?). As a monitor, you check the speaker's note while listening and offer any assistance he or she may need to complete the speech. For example, you may fill in a word or a phrase the speaker is having a hard time recalling or completing. Respond to your partner's questions and offer any additional comments and suggestions you may have. Switch roles after that. Conduct the entire process in Japanese as much as possible. Repeat this sequence a few more times with different partners. A sample dialogue between the speaker and the monitor is given below.*

A: 速かったですか。

B: ちょうどよかったです。
   でも、もう少しはっきり話してください。

A: はい。あのう、姿勢はよかったですか。

B: だいたいよかったです。
   でも、もう少し顔を上げてください。

A: あ、そうですか。 continued.

Stage 3 (Individual Work)

Practice your speech on your own again. This time make sure to take the comments that you have received into consideration. Record your speech digitally or on tape if possible.

Stage 4 (Trio Work)

Break up into groups of three. In your group, stand facing each other about 10 feet apart by forming a triangle. One person will make his or her speech while others listen. As a speaker, you will not only try to speak without seeing the note, but also make sure that you are "keeping in touch" with the audience by making occasional eye contact with both of the listeners. Repeat this sequence a few more times with different partners.

Stage 5 (Individual Work)

Practice your speech on your own one final time by taking the comments that you have received into consideration. Record your speech digitally or on tape if possible.

99

13 Practice hosting speeches

司会の練習をします
<small>しかい　れんしゅう</small>

In Virtual Reality you will be making a speech, one by one, and each speaker will be introduced by a host. There may be more than one host depending upon the number of speakers. The following exercise will help you serve as one of the hosts.

A. Read the note and study the expressions for introducing speakers. Then do the following exercise.

スピーカーを紹介してください。
<small>しょうかい</small>

ノート: Expressions to indicate an order

Expressions such as "first" "next" and "last" are useful when indicating sequential order. You will be using them in your next activity in which you will practice introducing speakers as a moderator.

最初のスピーカーはAさんです。
<small>さいしょ</small>
[Our first speaker is A *san*.]

次のスピーカーはBさんです。
<small>つぎ</small>
[Our next speaker is B *san*.]

最後のスピーカーはCさんです。
<small>さいご</small>
[Our last speaker is C *san*.]

1.

スピーカー
1	リサ・バーナム
2	ブライアン・タグチ
3	ペイジ・ジョーダン
4	ロバート・ウー

2.

スピーカー
1	ジェイ・マッカイ
2	フィリップ・チョー
3	ダナ・カーニー
4	リンダ・ジョンソン

最初のスピーカーは＿＿＿＿＿さんです。
<small>さいしょ</small>

次のスピーカーは＿＿＿＿＿さんです。
<small>つぎ</small>

次のスピーカーは＿＿＿＿＿さんです。

最後のスピーカーは＿＿＿＿＿さんです。
<small>さいご</small>

B. Practice introducing and thanking speakers by substituting the underlined parts with an appropriate greeting and the names of your classmates.

進行の練習をしましょう。
_{しんこう} _{れんしゅう}

始めのあいさつ   Opening greeting
_{はじ}

例 (Examples)

<u>こんにちは</u>。スピーチを始めましょう。
_{はじ}

スピーカーの紹介   Introduction of speakers
_{しょうかい}

例 (Examples)

Introducing the first speaker

最初のスピーカーは<u>A</u>さんです。じゃ、<u>A</u>さんどうぞ。
_{さいしょ}

Thanking the speaker

(After A's speech ends.)

ありがとうございました。

Introducing the next speaker

次のスピーカーは<u>B</u>さんです。<u>B</u>さんお願いします。
_{つぎ} _{ねが}

(After B's speech ends.)

<u>B</u>さん、ありがとうございました。

Introducing the next speaker who happens to be the moderator herself

次はわたしのスピーチです。聞いてください。
_き

(After her own speech, the moderator thanks the audience.)

Introducing the final speaker

最後のスピーカーは<u>C</u>さんです。<u>C</u>さんどうぞ。
_{さいご}

(After C's speech ends.)

ありがとうございました。

終わりのあいさつ   Closing greeting
_お

例 (Examples)

これでスピーチを終わります。
_お

New Kanji 4: 新出漢字 4

父

ON: フ **KUN:** ちち、(お)とう(さん)
父:ちち (one's own) father   お父さん:おとうさん father

ノ ハ グ 父

母

ON: ボ **KUN:** はは、(お)かあ(さん)
母:はは (one's own) mother   お母さん:おかあさん mother

ㄥ 口 口 母 母

兄

ON: キョウ、ケイ **KUN:** あに、(お)にい(さん)
兄:あに (one's own) older brother   お兄さん:おにいさん older brother

丨 冂 口 尸 兄

姉

ON: シ **KUN:** あね、(お)ねえ(さん)
姉:あね (one's own) older sister   お姉さん:おねえさん older sister

ㄑ 乄 女 女' 圹 圹 姉 姉

弟

ON: ダイ、テイ **KUN:** おとうと
弟:おとうと younger brother   兄弟:きょうだい siblings, brothers

丶 丷 丷 兰 肖 弟 弟

妹

ON: マイ **KUN:** いもうと
妹:いもうと younger sister   姉妹:しまい sisters

ㄑ 乄 女 女 奸 妹 妹 妹

私

ON: シ **KUN:** わたくし、わたし
私:わたし I (abbreviation of わたくし) 私:わたくし I

ㄧ 二 千 禾 禾 私 私

友

ON: ユウ **KUN:** とも
友:とも friend   友達:ともだち friends

一 ナ 方 友

Additional Kanji 2: 追加漢字 2
ついかかんじ

誕生日	たんじょうび、birthday　誕：**ON:**タン　　　　**KUN:**ー 生：**ON:**ジョウ、セイ **KUN:**うまれ(る) 誕生日が好きです。　I like my birthday.
例えば	たとえば、for example　例：**ON:**レイ　　**KUN:**たとえ(ば) 例えば、電車に乗っています。　For example, I am riding on train.
計画	けいかく、plan　　　　計：**ON:**ケイ　　　**KUN:**はか(る) 画：**ON:**ガ、カク **KUN:**えが(く) 新しい計画を作ります。　I am making new plan.
環境	かんきょう、environment　環：**ON:**カン　　**KUN:**たまき、わ 境：**ON:**キョウ **KUN:**さかい 環境にとてもいい。　It is great for the environment.
考える	かんがえる、think　　　　考：**ON:**コウ　　**KUN:**かんが(える) 考えることが多い。　I have so many thoughts.
発表	はっぴょう、presentation　発：**ON:**ハツ　　**KUN:**た(つ) 表：**ON:**ヒョウ **KUN:**おもて、あらわ(す) 発表をおこなう。　We make presentations.
売る	うる、sell　　　　　　　売：**ON:**バイ　　**KUN:**う(る) この本をたくさん売ることができるといいです 　　I hope you will be able to sell a great number of this book.
買う	かう、buy　　　　　　　買：**ON:**バイ　　**KUN:**か(う) 買うことにしますか。　Do you make up your mind to buy it?
成果	せいか、result　　　　　成：**ON:**セイ　　**KUN:**な(る) 果：**ON:**カ　　　**KUN:**は(て) 成果について話し合う。　We discuss the result.

FORM

1. Negative non-past form of い adjectives and な adjectives

～いです ⇒ ～くありません／くないです

For polite style, replace ～いです with either ～くありません or ～くないです. The latter sounds a bit stronger than ～くありません. For plain style just replace ～い with ～くない. Note that the negative form of いい (good) is よくない. いくない does not occur.

日本語は難しくありません。　　　Japanese language is not difficult.

天気はあまりよくありません。　　The weather isn't very good.

(な adjective)です ⇒ ～じゃありません／じゃないです

For polite style, replace ～です with either ～じゃありません or ～じゃないです. The latter sounds a bit stronger than ～じゃありません. For plain style just add ～じゃない.

この町は有名じゃありません。　　This town is not famous.

この町は静かじゃありません。　　The town isn't quiet.

2. Describing past states and conditions [1]

NOUN/な adj. ＋ です ⇒ NOUN/な adj. ＋ でした

～でした is the past tense of ～です.

田中さんは先生です/先生でした。　Ms. Tanaka is/was a teacher

リサさんは元気です/元気でした。　Lisa is/was healthy and spirited.

NOUN/な adj. ＋ じゃありません ⇒ NOUN/な adj. ＋ じゃありませんでした

For the negative, でした is added to じゃありません.

テストは木曜日じゃありませんでした。The test wasn't on Thursday.

3. Describing past states and conditions [2]

～い(です) ⇒ ～かった(です)

The past tense of い adjectives is obtained by replacing い with かった. The formal/polite ending です should remain unchanged regardless of the tense. ～かったでした does not occur. Also note that the past tense of いい(です) is よかった(です).

テストはやさしかったです。　　The test was easy.

昨日は寒かったです。　　　　　It was cold yesterday.

〜くありません ⇒ 〜くありませんでした
〜くない(です) ⇒ 〜くなかった(です)

For the negative past form, add でした to its nonpast counterpart 〜くありません or replace 〜くない(です) with 〜くなかった(です).

映画は長くありませんでした。　　The movie wasn't long.

ピザは安くなかったです。　　The pizza wasn't cheap.

4. Describing past actions and events

〜ました／〜ませんでした: Past Equivalent of 〜ます／〜ません

The past tense of a Japanese verb can be obtained by replacing ます with ました for polite affirmative, and ません with ませんでした for polite negative. While English verbs have three major tenses-the past, present, and future-Japanese verbs have only two-the past and nonpast. The nonpast tense in Japanese covers both present and future tenses in English. The past tense is used to indicate an action or state completed in the past.

昨日、6時に起きました。　　I woke up at 6 o'clock yesterday.

Q: パーティーへ行きましたか。　　Did you go to the party?

A1: はい、行きました。　　Yes, I did.

A2: いいえ、行きませんでした。　　No, I did not.

5. Asking how something was.

(〜は)どうでしたか/(〜は)どうだった

どうでしたか and its plain/informal equivalent, どうだった are used to ask someone how something was. パーティーはどうでしたか means "How was the party?"

Q: 週末はどうでしたか。　　How was your weekend?

A: とても、楽しかったです。　　It was very enjoyable.

Q: ダンスどうだった。　　How was the dance?

A: よかったよ。　　It was great.

6. Telling what you want to do: -たいです

Vます vs Vたい(です)

By replacing ます with たい, you can indicate your desire of wanting to do something. If you say, for example, たべたい instead of たべます, you mean "I want to eat." Since たべたい is plain and informal by itself, you have to add です at the end to make it polite and formal. Note that -たい(です) is used to express what the speaker wants to do and what the listener wants to do when used in a question. Unlike its English equivalent (want), it cannot be used to express what the third person wants to do.

Q: どこへ行きたいですか。 Where do you want to go?

A: 海へ行きたいです。 I want to go to the beach.

冬休みにスキーに行きたいです。 I want to go skiing during winter vacation.

<u>-をVたい vs -がVたい</u>

If -たい requires a direct object, you may use either を or が to mark the object. Use が when your desire to do something is high or urgent.

てんぷらが食べたい。 I want to eat *tempura*.

Q: あしたは何がしたいですか。 What do you want to do tomorrow?

A: 日本の映画が見たいです。 I want to watch a Japanese movie.

7. Asking someone to describe something: どんな-

どんな is used to make questions equivalent to "what kind of-?" or "what type of-?" in English. It is useful when you want to ask someone to describe something.

Q: リンダさんはどんな人ですか。 What kind of person is Linda?

A: とてもやさしい人です。 She is a very kind person.

Q: どんな夏休みでしたか。 What sort of summer vacation was it?

A: すばらしい夏休みでした。 It was a wonderful summer vacation.

Q: どんな車を買いたいですか。 What sort of car do you want to buy?

A: 大きいセダンを買いたいです。 I want to buy a large sedan.

8. Telling someone you want to become more skillful at X: Xがもっとじょうずになりたい(です)

じょうず is a *na* adjective and it means "skillful." Xがじょうず means (someone is) skillful at X. なりたい means "want to become" and もっと means "more."

日本語の会話がもっとじょうずになりたいです。

I want to become better at talking in Japanese.

スピーチがもっとじょうずになりたいです。

I want to become better at giving a speech.

9. Indicating an order by さいしょ, つぎ **and** さいご.

さいしょ, つぎ and さいご means "first," "next," and "last" respectively, and they are all nouns. "The first speaker" is さいしょのスピーカー, while "the final speaker" is さいごのスピーカー.

最初のスピーカーはスミスさんです。 The first speaker is Ms. Smith.

次のスピーカーはチョーさんです。 The next speaker is Mr. Cho.

最後のスピーカーはロメロさんです。 The last speaker is Ms. Romero.

10. Connectors それから、そして **and** でも

"Connectors" such as those below are useful in making your speech flow. They should sound familiar to you since they were introduced in *Haruichiban*.

それから "and then" "after that." それから is useful when stating something in sequence or making some additional statements

そして "and then" "after that" "having done all that." そして is similar to それから but it carries the implication of "having done all that.." Because of this そして is often used before the final statement in the sequence that may serve as a wrap-up and conclusion.

でも " but" "however. " でも is used to mean "but" or "however," but it should be placed in the beginning of a sentence.

11. "Hesitation sounds" and additional connectors

ええと is used to avoid an awkward pause or silence while the speaker is recalling or thinking what should be said next. It is also used when you start speaking in order to soften the tone of your speech.

あのう is used interchangeably with ええと, although it sounds more formal than ええと. あのう is also used to draw someone's attention. Often called "hesitation sounds" or "hesitation noises," both ええと and あのう are used only in speaking.

じゃ is used to develop a conversation based on what has been said and relates the current topic to what follows. It is also used to wrap up a conversation or a monologue. じゃ is used only in speaking. だから is the Japanese equivalent of "that is why," "so," and "therefore." It is usually used at the beginning of a sentence. ええと and あのう may be used consecutively depending upon the length of hesitation. あのう or ええと may be used with それから, でも, etc.

107

VOCABULARY

Functional Vocabulary

	Formal	Informal	English
Describing a non-past affirmative state	Noun/な Adj.です。	Noun/な Adj.だ。	It is -.
		い Adj.です。	い Adj.。　　　　It is -.
Describing a non-past negative state	Noun/な Adj.じゃありません。 Noun/な Adj.じゃないです。	Noun/な Adj.じゃない。	It isn't -.
	い Adj.くありません。 い Adj.くないです。	い Adj.くない。	It isn't -.
Describing a past affirmative state	Noun/な Adj.でした。	Noun/な Adj.だった。	It was -.
	い Adj.かったです。	い Adj.かった。	It was -.
Describing a past negative state	Noun/な Adj.じゃありませんでした。 Noun/な Adj.じゃなかったです。	Noun/な Adj.じゃなかった。	It wasn't -.
	い Adj.くありませんでした。 い Adj.くなかったです。	い Adj.くなかった。	It wasn't -.
Asking about a past state	Noun/な Adj.でしたか。	Noun/な Adj.だった？	Was it -?
	い Adj.かったですか。	い Adj.かった？	Was it -?
Describing past actions	- ました。/- ませんでした。	- た/- なかった。	I/you (etc.) did~/didn't do~.
Asking about past actions	- ましたか。	- た/だ？	Did you (etc.) do~?
Asking how something was	(Xは)どうでしたか。	(Xは)どうだった？	How was X?
Asking for descriptive information	どんなXですか。/- でしたか。	どんなX(だった)？	What kind of X is/was it?
Indicating what the speaker wants to do	Verb Stem ＋ たいです。	Verb Stem ＋ たい。	I want to ~.
Indicating what the speaker wants to be more skillful at	Xがもっとじょうずになりたいです。	Xがもっとじょうずになりたい。 I want to be better at X.	
Asking for support/boost	おうえんしてください。	おうえんして。	Please give me support. Please give me a boost.
Asking for cooperation	きょうりょくしてください。	きょうりょくして。	Please cooperate. Please lend me a hand.
Introducing the first speaker	さいしょのスピーカーはXさんです。	さいしょのスピーカーはX。	The first speaker is X.

	Formal	Informal	English
Introducing the next speaker	つぎのスピーカーはXさんです。	つぎのスピーカーはX。	The next speaker is X.
Introducing the final speaker	さいごのスピーカーはXさんです。	さいごのスピーカーはX。	The final speaker is X.
Asking someone if s/he can do something again	もういちどしてもいいですか。	もういちどやってもいい？	Can I do it again?
Asking someone if s/he can start from the beginning	はじめからしてもいいですか。	はじめからやってもいい？	Can I start all over again?
Asking someone to answer question #X	Xばんのこたえをおねがいします。	Xばんのこたえ(を)おねがい。	Please answer question #X
Asking someone if something is OK/correct	いいですか。	いい？	Is it OK/correct?

Notional Vocabulary

Connectors and Hesitation Sounds

それから	after that, and then
そして	and then, and finally
でも	but, however
だから	that is why
ええと	uh, well...
あのう	uh, well...
じゃ	well then

Countries and Places

アメリカ	USA, America
カナダ	Canada
メキシコ	Mexico
ハワイ	Hawaii
ボストン	Boston
ピッツバーグ	Pittsburgh
コンコード	Concord
ポートランド	Portland

Days of the Week

にちようび	日曜日	Sunday
げつようび	月曜日	Monday
かようび	火曜日	Tuesday
すいようび	水曜日	Wednesday
もくようび	木曜日	Thursday
きんようび	金曜日	Friday
どようび	土曜日	Saturday

なんようび	何曜日	what day of the week

Descriptive Words

まじめ（な）	真面目（な）	sincere, serious
げんき（な）	元気（な）	healthy, spirited
すてき（な）	素敵（な）	attractive
きれい（な）	綺麗（な）	clean, beautiful
むしあつい	蒸し暑い	hot and humid
いい	良い	good
うるさい	煩い	noisy
やさしい	優しい	gentle, kind
きびしい	厳しい	strict, demanding, harsh, severe
たのしい	楽しい	fun, enjoyable
すばらしい	素晴らしい	wonderful
いそがしい	忙しい	busy
たかい	高い	expensive, high (height)
やすい	安い	inexpensive
ながい	長い	long
みじかい	短い	short
おいしい	美味しい	delicious
まずい	不味い	awful (unpalatable)
おもしろい	面白い	interesting, entertaining
つまらない	詰まらない	boring
はやい	速い	fast
はやい	早い	early
おそい	遅い	slow, late
じょうず（な）	上手（な）	skillful

にがて（な）	苦手（な）	be poor at
じゅうよう（な）	重要（な）	important
たいへん（な）	大変（な）	hard, troublesome
スムーズ（な）		smooth

Exercise Directions

もんだい	問題	question, problem
こたえ	答え	answer
さんばん	三番	(Question) No.3
そうです		That's correct.
ちがいます/ちがう	違います	That's wrong.

Facilities and Stores

としょかん	図書館	library
ぎんこう	銀行	bank
ゆうびんきょく	郵便局	post office
えいがかん	映画館	movie theater
がっこう	学校	school
コンサートホール		concert hall
プール		swimming pool
ショッピングモール		shopping mall
みせ	店	store
レストラン		restaurant
デパート		department store

Family Terms

かぞく	家族	family
おじいさん	お祖父さん	(someone's) grandfather
	お爺さん	old man
おばあさん	お祖母さん	(someone's) grandmother
	お婆さん	old woman
おとうさん	お父さん	(someone's) father
おかあさん	お母さん	(someone's) mother
おにいさん	お兄さん	(someone's) older brother
おねえさん	お姉さん	(someone's) older sister
おとうとさん	弟さん	(someone's) younger brother
いもうとさん	妹さん	(someone's) younger sister
そふ	祖父	(one's own) grandfather
そぼ	祖母	(one's own) grandmother
ちち	父	(one's own) father
はは	母	(one's own) mother
あに	兄	(one's own) older brother
あね	姉	(one's own) older sister
おとうと	弟	younger brother
いもうと	妹	younger sister
しんせき	親戚	relative
いとこ		cousin
ぎりの -	義理の -	--in-law
ぎりのはは	義理の母	mother-in-law

Frequency Words

まいにち	毎日	every day
まいあさ	毎朝	every morning
よく		often
ときどき	時々	sometimes
あまり	余り	not often
ぜんぜん	全然	not at all

Grade Levels

がくねん	学年	grade level
いちねんせい	一年生	1st year student
		freshman
しょうがくいちねんせい	小学一年生	1st grader
		1st year elementary school student
ちゅうがくいちねんせい	中学一年生	7th grader
		1st year junior high student
こうこういちねんせい	高校一年生	10th grader
		1st year high school student
なんねんせい	何年生	what grade

Languages

にほんご	日本語	Japanese
えいご	英語	English
ちゅうごくご	中国語	Chinese
フランスご	フランス語	French
ことば	言葉	language, word

Miscellany

テレビ		television
でんわ	電話	telephone
いぬ	犬	dog
あき	秋	fall
ほん	本	book
クラブ		club
ポスター		poster
りょう	寮	dormitory
そうじ	掃除	cleaning, sweeping
たのしいこと	楽しい事	fun things/activities
ロック		rock (music)
クラシック		classical (music)
カントリー		country (music)
ラップ		rap (music)

Meals and Food

あさごはん	朝御飯	breakfast
ひるごはん	昼御飯	lunch
ばんごはん	晩御飯	supper, dinner
シーフード		seafood

ロブスター		lobster
ハンバーガー		hamburger
ピザ		pizza
コーヒー		coffee
みず	水	water
りょうり	料理	cooking, dish, food
イタリアりょうり	イタリア料理	Italian dish/food
メキシコりょうり	メキシコ料理	Mexican dish/food
フランスりょうり	フランス料理	French dish/food
タイりょうり	タイ料理	Thai dish/food
ちゅうごくりょうり	中国料理	Chinese dish/food
インドりょうり	インド料理	Indian dish/food
にほんりょうり	日本料理	Japanese dish/food

Order

さいしょ	最初	first, beginning
つぎ	次	next
さいご	最後	last, final

Personal Pronouns

わたし	私	I/me (semi-formal/formal)
ぼく	僕	I/me (masculine)
あたし		I/me (feminine)
あなた	貴方	You (feminine/semi-formal)
きみ	君	You (masculine)
かのじょ	彼女	she
かれ	彼	he

Persons

スピーカー		speaker
アドバイザー		advisor
カウンセラー		counselor
たんにんのせんせい	担任の先生	homeroom teacher
ともだち	友達	friend
コーチ		coach
キャプテン		captain
ガールフレンド		girlfriend
かのじょ	彼女	girlfriend
ボーイフレンド		boyfriend
かれ	彼	boyfriend
しかいしゃ	司会者	host, MC

Quantifiers

たくさん	沢山	many, a lot
すこし	少し	little, few
ぜんぜん	全然	not at all
だいたい	大体	for the most part

Question Word

どんな		what kind
いつ	何時	when
だれ	誰	who
だれと	誰と	with whom
なに	何	what
なんで	何で	by what means
どこ	何処	where
どう		how

Relative Time

きょねん	去年	last year
ことし	今年	this year
らいねん	来年	next year
おととい	一昨日	the day before yesterday
きのう	昨日	yesterday
きょう	今日	today
あした	明日	tomorrow
あさって	明後日	the day after tomorrow

Speech Organization

スピーチ		speech
くみたて	組み立て	structure, organization
はじめ	始め	beginning
なか	中	middle, main body
おわり	終わり	end
あいさつ	挨拶	greeting
なまえ	名前	name
きょねんのがっこう	去年の学校	last year's school
ことしのがっこう	今年の学校	this year's school
がくねん	学年	grade level
とし	年	age
じゅうろくさい	十六オ	sixteen years old
いっしょにいくひと	一緒に行く人	commuting partner
こうつう	交通	transportation
うち	家	home, hometown
プロフィール		profile
しゅっしん	出身	birthplace
こくせき	国籍	nationality
ことば	言葉	language
しゅみ	趣味	hobby
ジャズ	ジャズ	Jazz
なつやすみ	夏休み	summer vacation
さいこう	最高	superb, best
まあまあ		so-so
さいてい	最低	worst, awful
ねがいごと	願い事	wish
しんがっき	新学期	new academic period

111

VOCABULARY *(continued)*

もっと		more
じょうずになりたい	上手になりたい	
		want to become skillful
みなさん	皆さん	everyone
おうえん	応援	support, cheer, boost
きょうりょく	協力	cooperation

Speech Evaluation and Feedback

はっきり		clearly
スムーズ		smooth
せいかく	正確	accurate
おもしろい	面白い	interesting
こえ	声	voice
しせい	姿勢	posture
かお	顔	face
かおをあげる	顔を上げる	raise one's face
		look straight
ちょうどいい	丁度良い	just about right
ないよう	内容	content

Sports

テニス		tennis
バレーボール		volleyball
サッカー		soccer

Study of Japanese

かいわ	会話	conversation
はつおん	発音	pronunciation
スピーチ		speech
はっぴょう	発表	presentation
かんじ	漢字	kanji
かな	仮名	kana (hiragana, katakana)
しゅくだい	宿題	homework
べんきょう	勉強	studying
れんしゅう	練習	exercise, practice
げんこうようし	原稿用紙	composition paper
テキスト		textbook
せつぞくご	接続語	connector words

Transportation

こうつう	交通	transportation
バス		bus
タクシー		taxi
ちかてつ	地下鉄	subway
でんしゃ	電車	train
じてんしゃ	自転車	bicycle
ひこうき	飛行機	airplane
ふね	船	ship
あるいて	歩いて	on foot
くるま	車	car

Vacation/Weekend Destinations and Activities

なつやすみ	夏休み	summer vacation
しゅうまつ	週末	weekend
うみ	海	beach, ocean
やま	山	mountain
プール		swimming pool
ショッピングモール		shopping mall
みせ	店	store
レストラン		restaurant
キャンプ		camp
コンサート		concert
かいもの	買い物	shopping
パーティー		party
アルバイト		part time/summer job
えいが	映画	movie

Verbs

はじめます/はじめる	始めます	start
おわります/おわる	終わります	end
ちがいます/ちがう	違います	differ, be wrong
つくります/つくる	作ります	make
あります/ある	在ります	exist, have
います/いる	居ます	exist, have (living)
いきます/いく	行きます	go
きます/くる	来ます	come
かえります/かえる	帰ります	return, go home
します/する		do
やります/やる		do, perform
たべます/たべる	食べます	eat
のみます/のむ	飲みます	drink
はなします/はなす	話します	speak, talk
よみます/よむ	読みます	read
かきます/かく	書きます	write
みます/みる	見ます	watch, look
かいます/かう	買います	buy
およぎます/およぐ	泳ぎます	swim
おきます/おきる	起きます	wake up
ねます/ねる	寝ます	sleep
あげます/あげる	上げます	raise, lift
わかります/わかる	分かります	understand
まちがえます/まちがえる		
	間違えます	make mistakes
おねがいします/おねがいする		
	お願いします	request

1.7 Virtual Reality 実践
Presenting Speeches
スピーチをします

Overview

Are you ready to give your speech? You will do so in a setting similar to speech contests, although making this a real contest is up to you and your class. You will have an opportunity to check the rules and evaluation forms, choose hosts, and practice your speech one final time before presenting it. After the speech, you will conduct a self-evaluation and write your speech on a Japanese-style composition sheet (げんこうようし).

Preliminary Activities
前作業

14 Check rules — ルールの確認をします

15 Check evaluation forms — 評価用紙の確認をします

16 Choose hosts — 司会者を選びます

17 Last practice — 最後の練習をします

Main Activity
本作業

18 Present speeches — スピーチをします

Wrap-up Activities
後作業

19 Evaluate and reflect — 評価と振り返りをします

20 Make a hand-written script — 原稿用紙に書きます

14 Check rules ルールの確認をします

There will be a "second chance" rule in effect. You may not be able to help getting a bit nervous when you give your speech in front of others, and may end up losing track of your speech unexpectedly. If a situation such as this happens, you will be allowed to start your speech all over again just once. However, you will have to ask the host for permission to do so by using one of the following expressions. Make sure to study them beforehand.

Formal: 　もう一度してもいいですか。　[May I do it again?]

　　　　　始めからしてもいいですか。　[May I do it from the beginning?]

Informal: 　一度やってもいい。　[Do I it again?]

　　　　　始めからやってもいい。　[Do I it from the beginning?]

15 Check evaluation forms 評価用紙の確認をします

You will be evaluating your classmates' speeches based on four categories. They are as follows: enunciation, fluency, accuracy, and content and delivery. See the sample rubric below.

	いいえ	まあまあ	はい
Enunciation はっきり話しましたか。	Enunciation and pronunciation are unclear.	Enunciation and pronunciation are sometimes unclear.	Enunciation and pronunciation are clear and audible throughout.
Fluency スムーズでしたか。	Speaker lacks fluency and/or relies heavily on note.	Speaker fails to maintain fluency from time to time.	Speaker maintains fluency throughout, seldom relying on notes.
Accuracy 正確でしたか。	Speech has many grammatical or usage errors.	Speech has some grammatical or usage errors.	Speech has almost no grammatical or usage errors.
Content&Delivery 面白いスピーチでしたか。	Content is not interesting and/or is monotonously delivered.	Content is interesting and/or is inappropriately delivered.	Content is very interesting and/or very masterfully delivered.

16 Choose hosts

しかいしゃ えら
司会者を選びます

Choose a host to run the speech contest. You may choose more than one host depending upon the number of speakers. A possible alternative to choosing hosts is that each speaker will introduce the next speaker.

17 Last practice

さい ご れんしゅう
最後の練習をします

Practice your speech one last time. Make sure to keep the evaluation criteria in mind.

18 Present speeches

スピーチをします

It's time for the main activity. がんばって(Give it all you've got!).

Evaluate and reflect　　　評価と振り返りをします

How did you do? It is important that you look back on your performance and reflect upon it for your future reference and improvement. See evaluation forms that your classmates have filled out and ask for any comments and suggestions they may have. A reflective checklist such as the following will also be very helpful.

Checklist for Reflection	Yes absolutely positive				Don't think so
1. *I spoke loud enough, and clearly.*					
2. *I spoke fluently and smoothly.*					
3. *I faced the audience and maintained eye contact with them throughout.*					
4. *My speech was accurate with almost no grammatical or usage errors.*					
5. *I monitored my performance and made corrections appropriately when necessary.*					
6. *I changed rate and volume of my speech in order to convey my message in a lively and effective fashion.*					
7. *I was confident and comfortable during my speech.*					
8. *I think the audience found my speech interesting and easy to follow.*					
9. *I practiced hard to get ready for my performance.*					
10. *The quality of my performance was reflective of the quality of my preparation.*					
11. *CREATE YOUR OWN STATEMENT.*					

20 Make a hand-written script

げんこうようし　か
原稿用紙に書きます

Your final activity in this chapter is to write your speech on a Japanese-style composition sheet (げんこうようし). You may recall that you did a similar exercise when you made a self-introductory speech in *Haruichiban*. Below is a sample composition sheet for vertical writing. Each 400-character げんこうようし has 20 lines. On the first line, write the title of the composition. Your name occupies the second line. Skip the third line and start your composition on the fourth line, indenting one character space. Periods and commas occupy one character space each.

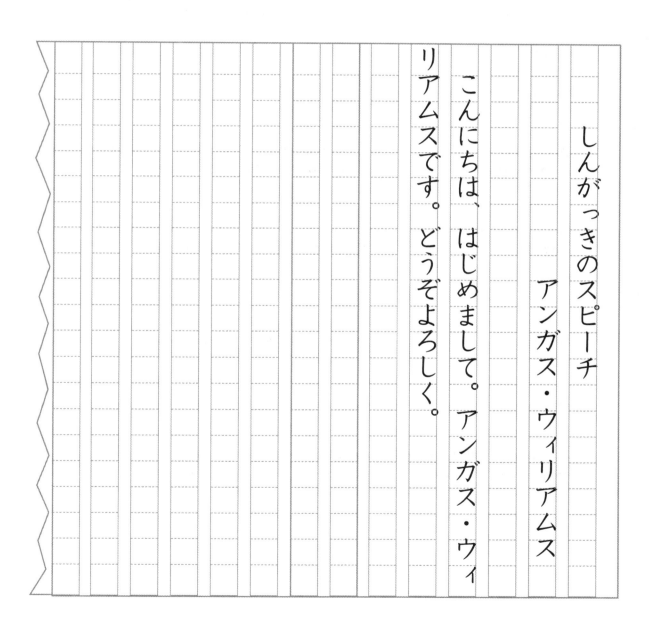

しんがっきのスピーチ

アンガス・ウィリアムス

こんにちは、はじめまして。アンガス・ウィリアムスです。どうぞよろしく。

SUM-UP

1. Which description did you choose to describe your summer vacation: (circle one)

    a. superb

    b. so - so

    c. worst

2. What differences did you find between your customs and Japanese customs during summer vacation?

3. Did you find any problems with the question and answer conversation?

4. During cooperative speech practice, were you aware of what the improvement needed to be made between Stage 1 (individual work) and Stage 4 (trio work) ?

5. Did you make any progress in your speaking presentation ability? Please rate your progress on a scale of 0 to 5. (0 = no progress, 5 = excellent progress)

0	1	2	3	4	5

6. Have you been able to use the writing strategy? Please rate your progress on a scale of 0 to 5. (0 = no progress, 5 = excellent progress)

0	1	2	3	4	5

7. Have you been able to refresh all items that you studied last year? Please rate your progress on a scale of 0 to 5. (0 = no progress, 5 = excellent progress)

0	1	2	3	4	5

ADDITIONAL VOCABULARY

Functional Vocabulary

Reported Speech

	formal	informal		
～といいます	～と言います	～という	～と言う	It said that~
～そうです	～そうです	～そうだ	～そうだ	I hear that ~
よんでいます	呼んでいます	よんでいる	呼んでいる	It is called that

Decision

ことにしました	事にしました	ことにした	事にした	I decided

Conditional

でかけますと	出掛けますと	でかけると	出掛けると	When you go out

Agreeing or Disagreeing Classroom Expressions

そうですね	そうだ(わ)ね	That's right.
そうですか	そうか	I see (with agreeable tone)
たってください	たって	(Please) stand up.

Notional Vocabulary

Summer Vacation

うみのひ	海の日	Marine day
けい	恵	name
しょうなんかいがん	湘南海岸	place name
ビーチバレー		beach volleyball
サーフィン		surfing
そのあと	その後	after that
すかわり	西瓜割り	breaking watermelon
えのしま	江ノ島	place name
あきはばら	秋葉原	place name
でんきや	電気屋	electronic shop
にっき	日記	diary
うる	売る	sell
にほんてき	日本的	Japanese style
ところ	所	place
そこで		so
あさくさ	浅草	place name
もの	物	things
かたな	刀	sword
ちよがみ	千代紙	Japanese paper
よろこぶ	喜ぶ	rejoice

Visiting Japan

こくさい	国際	international
Iこう	I校	I school
よぶ	呼ぶ	called
とる	撮る	to take (a photo)
だいすきです	大好きです	like much
とくに	特に	especially
でかける	出かける	going out
であいます	出会います	encounter
てはじめ	手始め	first of all
～ことにする		decide
そのころ	その頃	at that time
さくら	桜	cherry blossom
さきます	咲きます	bloom
しゃしんぶ	写真部	photo club

119

ADDITIONAL VOCABULARY (continued)

しけん	試験	exam
もつ	持つ	hold
おせわに	お世話に	kind help
おみやげ	お土産	souvenir
おちゃ	お茶	tea
つかれる	疲れる	tired
ふとん	布団	futon mats
しく	敷く	spread
てつだう	手伝う	help
しゃしん	写真	photo
おもい	重い	heavy
わかもの	若者	young people
おおい	多い	many, much

Mini Conversation 1:
ミニ会話 1

Travel to Japan: 日本へ旅行

会話 1 （空港で）

ホストマザー:	マイクさんですか。
マイク:	はい、これからお世話になります。
	よろしくお願いします。
ホストマザー:	荷物を持ちましょうか(1)。
マイク:	いいえ、重いですから(2)、私が持ちます。

会話 2 （ホストファミリーの家で）

マイク:	これはニューヨークのお土産です。
ホストマザー:	ありがとうございます。あけてもいいですか(3)。
マイク:	どうぞ。
ホストマザー:	わあ、きれいなチョコレートですね。
マイク:	今、これはニューヨークではやっています。家族はみんなこれが大好きです。
ホストマザー:	ひとつ食べてもいいですか。
マイク:	もちろん。
ホストマザー:	うーん、おいしい。

会話3（ホストファミリーの家で）

ホストマザー： お茶でも飲みますか。

マイク： いいえ、結構です。

ホストマザー： コーラもありますよ。

マイク： いいえ、疲れていますから今日は早く寝たいです。

ホストマザー： あ、そうですか。じゃあ、布団を敷きますからちょっと待ってください。

マイク： 手伝いましょうか。

ホストマザー： じゃあお願いします。

Dialogue 1 (At the airport)

Host mother: Are you Mike?
Mike: Yes, I am glad I can stay with you. Thank you very much.
Host mother: Shall I carry your luggage?
Mike: Thank you, but I'll do it because they are heavy.

Notes

- くうこう：airport
- これから：from now
- お世話になります：(lit.) Thank you in advance for taking care of me.
- よろしくお願いします：Nice to meet you. (when you meet the person for the first time)
- にもつ：luggage, what one carries
- おもい：heavy

Dialogue 2 (At home)

Mike: This is a souvenir from New York.
Host mother: Thank you so much. May I open it?
Mike: Sure.
Host mother: Wow, beautiful chocolates!
Mike: They are popular now in New York. My whole family likes them.
Host mother: May I have one?
Mike: Go ahead.
Host mother: Mmm, delicious!

Notes

- おみやげ：souvenir
- どうぞ：Go ahead.
- わあ：Wow!
- はやっている：popular
- もちろん：Of course. Sure.
- うーん：Mmm..

Dialogue 3 (At home)

Host mother: Would you like tea or something?
Mike: No, thank you.
Host mother: We also have coke.
Mike: No, I would like to go to sleep now because I am tired.
Host mother: Ok. Then I will prepare your futon. Please wait a little bit.
Mike: Shall I help you?
Host Thank you.

Notes

- 〜でも：〜 or other things
- 結構です：No, thank you.
- 疲れている：tired
- 早く：early
- 布団：futon
- (布団を)敷く：to place futon on the floor
- 手伝う：to help

Grammar Keys and Practice

(1) 〜ましょうか

〜ましょうか is equivalent to "shall I?" in English. The speaker expresses his/her will in choosing a decision.

> **1. Offer help to your host mother using ましょうか.**
>
> 野菜(Vegetable)を　切ります(cut) ⇒
>
> テーブルを　ふきます(wipe) ⇒

おさら(dish)を　洗_{あら}います(wash) ⇒

2. Reply to your friend's comment using ましょうか.

　　EX.

　　your friend: この宿題_{しゅくだい}(homework)は　難_{むず}かしい(difficult)です。

　　you:　　　　手伝_{てつだ}いましょうか。(Can I help you?)

　　your friend: この部屋_{へや}(room)は　少_{すこ}し(wash)　寒_{さむ}い(cold)です。

　　you: _____

　　your friend: この部屋_{へや}(room)は　少_{すこ}し　暑_{あつ}い(hot)です。

　　you: _____

　　your friend: この荷物_{にもつ}(baggage)は　重_{おも}い(heavy)です。

　　you: _____

Travel Practice 1

When you arrive at the airport in Japan, you will ask your host mother if you can help her, using ～ましょうか.

Travel Practice 2

When you arrive at your host family's house, you will ask your host mother if you are able to do certain things, using ～てもいいですか.

(2) ～から

～から means "because of" in English.

1. Make a sentence using ～から.　～からを使って一_{つか}つの文_{ぶん}にしましょう。

この本_{ほん}は　高_{たか}い(expensive)です。買_かいません(not buy)。⇒

頭_{あたま}(head)が　痛_{いた}い(hurt)です。早_{はや}く(early)　寝_ねます。⇒

日本の　アニメが　好きです。日本に来ました。⇒

2. Complete the sentence by stating the reason.　理由_{りゆう}を考_{かんが}えて文_{ぶん}を完成_{かんせい}させましょう。

_____から、日本語_{にほんご}を　勉強_{べんきょう}(study)しています。

_____から、今日は　学校_{がっこう}に　行きません。

_____から、この映画_{えいが}(movie)が　好_すきです。

(3) ～てもいいですか。

～てもいいですか means that you are seeking permission.

1. You are in the class. Ask for permission from the teacher using ～てもいいですか.

辞書_{じしょ}(dictionary)を　見_みる⇒

水_{みず}を　飲_のむ⇒

トイレに　行_いく⇒

Travel Practice 3

Form pairs. One person will be a host mother in Japan. The other will be an exchange student from outside of Japan. The exchange student will try to communicate with his host mother in Japanese and ask many permission questions with their reasonable matters.

Additional Kanji 3: 追加漢字 3
ついかかんじ

全部	ぜんぶ、all 全：**ON:**ゼン **KUN:**まった(く)、すべ(て) 部：**ON:**ブ **KUN:**べ 全部の答えを教えてください。 Please teach me the all answers.
旅行	りょこう、trip 旅：**ON:**リョ **KUN:**たび 行：**ON:**コウ **KUN:**い(く) どこかに旅行に行きたいです。 I want to go to a trip somewhere.
英語	えいご、English 英：**ON:**エイ **KUN:**一 語：**ON:**ゴ **KUN:**かた(る) 英語を教えてください。 Please teach me English.
勉強	べんきょう、study 勉：**ON:**ベン **KUN:**つとめ(る) 強：**ON:**キョウ **KUN:**つよ(い) 日本語を勉強します。 I study Japanese.
東京	とうきょう、Tokyo 東：**ON:**トウ **KUN:**ひがし 京：**ON:**キョウ、ケイ **KUN:**みやこ 東京駅はどこですか。 Where is Tokyo station?
泳ぐ	およぐ、swim 泳：**ON:**エイ **KUN:**およ(ぐ) この夏の間泳ぎましたか。 Did you swim for the summer ?
終わる	おわる、end/finish 終：**ON:**シュウ **KUN:**お(わる)、お(える) 夏休みは終わりましたか。 Is your summer vacation ended?
仕事	しごと、job 仕：**ON:**シ **KUN:**つか(える) 事：**ON:**ジ、ズ **KUN:**こと、ごと 仕事はなんですか。 What is your job?
週末	しゅうまつ、weekend 週：**ON:**シュウ **KUN:**一 末：**ON:**マツ **KUN:**すえ この週末に何をしますか。 What are you doing this weekend?

Chapter 2
Let's Teach
Your Lesson Plan!

Chapter 2: Let's Teach Your Lesson Plan!
レッスンプランを教えましょう

2.1 Introduction 序論

CHAPTER OBJECTIVES

AT THE END OF THIS SECTION, YOU WILL BE ABLE TO:

- plan and run student-led review sessions from start to finish
- choose a leader and select a topic for student-led review sessions
- check the progress of various tasks
- prepare several types of questions and exercises for the review sessions
- give instructions and lead language exercises
- prepare and conduct several types of warm-up exercises
- give directions for a simple physical workout
- greet the participants and introduce the topic in the review sessions
- deal with basic problems regarding class management
- conduct a question and answer session as a wrap-up
- conduct a purposeful evaluation of the review sessions
- make a list of things to do using the dictionary form of a verb
- tell someone not to do something
- recognize about 80 kanji and their basic compounds
- read and write 32 kanji and their basic compounds.

YOU WILL ALSO LEARN:

- about various types of questions and exercises
- basic instructional vocabulary
- about the dictionary form and the ない form of a verb
- how to make suggestions for consideration
- how to indicate an action in progress
- about the こそあど demonstrative words.

き せつげき

Let's Teach Your Lessen Plan!

おし
レッスンプランを教えましょう

Learning by Teaching

The focus of this chapter is on planning and conducting group review sessions on your prior studies of Japanese in Japanese. You will begin with a series of pre-production, where you and your classmates will divide into groups, choose topics, and make several activities. During the actual review sessions, each group will take turns to lead the class for discussions and exercises, and end with a brief Q and A session. This might sound intimidating but you don't need to worry, because you will be guided and given step-by-step instructions and you will practice thoroughly in the Mechanics section. You will soon discover how much you can learn by teaching one another!

A Fresh Take on Review

Your teaching experience in this chapter will enable you to design and conduct various review activities in the future. In the past your teacher might have created all the review sheets and offered you a thorough review class right before your tests. What you have learned is certainly a great asset of yours and you should have an active role in keeping your investment alive. So don't wait to be spoonfed-become an active manager of your learning!

Importance of Feedback and Reflection

You stood in front of the audience alone to deliver your speech in Chapter 1 and will do so as a group in this chapter to conduct a review session. In our daily lives we are also constantly "presenting" ourselves through words and actions, and this is how we communicate with our surrounding environment. Presentations are thus an integral part of *Ginga*, and they are followed by opportunities for feedback and reflection that are essential to improving your presentation skills. Feedback from the audience often includes reference to things that would have gone unnoticed otherwise and proves very valuable to you as a presenter. Watching a videotape of your presentation may be quite revealing as well. Let's not neglect feedback and reflection and let's strive to become masterful presenters by making good use of them.

Product 復習セッション

教案 (Lesson Plan)

トピック: 電話の表現　　グループの名前: ねこ

日にち: 10月18日　　時間: 10時5分-10時45分

ばしょ: 日本語の教室

始め (2分)	始めのあいさつをする (Opening greeting)		シャンタル
	トピックを紹介する (Introduction of topic)		シャンタル
	レッスンを紹介する (Introduction of lesson)		ホセ
中 (35分)	ウォームアップをする (Warm-ups)	(3分)	ホセ, ジェニー
	単語を紹介する (Introduction of words)	(2分)	ジェシカ
	表現を紹介する (Introduction of expressions)	(2分)	トム
	漢字を紹介する (Introduction of Kanji)	(2分)	シャンタル
	アクティビティーをする (Activities)	(23分)	みんな (all)
	質問に答える (Q and A)	(3分)	シャンタル
終り (3分)	まとめと確認をする (Wrap-up and confirmation)	(2分)	ジェニー　トム
	終りのあいさつをする (Closing greeting)	(1分)	シャンタル

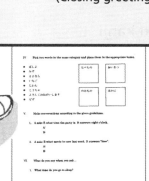

Process フローチャート

Mechanics

2.2 Group Development

1 Form groups
グループを作ります

2 Choose topics
トピックを選びます

3 Set a schedule
スケジュールを決めます

2.3 Structuring

4 Check the structure of a session
構成の確認をします

5 Check work progress
進行の確認をします

2.4 Session Prep I

6 Greeting and introduction
挨拶と紹介を準備します

7 Warm-up
ウォームアップを準備します

2.5 Session Prep II

8 Vocabulary and kanji
単語と表現と漢字を準備します

9 Activities
アクティビティーを準備します

10 Questions and answers
質問と答えを準備します

11 Closing
終わりの部分を準備します

12 Make a lesson plan
教案を作ります

13 Put everything in a folder
フォルダにまとめます

14 Practice class management
クラス運営の練習をします

15 Check folders
フォルダの確認をします

16 Check tasks
仕事の確認をします

17 Last practice
最後の練習をします

18 Conduct review sessions
復習セッションをします

19 Follow-up in English
フォローアップをします

20 Evaluate and reflect
評価と振り返りをします

Session Preparation III

2.6

Mechanics

2.7

Virtual Reality

Reflection

BASIC VOCABULARY 基礎語彙

グループをつくります
make
作ります

リーダーをえらびます
choose
選びます

スケジュールをきめます
decide
決めます

practice
練習します

プロジェクト ワーク

しごとをきめます
Decide on tasks

できましたか。

はい、できました。

いいえ、まだです。

confirm/check
確認します

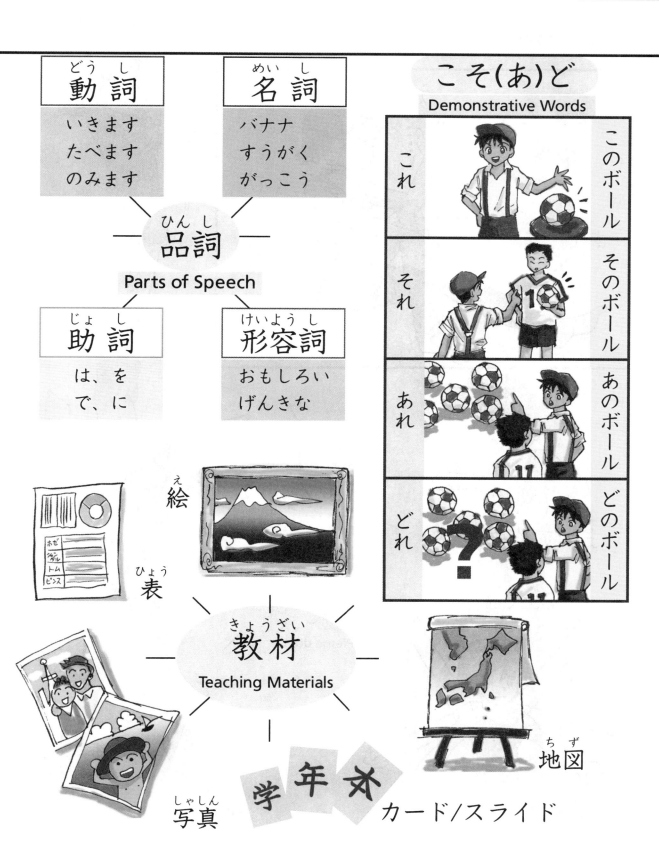

動詞（どうし）
いきます
たべます
のみます

名詞（めいし）
バナナ
すうがく
がっこう

こそ（あ）ど
Demonstrative Words

これ　このボール
それ　そのボール
あれ　あのボール
どれ　どのボール

品詞（ひんし）
Parts of Speech

助詞（じょし）
は、を
で、に

形容詞（けいようし）
おもしろい
げんきな

絵（え）

表（ひょう）

教材（きょうざい）
Teaching Materials

地図（ちず）

学年本

写真（しゃしん）

カード/スライド

133

(continued)

BASIC VOCABULARY

からだ
体

うで

くび

ひじ

ひざ…

あし

こし

のばしてください

ウォームアップの指示
しじ

まげてください

-てください
Please do -.

ひらいてください

まわしてください

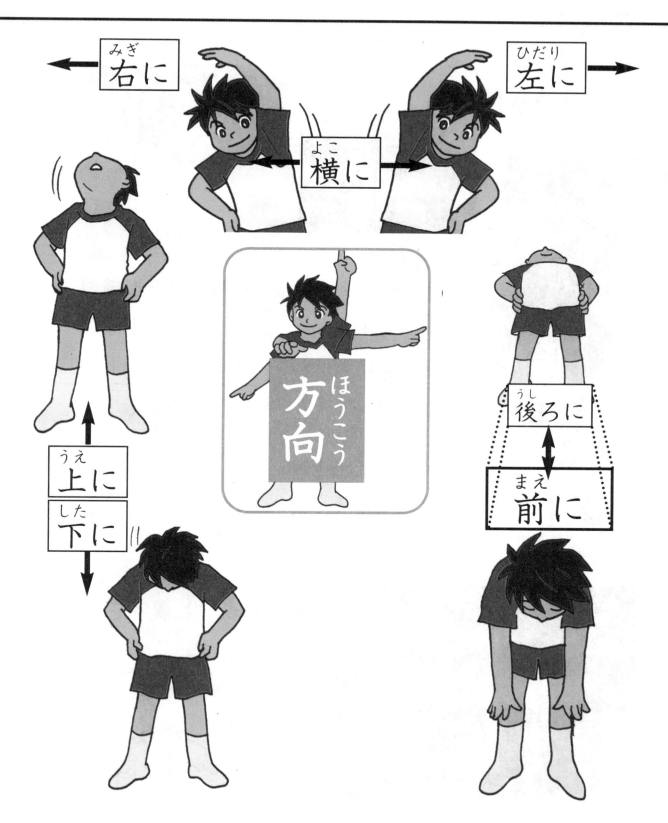

みぎ
右に

ひだり
左に

よこ
横に

ほうこう
方向

うえ
上に

した
下に

うし
後ろに

まえ
前に

ミーティングについて
ふくしゅう
復習しましょう。

ミーティングの
ろくしゅう

about-
-について

ふくしゅう
復習
review

きょうのレッスン
A,B,C,D...

Indicating order of activities

さいしょ
最初にAをします。

つぎ
次にBをします。

それからCをします。

さいご
最後にDをします。

たんご
単語
word

ひょうげん
表現
expression

かんじ
漢字
kanji

しょうかい
紹介
introduction

ひにち　　のみもの　のみます
じかん　　たべもの　たべます

てをあげてください　　時
おまかせします　　　　分
じゃ～にしましょう　　円

たんご　ひょうげん　かんじ
単語と表現と漢字を
しょうかい
紹介します。

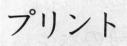

プリント
handout

配ります
distribute

指示
instructions

これからプリントを配ります。
最初に指示を読んでください。

はい。「ぎちょう」は
どういう意味ですか。

質問がありますか。

質問
question

三時はどう
ですか。

はい、いい
ですよ。

how about-?

-はどうですか

137

Dictionary form of verb

読む　する　書く　選ぶ　作る

plain/informal
nonpast
affirmative

Things to do today

日本語の本を読む
数学の宿題をする
レポートを書く
トピックを選ぶ

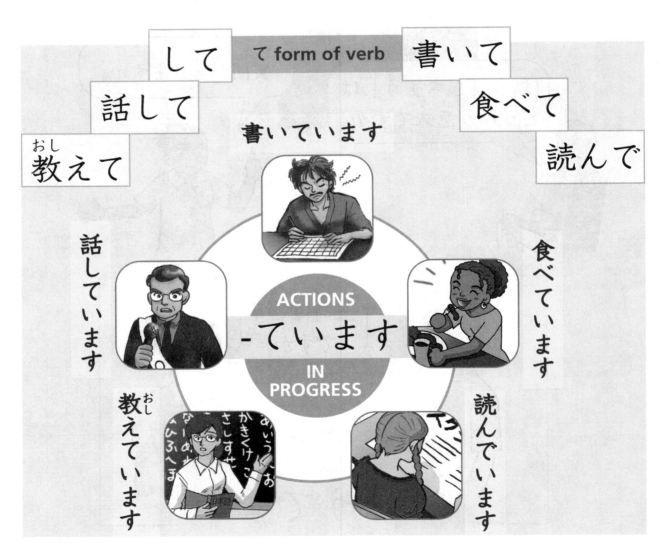

て form of verb

して　書いて
話して　食べて
教えて　読んで

書いています

話しています

教えています

食べています

読んでいます

ACTIONS
-ています
IN
PROGRESS

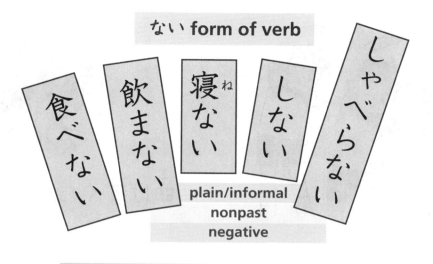

ない **form of verb**

食べない　飲まない　寝^ねない　しない　しゃべらない

plain/informal
nonpast
negative

-ないでください

Please do not do -.

食べ物^{もの}を食べないでください。

しゃべらないでください。

寝^ねないでください。

BASIC VOCABULARY

三<ruby>回<rt>かい</rt></ruby>曲<ruby>げ<rt>ま</rt></ruby>てください。

Day

-2   -1   0   +1   +2

おととい   <ruby>昨日<rt>きのう</rt></ruby>   <ruby>今日<rt>きょう</rt></ruby>   <ruby>明日<rt>あした</rt></ruby>   あさって

	Last~	*This~*	*Next~*
Year	<ruby>去年<rt>きょねん</rt></ruby>	<ruby>今年<rt>ことし</rt></ruby>	<ruby>来年<rt>らい</rt></ruby>
Month	<ruby>先月<rt>せんげつ</rt></ruby>	<ruby>今月<rt>こん</rt></ruby>	来月
Week	先<ruby>週<rt>しゅう</rt></ruby>	今週	来週

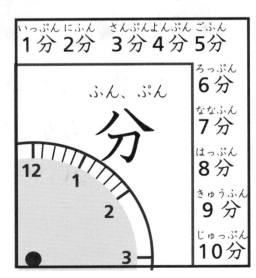

<ruby>1分<rt>いっぷん</rt></ruby> <ruby>2分<rt>にふん</rt></ruby> <ruby>3分<rt>さんぷん</rt></ruby><ruby>4分<rt>よんぷん</rt></ruby><ruby>5分<rt>ごふん</rt></ruby>	
ふん、ぷん	<ruby>6分<rt>ろっぷん</rt></ruby>
分	<ruby>7分<rt>ななふん</rt></ruby>
	<ruby>8分<rt>はっぷん</rt></ruby>
	<ruby>9分<rt>きゅうふん</rt></ruby>
	<ruby>10分<rt>じゅっぷん</rt></ruby>

2.2 Mechanics 組立て
<ruby>組<rt>く</rt></ruby><ruby>立<rt>み た</rt></ruby>て

Group Formation and Development
グループ作り
<ruby>作<rt>づく</rt></ruby>

Objectives

Form a group and choose a leader.
Choose the topic of a review session.
Make a review session schedule.

Overview

You now will start preparing for your group review session step by step. Since you will be doing this in Japanese, you will first need to make sure that you know the words, expressions, and sentence patterns that are essential to carrying out each of your tasks. What you have learned in *Haruichiban* will be very useful in this regard. You will be learning new items as well as some that have been introduced in Basic Vocabulary. After learning and practicing these items, your group will be able to complete the tasks.

1 **Make groups**　　　　グループを作ります

　1 **Form groups**　　　　グループになります

　2 **Choose leaders**　　　　リーダーを選びます

　3 **Enhance group spirit**　　　　グループの意識を高めます

2 **Choose topics**　　　　トピックを選びます

3 **Set the schedule**　　　　スケジュールを決めます

1   Make groups   グループを作ります

1   Form groups   グループになります

A. Follow your teacher's directions.   先生の指示に従いましょう。

Form groups under the guidance of your teacher.

2   Choose leaders   リーダーを選びます

A. Fill in the parentheses.

（　）に記号を入れてください。

Go over the following sample dialogues
about choosing a leader and match each of
them with the correct description by placing
the appropriate letter in each parenthesis.

1. (　　)

A: リーダーはだれがいいですか。

B: シャンタルさんがいいです。

A: Cさんは?

C: 私もシャンタルさんがいいです。

D: 私もシャンタルさんがいいです。

A: じゃ、シャンタルさんにしましょう。

3. (　　)

A: リーダーはだれがしますか。

B: 私がします。

A: ほかにいますか。 Anyone else?

C: 私がします。

A: Bさんがいいですか。それとも、C
さんがいいですか。

D: Cさんがいいです。

E: 私もCさんがいいです。

A: じゃ、Cさんにしましょう。

2. (　　)

A: リーダーはだれがしますか。

B: 私がします。

A: ほかにいますか。 Anyone else?

C: いいえ。

A: じゃ、Bさんお願いします。

4. (　　)

A: リーダーはだれがいいですか。

B: <u>シャンタル</u>さんがいいです。

A: Cさんは?

C: 私は<u>トム</u>さんがいいです。

A: じゃ、<u>シャンタル</u>さんの人、手をあげてください。

A: <u>4人</u>です。(after counting)

A: じゃ、<u>トム</u>さんの人、手をあげてください。

A: <u>2人</u>です。(after counting)

A: じゃ、<u>シャンタル</u>さんにしましょう。

5. (　　)

A: リーダーはだれがいいですか。

B: ええと、だれでもいいです。

A: Cさんは?

C: あのう、おまかせします。

A: Dさんは?

D: ええと、そうですねえ....。

A: じゃ、私がします。

いいですか。

B, C, D: はい、いいです。

---

a. A vote was being taken to decide on a nominated leader.

b. A person who nominated herself became a leader since no one else participated.

c. A person who was nominated became a leader since no one else was nominated.

d. A chair self-nominated herself since no one seemed willing to nominate anyone.

e. A leader will be chosen from two self-nominated candidates.

B. Practice conversations. 会話の練習をしましょう。

Now practice the five sample dialogues by replacing the underlined parts as well as Bさん and Cさん with names of your classmates.

C. Choose a leader. リーダーを選びましょう。

Have a group meeting and choose a group leader. A volunteer from each group will chair the meeting. Your experience with *Haruichiban* and the preceding practice should help you conduct the meeting entirely in Japanese.

D. Give your group a name in Japanese. 日本語で名前をつけましょう。

The newly chosen leader will take over the chair's role and lead a discussion in Japanese to create a name for your group. Your group may be named after an animal, a season, a color, a food, or a drink your group members like.

E. *Make a membership list.*

メンバーのリストを作りましょう。

Create an attractive membership list that includes the following.

グループの名前 (group name)

メンバーの名前 (members' names)

イラストや写真 (illustrations and/or photos)

---

3 **Enhance group spirit** グループの意識を高めます

A. *Play simple games.* やさしいゲームをしましょう。

Playing simple games in which groups compete against one another will encourage cooperation among group members and enhance group spirit.

ゲームの例 **1 (Sample Game 1)** ことば当てゲーム **Charades**

THINGS NEEDED: Sets of index cards on which a word from a certain category is written in both Japanese and English.

PROCEDURE:

1. Go get a set of cards from your teacher as a representative of your group.
2. Keep the cards face down and distribute evenly among the members.
3. Now look at the card(s) you are holding.
4. Have your group members make a circle and you go to the center.
5. Do gestures and make them guess the word on your card. They must raise their hands when ready and give their answers in Japanese.
6. When the word is correctly guessed, join the circle and ask another member to come to the center and repeat step 5 above. Note that words on the rest of the cards come from the same or a similar category as the first one.
7. Call your teacher when every word is correctly guessed. The group that does so first is the winner.

ゲームの例 2 (Sample Game 2)　"Feel that character" Game

THINGS NEEDED:

A list of about five hiragana or katakana characters for each group. Limit the number of characters used in this game to about 20, and the chosen characters should be known to everyone beforehand to ease the difficulty of guessing.

PROCEDURE:

1. Go get a list of characters from your teacher as a representative of your group.
2. Have your group form a straight line, with you standing at the end, seeing the back of the person in front of you. The person standing at the front of the line should be facing a whiteboard.
3. Go over your list but do not share it with your groupmates.
4. Upon hearing a signal from your teacher, use your index finger and write the first character on the list on the back of the person right in front of you up to three times. He or she then guesses the character and writes it on the back of the person in front of him or her. This will continue until the character reaches the person in the front of the line.
5. The person in front will go to the board and write the character.
6. Repeat steps 4-5 above with the rest of the characters.
7. The group that has written the characters on the board the fastest and most accurately is the winner.

ゲームの例 3 (Sample Game 3)　伝言ゲーム　"Deliver the message" Game

THINGS NEEDED:

Index cards on which a sentence is written in Japanese.

PROCEDURE:

1. Have your group form a straight line and stand in front of the line.
2. Go to your teacher and get a card. Read and memorize the sentence on the spot and give the card back to the teacher before going back to the line.
3. Whisper the memorized sentence to the next person on the line. He or she then whispers to the next person and this will be repeated down the line.
4. The person at the end of the line will say what he or she has heard aloud when called upon by the teacher.
5. Points will be awarded based on the accuracy of the message delivered down the line.

B. Evaluate the performance.　評価をしましょう。

Winning a competition is always exciting. However, other aspects of your performance are also very significant in our activities. They include cooperation among group members and the use of the Japanese language. The following sample evaluation form will allow you to reflect upon your performance as a group. Your teacher may also use it during the competition and pick a winning group based on their performance in all three areas listed in the form.

評価フォームの例 (Sample Evaluation Form)

		poor	fair	good	very good	excellent
Cooperation	協力	1	2	3	4	5
Concentration	集中力	1	2	3	4	5
Use of Japanese	日本語	1	2	3	4	5

2 | Choose topics 　　　　トピックを選<ruby>選<rt>えら</rt></ruby>びます

A. Brainstorming.　　ブレインストーミングをしましょう。

Sorting through what you have learned so far is the first step in establishing a topic for your review session. Have a brainstorming session with your group and write down any keywords you recall. Then write down any specific items, such as words and expressions you may recall, that are associated with each keyword. Prepare a blank mindmap beforehand and put これまでのべんきょう in the middle. これまで means "up to now."

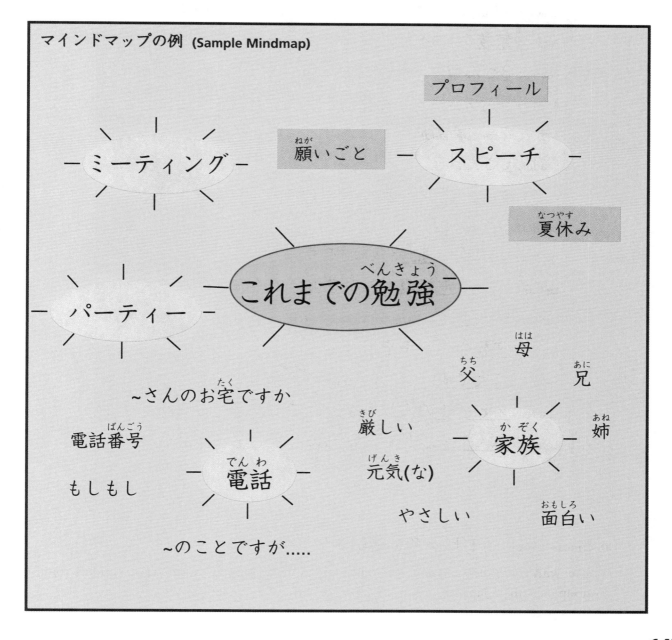

マインドマップの例 (Sample Mindmap)

B. Make a list of potential topic. トピックのリストを作りましょう。

Make a list of potential topics for your review session based on the brainstorming.

C. Conversation practice. 会話の練習をしましょう。

Go over the sample dialogue below and practice by substituting the underlined parts. This will help you prepare for your group meeting to decide upon your topic.

会話の例 (Sample Dialogue)

Leader: 復習セッションのトピックは何がいいですか。

A: 家族がいいです。

Leader: Bさんは？

B: 電話がいいです。

(C raises a hand)

Leader: Cさん。

C: 私は、スピーチがいいです。

Leader: Dさんは。

D: あのう、電話がいいです。

Leader: じゃ、電話の人、手を上げてください。

Leader: 四人です。*(after counting)*

Leader: 家族の人、手を上げてください。

Leader: 二人です。*(after counting)*

Leader: スピーチの人、手を上げてください。

Leader: 二人です。じゃ、電話にしましょう。

D. Choose a topic. トピックを選びましょう。

Meet with your group and choose a topic for your review session. Make sure to conduct your group meeting in Japanese.

3 | **Set the schedule** | スケジュールを決(き)めます

ノート: Relative Time Expressions

Scheduling involves constant reference to time. Let's learn some useful expressions so that you can use them in your meetings! Since you are scheduling events for the future, time expressions referring to the past may not be necessary. However, they are part of the basic terminologies for time and will be covered here.

A. Complete the following list. Use the vocabulary sections of this book and/or dictionaries as your resources.

リストを完成(かんせい)させてください。

		Last~	*This~*	*Next~*
Year		1.	今年(ことし)	来年(らいねん)
Month		先月(せんげつ)	2.	来月
Week		3.	今週(こんしゅう)	4.

		-2	*-1*	*today*	*+1*	*+2*
Day		5.	昨日(きのう)	今日(きょう)	明日(あした)	6.

B. Odd man out. Circle the one that doesn't belong in the group.

ちがうグループの単語(たん)を○（まる）で囲(かこ)みましょう。

1. あさって　　おととい　　　あした　　　きのう　　　こんげつ
2. きょねん　　きのう　　　　せんしゅう　あさって　　おととい
3. きょう　　　きょねん　　　こんしゅう　ことし　　　こんげつ
4. きのう　　　らいしゅう　　あした　　　あさって　　らいねん
5. せんげつ　　せんしゅう　　らいげつ　　らいねん　　さんがつ

C. Say the following in Japanese. 日本語で言(い)ってください。

EX. Wednesday, next week　　来週(らいしゅう)の水曜日

1. July, next year
2. September, this year
3. the 10th, last month
4. 9:00, the day after tomorrow
5. Tuesday, next week
6. Saturday, this week
7. the 8th, this month
8. April, last year
9. 1:00, tomorrow
10. the 6th, next month
11. Monday, last week
12. 4:30, the day before yesterday

149

ノート: Particle に to indicate a point of time

に

You already know that the particle に is used to mark a point of time. For example, 八時に means "at eight o'clock" and すいようびに means "on Wednesday." Beware that the particle に is not necessary when the "relative" time words introduced in this section such as "next week," "yesterday," and "last month" are used in a similar fashion. Compare the following.

土曜日に日本へ行きます。　　　来週日本へ行きます。

I will go to Japan on Saturday.　　　I will go to Japan next week.

D. Place に in those parentheses that require the particle to complete the sentences. Leave them blank if に is not necessary.

（　）は「に」ですか。それとも、ブランクですか。

1. 先週（　）ボストンで映画を見ました。

2. あさって（　）私のうちに来てください。

3. あさっての十時（　）私のうちに来てください。

4. 来月（　）車を買います。

5. 来年の三月（　）日本へ行きます。

6. 来週の木曜日（　）ミーティングがあります。

7. おととい（　）科学のレポートを書きました。

A tricky question. The following requires the particle に in one situation and will not require に in another situation. Can you explain why?

8. パーティーは来週（　）しましょう。

E. Check the review session schedule.　スケジュールをチェックしましょう。

Depending on the conditions of your school, the number of days and length of time spent on each session may vary. Consult your teacher beforehand and let her set the time schedule in this respect. See the sample schedule below.

復習セッションのスケジュール

	セッション1	セッション2	セッション3
日にち	10月18日	10月20日	10月22日
時間	10:05-10:45	9:10-9:50	11:00-11:40
場所	日本語の教室		
グループ			

F. Group meeting.　グループでミーティングをしましょう。

Meet with your group and choose a preferred date and time for your review session. The procedure of this meeting is similar to that of the topic selection meeting earlier.

G. Leaders' meeting.　リーダーのミーティングをしましょう。

Now the leaders shall gather and have a meeting to finalize the schedule. Your teacher will chair this meeting and deal with any conflicts that may occur.

H. Make a final confirmation.　確認しましょう。

Provide the information below and make sure to know when you are up for your session.

日にち:　　　　　　　時間:

場所:　　　　　　　　トピック:

Recognition Kanji 1: 認識漢字 1

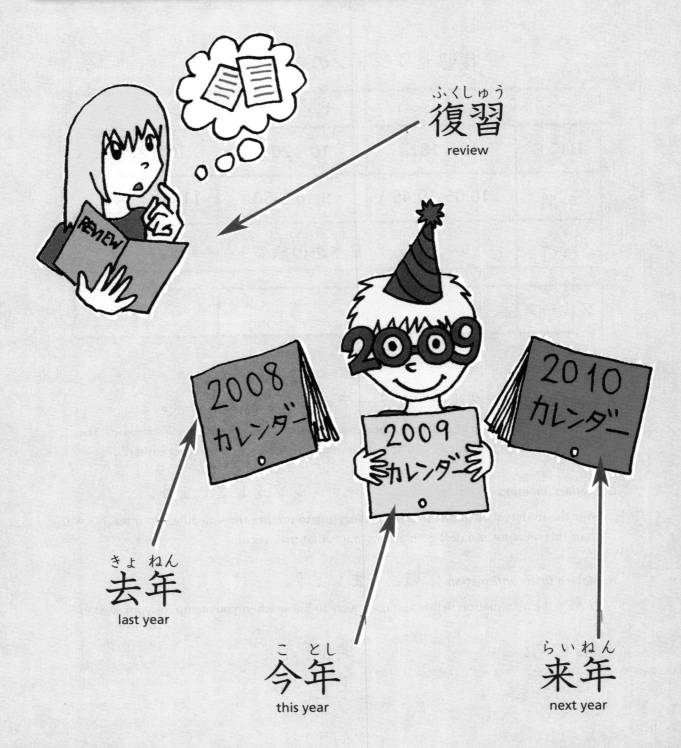

復習
ふくしゅう
review

去年
きょねん
last year

今年
ことし
this year

来年
らいねん
next year

JEM on Review: 復習<ruby>ふくしゅう</ruby>について

by Mary Ellen Jebbia

Overwhelmed?

When I started learning Japanese, I felt completely overwhelmed. Not only were there new words with new sounds, there was an entirely different written language! Quickly I learned that learning Japanese would take much discipline. Not to worry though- a simple 20 minutes spent reviewing everyday will help you master new phrases and *katakana* and *hiragana* quickly.

"Eat a duck I must"

Learning key phrases in Japanese might seem like a handful, but it is important to start the process of learning correct pronunciation as well as the structure of the language. In terms of pronunciation, a good way to learn is to say each phrase very slowly, syllable by syllable. For example, pronounce *hajimemashite* like this: *ha-ji-me-ma-shi-te*. This helps to break down the phrase so it doesn't seem so complicated. The next step is to use the proper intonation. Japanese doesn't have a stress syllable, so make sure to listen while you are in class to the proper inflection. When I started learning Japanese, I tried to remember phrases by making them sound like words in English. For example, to remember *itadakimasu*, I thought of "Eat a duck I must", and to remember *dooitashimashite*, I thought of "Don't touch my moustache." It sounds silly, but it helped!

Write and recite

To master *katakana* and *hiragana*, I found it very helpful to practice writing the characters while reciting the sound of the character. For example, when writing カ, say "*ka*" during each stroke. This helped me both in sight recognition and learning to write the characters. Studying flashcards with a partner is also helpful. When you start to read and write words in *katakana* and *hiragana*, it is a good idea to associate pictures with the words. This will help you start to see the words as words, and not as large strings of characters.

Let's lunch!

The best way to learn Japanese quickly and to feel comfortable using it is to practice as much as possible. Try and plan one lunch during the week with your classmates where you only speak Japanese. That way, you won't feel overwhelmed or slow because you'll all be in the same boat. It will be useful if your conversation revolves around phrases and vocabulary you have learned that week in class. For example, if you are studying school subjects, have a conversation about your favorite and least favorite subjects and why you like them. Apart from a formal lunch conversation, saying phrases like *ohayoo gozaimasu* and *o genki desu ka* to your classmates when you see them outside of class will help you feel more comfortable with the language.

Afraid of mistakes?

When you are in class, it is important to use Japanese whenever possible. When you aren't sure of something, you should always say *shitsumon ga arimasu* to your *sensei* and try your best to ask your question in Japanese. It is completely fine to make mistakes; in fact, it is good to make mistakes so you can learn the correct way to say something. If your classmates laugh, don't worry- it just makes class more fun!

Importance of self-teaching

My Japanese class was structured in a way, whereby my classmates and I did a good amount of self-teaching. We put on review sessions and the leader of the session would switch off. To review vocabulary and *kanji*, sometimes we played Memory, a card game in which you make two cards of each word or character, mix them all together, lay them all face down on a table, and flip two over at a time to see if you find a match. The object of the game is to remember the location of the words and characters so that you can find a match. Before you play this game, it is very helpful to study with flashcards. It is much easier to remember the location of a word if you recognize it easily. Other times in our sessions, we would make up worksheets with exercises. To help remember phrases, we would have to match the English meaning with the Japanese phrase. These are just a few examples of games and exercises you can try.

To me, the idea of self-teaching is very important. First of all, creating games and activities for your classmates forces you to learn and study. Even creating flashcards is a form of studying. Second, self-teaching gives you a framework for learning any language without relying too much on a teacher to help you learn the language. That way, during summer break and times when you might not be in class, you can continue to study. For me, this was also helpful when I studied abroad in Japan. I learned the most Japanese by practicing and making a habit of looking up new words and phrases I would hear, or new *kanji* I would see. In Japan even though I was taking language classes, I couldn't have learned as much Japanese if I hadn't taken initiative to learn outside of the classroom. Using this practice enriched my classes as well, because I could practice and perfect the language that I learned outside. On top of everything, the most important and most useful way to learn any language including Japanese is to practice. If you use your classroom time to learn new things and then practice what you learn outside, you'll no doubt have a great experience when you travel to Japan.

2.3 Mechanics 組立て

Structure and Work Progress
セッションの構成と進行

Objectives

Understand the structure of review session.
Practice monitoring work progress.
Learn about the dictionary form of verbs.

Overview

By the end of this section you will have a solid understanding of the structure of review sessions and will know how the leader may communicate with other members to check the progress of their work. New grammatical items in this section include the so-called "dictionary form" of verbs.

4 Check the structure of a session	構成の確認をする
1 Learn how to list actions	活動のリストの仕方を学ぶ
2 Check order of activities	活動の順序を確認する
5 Check the work progress	進行の確認をする
1 Check progress face-to-face	直接確認する
2 Check progress by e-mail	メールで確認する
3 Check progress by phone	電話で確認する

4 | **Check the structure of a session** | 構成の確認をする

1 | **Learn how to list actions** | 活動のリストの仕方を学ぶ

ノート: Dictionary Form of Verb　動詞の辞書形

affirmative

—

nonpast 動詞の

— 辞書形

—

plain/informal

Look at the preceding flow chart again and compare it with the chart in the beginning of the previous section. Do you notice any difference in style? Some of you might wonder why the sentences end with する and not with します. する is the plain and informal form of します and it is called the "dictionary form." The name comes from the fact that it is in this form that verbs are listed in various dictionaries. The dictionary form is used in casual conversations and other situations in which politeness and formality are not called for. One such situation is when listing things in the form of a chart or a memo. At this point, just remember the dictionary form for verbs is especially useful in this chapter. We will deal with the technical part of this form later on.

A. Consult an English-Japanese dictionary and complete the list below.

英和辞典を使って、リストを完成させてください。

あいます		meet	ききます		listen/ask
あそびます	あそぶ	play	きます		come
あらいます		wash	きめます		decide
あります	ある	exist/happen	こたえます	こたえる	answer
いいます		say	します		do
いきます		go	たべます		eat
います	いる	exist(living)	つくります		make
えらびます		choose	ねます	ねる	sleep
おきます		wake up	のみます		drink
おわります	おわる	end	はじめます		begin
かいます		buy	はなします	はなす	speak
かえります	かえる	go home	みます		watch/see
かきます		write	よみます		read

B. Fill in each parenthesis with a letter representing an appropriate ます form.

（　　）に記号を入れてください。

1. つくる （　　）　　2. きめる （　　　）　　3. する （　　　）

4. みる （　　）　　5. きく （　　）　　6. しょうかいする（　　）

7. えらぶ （　　）　　8. こたえる（　　）　　9. いう （　　　）

a. いいます	b. みます	c. しょうかいします
d. します	e. えらびます	f. ききます
g. こたえます	h. きめます	i. つくります

C. Complete the list on the right which is the "dictionary form version" of the list on the left.

Project Work	Project Work
グループを作ります	グループを作る
リーダーを選びます	リーダーを選ぶ
トピックを決めます	トピックを決める
スケジュールを決めます	
構成のチェックをします	
仕事を決めます	
アクティビティーを作ります	
教案を書きます	
練習をします	
復習セッションをします	

2 Check the order of activities　　活動の順序を確認する

It is necessary to know the basic structure of your session before starting to develop its content. You may recall that the concept of はじめ (beginning/introduction), なか (middle/main body), and おわり (end/conclusion) was introduced in *Haruichiban* and your session will be built on this three-part model. Go over the following sample.

復習セッション

トピック: 電話　　グループ: 猫

日にち: 10月18日　　時間: 10時5分-10時45分
場所: 日本語の教室

はじめのあいさつをする	**はじめ**	Greeting participants
トピックを紹介する		Introduction of topic
レッスンを紹介する		Introduction of lesson
ウォームアップをする	**なか**	Warm-ups
単語と表現と漢字を紹介する		Introduction of vocabulary and Kanji
アクティビティーをする		Activities
質問に答える		Questions & Answers
まとめと確認をする	**おわり**	Wrap-up
終りのあいさつをする		Last words

辞書形でリストを作りましょう。

A. Fill in each parenthesis with an appropriate letter.

( ) に記号を入れてください。

1. ひょうげん （　　）　2. あいさつ （　　）　3. トピック （　　）
4. はじめ　　（　　）　5. はっぴょう（　　）　6. まとめ　　（　　）
7. しょうかい（　　）　8. ふくしゅう（　　）　9. レッスン （　　）
10. おわり　　（　　）　11. たんご　　（　　）　12. しつもん （　　）

a. review	b. wrap-up	c. word	d. introduction
e. end	f. beginning	g. question	h. lesson
i. presentation	j. greeting	k. expression	l. topic

B. Confirm your understanding of the structure of your review session by putting a letter in each parenthesis to indicate the correct order of the session.

(）に記号を入れてください。

復習セッションの構成

1.（ *f* ）→ 2.（　　）→ 3.（　　）→ 4.（　　）→

5.（　　）→ 6.（　　）→ 7.（　　）→ 8.（　　）→ 9.（ *e* ）

a. 単語と表現と漢字を紹介する

b. まとめと確認をする

c. アクティビティーをする

d. ウォームアップをする

e. おわりのあいさつをする

f. はじめのあいさつをする

g. 質問に答える

h. トピックの紹介をする

i. レッスンを紹介する

---

5 | **Check work progress** | 進行の確認をする

You will soon start designing activities for your review session. Depending on the task, you might be working alone or with other group members. If you happen to be a leader, you are responsible for all the activities and will have to keep track of your members' progress. So let's practice how to confirm the progress and the completion of tasks beforehand.

1 | **Check progress face to face** | 直接確認する

ノート：Asking someone if something has been completed

Ｘができましたか

The past tense is often used to ask someone if something has been done and Ｘができましたか is especially useful in this respect. Ｘができました means "X has been done/completed."

<ruby>練習問題<rt>れんしゅうもんだい</rt></ruby>ができましたか。　(Lit.) Has the exercise been made/completed?

If your leader asks you the same question, your response will most likely be one of the following.

1. はい、できました。　Yes, it is done.

2. いいえ、まだです。　No, not yet.

3. いま、やっています。　I'm doing it right now.

ノート: Indicating actions in progress

〜ています

A verb form represented by きいて and よんで in きいてください and よんでください respectively is called the て(te) form. When the て(te) form of an action verb is immediately followed by います, it indicates that the action is in progress. きいています and よんでいます mean "I am listening," and "I am reading," respectively. You will learn more about the て(te) form in the next section.

<ruby>今<rt>いま</rt></ruby><ruby>漢字<rt>かんじ</rt></ruby>のカードを<ruby>作<rt>つく</rt></ruby>っています。　I am making Kanji cards now.

トムさんはお<ruby>昼<rt>ひる</rt></ruby>を<ruby>食<rt>た</rt></ruby>べています。　Tom is having his lunch.

A. Practice the following conversations by substituting the underlined parts.

<ruby>会話<rt>かいわ</rt></ruby>の<ruby>練習<rt>れんしゅう</rt></ruby>をしましょう。

<ruby>会話<rt>かいわ</rt></ruby>の<ruby>例<rt>れい</rt></ruby> A (Sample Dialogue A)

A: <u>アクティビティー</u>ができましたか。

B: はい、できました。 or

B: いいえ、まだです。 or

B: <ruby>今<rt>いま</rt></ruby>、やっています。 or
I'm doing it right now.

B: 今、作っています。
I'm making it right now.

やって is the て form of やります/やる, which is the more colloquial equivalent of します/する.

EX.　アクティビティー

1.　スピーチ

2.　<ruby>漢字<rt>かんじ</rt></ruby>のカード

3.　<ruby>単語<rt>たんご</rt></ruby>のリスト

4.　<ruby>表現<rt>ひょうげん</rt></ruby>のリスト

161

会話の例 B (Sample Dialogue B)

A: 漢字を書きましたか。
か ん じ

B: 今、書いています。
い ま

EX.	漢字を書きました、書いて
1.	リストを作りました、作って
2.	宿題をやりました、やって
3.	ビデオを見ました、見て
4.	リストを読みました、読んで

B. Practice the following conversation in which a leader checks with her group members in person about their work progress.

会話の練習をしましょう。
か い わ　れ ん し ゅ う

Face to Face の例 (Sample Dialogue)

シャンタル: ビンスさん、単語のリストができましたか。
た ん ご

ビンス: はい、できました。

シャンタル: 次は表現のリストですね。
つ ぎ　ひ ょ う げ ん

ビンス: はい、そうです。

シャンタル: ジェシカさんはカードですね。

ジェシカ: はい、そうです。

シャンタル: できましたか。

ジェシカ: あのう、今作っています。
い ま

シャンタル: じゃ、がんばってください。

ジェシカ: がんばります。

2 Check progress by e-mail

メールで確認する
か く に ん

A. Practice writing e-mail messages in which information about work progress has been exchanged.

メールを書きましょう。

メールの例 (Sample E-mail Exchange)

トムさん、

かんじとひょうげんのスライドができましたか。

しらせてください。(Let me know.)

シャンタル

リーダーのメール
Leader's e-mail

シャンタルさん、

かんじのスライドはできました。ひょうげんのスライドはまだです。これから、ジェシカさんと作ります。

がんばります。

トム

メンバーの返信
へんしん
Member's Reply

3 Check progress by phone

でんわ　かくにん
電話で確認する

A. Practice the following conversation in which a leader calls a group member at home to ask about her work progress.

でんわ　かいわ　れんしゅう
電話の会話を練習しましょう。

電話の例 (Sample Telephone Conversation)

 シャンタル　ジェニー

(dials Jenny's phone number)

→ もしもし。

ジョーンズさんのおたくですか。 → はい、そうです。

ジェニーさんいますか。 → はい。私です。

あ、こんばんは。シャンタルです。
あのう、復習セッションのことですが、
ふくしゅう
かんじ
漢字のリストはできましたか。 → はい、できました。

あ、そうですか。どうも、ありがとう。 → いいえ。

あした
じゃ、また、明日。 → おやすみなさい。

163

Recognition Kanji 2: 認識漢字 2

<ruby>認識漢字<rt>にんしきかんじ</rt></ruby>

<ruby>毎日<rt>まいにち</rt></ruby>
every day/daily

<ruby>毎月<rt>まいつき</rt></ruby>
every month/
monthly

<ruby>毎週<rt>まいしゅう</rt></ruby>
every week/
weekly

<ruby>毎年<rt>まいとし</rt></ruby>
every year/
annual

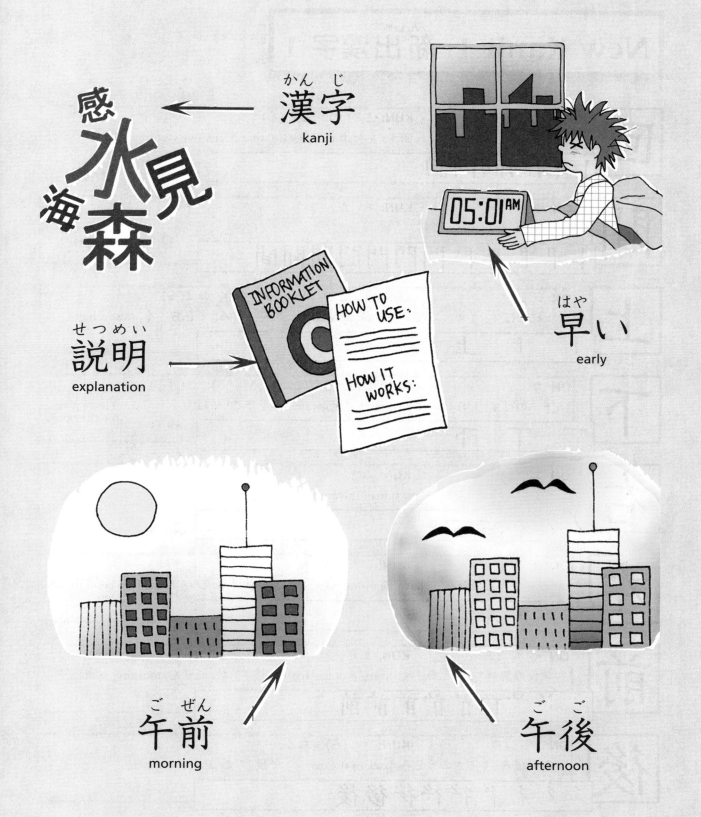

感
海水見
森

漢字
かんじ
kanji

05:01AM

早い
はや
early

説明
せつめい
explanation

INFORMATION
BOOKLET

HOW TO USE:

HOW IT WORKS:

午前
ごぜん
morning

午後
ごご
afternoon

165

New Kanji 1: 新出漢字 1

回
ON: カイ　　　　　　　　**KUN:** まわ(す)、まわ(る)
三回: さんかい　three times　回す: まわす　turn, rotate, spin (transitive verb)
丨 冂 冂 同 同 回

間
ON: カン　　　　　　　　**KUN:** あいだ、ま
時間: じかん　time
丨 冂 冂 冃 冃 門 門 門 門 間 間 間

上
ON: ジョウ　　　　　　　**KUN:** うえ、あ(がる)、あ(げる)、のぼ(る)
上にのばす: うえにのばす　stretch upward　　手を上げる: てをあげる　raise a hand
丨 卜 上

下
ON: カ、ゲ　　　　　　　**KUN:** した、くだ(さい)、さ(がる)、さ(げる)
下にのばす: したにのばす　stretch downward　本を下さい: ほんをください Please give me the book.
一 丁 下

右
ON: ユウ　　　　　　　　**KUN:** みぎ
本の右: ほんのみぎ　right side of the book　　右に曲げる: みぎにまげる bend to the right
ノ ナ ナ 才 右 右

左
ON: サ　　　　　　　　　**KUN:** ひだり
本の左: ほんのひだり　left side of the book　　左に曲げる: ひだりにまげる bend to the left
一 ナ ナ 左 左

前
ON: ゼン　　　　　　　　**KUN:** まえ
学校の前: がっこうのまえ　in front of the school　　午前: ごぜん　morning, a.m.
丶 丷 丷 产 产 前 前 前

後
ON: ゴ、コウ　　　　　　　**KUN:** うし(ろ)、あと
車の後ろ: くるまのうしろ　back of the car　　午後: ごご　afternoon, p.m.
ノ ク イ 彳 徏 徉 後 後 後

Language Note 2

Japanese Dictionaries

Japanese Language Dictionaries

When Japanese people hear an unfamiliar word and want to look it up in a dictionary, they reach for a こくごじてん ("national-language dictionary"). English speakers often call such a dictionary a Japanese-Japanese dictionary because both the words you look up and their detonations are in Japanese. A Japanese-Japanese dictionary lists words by their kana spelling, using katakana for words ordinarily written in katakana and hiragana for all other words.

The order of the words is determined by the conventional order of kana symbols, which is identical for hiragana and for katakana. The chart below displays the 46 basic hiragana symbols in their traditional arrangement. As the arrows show, the sequence within this arrangement follows the pattern for vertical Japanese writing: each column runs from top to bottom, and the columns run from right to left. In other words, the sequence goes あ い う え お か き く け こ and so on.

ん	わ	ら	や	ま	は	な	た	さ	か	あ
	り		み	ひ	に	ち	し	き	い	
	る	ゆ	む	ぶ	ぬ	つ	す	く	う	
	れ		め	へ	ね	て	せ	け	え	
	を	ろ	よ	も	ほ	の	と	そ	こ	お

A symbol with *dakuten* ("voicing dots") comes right after the same symbol without *dakuten*. For example, ざる (笊 "bamboo basket") will be listed right after さる (猿 "monkey"). A symbol with *handakuten* (the small circle) comes right after the same symbol with *dakuten*, so はん (判 "seal"), ばん (晩 "night"), and パン ("bread") will be listed in that order. Just as in English alphabetical order, if two words have the same first letter, their sequence depends on their second letters, and so on. For example, さかな (魚 "fish") comes before さばく (砂漠 "desert") because か comes before ば.

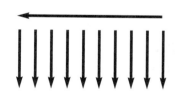

ひ

び　だくてん
　　"voicing dot"

ぴ　はんだくてん
　　"small circle"

A reduced-size symbol comes before a full-size symbol, so じゅう (十 "ten") comes before じゆう (自由 "freedom"), ファン ("sports fan") comes before ふあん (不安 "anxiety"), and かって (勝手 "selfish") comes before かつて (嘗て "formerly"). The katakana vowel-length indicator (ー) counts as equivalent to whatever vowel symbol would have the same sound. For example, スープ ("soup") is treated as if it were written スウプ, so it comes after すいようび (水曜日 "Wednesday") and before すえ (末 "end"), because い/イ, ぅ/ウ, and え/エ come in that order.

If two words have the same spelling except that one is listed in hiragana and the other in katakana, hiragana comes before katakana. As a result, めす(雌 "female) comes before メス ("scalpel").

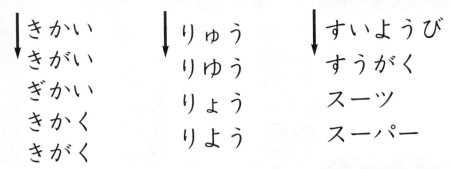

きかい
きがい
ぎかい
きかく
きがく

りゅう
りゆう
りょう
りよう

すいようび
すうがく
スーツ
スーパー

At this early stage in your study of Japanese, you don't have any use for a Japanese-Japanese dictionary, but the rules for sequencing words apply very widely. For instance, they apply to indexes, including the Japanese-English Index at the back of this book. As an exercise, try to put the following ten words in dictionary order.

EXERCISE 1	
くるま	(車 "car")
げき	(劇 "play")
こんど	(今度 "next time")
ゴルフ	("golf")
カラオケ	("karaoke")
こうえん	(公園 "park")
ケーキ	("cake")
コーヒー	("coffee")
くろ	(黒 "black")
からて	(空手 "karate")

EXERCISE 2	
バナナ	("banana")
はつおん	(発音 "pronunciation")
ひょう	(表 "chart")
ふくしゅう	(復習 "review")
パニック	("panic")
ぶんか	(文化 "culture")
ピッチャー	("pitcher")
ひよう	(費用 "expense")
はなび	(花火 "firework")
ひつよう	(必要 "necessary")

Bilingual Dictionaries

If you go into any large Japanese bookstore, you'll find dozens of えいわじてん ("English-Japanese dictionaries") and わえいじてん ("Japanese-English dictionaries"). The entry words in an English-Japanese dictionary are English, so they're always listed in English alphabetical order. The entry words in a Japanese-English dictionary are Japanese, and there are two main ways listing them. One way is to list them just as they'd be listed in a Japanese-Japanese dictionary: by kana spelling according to the rules explained above. The other way is to give the entry words in romanization and list them in alphabetical order.

Most Japanese-English dictionaries that use the kana method are aimed at Japanese-speaking users studying English, and most that use the romanization method are aimed at English-speaking users studying Japanese. The problem with the romanization method is that there's no universally accepted romanization system for Japanese, and different dictionaries follow different conventions.

へボン式[しき]	訓令式[くんれいしき]	日本式[にほんしき]	
し	shi	si	si
ち	chi	ti	ti
つ	tsu	tu	tu
ふ	fu	hu	hu
じ	ji	zi	zi
ぢ	ji	zi	di
づ	zu	zu	du
しゃ	sha	sya	sya
しゅ	shu	syu	syu
しょ	sho	syo	syo
じゃ	ja	zya	zya
じゅ	ju	zyu	zyu
じょ	jo	zyo	zyo
ぢゃ	ja	zya	dya
ぢゅ	ju	zyu	dyu
ぢょ	jo	zyo	dyo

The Romanization Maze

The table on the left shows how three most commonly used romanization systems, へボンしき (Hepburn system), くんれいしき (Japanese Ordinance system), and にほんしき ("Japan system") are different from one another. The rest are the same except for rules associated with "n" sound (ん), small つ, and long vowels. へボンしき is widely used both in and outside Japan. くんれいしき is a system developed by the Japanese government based on the other two. にほんしき, which was made in the late 19th century, was the least known until recently but the arrival of desktop word processing has brought this system back into action. For example, looking at the table, you may notice that the character ぢ is instantly obtainable only when an entry was made according to this system. You will be getting じ if your entries are based on the other systems. There are a fair amount of newer systems, which are a kind of derivation and variation of these three, as well as hybrid models.

Buying Dictionaries

As mentioned above, you don't have any use for a Japanese-Japanese dictionary at this stage in your study of Japanese. A Japanese-English dictionary or an English-Japanese dictionary would be more useful, and some publishers combine both into a single book. Before you spend your money on any dictionary though, you should ask your Japanese teacher for advice. Most bilingual dictionaries on the market are intended for customers whose native language is Japanese, and they can be nearly worthless to a beginning student of Japanese as a foreign language.

2.4 Mechanics 組立て

Review Session Preparation I
復習セッションの準備 I

Objectives

Be able to greet and introduce the topic of your review session.
Be able to give an overview of your session.
Be able to conduct assorted warm-up activities.

Overview

This is the first of three sections dealing with the contents of the review sessions. You will not only design activities, but also practice giving appropriate instructions. In this chapter we will focus on the first half of the sessions, from "Greeting participants" to "Introduction of vocabularies and kanji," as shown below.

6	Greeting and introduction	挨拶と紹介の準備をする
1	Greeting and introduction of topic	挨拶とトピックの紹介
2	Introduction of lesson	レッスンの紹介

7	Warm-up	ウォームアップの準備をする
1	Relaxation warm-up	リラックスのウォームアップ
2	Language warm-up	言葉のウォームアップ

6 **Greeting and introduction**　挨拶と紹介の準備をする

1 **Greeting and introduction of topic**　挨拶とトピックの紹介

ノート: To tell what something is about.

$$X について$$

X について means "about X."

これから、日本の歴史について話します。
I will talk about Japanese history.

リンダさんは夏休みについて書きました。
Linda wrote about her summer vacation.

A. Practice the following conversation by substituting the underlined part.

会話の練習をしましょう。

会話の例 (Sample Dialogue)

A: 何についてスピーチをしましたか。

B: <u>夏休み</u>についてスピーチをしました。

EX.	summer vacation
1.	my family
2.	my hobby
3.	last year's school
4.	my favorite food

B. Practice greeting your students and introducing your topic.

あいさつとトピックの紹介の練習をしましょう。

Practice in pairs. Substitute the first underlined part with another appropriate expression for greetings. You will introduce your topic in the second underlined part. Take turns between you and your partner while paying attention to each other's performance for accuracy. Afterwards, practice greeting and introducing topics as a team, in which you may be in charge of the greeting while your partner will take care of the introduction.

例 (Example)

あいさつ
Greeting

みなさん、<u>こんにちは。</u>
これから、去年の復習をしましょう。
(or復習セッションを始めます。)

トピックのしょうかい
Introducing the topic

今日は<u>ミーティング</u>について復習します。

171

An outline of your planned lesson will be given next. At this time you will practice giving such outlines by using the terms from the session structure introduction in the previous section.

ノート: Expressions to indicate something in sequence

When you describe something in sequence, expressions such as "first," "next," "and then," and "finally" are necessary. Effective use of them will make your instructions more cohesive and easier to follow. Look at the list below. Some of it should sound familiar to you from *Haruichiban*.

<ruby>始<rt>はじ</rt></ruby>めに〜します <ruby>最初<rt>さいしょ</rt></ruby>に〜します	first, to begin with, before anything else
<ruby>次<rt>つぎ</rt></ruby>に〜します それから〜します	next and then
<ruby>終<rt>お</rt></ruby>わりに〜します <ruby>最後<rt>さいご</rt></ruby>に〜します	finally

A. Practice saying the following schedule.　スケジュールを<ruby>言<rt>い</rt></ruby>ってください。

<ruby>来週<rt>らいしゅう</rt></ruby>の<ruby>月曜日<rt>よう</rt></ruby>	
1.	<ruby>音楽<rt>おんがく</rt></ruby>のクラスに<ruby>行<rt>い</rt></ruby>く
2.	<ruby>数学<rt>すうがく</rt></ruby>のテストをする
3.	ミーティングをする
4.	ポスターを<ruby>作<rt>つく</rt></ruby>る

EX.　<ruby>来週<rt>らいしゅう</rt></ruby>の<ruby>月曜日<rt>よう</rt></ruby>は：
<ruby>始<rt>はじ</rt></ruby>めに (or <ruby>最初<rt>さいしょ</rt></ruby>に)、<ruby>音楽<rt>おんがく</rt></ruby>のクラスに<ruby>行<rt>い</rt></ruby>きます。
<ruby>次<rt>つぎ</rt></ruby>に、<ruby>数学<rt>すうがく</rt></ruby>のテストをします。
<ruby>次<rt>つぎ</rt></ruby>に (or それから)、ミーティングをします。
<ruby>終<rt>お</rt></ruby>わりに (or <ruby>最後<rt>さいご</rt></ruby>に)、ポスターを<ruby>作<rt>つく</rt></ruby>ります。

1.

明日のミーティング	
1.	グループを作る
2.	リーダーを選ぶ
3.	トピックを決める
4.	スケジュールを決める
5.	教案を作る

2.

今日のクラス	
1.	単語の復習をする
2.	漢字のビデオを見る
3.	発音の練習をする
4.	会話の練習をする
5.	スピーチの練習をする

3.

品詞の勉強	
1.	名詞について勉強する
2.	動詞について勉強する
3.	形容詞について勉強する
4.	助詞について勉強する

4.

(Creat your own)	
1.	
2.	
3.	
4.	

B. Practice the entire はじめ part of a review session.

「はじめ」の部分を練習しましょう。

復習セッション	
1.	ウォームアップをする
2.	単語と表現と漢字を紹介する
3.	練習問題をする
4.	質問に答える
5.	まとめと確認をする

例 (Example)

みなさん、こんにちは。
これから、去年の復習をしましょう。
今日は電話について復習します。
始めにウォームアップをします。
次に単語と表現と漢字を紹介します。
　次に　　continued.

173

ノート: Two types of warm-up exercises:

Warm-up activities provide an opportunity for your classmates to break the ice, get ready, and call attention to group collaboration. You will practice conducting two types of warm-up activities. They are リラックスのウォームアップ ("relaxation warm-up"), and ことばの ウォームアップ ("language warm-up").

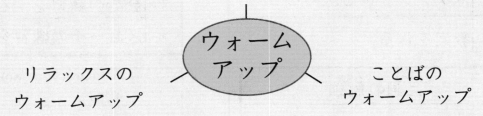

リラックスの　　　　　　ウォーム　　　　　　ことばの
ウォームアップ　　　　　アップ　　　　　　ウォームアップ

1 **Relaxation warm-up**　　　　　リラックスのウォームアップ

Warm-ups of this type could be a simple workout. You will learn words and expressions for indicating body parts and you will practice various workout directions using "〜てください."

A. Read the note on the て form first and then practice the following directions.

て<ruby>形<rt>けい</rt></ruby>を書きましょう。

EX. Please write.　　　かいてください。

1. Please stand.　　＿＿＿＿＿ください。

2. Please open.　　＿＿＿＿＿ください。

3. Please stretch.　　＿＿＿＿＿ください。

4. Please bend.　　＿＿＿＿＿ください。

5. Please rotate.　　＿＿＿＿＿ください。

6. Please sit down.　　＿＿＿＿＿ください。

7. Please say.　　＿＿＿＿＿ください。

8. Please listen.　　＿＿＿＿＿ください。

9. Please look.　　＿＿＿＿＿ください。

10. Please read.　　＿＿＿＿＿ください。

11. Please come.　　＿＿＿＿＿ください。

12. Please choose.　　＿＿＿＿＿ください。

ノート：て form of verb　動詞のて形

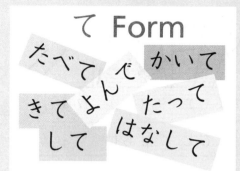

て Form

たべて かいて
よんで
きて たって
して はなして

-てください	Asking someone to do something
-ています	Indicating an action in progress

You must be familiar with expressions of requests such as たってください ("Please stand"), よんでください ("Please read") and もういちどいってください ("Please say that again"), since your teacher might have used them numerous times in class. The construction "〜てください" is the Japanese equivalent of "Please do such and such." A form represented by たって, よんで, and いって here is called the て (te) form. When this form is used by itself without ください, it simply takes away the formality and politeness the request carries. For example, たって is the informal/casual equivalent of たってください and is used among close friends and family members. The て form is also used in many sentence constructions, such as the "〜ています," which is used to indicate an action in progress and has appeared in the previous section. Formation of the て form follows several patterns and you will be learning about them later as well. For now, try to remember the て form of basic verbs. 〜てください is useful in giving directions and will be used repeatedly in warm-up exercises in this section.

USEFUL て FORM		ます form	て form は
ます form	**て form**	なします(speak)	はなして
おきます(wake up)	おきて	のばします(stretch)	のばして
ねます(sleep)	ねて	まわします(rotate, spin)	まわして
たべます(eat)	たべて	いきます(go)	いって
みます(look, watch, see)	みて	かえります(go home)	かえって
きめます(decide)	きめて	すわります(sit down)	すわって
まげます(bend)	まげて	つくります(make)	つくって
かきます(write)	かいて	たちます(stand up)	たって
ひらきます(open)	ひらいて	あいます(meet)	あって
よみます(read)	よんで	つかいます(use)	つかって
のみます(drink)	のんで	します(do)	して
えらびます(choose)	えらんで	きます(come)	きて

B. Fill in each parenthesis with a letter representing the appropriate body part.

（　　）に記号を入れてください。

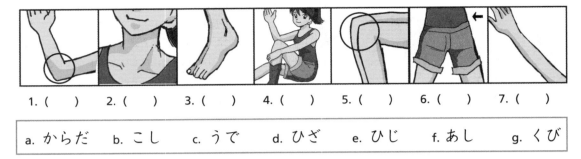

1. (　　) 　2. (　　) 　3. (　　) 　4. (　　) 　5. (　　) 　6. (　　) 　7. (　　)

a. からだ　　b. こし　　c. うで　　d. ひざ　　e. ひじ　　f. あし　　g. くび

C. Fill in each parenthesis with a letter representing the appropriate instruction.

（　　）に記号を入れてください。

1. (　　)　　　　　2. (　　)　　　　　3. (　　)　　　　　4. (　　)

5. (　　)　　　　　6. (　　)　　　　　7. (　　)

a. 腕を伸ばしてください。　　　　e. 足を開いてください。

b. ひじを曲げてください。　　　　f. 腕を回してください。

c. 首を回してください。　　　　　g. ひざを曲げてください。

d. 腰を曲げてください。

D. Do an exercise similar to one of those above with a partner or a group, actually showing the movements.

実際の動作で練習してください。

E. Fill in each parenthesis with a letter representing the appropriate direction.

（　）に記号を入れてください。

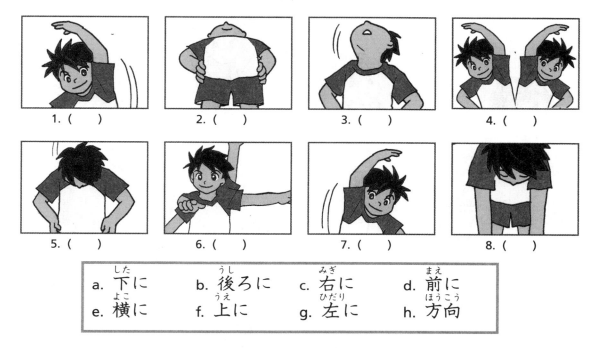

1. (　　)　　2. (　　)　　3. (　　)　　4. (　　)

5. (　　)　　6. (　　)　　7. (　　)　　8. (　　)

a. 下に	b. 後ろに	c. 右に	d. 前に
e. 横に	f. 上に	g. 左に	h. 方向

F. Fill in each parenthesis with a letter representing the appropriate instruction.

（　）に記号を入れてください。

1. (　　)　　2. (　　)　　3. (　　)　　4. (　　)

a. 体を横に曲げてください。　　c. 体/腰を後ろに曲げてください。

b. 腕を上に伸ばしてください。　　d. 体/腰を前に曲げてください。

G. Do an exercise similar to one of those above with a partner or a group, actually showing the movements.

実際の動作で練習してください。

H. What directions should you give if you want to have someone do the movements shown in the pictures below?

指示を作ってください。

1.

2.

3.

4.

5.

6.

7.

8.

9.

10.

11.

12.

13.

UP

DN

B

F

ノート: Asking to return to the original position

もどしてください

もどします(もどす) means "put back" or "return." If you want to ask workout participants to return to the previous position or posture, you may say もどしてください.

腕_{うで}を上_{うえ}に伸_のばしてください。戻_{もど}してください。

足_{あし}を開_{ひら}いてください。戻_{もど}してください。

ノート: Indicating repetition

〜回_{かい}

Xかい is the Japanese equivalent of "X times." If you want someone to read something twice, you may say 2かいよんでください. Xかい can be placed in the beginning of a sentence, though it is most commonly placed right before the predicate verb.

1回_{いっかい}, 2回_{にかい}, 3回_{さんかい}, 4回_{よんかい}, 5回_{ごかい}, 6回_{ろっかい}, 7回_{ななかい}, 8回_{はっかい}, 9回_{きゅうかい}, 10回_{じゅっかい}, 何回_{なんかい}

3回曲_{かいま}げてください。　　　　Bend three times.

体_{からだ}を3回曲げてください。　　Bend your body three times.

体を左_{ひだり}に3回曲げてください。　Bend your body to the left three times.

I. Practice indicating repetition of movements.

数_{かず} (number) の指示_{しじ}を練習_{れんしゅう}しましょう。

You may indicate repetition of movements in two ways. You may indicate repetitions after giving movement instructions, or give both instructions at once. Practice both ways, as shown in the example.

EX.
5 times

腕_{うで}を曲_まげてください。5回曲げてください。
or 腕_{うで}を5回曲げてください。

1. 4 times

2. 6 times

3. 3 times

4. 2 times

179

J. Practice in pairs or in small groups.　ペアか小グループで練習しましょう。

Create warm-up instructions and check if others can follow them appropriately.　Ask them to do one movement at a time initially, and gradually increase the degree of difficulty by giving instructions at once for a sequence of movements.

2 Language warm-up　　言葉のウォームアップ

Due to the cumulative nature of language learning, conducting constant reviews for past learning becomes an essential task.　Since you will have only a few minutes for this activity, preparing three to five simple review questions will be sufficient.

A. Go over the following and come up with one or two questions from each category.

質問を作りましょう。

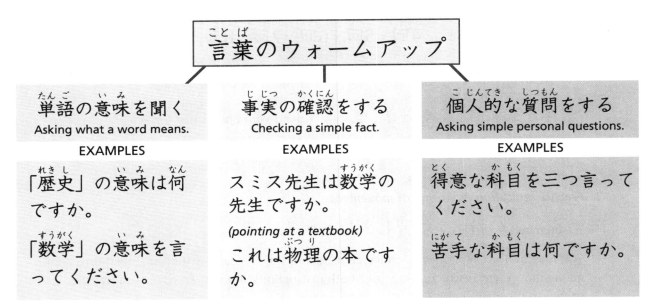

言葉のウォームアップ

単語の意味を聞く
Asking what a word means.

EXAMPLES

「歴史」の意味は何ですか。

「数学」の意味を言ってください。

事実の確認をする
Checking a simple fact.

EXAMPLES

スミス先生は数学の先生ですか。

(pointing at a textbook)
これは物理の本ですか。

個人的な質問をする
Asking simple personal questions.

EXAMPLES

得意な科目を三つ言ってください。

苦手な科目は何ですか。

B. Practice the entire warm-up section

ウォームアップを全部 (all of them) 練習しましょう。

The following sample instructions cover the entire process on how to conduct warm-up activities.　Practice with the sample instructions first.　Afterwards, continue to practice by substituting the underlined parts with similar activities you create.　The structure of the sample instructions is as follows and you may follow it in your review sessions

1. Indicating the beginning
2. Conducting a relaxation warm-up (3 movements)
3. Conducting a language warm-up (3-5 questions)
4. Indicating the end

ウォームアップの例 (Sample Warm-up Instructions)

Indicate the beginning of the warm -up

じゃ、ウォームアップをしましょう。

Indicate the beginning of the relaxation exercise

始めに、リラックスのウォームアップをします。

Ask the class to stand

みなさん、立ってください。

Instructions for relaxation exercise

最初に、腕を上に伸ばしてください。
次に、体を左に曲げてください。
3回曲げてください。(1, 2, 3...)
最後に、体を右に曲げてください。
3回曲げてください。(1, 2, 3...)
戻してください。(Go back to the original position.)
これで、終わります。

Indicate the beginning of the review warm-up

次に、言葉のウォームアップをしましょう。

Tell the class to answer the questions

質問に答えてください。

Ask questions (Review items: daily activities)

今日、何時に起きましたか。
何時に数学のクラスに行きますか。
何時にうちへ帰りますか。
何時に寝ますか。

いちばん
一番
first/best/
number one

かいわ
会話
conversation

もんだい
問題
problem

きせつ
季節
seasons

名詞
noun

動詞
verb

形容詞
adjective

助詞
propositional particle

学校から帰る。
私のお父さん。
日本へ行く。
君と僕は友達だ。

New Kanji 2: 新出漢字 2

(しんしゅつかんじ)

体

ON: タイ **KUN:** からだ

体:からだ body

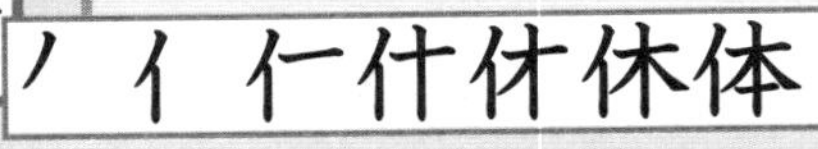

手

ON: シュ **KUN:** て

手: て hand 右手: みぎて right hand 左手: ひだりて left hand

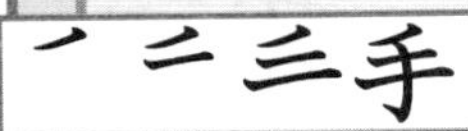

足

ON: ソク **KUN:** あし

足: あし leg, foot 右足: みぎあし right leg/foot 左足: ひだりあし left leg/foot

目

ON: モク **KUN:** め

目: め eyes 目的: もくてき goal

耳

ON: ジ **KUN:** みみ

耳: みみ ears

口

ON: コウ **KUN:** くち

口: くち mouth 人口: じんこう population

頭

ON: トウ **KUN:** あたま、かしら

頭:あたま head

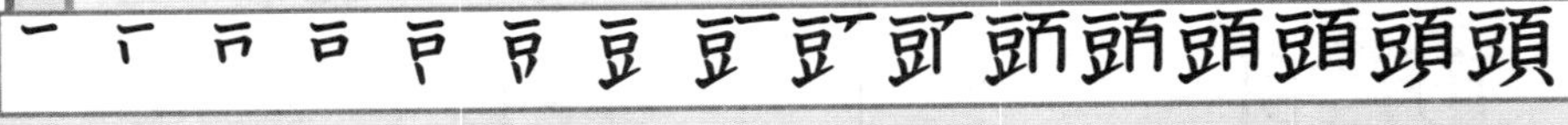

名

ON: メイ、ミョウ **KUN:** な

名: な name 名前: なまえ name 有名: ゆうめい famous

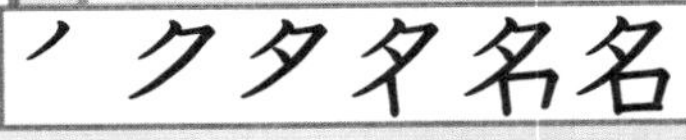

Reading 3:
読み物 3

Reading Dojo 2: Skimming
読解道場 2: スキミング

Skim It Part I: Finding the Appropriate Title & Word

A. Skim through the following articles and choose the appropriate title from the second box below.

1. ( )
旅行の予算は240ドルです。
ホテルが120ドルです。
バスと電車が70ドルです。
食べ物が50ドルです。

2. ( )
金曜日に焼き鳥セールをします。
だから、椅子とテーブルが必要です。
テントは必要じゃありません。

3. ( )
名前はジョーです。出身はボストンです。
住まいはダラスです。
趣味はテニスです。家族は5人です。

4. ( )
山中先生の発表は8じからです。
場所は講堂です。
トピックは日本の伝統スポーツです。

発表: presentation   場所: place   講堂: auditorium   住まい: residence
伝統: tradition   趣味: hobby

A. Personal profile   B. Event information   C. Budget report   D. Needs assessment

---

Skim It Part II: Finding the Visual Form

B. Skim through the following articles and choose the most appropriate visual form below.

1. ( )
あした、スミスさんの発表があります。場所は講堂です。時間は午後７時半です。トピックは相撲です。

A.   Tonight

スミス

7:30

B.   Tomorrow

スミス

7:30

C.   Tomorrow

スミス

7:30

2. (　　)
きょうは始めに図書室へ行きます。図書室で歴史のレポートを書きます。それから、講堂へ行きます。そのあと、コンピュータルームへ行きます。

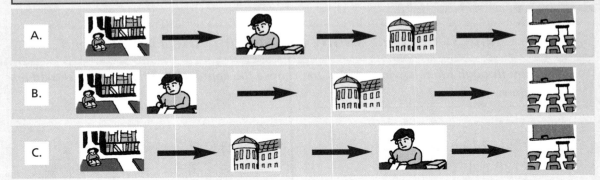

A.

B.

C.

Skim It Part III: Finding the Summary

C. Skim through the following articles and choose the best summary from the second box.

1. (　　)
トムは月曜日に柔道(じゅうどう)をします。火曜日に剣道(けんどう)をします。木曜日と金曜日に弓道(きゅうどう)をします。そして、日曜日に空手(からて)をします。

A. トムはすもうをします。　　B. トムは日本の伝統的(でんとうてき)スポーツがすきです。
C. トムは日本にいます。　　D. トムは柔道と剣道の選手(せんしゅ)です。

2. (　　)
サラは毎日サラダを食べます。よくバナナやリンゴやパイナップルも食べます。でも、ステーキやチキンやハンバーガーはぜんぜん食べません。

A. サラはサラダが好きです。　　B. サラはステーキがきらいです。
C. サラは元気です。　　D. サラはベジタリアンです。

Skim It Part IV: Finding the Summary Within Limited Time

D. Read the following story within three minutes, and choose the appropriate sentence that shows the biggest benefit of the "ウォーカーズギルト" club from the list below the story.

私たちの学校では5年前にウォーカーズギルドというクラブが出来た。最初5人だったメンバーは今250人だ。つまり、生徒ほぼ全員がメンバーなのだ。メンバーは毎月ハイキングやチャリティーウォークなどたくさんの行事に参加する。朝早く起きて、学校まで歩いて来る人も多くなった。車を使うことが少なくなったから、健康や環境にいいかも知れない。でも最大の成果はやはり歩くという健康的な活動を通じて生徒達の交流が深まったことである。毎年9月には新入生のための「ウエルカムウォーク」もある。これからもいろいろな歩く行事が増えて行くだろう

全員: all members　　行事: events　　参加: participate　　健康: health　　環境: environment
いいかも知れない: may be OK　　最大: the biggest　　成果: result　　活動: activity
交流: exchange　　深まる: deepen　　新入生: new student　　増える: increase

 a.　最初5人だったメンバーは今250人だ。

 b.　メンバーは毎月たくさんの行事に参加する。

 c.　健康的な活動を通じて生徒達の交流が深まった。

 d.　これからもいろいろな歩く行事が増えて行く。

Skim It Part V: Finding the Important Message Within Limited Time

E. Skim the message from the captain of our volleyball team who is so busy for preparing for the tournament.

きのうの練習ではサーブとサーブレシーブはよくできたけど、アタックがあまりうまくできなかったと思います。トーナメントは来週だけど、ちょっと心配です。コーチも心配だと言っていました。それで、明日は休みの日だけど、2時から4時まで練習することにしました。だから、2時にジムに来てください。お願いします。

練習: practice　　心配: worry

You are very busy right now preparing for an upcoming math test. You just received an e-mail message of "high importance" from the captain for your Japanese volleyball team. Skim the message and get the gist of it. Then choose the most crucial information in the message form below.

 a.　来週トーナメントがあります。

 b.　コーチが心配しています。

 c.　明日2時からジムで練習があります。

 d.　サーブとサーブレシーブがよくできました。

 e.　明日は休みの日です。

2.5 Mechanics 組立て
<ruby>組<rt>く</rt></ruby><ruby>立<rt>た</rt></ruby>て

Review Session Preparation II
<ruby>復習<rt>ふくしゅう</rt></ruby>セッションの<ruby>準備<rt>じゅん び</rt></ruby> II

Objectives

Be able to introduce words, expressions, and kanji that will appear in your session.
Prepare several different types of exercises for your review session.
Practice conducting exercises in Japanese.

Overview

In this section you will first decide how to introduce words, expressions, and kanji that are essential in your session, and then practice introducing them. Next you will move onto the "activities" portion of your session. You will create several different types of activities that are relevant to your session and practice conducting them entirely in Japanese, spending a good deal of time collaborating and making teaching materials as well as exercises. It is important that you communicate in Japanese as much as possible throughout the process and refrain from chatting in English.

8	**Vocabulary and kanji**	単語と表現と漢字の準備をする
1	Select visuals	ビジュアルを選ぶ
2	Learn useful expressions	役に立つ表現を学ぶ
3	Make visuals	ビジュアルを作る
4	Practice giving directions	指示の練習をする

9	**Activities**	アクティビティーの準備をする
1	Worksheet/slide style	ワークシート/スライド型
2	Read aloud style	音読型
3	Skit style	スキット型
4	Role play style	ロールプレイ型

9 Vocabulary and kanji　　単語と表現と漢字

1 Select visuals　　ビジュアルを選ぶ

A. Make a list.　リストを作りましょう

List up any key vocabulary, expressions and kanji for your review session. The lists serve as a common ground upon which group members prepare their lesson.

B. Think about using visual aids.　ビジュアルについて考えましょう。

Use of visual aids will enable you to effectively introduce and practice words, expressions and kanji.

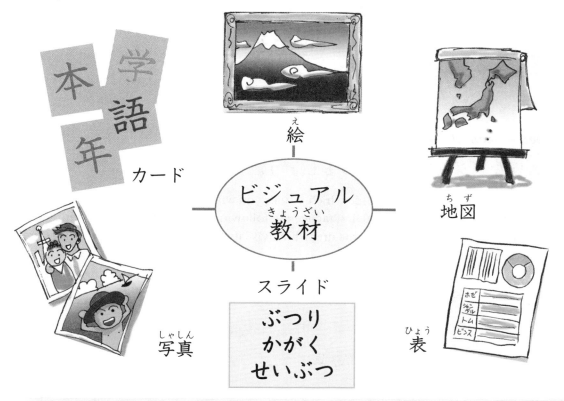

本　学　語　年　カード

絵

ビジュアル教材

地図

写真

スライド

ぶつり
かがく
せいぶつ

表

ノート: Suggesting something

Xはどうですか

Xはどうですか means "How about X." It is useful in making suggestions in various decision making situations. It is also useful in asking someone for his or her countersuggestion, opinion, or response.

A: トピックは何がいいですか。　　What is a good topic?

B: 家族はどうですか。　　How about family?

C. *Practice making suggestions.* 提案の練習をしましょう。

Substitute (1) with one of the following word in the box and (2) with any suitable word given the change in (1).

何曜日
どこ
何時

会話の例 (Sample Dialogue)

A: パーティーは (1)何日がいいですか。

B: (2)六日はどうですか。

C: あ、いいですね。

A: Dさんはどうですか。

D: 私も (2)六日がいいです。

A: じゃ、(2)六日にしましょう。

D. *Decide upon what types of visuals you will need.*

必要なビジュアルを決めましょう。

Meet with your group and decide which visuals you will be using in your session. You may use more than one type of visual. Practice the following conversation beforehand. Also decide who will be in charge of making which visuals. Make sure to conduct your entire meeting in Japanese.

会話の例 (Sample Dialogue)

A: どんなビジュアルが必要ですか。

B: カードが必要です。それから、絵も必要です。

A: 写真はどうですか。

C: 写真は必要じゃありません。

A: じゃ、表はどうですか。

D: 家族の単語の表を作りましょう。

A: 地図は必要ですか。

D: いいえ。

E. Make a list.　リストを作りましょう。

Make a list of the visuals your group will be making and the names of the persons in charge.

ビジュアルのリスト

1. 漢字のカード (Kanji cards)　　　　　ホセ

2. 形容詞のカード (Adjective cards)　　シャンタル

3. 家族の絵 (Pictures of family members)　トム

4. 家族の単語の表 (Family term chart)　ジェニー

---

2 **Learn useful expressions**　　　役に立つ表現を学ぶ

Before you start making your visuals, let's learn some expressions that will help you communicate with each other in Japanese while making the visuals. Make sure to limit your conversation to those matters related to your task and refrain from chatting in English. Go over the following expressions.

日本語 (Formal)	英語	日本語 (Informal)
サラさん、青いマーカーはありますか。	Sara. Do you have a blue marker?	サラ、青いマーカーある?
トムさん、それを取ってください。	Tom. Pass that one to me.	トム、それ取って。
ボブさん、このペンを使ってもいいですか。	May I use this pen, Bob?	ボブ、このペン使ってもいい?
何色ですか。	What color (do you want)?	何色?
これでいいですか。	Is this alright?	これでいい?
できましたか。	Are you done?	できた?

A. Practice using some of the expressions.　　表現の練習をしましょう。

会話の例 A Formal

A: リンダさん。それを取ってください。

B: どれですか。

A: その赤いマーカーです。

EX. 赤いマーカー
1. 青いカード
2. 緑のペン
3. 電車の写真

会話の例 B Informal

A: リンダ、このペン使ってもいい。

YES　　　　　　　　　　　　　　NO

B: うん、いいよ。　　B: ごめん、今はだめ。

A: ありがとう。　　　A: あ、そう。

EX. ペン
1. はさみ (scissors)
2. 紙 (a sheet of paper)
3. のり (glue)

3　Make visuals　　　　ビジュアルを作る

Now start making your visuals. Remember you will be speaking in Japanese as much as possible.

4　Practice giving instructions　　　指示の練習をする

A. Go over the examples below and create simple instructions of your own.

指示を作りましょう。

指示の例 (Sample Instructions)

1. 単語 (Ask students to look at pictures and say what they are.)
   これは何ですか。絵を見てください。それから、言ってください。

2. 表現 (Ask students to listen to an expression and give its meaning.)
   表現を聞いてください。そして、意味を言ってください。

3. 漢字 (Ask students to look at flash cards and read kanji on them.)
   漢字のカードです。読んでください。

B. Practice the entire section.

このセクションを全部 (all of them) 練習しましょう。

Do the run-through of this section in which your group will introduce words, expressions and kanji.

紹介の例 (Example)

Indicate the beginning	これから、単語と表現と漢字を紹介します。
Give instructions about introduction of words	最初は単語です。絵を見てください。それから、言ってください。
Give instructions about introduction of expressions	次は表現です。聞いてください。そして、意味を言ってください。
Give instructions about introduction of kanji	最後は漢字です。カードを読んでください。
Thank the students for their cooperation and announce the end	はい、ありがとうございました。これで、終わります。

If you think the above procedure is too monotonous, you may think of a more challenging procedure. For example, you can involve more students during your activities by doing things such as the following.

- Ask your students for assistance.
  マイクさん、このしゃしんをみせてください
  (Mike, please show/hold up this picture.)

- Distribute vocabulary or kanji cards and have them lead a review activity about the items on their cards.

You will prepare three or four different styles of activities listed below. Written directions in English may accompany each activity. You may either do all four or the first two plus a skit or role play.

ACTIVITIES		
	Worksheet/Digital style	ワークシート／デジタル型
	Read Aloud style	音読型
	Skit style	スキット型
	Role Play style	ロールプレイ型

1 **Worksheet/digital style** ワークシート／デジタル型

You will start with a worksheet or digital slide based activity. You may create a series of exercises on a worksheet or present them digitally using a slide software. Your exercises may include both those that can be answered by a letter or number such as vocabulary matching and those that can be answered by word or sentence such as grammatical completion and translation. Keep in mind that this activity may be useful in facilitating your subsequent activities such as a role play.

例 A (Example A)

Draw a line from the verbs on the left to their English equivalents on the right.

1. えらぶ　　　　　　•　　• introduce
2. きめる　　　　　　•　　• decide
3. つくる　　　　　　•　　• choose
4. しょうかいする　•　　• answer
5. こたえる　　　　　•　　• make

例 B (Example B)

Rearrange the words in parentheses in a correct order and read the entire sentences.

1. キムさん (せんせい／の／は／にほんご) です。

2. ジェニーさんは (いもうと／で／と／バス) がっこうにいきます。

例 C (Example C)

You are on the phone. Ask the other party:

1. if you have called the Moriyama residence.
2. if Midori is at home.
3. what time Midori will return.
4. what Midori's cell phone (けいたい) number is.

A. Now you will practice conducting the activity you just made. First, ask your classmates to do the exercises according to the written instructions given in English. Then call upon your students for responses. As you hear their responses, you may make corrections if necessary or check with the rest of your class. Practice in your group.

グループで練習しましょう。

指示の例 (Sample Instructions)

Indicate the beginning of exercises

じゃ、練習問題をしましょう。

Distribute a worksheet

これから、ワークシートを配ります。

Ask classmates to quietly read the instructions

始めに指示を読んでください。静かに、読んでください。

会話の例 (Sample Dialogue)

The leader calls upon Nina

L: ニーナさん、2の1をお願いします。

Nina responds by a word

N: はい、「電話」は名詞です。

The leader affirms Nina's response

L: はい、そうです。よくできました。

Choose one word you think is correct and then read the entire sentence.

1. 「電話」は (名詞/動詞/形容詞/助詞) です。
2. 「決める」は (名詞/動詞/形容詞/助詞) です。
3. 「すてきな」は (名詞/動詞/形容詞/助詞) です。
4. 「へ」は (めいし/どうし/けいようし/じょし) です。

B. Practice checking your students' response. 答<ruby>え<rt>こた</rt></ruby>のチェックをしましょう。

After making sure that instructions have been followed correctly, you must check answers and make corrections if necessary before moving onto the next one.

Fill in each parenthesis with an appropriate letter.

( )に<ruby>記号<rt>きごう</rt></ruby>を<ruby>入<rt>い</rt></ruby>れてください。

Go over the following sample dialogues about checking answers and match each of them with a description by placing the appropriate letter in each parenthesis.

---

1. (　　)

L: <u>サラさん</u>、<u>1の1</u>の<ruby>答<rt>こた</rt></ruby>えは<ruby>何<rt>なん</rt></ruby>ですか。

S: ええと、<u>b</u>です。

L: いいですか。

C: はい、いいです。

L: そうですね。<ruby>正<rt>ただ</rt></ruby>しい答えは<u>b</u>です。

---

2. (　　)

L: <u>サラさん</u>、<u>1の1</u>の<ruby>答<rt>こた</rt></ruby>えは<ruby>何<rt>なん</rt></ruby>ですか。

S: ええと、<u>b</u>です。

L: はい、そうです。
<ruby>正<rt>ただ</rt></ruby>しい答えは<u>b</u>です。

---

3. (　　)

L: <u>ビルさん</u>、<u>1の1</u>をお<ruby>願<rt>ねが</rt></ruby>いします。

B: はい、<ruby>答<rt>こた</rt></ruby>えは<u>a</u>です。

L: いいですか。

C: いいえ、<ruby>違<rt>ちが</rt></ruby>います。

L: じゃ、どれですか。

C: <u>b</u>です。

L: そうですね。<ruby>正<rt>ただ</rt></ruby>しい答えは b です。

---

4. (　　)

L: <u>ビルさん</u>、<u>1の1</u>の<ruby>答<rt>こた</rt></ruby>えを<ruby>言<rt>い</rt></ruby>ってください。

B: ええと、<u>a</u>です。

L: <u>a</u>じゃありません。
<ruby>正<rt>ただ</rt></ruby>しい答えは<u>b</u>です。

---

5. (　　)

L: <u>ビルさん</u>、<u>1の1</u>の<ruby>答<rt>こた</rt></ruby>えは<ruby>何<rt>なん</rt></ruby>ですか。

B: ええと、<u>a</u>です。

L: そうですか。ニーナさん。

N: いいえ、<u>b</u>です。

L: そうですね。<ruby>正<rt>ただ</rt></ruby>しい答えは<u>b</u>です。

---

a. A correct answer was given and the leader confirmed it by herself.

b. A wrong answer was given and the leader asked the class to give a correct answer.

c. A wrong answer was given and the leader called upon another student.

d. A correct answer was given and the leader asked the class to confirm it.

e. A wrong answer was given and the leader immediately gave the correct answer.

Conversation practice. 会話の練習をしましょう。

Now practice the five sample dialogues given above by replacing the underlined parts.

C. *See the flow chart.* フローチャートを見ましょう。

The following flow chart will be helpful when you practice checking whether or not instructions have been correctly followed and whether or not correct answers have been given

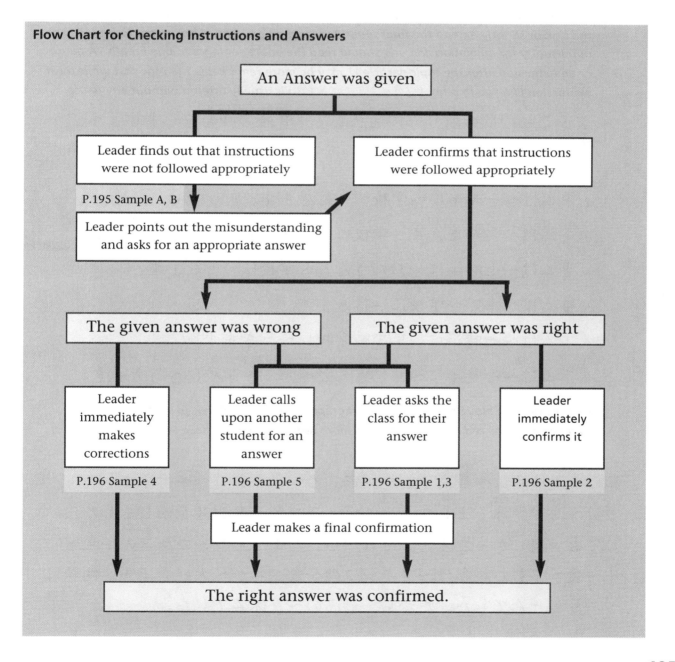

Flow Chart for Checking Instructions and Answers

An Answer was given

Leader finds out that instructions were not followed appropriately

P.195 Sample A, B

Leader points out the misunderstanding and asks for an appropriate answer

Leader confirms that instructions were followed appropriately

The given answer was wrong

The given answer was right

Leader immediately makes corrections

P.196 Sample 4

Leader calls upon another student for an answer

P.196 Sample 5

Leader asks the class for their answer

P.196 Sample 1,3

Leader immediately confirms it

P.196 Sample 2

Leader makes a final confirmation

The right answer was confirmed.

Do you always speak clearly in class? Does your teacher have a problem understanding your Japanese even if you are sure it's correct? We are prone to lack articulation in class from time to time and as a teacher you need to make sure that both you and your students are speaking clearly and loud enough. Offering an activity which involves reading something aloud will serve as en effective reminder about the importance of articulation.

A. Practice reading aloud the following sentences. They are broken up by a unit of articulation called bunsetsu and "〜" is placed after every bunsetsu. You may either slightly pause at the sign or slightly extend the final sound before the sign. This is not meant to provide an opportunity for inhalation and you should read the entire sentence in one breath. A pause or an extension after the topic particle は *may be more remarkable than the rest while a set expression like "go to school" (*がっこうにいきます*) is usually uttered without any pause.*

<ruby>文節<rt>ぶんせつ</rt></ruby>ごとの<ruby>間<rt>ま</rt></ruby>の<ruby>取<rt>と</rt></ruby>り<ruby>方<rt>かた</rt></ruby>に<ruby>注意<rt>ちゅうい</rt></ruby>して、<ruby>音読<rt>おんどく</rt></ruby>の<ruby>練習<rt>れんしゅう</rt></ruby>をしましょう。

1. トムは〜<ruby>学校<rt>がっこう</rt></ruby>に〜<ruby>行<rt>い</rt></ruby>きます。
2. トムは〜<ruby>七時半<rt>しちじはん</rt></ruby>に〜<ruby>学校<rt>がっこう</rt></ruby>に〜<ruby>行<rt>い</rt></ruby>きます。
3. トムは〜お<ruby>姉<rt>ねえ</rt></ruby>さんと〜<ruby>学校<rt>がっこう</rt></ruby>に〜<ruby>行<rt>い</rt></ruby>きます。
4. トムは〜<ruby>七時半<rt>しちじはん</rt></ruby>に〜お<ruby>姉<rt>ねえ</rt></ruby>さんと〜<ruby>学校<rt>がっこう</rt></ruby>に〜<ruby>行<rt>い</rt></ruby>きます。
5. トムは〜<ruby>車<rt>くるま</rt></ruby>で〜<ruby>学校<rt>がっこう</rt></ruby>に〜<ruby>行<rt>い</rt></ruby>きます。
6. トムは〜<ruby>七時半<rt>しちじはん</rt></ruby>に〜<ruby>車<rt>くるま</rt></ruby>で〜<ruby>学校<rt>がっこう</rt></ruby>に〜<ruby>行<rt>い</rt></ruby>きます。
7. トムは〜<ruby>七時半<rt>しちじはん</rt></ruby>に〜お<ruby>姉<rt>ねえ</rt></ruby>さんと〜<ruby>車<rt>くるま</rt></ruby>で〜<ruby>学校<rt>がっこう</rt></ruby>に〜<ruby>行<rt>い</rt></ruby>きます。

B. Practice reading aloud the following paragraph. Keep in mind that pauses or sound extensions at the red "〜" signs may be more remarkable than those at the blue "〜" signs.

<ruby>私<rt>わたし</rt></ruby>の〜<ruby>夏休<rt>なつやす</rt></ruby>みは〜<ruby>最高<rt>さいこう</rt></ruby>でした。<ruby>家族<rt>かぞく</rt></ruby>と〜メキシコへ〜<ruby>行<rt>い</rt></ruby>きました。<ruby>毎日<rt>まいにち</rt></ruby>〜<ruby>海<rt>うみ</rt></ruby>で〜<ruby>泳<rt>およ</rt></ruby>ぎました。<ruby>夜<rt>よる</rt></ruby>、ディスコで〜ダンスを〜しました。とても〜<ruby>楽<rt>たの</rt></ruby>しかったです。それから、たくさん〜メキシコの〜<ruby>食<rt>た</rt></ruby>べ<ruby>物<rt>もの</rt></ruby>を〜<ruby>食<rt>た</rt></ruby>べました。<ruby>私<rt>わたし</rt></ruby>は〜メキシコの〜<ruby>食<rt>た</rt></ruby>べ<ruby>物<rt>もの</rt></ruby>が〜<ruby>大好<rt>だいす</rt></ruby>きです。<ruby>問題<rt>もんだい</rt></ruby>は〜ありませんでした。だから、<ruby>最高<rt>さいこう</rt></ruby>の〜<ruby>夏休<rt>なつやす</rt></ruby>みでした。

C. There may be more than a handful of activities in which ondoku (reading aloud) can be effectively incorporated. At this time we introduce two. One focuses on ondoku itself and the other is a listening activity in which your students will answer questions after listening to your ondoku presentation. You may do one or both of them and you will need to make two different paragraphs if you are going to do both. Start your preparation according to the flow chart below.

フローチャートに従ってアクティビティーの準備をしましょう。

Write a short paragraph such as the one you practiced reading aloud in the previous section.

前のセクションのような文章を作ってください。

Place "〜" for major pauses or sound extension and "˜" for minor ones and have your teacher check the script.

主な間には「〜」を、それ以外の間には「〜」を書き入れてください。

Practice reading your paragraph aloud with appropriate pauses or sound extension.

間の取り方に注意して、音読の練習をしてください。

For *ondoku* 音読の場合

Either print the paragraph for distribution to your students or prepare a slide that shows the entire paragraph.

文章のプリント、またはスライドを用意してください。

For *listening* 聴解の場合

Create several questions about your paragraph to check the students' comprehension and either print the questions for distribution or make a slide.

文章の内容についての質問を作って、プリントまたはスライドにしてください。

199

D. Practice giving directions. 指示の練習をしましょう。

For *ondoku* 音読の場合

	指示の例 (Sample Instructions)
Indicate the beginning of ondoku exercises	音読の練習をします。
Distribute a worksheet	これから、プリントを配ります。
Tell students to first listen to a model and then practice reading a paragraph in the handout	最初に私がプリントの文章を読みます。よく聞いてください。それから、大きい声で読んでください。

For *listening* 聴解の場合

	指示の例 (Sample Instructions)
Indicate the beginning of a listening exercises	聴解の練習をします。
Distribute a worksheet	これから、プリントを配ります。
Tell students to first look at the questions and then carefully listen and answer the questions based on what they heard	最初にプリントの質問を見てください。次に私が読む文章をよく聞いてください。最後に、プリントの質問に答えてください。

3 Skit style　　　　　　　　スキット型

Skits are useful in practicing Japanese in a contextualized, interactive and purposeful mode. The fact that conversations are prepared in advance will allow you to pay careful attention to articulation, emotion, movements and gestures. Skits are also effective to raise your sociocultural awareness in language learning.

A. Practice the following dialogue between Mike and his Japanese host mother. This is his first day in Japan and with his host family. Think about his and his host mother's feeling and mind-set when you practice this dialogue.

登場人物の気持ちも考えながら、次の会話を練習しましょう。

登場人物 (Characters)	時間 (Time)	場所 (Place)
マイクとホストマザー	午後八時ごろ	ホストファミリーの家

ホストマザー： お茶でも飲みますか。

マイク： いいえ、結構です。

ホストマザー： コーラもありますよ。

マイク： いいえ、疲れていますから、今日は早く寝たいです。

ホストマザー： あ、そうですか。じゃあ、布団を敷きますから、ちょっと待ってください。

マイク： 手伝いましょうか。

ホストマザー： じゃあ、お願いします。

B. *Now make a skit relevant to the topic of your review session. Provide information about characters, time and place. Also give any additional information you and your students should know in English.*

スキットを作りましょう。

登場人物 (Characters)	時間 (Time)	場所 (Place)

C. *Assign roles and practice the skit you just made in your group. See the following conversation and conduct the entire practice session in Japanese.*

役割を決めて、スキットを練習しましょう。

会話の例 (Sample Dialogue)

Leader: 役の割り当てをしましょう。役は二つあります。

だれが__A__の役をしますか。

Jessica: __ホセ__さんがいいです。

continued to the next page

Leader: <u>ホセ</u>さん、いいですか。

Jose: はい、いいです。

Leader: じゃ、<u>ホセ</u>さんお願_{ねが}いします。

次は **B** の役_{やく}です。だれがしますか。

Jenny: 私がします。

Leader: ほかにいますか。(No one responds.)

じゃ、<u>ジェニー</u>さんお願_{ねが}いします。

Leader: <u>ビンス</u>さんと<u>ジェシカ</u>さんは、二人の
演技_{えんぎ}をモニターしてください。

As you see two performers and
two monitors are named in
this sample dialogue. You
may switch roles and decide
who will be performing in
your review session.

役_{やく} role　　割_わり当_あて assignment　　演技_{えんぎ} acting

**D. Practice giving directions in your review session. This time you assign roles rather than
asking your students their preference in order to save time.**

指示_{しじ}の練習_{れんしゅう}をしましょう。

指示の例 (Sample Instructions)

Indicate the beginning of a skit activity	スキットをします。
Distribute the skit	これから、スキットを配_{くば}ります。
Tell students to first see the presentation and then to perform the skit	最初_{さいしょ}に私達_{たち}が発表_{はっぴょう}します。それから、皆_{みな}さんが演技_{えんぎ}をしてください。
Assign every student a role A or B and ask them to practice for one minute	トムさんとジェニーさん、**A**の役_{やく}をやってください。サラさんとサムさん、**B**の役_{やく}をやってください。これから、1分練習_{れんしゅう}してください。
Ask one pair to go ahead and present their skit first	じゃ、トムさんとサラさんお願_{ねが}いします。

Role Play style ロールプレイ型

Role plays are also useful in practicing Japanese in a contextualized, interactive and purposeful mode. Unlike skits, participants in a role play will be asked to construct their own utterance and deal with the unpredictable and open-ended nature of real-life communication. Therefore, role plays are more challenging than skits and will provide your students a valuable opportunity to see if they can put what they have learned into practical use.

A. Read the following role cards and complete the chart. "M" or "F" underneath a title indicates gender. "M/F" means that the role can be either male or female. Male/man and female/woman are おとこ *and* おんな *respectively. Also note that more than one person can play the same role in Role Play 1.*

ロールカードを読んで情報を書き入れましょう。

ロールプレイ1

Role A: An American High School Student (M/F)

It's 8:30 in the evening and you are at a nearby park for an event sponsored by a local Japanese youth organization. It is very hot and humid. Go around the area and introduce yourself to some Japanese participants. Exchange the following information with them: birthplace, school, age, grade level, favorite sport, favorite music, and favorite movie.

ロールプレイ1

Role B: A Japanese High School Student (M/F)

You are a Japanese high school student who has been in the US on a short exchange program. It's 8:30 in the evening and you are at a nearby park for an event sponsored by a local Japanese youth organization. It is very hot and humid. Go around the area and introduce yourself to other participants. Exchange the following information with them: birthplace, school, age, grade level, favorite sport, favorite music, and favorite movie.

	Name/Title/Age	Gender	じかん	ばしょ	てんき
Role A.	アメリカ人の高校生	男／女			
Role B					むしあつい

ロールプレイ2

Role A: Midori Suzuki (F)

You are Midori Suzuki, a high school exchange student from Japan. You live with your Japanese aunt. It's 11:00 in the morning on a sunny Sunday. John who is a classmate of yours calls you at home. As a school newspaper reporter, he is writing an article about the daily lives of some foreign exchange students at his school. He will ask you about your daily activities. Carry out a conversation by responding to his questions.

ロールプレイ2

Role B: John Nelson (M)

You are John Nelson. As a reporter of your school newspaper, you are writing an article about the daily lives of some foreign exchange students at your school. It's 11:00 in the morning on a sunny Sunday. You call Midori Suzuki, an exchange student from Japan who lives with her Japanese aunt. After greeting appropriately, ask her questions regarding her daily activities. Take notes as you hear her responses. Make sure that you have accurate information before moving onto your next question.

	Name/Title/Age	Gender	じかん	ばしょ	てんき
Role A.		女 (おんな)			
Role B					

B. Meet with your group and design a role play. Create roles by filling in the following chart. The example below is for the role of Midori Suzuki from Role Play 3 in the previous exercise. Conditions regarding time, place and weather should be the same for every role except for role plays that deal with telephone communication. Keep the number of roles under 3 and try to make the "workload" even for each role.

ロールプレイを作りましょう。

	Name/Title/Age	Gender	What he or she will be doing	じかん, ばしょ, てんき
EX.	Midori Suzuki (A Japanese exchange student)	Female	Answer a phone call from a school newspaper reporter and respond to his questions about her daily activities.	11:00 a.m. Home Sunny
Role A				
Role B				
Role C				

C. Make role cards based on the chart you have made. Use the cards shown earlier as a model.

ロールカードを作りましょう。

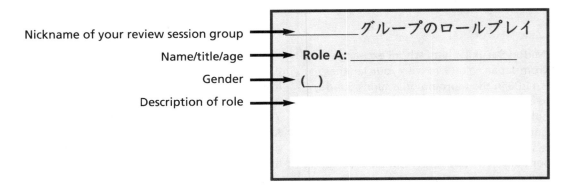

Nickname of your review session group → _________グループのロールプレイ

Name/title/age → **Role A:** ________________

Gender → (__)

Description of role →

D. Practice the role play just made in your group. Make sure that your role play is "playable" and make adjustments if any. Conduct the entire practice session in Japanese and see the sample dialogue in the skit section if necessary.

グループでロールプレイを練習しましょう。

E. Now practice conducting the entire role play activity part of your review session.

ロールプレイのセッションを練習しましょう。

会話の例 (Sample Dialogue)

Briefly explain all the roles and present the role play in class.

ロールプレイの説明をしてから、発表する。

L: これから、ロールプレイをします。役は2つあります。すずきみどりとジョン・ネルソンです。すずきみどりさんは日本の高校生ですが、いまアメリカの高校で勉強しています。ジョンさんから電話が来ました。ジョンさんはみどりさんの高校生活について質問したいです。最初に私達が発表します。

[Presentation by the teaching group takes place.]

Prepare enough sets of role cards and randomly distribute them to the students.

生徒全員にロールカードを配る。

L: じゃ、ロールカードを配ります。パートナーを見つけて練習してください。

[Students practice the role play with a partner.]

Have students find a partner and practice.

パートナーを見つけて練習してもらう。

Have them perform the role play one pair at a time.

発表してもらう。

L: じゃ、AさんとBさん、ロールプレイを発表してください。よろしくお願いします。

[Student A and B present the role play.]

Offer advice.

アドバイスをする。

L: よくできました。Aさん、もう少しはっきり話してください。発音はよかったです。Bさん、もう少しスムーズに話してください。演技は上手でした。じゃ、次にCさんとDさんお願いします。

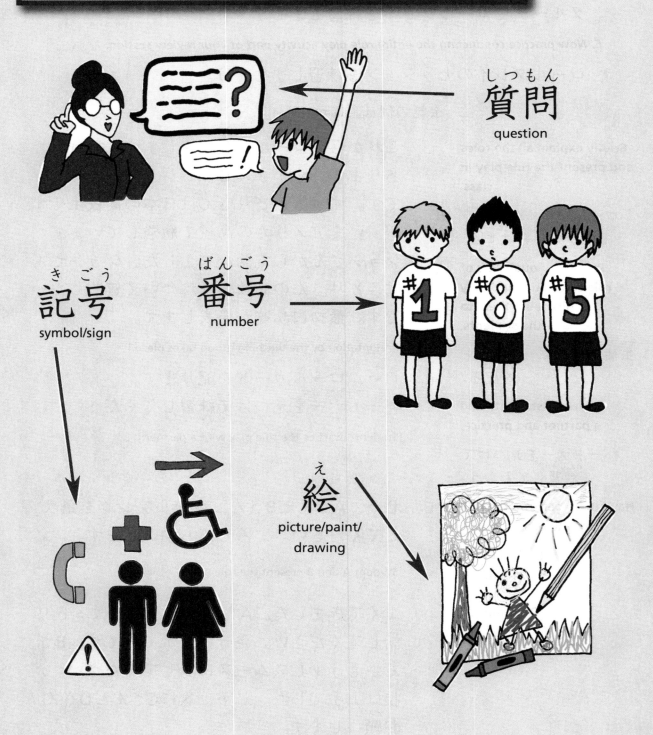

しつもん
質問
question

きごう
記号
symbol/sign

ばんごう
番号
number

え
絵
picture/paint/
drawing

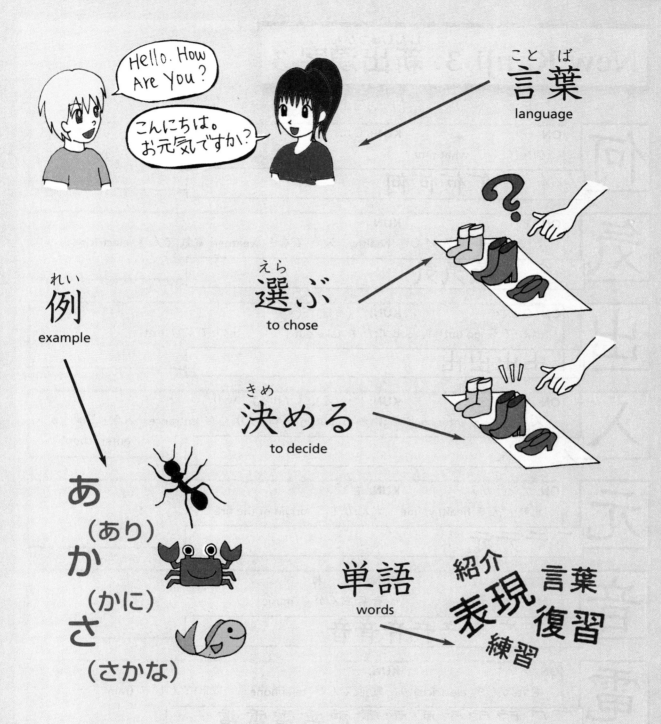

言葉
（こと ば）
language

例
（れい）
example

選ぶ
（えら）
to chose

決める
（きめ）
to decide

あ
（あり）

か
（かに）

さ
（さかな）

単語
words

紹介
表現
練習
言葉
復習

New Kanji 3: 新出漢字 3

何
ON: イチ　　　　　　**KUN:** なに、なん
何時:なんじ　what time?
ノ イ イ 行 行 行 何

気
ON: キ　　　　　　**KUN:** ―
気:き　mind　元気:げんき　healthy　天気:てんき　weather　電気:でんき　electricity
ノ ケ 气 気 気 気

出
ON: シュツ　　　　　　**KUN:** で(る)、だ(す)
出る:でる　go out　　　出す:だす　take out　　　　　出口:でぐち　exit
丨 屮 屮 出 出

入
ON: ニュウ　　　　　　**KUN:** はい(る)、い(れる)、いり
入る:はいる enter　入れる:いれる　put in　入口:いりぐち entrance　入学:にゅうがく
enter school
ノ 入

元
ON: ゲン、ガン　　　　　　**KUN:** もと
元気:げんき healthy, fine　　火元:ひもと　origin of the fire
一 二 テ 元

音
ON: オン　　　　　　**KUN:** おと、ね
音:おと sound　　　　　音楽:おんがく　music
丶 立 サ 立 立 产 音 音 音

電
ON: デン　　　　　　**KUN:** ―
電気:でんき electricity　　電話:でんわ telephone　　電車:でんしゃ train
一 一 戸 戸 雨 雨 雨 雨 雪 雪 雪 雷 電

国
ON: コク、コッ　　　　　　**KUN:** くに
国:くに country　　外国:がいこく foreign country　　国家:こっか state
丨 冂 冂 匡 用 国 国 国

Reading 4:
読み物 4

Photography Club: 写真部

1. こんにちは、海野　恵です。私は横浜に住んでいます。横浜国際教育高校の2年生で16才です。学校の別の名前はI校です。私は写真を撮ることが大好きです。特に、人や風景の写真を撮るのが面白いです。写真を撮りに出かけます。そこで、色々な人に出会います。そこで、今日は学校で写真を撮ることにしました。

2. この写真は4月に撮った物です。日本の学校の始まりは4月です。その頃は、日本では、桜が咲きます。色々な学校で桜が咲きます。たくさんの桜が咲いて、学校はとてもきれいです。クラブ活動も4月から始まります。だから、写真部に入りました。写真部では毎日写真を撮ります。写真部はとても面白い人が多いです。

A. Scan the following words. 次の文をスキャンして、以下の言葉を探しなさい。

1. Scan the first story, quickly find the following words and circle them.

   a. 横浜　　b. 学校　　c. 写真

   d. 色々な　e. 出会う　f. 面白い

2. Scan the second story, quickly find the following words and circle them.

   a. 桜　　　b. 始まり　c. 活動　　d. 出会う　e. 写真部　f. 面白い

   g. 楽しい　h. 写真を撮る

B. Do the previous stories include the reference to information listed below? Scan them and find out as quickly as possible. スキャンして適切な言葉を選んでください。

1. Skim through the first story and find out what kind of pictures of objects Kei has most interesting. Circle all that apply.

   people, architecture, classrooms, scenery, animals, food

2. Skim through the second story and find out what Kei did in April other than taking pictures.

   joined her school's photography club, joined her school's international contest, joined her International exchange program, joined her charry blossom club

C. Practice skimming through the stories.

1. Skim through the stories and choose key words from the following.
キーワードを下から探して選んでください。

First story **16才、風景、横浜、写真、学校、人**

Second story **学校、写真、桜、人、場所、クラブ活動**

2. Read the following sentences within three minutes and sum up what the author wants to say. 3分以内でどの文が適格な要点かを4つの文から選んでください。

First a. 恵さんは横浜に住んでいます。

story b. 恵さんの学校はI校です。

c. 恵さんは写真を撮ることが大好きです。

d. 恵さんは色々な人に出会います。

Second a. 恵さんの写真は桜の花です。

story b. 日本の学校の始まりは4月です。

c. 恵さんのクラブ活動は面白いです。

d. 恵さんは写真が好きなので、写真部に入りました。

D. Link three items in the vocabulary list below.
線を結んで、漢字／語彙のリストを完成させてください。

単語	読み	意味
Ex. 同じ ⟷	おなじ ⟷	same
1. 写真	いろいろな	everyday
2. 色々な	まいにち	photo
3. 毎日	しゃしん	many
4. 多い	おおい	various

E. Analyze the following kanji and write the English definition below.
例のように下の語彙のリストを完成させてください。

単語	知っている漢字	その意味	英語
Ex. 国際科	国、科目	nation, subject	international studies
1. 大好き	大、好き	_____	_____
2. 出会う	出る　会う	_____	_____
3. 海野	海　野	_____	_____
4. 面白い人	面　白い　人	_____	_____

F. Check whether the following statement is true or false.

内容の正しいものを選びなさい。

1. この高校に写真部がある。 (本当、嘘)
2. この人は風景や人を撮るのが好きです。 (本当、嘘)
3. この高校の写真部は面白い人が多い。 (本当、嘘)
4. この高校の写真部は中学と同じである。 (本当、嘘)

G. Form a group and answer the guided questions in Japanese.

グループで日本語で答えてください。

1 この学校の写真部はどんなクラブだと思いますか。
2. あなたの高校の写真部とこの高校の写真部を比べてみて、どう思いますか。

1. こんにちは、海野 恵です。私は横浜に住んでいます。横浜国際教育高校の2年生で16才です。学校の別の名前はI校です。私は写真を撮ることが大好きです。特に、人や風景の写真を撮るのが面白いです。写真を撮りに出かけます。そこで、色々な人に出会います。そこで、今日は学校で写真を撮ることにしました。

横浜：city name　住んでいます：live in
横浜国際教育高校：Yokohama international Educational School　別：another
I校：I school　写真：photo　撮る：take　大好きです：like very much
特に：especially　風景：landscape　写真を撮る：taking a picture
面白い：interesting　出かける：go out　そこで：at that　色々な：various
出会います：encounter　撮ることにしました：decided to take

2. この写真は4月に撮った物です。日本の学校の始まりは4月です。その頃は、日本では、桜が咲きます。色々な学校で桜が咲きます。たくさんの桜が咲いて、学校はとてもきれいです。クラブ活動も4月から始まります。だから、写真部に入りました。写真部では毎日写真を撮ります。写真部にはとても面白い人が多いです。

撮った物：things taken　学校の始まり：beginning of school　その頃：that time
桜が咲きます：cherry blossoms bloom　色々な学校：various schools
クラブ活動：club activity　始まります：begin　次の写真：next photo
写真部：photography club　面白い人：interesting person　多い：many

Additional Kanji 4: 追加漢字 4

深まる	ふかまる、deepen　　深：**ON:**シン　　　**KUN:**ふか(まる) 交流を深めるためにパーティーを開く。 We have a party to deepen exchange.
新入生	しんにゅうせい　　　　新：**ON:**シン　　**KUN:**あたら(しい) new student　　　　　入：**ON:**ニュウ　**KUN:**い(れる)、はい(る) 生：**ON:**セイ　　**KUN:**うま(れる) 新入生はどこですか。　Where are new students?
増える	ふえる、increase　　増：**ON:**ゾウ　　**KUN:**ふ(える)、ま(す) 宿題は増えましたか。 Did you gen an increase your home work load?
交流	こうりゅう、exchange　交：**ON:**コウ　　**KUN:**まじ(わる)、まじ(る) 流：**ON:**リュウ　**KUN:**なが(れる) 交流を深めるためにパーティーを開く。 We have a party to deepen exchange.
講堂	こうどう、auditorium　講：**ON:**コウ　　　**KUN:** 一 堂：**ON:**ドウ　　　**KUN:** 一 講堂の場所を教えて。　Tell me the location of auditorium.
始まる	はじまる、begin, start　始：**ON:**シ　　　　**KUN:**はじ(まる) 英語のクラスが始まる。　English class begins.
全員	ぜんいん、all members　全：**ON:**ゼン　　**KUN:**まった(く)、すべ(て) まっと(う) 員：**ON:**イン　　**KUN:** 一 全員が電車に乗っています。　All members are together on a train.
参加	さんか、participate　　参：**ON:**サン　　　**KUN:**まい(る) 加：**ON:**カ　　　　**KUN:**くわ(える) 旅行に参加したいです。　I want to participate in trip.
健康	けんこう、health　　　健：**ON:**ケン　　　**KUN:**すこや(か) 康：**ON:**コウ　　　**KUN:**やす(らか)、やす(い) 健康でいますか。　Do you stay healthy?

2.6 Mechanics 組立て
<ruby>組<rt>く</rt></ruby><ruby>立<rt>み</rt></ruby>て

Review Session Preparation III
復習セッションの準備 III

Objectives

Be able to answer questions of the review session participants.
Be able to appropriately wrap up your session.
Make a lesson plan of your session.
Prepare a folder containing all the materials and information necessary for your session.
Be able to deal with basic class management issues that may occur during your review session.

Overview

In this section you will first prepare the last portion of the なか part of the session ("questions and answers") and the entire おわり part. After that you will make a lesson plan based on what you have prepared. Finally you will sort all the materials and put them in a folder along with your lesson plan. You will also practice dealing with basic issues concerning classroom management.

10	Questions and answers	質問と答えを準備する
11	Closing	終わりの部分を準備する
1	Wrap-up and confirmation	まとめと確認をする
2	Last words	終わりの挨拶をする
12	Make a lesson plan	教案を作る
13	Put everything in a folder	フォルダにまとめる
14	Practice class management	クラス運営の練習をする
1	Identify problems	問題を確認する
2	Deal with problems	問題に対処する

Suppose you want to ask your teacher a question regarding a word written on the board. The teacher is standing right by the board and you are sitting further away from it. In English you may say to him or her "What does that word mean?" Japanese equivalents of "this" and "that" are known as "*ko-so-a-do,*" and this is what you will learn first in this section.

ノート: *ko-so-a-do*
こそあど<ruby>言葉<rt>ことば</rt></ruby>

	demonstrative pronouns <ruby>指示代名詞<rt>し じ だいめい し</rt></ruby>	demonstrative adjectives <ruby>指示形容詞<rt>し じ けいよう し</rt></ruby>
こ－series close to the speaker	これ	この+<ruby>名詞<rt>めい し</rt></ruby> (Noun)
そ－series close to the listener	それ	その+名詞 (Noun)
あ－series far from both	あれ	あの+名詞 (Noun)
ど－series question words	どれ	どの+名詞 (Noun)

As you can see from the table above Japanese equivalents of words such as "this" and "that" follow a systematic pattern known as こそあど *ko-so-a-do*. You already know ど- series such as どれ, どちら, どこ as question words. こ- series refer to an object that is close to the speaker. そ- series refer to an object that is close to the listener. あ- series of words refer to an object that is far from both sides. この, その, あの, and どの precede nouns they modify. Compare the following:

これをください。
Please give me this one.

その本をください。
Please give me that book.

A: この<ruby>漢字<rt>かん じ</rt></ruby>を<ruby>読<rt>よ</rt></ruby>んでください。
　Please read this kanji.

B: それは、ええと「ひゃくまん」。
　That one is...uh... it's *hyakuman.*

A. Fill in an appropriate こ、そ、**or** ど **word according to the picture.**

（　）に「こそあど」言葉を入れてください。

1. （　　）ボール

2. （　　）

3. （　　）ボール?

4. （　　）ボール

5. （　　）

6. （　　）?

7. （　　）ボール

8. （　　）

B. Choose an appropriate こそあど **word to complete each conversation.**

正しい「こそあど」言葉をまる〇で囲んでください。

1. A was given an index card with a kanji on it. He points at the kanji and says to B:

A: (その、この、あれ、これ) 漢字はどういう意味ですか。

B: (その、どの、どれ、それ) は"hundred"です。

2. A asks B which problem he should do. B points at a matching problem.

A: (どれ、それ、どの、これ) 問題をしますか。

B: (この、どの、あれ、それ) マッチングの問題をしてください。

3. A asks B to read a kanji on the board. A is away from the board, but B is right by it.

A: あのう、(その、この、それ、これ) 漢字を読んでください。

B: (その、この、それ、これ) 漢字ですね。「せんせい」です。

4. A asks B which one is his card. B responds by saying "this one."

A: Bさんのカードは(その、どれ、それ、どの) ですか。

B: (その、この、それ、これ) です。

ノート: Four types of questions

The mindmap in this note shows four types of questions that will most likely appear during review sessions. Useful constructions for each type are listed underneath. "Questions" here include those non-question statements that may be used for help-seeking purposes, such as Xが わかりません (I don't understand X).

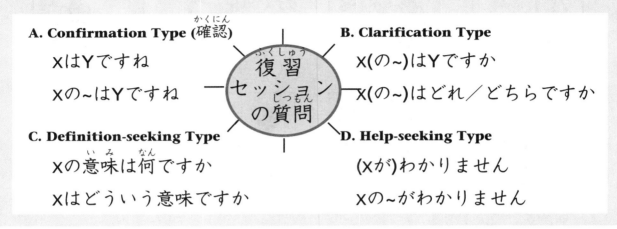

A. Confirmation Type (確認)

XはYですね

Xの~はYですね

B. Clarification Type

X(の~)はYですか

X(の~)はどれ／どちらですか

復習
セッション
の質問

C. Definition-seeking Type

Xの意味は何ですか

Xはどういう意味ですか

D. Help-seeking Type

(Xが)わかりません

Xの~がわかりません

C. *To which type (A - D in the preceding note) does each of the following questions belong?*

質問のタイプはどれですか。

1. (　) その単語の意味は"cute"ですね。
2. (　) その文の意味がわかりません。
3. (　) 「ひゃく」の漢字はどれですか。
4. (　) 「かわいい」は形容詞ですか。
5. (　) その表現はどういう意味ですか。

D. *Practice answering the four types of questions.*

質問に答える練習をしましょう。

1. Confirmation type

会話の例 A (Sample Dialogue A)

A: (Pointing at a kanji on the board) その漢字は「せんせい」ですね。

B: はい、そうです。

会話の例 B (Sample Dialogue B)

A: 「<u>かぞく</u>」の意味^{いみ}は"<u>residence</u>"ですね。

B: いいえ、ちがいます。"<u>Family</u>"です。

2. Clarification type

会話の例 A (Sample Dialogue A)

A: 「<u>すき</u>」は<u>形容詞</u>ですか。　　B: はい、そうです。

会話の例 B (Sample Dialogue B)

A: 「すい」の漢字はどれですか。

B: (Pointing at a kanji on the board) この漢字です。

3. Definition-seeking type

会話の例 (Sample Dialogue)

A: 「<u>むらさき</u>」の意味は何ですか。

B: 「<u>むらさき</u>」の意味は"<u>purple</u>"です。

4. Help-seeking type

会話の例 (Sample Dialogue)

A: (While listening to an instruction) あのう、わかりません。

B: じゃ、もう一度言います。　[I will say it once again.]

or

B: じゃ、英語で言います。　[I will say it in English.]

217

11 Closing

終わりの部分を準備する

1 Wrap-up and confirmation

まとめと確認をする

Your session is nearing the end. You have done all the activities and answered the students' questions. It's time for you to make sure that the students have followed and understood your presentation.

ノート: Ideas for wrap-up and confirmation

There are several effective ways of conducting your wrap-up and confirmation part. Two of them are indicated below.

1. Using visual aids

Give some type of visual reminder toward the end of the session that will help your students effectively organize what they have learned and leave them with a lasting memory of your session.

2. Asking questions

Ask questions to check your students' understanding as another effective way to end your session. You may also ask them to respond to your requests.

この単語はどういう意味ですか。

(showing several kanji) 「きん」はどれですか。

電話の表現を五つ言ってください。

動物の名前を五つ言ってください。

A. Prepare visual aids and practice conducting a wrap-up activity. You may use the visual aids you have made to introduce the vocabulary and kanji earlier.

ビジュアル教材を使って、まとめの練習をしましょう。

B. Make questions to check your students' understanding of the materials covered in your session and practice conducting a wrap-up activity.

質問を作って、まとめの練習をしましょう。

2 Last words　　　　終わりの挨拶をする

A. Practice a closing greeting to your students and bring your session to a close.

終わりのあいさつを練習しましょう。

例 (Example)

これで「電話の表現」の復習セッションを
終わります。ありがとうございました。

12 Make a lesson plan　　　　教案を作る

A lesson plan is a brief description of each activity in your session. Your lesson plan should follow the structure of your session and should include information regarding time allocation and names of persons in charge of particular activities.

A. Make a lesson plan.　　教案を作りましょう。

Review the sample lesson plan and then create your own. You do not need to provide information regarding time allocation and persons in charge yet. Make any necessary adjustments to accommodate your additional exercises.

B. Group meeting.　　グループでミーティングをしましょう。

Allocate time for each activity and decide who will be in charge of conducting each part. Make sure to do this in Japanese. Afterwards, write all this information on your lesson plan.

13 Put everything in a folder　　　　フォルダにまとめる

A. Gather all the materials you have made for your session and put them in a folder along with your lesson plan.

教材と教案をを一つのフォルダに入れてください。

219

教案: Lesson Plan

トピック: 電話の表現　　　グループ: 猫

日にち: 10月18日　　時間: 10時5分-10時45分

場所: 日本語の教室

始め	(2分)	始めのあいさつをする (Opening greeting)		シャンタル
		トピックを紹介する (Introduction of topic)		シャンタル
		レッスンを紹介する (Introduction of lesson)		ホセ
中	(35分)	ウォームアップをする (Warm-ups)	(3分)	ホセ、ジェニー
		単語を紹介する (Introduction of words)	(2分)	ジェシカ
		表現を紹介する (Introduction of expressions)	(2分)	トム
		漢字を紹介する (Introduction of kanji)	(2分)	シャンタル
		アクティビティーをする (Activities)		
		◎ワークシート/デジタル型 (Worksheet/digital slide style)	(5分)	ホセ、トム
		◎音読型 (Read aloud style)	(5分)	ジェシカ、シャンタル
		◎スキット型 (Skit style)	(6分)	みんな
		◎ロールプレイ型 (Role play style)	(7分)	みんな
		質問に答える (Answering questions)	(3分)	シャンタル
終り	(3分)	まとめと確認をする (Wrap-up and confirmation)	(2分)	ジェニー、トム
		終わりのあいさつをする (Closing greeting)	(1分)	シャンタル

14 Practice class management　クラス運営の練習をする

During the course of your review session, you may encounter a situation in which your students are not as focused as they should be or they are doing something they shouldn't be doing. In such a situation you will need to ask them to correct their behavior. You will be learning some useful expressions that will enable you to do that.

1 Identify problems　問題を確認する

A. Brainstorming.　ブレインストーミングをしましょう。

Think about some likely situations which may call for your immediate attention. The scope of "problems" may differ according to classes so create a mindmap like the one below with your own situation in mind.

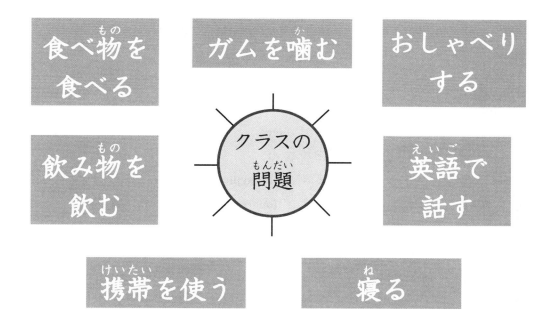

食べ物を食べる　ガムを噛む　おしゃべりする

飲み物を飲む　クラスの問題　英語で話す

携帯を使う　寝る

B. Make a list.　リストを作りましょう。

Make a list of probable situations based on your brainstorming.

2 Deal with problems 　　問題に対処する

Your initial reaction upon observing someone's inappropriate behavior will be telling him or her to refrain from what he or she has been doing. You will learn a useful sentence structure for this and will be introduced to the so-called ない form of a verb that is included in the structure.

negative

動詞の
ない形

plain/informal

ノート: ない Form of Verb 　　動詞のない形

The so-called ない form is a plain, nonpast, and negative form of a verb. In other words, it is the plain/informal counterpart of -ません. This is the second plain form to be introduced. You already know the dictionary form which is a plain, nonpast, and affirmative form. These plain forms are used not only in casual conversations but also to make many sentence constructions. The ない form is introduced here since it is used in a construction for telling someone not to do something. Note that the ない form of あります is just ない.

A. Take a guess and fill in the box with the appropriate ない form.

リストを完成させてください。

Plain nonpast negative ない form	Polite nonpast affirmative ます form	Plain nonpast affirmative Dictionary form
まげない	まげます (bend)	まげる
	たべます (eat)	たべる
ない	あります (exist, be [inanimate])	ある
ひらかない	ひらきます (open)	ひらく
	かきます (write)	かく
たたない	たちます (stand up)	たつ
はなさない	はなします (speak)	はなす
かまない	かみます (chew)	かむ
	のみます (drink)	のむ
すわらない	すわります (sit)	すわる
	かえります (return, go home)	かえる
つかわない	つかいます (use)	つかう
あそばない	あそびます (play)	あそぶ
しない	します (do)	する
こない	きます (come)	くる

B. Fill in each parenthesis with a letter representing the appropriate ます *form.*

（　　）に記号を入れてください。

1. かかない　（　　）　2. しない　　（　　）　3. かまない　　　（　　）
4. のまない　（　　）　5. ねない　　（　　）　6. はなさない　　（　　）
7. みない　　（　　）　8. こない　　（　　）　9. つかわない　　（　　）
10. たたない　（　　）　11. まげない　（　　）　12. ひらかない　　（　　）
13. たべない　（　　）　14. よまない　（　　）　15. まわさない　　（　　）

---

a. たちます　　　b. ひらきます　　c. たべます

d. みます　　　　e. はなします　　f. のみます

g. よみます　　　h. ねます　　　　i. きます

j. まわします　　k. かみます　　　l. つかいます

m. します　　　　n. かきます　　　o. まげます

C. Change the following into the ない *form.*　　ない形の練習をしましょう。

As an alternative, one student may orally give either the ます form or the dictionary form of a verb, and another student sitting next to him or her can give the ない form of that verb.

Ex. 食べます→食べない

1. します→　　　　　　　　　2. 曲げます→
3. 話します→　　　　　　　　4. 座ります→
5. 立ちます→　　　　　　　　6. 書きます→
7. 飲みます→　　　　　　　　8. 開きます→
9. 見ます→　　　　　　　　　10. 伸ばします→
11. 読みます→　　　　　　　　12. 寝ます→
13. 使います→　　　　　　　　14. 回します→
15. 来ます→

223

ノート: Telling someone not to do something

ないForm of V + でください

～ないでください is used to tell someone not to do something. A judge or a leader overseeing the progress of bingo or some other games may use this construction when he or she wants to warn a player who is not following the rules or whose conduct is not appropriate.

英語で話さないでください。　Please do not speak in English.
携帯を使わないでください。　Please do not use cellular phones.

D. Practice making ～ないでください sentences using the verbs that appeared in the preceding exercise.

「～ないでください」の文を作りましょう。

E. Conversation practice　会話の練習をしましょう。

Substitute the underlined part with an appropriate warning according to each picture.

会話の例 (Sample Dialogue)
A: 英語で話さないでください。　　B: あ、すみません。

EX.

1.

2.

3.

4.

5.

6.

224　*Reflection / Chapter 2*

FORM

1. Dictionary form of a verb

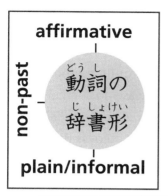

The so-called dictionary form of a verb is a plain and informal counterpart of the ます form. The name comes from the fact that it is in this form that verbs are listed in various dictionaries. The dictionary form is used in casual conversations and other situations in which politeness and formality are not called for. One such situation is when you simply list something in the form of a chart or a memo. Therefore, once you know the dictionary form, you can use it when you make a flow chart, a things-to-do list, index cards, and so on.

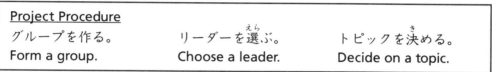

Project Procedure

グループを作る。　　リーダーを選ぶ。　　トピックを決める。

Form a group.　　　Choose a leader.　　Decide on a topic.

2. ない form of a verb

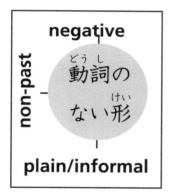

The so-called ない form is a plain, nonpast and negative form of a verb. In other words, it is the plain/informal counterpart of -ません. This is the second plain form to be introduced. You already know the dictionary form which is a plain, nonpast and affirmative form. These plain forms are used not only in casual and informal conversations, but also to make many sentence constructions and idiomatic expressions. The ない form is introduced here since it is used in telling someone not to do something. There is a way to create the ない form from the ます form or the dictionary form. However, more information on Japanese verbs is needed to do that. At this point, just remember the ない form of some useful verbs.

3. て form of a verb

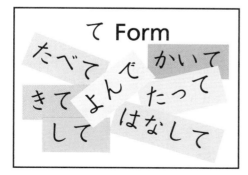

A form represented by 〜てas in たって, よんで, and きいて is called the て (te) form. This form can be used by itself to make a casual request. For example, たって is the informal/casual equivalent of たってください (Please stand) and is used among close friends and family members. The て form is also used in many sentence constructions.

3. Asking someone to do something

〜てください

Directions such as 立ってください ("Please stand"), よんでください ("Please read") and もういちどいってください ("Please say that again") have been used quite frequently. The construction "〜てください" is the Japanese equivalent of "Please do such and such." These expressions use the て (te) form of verbs. When this て (te) form is used by itself without ください, it simply takes away the formality and politeness the request carries. For example, 立って is the informal/casual equivalent of 立ってください and is used among close friends and family members. Formation of the て form follows several patterns and you will be learning about them later as well. For now, try to remember the て form of basic verbs.

立^たってください。　　　　　　Please stand up.

足を開^{ひら}いてください。　　　　Please spread your legs apart.

手を前に伸^のばしてください。　　Please extend your arms forward.

4. Asking someone not to do something

〜ないでください

The construction "〜ないでください" is the Japanese equivalent of "Please do NOT do such and such." It is a negative counterpart of "〜てください." The ない form of a verb precedes でください. While it is perfectly alright to use this construction when you ask your student not to do something in a classroom situation, "〜ないでください" will sound too strong if you use it in social interactions, especially with people older or higher in relative social status than you. There are certainly better expressions for such an occasion. Until you learn them, make sure to say すみませんが... ("I am sorry but..") first when you must use the construction, and say it softly.

新聞^{しんぶん}を読まないでください。　　Please don't read newspapers.

英語^{えいご}で話さないでください。　　Please don't speak in English.

食べ物^{もの}を食べないでください。　　Please do not eat food.

5. こそあど (Demonstrative words)

The Japanese equivalent of words such as "this" and "that" follow a systematic pattern known as こそあど. For example, an object closest to the speaker is referred to as これ (this one) while one closest to the listener is referred to as それ (that one). An object which is away from both the speaker and the listener is あれ (that one over there) and the interrogative form is どれ (which one). この, その, あの and どの precede nouns they modify.

	demonstrative pronouns しじだいめいし 指示代名詞	demonstrative adjectives しじけいようし 指示形容詞
こ―series close to the speaker	これ	この + 名詞 (Noun)
そ―series close to the listener	それ	その + 名詞 (Noun)
あ―series far from both	あれ	あの + 名詞 (Noun)
ど―series question words	どれ	どの + 名詞 (Noun)

6. Actions in progress

Vています

The construction "Vています" (the て form of an action verb + います) is used to indicate the progression of an action.

妹は映画を見ています。 My younger sister is watching a movie.

今、何をしていますか。 What are you doing right now?

A: 昨日の8時ごろ何をしていましたか。

What were you doing around 8 o'clock yesterday?

B: ええと、寮でテレビを見ていました。

Well, I was watching TV in my dorm.

7. Making suggestions: How about-?

Xはどうですか

The construction "Xはどうですか" is used to ask someone his or her opinion, feeling, or assessment of X (a noun). It is also very useful when making a suggestion in decision-making situations. "がっこうはどうですか" may mean "How is your school?"

or "How about the school?" depending upon the context. "Xはどう?" is informal.

木曜日はどうですか。	How about Thursday?
ピザはどうですか。	How about pizza? (in decision making)
	How is your pizza?/How do you like it?

8. Giving the order of actions or events

When you describe something in sequence, expressions such as "at first," "next," "and then," and "finally" are included. Effective use of these expressions will make your description cohesive and easy to follow. See the list below. Some of the items on the list may sound familiar to you since similar words appeared in *Haruichiban*.

始めに〜します 最初に〜します	first, to begin with, before anything else	始めは〜です 最初は〜です
次に〜します	next	次は〜です
それから〜します	and then	それから〜です
終わりに〜します 最後に〜します	finally	終わりは〜です 最後は〜です

9. Indicating repetition and frequency

Xかい is the Japanese equivalent of "X times." If you want someone to read something twice, you may say 2かいよんでください. Xかい can be placed in the beginning of a sentence, though it is most commonly placed right before the predicate verb.

ひざを二回曲げてください。	Bend your knees twice.
映画を五回見ました。	I saw the movie five times.

10. Particles に to indicate a point of time and について To tell what something is about

The particle に is used to mark a point of time. Beware that the particle に is not necessary for certain "relative" time words introduced such as "next week," and "yesterday."

八時におきます。	I will wake up at 8 o'clock.

Xについて means "about X."

日本の歴史について話します。	I will talk about Japanese history.

VOCABULARY

Functional Vocabulary

	Formal	Informal	English
Identifying today's topic	きょうのトピックはXです。	きょうのトピックはX。	Today's topic is X.
Indicating actions X, Y, Z in sequence	はじめにXをします。 つぎにYをします。 おわりにZをします。	はじめにXをする。 つぎにYをする。 おわりにZをする。	(You) do X first. (You) do Y next. Finally, (you) do Z.
Asking someone if X is done	Xができましたか。	Xできた。	Is X done?/Have you done X?
Telling someone X is done	Xができました。	Xができた。	X is done.
Telling someone X is not yet done	Xはまだです。	Xはまだ(だ)。	X is not yet done.
Telling someone X is in progress	Xをしています。 Xをやっています。	Xをしている。 Xをやっている。	(Someone is) doing X.
Encouraging someone to try his or her best	がんばってください。	がんばって。	Give it all you've got.
Suggesting something to someone	Xはどうですか。	Xはどう。	How about X?
Asking someone to do something	てください。	て(くれ)。	Please do -.
Asking someone not to do something	ないでください。	ないで(くれ)。	Please do not do -.
Asking someone to do Question 1 in Section 2	2の1をおねがいします。	2の1(を)おねがい。	Please do Question 1 in Section 2.
Asking for questions	しつもんがありますか。	しつもん(が)ある(か)。	Do you have any questions?
Asking someone if there is anything else	ほかにありますか。	ほか(に)ある。	Is there anything else (on your mind)?
Asking someone to put a symbol in the parenthesis	かっこにきごうをいれてください。	- いれて(くれ)。	Please put a symbol in the (　).
Asking someone to stretch his/her arms forward	うでをまえにのばしてください。	- のばして(くれ)。	Please stretch your arms forward.
Asking someone to stretch his/her arms three times	うでを3かいのばしてください。	- 3かいのばして(くれ)。	Please stretch your arms three times.
Asking someone to undo the previous action	もどしてください。	- もどして(くれ)。	Please return to the original position.

229

VOCABULARY *(continued)*

Asking someone to be quiet	しずかにしてください。	しずかにして(くれ)。	Be quiet, please.
Asking a confirmation type question	XはYですね。	XはY(だ)ね。	X is Y, isn't it?
Asking a clarification type question	XはYですか。	XはY。	Is X Y?
Asking a definition-seeking type question	Xのいみはなんですか。 XはどういういみですかВ。	Xのいみはなに。 XはどういういみВ。	What is the meaning of X? What do you mean by X?
Seeking help type question	Xがわかりません。	Xがわからない。	I don't understand X.

Notional Vocabulary

Body Parts

からだ	体	body
あし	足	leg, foot
くび	首	neck
うで	腕	arm
こし	腰	waist
て	手	hand
ひざ	膝	knee
ひじ	肘	elbow

Class Management/Problem Solving

クラスうんえい	クラス運営	classroom management
もんだい	問題	problem
ガムをかみます/-かむ	ガムを噛む	chew gum
ぼうしをかぶります/-かぶる	帽子を被る	wear a hat, cap
けいたい	携帯	cell phone
つかいます/つかう	使う	use
おしゃべりをします/-する		chat
しずかにします/-する	静かにする	be quiet, calm down

Demonstrative Words

これ	this one
この -	this -
それ	that one
その -	that -
あれ	that one over there
あの -	that - over there
どれ	which one
どの -	which -

Directions of Movements

ほうこう	方向	directions
みぎに	右に	to the right
ひだりに	左に	to the left
うえに	上に	up
したに	下に	down
まえに	前に	forward
うしろに	後ろに	backward
よこに	横に	to the side

Evaluation

ひょうか	評価	evaluation
きょうりょく	協力	cooperation
しゅうちゅう	集中	concentration

Forms, Parts of Speech

ひんし	品詞	parts of speech
めいし	名詞	noun
どうし	動詞	verb
けいようし	形容詞	adjective
じょし	助詞	particle
じしょけい	辞書形	dictionary form
ますけい	ます形	*masu* form
ないけい	ない形	*nai* form
てけい	て形	*te* form
ぶん	文	sentence

Order, Sequence

はじめに	始めに	at first, to begin with
さいしょに	最初に	at first, to begin with
つぎに	次に	next
それから		and then
おわりに	終わりに	finally
さいごに	最後に	finally
まえさぎょう	前作業	preliminary activities
ほんさぎょう	本作業	main activities
あとさぎょう	後作業	wrap-up activities

Physical Exercises/Warm-Up

たちます/たつ	立つ	stand
すわります/すわる	座る	sit down
まげます/まげる	曲げる	bend
のばします/のばす	伸ばす	stretch
まわします/まわす	回す	spin, turn, rotate
ひらきます/ひらく	開く	open, spread
もどします/もどす	戻す	undo, return
-かい	-回	- times
リラックス		relaxation
たいそう	体操	exercises, gymnastics
かず	数	number

Question Types and Instructions

マッチング		matching
もんだい	問題	question
しじ	指示	instructions
せつめい	説明	explanation, description
いみ	意味	meaning
こたえ	答え	answer
れい	例	example
きごう	記号	sign, symbol, mark
ただしい	正しい	right, correct
ことば	言葉	language, word
ぶん	文	sentence
じゅんばん	順番	order, sequence
ばんごう	番号	number
えらびます/えらぶ	選ぶ	choose
いれます/いれる	入れる	put in
くばります/くばる	配る	distribute
かいわ	会話	conversation
れんしゅうします/-する	練習する	practice
ぜんぶ	全部	all
いいます/いう	言う	say

これから — from now
タイプ — type
チェックします/する — check

Relative Time

きのう	昨日	yesterday
おととい	一昨日	the day before yesterday
きょう	今日	today
あした	明日	tomorrow
あさって	明後日	the day after tomorrow
きょねん	去年	last year
ことし	今年	this year
らいねん	来年	next year
せんしゅう	先週	last week
こんしゅう	今週	this week
らいしゅう	来週	next week
せんげつ	先月	last month
こんげつ	今月	this month
らいげつ	来月	next month
とき	時	time

Review Sessions

ふくしゅう	復習	review
セッション		session
もくてき	目的	objective, purpose
ひにち	日にち	date
じかん	時間	time
ばしょ	場所	place
プロジェクト		project
リーダー		leader
グループ		group
メンバー		member
トピック		topic
これまで		up to now
せいと	生徒	student
えらびます/えらぶ	選ぶ	choose
しごと	仕事	task, job
しんこう	進行	progress
かつどう	活動	action, activity
リスト		list
つくります/つくる	作る	make
(-の)つくりかた	作り方	how to make -
(-に)なります/なる		become -
かくにんします/-する	確認する	confirm, check
ちょくせつ	直接	directly
スケジュール		schedule

231

VOCABULARY *(continued)*

きめます/きめる	決める	decide
したがいます/したがう	従う	follow, obey
できます/できる	出来る	be done, be finished
たかめます/たかめる	高める	heighten, enhance
いしき	意識	consciousness
まだ	未だ	(not) yet, still
きょうあん	教案	lesson plan
リハーサル		rehearsal
メール		electronic mail
へんしん	返信	reply
がんばります/がんばる	頑張る	try one's best
ジェスチャー		gesture
かきとり	書き取り	dictation
フローチャート		flow chart
たいしょします/たいしょする		
	対処する	cope, deal with
まとめます/まとめる	纏める	put together, summarize

Structure of Review Sessions

こうせい	構成	structure
あいさつ	挨拶	greeting
プログラム		program
しょうかい	紹介	introduction
じゅんび	準備	preparation
ウォームアップ		warm-up
たんご	単語	words
ひょうげん	表現	expressions
れんしゅうもんだい	練習問題	exercise
しつもん	質問	question
こたえる	答える	answer (verb)
まとめ		wrap-up
かくにん	確認	confirmation, checking
フォローアップ		follow-up
ひょうか	評価	evaluation
ふりかえり	振り返り	feedback

Activities

かた	型	style, form
ワークシート		worksheet
デジタル		digital
スライド		slide
おんどく	音読	reading aloud
ちょうかい	聴解	listening comprehension
スキット		skit
ロールプレイ		role play
やく	役	role
わりあて	割り当て	assignment, allotment

おとこ	男	male, man
おんな	女	female, woman
えんぎ	演技	acting, performance
わたしたち	私達	we
くばります/くばる	配る	distribute

Teaching Materials

きょうざい	教材	teaching materials
ビジュアル		visuals, visual aid
え	絵	picture, painting
しゃしん	写真	photo
ちず	地図	map
ひょう	表	chart, list, table
カード		card
リスト		list
ポスター		poster
ロールカード		role card
はさみ	鋏	scissors
かみ	紙	paper
マーカー		marker
のり	糊	glue
ビデオ		video
プリント		handout

New Kanji 4: 新出漢字 4

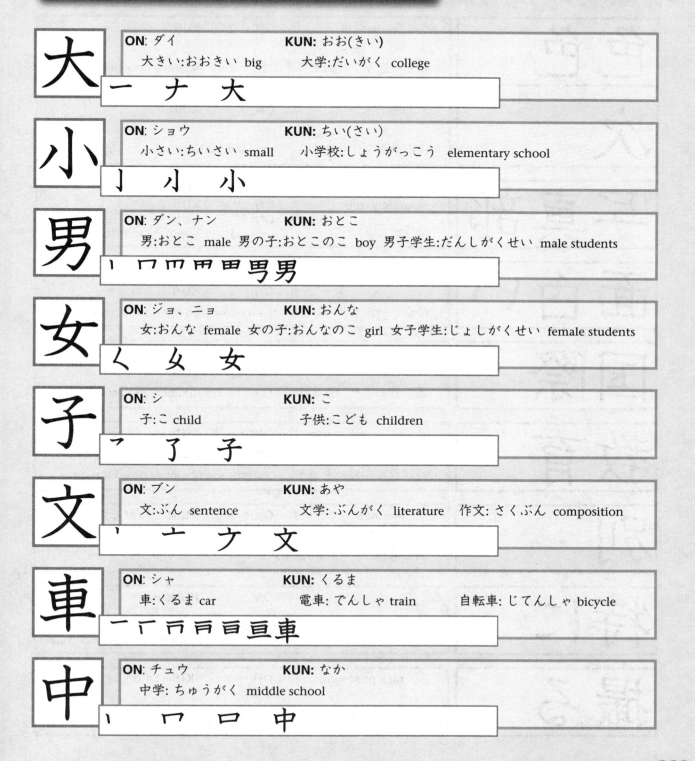

大
ON: ダイ　　　　　　**KUN:** おお(きい)
大きい:おおきい　big　　　大学:だいがく　college
一 ナ 大

小
ON: ショウ　　　　　　**KUN:** ちい(さい)
小さい:ちいさい　small　　小学校:しょうがっこう　elementary school
亅 小 小

男
ON: ダン、ナン　　　　**KUN:** おとこ
男:おとこ　male　男の子:おとこのこ　boy　男子学生:だんしがくせい　male students
丨 口 田 田 田 男 男

女
ON: ジョ、ニョ　　　　**KUN:** おんな
女:おんな　female　女の子:おんなのこ　girl　女子学生:じょしがくせい　female students
く 夕 女

子
ON: シ　　　　　　　　**KUN:** こ
子:こ　child　　　　　子供:こども　children
フ 了 子

文
ON: ブン　　　　　　　**KUN:** あや
文:ぶん　sentence　　　文学:ぶんがく　literature　　作文:さくぶん　composition
丶 亠 ナ 文

車
ON: シャ　　　　　　　**KUN:** くるま
車:くるま　car　　　　電車:でんしゃ　train　　　自転車:じてんしゃ　bicycle
一 ㄏ 戸 百 百 亘 車

中
ON: チュウ　　　　　　**KUN:** なか
中学:ちゅうがく　middle school
丶 丨 口 口 中

Additional Kanji 5: 追加漢字 5

色色	いろいろ、various　　色：**ON**:シキ　　**KUN**:いろ 新しい色々な計画を作ります。　I am making a new various plans.
次	つぎ、next　　　　　次：**ON**:ジ　　　**KUN**:つぎ 次の計画を作ります。　I am making a next plan.
写真部	しゃしんぶ　　　　写：**ON**:シャ　**KUN**:うつ(す) photography club　真：**ON**: シン　**KUN**:ま 　　　　　　　　部：**ON**: ブ　　**KUN**: べ 写真部に参加します。　I participate in a photography club.
面白い	おもしろい、interesting 面：**ON**:メン　　**KUN**:おも 　　　　　　　　　白：**ON**:ハク　**KUN**:しろ(い) 面白い計画を作ります。　I am making an interesting plan.
国際	こくさい、international 国：**ON**:コク　　**KUN**:くに 　　　　　　　　際：**ON**:サイ　　**KUN**:きわ 国際計画に参加します。　I join an international project.
教育	きょういく、education 教：**ON**:キョウ　**KUN**:おし(える) 　　　　　　　育：**ON**:イク　　**KUN**:そだ(つ) 親は教育にお金を使う。　Parents spend money on education.
別	べつ、another　　　　別：**ON**:ベツ　　**KUN**:わか(れる) 別の名前は。　Another name?
特に	とくに、especially　　特：**ON**:トク　　**KUN**: 一 特になにかかさがしていますか 　　　　　　　　　Are you looking for something in particular?
撮る	とる、take photographs 撮：**ON**:サツ　　**KUN**:と(る) 新しい写真を撮ります。　I am taking new photographs.

2.7 Virtual Reality 実践
<ruby>実践<rt>じっせん</rt></ruby>

Conducting Review Sessions
復習セッションをする
<ruby>復習<rt>ふくしゅう</rt></ruby>セッションをする

Overview

It's now time to show off your teaching skills. This section begins with preliminary activities in which you will check your folder and your assigned tasks to make sure that you are ready to start your session. Remember this is a collaborative project and good communication and teamwork are essential to your success. Do some more practice with this in mind. After the review session, you will have an opportunity to have a follow-up session with your classmates and to do some evaluation.

	15 Check folders	フォルダをチェックする
Preliminary Activities 前作業 <ruby>前作業<rt>まえさぎょう</rt></ruby>	**16** Check each other's tasks	仕事の確認をする <ruby>仕事<rt>しごと</rt></ruby>の<ruby>確認<rt>かくにん</rt></ruby>をする
	17 Last practice	最後の練習をする <ruby>最後<rt>さいご</rt></ruby>の<ruby>練習<rt>れんしゅう</rt></ruby>をする
Main Activity 本作業	**18** Conduct review sessions	復習セッションをする <ruby>復習<rt>ふくしゅう</rt></ruby>セッションをする
Wrap-up Activities 後作業 <ruby>後<rt>あと</rt></ruby>	**19** Follow-up in English	フォローアップをする
	20 Evaluate and reflect	評価と振り返りをする <ruby>評価<rt>ひょうか</rt></ruby>と<ruby>振<rt>ふ</rt></ruby>り<ruby>返<rt>かえ</rt></ruby>りをする

15 Check folders

フォルダをチェックする

Check the folder to see that all the materials are in order and ready for use. Also go over the lesson plan to make sure that everyone is fully aware of how the session will proceed.

16 Checking each other's tasks

仕事の確認をする

Check all the individual and group tasks for your review session and make sure that you know your roles.

17 Last practice

最後の練習をする

Practice conducting the review session one last time with particular attention to teamwork.

18 **Conduct review sessions**　　復習_{ふくしゅう}セッションをする

| 復習_{ふくしゅう}セッションの構成_{こうせい} | **Structure of Review Session** |

はじめのあいさつをする トピックの紹介_{しょうかい}をする レッスンを紹介する	**はじめ**	Greet participants Introduce the topic Introduce the lesson
ウォームアップをする 単語_{たん}と表現_{ひょうげん}と漢字_{かんじ}を紹介する アクティビティーをする 質問_{しつもん}に答_{こた}える	**なか**	Do warm-up Introduce words, expressions, and kanji Conduct the activities Answer questions
まとめと確認_{かくにん}をする おわりのあいさつをする	**おわり**	Do wrap-up and confirmation Greeting

19 **Follow-up in English**　　　フォローアップをする

At the conclusion of the review session, have a follow-up session with your classmates. Solicit questions and feedback from them and clarify any confusions or miscommunications you might have had during your session.

20 **Evaluate and reflect**　　　評価と振り返りをする

The follow-up session is meant to be very helpful to you in reflecting upon your performance individually as well as collectively. Filling out a checklist such as the one below will also help you identify your strengths and weaknesses.

Reflective Checklist for Review Session

	Yes absolutely positive			Don't think so
1. I was extremely cooperative and effective in keeping myself and others on task during the preparation.				
2. I spoke Japanese during the preparation and encouraged others to do so.				
3. I think my group had an excellent work ethic and was fully prepared for the review session.				
4. I gave all the instructions in a clear voice and at an appropriate rate throughout the review session.				
5. I spoke fluently and made almost no grammatical or usage mistakes during the review session.				
6. I made eye contact with every participant and paid a good deal of attention to how they were doing.				
7. I used visuals and handouts in a timely and effective manner.				
8. I appropriately responded to the participants' questions.				
9. I kept excellent posture and did not make myself look sloppy throughout the review session.				
10. I exercised good class management skills when such skills were called for.				
11. I think my group did an excellent job as a team during the review session.				
12. I think the review session was extremely successful on the whole.				
13. CREATE YOUR OWN STATEMENT.				

SUM-UP

1. *What differences did you find between your lesson plan and actual lesson during the review session?*

2. *The way you conducted your review session in Japanese was: (circle one)*

    a. formal

    b. informal

    c. casual

    d. emotional

3. *What do you think about your review session?*

4. *What is the difference between Japanese grammar and your language grammar?*

5. *Did you make any progress in your teaching ability? Please rate your progress on a scale of 0 to 5. (0 = no progress, 5 = excellent progress)*

0	1	2	3	4	5

6. *Were you able to use your presentation skills when you did your presentation? Please rate your progress on a scale of 0 to 5. (0 = no progress, 5 = excellent progress)*

0	1	2	3	4	5

7. *Were you able to use the class management strategy as necessary during your lesson? Please rate your progress on a scale of 0 to 5. (0 = no progress, 5 = excellent progress)*

0	1	2	3	4	5

ADDITIONAL VOCABULARY

Functional Vocabulary

Te Form Plus

つくってくれます	作ってくれます	つくってくれる	作ってくれる	will make it for me
べんきょうしておきます	勉強しておきます	べんきょうしておく	勉強しておく	(I will) study before hand
かんがえてみます	考えてみます	かんがえてみる	考えてみる	try to think

Auxiliary Verb

りかいしなくてはなりません	理解しなくては なりません	りかいしなくては ならない	理解しなくては ならない	(You) must understand
しなければなりません		しなければならない		(You) must do it.

Connectors

し		and~
ので		because~
とき	時	When ~
べんきょうしたあと	勉強した後	after studying
べんきょうするまえ	勉強する前	before studying
それにたいして	それに対して	In regards to that

Question Word Plus

いつか		Some day
なんども	何度も	many times

Agreeing or disagreeing classroom expressions

そうですね	*Soo desu ne*	そうだ(わ)ね	*Soo da(wa) ne*	That's right.
し	*Soo desu ka*	し	*Soo ka*	I see (with agreeable tone)

Notional Vocabulary

School

いちじかんめ	一時間目	the first period
こくご	国語	language arts
しゃかいか	社会科	social studies
じゅぎょう	授業	class
おこなう	行う	do
りか	理科	science
げいじゅつ	芸術	art
いどうする	移動する	move
ねている	寝ている	sleeping
たべることができる	食べることができる	can eat
もってくる	持ってくる	bring
べんとう	弁当	lunch box
アメフト		American football
ほか	他	other
わだい	話題	topic
チアリーダー		cheer leader
ほうかご	放課後	afterschool
ぜんこくたいかい	全国大会	national competition
なんども	何度も	many times

べんきょうする	勉強する	study
でている	出ている	entry
ごろ	頃	around
じゅく	塾	cram school
つく	着く	arrive
さきに	先に	ahead, before, earlier
せいと	生徒	student
いっしょうけんめい	一生懸命	work hard
となり	隣	next to
コンビニ		convenience store

Extracurricular Activities

しがけん	滋賀県	Prefecture name
なかた	中田	name
まさこ	雅子	name
うまれる	生まれる	be born
こうこう３ねんせい	高校三年生	high school third year student
１８さい	１８才	18 years old
ながはま	長浜	place name
は	歯	tooth
みがく	磨く	brush

にきび	面皰	pimple
きをつける	気を付ける	take care/ be careful
かお	顔	face
あらう	洗う	wash
せいふく	制服	uniform
きる	着る	wear
しゅるい	種類	kind, type
なる	成る	become
にんき	人気	popular
かばん	鞄	bag
わたしたち	私達	we
のる	乗る	ride
ので		because~
とき	時	when~
ぬぐ	脱ぐ	take off
うわばき	上履き	shoes for indoor
しなければなりません		must do
じゅんび	準備	preparation
ざっし	雑誌	magazine
れんしゅう	練習	practice
だいがく	大学	college
つよい	強い	strong
つくってくれます	作ってくれます	will make it for me
そのとき	その時	that time
そのあいだ	その間	during that time

よしゅう	予習	preview
べんきょうしたあと	勉強した後	after studying
べんきょうするまえ	勉強する前	before studying
みなおす	見直す	look over
それにたいして	それに対して	in regards to that
べんきょうしておく	勉強しておく	study beforehand
クラスない	クラス内	in the class
はんせい	反省	think over, reflect
うんどうかい	運動会	field day
ぶんかさい	文化祭	annual school cultural festival
かいぎ	会議	meeting
はんせいかい	反省会	meeting for reflection
かいけつ	解決	solution
すぎる	過ぎる	over, too excess
ほうほう	方法	method
いしけってい	意志決定	decision making
いけん	意見	opinion
とりいれる	取り入れる	borrow, introduce
さんぎょうかい	産業界	industrial world
かいぜん	改善	improve, reform
かんけい	関係	relationship
かんがえてみる	考えてみる	try to think
れんしゅう	練習	practice
だいがく	大学	college
つよい	強い	strong

In Japan

ねむい	眠い	sleepy
あくびする	欠伸する	yawn
さっぱりした	さっぱりした	feel refreshed
わしょく	和食	Japanese style food
ようしょく	洋食	Western style food
さら	皿	dish
しょうゆ	醤油	soy sauce
よう	用	for
みそしる	味噌汁	miso soup
スプーン		spoon
どうやって		how about
きょうかしょ	教科書	textbook
ハンカチ		handkerchief
わすれる	忘れる	forget
わすれもの	忘れ物	something you forget

Reviewing

ふくしゅう	復習	review

Mini Conversation 2: ミニ会話2

Travel to Japan: 日本へ旅行

会話1 （到着の翌朝）

マイク： おはようございます。

ホストマザー： おはよう。朝ご飯を食べますか。

マイク： はい。あああああ眠い！（あくびをする）

ホストマザー： (笑う)まだ時差ぼけですね。じゃあご飯を食べる前(1)に
シャワーを浴びますか。

マイク： はい、そうします。 (Mike takes a shower and comes out of the bathroom.)

マイク： ありがとうございました。さっぱりしました。

ホストマザー： よかった。じゃあ朝ご飯を食べましょうか。

会話2

ホストマザー： 和食と洋食、どっちがいい？

マイク： 和食にします。
・ （ご飯がでてくる）お皿がたくさんありますね。

ホストマザー： ええ、この小さいお皿はおしょうゆ用ですよ。

マイク： これは味噌汁ですね。あのう、スプーンがありませんが
どうやって飲みますか。

ホストマザー： (Putting her mouth directly to the bowl) こうやって飲んでください。

会話3

マイク：　　　　明日から学校がありますから準備を<u>しなければなりません</u>(2)。

ホストマザー：何を持っていきますか。

マイク：　　　　教科書、ノート、お弁当、ハンカチ。

ホストマザー：忘れ物はありませんか。上履きを入れましたか。

マイク：　　　　忘れていました。上履きはアメリカにありませんから。

ホストマザー：持っていますか。

マイク：　　　　いいえ、買わなければなりません。

ホストマザー：じゃあ、昼ご飯を<u>食べてから</u>(3)デパートに行きましょう。

Dialogue 1 (The next morning after Mike arrived in Japan)

Mike:　Good morning.
Host mother: Good morning. Do you want to eat breakfast?
Mike:　Yes. Uhhh, I'm sleepy! (He yarns)
Host mother: (laughing) You still have jet lag. Would you like to take a shower before having breakfast?
Mike:　Yes, I will do so.
(Mike takes shower and comes out of the bathroom.)
Mike:　Thank you. I feel refreshed.
Host mother: Good. Now let's have breakfast.

Dialogue 2

Host mother: Which would you prefer, Japanese or Western breakfast?
Mike:　I will go with Japanese. (The host mother serves breakfast) There are a lot of plates.
Host mother: Ah huh, this small plate is for soy sauce.
Mike:　This is miso soup, isn't it? Uh, there is no spoon. How would I eat it?
Host mother: (Putting her mouth directly to the bowl) Eat like this.

Dialogue 3

Mike:　I am going to school tomorrow, so I have to prepare for it.
Host mother: What are you going to take with you?
Mike:　Textbooks, notebooks, lunch, a handkerchief.
Host mother: Is there anything you are missing? Have you put indoor shoes?
Mike:　I have forgotten about them, because we don't use anything like those in the States.
Host mother: Do you have indoor shoes?
Mike:　No, I have to buy a pair.
Host mother: Let's go to the supermarket after haveing lunch.

Notes

- 到着：arrival
- 翌朝：the next morning
- あくび：yawn
- あくびをする：to yawn
- まだ：still
- 時差ぼけ：jet lag
- 時差ぼけだ：One has jet lag
- 前に：before
- 浴びる：to bathe
シャワーを浴びる：to take a shower
- さっぱりする：to be refreshed

Notes

- 和食：Japanese style meal
- 洋食：Western style meal
- どっちがいい：Which would you prefer?
- (お)しょうゆ：soy sauce
- ～用：for~, to be used for ~
- 味噌汁：miso soup
- どうやって+V：how do you V?
- こうやって+V：V in this way.
e.g. こうやって飲みます=(We) drink like this.

Notes

- 準備をする：to prepare
- 持っていく：to take something with oneself (to another place)
- お弁当：lunch box, Japanese bento
- ハンカチ：handkerchief
- 忘れ物：something you forget, something you left
忘れ物がある：to forget to take something
- 上履き：shoes for inside of a building

Grammar Keys and Practice

(1) dictionary form+前^{まえ}に

dictionary form+ 前^{まえ}に means before an action. Look at the following sample sentences.

Say it in Japanese. 日本語^{にほんご}で言^いいましょう。

Before having a meal, I wash my hands.

Before watching TV, I do my homework.

Before entering the house, (we) take off our shoes

(2) ～てから

～てから means after one action is done the next action will follow.

Make a single sentence using the following example. 例^{れい}にならって、一^{ひと}つの文^{ぶん}にしましょう。

EX. シャワーをあびます (take)。寝^ねます。⇒シャワーをあびてから寝^ねます。

1. メールをチェックします。でかけます (go out)。⇒
2. 歯^は (teeth) をみがきます。学校^{がっこう}に行きます。⇒
3. くつ (shoes) をぬぎます。うちに入ります。⇒

(3) ～なければなりません

～なければなりません is equivalent to "must" and "have to" in English.

1. Rewrite the sentence using ～なければなりません using the following example.

例^{れい}にならって、「～なければなりません」を使って文を書^かき換えましょう。

EX. 明日^{あした}、早^{はや}く起^おきます。⇒ 明日^{あした}、早^{はや}く起^おきなければなりません。

1. 両親^{りょうしん} (parents) に電話^{でんわ}をかけます。⇒
2. 辞書^{じしょ} (dictionary) を買^かう。⇒
3. 宿題^{しゅくだい} (home work) をする。⇒

2. Make an extended sentence using the following example.

例^{れい}にならって、文を付^つけ加^{くわ}えましょう。

EX. 明日、テストがあります。⇒ 明日、テストが
ありますから、勉強^{べんきょう}しなければなりません。

1. かぜ (catch cold) です。⇒
2. 来週^{らいしゅう}、日本に行きます。⇒
3. 部屋^{へや} (room) がきれいじゃありません。⇒

> **Travel Practice 1**
>
> When you arrive at your host family, you will ask your host mother if you are able to do certain things , using ～なければなりませんか with ～前^{まえ}に or ～てから.

> **Travel Practice 2**
>
> Form pairs. One person will be a host mother in Japan. The other will be an exchange student from outside of Japan. The exchange student will try to communicate with his host mother in Japanese and ask about possible responsibilities.

> **Travel Practice 3**
>
> Create another activity describing host family life. Be sure that the activity is interesting, and integrates cultural issues.

UNIT 3 REVIEW THROUGH GAMES

ゲームで復習

I. Verb Form Memory Game　動詞の神経衰弱
<small>どうし　しんけいすいじゃく</small>

Playing the memory game (also known as the game of concentration) is a fun and effective way of reviewing words, short expressions, and kanji with your classmates. In an ordinary game a deck of cards is placed face-down in rows and players try to find two identical cards. Here we will attempt a modified version in which players will try to collect three different forms (the ない form, the dictionary form, and the て form) of the same verb to score a point. Only Japanese will be used throughout the game.

1. Break up into groups of five.　五人のグループに分かれる。
<small>わ</small>

The number of players per game is five, though it may change according to the size of your class. Listen to your teacher's instructions and break up into groups.

2. Make cards.　カードを作る。

Things needed （ひつよう　もの） (必要な物)	1. Blank index cards (インデックスカード) 2. Markers　　　　　　（マーカー）

You will use a set of 45 cards representing the ない form, the dictionary form, and the て form of the 15 verbs shown below in sets of three. Everyone in your group should be in charge of one of the sets (A-E) and make 9 cards each.

始めます <small>た</small> 立ちます あります	食べます <small>えら</small> 選びます 書きます	言います 読みます 答えます	行きます 来ます <small>お</small> 終わります	作ります 話します します
A.	**B.**	**C.**	**D.**	**E.**

245

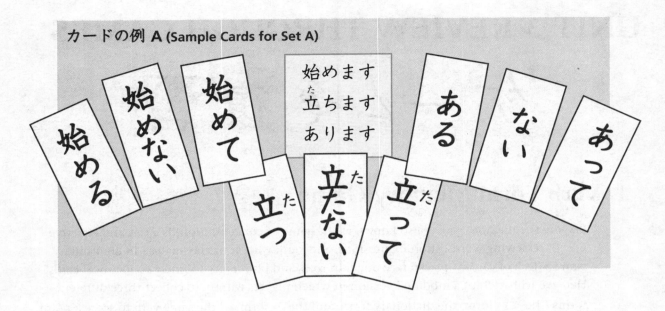

カードの例 A (Sample Cards for Set A)

始める　始めない　始めて　始めます／立ちます／あります（た）　ある　ない　あって

立つ（た）　立たない（た）　立って（た）

3. Check rules and procedure. ルールと進行の確認をする。
<small>しんこう　かくにん</small>

Rules and Procedure:

1. Shuffle the cards and place them face-down in rows.
2. Take turns and try to collect a set of three cards indicating the ない form, the dictionary form, and the て form of the same verb by turning over 3 cards in succession. You will lose your turn when you turn over a set of different cards.
3. Read what is written on a card right after you turn it over.
4. Place the cards you have collected face up in front of you.
5. The game ends when all the cards have been collected and a player with the most cards is declared a winner.

4. Decide who will play first. 順番を決める。
<small>じゅんばん　き</small>

Decide who will turn over a card first in the game by *janken*. The remaining order may also be determined by *janken* and the players should be seated accordingly.

5. Practice useful expressions. 役<small>やく</small>に立<small>た</small>つ表現<small>ひょうげん</small>の練習<small>れんしゅう</small>をする。

Your game will be conducted entirely in Japanese. Practice the following expressions and use them during the game as much as you can. In the informal section on the right, female speech and male speech is indicated in red and blue respectively.

日本語 (Formal)	英語<small>えいご</small> (Informal)	日本語 (Informal)
次<small>つぎ</small>は誰<small>だれ</small>の番<small>ばん</small>ですか。	Who is next?	次誰<small>つぎだれ</small>の番<small>ばん</small>?
私の番です。	It's my turn.	私/僕<small>ぼく</small>の番<small>ばん</small>。
リンダさんの番ですよ。	Hey, it's Linda's turn.	リンダの番<small>ばん</small>だよ。
それを裏返<small>うらがえ</small>してください。	Turn that one over.	それ裏返<small>うらがえ</small>して。
それを取<small>と</small>ってください。	Pass that one to me.	それ取<small>と</small>って。
それを戻<small>もど</small>してください。	Put that one back.	それ戻<small>もど</small>して。
それを置<small>お</small>いてください。	Put that one down.	それ置<small>お</small>いて。
あ、間違<small>まちが</small>えました。	Oh I made a mistake.	あ、間違<small>まちが</small>えた。
惜<small>お</small>しかっです。	It was so close.	惜<small>お</small>しかった。
信<small>しん</small>じられません。	Unbelievable.	信<small>しん</small>じられない。
すごいですね。	Awesome.	すごいね。
興奮<small>こうふん</small>しないでください。	Don't get too excited.	興奮<small>こうふん</small>しないで。
ずるをしないでください。	Don't cheat.	ずるしないで。
カードを数<small>かぞ</small>えてください。	Count your cards.	カード数<small>かぞ</small>えて。
何組<small>なんくみ</small>ありますか。	How many sets (of cards) do you have?	何組<small>なんくみ</small>ある?
六組<small>ろっ</small>あります。	I have six sets.	六組<small>ろっ</small>ある。
トムさんの勝<small>か</small>ちですね。	Tom is the winner.	トムの勝<small>か</small>ちだね。
おめでとうございます。	Congratulations!	おめでとう。
もう一度<small>いちど</small>やりましょう。	Let's play another game.	もう一度<small>いちど</small>やろう。
もう一度しましょう。	Let's play another game.	もう一度しよう。

6. Play the game. ゲームをする。

II. Let's Say It Together　一緒に言おう

In this game, players are given a card on which a sentence is written in Japanese. Standing in a circle facing one another, participants simultaneously say their sentence and try to find a player who might have said exactly the same thing as them. It's an exciting game that will help you not only review different sentence patterns but also pronounce Japanese as clearly as you can and listen carefully to what other people are saying at the same time.

いっしょにいおう can be played by a group of any size as long as it consists of even number of players. The larger the group, the more challenging and exciting the game may become. Perhaps, 10-14 players may be most appropriate at this stage, and examples we use here are based on 12 players.

1. Make cards.　カードを作る。

Things needed (必要な物)	1. Blank index cards (インデックスカード) 2. Markers　　　　　　　(マーカー)

Create 6 similar sentences using the constructions you have learned so far. Write each sentence on an index card. You need to make 2 of the same kind for each sentence, 12 cards altogether.

文とカードの例 (Sample Sentences and Cards)

1. 腕を上に三回伸ばしてください。

2. 腕を上に伸ばさないでください。

3. 腕を上に三回伸ばしたいです。

4. 腕を上に何回伸ばしましたか。

5. 腕を上に伸ばしています。

6. 腕を上に三回伸ばしてもいいです。

うでを上に三回伸ばしてください。

うでを上に三回伸ばしてください。

うでを上に三回伸ばしてもいいです。

うでを上に三回伸ばしてもいいです。

2. Check rules and procedure. ルールと進行の確認をする。

Rules and Procedure:

1. Get a card from your teacher, and silently read and memorize the sentence on the card.
2. Stand in a circle facing each other and wait for a signal by the teacher.
3. As soon as you get the signal, say the memorized sentence clearly and loudly.
4. Listen to what your classmates are saying in the meantime and move over to the side of another player who you think has said the same sentence as your own.
5. Wait for your teacher's next signal without checking each other's card.
6. After the signal, you and your partner say the sentence in unison to verify the match.
7. Repeat steps 2-6 above for those who had the wrong match or could not find their partner.

---

3. Play the game. ゲームをする。

Unit 4:
Environment

The Japanese word for environment is 環境, comprising this word, 環 and 境, represent "ring/circle" and "boundary/condition" respectively. 環境 is therefore etymologically similar to its English counterpart, as the word environment also represents a state of being surrounded or being "in the circle." So the environment is everything that surrounds us and what we interact with in our daily life. In the next two chapters you will turn your attention to two thigs that comprise your immediate surroundings: your town and your school.

In Chapter 3 you will learn how to construct paragraphs and write about your home town, including its weather. In Chapter 4 you will create a photo book, introducing your school and featuring those facilities and buildings that are of particular significance to you.

During the course of this study, you will learn ho to develop logical and cohesive paragraphs and accumulate a good deal of useful words and expressions for describing your environment. This will prepare you to deal with some of the more global issues and concerns relating to our environment discussed in our later units.

You must be quite familiar with your hometown and your school. Let's have another look at them at this time and think about how to showcase them effectively in Japanese.

Photo: Tsukasa Yokozawa "On the Margin" 1999

Chapter 3
Let's Write About Your Town!

Photo: Tsukasa Yokozawa "Spilt Milk #2" 2001

Chapter 3: Let's Write About Your Town!

町について書きましょう

3.1 Introduction 序論
<ruby>じょろん</ruby>

CHAPTER OBJECTIVES

AT THE END OF THIS SECTION, YOU WILL BE ABLE TO:

- write a logical and coherent paragraph about a topic related to your town

- understand the basic structure of a paragraph

- describe basic features of your town by referring to its weather, public facilities, and landscape, among other things

- indicate the existence of something or someone

- express levels of quantity and frequency using adverbs

- create and use plain-style sentences as a noun modifier

- make comparative statements and answer comparative questions

- count different types of objects by using appropriate counters

- build up substantial vocabulary that is useful in describing various aspects of a town

- learn or review vocabulary by playing bingo games

- look up a new word in the dictionary

- express English units of measurement in Japanese, and convert between the English system and the metric system

- recognize about 32 kanji and their basic compounds

- give numeric information including fractions

- read and write 24 kanji and their basic compounds.

YOU WILL ALSO LEARN:

- about the basic structure of a paragraph

- two paragraph development tactics

- about Japanese positional words and counters

- useful expressions for various aspects of town

- about Japanese language accent

- about Japanese numerical progression and units of measurements (metric system).

Let's Write About Your Town!
町について書きましょう

Writing Paragraphs

This chapter is primarily about paragraph writing. After studying some useful sentence constructions, you will learn about the basic structure that you will follow at this time to create logical and coherent paragraphs. You may find the structure easy to follow since it is quite similar to what you follow when constructing descriptive or expository paragraphs in English. This is not to say that patterns of writing in Japanese are the same as those in English, and you will learn more about this in later volumes of *Kisetsu*. In the meantime, following the familiar structure will help you to make a solid initial step toward your successful writing career in Japanese.

TOPIC SENTENCE

SUPPORTING SENTENCES

Paragraph Development Tactics

There are two useful paragraph development tactics you should know about. Fortunately, they are basically the same as something you learned already in Volume 1 of *Kisetsu*. You may recall that in Chapter 4 of *Haruichiban* you were introduced to the attribution tactic and the analogy tactic to extend your social conversation. (See *Haruichiban* p. 260.) These tactics are applicable to writing as well, and you will practice developing your paragraph with these tactics in mind.

TOPIC SENTENCE

SUPPORTING SENTENCES

Describing Your Town

You will be practicing paragraph development by writing about some aspect of your town. This is the first chapter in Unit 4 and its theme is the environment. In the previous unit, your resources mainly came from your classroom or your own personal experiences. In this chapter, you will turn your attention to your surrounding environment. You may have some unexpected discoveries and renewed appreciation about your town and community while you think about how you want to present them to others. Also you will be able to build up substantial vocabulary about such town themes as the weather, public and entertainment facilities, nature and landscape, as well as stores. Furthermore, you will have an opportunity to compare your town with some Japanese towns. So get ready to reacquaint yourself with your town while improving your writing skills!

Product

町<ruby>まち</ruby>のパラグラフ

Paragraphs about your town

ジョイタウンの冬<ruby>ふゆ</ruby>の天気<ruby>てんき</ruby>

MAIN PARAGRAPH	TOPIC SENTENCE	ジョイタウンの冬はかなり厳しいです。寒い日がたくさんあります。気温は摂氏0度くらいです。1月と2月は湖が凍ります。よくダウンコートが必要です。それに、雪もけっこう降ります。去年は雪の日が20日くらいありました。吹雪もけっこうありました。雪は全部で1メートル50センチくらい降りました。

MAIN PARAGRAPH

TOPIC SENTENCE

SUPPORTING SENTENCE 1

EXAMPLE 1
EXAMPLE 2
EXAMPLE 3

SUPPORTING SENTENCE 2

EXAMPLE 1
EXAMPLE 2
EXAMPLE 3

"SUM-UP" PARAGRAPH

"SUM-UP" COMPARATIVE STATEMENTS

ジョイタウンの冬はかなり厳<ruby>きび</ruby>しいです。寒<ruby>さむ</ruby>い日がたくさんあります。気温<ruby>きおん</ruby>は摂氏<ruby>せっし</ruby>0度<ruby>ど</ruby>くらいです。1月と2月は湖<ruby>みずうみ</ruby>が凍<ruby>こお</ruby>ります。よくダウンコートが必要<ruby>ひつよう</ruby>です。それに、雪<ruby>ゆき</ruby>もけっこう降<ruby>ふ</ruby>ります。去年<ruby>きょねん</ruby>は雪<ruby>ゆき</ruby>の日が20日<ruby>にち</ruby>くらいありました。吹雪<ruby>ふぶき</ruby>もけっこうありました。雪は全部<ruby>ぜんぶ</ruby>で1メートル50センチくらい降<ruby>ふ</ruby>りました。

ジョイタウンの冬は稚内<ruby>わっかない</ruby>の冬ほど厳<ruby>きび</ruby>しくありません。でも、東京<ruby>とうきょう</ruby>の冬より厳しいです。たぶん、長野<ruby>ながの</ruby>の冬と同<ruby>おな</ruby>じくらい厳しいでしょう。

Process フローチャート

3.2		**1**	**Building up vocabulary**	語彙を構築する
3.3	Mechanics	**2**	**Sentence construction: Part 1**	文を作る その1
3.4		**3**	**Sentence construction: Part 2**	文を作る その2
		4	**Paragraph construction: Part 1**	パラグラフを作る その1
3.5		**5**	**Paragraph construction: Part 2**	パラグラフを作る その2
		6	**Paragraph development**	パラグラフをより詳しく書く
3.6		**7**	**Draw comparisons**	比較をする
3.7		**8**	**Write about the winter weather**	冬の天気について書く
3.8	Virtual Reality	**9**	**Decide upon a topic**	トピックを決める
		10	**Learn vocabulary**	語彙を学ぶ
		11	**Confirm the structure**	構造の確認をする
		12	**Create your work**	作品を書く
		13	**Evaluate and reflect**	評価と振り返りをする
		14	**Make a hand-written version**	原稿用紙に書く

BASIC VOCABULARY　基礎語彙

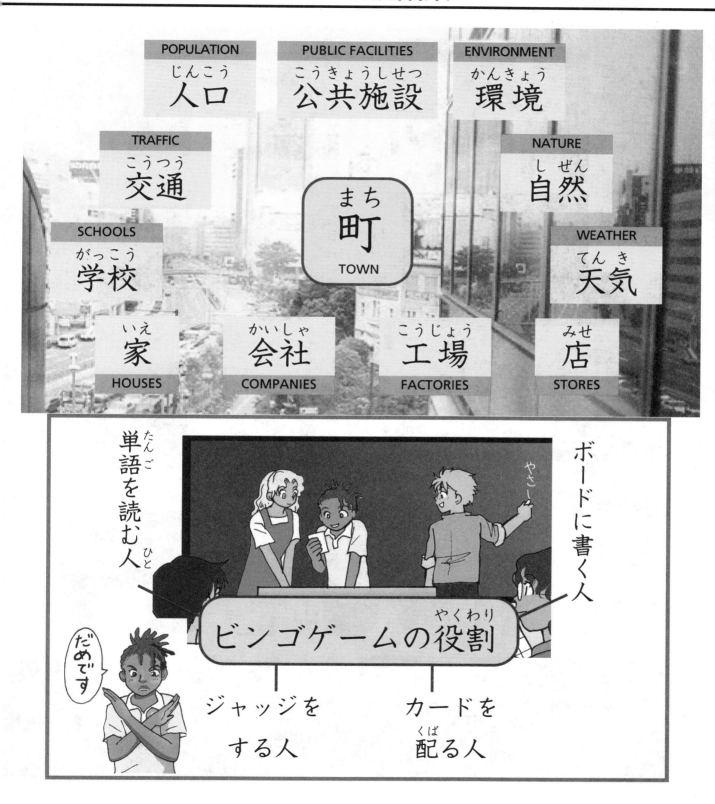

POPULATION
人口

PUBLIC FACILITIES
公共施設

ENVIRONMENT
環境

TRAFFIC
交通

NATURE
自然

まち
町
TOWN

SCHOOLS
学校

WEATHER
天気

家
HOUSES

会社
COMPANIES

工場
FACTORIES

店
STORES

ビンゴゲームの役割

単語を読む人

ボードに書く人

ジャッジをする人

カードを配る人

だめです

PUBLIC FACILITIES

公共施設（こうきょうしせつ）

駅（えき）

空港（くうこう）

港（みなと）

消防署（しょうぼうしょ）

病院（びょういん）

公民館（こうみんかん）

警察（けいさつ）

交番（こうばん）

図書館（としょかん）

美術館（びじゅつかん）

NATURE

自然（しぜん）

川（かわ）

山（やま）

池（いけ）

滝（たき）

森（もり）

木（き）

林（はやし）

体育館（たいいくかん）

遊園地（ゆうえんち）

ENTERTAINMENT FACILITIES

娯楽施設（ごらくしせつ）

公園（こうえん）

動物園（どうぶつえん）

郵便局（ゆうびんきょく）

POST OFFICE
郵便局

映画館（えいがかん）

MOVIE

畑（はたけ）

田（た） or（田んぼ）

海（うみ）

湖（みずうみ）

砂漠（さばく）

海岸（かいがん）

261

レストラン

スーパー

くすりや
薬屋

みせ
店
STORES

くだものや
果物屋

パンや
パン屋

ほんや
本屋

はなや
花屋

さかなや
魚屋

しょうてんがい
商店街

にくや
肉屋

おもちゃや
おもちゃ屋

やおや
八百屋

ケーキや
ケーキ屋

デパート

コンビニ

カフェテリア

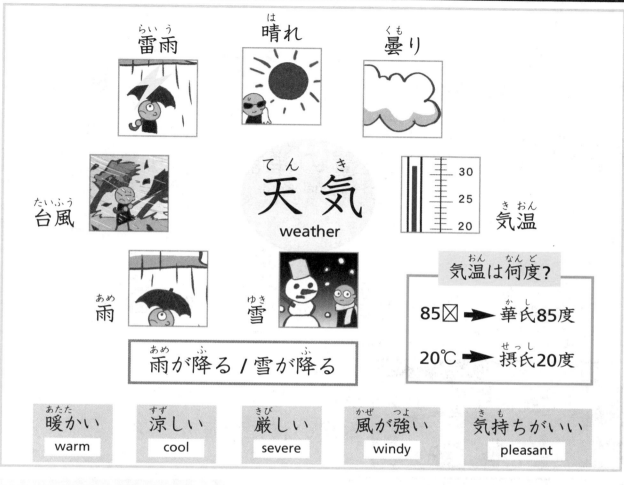

雷雨（らいう）

晴（は）れ

曇（くも）り

台風（たいふう）

天気（てんき）
weather

気温（きおん）

雨（あめ）

雪（ゆき）

気温は何度？（おん なん ど）

85° ➡ 華氏85度（か し）

20℃ ➡ 摂氏20度（せっ し）

雨が降る / 雪が降る（あめ が ふ / ゆき が ふ）

暖かい（あたた）	涼しい（すず）	厳しい（きび）	風が強い（かぜ つよ）	気持ちがいい（き も）
warm	cool	severe	windy	pleasant

方角（ほうがく）　direction

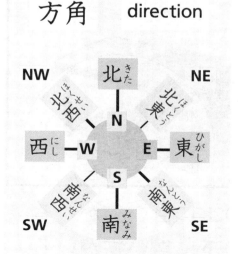

NW　北（きた）　NE
北西（ほくせい）
西（にし）　W　N　E　東（ひがし）
S
南西（なんせい）
SW　南（みなみ）　SE
北東（ほくとう）
南東（なんとう）

Expressing uncertainty or probability
-でしょう　it will probably be -

札幌（さっぽろ）の明日（あした）の天気（てんき）は晴（は）れでしょう。それから、暖（あたた）かいでしょう。

BASIC VOCABULARY

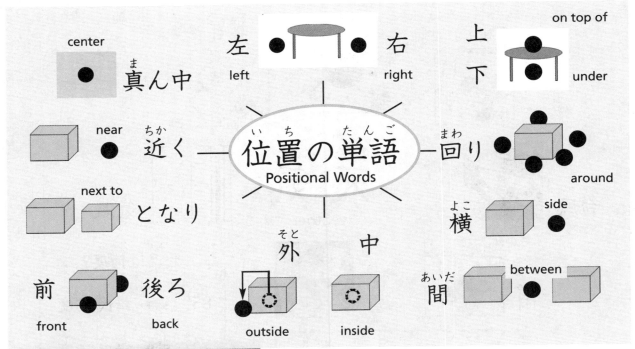

center
真ん中 (ま)

左 left ● 右 right

上 下 on top of / under

位置の単語 (い ち た ん ご)
Positional Words

near 近く (ちか)

回り (まわ) around

next to となり

横 (よこ) side

外 (そと) 中

前 後ろ front back

outside inside

間 (あいだ) between

魚屋のとなりに本屋があります。(さかなや)
本屋の横に魚屋がある。(よこ)

くるまのうしろ

まえ

車の前に男の子がいます。
車の後ろに女の子がいます。

うえ

した

机の上に白い猫がいる。(つくえ / しろ / ねこ)
机の下に黒い猫がいる。(くろ)

本　ほん、ぼん　ぽん

long/ slender objects, (video/audio tapes, trees)

軒　けん、げん

houses, stores, restaurants etc.

台　だい

machines, appliances (cars, trucks, buses)

個　こ

any objects esp. small and solid ones

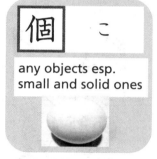

じょすうし
助数詞
Counters

頭　とう

big animals (horse, tiger, etc.).

枚　まい

thin/flat objects (CDs, paper, T shirts, etc.)

冊　さつ

bound objects (books, notebooks, magazines, etc.)

匹　ひき、びき　ぴき

small animals (dogs, cats, mice, etc.).

なんぼん
ペンが**何本**ありますか。

とら　とう
虎が**何頭**いますか。

じてんしゃ　だい
自転車が**何台**ある？

形容詞
けいようし

広い
ひろ

狭い
せま

大きい
おお

小さい

遠い
とお

近い
ちか

少ない
すく

多い
おお

ごはん　ごはん

静か(な)
しず

高い
たか

低い
ひく

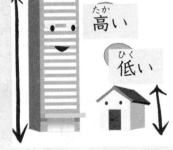

うるさい

CLEAN

きれい(な)

汚い
きたな

比較
ひかく

XはYより-です。

X is - than Y.

XはYほど-じゃ/
くありません。

X is not as - as Y.

私の町の冬は
まち
東京の冬より
とうきょう
寒いです。
さむ

私の町の冬は
東京の冬ほど
寒くありませ
ん。

新<ruby>新<rt>あたら</rt></ruby>しい　　<ruby>古<rt>ふる</rt></ruby>い

NEW

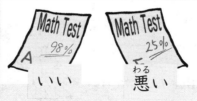

Math Test A 98%　　いい

Math Test 25%　　<ruby>悪<rt>わる</rt></ruby>い

<ruby>安<rt>やす</rt></ruby>い

300円

<ruby>高<rt>たか</rt></ruby>い

1000円

<ruby>重<rt>おも</rt></ruby>い　1000 kg

<ruby>軽<rt>かる</rt></ruby>い　5 kg

<ruby>強<rt>つよ</rt></ruby>い

30 wins
3 losses

<ruby>弱<rt>よわ</rt></ruby>い

3 wins
30 losses

<ruby>便利<rt>べんり</rt></ruby>(な)

SUPER

<ruby>不便<rt>ふべん</rt></ruby>(な)

<ruby>明<rt>あか</rt></ruby>るい　　　<ruby>暗<rt>くら</rt></ruby>い

私の<ruby>町<rt></rt></ruby>の<ruby>夏<rt>なつ</rt></ruby>は<ruby>東京<rt></rt></ruby>の夏と<ruby>気温<rt>おん</rt></ruby>がほぼ<ruby>同<rt>おな</rt></ruby>じです。

私の町の夏は東京の夏と同じくらい<ruby>蒸<rt>む</rt></ruby>し<ruby>暑<rt>あつ</rt></ruby>いです。

XはYと(ほぼ)同じです。

X is (just about) the same as Y.

XはYとZが(ほぼ)同じです。

X is (just about) the same as Y in terms of Z.

XはYと同じくらい‐です。

X is just about as ‐ as Y.

267

BASIC VOCABULARY

バナナとりんごと
どちらがいいですか。

りんごの方が
いいです。

Answering comparative questions

Xのほうが-です

Indicating potentiality or ability: what one can/cannot do

Dictionary Form of V+ことができる

ピクニックに
行くことが
できます。

ピクニックに
行くことが
できません。

論理的に (ろんりてき) logically
書きましたか。

in an interesting manner
面白く (おもしろ)
書きましたか。

パラグラフ
の評価 (ひょうか)
Paragraph Writing
Evaluation

詳しく (くわ) in detail
書きましたか。

accurately
正確に (せいかく)
書きましたか。

3.2 Mechanics 組立て
くみ た

Vocabulary Building
語彙の構築
ご い　こうちく

Objectives

Build up vocabulary for describing a town through cooperative exercises and games.
Learn about and practice making noun-modifying clauses.
Prepare and play bingo games entirely in Japanese.

Overview

This section focuses on the learning of vocabulary you will need to describe your town. Having done review sessions, you should be able to conduct in Japanese some simple activities, such as matching exercises. You will also prepare and play bingo games, and this will be done in Japanese as much as possible.

1	**Build up vocabulary**	語彙を構築する
1	**Conduct exercises**	練習問題をする
2	**Play bingo games**	ビンゴゲームをする

自然
施設
天気
店
形容詞

1 Build up vocabulary
<ruby>語<rt>ご</rt></ruby><ruby>彙<rt>い</rt></ruby>を<ruby>構築<rt>こうちく</rt></ruby>する

1 Conduct exercises
<ruby>練習問題<rt>れんしゅうもんだい</rt></ruby>をする

A. Match the images with the words by filling each parenthesis with the appropriate letter.

<ruby>絵<rt>え</rt></ruby>と<ruby>単語<rt>たんご</rt></ruby>をマッチさせてください。

1. (   )   2. (   )   3. (   )   4. (   )   5. (   )

6. ( )   7 (   )   8. (   )   9. (   )   10. (   )

a. 川（かわ）	b. 砂漠（さばく）		
c. 森（もり）	d. 海岸（かいがん）		
e. 田（た）	f. 畑（はたけ）		
g. 池（いけ）	h. 湖（みずうみ）		
i. 山（やま）	j. 林（はやし）		

1. (   )   2. (   )   3. (   )   4. (   )   5. (   )

6. (   )   7. (   )   8 (   )   9. (   )   10. (   )

11. (   )   12. (   )   13. (   )   14. (   )   15. (   )

a. 郵便局（ゆうびんきょく）	b. 映画館（えいがかん）	c. 公園（こうえん）	d. 消防署（しょうぼうしょ）	e. 商店街（しょうてんがい）
f. 警察（けいさつ）	g. 動物園（どうぶつえん）	h. 公民館（こうみんかん）	i. 駅（えき）	j. 遊園地（ゆうえんち）
k. 美術館（びじゅつかん）	l. 病院（びょういん）	m. 空港（くうこう）	n. 体育館（たいいくかん）	o. 港（みなと）

B. Fill in the parenthesis with the letter of the store on the right which sells the items on the left. 次の品物はどの店にありますか。

1.	carrots, bell pepper, onions	( )	a. コーヒーショップ
2.	pork chops, ham, drumsticks	( )	b. さかなや
3.	roses, lilies, carnations	( )	c. ほんや
4.	clothes, cosmetics, jewelry	( )	d. パンや
5.	medicine, cosmetics, candies	( )	e. はなや
6.	books, magazines, newspapers	( )	f. スーパー
7.	groceries, magazines, pet food	( )	g. やおや
8.	iced coffee, tea, coke, cakes	( )	h. デパート
9.	white bread, croissant, sandwiches	( )	i. ドラッグストア
10.	shrimps, cod fish, scallops	( )	j. にくや

C. Match the images with the words by filling each parenthesis with the appropriate letter. 絵と単語をマッチさせてください。

1.(　) 2.(　)　　3.(　) 4.(　)　　5.(　) 6.(　)　　7.(　) 8.(　)

9.(　) 10.(　)　　11.(　) 12.(　)　　13.(　) 14.(　)　　15.(　) 16.(　)

17.(　) 18.(　)　　19.(　) 20.(　)

a. うるさい	b. おおきい	c. やすい	d. ふるい	e. くらい
f. すくない	g きれい(な)	h. べんり(な)	i. おおい	j. ひくい
k. きたない	l. しずか(な)	m. あかるい	n. たかい	o. せまい
p. ふべん(な)	q. あたらしい	r. ちいさい	s. ひろい	

271

D. Where will you most likely go if you want to do the following?

どこへ行きますか。

1. See some famous artwork _____
2. Play basketball with friends _____
3. Catch a flight to Tokyo _____
4. Ride a roller coaster _____
5. Consult a medical doctor _____
6. Catch a train _____
7. Buy some stamps _____
8. Participate in a town meeting _____
9. Watch a big screen movie _____
10. Catch a ferryboat _____

E. Group Work - Break up into small groups.   小グループになってください。

Objective: Learn more basic vocabulary.

Activities:

1. Meet with your group and study those words in Basic Vocabulary that have not appeared in this section so far, such as the weather terms.
2. Make a matching exercise using 12 words in which the majority of them are new. You may choose to make a different type of exercise if you like.
3. Conduct the exercise you have made in front of the class.

F. Give a short vocabulary test to one another.   短い語彙のテストをしましょう。

Procedure:

1. List 10 words that you want to ask your classmates to say in Japanese.
2. Go find a classmate and test his or her vocabulary. Record the number of his or her correct answers before you go find another test-taker.
3. Report the results to the class.
4. The student who has the best overall record will be declared a winner.

Variation:

You may ask for both oral and written answers to make the tests more challenging, though you may want to reduce the number of words on the test in such a format.

2 **Play bingo games** ビンゴゲームをする

Have you enjoyed playing memory games in the Unit 1 Review? Were you able to conduct the entire activity in Japanese? This time you will be playing bingo games to build up your vocabulary and you are also expected to use Japanese throughout the activity.

A. Break up into small groups. Meet with your group members and decide upon the theme of your bingo game.

グループでビンゴのテーマを決めましょう。

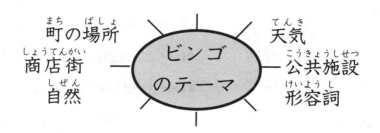

町の場所　　天気
商店街　　公共施設
自然　　形容詞

ビンゴのテーマ

会話の例 (Sample Dialogue)

A: 今日のリーダーはだれがしますか。

B: 私がします。

A: じゃ、Bさんお願いします。

B: みなさん、今日のビンゴのテーマは何がいいですか。

C: わたしは自然がいいです。

B: Dさん、どうですか。

D: はい。私は公共施設がいいです。

B: はい。ほかにありますか。 (Anything else?)

(No further suggestions offered)

B: じゃ、自然がいい人、手をあげてください。

B: 1, 2 ,3…. 自然がいい人は5人です。

B: じゃ、公共施設がいい人、手をあげてください。

B: 1, 2 ,3…. 公共施設がいい人は10人です。

B: じゃ、公共施設にしましょう。

ノート：Modifying a noun by a sentence (文による名詞の修飾)

ゲームをする人　　自然がいい人

In Japanese, a noun can be modified not only by an adjective but also by a plain style sentence. When such modification occurs, the sentence is placed before the noun it modifies. ゲームをするひと means "the person who plays a game." しぜんがいいひと means "the person who prefers nature." See the following sentences and make note of the difference between the Japanese examples and their English counterparts.

ゲームをする人	Those (people) who play a game
寝る場所	Place where one/I will go to bed/goes to bed
トムさんが来る時間	Time when Tom will come
ゲームがいい人	Those (people) who prefer a game
ゲームが好きな人	Those (people) who like a game

Note that the subject within the noun-modifying sentence is usually marked by が as in トムがくるじかん and しぜんがいいひと.

B. Choose an appropriate English equivalent for the following.

（　　）に記号を入れてください。

1. カードを読む人	（　）	a. people who play the game
2. 勉強している人	（　）	b. people who distribute cards
3. カードを配る人	（　）	c. people who are in town
4. ゲームをする人	（　）	d. place where I watch T.V.
5. 学校に行く人	（　）	e. people who read cards
6. 寝る場所	（　）	f. people who drink cola
7. テレビを見る場所	（　）	g. place where one sleeps
8. 町にいる人	（　）	h. person who is sleeping
9. 寝ている人	（　）	i. people who go to school
10. コーラを飲む人	（　）	j. people who are studying

C. Choose an appropriate English equivalent for the following.

（　　）に記号を入れてください。

1.	すしがいい人	（　）	a. people who are smart
2.	日本語が好きな人	（　）	b. people who like Japanese
3.	町がきらいな人	（　）	c. store/eatery in which pasta is cheap
4.	頭がいい人	（　）	d. store/eatery in which pizza is delicious
5.	ピザがおいしい店	（　）	e. people who prefer sushi
6.	パスタが安い店	（　）	f. people who dislike the town

D. Meet with your group and decide upon who will be in charge of the following specific tasks during the game. As always, go over the sample dialogue and conduct your meeting entirely in Japanese.

次の手順で仕事の役割を決めてください。

会話の例 (Sample Dialogue)

A: 単語を読む人はだれですか。

B: アリアさんです。

A: じゃ、アリアさんお願いします。

A: 次にジャッジをする人はだれですか。　continued.

仕事 (tasks)	役割り (roles)	名前
単語を読む	単語を読む人	アリア
ジャッジをする	ジャッジをする人	ステファニー
カードを配る		
ボードに書く		

275

E. *Individually practice the following expressions by substituting the underlined words. They are useful when you give instructions about the bingo game to the players.*

指示の表現を練習しましょう。

1. **X を配ります。**　　I am going to distribute X.

   EX. ビンゴシートを配ります。

   1. 漢字のリスト　　　　　2. 単語のテスト　　　　　3. 今日の宿題

2. **Y に書いてください。**　　Please write (something) on/in Y.

   EX. ビンゴシートに書いてください。

   1. ホワイトボード　　　　2. ノート　　　　　　　3. 紙 (paper)

3. **Z をまるで囲んでください。**　　Please circle Z.

   EX. 形容詞をまるで囲んでください。

   1. 動詞　　　　　　　　　2. 名詞　　　　　　　　3. 科目の単語

4. **これから、X を配ります。配る人、お願いします。**

   Now, we are going to distribute X. The person slated to distribute X. Please do it.

   EX. ビンゴシートを配ります。配る人お願いします。

   1. 漢字のリスト　　　　　2. 単語のテスト　　　　　3. 今日の宿題

5. **Y がありますか。Y がある人、手を上げてください。**

   Do you have Y? Those who have Y, please raise your hand.

   EX. ビンゴシートがありますか。

   1. ワークシート　　　　　2. ノート　　　　　　　3. 紙 (paper)

6. Zがありますか。Zがない人、手を上げてください。

Do you have Z? Those who don't have Z, please raise your hand.

EX. ビンゴシートがありますか。

ビンゴシートがない人、手を上げてください。

1. 単語のリスト　　　　2. 漢字のカード

F. Pair up and practice the conversation used for the beginning part of the bingo game.

ビンゴの始めの会話を練習しましょう。

会話の例 (Sample Dialogue)

Leader indicates the theme and distributes bingo sheets.

L: ビンゴをしましょう。自然と天気のビンゴです。始めに、ビンゴシートを配ります。(シートを)配る人お願いします。

Leader makes sure that everyone has a sheet.

L: みなさん、シートがありますか。

(シートが)ない人は手を上げてください。

Leader distributes a list of words to be added on their bingo sheets.

L: 次に、リストを配ります。(リストを)配る人お願いします。リストの単語をビンゴシートに書いてください。

Leader makes sure that everyone has filled out their sheet and players respond.

L: できましたか。

P: はい、できました。

or いいえ、まだです。ちょっと待ってください。

L: まだ書いている人、いますか。

P: いいえ、いません。

Leader indicates the beginning of game and asks players to circle words they hear on their sheet.

L: じゃ、始めましょう。単語を言います。その単語をまる(○)で囲んでください。いいですか。

Players respond.

P: はい。or すみません、もう一度お願いします。

277

G. Go over the following conversation used during the bingo game.

ビンゴゲームの会話を練習しましょう。

Leader reads words.

Game continues until a player who has covered all the squares in a row says "bingo."

会話の例 (Sample Dialogue)

L: 最初は、「さばく」です。
次は、「みずうみ」です。

P: ビンゴ!

Judge checks the player's sheet and congratulates him or her on winning the game. Leader then announces the end of the game.	Judge checks the player's sheet and congratulates him or her. The game continues to determine the second place. つづけましょう means "Let's continue."	Judge checks the player's sheet and finds an error. The game continues as a result.
J: あ、ビンゴですね。おめでとうございます。 L: これで、自然のビンゴを終わります。	J: あ、ビンゴですね。おめでとうございます。 L: 続けましょう。次は「あめ」です。	J: これは、ビンゴじゃありません。 L: 続けましょう。次は「あめ」です。

H. Make a bingo sheet.

ビンゴシートを作りましょう。

You will need either 16 or 25 words and/or expressions for your bingo game: 16 words and 25 words will make a 4 x 4 sheet and a 5 x 5 sheet respectively. Suppose you have chosen 16 words for the game. Make a 4 x 4 bingo sheet first and fill 8 of the 16 slots. Then prepare a list of the 8 remaining words. You will be asking your classmates to fill empty slots on their sheet before starting a game. The sample below is based on a bingo game about nature.

I. Let's play bingo! ビンゴをしましょう。

もり			
さばく		やま	くもり
	かいがん		ゆき
いけ		はれ	

みずうみ	うみ
はやし	かわ
しぜん	あめ
はたけ	たいふう

Recognition Kanji 1: 認識漢字 1

みせ
店
shop

いえ
家
house

こうじょう
工場
factory

会社
company/corporation

東西南北
All directions
(east-west-south-north)

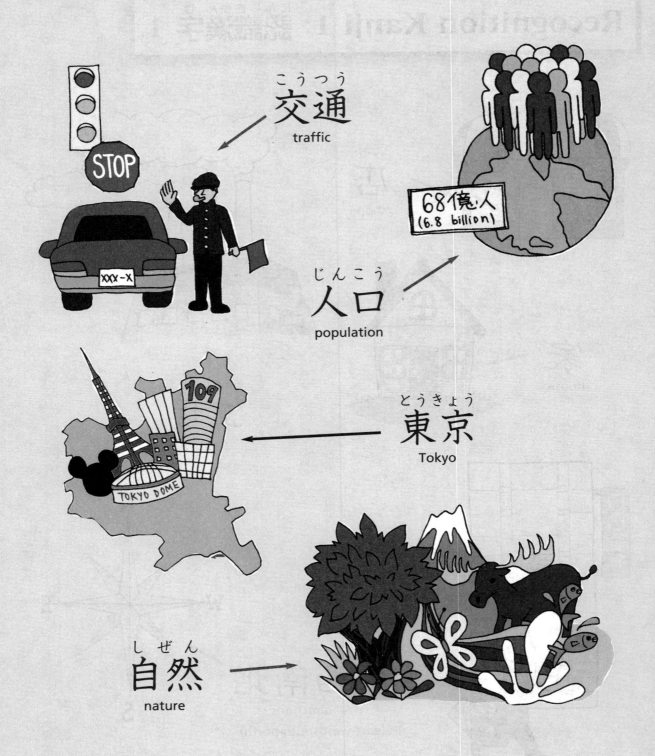

こうつう
交通
traffic

じんこう
人口
population

68億人
(6.8 billion)

とうきょう
東京
Tokyo

しぜん
自然
nature

Culture Note 3

JEM on Japanese Cities:
日本の都市

by Mary Ellen Jebbia

Tokyo is the capital city of Japan, and for good reason. Tokyo is one of the most urban cities in the world. It is a crowded, bustling hub of modern culture. I enjoyed my time in Tokyo immensely. I stayed in a place called Iidabashi, only about five minutes from Tokyo Tower and the Imperial Palace. I took the Sobu line train to get to school every morning. The train station was only about a five minute walk from my host family's apartment. In Tokyo, you can find anything you might imagine, from new technology to sports stadiums to fashion to fancy food. The Tokyo dialect serves as the standard for the Japanese language.

On the contrary, Kyoto is a city torn between contemporary and traditional culture. Near Kyoto train station, you can find many things you would find in Tokyo: game centers, karaoke boxes, nice restaurants, fast food, shopping, and tourist attractions like the Kyoto Tower. In other parts of Kyoto, however, you will find the Imperial Palace, Kinkakuji (the Golden Pavilion), tons of temples and shrines, and other cultural sights that show Japan's rich history. Close to Kyoto is a city called Nara, which served as Japan's capital city from 710 to 794. Nara is famous for Inokashira koen, a large park where hundreds of wild deer roam around. You have to be careful though- the deer are quite friendly and will probably walk right up to you! In the following paragraphs, I provide four snapshots of areas within Tokyo, Kyoto, and finally Nagoya that will give you a better feel for some aspects of Japanese culture.

Shibuya is a very famous area for young people in the center of Tokyo. Huge shopping centers, massive crowds of people, and lights and advertisements are a staple of this district. Usually I would take the train with some friends from school (it was only a 25 minute ride) and we would go shopping or get some coffee at a little shop. Shibuya is a great place to go for people watching as well. I remember going to a concert in Shibuya on a Saturday night and enjoyed seeing the young people dressed up in the newest fashions almost as much as the concert itself. Many businessmen go out to eat after work, and the train station at Shibuya connects to tons of different train lines.

A similar but smaller area than Shibuya is Harajuku, famous for the Harajuku Girls that crowd into Harajuku on Sundays wearing colorful costumes that make you feel as though you've stepped into a circus. Both Shibuya and Harajuku merit a visit if you are in Tokyo, especially if you want to see a new culture that is emerging among the Japanese youth.

A more suburban area of Tokyo is called Musashi-koganei, which is right off the Chuou train line. Compared to American suburbs, Musasi-koganei is still quite urban- stores line the big streets and houses cramp together. The houses are a bit more traditional; most of them have rooms with tatami mats and kitchen tables that require you to sit on the floor. The area also has a more suburban feel because most of the residences are houses, whereas in the very urban areas, you will only find apartments. Musasi-koganei is a fine place to live if you are looking for a quieter area not too far from the center of the city.

Kiyomizu is in my opinion the most beautiful area in Japan. The first time I went, I trekked almost a mile up a mountain road in the rain and you could see the humidity rising like steam. I remember being extremely frustrated and wondering why I was doing this, but I forgot all my complaints when I arrived at the foot of the temple. Kiyomizu Temple is perched atop a mountain right above Kyoto, and the view is breathtaking. If you stand on the veranda, you can see all of Kyoto on a clear day, as well as the gorgeous greenery surrounding the area. If you visit in the winter, you will be able to see snow coating the mountains. On the road leading up to Kiyomizu Temple, little shops and restaurants crowd next to each other, selling souvenirs and mochi, a treat made out of rice and bean paste famous in Kyoto. When you visit the temple, you may learn about a legend within the temple. Outside the temple, there are two rocks about twenty feet apart from each other. The legend says that if you are able to walk from one rock to the other with your eyes closed, you will find your true love. Kiyomizu is a great example of a more traditional area of Kyoto, one that shows the rich beauty of historic Japan.

Nagoya is Japan's third largest city. The people in Nagoya are quite friendly, especially to those from Los Angeles, their sister city. Like Tokyo, it is quite urban- but if you stay long enough, you can feel the comfort of a smaller town without having to leave the buzz of a big city. Nightlife in Nagoya is fantastic, with restaurants and karaoke bars on almost every corner. Nanzan University is one of Japan's only Christian universities and boasts one of the best international student programs in Japan. Nanzan houses a beautiful campus, very close to a large monastery in a more suburban area. Nagoya is a great place to visit after you have seen Tokyo and Kyoto to get a more in-between flavor of contemporary and traditional Japanese culture.

3.3 Mechanics 組立て
Sentence Construction
簡単な存在の文

Objectives

Make sentences that indicate the existence of something or someone.
Make sentences that indicate the location or the relative position of something or someone.
Make sentences with the topic of a potential paragraph in mind.

Overview

First, you will learn to make simple sentences that indicate the existence of something or someone. Next, you will practice indicating the location or the relative position of something or someone. You will also practice making sentences on the topic of your potential paragraph in mind and enhance your understanding of the particle は which plays a crucial role at this stage.

| 2 | Sentence construction: Part 1 | 文を作る その1 |

1	Indicate the existence of something	存在を表わす短い文
2	Add locational information	場所の情報を加える
3	Add positional information	位置の情報を加える
4	Set topic appropriately	テーマを考えて文を作る

町の北東には遊園地があります。
町の南東にはスポーツセンターがあります。

町の北西にはきれいな湖がある。
町の南西には大きい商店街がある。

2 Sentence construction: Part 1 　文を作る その1

1 Indicate the existence of something 　存在を表す短い文

ノート: Expressing the existence of something or someone

X1がある/あります

X2がいる/います

X1がある/あります and X2がいる/います are used to express the existence of an inanimate object X1 and that of an animate object X2 respectively. Animate objects include humans and animals.

山がある/あります。　　There is a mountain.

コーチがいる/います。　There is a coach.

A. Circle the one that you think is correct. 　正しいものをまるで囲みましょう。

1. 病院が (いる、ある)。
2. 先生が (いる、ある)。
3. 池が (いる、ある)。
4. 犬が (いる、ある)。

B. Make short sentences X1がある **and** X2がいる **based on the map below.**

地図を見てください。そして、町の短い文を作ってください。

例 (Examples)

図書館がある。

ねずみがいる。

2 Add locational information

ばしょ じょうほう くわ
場所の情報を加える

ノート: Expressing location of something or someone

YにX1がある/あります

YにX2がいる/います

These are patterns used to express the object X's existence in the place Y. It corresponds to "There is X at/in Y" in English. The one on the top is for inanimate objects while the one on the bottom is for animate objects. The particle に is used here to indicate the location of something or someone's existence.

まち どうぶつえん
トムさんの町に動物園がありますか。 Is there a zoo in your town, Tom?

動物園にどんな動物がいますか。 What sort of animals are there in the zoo?

A. Pair Work: *One student will use Map A below and the other will use Map B on next page.*

ひとり ちず
一人は地図Aを使ってください。もう一人は地図Bを使いましょう。

Your map shows the same part of a town as your partner's map. It is missing different buildings and facilities however, and they are listed beside the map. Find out their locations from your partner and indicate them on your map.

会話の例 (Sample Dialogue)

えいがかん
A: どこに映画館がありますか。

B: 映画館ですか。ええと、クイーンズストリートにあります。

Map A

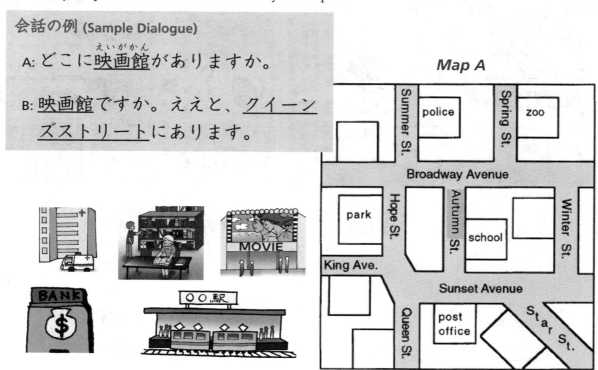

285

Map B

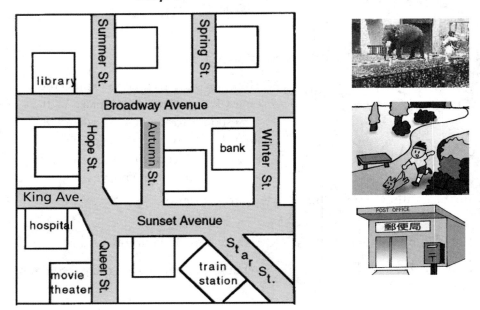

B. **Read the descriptions about** しろやままち **and** しずかむら **practice making similar descriptions by substituting the underlined part.**

例を見て入れ替えてください。

しろやままち
城山町

しず　むら
静か村

例 (Examples)

しろやままち　もり
城山町に森があります。

しず　むら　うみ
静か村に海があります。

城山町の森にへびがいます。

しず　むら　くうこう
静か村に空港がありません。

C. Find "short sentences" (*X1 が / は / も あります and X2 が / は / も います*) in the following paragraph and underline them. *Underline in yellow for X* が / は / も *and underline in black for* あります / います.

次のように短い文をさがして、下線を引いてください。黄色は
Xが / は / も、黒はあります / います。

EX.

私の町の公共施設は最高です。大きい図書館に好きな本がたくさんあります。面白い本もたくさんあります。それから、広い公園に木がたくさんあります。ジョギングコースもあります。

1.

私の町は静かです。森がたくさんあります。大きい山がたくさんあります。それから、天気もいいです。公共施設がたくさんあります。図書館もいろいろな所にあります。だから、私の町が好きです。

いろいろ(な) various

2.

私の町の商店街は最高です。新しい八百屋があります。おいしいパン屋もあります。それから、安い肉屋もあります。本屋に面白い本もたくさんあります。だから、私はよく商店街に行きます。

3.

私の学校はすばらしいです。新しい施設がたくさんあります。おもしろい科目もたくさんあります。いい先生もたくさんいます。いろいろなクラブもあります。それから、カフェテリアの食べ物もおいしいです。

4.

私の町の交通は便利だ。広い空港がある。新しい高速道路もある。それから、電車の駅もたくさんある。駅はきれいだ。地下鉄はない。でも、バスは多い。私は毎日電車とバスで学校へ行く。

高速道路 expressway

287

ノート：Expressing the position of something or someone

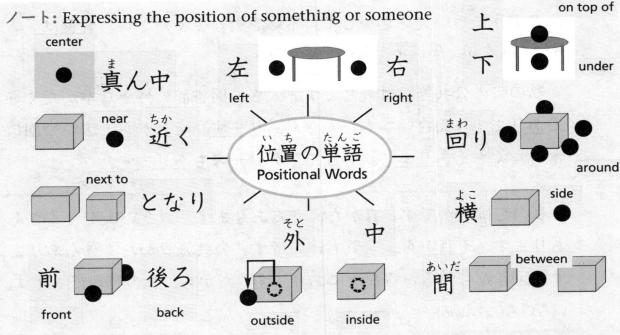

YのPにX1がある/あります

YのPにX2がいる/います

These are patterns used to express the object X's relative position in reference to Y. P indicates a positional word. The one on the left is for inanimate objects while the one on the right is for animate objects

<ruby>図書館<rt>としょかん</rt></ruby>の<ruby>前<rt>まえ</rt></ruby>に<ruby>花屋<rt>はなや</rt></ruby>があります。　There is a flower shop in front of the library.

テーブルの<ruby>上<rt>うえ</rt></ruby>に<ruby>犬<rt>いぬ</rt></ruby>がいます。　There is a dog on the table.

A. Circle the appropriate positional word.
<ruby>適切<rt>てきせつ</rt></ruby>な<ruby>位置<rt>いち</rt></ruby>の<ruby>単語<rt>たんご</rt></ruby>をまるで<ruby>囲<rt>かこ</rt></ruby>んでください。

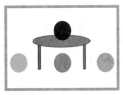

1. テーブルの (上、下、右、左) にピンクのボールがあります。

2. テーブルの (上、下、右、左) にみどりのボールがあります。

3. テーブルの (上、下、右、左) にオレンジのボールがあります

4. テーブルの (上、下、右、左) に<ruby>黒<rt>くろ</rt></ruby>いボールがあります。

5. 箱の (中、下、外、間) にねこがいます。

6. 箱の (中、下、外、前) にねずみがいます。

7. 車の(回り、前、となり、後ろ) に女の子がいます。

8. 車の(回り、前、となり、後ろ) に男の子がいます。

9. 部屋の(回り、真ん中、近く、間)にランプがあります。

10. 噴水の(回り、真ん中、間) に木とベンチがあります。

11. ベンチとベンチの(回り、横、間)に噴水があります。

B. Look at the map and indicate the existence and relative position of something or someone.

地図を見て、あるものとその位置を表す文を作りましょう。

例 (Examples)

病院のとなりに公園がある。

公園の前に肉屋がある。

C. Complete the following list.

リストを完成させてください。

1. ☐ east
　西(にし) west
2. ☐ south
3. ☐ north

北東(ほくとう) northeast
4. ☐ northwest
5. ☐ southeast
　南西(なんせい) southwest

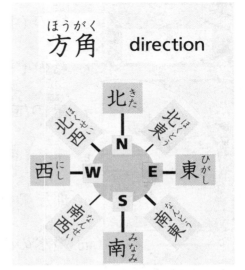

方角(ほうがく) direction

D. Create sentences that indicate the existence and direction of something or someone.

絵を見て、存在(そんざい)と方角(ほうがく)を表(あらわ)す文(ぶん)を作ってください。

例 **(Example)**

学校(がっこう)の北(きた)に山(やま)があります。町(まち)の東(ひがし)に畑(はたけ)があります。

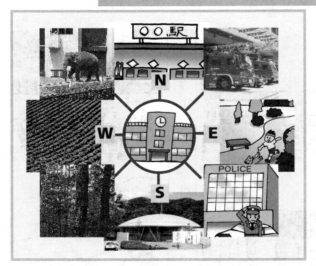

E. Create sentences that indicate the existence and direction of something or someone based on the collected data about your town or school. Use YのDにX1があります and YのDにX2がいます. "D" represents a directional word such as "north" and "southwest."

あなたの町(まち)か学校(がっこう)のデータを使って、そこにあるものとその方角(ほうがく)を表(あらわ)す文(ぶん)を作ってください。「YのDにX1があります」と「YのDにX2がいます」を使ってください。Dは方角(ほうがく)の単語(たんご)です。

4 Set topic appropriately

テーマを考えて文を作る

So far you have created sentences that indicate the existence and location, position or direction, of something or someone by using -に-が あります/います. These sentences convey the message objectively but in a rather isolated fashion. When you start thinking of creating a paragraph based on these sentences, you will need to make some modifications so that they sound connected and coherent. Use of the topic particle は becomes important at this stage.

ノート: Particle は (wa) (助詞の 「は」)

は

は as a topic marker

You already learned that the particle は is used to mark the topic of a sentence. For example, in わたしのがっこうはあたらしいです (My school is new.), わたしのがっこう (my school) is considered the topic since it is what this sentence is all about, and therefore it is marked by は.

は as a contrastive element marker

The particle は is also known as a contrastive element marker and it marks an item which the speaker is contrasting or comparing with something else. Such contrast and comparison is done rather implicitly in many occasions. When someone says コーヒーはのみません (I don't drink coffee), for example, she is implying, knowingly or unknowingly, that she may drink many beverages other than coffee. Implicit contrast or comparison such as this occurs often, especially in negative sentences. For example, トニーのうちのちかくにやまがあります。でも さばくはありません (There are mountains in Tony's neighborhood. However, there aren't any deserts), implies that Tony's neighborhood is blessed with many natural and other fine features, even though it does not have any deserts.

Compare the following.

YにXがあります	This is a pattern used to express the object X's existence in the place Y. It corresponds to "There is X at/in Y" in English.
TXはYにあります	In this pattern, the object X is identified as a topic and its locational information is given subsequently. (TX = Topic X)

メーン州に私達の町があります。

私達の町はメーン州にあります。

Both of these sentences indicate that the writer's town is located in the state of Maine. However, the first sentence does not have a topic and simply expresses a fact. The second sentence, on the other hand, has a topic which is わたしたちのまち ("our town") and sounds like more information about this topic will follow. In ピラミッドはエジプトにあります, ピラミッド (the pyramids) is the topic and the sentence means "As for the pyramids, they are in Egypt." Suppose you want to talk about "what sites are in Egypt" rather than "the pyramids." In that case, you need to make "what sites are in Egypt" the topic of your sentence. エジプトにはピラミッドがあります literally means "As for what are in Egypt, there are pyramids." Note that the location particle に remains and is immediately followed by the topic particle は, resulting in a "double particle" situation.

Compare the following.

TYにはXがありますハいます

私達の町に有名な遊園地があります。　　　有名な　famous

私達の町には有名な遊園地があります。　　遊園地　amusement park

Let's review the three patterns for expressing existence.

1. YにXがあります／います。　　Expressing X's existence in Place Y.

2. TXはYにあります／います。　　Expressing Topic X's existence in Place Y.

3. TYにはXがあります／います。　　Expressing X's existence in Topic/Place Y.

A. Check a box next to the most appropriate sentence in each of the following situations.

どれが正しいですか。チェックしてください。

1. You are telling your host parents about your hometown and want to point out that it has beautiful lakes.

　☐ a. 私達の町にきれいな湖があります。

　☐ b. きれいな湖は私達の町にあります。

　☐ c. 私達の町にはきれいな湖があります。

2. Your host parents are asking you about Yellowstone National Park. You want to say that Yellowstone National Park is in Wyoming.

　☐ a. ワイオミングにイエローストーン国立公園があります。

　☐ b. イエローストーン国立公園はワイオミングにあります。

　☐ c. ワイオミングにはイエローストーン国立公園があります。

3. You are telling a Japanese exchange student about things she may find useful in your school. You just want to point out that there are computers in the library.

☐ a. 図書館にコンピューターがあります。

☐ b. コンピューターは図書館にあります。

☐ c. 図書館にはコンピューターがあります。

B. Let's describe Tony's, Sally's, and your neighborhood by using -には-が あります.

トニーさんとサリーさんのうちの近くには何がありますか。何が
ありませんか。あなたのうちの近くはどうですか。

例 (Example)

トニーさんのうちの近くには八百屋が
あります。でも、果物屋はありません。

トニー	○	×	×	○	×	○	×	×
サリー	×	○	○	×	○	×	×	○
あなた								

C. Let's role play using this example.

例を見ながらロールプレイをしましょう。

会話の例 (Sample Dialogue)

A: ソーホーにはどんな学校がありますか。

B: 古い学校があります。

Role A : Information seeker

You are thinking of relocating yourself and are looking for a good town to live in. You are talking on the phone to an employee of a town called SOHO. Ask him what kind of school, hospital, park, restaurants, and natural features the town of SOHO has.

Role B : SOHO town official

You are an employee of a town called SOHO. You are talking on the phone to someone who is thinking of moving to SOHO in the near future. Answer her questions.

293

D. Look at the sentences and find the topic (TYには) and "short sentences" (X1が / も ある and X2が / も いる). Then circle the former with red and underline the latter.

下の文を見て、トピックと存在の文を探して、例のように赤マルと下線をつけてください。

1. （私の学校の回りには）公共施設がたくさん<u>あります</u>。大きい図書館があります。その図書館には好きな本がたくさんあります。動物園もあります。そこにはライオンがいます。さるもいます。動物園は楽しいです。それから、大きい公園もあります。公園には池があります。川もあります。ほかに、公民館もあります。公民館には小さいコンサートホールがあります。デイケアセンターや動物の病院もあります。

デイケアセンター　day care center

2. （私の町には）娯楽施設がたくさん<u>ある</u>。町の北東には遊園地がある。遊園地にはいろいろな乗り物がある。子供がよく遊ぶ。北西には大きいショッピングモールがある。便利だ。この施設には映画館が五つある。多くの人が映画を見に行く。南東にはスポーツセンターがある。スポーツセンターにはテニスコートがたくさんある。このセンターはきれいだ。それから、南西には大きい商店街がある。この商店街にはゲームセンターがたくさんある。だから、楽しい。

のりもの　ride

E. Create sentences that indicate the existence and direction of something or someone based on the collected data about your surroundings (school or town). Use Y の D には X1 があります and Y の D には X2 がいます. "D" represents a directional word.

あなたの学校か町のデータを使って、そこにあるものとその方角を表す文を作ってください。「YのDにはX1があります」と「YのDにはX2がいます」を使ってください。Dは方角の単語です。

Recognition Kanji 2: 認識漢字 2

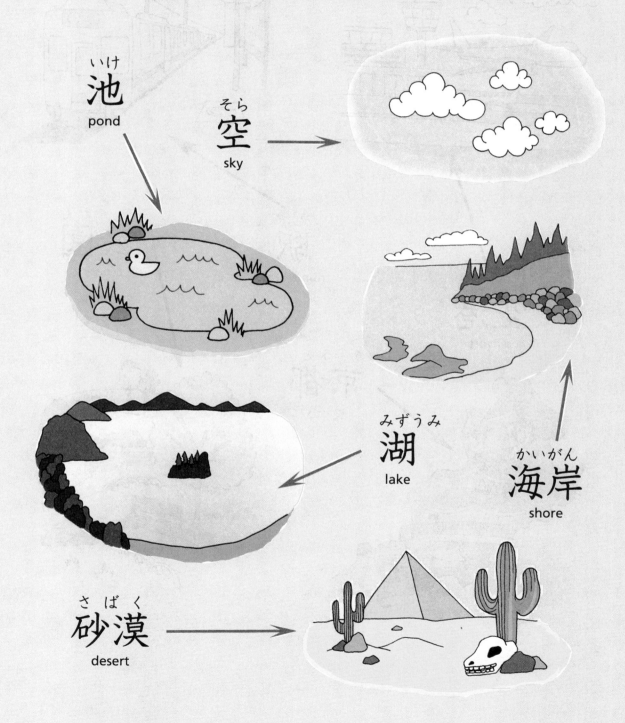

いけ
池
pond

そら
空
sky

みずうみ
湖
lake

かいがん
海岸
shore

さばく
砂漠
desert

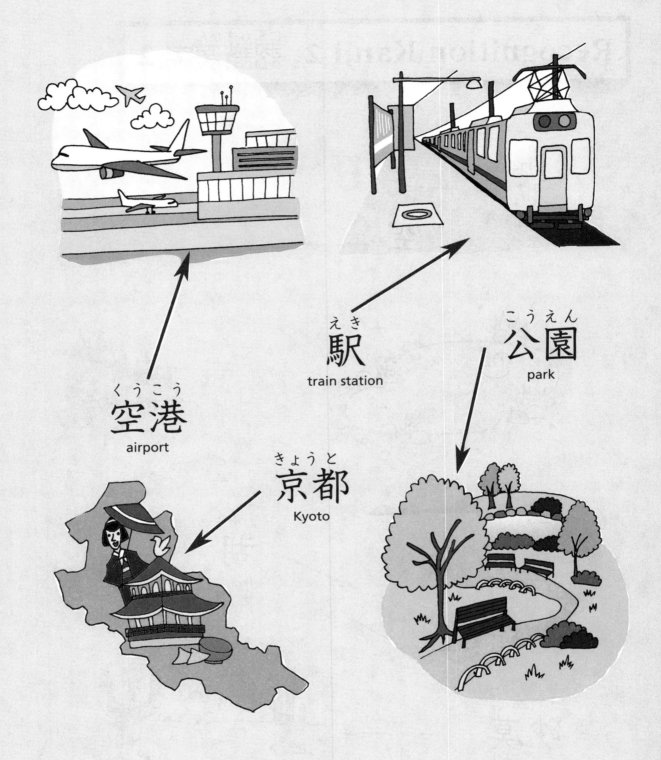

くうこう
空港
airport

えき
駅
train station

こうえん
公園
park

きょうと
京都
Kyoto

New Kanji 1: 新出漢字 1
しんしゅつかんじ

田

ON: デン　　　　　**KUN**: た

田: た rice field　　水田: すいでん rice paddy, rice field

一 冂 冊 用 田

林

ON: リン　　　　　**KUN**: はやし

林: はやし woods

一 十 オ オ 木 村 材 林

森

ON: シン　　　　　**KUN**: もり

森: もり woods, forest (thicker and larger than はやし)　森林: しんりん woodland, forest

一 十 オ 未 未 杢 柔 森 森 森 森

山

ON: サン　　　　　**KUN**: やま

山: やま mountain　　富士山: ふじさん Mt. Fuji (the highest mountain in Japan)

丨 山 山

川

ON: セン　　　　　**KUN**: かわ

川: かわ river　　信濃川: しなのがわ Shinano River (the longest river in Japan)

丿 川 川

海

ON: カイ　　　　　**KUN**: うみ

海: うみ ocean, sea　海岸: かいがん seashore　カリブ海: かりぶかい Caribbean Sea

丶 氵 氵 氿 汽 汢 海 海 海

町

ON: チョウ　　　　**KUN**: まち

町: まち town

一 冂 冊 用 田 町 町

店

ON: テン　　　　　**KUN**: みせ

店: みせ shop, store　　　　本店: ほんてん main store, headquarters

丶 广 广 广 庁 店 店

297

Language Note 3

Vowel Reduction vs Devoiced Vowels

Vowel reduction

You may remember learning about the fact that Japanese has pitch accent and English has stress accent. In languages with stress accent, vowels in unstressed syllables are often pronounced with an indistinct quality known as schwa. For example, except in unnaturally careful pronunciation, the first and last vowels in the English word *convicted* are pronounced with this schwa quality. Notice that the stress in *convicted* is on the middle syllable: *conVICTed*. A technical term for this tendency to have schwa in unstressed syllables is vowel reduction, and many native speakers of English carry it over into their Japanese pronunciation. The problem is that vowel reduction is completely alien to Japanese. There's no tendency for the five Japanese vowel qualities to become less distinct from each other in certain syllables, and a person who substitutes schwa for the correct Japanese vowels can be very hard to understand.

Devoiced vowels

Although Japanese doesn't have vowel reduction, the short vowels *i* and *u* are often devoiced, which sometimes makes them sound to an English speaker as if they've completely disappeared. Ask your teacher or another speaker of Japanese to pronounce the following words for you, and pay careful attention to the vowels. The devoiced vowels are indicated by outline letters in the romanization.

ashita	tomorrow	*shukudai*	homework
kitanai	dirty	*tesuto*	test
chikai	near	*tsukue*	desk
hitori	one person	*futari*	two people

A devoiced vowel is just a vowel pronounced without voicing, and as you already know, voicing is the buzz caused by rapid vibration of your vocal cords. If you place the fingers of one hand on the side of your neck while you pronounce a long Japanese aaaaa sound, you'll feel the vibration of your vocal cords through your skin.

If you whisper the vowel, though, you won't feel or hear any vibration, because you suppress voicing when you whisper. A devoiced vowel sounds very much like a whispered vowel.

So when exactly can you expect i or u to be devoiced? It's most likely to happen when the vowel is surrounded by consonants that are pronounced without voicing. Using *ashita* ("tomorrow") to illustrate, you'll notice that both the consonant before the devoiced vowel (*sh*) and the consonant after it (*t*) are pronounced without voicing, and the same is true in all the other examples listed above. In fact, these words sound unnaturally precise if all their vowels are voiced.

It's also typical for an i or u to be devoiced between a consonant without voicing and a pause. For example, since a verb form like *tabemasu* is often the last word in a sentence, it often comes right before a pause. The consonant before u is *s*, which is pronounced without voicing, and as you've probably noticed, the pronunciation *tabemasu* is very common.

When an *i* or *u* appears in the circumstances described above, devoicing is a strong tendency, but it isn't a hard and fast rule. We won't go into all the complications here. The point is just to draw your attention to devoiced vowels. As always, the best strategy is to pay careful attention to native speakers of Japanese and imitate their pronunciation as closely as you can.

3.4 Mechanics 組立て
Basic Paragraph Construction
パラグラフ作りの基礎を学ぶ

Objectives

Indicate the number or relative quantity of things that exist.

Understand the basic structure of a paragraph.

Make simple paragraphs consisting of a topic sentence and several supporting sentences.

Overview

Continuing with the sentence construction you started in the previous section, you will first learn how to indicate the number or quantity of things that exist. Next you will check the basic structure of a paragraph and practice identifying both the topic and the supporting sentences. Finally you will be creating a simple paragraph about your town or school consisting of a topic sentence and two supporting sentences.

3 Sentence construction: Part 2 文を作る その2

1 Indicate quantity by numbers ものの量を数で表す

2 Indicate quantity by adverbs ものの量を副詞で表す

4 Paragraph construction Part 1 パラグラフを作る その1

1 Understand the basic structure 基本構造を理解する

2 Make simple paragraphs 簡単なパラグラフを作る

3 Sentence construction: Part 2　　文を作る その2

1 Indicate quantity by numbers　　数に関する情報を加える

ノート: Counting in Japanese (数の表現)

Unlike English, in which numeral progression takes place every third digit, the numbers in Japanese have numeral progression after the fourth digit. In English, you read numbers of four, five, and six figures using thousand: 1000 is one thousand, 10000 is ten thousand and 100000 is one hundred thousand, etc. After that, the number reaches the million range and stays in that range for three more digits before it moves up to billions. In Japanese, on the other hand, 10000 is いちまん and this まん unit covers the next three figures: 100000 is じゅうまん, 1000000 (one million) is ひゃくまん and 10000000 (ten million) is いっせんまん. After that a new unit called おく comes in. 100000000 (one hundred million) is いちおく in Japanese.

にほんご	1000 100 10 1 おく UNIT	1000 100 10 1 まん UNIT	1000 100 10 1
	5 5 7 6 5 8 2 4 3 2 1 9		
えいご	**5 5 7 6 5 8 2 4 3 2 1 9**		
	BILLION 100 10 1	MILLION 100 10 1	THOUSAND 100 10 1　　100 10 1

A. Read the explanation above and practice reading the following numbers.

ノートの説明を読んで、数の練習をしてください。

EX1. **6912**　　ろくせんきゅうひゃくじゅうに

EX2. **348005**　　さんじゅうよんまんはっせんご

1. **283**　2. **967**　3. **7460**　4. **1318**　5. **4894**　6. **6050**

7. **3507**　8. **2850**　9. **91620**　10. **10329**　11. **78006**　12. **40222**

13. **30178**　14. **195622**　15. **120020**　16. **354885**

17. **781069**　18. **410771**　19. **1500000**　20. **26280000**

B. In Japanese different "counters" are used to count different things. Study eight such counters and complete the list below.

助数詞を勉強して表を完成させてください。

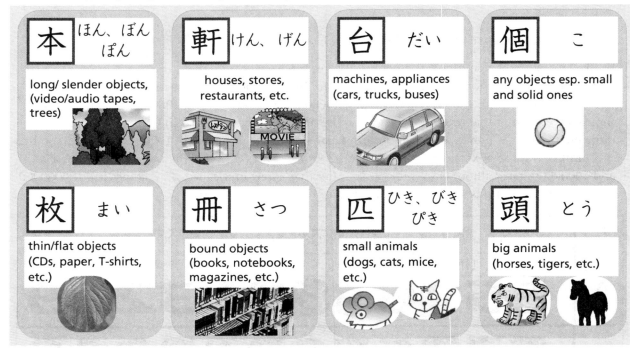

	本 (ほん, ぼん, ぽん)	軒 (けん, げん)	台 (だい)	枚 (まい)	匹 (ひき, びき, ぴき)	頭 (とう)	個 (こ)	冊 (さつ)
1	いっぽん	いっけん	いちだい	いちまい	いっぴき	＿＿＿	いっこ	いっさつ
2	にほん	にけん	にだい	にまい	＿＿＿	＿＿＿	にこ	にさつ
3	さんぼん	さんげん	＿＿＿	＿＿＿	さんびき	さんとう	さんこ	さんさつ
4	よんほん	＿＿＿	＿＿＿	よんまい	＿＿＿	＿＿＿	よんこ	よんさつ
5	＿＿＿	ごけん	＿＿＿	＿＿＿	ごひき	＿＿＿	＿＿＿	＿＿＿
6	ろっぽん	＿＿＿	ろくだい	＿＿＿	ろっぴき	ろくとう	ろっこ	ろくさつ
7	＿＿＿	ななけん	ななだい	＿＿＿	＿＿＿	＿＿＿	＿＿＿	＿＿＿
8	＿＿＿	＿＿＿	はちだい	はちまい	＿＿＿	＿＿＿	＿＿＿	＿＿＿
9	きゅうほん	きゅうけん	＿＿＿	＿＿＿	きゅうひき	きゅうとう	きゅうこ	きゅうさつ
10	じゅっぽん	＿＿＿	じゅうだい	＿＿＿	＿＿＿	＿＿＿	じゅっこ	じゅっさつ
?	なんぼん	なんげん	なんだい	なんまい	なんびき	なんとう	なんこ	なんさつ

C. Match the counters on the left with the corresponding item on the right.

助数詞の復習です。左と右をマッチさせてください。

1. いっとう、にとう、さんとう　（　　）　　　　a. Counting sheets of paper

2. いっぽん、にほん、さんぼん　（　　）　　　　b. Counting people

3. いっさつ、にさつ、さんさつ　（　　）　　　　c. Counting eggs

4. いちにち、ふつか、みっか　　（　　）　　　　d. Counting days

5. いちまい、にまい、さんまい　（　　）　　　　e. Counting trees

6. いっけん、にけん、さんげん　（　　）　　　　f. Counting large animals

7. いっこ、にこ、さんこ　　　　（　　）　　　　g. Counting houses

8. ひとり、ふたり、さんにん　　（　　）　　　　h. Counting books

D. Circle the one you think is correct. 正しいものをまる(○)で囲みましょう

1. 男の人が (さんにん、さんだい、さんまい、さんさつ) います。

2. バスが (さんにん、さんだい、さんまい、さんげん) あります。

3. レストランが (ごさつ、ごだい、ごけん、ごまい、ごほん) あります。

4. 動物園にさるが (ごとう、ごだい、ごひき、ごまい、ごこ) います。

5. 日本語の本が (ごさつ、ごだい、ごひき、ごまい、ごほん) ある。

6. 公園に木が (ごとう、ごだい、ごけん、ごまい、ごほん) ある。

7. 青いボールが (にまい、にさつ、にこ、にとう、にけん) ある。

8. テーブルの上に写真が (にさつ、にだい、にまい、にほん) ある。

9. 町のバスは一時間に (にさつ、にだい、にけん、にほん) ある。

10. 動物園にうまが (ごとう、ごだい、ごひき、ごまい、ごこ) いる。

E. Pair Work.　ペアワークをしましょう。

Procedure:
1. One of the pairs says the name of an object followed by the particle が. Information regarding its location may be added.
2. His or her partner quickly finishes the sentence by indicating the quantity of the object using the appropriate counter.
3. Switch roles and continue.
4. You may make this a game and have a class tournament in which a person who makes a mistake or cannot create the predicate within 3 seconds first will be eliminated and one winner will be declared at the end.

ノート：Indicating what and how many something or someone exists

X1がQある/あります　　X2がQいる/います

X1がQある and X2がQいる are used to indicate how many X1 (inanimate object) and X2 (animate object) exist. "Q" (quantity) consists of a number and an appropriate counter. For example, if X1 is a car and X2 is a cow, the counter wil be だい and とう respectively.

動物園にライオンが4頭います。　　There are five lions in the zoo.

教室にコンピューターが5台あります。　　There are five computers in the classroom.

F. Practice the following conversation by substituting the underlined parts according to the information on the chart. Use the appropriate counters.

表を見て、会話を練習しましょう。

会話の例 (Sample Dialogue)

A: 図書館にDVDが何枚ありますか。

B: 2500枚あります。

OBJECT	LOCATION	QUANTITY
DVD	LIBRARY	2500
Tiger	ZOO	6
Book	CLASSROOM	140
Computer	SCHOOL	70
Salmon	FISH MARKET	3
Pen	ON THE TABLE	8
Egg	ON THE TABLE	4
CD	ON THE TABLE	15
Restaurant	SHOPPING	9

G. Tell how many men (おとこのひと) and/or women (おんなのひと) there are in the location indicated in each picture.

次の場所に男の人は何人いますか。女の人は何人いますか。

EX1.
ほんや

EX2.
きょうしつ

例 (Examples)

1. 本屋には男の人が二人います。
2. 教室には男の人が三人と女の人が二人います。

1.
ジム

2.
ゆうびんきょく

3.
カフェテリア

4.
グラウンド

H How many were there?

何人(何台, 何匹 etc.)いましたか／ありましたか。

Procedure:

1. Bring a picture that contains a certain number of several different objects.
2. Go around the class and show your picture to someone for a few seconds.
3. Ask him or her the number of a certain kind of object in the picture.

2 Indicate quantity by adverbs — もの の<ruby>量<rt>りょう</rt></ruby>を<ruby>副詞<rt>ふくし</rt></ruby>で<ruby>表<rt>あらわ</rt></ruby>す

This time you will comment about the quantity of something by using adverbs. Unlike nouns, adverbs tend to be relative and subjective in their implication. For example, 15 students in a class may be described as "many" when the average size of a class in that school is under 10. Because of this you must do some careful examination before you choose an adverb to use in your description. Let's begin with the study of some useful adverbs to indicate a relative quantity.

ノート: Useful adverbs for indicating relative quantity (<ruby>量<rt>りょう</rt></ruby>を<ruby>表<rt>あらわ</rt></ruby>す<ruby>副詞<rt>ふくし</rt></ruby>)

A list of useful quantifiers is given on the right. The numbers represent a rating for each word with 6 being "many" and 0 being "not at all." Both あまり and、ぜんぜん are followed by the negative predicate. The following examples show how these words can be used in some of the sentence patterns introduced so far. Note the location of the quantifiers as you go through the examples. Note that many of these adverbs can also indicate frequency of an activity or degree of a condition such as あまりいかない (doesn't go often) or かなりあつい (considerably hot).

6	たくさん (a lot)
5	かなり (considerably)
4	けっこう (fairly)
3	まあまあ (so-so)
2	すこし (a little)
1	あまり (not so much)
0	ぜんぜん (not at all)

<ruby>私<rt>わたし</rt></ruby>の<ruby>町<rt>まち</rt></ruby>にはコーヒーショップがたくさんあります。
My town has a lot of coffee shops.

ジョンさんはコーヒーをかなり<ruby>飲<rt>の</rt></ruby>みました。
John drank a considerable amount of coffee.

その<ruby>商店街<rt>しょうてんがい</rt></ruby>には<ruby>花屋<rt>はなや</rt></ruby>がけっこうあります。
There are a fair amount of flower shops in that shopping district.

<ruby>私<rt>わたし</rt></ruby>の<ruby>町<rt>まち</rt></ruby>にはパン<ruby>屋<rt>や</rt></ruby>がまあまああります。
There are a so-so number of bakeries in my town.

<ruby>西山<rt>にしやま</rt></ruby>町にはデパートが<ruby>少<rt>すこ</rt></ruby>しあります。
Nishiyama-machi (town of Nishiyama) has a few department stores.

マイクさんはコーヒーをあまり<ruby>飲<rt>の</rt></ruby>みません。
Mike does not drink much coffee.

その<ruby>動物園<rt>どうぶつえん</rt></ruby>にはパンダがぜんぜんいません。
There are no panda bears at all in that zoo.

As you can see, quantifiers are usually placed after the noun whose quantity is mentioned and before the predicate verb.

A. How many or how few of the following stores does the town of Tajima have? Circle the correct rating for each store by using the five point scale (5 = many, 0 = not at all) according to the given descriptions.

田島_{たじま}には次_{つぎ}の店_{みせ}がどのぐらいありますか。

EX. 田島_{たじま}には魚屋_{さかなや}が
たくさんあります。

1. 田島には本屋_{ほんや}が
あまりありません。

2. 田島には八百屋_{やおや}が
けっこうあります。

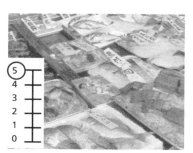

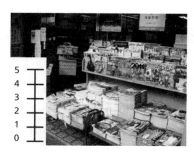

3. 田島には肉屋_{にく}がぜん
ぜんありません。

4. 田島にはすし屋が
少_{すこ}しあります。

5. 田島には果物屋_{くだもの}が
かなりあります。

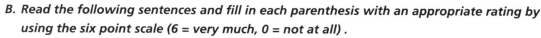

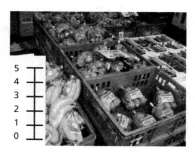

B. Read the following sentences and fill in each parenthesis with an appropriate rating by using the six point scale (6 = very much, 0 = not at all).

次の文_{ぶん}を読んで程度_{ていど}の数字_{すうじ}を書いてください。

EX. （ ６ ）月曜日_{よう}はたくさん仕事_{しごと}があります。　　　仕事 work

1. （　　）七月と八月はけっこう暑_{あつ}いです。

2. （　　）バスはあまり便利_{べんり}じゃありません。

3. （　　）川の水は少_{すこ}し汚_{きたな}いです。

4. （　　）その山はかなり高_{たか}いです。

5. （　　）このピザはぜんぜんおいしくありません。

6. （　　）その映画_{えいが}はまあまあ面白_{おもしろ}いです。

307

4 Basic paragraph construction　パラグラフ作りの基礎を学ぶ

1 Understand the basic structure　基本構造を理解する

A. Group Work - Break up into groups of three.

グループワークです。三人のグループになってください。

Objective:
Make a short paragraph based on a few keywords and confirm your knowledge about basic paragraph writing.

Procedure:
1. Examine the mindmaps below and make a few similar ones.
2. Share your knowledge of the basic structure of a paragraph with your group and make sure to have a general consensus about it.
3. Make a paragraph consisting of three to six sentences based on one of your mindmaps. Prepare up to three paragraphs.
4. Write two of your paragraphs on the board.
5. Read other groups' paragraphs and compare them with yours.
6. Exchange comments and opinions about each other's work.
7. Meet with your group and make adjustments to your work if needed.
8. Go over "Paragraph 101" on the following page and another note on paragraph development that follows in the Make Simple Paragraphs section.

マインドマップの例 (Sample Mindmaps)

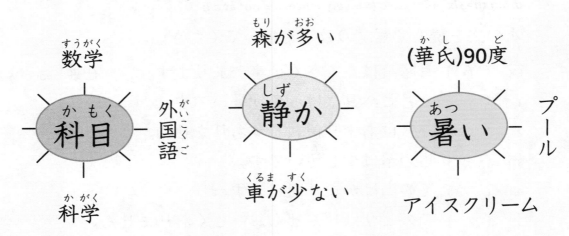

ノート: Paragraph 101 (パラグラフ入門)

1. Introduction

A paragraph represents a constellation of thought or ideas using a group of sentences. Each culture or language has its own logical pattern by which thoughts and ideas are organized and expressed. For example, Japanese poetic tradition has different systematic patterns from English expository writing and we hope you will have an opportunity to learn about this in the later volumes of *Kisetsu*. For now, you will practice writing a paragraph in Japanese by following the same format as you would follow in expository writing in English. In Japan many scholastic, business, and scientific writings are done according to this format.

2. Topic sentences and supporting sentences

A typical paragraph consists of a topic sentence and several supporting sentences. The topic sentence clearly states the main idea of the paragraph, and the supporting sentences effectively uphold and reinforce the main idea. Look at the following examples. Although they are very simple paragraphs, they clearly illustrate the close relationship between the topic sentence and the supporting sentences.

TOPIC SENTENCE → 谷川市には公共施設がたくさんあります。

There are many public facilities in Tanigawa City.

SUPPORTING SENTENCE 1 → 図書館は 12 あります。

There are 12 libraries.

SUPPORTING SENTENCE 2 → 病院も 20 あります。

There are 20 hospitals.

SUPPORTING SENTENCE 3 → それから、公園も 25 あります。

In addition, there are 25 public parks.

These three supporting sentences add details about the main idea expressed in the topic sentence.

309

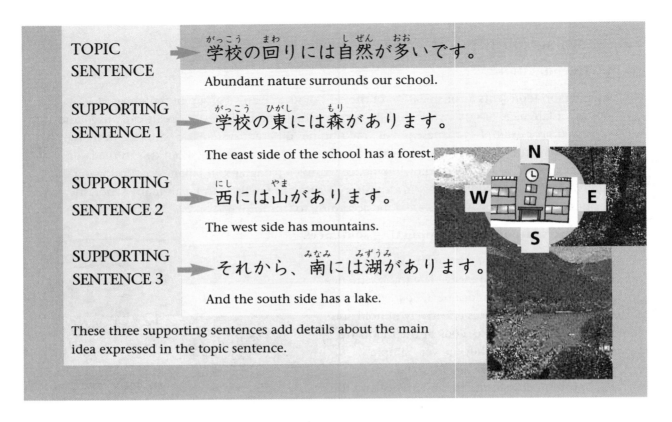

TOPIC SENTENCE	学校の回りには自然が多いです。
	Abundant nature surrounds our school.
SUPPORTING SENTENCE 1	学校の東には森があります。
	The east side of the school has a forest.
SUPPORTING SENTENCE 2	西には山があります。
	The west side has mountains.
SUPPORTING SENTENCE 3	それから、南には湖があります。
	And the south side has a lake.

These three supporting sentences add details about the main idea expressed in the topic sentence.

B. Choose the most appropriate topic sentence for each paragraph below and fill in each brackets with the letter of your choice.

トピックセンテンスはどれですか。下から選んでください。

EX.
supporting sentences

TOPIC SENTENCE　[**f**]

小学校は15校あります。中学は10校あります。それから、高校も8校あります。

1.

TOPIC SENTENCE　[　]

スーパーは5軒 あります。薬屋も6軒 あります。コンビニも7軒あります。

2.

TOPIC SENTENCE　[　]

教室には絵が2枚 あります。表も3枚 あります。それから、地図も1枚 あります。

3.

TOPIC SENTENCE　[　]

学校の西には病院があります。南には図書館があります。それから、北には美術館があります。

4. TOPIC SENTENCE [　]

フランス語の先生は7人いる。ドイツ語の先生は5人いる。それから、中国語の先生も4人いる。

5. TOPIC SENTENCE [　]

月曜日に数学のテストがある。水曜日に歴史と科学のテストがある。そして、金曜日に日本語のテストがある。

a. 日本語の教室にはいろいろな教材がたくさんあります。
b. トムさんの学校には外国語の先生がたくさんいる。
c. 商店街には日本食のレストランがたくさんあります。
d. 学校の回りには公共施設がたくさんあります。
e. 私の家の回りには便利な店がたくさんあります。
f. 私の町には学校がたくさんあります。
g. 来週はテストが多い。

C. *Create two sentences to support each topic sentence below.*

サポートセンテンスを二つ作ってください。

EX. 谷川市には学校がたくさんあります。　　TOPIC SENTENCE

(1) 中学は20校あります。 (2) 高校も15校あります。

1. 私の町には公共施設がたくさんあります。

(1)_____ (2)_____

2. 私の学校には外国語の先生がたくさんいます。

(1)_____ (2)_____

3. 私の町の回りは自然が多いです。

(1)_____ (2)_____

4. 私の家の回りは交通が便利だ。

(1)_____ (2)_____

311

2 Make simple paragraphs

簡単^{かんたん}なパラグラフを作^{つく}る

ノート: Paragraph Development Tactics

Tactic A (Attribution) "Bits and pieces" approach

There are two useful paragraph development tactics you will be learning in this chapter and the first one is called the attribution tactic or the "bits and pieces" approach. In fact, all the sample paragraphs in this section have been developed by this tactic. In the example on the right, としょかん, びょういん and こうえん are "bits and pieces" of こうきょうしせつ.

谷川市^{たにがわし}には公共施設^{こうきょうしせつ}がたくさんあります。図書館^{としょかん}は12あります。病院^{びょういん}も20あります。それから、公園^{こうえん}も25あります。

TOPIC SENTENCE

SUPPORTING SENTENCES

A. Read the note above and make several paragraphs using the attribution tactic. You may write about your town or school, and your topic sentence may end with ～がたくさんあります／います *or* ～がおおいです.

上のノートを読んでから、幾^{いく}つかパラグラフを作ってください。トピックセンテンスは「～がたくさんあります／います」か「～がおおいです」にしてください。

Recognition Kanji 3: 認識漢字 3

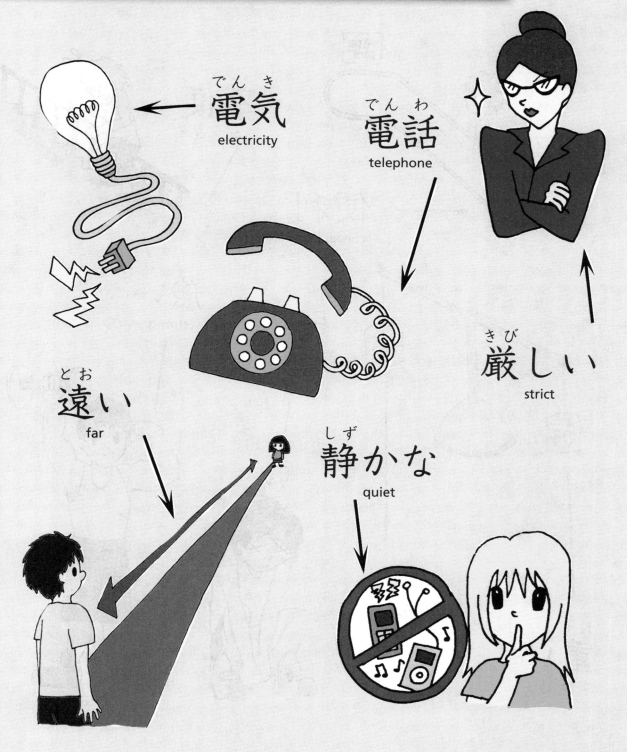

でんき
電気
electricity

でんわ
電話
telephone

きび
厳しい
strict

とお
遠い
far

しず
静かな
quiet

New Kanji 2: 新出漢字 2
しんしゅつかんじ

天
ON: テン　　　　　　**KUN**: あま
天: てん heaven　　天の川: あまのがわ the Galaxy, the Milky Way　　天文学: てんもんがく astronomy
一　二　チ　天

度
ON: ド　　　　　　**KUN**: 一
３０度: ３０ど 30 degree　　温度: おんど temperature
、　亠　广　户　产　产　产　庐　度

晴
ON: セイ　　　　　　**KUN**: は(れ)、は(れる)
晴れ: はれ sunny　　晴れる: はれる become clear　　晴天: せいてん clear weather
｜　冂　月　日　日一　日十　日キ　晴　晴　晴　晴　晴

雨
ON: ウ　　　　　　**KUN**: あめ
雨: あめ rain　　雨がふる: あめがふる to rain　　雨天: うてん rainy weather
一　厂　冂　币　雨　雨　雨　雨

雪
ON: セツ　　　　　　**KUN**: ゆき
雪: ゆき snow　　大雪: おおゆき heavy snow
一　广　户　币　而　雨　雨　雪　雪　雪

暑
ON: ショ　　　　　　**KUN**: あつ(い)
暑い: あつい hot (weather)
一　冂　日　日　旦　早　显　昇　昇　暑　暑　暑

寒
ON: カン　　　　　　**KUN**: さむ(い)
寒い: さむい cold (weather)
、　宀　宀　宀　中　审　审　軍　寒　寒　寒

化
ON: カ　　　　　　**KUN**: ば(ける)
文化: ぶんか culture　　化ける: ばける change, disguise　　化学: かがく chemistry
変化: へんか change
ノ　イ　仁　化

315

Reading 5:
読み物 5

Reading Dojo 3: Schema Strategy
読解道場 3: 話題ストラテジー

Reading Signal Strategy Part I: Using Formal Order Language Schema

A schema is a mental structure that we use to organize and simplify our knowledge of the world around us.

A. Formal schema: Check the language schema for order relation words such as "at first/beginning," precedes "next/and then."

来週の月曜日のスケジュールは、始めに、音楽のクラスにいきます。次に、数学のテストをします。それから、ミーティングをします。最後に日本語のクラスがあります。

来週の月曜日の日本語クラスの発表のスケジュールは、始めに、ワークシート／デジタル型のクラスの発表をします。次に、スキット型のクラスの発表をします。それから、ロールプレー型のクラスの発表をします。最後に音読型のクラスの発表をします。

型: form

来週の水曜日の復習セッションのスケジュールは、始めに、ウォームアップをする。次に、単語と表現と漢字を紹介する。次に練習問題をする。それから、パワーポイントで発表をする。最後に質問に答える。

復習: reviewing　　紹介: introduce

Signal schema: Check the signal word and choose the appropriate word from the parenthesis in the sum up sentence.

シグナルワード(signal word)：

　　まず、一日中、始め、こんにちは、色々な、次に、それから、最後に

1. 来週の月曜日のスケジュールに（音楽、数学、英語、日本語）があります。
2. 来週の（日本語、英語）の月曜日のスケジュールにはスキットがあります。
3. 来週の水曜日の復習セッションは（最後に、最初に、次ぎに）質問があります。

Reading Signal Strategy Part II: Using Formal Demonstrative Word Schema

D. Formal schema: Check the language schema for demonstrative words such as "this around," "this town," and "this country," and find these images.

この辺はこの町の中でも特ににぎやかな所だ。道路が左と右に分かれ、真ん中のビルには巨大なスクリーンがあり、コマーシャルやニュースが流れている。この国の他の町に比べてタクシーがずっと多いし、歩いている人もたくさんいる。左の道にも右の道にも大きなホテルやレストラン、店、劇場などが立ち並んでいる。そして、世界中から観光客が来ていて、いろいろな外国語を聞くこともできる。

道路：road　劇場：theater　観光客：tourist

The above story is a description of a place somewhere in the United States. Read it until you understand what このへん (this area) and このまち (this town) refer to and fill in the blanks below.

このへん＝＿＿＿＿＿＿　　このまち＝＿＿＿＿＿＿

Were you able to figure out the place in question before reaching the end of the story? If so, how did you do that? Did you have any previous knowledge about the place? Share your experience with your classmates and think about what else might have enhanced your comprehension.

Choose the word: この町は（小さい、いなか、大都市、小都市）です。

Writer's opinion: この人は（おしゃべり、宿題して、ねて、あるいて）います。

Reading Signal Strategy Part III: Using Prior Knowledge Content Schema

E. Examine the following sentences and choose the appropriate words in the parenthesis by using your prior knowledge and experience.

1. 私たちの頭の中は小さな図書館です。図書館には（子供、本、先生）がたくさん（います、あります、かります。）

2. わたしの学校はかえるの学校です。かえるの学校は（しずかな、うるさい、あたまがいい）子供が　たくさん（います、あります、かえります。）

3. アニカさんの足はカンガルーのようです。カンガルーは（足、頭、手）がとても（おそい、はやい、おおきい）。　　　　　　　ようです：seem

4. 私たちの頭の中は小さな町ににています。町には（動物、子供、道）がたくさん　（います、あります、かります。）　　　にています：look like

F. When you start to read the sentences, you should imagine what kind of topic by checking its title and the first sentence using the schema. Provide a framework for future understanding and choose the appropriate word to complete the sum up sentence below.

夏休みの日記

マイク君は東京で日本的な所へ行きたいと言っていました。そこで、7月23日に浅草に行きました。そこには、いろいろな日本的な物が売っています。だから、マイク君は日本の刀や千代紙を買って、とても喜んでいました。

Title: _____

The first sentence: _____

マイク君は（東京、横浜、京都）へ行って、（買物、スポーツ、コンサート）をしている。

写真部

この写真は4月に撮った物です。日本の学校の始まりは4月です。その頃は、日本では、桜が咲きます。色々な学校で桜が咲きます。たくさんの桜が咲いて、学校はとてもきれいです。クラブ活動も4月から始まります。だから、写真部に入りました。写真部では毎日写真を撮ります。写真部にはとても面白い人が多いです。

Title: _____

The first sentence: _____

恵さんは（映画部、写真部）へ入って、桜を（かいて、とって、よんで、はじまって）いる。

3.5 Mechanics 組立て
くみ た

Paragraph Development
パラグラフをより詳しく書く
くわ

Objectives

Develop a paragraph by adding a few examples to each supporting sentence.

Be able to link two sentences with the て form.

Be able to express what one can do or cannot do.

Overview

This section begins with the study of a new sentence construction by which you can indicate what one can do or cannot do. Then you will learn more about paragraph development and will be introduced to the second paragraph development tactic called the analogy tactic or the layer approach. The construction you learned in the beginning will be useful at this stage.

| 5 Paragraph construction: Part 2 | パラグラフを作る その2 |

| 1 Indicate what one can do | 可能なことを表す文を作る |
か のう あらわ ぶん

| 2 Make simple paragraphs | 簡単なパラグラフを作る |
かんたん

| 6 Paragraph development | パラグラフをより詳しく書く |
くわ

| 1 Expand the basic structure | 基本構造を拡大する |
き ほんこうぞう かくだい

| 2 Make detailed paragraphs | 詳しいパラグラフを作る |
くわ

1 | Indicate what one can do | 可能なことを表す文を作る

So far most of the sample paragraphs you have read are about towns and schools. You have also made a simple paragraph about your own town or school. When you write about places and facilities like these, your readers may find it helpful to know what they can or cannot do there. With this in mind let's learn the constructions below.

ノート: Potential statements in Japanese

Dictionary Form of V + ことができます

The construction above makes an English equivalent of "one can do such and such" or "it is possible to do such and such." It expresses potentiality or ability though we will use it mainly to indicate the former. You can make this negative by simply replacing できます with できません.

その川の水はきれいです。だから、泳ぐことができます。
Water in that river is clean. So you can swim.

その川の水は汚いです。だから、泳ぐことができません。
Water in that river is dirty. So you cannot swim.

Xをすることができます vs Xができます

Some actions in Japanese are expressed by placing (を)します right after a noun. テニスをします (to play tennis) べんきょうをします (to study) and スピーチをします (to make a speech) are among them. If you follow the formula introduced above, "can play tennis" will be テニスをすることができます. However, you may drop をすること and just say テニスができます which basically means the same thing.

土曜日にはダンスやパーティーができます。
We can have dances or parties on Saturdays.

雨の日はテニスができません。
We cannot play tennis on rainy days.

A. Match the following -masu form with its dictionary form.

動詞のます形と辞書形をマッチさせてください。

1. いきます （　） 2. たべます （　） 3. みます （　）
4. します （　） 5. えらびます（　） 6. ききます （　）
7. のみます （　） 8. はなします（　） 9. つくります（　）
10. かいます （　） 11. つかいます（　） 12. およぎます（　）

a. はなす	b. みる	c. きく	d. つかう
e. えらぶ	f. かう	g. する	h. つくる
i. たべる	j. およぐ	k. いく	l. のむ

B. Change the underlined part as shown in the example.

例のように下線の部分を置き換えてください。

EX1. 学校へバスで行きます。→ バスで行くことができます。
EX2. 公園でキャンプをします。→ キャンプができます。

1. 学校ですしを食べます。→
2. 図書館で日本の雑誌を読みます。→　　雑誌 magazine
3. 学校で科目を選びます。→
4. ホテルでパーティーをします。→
5. 質問に英語で答えます。→
6. 教室で日本語のパソコンを使います。→
7. 先生の名前を漢字で書きます。→
8. その店で電話を買います。→
9. 好きな科目を選びます。→
10. その工場でカメラを作ります。→

C. Change the sentences that appeared in the previous section into questions and then practice asking and answering the questions.

前のセクションの文を質問文にして、会話の練習をしましょう。

会話の例 (Sample Dialogue)

A: 学校にバスで行くことができますか。

B: はい、できます。 or いいえ、できません。

D. Practice the following conversation according to the information given below about what B could or could not do at her junior high school.

会話の練習をしましょう。

会話の例 (Sample Dialogue)

A: 中学でコーヒーを飲むことができましたか。

B: はい、できました。

A: じゃ、すしを買うことができましたか。

B: いいえ、できませんでした。

EX1

EX2

1.

2.

3.

4.

5.

6.

ノート: Indicating benefit

Xのための Y

X (Noun 1) のための **Y (Noun 2)**

The above formula corresponds to "Y which is designed/meant for X."

「春一番<ruby>春一番<rt>はるいちばん</rt></ruby>」は中学生と高校生のための教科書<ruby>教科書<rt>きょうかしょ</rt></ruby>です。

Haruichiban is a textbook intended for junior high and high school students.

たとえば

ノート: Indicating examples

「春一番<ruby>春一番<rt>はるいちばん</rt></ruby>」は日本語を習<ruby>習<rt>なら</rt></ruby>うための教科書<ruby>教科書<rt>きょうかしょ</rt></ruby>です。たとえば、よく中学生と高校生が使います。

Haruichiban is a textbook intended for leaning Japanese. For example, junior high and high school students use it a lot.

E. Practice the following development according to the information about what B could or could not do at school given below.

練習<ruby>練習<rt>れんしゅう</rt></ruby>をしましょう。

会話の例 (Sample Dialogue)

A: この学校<ruby>学校<rt>がっこう</rt></ruby>は<u>音楽<ruby>音楽<rt>おんがく</rt></ruby>のための</u>学校ですね。たとえば、どんなことができますか。

B: そうですね。 たとえば、<u>オーケストラをすること</u>や<u>コーラスをすること</u>ができます。

A: ああ、そうですか。ありがとうございます。

Ex. 音楽<ruby>音楽<rt>おんがく</rt></ruby>　　1. 芸術<ruby>芸術<rt>げいじゅつ</rt></ruby>　　2. 体育<ruby>体育<rt>たいいく</rt></ruby>　　3. 科学<ruby>科学<rt>かがく</rt></ruby>

4. 福祉<ruby>福祉<rt>ふくし</rt></ruby> social welfare　　　　5. 国際教育<ruby>国際教育<rt>こくさいきょういく</rt></ruby> International education

---

F. Ask your classmates some questions about what they could or could not do either at their elementary or junior high school.

クラスメートに聞きましょう。

2 Make simple paragraphs

<ruby>簡単<rt>かんたん</rt></ruby>なパラグラフを作る

ノート: Paragraph Development Tactics

Tactic B (Analogy) "Layer" approach

The analogy tactic or the "layer" approach is the second paragraph development tactic. In this tactic, you will create supporting sentences that not only add details but also connote the same or similar message expressed in the topic sentence. Let's go over some sample paragraphs developed by this tactic.

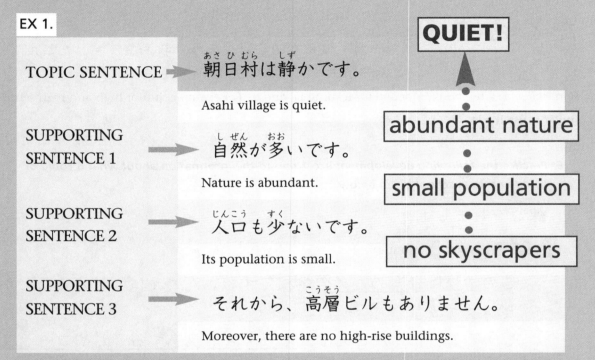

EX 1.

TOPIC SENTENCE → 朝日村は静かです。

Asahi village is quiet.

SUPPORTING SENTENCE 1 → 自然が多いです。

Nature is abundant.

SUPPORTING SENTENCE 2 → 人口も少ないです。

Its population is small.

SUPPORTING SENTENCE 3 → それから、高層ビルもありません。

Moreover, there are no high-rise buildings.

QUIET!

abundant nature

small population

no skyscrapers

All the supporting sentences above not only provide some details about Asahi village but also imply how quiet the village is. Abundant nature, small population, and the absence of skyscrapers are easily considered characteristics of a quiet place, and reference to such features effectively reinforce the claim made in the topic sentence. Look at two more sample paragraphs on the following page. You will notice that they too have been developed by the analogy tactic.

continued to the next page

EX 2.

CONVENIENT!

TOPIC SENTENCE → 私の町の図書館は便利です。

good location

The library in my town is convenient.

can borrow DVDs

SUPPORTING
SENTENCE 1 → 駅の前にあります。

can read Japanese newspapers

It is located in front of the train station.

SUPPORTING
SENTENCE 2 → いろいろな映画のDVDを借りることができます。

We can borrow various movies on DVD.　　かりる/かります borrow

SUPPORTING
SENTENCE 3 → それから、日本語の新聞を読むこともできます。

Moreover, we can read Japanese language newspapers.

INCONVENIENT!

EX 3.

TOPIC SENTENCE → 私の家の近くは不便です。

no supermarkets

My neighborhood is inconvenient.

no train stations

SUPPORTING
SENTENCE 1 → スーパーやコンビニが
ありません。

no post office

There are neither supermarkets nor convenience stores.

SUPPORTING
SENTENCE 2 → 電車や地下鉄の駅もありません。

There are no train or subway stations.

SUPPORTING
SENTENCE 3 → それから、郵便局もありません。

Moreover, there is no post office.

continued to the next page

It should be noted that both attributive and analogical supporting sentences can follow the same topic sentence. See the following example.

EX.

TOPIC
SENTENCE → 私の町の冬は寒いです。

Winters in my town are cold.

SUPPORTING
SENTENCE 1 → 1月の気温は華氏35度です。

The temperature in January is 35 degrees (Fahr).

TACTIC A
(Attribution)

SUPPORTING
SENTENCE 2 → 2月の気温は華氏30度です。

The temperature in February is 30 degrees (Fahr).

SUPPORTING
SENTENCE 3 → それから、雪もたくさん降ります。

Moreover, it snows a lot.

TACTIC B
(Analogy)

A. Classify the following paragraphs into three groups based on how they have been developed. Insert the appropriate paragraph-representing number in the brackets.

パラグラフを次の三つのタイプに分類してください。

1. Made by Tactic A (Attribution): [   ]
2. Made by Tactic B (Analogy): [   ]
3. Made by Tactic A and B (Hybrid): [   ]

1.
日本語の勉強は面白いです。
会話の練習は楽しいです。漢字
の勉強も大好きです。そして、
単語のゲームも楽しいです。

2.
トムさんの寮は静かです。テレ
ビやステレオがありません。う
るさい生徒もいません。好きな
時間に勉強することができます。

3.

スミスさんは忙しいです。朝と昼は会社にいます。夜は学校に行きます。あまり寝ません。

4.

学校の回りは不便です。公共施設がありません。商店街もありません。駅も遠いです。

5.

私の家の回りはうるさいです。家の前にはディスコがあります。後ろには工場があります。それから、横には駅があります。

6.

学校は楽しいです。毎日友達と会うことができます。日本語を勉強することもできます。クラブもたくさんあります。

7.

去年の夏休みは最高でした。6月はサッカーのキャンプに行きました。7月は日本に行きました。そして、8月は好きなアニメをたくさん見ました。

8.

去年の夏休みは最高だった。毎日、海やプールで泳いだ。おいしい食べ物もたくさん食べた。好きな時間に寝ることもできた。

9.

私の町の夏は暑い。7月の気温は華氏85度だ。8月の気温は華氏90度だ。毎日プールで泳ぐ人がたくさんいる。

10.

コンビニは便利だ。食べ物を買うことができる。雑誌を読むこともできる。それから、ATMもある。

B. Create the third supporting sentence by using the paragraph development tactic indicated in the parenthesis.

三つ目のサポートセンテンスを作ってください。

EX1. 私の家の回りには自然が多いです。　(Tactic A: Attribution)

(1) 家の前には山があります。

(2) 後ろには森があります。

(3) それから、横には川があります。

EX2. 私の町の図書館は便利です。　　　(Tactic B: Analogy)

(1) 外国の新聞や雑誌がたくさんあります。

(2) 日本語の本を読むこともできます。

(3) それから、地下鉄で行くこともできます。

EX3. 私の家の回りは静かです。　　　　(Hybrid)

(1) 家の前には山があります。

(2) 後ろには森があります。

(3) それから、高層ビルもありません。

1.　去年の夏休みは最高でした。　　　(Tactic A: Attribution)

(1) 6月はパーティーがたくさんありました。

(2) 7月は楽しいキャンプに行きました。

(3) それから、＿＿＿＿＿＿＿＿＿＿＿＿＿＿＿。

2.　去年の夏休みは最低でした。　　　(Tactic B: Analogy)

(1) 毎日つまらないアルバイトをしました。

(2) ハワイに行くこともできませんでした。

(3) それから、＿＿＿＿＿＿＿＿＿＿＿＿＿＿＿。

3.　私の家の近くは便利です。　　　　　　(Tactic B: Analogy)

　(1) コンビニがたくさんあります。

　(2) 電車や地下鉄の駅も近いです。

　(3) それから、＿＿＿＿＿＿＿＿＿＿＿＿＿。

4.　私の町の夏はとても暑いです。　　　　　(Hybrid)

　(1) 7月の気温は華氏90度です。

　(2) 8月の気温は華氏95度です。

　(3) それから、＿＿＿＿＿＿＿＿＿＿＿＿＿。

5.　夏休みにアルバイトをする友達がたくさんいます。　(Tactic A: Attribution)

　(1) 花屋でアルバイトをする人は5人います。

　(2) 本屋でアルバイトをする人は6人います。

　(3) それから、＿＿＿＿＿＿＿＿＿＿＿＿＿。

C. *Create one paragraph using Tactic A (attribution or the "bits and pieces" approach), two paragraphs using Tactic B (analogy or the "layer" approach), and one paragraph using both tactics (hybrid). Write about your town or school and your topic sentence may end with ～ がたくさんあります／います, ～がおおいです, ～はべんり／ふべんです, ～はさいこう／さいていです, ～はしずか／うるさいです, etc.*

タクティックAを使ったパラグラフを一つ、タクティックBを使ったパラグラフを二つ、AとBを両方 使ったパラグラフを一つ作ってください。町か学校についてで、トピックセンテンスは「～がたくさんあります／います」「～が多いです」「～は便利／不便です」「～は最高／最低です」「～は静か／うるさいです」等を使ってください。

1 **Expand the basic structure**　基本構造を拡大する

ノート：Topic, support, example: A three-tier structure

As you know, a basic paragraph consists of a topic sentence and several supporting sentences. The information provided by this simple structure tends to be rather limited and you can provide more details by elaborating upon each supporting sentence. This means that you will be making additional sentences that "support the supporting sentences." Let's call these sentences "examples." See the following:

TOPIC SENTENCE ► 私の町の公民館は楽しいです。

The community center in my town is a fun place.

SUPPORTING
SENTENCE 1 ► 若者のための催しがたくさんあります。young people

There are many events for young people.　もよおし event

EXAMPLE 1
EXAMPLE 2 ► たとえば、先月、ファッションショーがありました。今月はロックコンサートがあります。

For example, we had a fashion show last month.
We will have a rock concert this month.　たとえば for example

SUPPORTING
SENTENCE 2 ► それに、毎週、映画を見ることができます。それに furthermore

Furthermore, we can watch a movie every week.

EXAMPLE 1
EXAMPLE 2 ► 今週の映画は「カサブランカ」です。
来週の映画は「ゴジラ」です。

This week's movie is "Casablanca."
Next week's movie is "Godzilla."

SUPPORTING
SENTENCE 3 ► 面白いクラスもたくさんあります。

There are many interesting classes as well.

EXAMPLE 1
EXAMPLE 2 ► たとえば、木曜日にヨガのクラスがあります。
金曜日に折り紙のクラスがあります。

For example, there are Yoga classes on Thursdays.
There are *origami* classes on Fridays.

TOPIC SENTENCE

私の家の回りはうるさいです。

My neighborhood is noisy.

SUPPORTING SENTENCE 1

家の前にはディスコがあります。

There is a disco in front of my house.

EXAMPLE 1
EXAMPLE 2

ディスコは午前2時までです。

よくハードロックのコンサートもあります。

The disco is open until 2:00 a.m.
They often have hard rock concerts there.

SUPPORTING SENTENCE 2

家の後ろには工場があります。

There is a factory behind our house.

EXAMPLE 1
EXAMPLE 2

工場は午後8時までです。

大きいトラックがたくさん来ます。

The factory is in operation until 8:00 p.m.
Many large trucks come to the factory.

SUPPORTING SENTENCE 3

それから、横には駅があります。

There is a train station on the side of our house.

EXAMPLE 1
EXAMPLE 2

電車は24時間あります。

毎日10万人がこの駅を使います。

Trains run 24 hours (a day).
One hundred thousand people use the station everyday.

Don't lose sight of the topic sentence

As you can see from these two paragraphs, examples tend to be specific and concrete. You can rely on the two paragraph development tactics you have learned to create these examples. You may notice that Tactic A (Attribution, the "bits and pieces" approach) was used in the first paragraph while Tactic B (Analogy, the "layer" approach) was used in the second. It is important to keep in mind that whatever examples you give must be in line with the main idea expressed in the topic sentence. Seemingly useful information may often be a mismatch because it does not relate well to the topic sentence.

A. *One of the three examples in each paragraph is inappropriate. Find it and circle the number representing the sentence.*

適切でない例を選んでください。

EX. TS 私の町の公民館は楽しいです。

SS1 若者のための催しがたくさんあります。

EX (1) たとえば、先月、ファッションショーがありました。

(2) 今月はロックコンサートがあります。

(3) 催しは午後7時からです。

#3 is inappropriate here because telling what time these events start has little to do with telling the "fun" nature of the community center.

1. TS 私の学校には外国語の先生がたくさんいます。

SS1 フランス語の先生は10人います。

EX (1) とてもやさしい先生です。

(2) 男の先生は4人います。

(3) 女の先生は6人います。

2. TS 私の家の回りはうるさいです。

SS1 家の前には工場があります。

EX (1) 夜のシフトもあります。　　　　　よるのシフト night shift

(2) アメリカの会社の工場です。

(3) 大きいトラックがたくさん来ます。

3. TS 私の町にはいい公共施設があります。

SS1 図書館は便利です。

EX (1) 外国映画のDVDを見ることができます。

(2) 日本語の本や新聞はありません。

(3) 駅の近くにあります。

2 Make detailed paragraphs　　詳しいパラグラフを作る

A. Complete the following paragraphs by creating a couple of examples for each supporting sentence. Make use of expressions such as たとえば *(for example).*

例を作ってパラグラフを完成させてください。

1.

TOPIC SENTENCE	スミスさんは忙しいです。
	Mr. Smith is busy.
SUPPORTING SENTENCE 1	朝と昼は会社にいます。
	He spends his morning and day at his company.
EXAMPLE 1 EXAMPLE 2	
SUPPORTING SENTENCE 2	そして、夜は学校に行きます。
	He goes to school at night.
EXAMPLE 1 EXAMPLE 2	

2.

TOPIC SENTENCE	去年の夏休みは最高でした。
	My last year's summer vacation was super.
SUPPORTING SENTENCE 1	家族といろいろな所へ行きました。
	I went to various places with my family.
EXAMPLE 1 EXAMPLE 2	
SUPPORTING SENTENCE 2	よくスポーツや買い物もしました。
	I often played sports or did shopping.
EXAMPLE 1 EXAMPLE 2	

B. Practice developing paragraphs by creating two supporting sentences and two examples for each supporting sentence.

パラグラフを完成させてください。

1.

TOPIC SENTENCE	私の家の回りは便利です。	
	My neighborhood is convenient.	
SUPPORTING SENTENCE 1		
EXAMPLE 1		
EXAMPLE 2		
SUPPORTING SENTENCE 2		
EXAMPLE 1		
EXAMPLE 2		

2.

TOPIC SENTENCE	去年の夏休みは最低でした。	
	My last year's summer vacation was the worst ever.	
SUPPORTING SENTENCE 1		
EXAMPLE 1		
EXAMPLE 2		
SUPPORTING SENTENCE 2		
EXAMPLE 1		
EXAMPLE 2		

C. Write some detailed paragraphs about your town. They should consist of a topic sentence, at least two supporting sentences, and at least two examples for each supporting sentence.

自分の町についての詳しいパラグラフを書いてください。トピックセンテンスは一つ、サポートセンテンスは二つ以上、そして例は一つのサポートセンテンスに対して二つ以上作ってください。

Recognition Kanji 4: 認識漢字 4

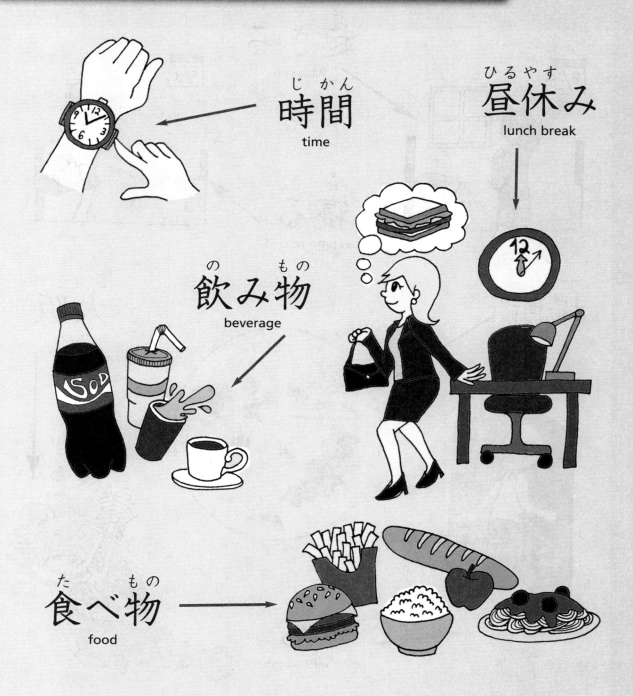

時間
time

昼休み
lunch break

飲み物
beverage

食べ物
food

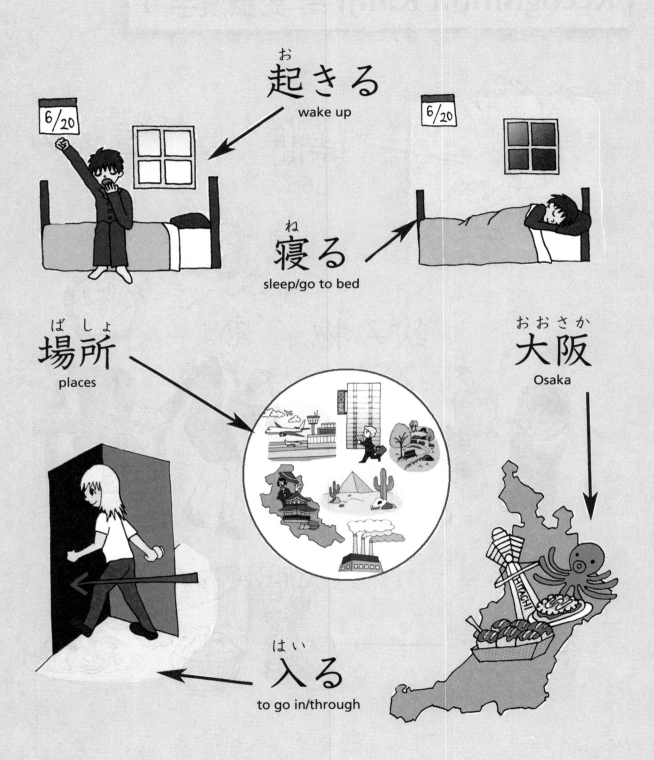

お
起きる
wake up

ね
寝る
sleep/go to bed

ば しょ
場所
places

おおさか
大阪
Osaka

はい
入る
to go in/through

New Kanji 3: 新出漢字 3
しんしゅつかんじ

校

ON: コウ　　　　　　　**KUN**: ―
学校: がっこう　school　　校門: こうもん　school gate

一 十 才 木 朴' 术' 栌 栌 栌 校

島

ON: トウ　　　　　　　**KUN**: しま
島: しま　island　　半島: はんとう　peninsula　　小島: こじま　small island

' イ 宀 戸 自 皀 鳥 鳥 島 島

石

ON: セキ　　　　　　　**KUN**: いし
石: いし　stone　　石油: せきゆ　oil, petroleum

一 ア イ 石 石

平

ON: ヘイ、ビョウ　　　　**KUN**: ひら、たいら
平ら: たいら　flat　　平和: へいわ　peace　　平等: びようどう　equality

一 ア ア 平 平

野

ON: ヤ　　　　　　　　**KUN**: の
野: の　field　　平野: へいや　plain

一 冂 日 日 甲 里 里 野' 野' 野 野

道

ON: ドウ　　　　　　　**KUN**: みち
道: みち　street　　北海道: ほっかいどう　Hokkaido

、 ソ ソ 并 产 首 首 首 首 道 道

市

ON: シ　　　　　　　　**KUN**: いち
市: し　city　　市長: しちょう　mayor of the city　市場: いちば　market

' 宀 广 方 市

村

ON: ソン　　　　　　　**KUN**: むら
村: むら　village　　村長: そんちょう　mayor of the village

一 十 才 木 村 村 村

Reading 6:

New York Tour Guide:
ニューヨーク観光案内

1. 今日は。これからニューヨークの観光案内をします。グリニッチ・ビレッジでは、いろいろなことができます。まず、始めに、朝はグリニッチ・ビレッジのコーヒーショップやカフェでコーヒーとベーグルを食べましょう。グリニッチ・ビレッジでは色々な小さい店があります。ウインドーショッピングも楽しいです。次に、ワシントン・スクエアー・パークに入って、音楽を聞きます。色々なグループの音楽を聞くことができます。お昼はピザ屋でピザを食べましょう。それから、イースト・ビレッジに行く前にニューヨーク大学を見学してみてください。最後に、夜はビレッジでジャズ等を聞きましょう。

A. First, scan the articles and see how the following words are spelled. Then circle the one with the correct spelling below.

1. New York: ニュヨク、ニュヨーク、ニュヨークー 、ニューヨーク

2. Greenwich Village:
グリニッチ・ビレッジ、
グリッチ・ビレジッ、
グッリニチ・ビッレジ、
グリニチ・ビレージ

3. Central Park: セントラル・パク、
セントラル・パーク、
セントラル・パーク、
セントラ・パーク、
セントラル・パーク

2. セントラル・パークは一日中遊べます。野外のコンサートもたくさんあります。ピクニックもできるし、ジョギングやサイクリングもできるし、動物園もあります。それから、色々なイベントがあります。たとえば、ジャパンデーでは、日本からの有名な音楽家のショーや盆踊りがあります。日本語を習っている高校生もイベントに参加しています。

B. Skim through the articles and choose the highest frequent word.

1. Greenwich Village:
今日は、最後、食べる、朝、店、
大学、音楽

2. Central Park:
学校、動物園、桜、日本語、
遊ぶ、ジョッキング

C. *Examine the following sentences and choose the appropriate words in the parenthesis by using your prior knowledge and experience.*

1. ニューヨークはアメリカの（西、東、南、北）にある（大きな、小さな、）町である。

2. セントラルパークは町の（右、左、真ん中、外、回り、向こう）にある。

D. *Check the language schema for order relation words such as "at first/beginning," "next/and then," and "at last/finally."*

シグナルワード(signal words)：
まず、一日中、始め、こんにちは、色々な、次に、それから、最後に

E. *When you start to read the articles, you should imagine what the topic is and how it is developed in the article by checking its title and the first sentences.*

Title: _____

1. First sentence: _____

2. First sentence: _____

After checking the title and the first the sentences, read the previous articles within 3 minutes and sum up what the author wants to say.

1. a. ニューヨークの交通についてです。

　 b. ニューヨーク大学は新しい学校です。

　 c. グリニッチ・ビレッジはいろいろな観光ができます。

　 d. グリニッチ・ビレッジは古い町です。

2. a. セントラルパークにはお金が必要です。

　 b. セントラルパークでは色々あそぶことができます。

　 c. セントラルパークは日本にあります。

　 d. セントラルパークの観光は朝早いです。

F. *Link three items in the vocabulary list below.*

単語	読み	意味
Ex. 同じ ⟷	おなじ ⟷	same
1. 楽しい	いちにちじゅう	zoo
2. 話	はなし	sight seeing
3. 音楽	おんがく	music
4. 店	どうぶつえん	noon
5. 昼	ばしょ	park
6. 観光	みせ	place
7. 案内	こうえん	shop
8. 場所	ひる	story

339

9.	公園	たのしい	fun
10.	動物園	かんこう	all day
11.	一日中	あんない	guide

G. Check whether the following information is true or false.

1. グリニッジ・ビレッジは小さい店がたくさんある。 (本当、嘘)

2. ワシントン・スクエアーは町の中にある。 (本当、嘘)

3. セントラル・パークには動物園がある。 (本当、嘘)

H. Form a group and answer these guided questions in Japanese.

1. グリニッジ・ビレッジの朝のカフェで何を食べるといいですか。

2. ワシントン・スクエアー・パークはどんな公園ですか。

3. セントラル・パークではどんなことができると思いますか。

---

1. 今日は。これからニューヨークの観光案内をします。グリニッチ・ビレッジでは、いろいろなことができます。まず、朝はグリニッチ・ビレッジのコーヒーショップやカフェでコーヒーとベーグルを食べましょう。コーヒーショップやカフェは楽しい所です。グリニッチ・ビレッジでは色々な小さい店があります。ウインドーショッピングも楽しいです。それから、ワシントン・スクエアー・パークに入って、音楽を聞きます。色々なグループの音楽を聞くことができます。お昼はピザ屋でピザを食べましょう。イースト・ビレッジに行く前にニューヨーク大学を見学してください。最後に、夜はビレッジでジャズ等を聞きましょう。

観光：sightseeing　　案内：guide　　グリニッチ・ビッレジ：Greenwich Village　　ワシントン・
スクエアー・パーク：Washington Square Park　　通る：pass by　　ベーグル：bagel　　店：shop
ウインドー・ショッピング：window shopping　　行く前：before going　　見学：visit　　等：etc.

2. セントラル・パークは一日中遊べます。野外のコンサートもたくさんあります。ピクニックもできるし、ジョギングやサイクリングもできるし、動物園もあります。それから、色々なイベントがあります。たとえば、ジャパンデイでは、日本からの有名な音楽家のショーや盆踊りがあります。日本語を習っている高校生もイベントに参加しています。

一日中：all day　　遊ぶ：play　　野外：outside　　動物園：zoo　　音楽家：musician
盆踊り：bon dance　　参加：join　　ジャパンデイ：Japan Day　　ショー：performance
イベント：event　　有名：famous　　習う：learn

3.6 Mechanics 組立て
Drawing comparison
比較をする

Objectives

Learn useful weather terms and describe various weather conditions.
Make both affirmative and negative comparative statements.
Make similarity statements.

Overview

It is important that the message in your writing will effectively be delivered to its readers. Use of comparative data or information is helpful in this regard. For example, your readers may relate to your writing better if you describe your town while occasionally comparing it with their own town or any other town they may be more familiar with. When you describe your school as "old," you may also want to point out that it is actually older than a famous school or building that your potential readers may know. In this section you will learn how to make comparative sentences and practice making paragraphs taking a comparative perspective into consideration. Since you will be writing about the weather in the next section, we will be using weather data and conditions among other things as objects of comparison. Thus we will begin the section by learning some useful weather terms.

7	Draw comparisons	比較をする
1	Describe weather conditions	天気の描写をする
2	Make comparative statements: Part 1	比較の文を作る 1
3	Make similarity statements	相似の文を作る
4	Make comparative statements: Part 2	比較の文を作る 2

7 Make comparisons 比較をする

1 Describe weather conditions 天気の描写をする

A. Fill in the blanks with an appropriate word from below.

正しいことばを下のリストから選んでください。

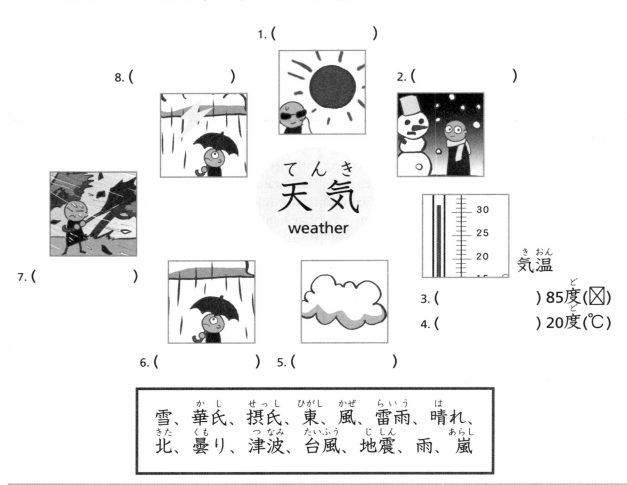

1. ( )

8. ( )

2. ( )

7. ( )

てんき
天気
weather

気温

3. ( ) 85度(☒)
4. ( ) 20度(℃)

6. ( ) 5. ( )

雪、華氏、摂氏、東、風、雷雨、晴れ、
北、曇り、津波、台風、地震、雨、嵐

ノート: How to read temperatures in Japanese (気温の読み方)

In Japan、きおん (atmospheric temperature) is measured by せっし (the Celsius or centigrade scale). According to this scale, the freezing point is 0 degree and the boiling point is 100 degrees. ど corresponds to "degrees" in English. If you just say, for example, 25ど (25 degrees), people assume that you mean "25 degrees centigrade." When indicating a temperature by the Fahrenheit scale, you need to place かし before the temperature (かし80ど). It should be noted, however, that most Japanese are not familiar with the Fahrenheit scale.

Continue on next page

How to convert 華氏(かし) to 摂氏(せっし) and vice versa

$$(かし - 32) \div 1.8 = せっし$$

For example, 95 degrees Fahrenheit is 35 degrees Celsius.

$$(95 ℉ - 32) \div 1.8 = 35 ℃$$

$$せっし \times 1.8 + 32 = かし$$

For example, 10 degrees Celsius is 50 degrees Fahrenheit.

$$10 ℃ \times 1.8 + 32 = 50 ℉$$

ノート: Additional useful words and expressions

雨(あめ)が降(ふ)る

Rain falls

ふる(ふります) means "fall" or "pour" and it is usually used with あめ, ゆき and other weather phenomena such as hail, and sleet. やむ(やみます) means "stop" or "cease" and あめがやむ means "it stops raining."

風(かぜ)が強(つよ)い

Windy

かぜ means "wind" and つよい means "strong."

地震(じしん)

Earthquake

じしん frequently occurs in Japan since the archipelago is situated in an area where several continental and oceanic plates meet. じしんがある means "have an earthquake" or "an earthquake occurs."

晴(は)れの日(ひ)

Sunny day

はれのひ means "sunny day." くもりのひ, あめのひ, and ゆきのひ mean "cloudy day," "rainy day," and "snowy day," respectively.

凍(こお)る

freeze

こおる(こおります) means "freeze." みずうみがこおる means "The lake freezes/is covered with ice." You may also say みずうみにこおりがはる. こおり means "ice." and はる(はります) means "stretch" or "tighten."

吹雪(ふぶき)

Snowstorm

気持(きも)ちがいい

feel good, pleasant

梅雨(つゆ)

Rainy season

In most areas in Japan, it begins in June and lasts until mid-July.

湿度(しつど)

humidity

しつどがたかい means "Humidity is high."

風(かぜ)が吹(ふ)く

Wind blows

ふく(ふきます) means "blow." This verb is also used to mean "play" when coupled with a wind or pipe instrument.

津波(つなみ)

Tsunami

A giant ocean wave caused primarily by undersea earthquakes and volcanic eruptions.

B. Can you quickly convert かし to せっし and vice versa?

気温の変換ができますか。

1. 89°Fは (42, 50, 32)°Cです。
2. 25°Cは (57, 77, 97)°Fです
3. –6°Fは (–21, –50, 11)°Cです
4. –5°Cは (23, –13, 33)°Fです。
5. 華氏100度は摂氏 (28, 38, 48) 度です。
6. 摂氏100度は華氏 (112, 212, 312) 度です。

C. Choose an appropriate English description to match each Japanese description.

日本語と英語をマッチさせてください。

1. ( ) 今、雪が降っています。 a. The humidity isn't high.
2. ( ) 地震がありました。 b. The south wind is blowing today.
3. ( ) 明日は風が強いです。 c. There was an earthquake.
4. ( ) 今日は暖かいです。 d. There are many sunny days.
5. ( ) 湿度は高くありません。 e. It's snowing now.
6. ( ) 晴れの日がたくさんあります。 f. The lake has frozen.
7. ( ) 雷雨がありました。 g. It will be windy tomorrow.
8. ( ) 日本は今、梅雨です。 h. It rained yesterday.
9. ( ) 昨日雨がふりました。 i. There are a few cloudy days.
10. ( ) 今日は南の風が吹いています。 j. It's warm today.
11. ( ) 湖が凍りました。 k. Japan is in a rainy season now.
12. ( ) 曇りの日は少ないです。 l. There was a thunderstorm.

D. Have a conversation based on the data given below about world weather.

世界の天気についてクラスメートと話しましょう。

<small>せ か い</small>

世界の天気

<small>せ か い</small>

トロント (Toronto)	CLOUDY	33℉ (1℃)	COLD	NO WIND
モスクワ (Moscow)	SNOW	22℉ (-5℃)	COLD	WINDY
ジャカルタ (Jakarta)	RAIN	84℉ (29℃)	MUGGY	NO WIND
ツーソン (Tuson)	SUNNY	82℉ (28℃)	HOT	NO WIND
東京 (とうきょう)	CLOUDY	41℉ (5℃)	COOL	WINDY
シドニー (Sydney)	SUNNY	72℉ (22℃)	WARM	WINDY

会話の例 (Sample Dialogue)

A: モスクワはどんな天気ですか。

B: 雪です。寒いです

A: 気温は何度ですか。
<small>き おん</small>

B: 華氏22度です。
<small>か し</small>

A: 華氏22度は摂氏何度ですか。
<small>か し</small> <small>せっ し</small>

B: ええと、摂氏マイナス5度です。
<small>せっ し</small>

A: じゃ、寒いですね。風は強いですか。
<small>かぜ</small> <small>つよ</small>

B: はい、強いです。

E. Check the current weather conditions of various places in the world and report them to class.

世界の天気について調べて報告しましょう。

<small>せ か い</small> <small>しら</small> <small>ほうこく</small>

345

2 Make comparative statements: Part 1　比較の文を作る その1

Since comparative statements often include adjectives, we will review some old and learn some new adjectives before we practice making comparisons. Go over the Basic Vocabulary again before you proceed.

A. Fill in each parenthesis with a letter representing an appropriate adjective.

(　) に記号を入れてください。

a. ながい	b. ひくい	c. おもい	d. みじかい	e. あたたかい
f. おおい	g. たかい	h. あかるい	i. しずか(な)	j. よわい
k. ふべん(な)	l. ひろい	m. すずしい	n. べんり(な)	o. つよい
p. くらい	q. きびしい	r. ふるい	s. せまい	t. すくない
u. おおきい	v. うるさい	w. ちいさい	x. かるい	y. やすい
z. あたらしい				

B. Fill in the parenthesis with the letter of the adjective in the box that means the opposite of the adjectives below.

はんたい　　い　み　けいようし　　えら
反対の意味の形容詞を選んでください。

1. いい　　　（　　）　2. うるさい　（　　）　3. つめたい　（　　）
4. ひろい　　（　　）　5. あたたかい（　　）　6. やすい　　（　　）
7. おおい　　（　　）　8. よわい　　（　　）　9. みじかい　（　　）
10. かるい　（　　）　11. きれい(な)（　　）　12. とおい　　（　　）
13. くらい　（　　）　14. べんり(な)（　　）　15. ひくい　　（　　）

a. すくない	b. ちいさい	c. ながい	d. ちかい	e. しずか(な)
f. いそがしい	g. あかるい	h. あつい	i. わるい	j. きたない
k. すずしい	l. ふべん(な)	m. ながい	n. たかい	o. せまい
p. おいしい	q. やさしい	r. おもい	s. つよい	t. すてき(な)

C. Practice the following conversation by substituting the underlined parts according to the pictures.

かい わ　　れんしゅう
会話の練習をしましょう。

EX.1　　　　　EX.2　　　　　1.　　　　　　2.

　　　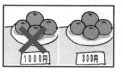

3.　　　　　　4.　　　　　　5.　　　　　　6.

会話の例 (Sample Dialogue): い adjective and な adjective

せま
A: 狭いですか。　B: いいえ、狭くありません。広いです。
　　　　　　　　　　　　せま　　　　　　　　ひろ

しず
A: 静かですか。　B: いいえ、静かじゃありません。うるさいです。
　　　　　　　　　　　　しず

ノート: Comparative Statement (X is - than Y) (比較する)

XはYより_

The above is a simple construction for making a comparative statement. It corresponds to "X is more(less) ～ than Y" in English. See the examples below.

テキサスはフロリダより大きいです。　　Texas is larger than Florida.
X [Texas]　　Y [Florida]　- [large]

東京(とうきょう)はボストンより人口(じんこう)が多(おお)いですか。Is Tokyo more populated than Boston?
X [Tokyo]　　Y [Boston]　- [more populated]

D. Circle an appropriate adjective based on the information given below.

情報(じょうほう)に基(もと)づいて適切(てきせつ)な形容詞(けいようし)を○(まる)で囲(かこ)んでください。

1. バスは電車(でんしゃ)より (高(たか)い、安(やす)い) です。

2. オレゴンはアイオワより (大きい、小さい) です。

3. 郵便局(ゆうびんきょく)は病院(びょういん)より (遠(とお)い、近(ちか)い) です。

4. ナイロビはベルリンより人口(じんこう)が (多(おお)い、少(すく)ない) です。

5. リバー高校(こうこう)はレイク高校より (新(あたら)しい、古(ふる)い) です。

6. イースト川はウエスト川より (長(なが)い、短(みじか)い) です。

7. ノース公園(こうえん)はサウス公園より (広(ひろ)い、狭(せま)い) です。

1. 250円(えん)
 200円

2. オレゴン 251400 sq.km.
アイオワ 145800 sq.km

3. Distance from school
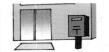
250メートル 600メートル

4. ナイロビの人口(じんこう)　　2143000人
ベルリンの人口　　3387000人

5. リバー高校(こうこう) *est.* 1975
レイク高校 *est.* 1990

6. イースト川 72420メートル
ウエスト川 90000メートル

7. ノース公園(こうえん) 53300 sq.m
サウス公園 33500 sq.m

ノート: Answering comparative questions

-のほうがAdj.です

～のほうが is used to answer comparative questions.

Q: 電車とバスとどちらが速いですか。

A: 電車の方が速いです。　Trains are faster.

Q: 夏休みと春休みとどちらが長いですか。

A: 夏休みの方が長いです。　The summer vacation is longer.

E. Practice asking and answering cooperative questions according to the given information.

比較の質問と答えの練習をしてください。

会話の例 (Sample Dialogue)

Q: 電車とバスとどちらが高いですか。

A: 電車の方が高いです。

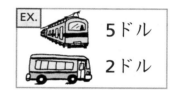
EX. 5ドル / 2ドル

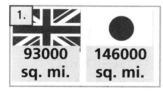
1. 93000 sq. mi. / 146000 sq. mi.

2.

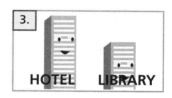
3. HOTEL LIBRARY

4. SINCE 1915 / MOVIE 1940

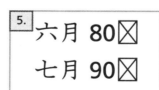
5. 六月 80⊠ / 七月 90⊠

6.

Suggested additional work

Procedure:

1. Break up into small groups and collect some comparative data about any interesting topic.
2. Make five comparative questions based on the collected data.
3. Have a little "quiz show" in which you ask your questions to other groups.

F. Create five comparative sentences about some aspects of your town or school using "X は Y より -."

みなさんの町か学校について、比較の文を五つ作ってください。

> 例 (Examples)
>
> 私の学校の体育館は図書館より新しいです。
> 私の町はとなりの町より自然が多いです。

2 Make similarity statements　　相似の文を作る 1

ノート: Indicating similarity between two items

| XはYと(ほぼ)同じです。 | X is (just about) the same as Y. |

X は Y とおなじです means "X is the same as Y." ほぼ is an adverb and corresponds to "just about" in English. It corresponds to "X is the same ~ as Y."

私の町の人口はホノルルの人口とほぼ同じです。
The population of my town is just about the same as that of Honolulu.

| XはYとZが(ほぼ)同じです。 | X is (just about) the same as Y in terms of Z. |

In this construction the subject being compared is marked by the particle が and placed before (ほぼ) おなじです. The sentence above can be written using this construction with じんこう (population) being "Z."

私の町はホノルルと人口がほぼ同じです。
My town has just about the same population as Honolulu.

| XはYと同じくらい - です。 | X is just about as - as Y |

私の町はホノルルと同じくらい暑いです。
My town is just as hot as Honolulu.

A. Circle the appropriate word in each parenthesis.

適切なことばを○で囲んでください。

1. 日本の100円はアメリカの (1, 10, 100) ドルとほぼ同じです。

2. 華氏85度は摂氏 (20, 30, 40) 度とほぼ同じです。

3. 昨日は今日と気温が同じ位 (安、低、長) かったです。

4. シカゴはニューヨークと同じ位 (大きい、小さい、短かい) です。

5. フランスは (イギリス、日本、カナダ) と人口がほぼ同じです。

6. 私の学校は8時に始まります。あなたの学校と同じですか。

   そうですね、(同じです、ほぼ同じです、違います)。

B. Practice the following conversation by replacing the underlined part according to the pictures. Use ほぼ (just about) when answering 6-8.

絵を見て、下線の部分を入れかえて練習しましょう。

EX.	1.	2.	3.	4.
$1 $1	七月 28℃ 八月 28℃	中学生 25人 高校生 25人	一月 26⊠ 二月 26⊠	四月 20℃ 九月 20℃

5.	6.	7.	8.
 東公園 53300 sq.m 西公園 53300 sq.m	男の人 58人 女の人 60人	$2 $2.20	三月 48⊠ 十月 46⊠

会話の例 (Sample Dialogue)

A: <u>電車とバスとどちらが安い</u>ですか。

B: そうですね。、<u>電車はバスと同じ</u>です。

C. Practice the following conversation by replacing the underlined part according to the pictures.

絵を見て、下線の部分を入れかえて練習しましょう。

EX. 195円 / 200円

1. 値段 price — 240円 / 230円

2. 一月 -3°C / 二月 -4°C

3. 気温 temp — 三月 10°C / 十月 11°C

4. サウス中学 1104人 / イースト中学 1099人 — 生徒の数 number of students

5. 東高校 1104人 / 西高校 1099人

会話の例 (Sample Dialogue)

A: <u>電車</u>と<u>バス</u>とどちらが<u>安い</u>ですか。

B: そうですね。、<u>電車</u>は<u>バス</u>と<u>値段</u>がほぼ同じです。

D. Practice the following conversation by replacing the underlined part according to the chart.

表を見て、下線の部分を入れかえて練習しましょう。

	A町	B町
人口	5万3千人	5万4千人
8月の気温	摂氏27度	摂氏28度
本屋の数	8軒	9軒

会話の例 (Sample Dialogue)

A: A町とB町とどちらが<u>人口が多い</u>ですか。

B: そうですね。同じくらい<u>多い</u>です。

でしょう

ノート: Expressing uncertainty or probability

When you end your speech with でしょう rather than です, you indicate that what you have said may well happen or be the case, but not for certain. テストはあしたでしょう and あしたはさむいでしょう mean "The test will probably be tomorrow" and "It will probably be cold tomorrow," respectively. でしょう can also follow a plain form of a verb such as the dictionary form. For example, サラはダンスにいくでしょう means "Sara will go to the dance in all likelihood." In Japan you may hear this ending often in a weather forecast on TV or radio. It is also convenient to use this ending when you give an uncertain answer or simply want to avoid being too definitive. たぶん is an adverb that corresponds to "probably" or "perhaps" and is often used with -でしょう in daily conversations.

Q: テキサスとカリフォルニアとどちらが大きいですか。

A: たぶん、ほぼ同じでしょう。 It's probably just about the same.

E. Forecast tomorrow's weather according to the given data using -でしょう.

「でしょう」を使って、天気予報をしましょう。

EX. muggy 1. cool 2. cold 3. windy 4. warm 5. pleasant

例 (Example)

明日は晴れでしょう。そして、蒸し暑いでしょう。

F. Practice making a comparative question and answering with -でしょう.

比較の質問を作って、「でしょう」で答える練習をしましょう。

会話の例 (Sample Dialogue)

A: 電車とバスとどちらが安いですか。

B: たぶん、電車はバスとほぼ同じでしょう。

G. *Make six "similarity sentences" about aspects of your town or school using "X* は Y と (ほぼ) *おなじです," "X* は Y と Z が (ほぼ) *おなじです," and "X* は Y とおなじくらい -です." *Make use of the* -でしょう *ending as well.*

みなさんの町か学校について、「X は Y と (ほぼ) 同(おな)じです」「X は Y と Z が (ほぼ) 同じです」「X は Y と 同じくらい - です」を使って文(ぶん)を六つ作ってください。「- でしょう」も使ってください。

例 (Examples)

私の町の人口(じんこう)は広島(ひろしま)の人口とほぼ同(おな)じです。

The population in my town is just about the same as the population in Hiroshima.

私の町はホノルルと夏の気温(きおん)がほぼ同じでしょう。

Summer temperatures are probably just about the same in my town and Honolulu.

私の学校のカフェテリアのパスタはレストランのパスタと同じくらいおいしいです。

Pasta at my school's cafeteria is as delicious as those at the restaurants.

 4 **Make comparative statements: Part 2**   比較(ひかく)の文(ぶん)を作る その2

ノート: Comparative statement

XはYほど+ Negative Form of Adjective

The construction above makes an English equivalent of "X is not so much - as Y."

ノース公園(こうえん)はサウス公園ほど広(ひろ)くありません。

North Park is not as spacious as South Park.

トムさんの寮(りょう)はリンダさんの寮ほど静(しず)かじゃありません。

Tom's dorm is not as quiet as Linda's dorm.

Compare the following:

<ruby>数<rt>すう</rt>学<rt>がく</rt></ruby>のテストは<ruby>化<rt>か</rt>学<rt>がく</rt></ruby>のテストほど<ruby>難<rt>むず</rt></ruby>かしくありません。

Math tests are not as difficult as chemistry tests.

<ruby>数<rt>すう</rt>学<rt>がく</rt></ruby>のテストは<ruby>化<rt>か</rt>学<rt>がく</rt></ruby>のテストよりやさしいです。

Math tests are easier than chemistry tests.

Both sentences basically indicate the same thing. However, the first sentence tends to imply that the math tests are also difficult, but they are not as difficult as the (super difficult) chemistry tests. The second sentence, on the other hand, will not warrant the same assumption partly because of the presence of やさしい. Keep this difference in mind. You will be able to choose a construction that is more suitable to your claim.

A. Rewrite the following comparative sentences by using "X は Y ほど-く/じゃありません."

「XはYほど-く/じゃありません」を使って<ruby>書<rt>か</rt></ruby>き換えてください。

EX. <ruby>月<rt>よう</rt></ruby><ruby>曜<rt>よう</rt></ruby>日は<ruby>水<rt>よう</rt></ruby><ruby>曜<rt>よう</rt></ruby>日より<ruby>忙<rt>いそが</rt></ruby>しいです。

→<u><ruby>水<rt>よう</rt></ruby><ruby>曜<rt>よう</rt></ruby>日は<ruby>月<rt>よう</rt></ruby><ruby>曜<rt>よう</rt></ruby>日ほど忙しくありません。</u>

1. 二月は三月より寒いです。 → 三月は＿＿＿＿＿＿。

2. <ruby>八<rt>や</rt>百<rt>お</rt>屋<rt>や</rt></ruby>はパン屋より<ruby>近<rt>ちか</rt></ruby>いです。 → <ruby>八<rt>や</rt>百<rt>お</rt>屋<rt>や</rt></ruby>は＿＿＿＿＿＿。

3. 男の人は女の人より<ruby>多<rt>おお</rt></ruby>いです。 → 女の人は＿＿＿＿＿＿。

4. 私の<ruby>部<rt>へ</rt>屋<rt>や</rt></ruby>は<ruby>弟<rt>おとうと</rt></ruby>の部屋より<ruby>明<rt>あか</rt></ruby>るいです。 → 弟の部屋は＿＿＿＿。

5. <ruby>地<rt>ち</rt>下<rt>か</rt>鉄<rt>てつ</rt></ruby>はバスより<ruby>便<rt>べん</rt>利<rt>り</rt></ruby>です。 → バスは＿＿＿＿＿＿。

6. 高校のサッカーチームは中学のサッカーチームより<ruby>強<rt>つよ</rt></ruby>いです。

→ 中学のサッカーチームは＿＿＿＿＿＿。

Suggested additional work

Procedure:

1. Individually make three more "X は Y より-" statements and convert them to "Y は X ほど-."

2. Read your original statements to a classmate and check if he or she can do the same conversion successfully. Find another classmate to do the same.

B. Practice the following conversation by replacing the underlined part according to the pictures.

絵を見て、下線の部分を入れ換えて練習しましょう。

more strict ←————————————————————→ less strict

会話の例 (Sample Dialogue)

A: テニスのコーチは厳しいですか。

B: はい、音楽の先生より厳しいです。でも、担任の先生ほど厳しくありません。

C. Continue to practice conversations similar to the one above by using some real life examples at your school.

あなたの学校を例にして、上の会話をもっと練習してください。

D. Make five sets of comparative statements. Each set should consist of two sentences: "X は Y より-です. でも, X は Zほど-く/じゃありません." You may write about your town, school, or any other topic you like.

「X は Y より- です。でも、X は Z ほど-く/じゃありません。」という二つの文でできたものを五つ作ってください。町、学校かあなたの好きなトピックについて書いてください。

例 (Examples)

数学のクラスは英語のクラスより宿題が多いです。
でも、数学のクラスは日本語のクラスほど宿題が多くありません。
数学のクラスは英語のクラスより宿題が多い。しかし、数学のクラスは日本語のクラスほど宿題が多くない。

Recognition Kanji 5: 認識漢字 5
<ruby>認識漢字<rt>にんしきかんじ</rt></ruby>

勉強
べんきょう
study

復習
ふくしゅう
review

表現
ひょうげん
expression

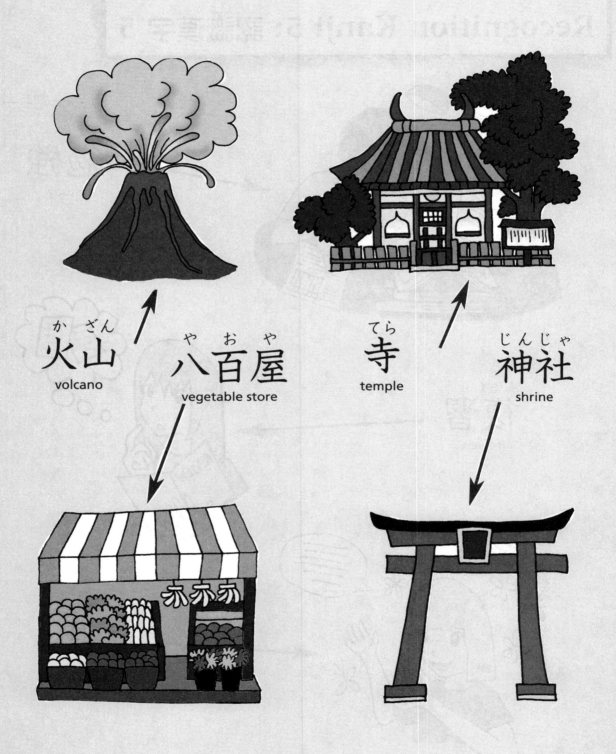

<ruby>火<rt>か</rt>山<rt>ざん</rt></ruby>
volcano

<ruby>八<rt>や</rt>百<rt>お</rt>屋<rt>や</rt></ruby>
vegetable store

<ruby>寺<rt>てら</rt></ruby>
temple

<ruby>神社<rt>じんじゃ</rt></ruby>
shrine

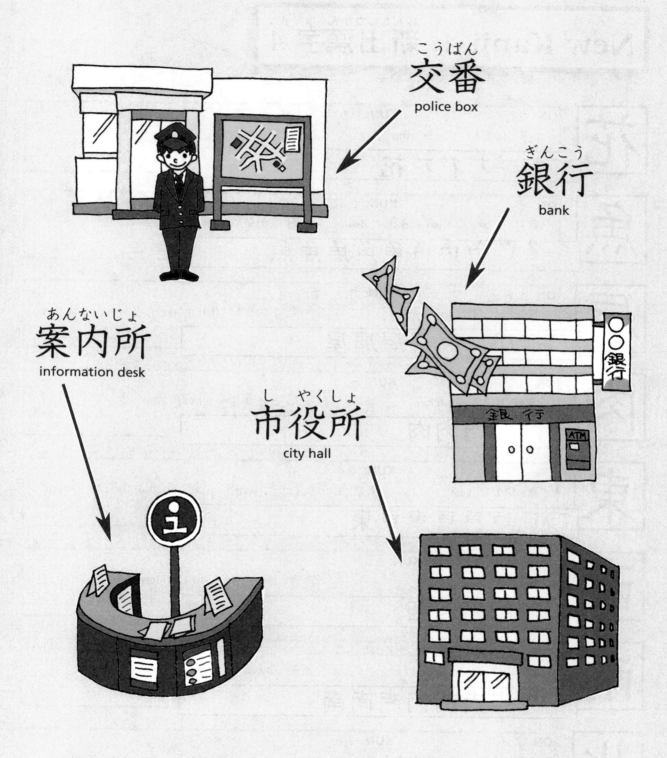

こうばん
交番
police box

ぎんこう
銀行
bank

あんないじょ
案内所
information desk

し やくしょ
市役所
city hall

花
ON: カ **KUN**: はな
花屋: はなや flower shop 花器: かき vase
一 十 廾 艹 艹 艼 花 花

魚
ON: ギョ **KUN**: さかな
魚貝: ぎょかい fish and shell fish 魚屋: さかなや fish market
ｱ ｸ ｸ ｸ 呂 呙 角 甾 角 魚 魚

屋
ON: オク **KUN**: ヤ
花屋: はなや flower shop 魚屋: さかなや fish market
一 コ 尸 尸 尸 居 居 屋 屋

肉
ON: ニク **KUN**: 一
肉屋: にくや butcher 牛肉: ぎゅうにく beef
一 冂 内 内 肉 肉

東
ON: トウ **KUN**: ひがし
東: ひがし east 東京: とうきょう Tokyo 東洋: とうよう The Orient
一 ｢ 戸 百 百 申 東 東

西
ON: セイ、ザイ **KUN**: にし
西: にし west 西洋: せいよう The Occident
一 ｢ 而 西 西 西

南
ON: ナン **KUN**: みなみ
南: みなみ south 南国: なんごく southern country
一 十 古 古 市 市 南 南 南

北
ON: ホク,ボク **KUN**: きた
北: きた north 北国: きたぐに northern provinces 北海道: ほっかいどう Hokkaido
一 ｜ ｜ 北 北

Reading 7:
読み物 7

Yokohama Tour Guide:
よこはまかんこうあんない
横浜観光案内

---

1. 港未来21地区は、未来があるので、私の好きな場所です。ビルがたくさんあって、ベイブリッジが見えて、とても現代的です。これらのビルには国連関係のオフィスがたくさん入っていて、国際的です。

未来: future　　現代的: modern
国際的: international　　国連関係: related UN

---

2. 船や港が見える山下公園の辺りには明治時代から昭和の初めのころの建物があります。博物館などもあるので、その時代のことを知ることができます。

明治時代: Meiji era　　昭和の初め: early part of the Showa era(1926-1989)　　博物館:museum

---

---

3. 横浜には中国のような中華街があります。そこは、中国の物を売っている店や、中国語で注文する中国料理店がたくさんある商店街です。中国語を中心にした国際学校もあります。ですから、ここに入ると日本にいるより中国にいる感じがします。

注文: order　　感じ: feeling

A. Scan the following words.

1. Find the key words which are referring to a place.

　　横浜　　　港未来21地区　　　山下公園　　　中国人　　　博物館　　　商店街

2. Find the similar Kanji which is referring to a place.

　　a. 公園：図書館、建物、動物園　　　　b. 博物館：図書館、川、運動場

　　c. 国連：町、山、国

3. Find the Kanji with the same radical of the Kanji in red.

　　a. 港：海、空、土地　　　　b. 場：港、時、地

　　c. 園：店、船、国　　　　d. 時：明治、昭和、国際

4. Find the same content of the Kanji in red.

　　a. 商店街：本屋、図書館、公園　　b. 横浜：中華街、飛行場、温泉
　　（しょうてんがい）　　　　　　　　　（よこはま）

B. Go over through the previous articles and choose the important key word.

1. 港未来21地区：　　昭和、好きな場所、時代、音楽、国連関係、現代的、料理
2. 山下公園：　　　　船、動物園、国連、日本語、遊ぶ、明治時代、建物、山下公園
　　　　　　　　　　　　　（どうぶつえん）　　　　　　　（あそ）
3. 中華街：　　　　　国際学校、中国語、日本語、中国、中国料理店、材料

C. Examine the following sentences and choose the appropriate words in the parenthesis by using your prior knowledge and experience.

1. ベイブリッジは港未来21地区の（上、下、前、中）にある（大きな、小さな）橋である。
2. 山下公園の（右、左、真ん中、外、回り、向こう）に古い建物がある。
　　　　　　　　　　（まん なか、そと、まわ、むこ）
3. 横浜の中華街の（右、左、中、外、回り、向こう）に国際学校ある。
　　　　　　　　　　　　　（なか、そと、まわ、むこ）

D. When you start to read the sentences, you should imagine what kind of topic and how it's developed by checking its title and the first sentence. Fill out the lines below.

Title:_____

1. First sentence:_____

2. First sentence:_____

3. First sentence:_____

After checking the title and the first sentences, read the previous articles within 3 minutes and sum up what the author wants to say.

1. a. 港未来21地区の交通についてです。
　　　　　　　　　（こうつう）
　 b. ベイブリッジは古い橋です。
　 c. 港未来21地区は現代的で国際的です。
　 d. 港未来21地区は古い町です。

2. a. 山下公園は昭和にできました。
　 b. 山下公園には動物園があります。
　　　　　　　（どうぶつえん）
　 c. 山下公園の回りには古い建物があります。
　 d. 山下公園は日本の明治にあります。

3. a. 中国人の観光は横浜にたくさん来ます。
　 b. 横浜の中華街では中国語のガイドが必要です。
　　　　　　　　　　　　　　　　　　　（ひつよう）
　 c. 中国には国際学校がたくさんあります。
　 d. 横浜の中華街には中国料理店や中国のものがたくさんあります。

E. Link three items in the vocabulary list below.

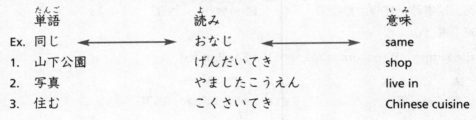

単語	読み	意味
（たんご）	（よ）	（いみ）
Ex. 同じ ⟷	おなじ ⟷	same
1. 山下公園	げんだいてき	shop
2. 写真	やましたこうえん	live in
3. 住む	こくさいてき	Chinese cuisine

4.	場所	めいじじだい	Chinese language
5.	現代的	しょうわじだい	Meiji era
6.	国際的	みせ	Showa era
7.	明治時代	ばしょ	photo
8.	昭和時代	しゃしん	place
9.	中国料理	ちゅうごくご	Yamashita Park
10.	中国語	ちゅうごくりょうり	contemporary
11.	店	すむ	international

3. Check whether the following information is true or false.

1. 港未来21地区に国連関係のオフィスがある。 （本当、嘘）
2. 山下公園の前に海がある。 （本当、嘘）
3. 横浜には中国人がたくさんいる。 （本当、嘘）

4. Form a group and answer these guided questions in Japanese.

1. この人は横浜のどこを紹介したいと思っていますか。
2. この人はどうして港未来21地区が好きなのでしょうか。
3. 山下公園の回りの建物はいつ建てられたのでしょうか。
4. 中華街はどんな店があると思いますか。

---

1. 港未来21地区は、未来があるので、私の好きな場所です。ビルがたくさんあって、ベイブリッジが見えて、とても現代的です。これらのビルには国連関係のオフィスがたくさん入っていて、国際的です。

港未来21地区：Minato Mirai 21 district　未来：future　ビル：building
並ぶ：stand in line　ベイブリッジ：name of bridge　見える：can see
現代的：contemporary　国連関係：related UN　国際的：international

2. 船や港が見える山下公園の辺りには明治時代から昭和の初めのころの建物が残っています。また、博物館などもあるので、その時代のことを知ることができます。

山下公園：name of park　辺り：vicinity　明治時代：Meiji era (1869 -1912)
昭和の初めのころ：early part of the Showa era(1926-1989)　建物：building　残る：leave
博物館：museum　など：etc.　知る：know

3. 横浜には中国のような中華街があります。そこは、中国の物を売っている店や、中国語で注文する中国料理店がたくさんある商店街です。中国語を中心にした国際学校もあります。ですから、ここに入ると日本にいるより中国にいる感じがします。

中華街：Chinatown　中国料理：Chinese food　材料：ingredients

出会い

であい、encounter　　　　出：**ON:**シュツ　**KUN:**で(る)、だ(す)
　　　　　　　　　　　　会：**ON:**カイ　**KUN:**あ(う)
出会いがいっぱいあります。　There will be many encounters.

風景

ふうけい、landscape　　　　風：**ON:**フウ　**KUN:**かぜ
　　　　　　　　　　　　　景：**ON:**ケイ　**KUN:**一
風景の写真を撮りました。　I took pictures of the scenery.

日本的

にほんてき、Japanese style 日：**ON:**ニチ　**KUN:** ひ、か
　　　　　　　　　　　　　本：**ON:**ホン　**KUN:**もと
　　　　　　　　　　　　　的：**ON:**テキ　**KUN:**まと
日本的なスタイルを作ります。　I am making Japanese style.

観光客

かんこうきゃく、　　　　観：**ON:**カン　**KUN:**み(る)
　visiter, tourist　　　　光：**ON:**コウ　**KUN:**ひかり、ひか(る)
　　　　　　　　　　　　客：**ON:**キャク　**KUN:**一
観光客が日本的な物を買います。
　　　　　　　　Tourists buy Japanese style souvenirs.

音読型

おんどくがた、　　　　　音：**ON**オン　　**KUN:** おと
　reading aloud type　　読：**ON:**ドク　**KUN:**よ(む)
　　　　　　　　　　　　型：**ON:**ケイ　**KUN:** かた
音読型で発表します。　I present by reading aloud type.

道路

どうろ、road　　　　　道：**ON**ドウ　**KUN:** みち
　　　　　　　　　　　路：**ON:**ロ　　**KUN:**じ、みち
道路で車を運転します。　I drive a car on the road.

劇場

げきじょう、theater　　劇：**ON:**ゲキ　**KUN:** 一
　　　　　　　　　　　場：**ON:**ジョウ　**KUN:**ば
劇場に出かけます。　I am going to the theater.

見学

けんがく、visit, take a tour 見：**ON:**ケ　**KUN:**み(る)
　　　　　　　　　　　　学：**ON:**ガク　**KUN:**まな(ぶ)
工場見学に参加します。　I join the factory tour.

遊ぶ

あそぶ、play　　　　　　遊：**ON:**ユウ　**KUN:** あそ(ぶ)

友だちと遊ぶのが好きです。　I like playing with my friends.

3.7 Mechanics 組立て
<ruby>組<rt>く</rt>立<rt>み</rt>て<rt>た</rt></ruby>

Writing about weather

天気について書く

Objectives

Describe winter weather in your area.

Create a "sum-up" paragraph by using comparative statements.

Evaluate your writing based on several criteria.

Overview

In this section you will write about winter weather in your town or another place you are familiar with. Let's assume that the potential readers of your writing are Japanese. This means that you will be using the Celsius scale and the metric system when referring to various weather data. Other than a main paragraph consisting of the three elements you have learned, you will be creating a few "sum-up" statements and place it at the end. Because our focus is still on the structural aspect, we will narrow the scope of our topic at this time and base it on how severe the winter is, and examine the degree of severity based on the temperature and the amount of snowfall. We know many of you are leading a very active life and may be tempted to describe the more active and fun side of the season. But building a solid foundation is critical to your future success as a creative writer. Also, those of you who live in the tropical zone or in the Southern Hemisphere may be wondering if judging the severity of winter based on the aforementioned criteria is relevant in your area. Consult your teacher and make some adjustments if you wish.

8	**Write about the weather**	冬の天気について書く
1	**Check the organization**	構成のチェックをする
2	**Create a topic sentence**	トピックセンテンスを作る
3	**Create supporting sentences**	サポートセンテンスを作る
4	**Create examples**	例を作る
5	**Make a "sum-up" paragraph**	まとめのパラグラフを作る
6	**Conduct an evaluation**	評価をする

1 Check the organization of your writing 構成(こうせい)のチェックをする

As noted in the overview you will be creating a "sum-up" paragraph in addition to a main paragraph. Your main paragraph will consist of a topic sentence, two supporting sentences, and three examples for each supporting sentence. Look at "My Draft" below and familiarize yourself with the organization of your writing. You will fill the empty slots as you create each corresponding part.

X町(まち)の冬(ふゆ)の天気(てんき) My Draft

Main Paragraph	TOPIC SENTENCE	
	SUPPORTING SENTENCE 1	
	EXAMPLE 1 EXAMPLE 2 EXAMPLE 3	
	SUPPORTING SENTENCE 2	
	EXAMPLE 1 EXAMPLE 2 EXAMPLE 3	
"Sum-up" Paragraph	"SUM-UP" STATEMENTS	

2 **Create a topic sentence**　　　　トピックセンテンスを作<ruby>作<rt>つく</rt></ruby>る

A. Write down the name of a place you will be writing about. It could be your current town or any other town you think you have the sufficient information to describe.

<ruby>冬<rt>ふゆ</rt></ruby>の<ruby>天気<rt>てんき</rt></ruby>について<ruby>書<rt>か</rt></ruby>く<ruby>町<rt>まち</rt></ruby>を<ruby>決<rt>き</rt></ruby>めましょう。

町の名前: ＿＿＿＿＿＿＿＿＿＿＿＿＿＿＿

*B. First, choose an appropriate response to the following questions based on your own experience and knowledge. Next, add the points in parenthesis according to your choices and write the total in the box below. The town you write about is referred to as X*まち *(Town X).*

<ruby>質問<rt>しつもん</rt></ruby>を<ruby>読<rt>よ</rt></ruby>んで、<ruby>一番適切<rt>いちばんてきせつ</rt></ruby>な<ruby>答<rt>こた</rt></ruby>えを<ruby>選<rt>えら</rt></ruby>んでください。

1. X<ruby>町<rt>まち</rt></ruby>の<ruby>冬<rt>ふゆ</rt></ruby>は<ruby>寒<rt>さむ</rt></ruby>いですか。

   A. はい、とても寒いです。(5)

   B. はい、かなり寒いです。(4)

   C. はい、まあまあ寒いです。(3)

   D. はい、あまり寒くありません。(2)

   E. はい、ぜんぜん寒くありません。(1)

2. X<ruby>町<rt>まち</rt></ruby>の冬は<ruby>雪<rt>ゆき</rt></ruby>が<ruby>多<rt>おお</rt></ruby>いですか。

   F. はい、とても多いです。(5)

   G. はい、かなり多いです。(4)

   H. はい、まあまあ多いです。(3)

   I. はい、あまり多くありません。(2)

   J. はい、ぜんぜん多くありません。(1)

Total Points

とても (very much)
かなり (considerably)
まあまあ (moderately)
あまり (not so much)
ぜんぜん (not at all)

In case you forgot...

367

C. *Review the following chart to determine which of the five sentences may be most appropriate as your topic sentence based on your total points from the previous section.* きびしい *(strict) also means "harsh" or "severe" and* たいへん *means "greatly" or "extremely."*

表を見てトピックセンテンスを決めましょう。

Total points ごうけいてん 合計点	Potential topic sentence starting with: X町の冬の天気は・・・
10	・・たいへん厳しいです。
9	
8	・・かなり厳しいです。
7-6	・・まあまあ厳しいです。
5	・・あまり厳しくありません。
4	
3	・・ぜんぜん厳しくありません。
2	

My topic sentence is:

3 Create supporting sentences

サポートセンテンスを作る

A. You have written your topic sentence and have therefore set forth the main idea of your writing. The next step is to create supporting sentences. Let's make just two of them at this time. The first one should make a reference to "how cold" and the second one to "how snowy." These correspond to the two questions you have answered in the beginning. Keep in mind that you will be adding examples to each supporting sentence later.

サポートセンテンスを二つ作りましょう。

サポートセンテンス1の例 (Examples for Supporting Sentence 1)	サポートセンテンス2の例 (Examples for Supporting Sentence 2)
毎日とても寒いです。 寒い日がたくさんあります。 寒い日がけっこうあります。 寒い日があまりありません。 あまり寒くありません。 ぜんぜん寒くありません。	雪がたくさん降ります。 雪の日がかなり多いです。 雪の日がけっこうあります。 雪があまり降りません。 雪の日が少ないです。 雪がぜんぜん降りません。

My supporting sentences are:

1.

2.

B. Take a close look at your second supporting sentence and see if it contrasts with your first one. Make the following adjustments to the sentence depending upon the outcome.

二番目のサポートセンテンスを調整しましょう。

Does it contrast?

YES Place でも in the beginning and change the particle が into は which will serve as a contrasting element marker.

NO Place それに (furthermore) in the beginning and change the particle が into も.

369

対照的な場合の例 (Examples for Contrasting Situations)	対照的じゃない場合の例 (Examples for Non contrasting Situations)
1. 毎日とても寒いです。 2. でも、雪はあまり降りません。	1. 毎日とても寒いです。 2. それに、雪もたくさん降ります。
1. あまり寒くありません。 2. でも、雪の日はけっこうあります。	1. 寒い日がけっこうあります。 2. それに、雪の日もかなりあります。

C. Fill in the appropriate slots in "My Draft" in the beginning of this section with your topic and supporting sentences.

このセクションの始めの"My Draft"の該当部分にトピックセンテンスとサポートセンテンスを書きましょう。

TOPIC SENTENCE	ジョイタウンの冬はかなり厳しいです。
SUPPORTING SENTENCE 1	寒い日がたくさんあります。
EXAMPLE 1 **EXAMPLE 2** **EXAMPLE 3**	
SUPPORTING SENTENCE 2	それに、雪もけっこう降ります。
EXAMPLE 1 **EXAMPLE 2** **EXAMPLE 3**	
"SUM-UP" PARAGRAPH	

SAMPLE

4 **Create examples**

<ruby>例<rt>れい</rt></ruby>を<ruby>作<rt>つく</rt></ruby>る

We now deal with examples that will add details to each supporting sentence. At this stage you are more likely to provide specific data and we will begin by familiarizing ourselves with the metric system. The Celsius or the centigrade system for measuring temperatures has been introduced earlier in the chapter and you may want to read the information once again before you proceed.

A. Circle the appropriate adjective.　<ruby>正<rt>ただ</rt></ruby>しい<ruby>形容詞<rt>けいようし</rt></ruby>を○で<ruby>囲<rt>まる</rt></ruby>みましょう。

1. 1センチ(cm)は1インチ(in)より (<ruby>長<rt>なが</rt></ruby>い、<ruby>短<rt>みじか</rt></ruby>い) です。

2. 1フィート(ft)は1メートル(m)より (長い、短い) です。

3. 100ミリ(mm)は1メートル(m)より (長い、短い) です。

4. 5インチ(in)は10センチ(cm)より (長い、短い) です。

5. 10ヤード(yd)は10メートル(m)より (長い、短い) です。

B. Complete the following conversion charts.　<ruby>次<rt>つぎ</rt></ruby>の<ruby>表<rt>ひょう</rt></ruby>を<ruby>完成<rt>かんせい</rt></ruby>させてください。

1. <u>English to metric</u>

When you know:	You can find:	If you multiple by:
インチ[in]	センチ(メートル) [cm]	2.5
フィート[ft]	センチ(メートル) [cm]	

2. <u>Metric to English</u>

When you know:	You can find:	If you multiple by:
センチ(メートル) [cm]	インチ[in]	0.4
センチ(メートル) [cm]	フィート[ft]	

ノート: Measuring amount of precipitation

The following units of measurement are usually used to indicate the amount of precipitation and snow accumulation. センチメートル and ミリメートル are usually referred to as just センチ and ミリ respectively.

メートル (meters)
センチメートル (centimeters): one hundredth meter
ミリメートル (millimeters): one thousandth meter

1メートル=1m
100センチ=1cm
1000ミリ=1mm

371

C. Group Competition - Break up into groups of three.

グループ対抗競争です。三人のグループになってください。

Objective:

Practice converting from Fahrenheit to Celsius and vice versa, and from inches to millimeters and vice versa.

Procedure:

1. Group members cooperate and complete both Chart A and Chart B.
2. The group that finishes their task fastest and most accurately wins the competition.

Monthly Highest Temperature and Amount of Precipitation: Beijing, China

Chart A		1月	2月	3月	4月	5月	6月	7月	8月	9月	10月	11月	12月
最高気温	°F☒		39		68		86		84	79		50	37
降水量	inches		0.28		0.75		3.07		8.35	2.24		0.28	0.12

Chart B		1月	2月	3月	4月	5月	6月	7月	8月	9月	10月	11月	12月
最高気温	°C	1		11	20	26		31		26	19		3
降水量	centi-meters	0.3		0.9	1.9	3.3		19.3		5.7	2.4		0.3

ノート: How to read decimals

When you read fractions, you say "てん" to indicate the presence of a decimal point. For example 3.5 is "さんてんご" in Japanese. Numbers after the decimal point is read one by one, just like phone numbers.

0.3 (れいてんさん)   **104.5** (ひゃくよんてんご)

2.78 (にいてんななはち)   **16.47** (じゅうろくてんよんなな)

D. Conduct research and find out the average monthly temperature and amount of snowfall in your town from November to February, and indicate them by Celsius and by centimeter.

自分の町の11月から2月までの月別気温と積雪量を調べて、気温は摂氏、積雪量はセンチで示してください。

E. As mentioned before, examples add details to each supporting sentence. They should also uphold and reinforce the topic sentence. Any statement that doesn't do that will not qualify, no matter how informative it may sound. See the mindmap below and cross out any irrelevant or ineffective examples.

適切でない例を線で消してください。

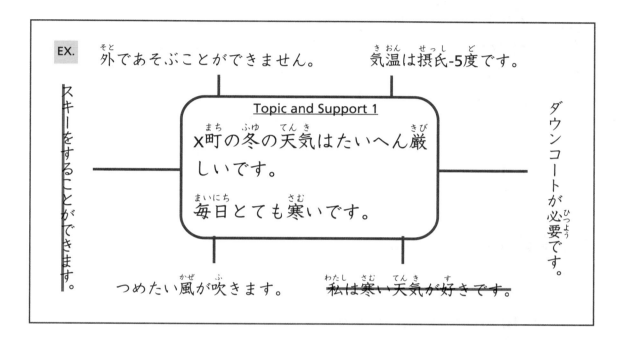

EX.

外であそぶことができません。　　気温は摂氏-5度です。

スキーをすることができます。

Topic and Support 1

X町の冬の天気はたいへん厳しいです。

毎日とても寒いです。

ダウンコートが必要です。

つめたい風が吹きます。　　私は寒い天気が好きです。

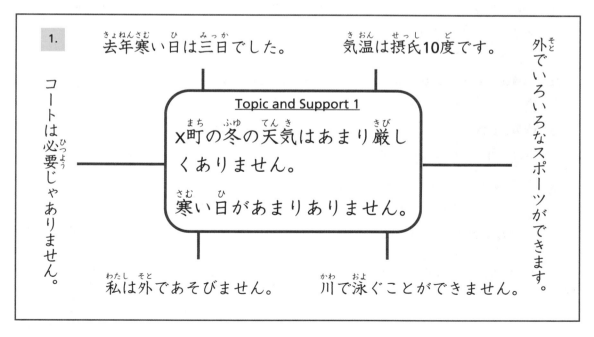

1.

去年寒い日は三日でした。　　気温は摂氏10度です。

コートは必要じゃありません。

Topic and Support 1

X町の冬の天気はあまり厳しくありません。

寒い日があまりありません。

外でいろいろなスポーツができます。

私は外であそびません。　　川で泳ぐことができません。

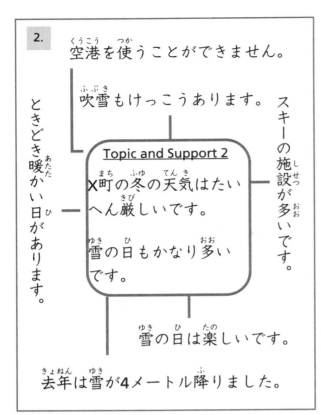

2.
空港を使うことができません。

吹雪もけっこうあります。

ときどき暖かい日があります。

スキーの施設が多いです。

Topic and Support 2
X町の冬の天気はたいへん厳しいです。
雪の日もかなり多いです。

雪の日は楽しいです。

去年は雪が4メートル降りました。

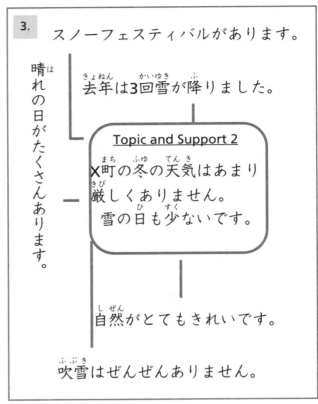

3.
スノーフェスティバルがあります。

去年は3回雪が降りました。

晴れの日がたくさんあります。

Topic and Support 2
X町の冬の天気はあまり厳しくありません。
雪の日も少ないです。

自然がとてもきれいです。

吹雪はぜんぜんありません。

ノート: Tips for making examples

You may use the following factors to create examples for your winter weather description.

1. **Data and statics**

   EX. The number of snowy days, total snow accumulation, and average temperature.

2. **Notable phenomena and happenings**

   EX. Lakes freezing, airport closing, and schools having snow days.

3. **What people can do and/or cannot do**

   EX. Being able/unable to play outdoors or ride bicycles.

4. **What is or isn't necessary**

   EX. Needing or not needing heavy coats and other winter gear.

5. **Comparative reference**

   We will save this for use in the "sum-up" paragraph at this time.

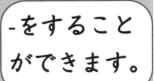

-をすることができます。

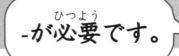

-が必要です。

F. Fill in the appropriate slots in "My Draft" in the beginning of this section with your examples.

セクション始めの"My Draft"の該当部分に例を書きましょう。

TOPIC SENTENCE	ジョイタウンの冬はかなり厳しいです。
SUPPORTING SENTENCE 1	寒い日がたくさんあります。
EXAMPLE 1 EXAMPLE 2 EXAMPLE 3	気温は摂氏0度ぐらいです。1月と2月は湖が凍ります。よくダウンコートが必要です。
SUPPORTING SENTENCE 2	それに、雪もけっこう降ります。
EXAMPLE 1 EXAMPLE 2 EXAMPLE 3	去年は雪の日が20日ぐらいありました。吹雪もけっこうありました。雪は全部で1メートル50センチぐらい降りました。
"SUM-UP" PARAGRAPH	

SAMPLE

4 Create a "sum-up" paragraph　　まとめのパラグラフを作る

As mentioned earlier, you will create a short "sum-up" paragraph. This is helpful in ensuring that your readers have understood your main points. In this exercise, you will make the paragraph by using comparative sentences. Comparing the severity of winter weather in your town and places your readers know well may enhance their comprehension and reinforce your main idea. Let's proceed with the assumption that your potential readers are familiar with the general and regional climate in Japan.

A. To make a meaningful comparison, you need some data about winter weather in Japan. Luckily you will be provided such data at this time. First, study the map and the chart on the next page and then determine whether or not the following statements are true or false. Fill in each parenthesis with either ○ (まる) for true or × (ばつ) for false.

最初に次のページの地図と表を見てください。それから、正しい文には○、正しくない文には×をつけましょう。

375

Average winter monthly temperature and

(日本各地の冬の月別平均気温と

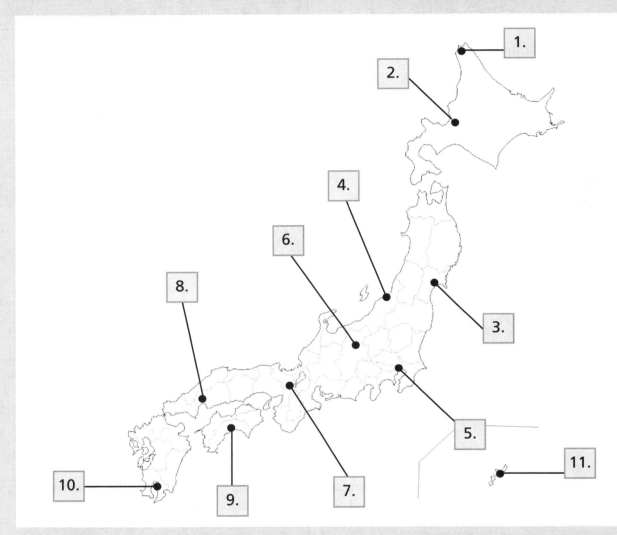

1.（　）札幌の冬は高知より厳しいです。

2.（　）仙台の冬は新潟ほど雪が多くありません。

3.（　）長野は稚内と同じくらい寒いです。

4.（　）東京と広島は2月の気温がほぼ同じです。

snowfall of various places in Japan

せきせつりょう
積雪量)

# on map	Place	12月	1月	2月	12月	1月	2月
1.	わっかない 稚内	-2.0	-5.0	-5.1	40	66	78
2.	さっぽろ 札幌	-1.0	-4.1	-3.5	44	73	98
3.	せんだい 仙台	4.3	1.5	1.7	17	11	13
4.	にいがた 新潟	5.3	2.6	2.5	11	30	30
5.	とうきょう 東京	8.5	5.8	6.1	0	3	5
6.	ながの 長野	1.9	-0.7	-0.3	15	22	24
7.	きょうと 京都	6.9	4.6	4.8	2	3	4
8.	ひろしま 広島	7.5	5.3	5.7	1	3	4
9.	こうち 高知	8.2	6.2	6.9	0	0	1
10.	かごしま 鹿児島	10.4	8.3	9.3	0	2	2
11.	なは 那覇	18.4	16.6	16.6	0	0	0

Based on the 1971- 2000 cumulative data by the Japan Meteorological Agency.

5. （　　）那覇の冬は鹿児島の冬ほど暖かくありません。

6. （　　）京都は広島と同じくらい雪が少ないです。

7. （　　）長野の冬は東京の冬より厳しいです。でも、新潟の冬ほど厳しくありません。

B. Make your own sum-up paragraph by comparing your town with a few of the Japanese towns. Then fill in the appropriate slots in "My Draft" in the beginning of this section with your creation.

セクション始めの"My Draft"の該当部分にまとめのパラグラフを書きましょう。

<table>
<tr><td rowspan="8">SAMPLE</td><td>TOPIC SENTENCE</td><td>ジョイタウンの冬はかなり厳しいです。</td></tr>
<tr><td>SUPPORTING SENTENCE 1</td><td>寒い日がたくさんあります。</td></tr>
<tr><td>EXAMPLE 1
EXAMPLE 2
EXAMPLE 3</td><td>気温は摂氏0度ぐらいです。1月と2月は湖が凍ります。ダウンコートが必要です。</td></tr>
<tr><td>SUPPORTING SENTENCE 2</td><td>それに、雪もけっこう降ります。</td></tr>
<tr><td>EXAMPLE 1
EXAMPLE 2
EXAMPLE 3</td><td>去年は雪の日が20日ぐらいありました。吹雪もけっこうありました。雪は全部で1メートル50センチぐらい降りました。</td></tr>
<tr><td>SUM-UP PARAGRAPH</td><td>ジョイタウンの冬は稚内の冬ほど厳しくありません。でも、東京の冬より厳しいです。たぶん、長野の冬と同じくらい厳しいでしょう。</td></tr>
</table>

C. Read your entire creation once again and make any corrections or adjustments if needed.

自分の作品をもう一度読んで、必要なら修正してください。

4 Conduct an evaluation

評価をする

ノート: Criteria for Evaluation (評価の基準)

Conducting self-peer-evaluations of your work is very useful in developing your writing skills. Self-evaluation will enable you to assess your own work from an objective standpoint, and peer-evaluation may help you notice those things that would otherwise go unnoticed. At this time you will be evaluating your work and your classmates' work based on four criteria. They are as follows: coherence, details, accuracy, and content.

1. Logical sequence

   In this criterion, you will check whether or not the relationship between the topic sentence, supporting sentences, and examples is logical and smooth. In a logically sequenced work, the topic sentence is well supported and the main idea is effectively delivered. The text flows smoothly and sounds convincing.

2. Details

   In this criterion, the focus is on the examples. You will check that all the examples are selected and presented appropriately. Good examples effectively add details to the topic and the supporting sentences. Effective use of comparative statements in the sum-up paragraph should be examined as well.

3. Accuracy

   This includes all the technical errors. You should point out any problems with grammar, spelling, kanji, and usage.

4. Content

   You will check how interesting and appealing the content of the writing is. You will also check if there are any factual errors. Factual errors may not be easily identified, but keep an eye on any outrageous claims or information that is simply hard to believe.

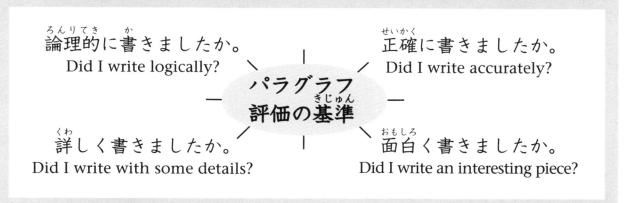

論理的に書きましたか。
Did I write logically?

正確に書きましたか。
Did I write accurately?

パラグラフ
評価の基準

詳しく書きましたか。
Did I write with some details?

面白く書きましたか。
Did I write an interesting piece?

A. Conduct self-and peer-evaluations of your work by using the rubric below.

自己評価、ピア評価をしましょう。

	はい、たいへん	はい、だいたい	はい、まあまあ	いいえ、あまり
Logical sequence ろんりてきに書きましたか。	The information sequence is always logical, coherent, and easy to follow.	The information sequence is mostly logical, coherent, and easy to follow.	The information sequence is not always logical, coherent, and easy to follow.	The information sequence is problematic and not easy to follow.
Details くわしく書きましたか。	All examples are very appropriate and they effectively add details to the topic and supporting sentences.	Most examples are appropriate and they effectively add details to the topic and supporting sentences.	Examples are adequate and they add details to the topic and supporting sentences.	Examples are not very adequate and do not always match well with the topic and supporting sentences.
Accuracy せいかくに書きましたか。	The text has little or no grammatical, spelling, and usage errors.	The text has little grammatical, spelling, and usage errors, for the most part.	The text has more than a few grammatical, spelling, and usage errors.	The text has many content, grammatical, spelling, and usage errors.
Content おもしろく書きましたか。	The content is very interesting and masterfully elaborated. It also has no factual errors.	The content is interesting and well-elaborated, for the most part. It also has no factual errors.	The content is moderately interesting and adequately elaborated. It also may contain a few factual errors.	The content is not very interesting and not well-elaborated. It also may contain many factual errors.

B. Create a vertical and hand-written version of your writing by using げんこうようし.

原稿用紙に書きましょう。

ジョイタウンの冬の天気

　　　　　　　　　　ジャッキー・サンズ

　ジョイタウンの冬はかなり厳しいです。寒い日がたくさんあります。気温は、摂氏〇度くらいです。一月と二月は湖が凍ります。ダウンコートが必要です。それに雪もけっこう降ります。去年の雪の日は二十日くらいありました。吹雪もけっこうありました。雪は全部で一メートル五十センチぐらいありました。

381

Recognition Kanji 5: 認識漢字 5

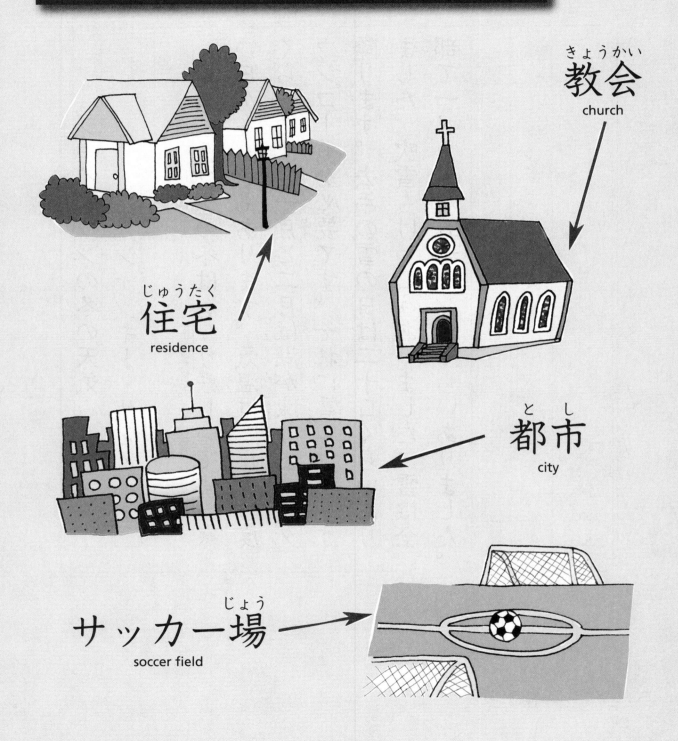

じゅうたく
住宅
residence

きょうかい
教会
church

と　し
都市
city

サッカー場
じょう
soccer field

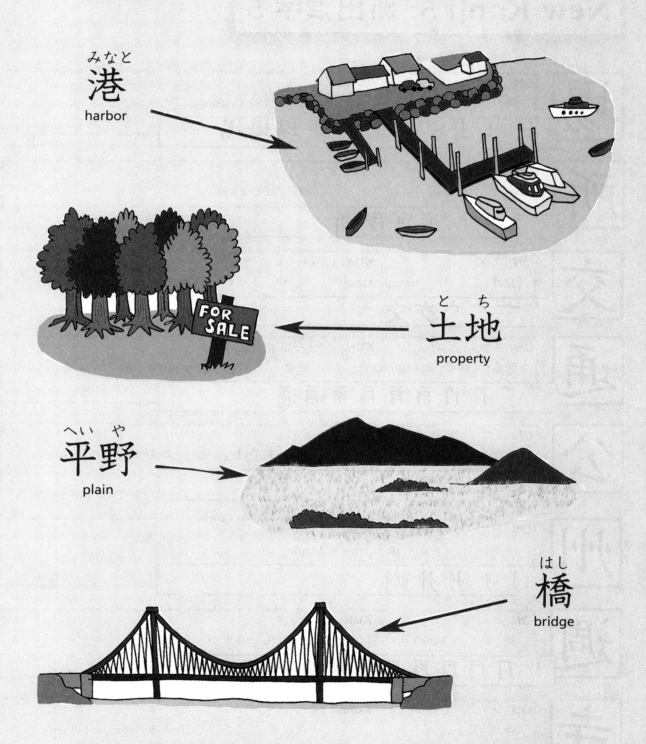

みなと
港
harbor

と　ち
土地
property

FOR SALE

へい　や
平野
plain

はし
橋
bridge

New Kanji 5: 新出漢字 5

場
ON: ジョウ　　**KUN**: ば
場: ば place　　　　　　場所: ばしょ place
一 十 土 圵 圴 坍 坍 垻 垻 垻 場 場

所
ON: ショ　　**KUN**: ところ
所: ところ place　　　　場所: ばしょ place
一 ニ ヲ 戸 戸 所 所 所

交
ON: コウ　　**KUN**: まじ(わる)
交通: こうつう transportation　　交わる: まじわる cross
` 一 六 六 交 交

通
ON: ツウ　　**KUN**: とお(る)、かよ(う)
通る: とおる pass through　　交通: こうつう transportation 通う: かよう
　　　　　　　　　　　　　　　　　　　　　　　　commute
フ マ マ 丙 月 甬 甬 甬 通 通

公
ON: コウ　　**KUN**: おおやけ
公園: こうえん park　　　　公: おおやけ public　公立: こうりつ public
ノ 八 公 公

州
ON: シュウ　　**KUN**: す
メーン州: メーンしゅう State of Maine
` リ 少 州 州 州

週
ON: シュウ　　**KUN**: ー
週: しゅう week　　　　週末: しゅうまつ weekend
ノ 刀 月 月 用 周 周 周 週 週 週

寺
ON: ジ　　**KUN**: てら
寺: てら temple　　　　東大寺: とうだいじ Todaiji (Japanese old temple)
一 十 土 丰 寺 寺

Additional Kanji 7: 追加漢字 7

野外	やがい、outdoors　　　　　野：ON:ヤ　　　KUN:の 外：ON:ガイ　　KUN:そと、ほか 野外のスポーツがすきです。　I like playing outdoor sports.
動物園	どうぶつえん、zoo　　　　動：ON:ドウ　　KUN:うご（く）、 物：ON:ブツ　　KUN:もの 園：ON:エン　　KUN:その 動物園に行きます。　I am going to the zoo.
有名	ゆうめい、famous　　　　有：ON:ユウ　　KUN:あ（る） 名：ON:メイ　　KUN:な これは有名な動物園です。　This is a famous zoo.
習う	ならう、learn　　　　　習：ON:シュウ　KUN:なら（う） 日本語を習います。　I am learning Japanese.
盆踊り	ぼんおどり、bon dance　　盆：ON:ボン　　KUN:ー 踊：ON:ヨウ　　KUN:おど（り） 盆踊りをします。　I am doing a bon dance..
未来	みらい、future　　　　　未：ON:ミ　　　KUN:いま（だ）、ま（だ） 来：ON:ライ　　KUN:く（る）、きた（る） 未来の計画を作ります。　I am making a future plan.
地区	ちく、district　　　　　地：ON:チ、ジ　KUN:つち 区：ON:ク　　　KUN:ー 原宿はおしゃれな地区です。　Harajuyu is a fashionable district.
辺り	あたり、around　　　　　辺：ON:ヘン　　KUN:あた（り） この辺りにあたらしいおしゃれな地区があります。 There is a new fashionable district around here.
時代	じだい、era　　　　　　時：ON:ジ　　　KUN:とき 代：ON:ダイ　　KUN:かわ（る） 新しい時代を作ります。　I am making a new era

FORM

1. Indicating existence of an object: 〜が います and 〜が あります

The verb います is used to express the existence of animate objects such as people and animals. あります on the other hand, is used to express the existence of any inanimate object ranging from concrete things, such as a "clock" and "umbrella" to abstract things, such as "ideas" and "plans."

These objects are marked by the particle が.

Subject	Particle が	Verb
高校生 (animate)〔こうこうせい〕	が	います (いる)。
テレビ (inanimate)	が	あります (ある)。

女の子が います。〔おんな こ〕　　There is a girl.

新しい車が あります。〔あたら くるま〕　　There is a new car.

It should be noted that います and あります may express either mere existence (there is -) or existence and possession (I have -), depending on the context. For example, ひろいへやがあります may mean either, "There is a spacious room (somewhere)," or "I have/own a spacious room."

2. Indicating location of existence with the particle に.

The particle に is used to mark the location of existence. For example, としょかんに います means "(someone) is in the library," and カフェテリアに あります means "(something) is in the cafeteria."

<u>TXは Yに います、TXは Yに あります</u>

This is a pattern used to say "(Speaking about X) X is in such and such a place (Y)."

Because it is marked by the topic particle は ("TX" above represents "Topic"), X has to be something or someone specific and easily recognizable by the listener.

Topic	Particle は	Location	Particle に	Verb
トムさん	は	図書館〔としょかん〕	に	います (いる)。
ピラミッド	は	エジプト	に	あります (ある)。

ディズニーワールドは フロリダに あります。　Disney World is in Florida.

ジェニーさんは 東京に います。〔とうきょう〕　Jenny (whom we all know) is in Tokyo.

<u>Yに Xが います、 Yに Xが あります</u>

This is a pattern which corresponds to "There is an X in such and such a place (Y)." In this construction, the location of an object is stated first and it is followed immediately by the locational particle に and then by います／あります.

Location	Particle に	Subject	Particle が	Verb
学校 (がっこう)	に	高校生 (こうこうせい)	が	います （いる）。
教室 (きょうしつ)	に	テレビ	が	あります （ある）。

This pattern is often used under the following circumstances.

a. When the speaker wants to indicate the existence of something or someone in a situation such as giving directions.

A: あそこに 本屋 (ほんや) が あ20ますね。   There is a bookstore over there, you see?

B: ええ、 あります。   Yes, there is.

b. In questions concerning the existence of something, question words, such as なに and だれ, are the subject.

A: 24番教室 (ばんきょうしつ) に だれが いますか。 Who is in Classroom 24?

B: 石川先生 (いしかわせんせい) が います。   Ishikawa sensei is there.

<u>TYには Xが います、 TYには Xが あります</u>

The difference between this pattern and the previous one is that its topic is a place rather than an item or a person. In this pattern a word indicating the place is mentioned first and is immediately followed by the location particle に. The topic particle は comes next resulting in a "double particle" situation in which に and は are right next to each other. This is because the topic is considered not "the place Y" but "in the place Y." The entire construction corresponds to "As for what is in place Y, there is X."

Topic	DP には	Subject	Particle が	Verb
私の町 (わたし まち)	には	外国人 (がいこくじん)	が	たくさんいます （いる）。
私の町 (わたし まち)	には	映画館 (えいがかん)	が	たくさんあります （ある）。

ニューヨークには大きいホテルがあります。

In New York there are big hotels. / New York has big hotels.

3. Indicating location with positional words

<u>TXは〜の (positional word) にいます、TXは〜の (positional word) にあります</u>

This is a pattern used to say "(Speaking about X) X is in the position of such and such a place." Since it is marked by the topic particle は ("TX" = "Topic X"), X has to be something or someone specific and easily recognizable by the listener.

Topic	Particle は	Location	Particle の	Position	Particle に	Verb
先生	は	ドア	の	前	に	います (いる)。
花屋	は	パン屋	の	となり	に	あります (ある)。

私の家は駅の近くにあります。　My house is located near the train station.

<u>〜の (positional word) にXがいます、〜の (positional word) にXがあります</u>

This pattern adds positional information to YにXがいます and YにXがあります.

Location	Particle の	Position	Particle に	Subject	Particle が	Verb
つくえ	の	下	に	ねこ	が	います (いる)。
学校	の	前	に	本屋	が	あります (ある)。

私の家の近くに駅があります。　There is a train station near my house.

4. Adding numerical information to expressions of existence.

Numerical information may be given with expressions of existence and such information is usually placed right before います and あります.

Location	Particle に(は)	Subject	Particle が	Quantity	Verb
学校	に (は)	先生	が	35人	います (いる)。
石山町	に (は)	病院	が	四つ	あります (ある)。

A: Bさんの町には図書館がいくつありますか。

How many libraries are there in your town?

B: 私の町には図書館が三つあります。　My town has three libraries.

5. Counters

When counting things in Japanese, the so-called "counters" are placed after a number and different counters are used depending on the type of things being counted. Here are some useful counters.

まい	（枚）	thin and flat objects such as papers, stamps, CDs, DVDs, and plates
ほん	（本）	cylindrical, long objects such as pencils, sticks, rods, and poles
けん	（軒）	stores, restaurants, and houses
だい	（台）	machines & vehicles, such as cars, computers and bicycles
ひき	（匹）	small animals, such as cats, dogs, fish, and insects
とう	（頭）	large animals, such as horses, cows and elephants
さつ	（冊）	bound object, including books, note-books, and magazines
こ	（個）	any object, especially small and solid ones, such as balls and eggs
ど	（度）	temperature

	ほん, ぼん, ぽん 本	けん, げん 軒	だい 台	まい 枚	ひき, びき, ぴき 匹	とう 頭	こ 個	さつ 冊
1	いっぽん	いっけん	いちだい	いちまい	いっぴき	いっとう	いっこ	いっさつ
2	にほん	にけん	にだい	にまい	にひき	にとう	にこ	にさつ
3	さんぼん	さんげん	さんだい	さんまい	さんびき	さんとう	さんこ	さんさつ
4	よんほん	よんけん	よんだい	よんまい	よんひき	よんとう	よんこ	よんさつ
5	ごほん	ごけん	ごだい	ごまい	ごひき	ごとう	ごこ	ごさつ
6	ろっぽん	ろっけん	ろくだい	ろくまい	ろっぴき	ろくとう	ろっこ	ろくさつ
7	ななほん	ななけん	ななだい	ななまい	ななひき	ななとう	ななこ	ななさつ
8	はっぽん	はっけん	はちだい	はちまい	はっぴき	はっとう	はっこ	はっさつ
9	きゅうほん	きゅうけん	きゅうだい	きゅうまい	きゅうひき	きゅうとう	きゅうこ	きゅうさつ
10	じゅっぽん	じゅっけん	じゅうだい	じゅうまい	じゅっぴき	じゅっとう	じゅっこ	じゅっさつ
?	なんぼん	なんげん	なんだい	なんまい	なんびき	なんとう	なんこ	なんさつ

6. **Negative form of い Adjective** い **adj.** くありません、い **adj.** くない **(です)**

Unlike their English counterparts, Japanese adjectives change their form according to style (plain/polite), tense (non-past/past), and affirmation/negation. The negative form of い adjectives can be obtained by replacing 〜い with 〜くない for plain style, and replacing 〜いです with either 〜くないです or 〜くありません for polite style. 〜くないです sounds a bit stronger than 〜くありません. Note/ Remember the adjective いい becomes よくありません. いくありません does not occur.

映画はあまり長くありません。　The movie is not very long.

明日はぜんぜん忙しくないです。I am not busy at all tomorrow.

7. **Making a comparative statement X** は **Y** より〜

The above construction is used to make a comparative statement in which you compare the first item X, which is also the topic of the sentence, to the second item Y. It corresponds to "X is more - than Y" in English.

北海道は九州より広いです。　　Hokkaido is more spacious than Kyushu.

春休みは冬休みより長いですか。

Is the spring break longer than the winter break?

8. **Answering a comparative question X/Y** のほうが〜

〜のほうが is used to answer comparative questions. Place your choice before のほうが, and end your response by putting an applicable description after のほうが.

A: 夏休みと冬休みとどちらが長いですか。

Which is longer - the summer break or winter break?

B: 夏休みの方が長いです。　　The summer break is longer.

9. **Similarity statements: X** は **Y** と(ほぼ)同じです。**X** は **Y** と **Z** が (ほぼ) 同じです。**X** は **Y** と同じくらい〜です。

The three constructions above correspond to "X is (just about) the same as Y," "X is (just about) the same as Y in terms of Z," and "X is as~ as Y" in English, respectively. See the examples below.

今日の気温は昨日の気温と(ほぼ)同じです。

Today's temperature is (just about) the same as yesterday's temperature.

東京はニューヨークと人口が(ほぼ)同じですか。

Does Tokyo have (just about) the same amount of population as New York?

シンガポールはハワイと同じくらい暑いですか。

Is it as hot in Singapore as it is in Hawaii?

10. Comparative statement: X は Y ほど + negative form of adjective

The construction above makes an English equivalent of "X is not so much - as Y."

図書館は体育館ほど広くありません。

> The library is not as spacious as the gym.

トムさんの寮はリンダさんの寮ほど静かじゃありません。

> Tom's dormitory is not as quiet as Linda's dormitory.

Compare the following:

数学のテストは化学のテストほど難かしくありません。

> Math tests are not as difficult as chemistry tests.

数学のテストは化学のテストよりやさしいです。

> Math tests are easier than chemistry tests.

Both sentences basically indicate the same thing. However, the first sentence tends to imply that the math tests are also difficult, but they are not as difficult as the (super difficult) chemistry tests. The second sentence, on the other hand, will not warrant the same assumption, partly because of the presence of やさしい. Keep this difference in mind and you will be able to choose a construction that is more suitable to your claim.

11. Adverbs for indicating degree or extent of a state

A list of useful adverbs is given below. The numbers represent a rating for each word with 6 being "very much" and 0 being "not at all." Both あまり and ぜんぜん are followed by the negative predicate. You may notice that most of the quantifiers introduced earlier can also be used to indicate degree or extent of a state. まあまあ may be used by itself.

6 —	とても (very much)
5 —	かなり (considerably)
4 —	けっこう (fairly)
3 —	まあまあ (so-so)
2 —	すこし (a little)
1 —	あまり (not so much)
0 —	ぜんぜん (not at all)

月曜日はかなり忙しいです。
> I am quite busy on Mondays.

A: 雪の日は多いですか。
> Do you have many snowy days?

B: はい、けっこう多いです。
> Yes, we have a fair number of snowy days.

C: いいえ、あまり多くありません。
> No, we don't have many snowy days.

12. Expressing uncertainty or probability: -でしょう

When you end your speech with でしょう rather than です, you indicate that what you have said may well happen to be the case, but not for certain. テストはあしたでしょう and あしたはさむいでしょう mean "The test will probably be tomorrow" and "It will probably be cold tomorrow" respectively. でしょう can also follow a plain form of a verb, such as the dictionary form. For example, サラはダンスにいくでしょう means "Sara will go to the dance in all likelihood." たぶん is an adverb that corresponds to "probably" or "perhaps" and is often used with -でしょう in daily conversations.

明日の天気はくもりでしょう。	It will probably be cloudy tomorrow.
A: 明日も雪が降りますか。	Will it snow again tomorrow?
B: たぶん、降るでしょう。	Yes, it will snow most likely.

13. Making potential statements: Dictionary Form of Verb + ことができます

The construction above makes an English equivalent of "one can do such and such." You can make this negative by simply replacing できます with できません.

その川の水はきれいです。だから、泳ぐことができます。

        The water in the river is clean. So you can swim.

その川の水は汚いです。だから、泳ぐことができません。

        The water in the river is dirty. So you cannot swim.

14. Modifying nouns by plain-style sentences

あかいくるま (a red car), きびしいコーチ (a strict coach), すてきなひと (an attractive person) -- these are examples of a noun being modified by an adjective. あかい, きびしい and すてきな are added to provide specific information about くるま, コーチ, and ひと respectively. In Japanese, a noun can be modified not only by an adjective but also by a sentence. When such modification occurs, the sentence is placed before the noun it modifies. For example, if you want to say "time when one goes to school" in Japanese, you have to place the "one goes to school" part in its plain form (the dictionary form in this example) before "time." A sentence modifying a noun is called the relative clause, and the noun being modified is called the head noun. There is no need to find a Japanese equivalent of a clause introducing pronouns, such as "when" in "time when one goes to school" in Japanese, since the Japanese relative clause construction does not require such pronouns. Compare the following.

When the subject needs to be specified within a relative clause, it should be marked by が. の is also possible but let's concentrate on が at this time.

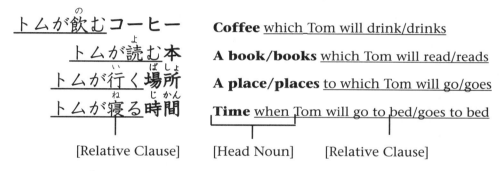

15. Topic sentences and supporting sentences

A paragraph represents a constellation of thought or ideas using a group of sentences. Each culture or language has its own logical pattern by which thoughts and ideas are organized and expressed. For example, Japanese poetic tradition has different systematic patterns from English expository writing and we hope you will have an opportunity to learn about this in the later volumes of Kisetsu. For now, you will practice writing a paragraph in Japanese by following the same format as you would follow in expository writing in English. In Japan many scholastic, business, and scientific writings are done according to this format. A typical paragraph consists of a topic sentence and several supporting sentences. The topic sentence clearly states the main idea of the paragraph, and the supporting sentences effectively uphold and reinforce the main idea.

VOCABULARY

Functional Vocabulary

	Formal	Informal	English
Indicating existence of X1 (animate) and X2 (inanimate) in Place Y	YにX1がいます。	YにX1がいる。	There is X1 at/in Y.
	YにX2があります。	YにX2がある。	There is X2 at/in Y.
Indicating existence of Topic X1 (animate) and Topic X2 (inanimate) in Place Y	TX1はYにいます。	TX1はYにいる。	TX1 is at/in Y.
	TX2はYにあります。	TX2はYにある。	TX2 is at/in Y.
Indicating existence of X1 and X2 in Topic Place Y	TYにはX1がいます。	TYにはX1がいる。	At/in TY, there is X1.
	TYにはX2があります。	TYにはX2がある。	At/in TY, there is X2.
Indicating relative position of X1 and X2 in reference to Y	YのPWにX1がいます。	YのPWにX1がいる。	There is X1/X2 in such and such a position in reference to Y.
	YのPWにX2があります。 (PW = positional word)	YのPWにX2がある。	
Indicating relative position of Topic X1 and Topic X2 in reference to Y	TX1はYのPWにいます。	TX1はYのPWにいる。	TX1/TX2 is in such and such a position in reference to Y.
	TX2はYのPWにあります。 (PW = positional word)	TX2はYのPWにある。	
Describing non-past negative state	い-adj.(root) くありません。	い-adj.(root) くない。	It is not i-adjective.
	い-adj.(root) くないです。		
	な-adj. じゃありません。	な-adj. じゃない。	It is not na-adjective
Comparative statements	TXはYより い-adj. です。	TXはYより い-adj. 。	TX is more i-adj. than Y.
	TXはYより な-adj. です。	TXはYより な-adj. 。	TX is more na-adj. than Y.
	TXはYほど negative adj。	TXはYほど negative adj。	TX is not as adj. as Y.
Answering comparative questions	X のほうが い-adj. です。	X のほうが い-adj. 。	X is more i-adj. (than Y).
	X のほうが な-adj. です。	X のほうが な-adj.だ。	X is more na-adj. (than Y).
Potential statement	V(dict.) -ことができます。	V(dict.) -ことができる。	be able to ~ verb
Similarity Statements	XはYと(ほぼ)おなじです。	XはYと(ほぼ)おなじだ。	X is (just about) the same as Y.
	XはYとZが(ほぼ)おなじです。	XはYとZが(ほぼ)おなじだ。	X is (just about) the same as Y in terms of Z.

	Formal	Informal	English
Similarity statement	XはYとおなじくらい-です。	XはYとおなじくらいだ。	X is as~ as Y.
Indicating uncertainty or probability	-でしょう。	-だろう。	It is probably -.

Notional Vocabulary

Administrative Units

まち	町	town
し	市	city
むら	村	village

Animals

どうぶつ	動物	animal
いぬ	犬	dog
ねこ	猫	cat
ライオン		lion
へび	蛇	snake
うま	馬	horse
うさぎ	兎	rabbit
さる	猿	monkey
とら	虎	tiger

Adverbs

たくさん	沢山	many, a lot
かなり	可成り	considerably
けっこう	結構	a fair amount
まあまあ		a so-so amount
すこし	少し	a little
あまり (neg. predicate)	余り	not much
ぜんぜん (neg. pred.)	全然	not at all
たとえば	例えば	for example

Bingo Games

たんご	単語	word
くばる	配る	distribute
まるでかこむ	円で囲む	put a circle
てをあげる	手を上げる	raise a hand
ジャッジをする		judge (verb)
ボードにかく	ボードに書く	write on a board
ビンゴシート		bingo sheet

リーチ		reach
リスト		list
やくわり	役割	role
はじめに	始めに	first (of all)
つぎに	次に	next
まだ		still
おめでとう		congratulations

Categories for describing towns

がっこう	学校	school
しせつ	施設	facilities
しぜん	自然	nature
てんき	天気	weather
れきし	歴史	history
かんきょう	環境	environment
じんこう	人口	population
こうつう	交通	transportation
みせ	店	store
いえ	家	house
かいしゃ	会社	company
こうじょう	工場	factory

Connection Words

それから	after that, and then
そして	and then
それに	furthermore
でも	but, however
だから	that is why

Counters

ほん、ぼん、ぽん	本	long cylindrical items
まい	枚	thin, flat items
けん、げん	軒	stores, houses
だい	台	machines items

ひき、びき、ぴき	匹	small animals
とう	頭	large animals
さつ	冊	bound items
こ	個	any solid object
じかん	時間	hours
ふん、ぶん、ぷん	分	minutes
にち、か	日	days
じょすうし	助数詞	counters

Descriptive Words

あたらしい	新しい	new
ふるい	古い	old
しずか(な)	静か(な)	quiet
うるさい	煩い	noisy
いい	(良い)	good
よい	良い	good
わるい	悪い	bad
あかるい	明るい	light, bright
くらい	暗い	dark
あたたかい	暖かい	warm
すずしい	涼しい	cool
きれい(な)	綺麗(な)	clean, beautiful
きたない	汚い	dirty
たかい	高い	expensive, high
やすい	安い	inexpensive, cheap
ひくい	低い	low (vertical length)
おおきい	大きい	large, big
ちいさい	小さい	small
やさしい	優しい	kind
やさしい	易しい	easy
むずかしい	難しい	difficult
ひろい	広い	spacious, wide
せまい	狭い	narrow, cramped
ながい	長い	long
みじかい	短い	short
はやい	速い	fast
おそい	遅い	slow, late
ちかい	近い	near
とおい	遠い	far away
おいしい	美味しい	delicious
まずい	不味い	bad-tasting
おおい	多い	many, much
すくない	少ない	few, little
おもしろい	面白い	interesting
つまらない	詰らない	boring
ただしい	正しい	correct
つよい	強い	strong

よわい	弱い	weak
きびしい	厳しい	severe, strict, harsh
すばらしい	素晴しい	wonderful
くわしい	詳しい	detailed, be versed
きもちがいい	気持ちがいい	pleasant
くろい	黒い	black (adj.)
あおい	青い	blue (adj.)
ゆうめい(な)	有名(な)	famous
いろいろ(な)	色々(な)	various
じゅうよう(な)	重要(な)	important
ひつよう(な)	必要(な)	necessary
せいかく(な)	正確(な)	accurate
ろんりてき(な)	論理的(な)	logical
べんり(な)	便利(な)	convenient
ふべん(な)	不便(な)	inconvenient

Dining and Restaurants

レストラン		restaurant
コーヒーショップ		coffee shop
りょうり	料理	food, cooking
イタリアりょうり	イタリア料理	Italian food, cuisine
インドりょうり	インド料理	Indian food, cuisine
メキシコりょうり	メキシコ料理	Mexican food, cuisine
パスタ		pasta
ねだん	値段	price

Directions

ほうがく	方角	direction
ひがし	東	east
にし	西	west
みなみ	南	south
きた	北	north
ほくとう/とうほく	北東/東北	northeast
なんとう/とうなん	南東/東南	southeast
ほくせい/せいほく	北西/西北	northwest
なんせい/せいなん	南西/西南	southwest

Events and Gatherings

ぎょうじ	行事	event
もよおし	催し	gathering, event
ファッションショー		fashion show
ロックコンサート		rock concert
スノーフェスティバル		snow festival
ヨガ		yoga
おりがみ	折り紙	*origami*

「カサブランカ」	(movie title)	"Casablanca"
「ゴジラ」	(movie title)	"Godzilla"
タウンミーティング		town meeting
キャンプ		camp
ダンス		dance
パーティー		party

Existence (Verbs)

| います／いる | 居る | exist (animate) |
| あります／ある | 在る（有る） | exist, (have) (inanimate) |

Facilities

しせつ	施設	facilities
こうきょうしせつ	公共施設	public facilities
ごらくしせつ	娯楽施設	entertainment facilities
としょかん	図書館	library
こうばん	交番	police box
けいさつ	警察	police
ゆうびんきょく	郵便局	post office
しょうぼうしょ	消防署	fire station
えき	駅	train station
びょういん	病院	hospital
びじゅつかん	美術館	fine art museum
こうみんかん	公民館	community center
たいいくかん	体育館	gymnasium
プール		swimming pool
ぎんこう	銀行	bank
えいがかん	映画館	movie theater
こうえん	公園	public park
こうどう	講堂	auditorium
どうぶつえん	動物園	zoo
ゆうえんち	遊園地	amusement park
しょうてんがい	商店街	shopping arcade
トイレ		toilet, bathroom
こうじょう	工場	factory
くうこう	空港	airport
こうそうビル	高層ビル	high-rise building
こうそくどうろ	高速道路	highway
かいしゃ	会社	company
(お)てら	寺	temple
じんじゃ	神社	shinto shrine
ショッピングモール		shopping mall
ディスコ		disco
デイケアセンター		day care center
ゲームセンター		game center
スポーツセンター		sports center

テニスコート		tennis court
ヘルスクラブ		health club
ジョギングコース		jogging course
ジム		gym
コンサートホール		concert hall
ボウリングじょう	ボウリング場	bowling alley
りょう	寮	dormitory
ようちえん	幼稚園	kindergarten

Geography

イギリス		England
カナダ		Canada
フランス		France
アイオワ		Iowa
オレゴン		Oregon
カリフォルニア		California
テキサス		Texas
ニューヨーク		New York
ハワイ		Hawaii
フロリダ		Florida
メーンしゅう	メーン州	(state of) Maine
ワイオミング		Wyoming
シカゴ		Chicago
ツーソン		Tuson
ボストン		Boston
ホノルル		Honolulu
シドニー		Sydney
ジャカルタ		Jakarta
トロント		Toronto
ナイロビ		Nairobi
ベルリン		Berlin
モスクワ		Moscow
イエローストーンこくりつこうえん		
イエローストーン国立公園		Yellowstone National Park
ところ	所	place
ちず	地図	map

Japanese Cities

わっかない	稚内	Wakkanai
さっぽろ	札幌	Sapporo
せんだい	仙台	Sendai
にいがた	新潟	Niigata
とうきょう	東京	Tokyo
ながの	長野	Nagano
きょうと	京都	Kyoto
ひろしま	広島	Hiroshima

こうち	高知	Kochi
かごしま	鹿児島	Kagoshima
なは	那覇	Naha

Measurement

～ど	～度	- degree
メートル		meter
ミリ（メートル）		millimeter
センチ（メートル）		centimeter
インチ		inch
フィート		foot

Miscellaneous words

アルバイト		part-time job
テーブル		table
ボール		ball
ピンク		pink
みどり	緑	green
オレンジ		orange
ふんすい	噴水	fountain
ベンチ		bench
ランプ		lamp
ラジカセ		radio/cassette player
シャツ		shirt
ざっし	雑誌	magazine
きょうざい	教材	teaching materials
しゅくだい	宿題	homework
ひかく	比較	comparison
よるのシフト	夜のシフト	night shift
トラック		truck
のりもの	乗り物	ride, vehicle
クーラー		air conditioner
みず	水	water
はな	花	flower
だいたい	大体	for the most part
ぜんぶ	全部	all, the whole
かもく	科目	academic subject
ダウンコート		down coat
DVD	ディーブイディー	digital versatile disc
CD	シーディー	compact disc

Nature and Environment

しぜん	自然	nature
かんきょう	環境	environment
やま	山	mountain
うみ	海	sea, ocean, beach
かわ	川	river
もり	森	forest
き	木	tree
みずうみ	湖	lake
いけ	池	pond
たき	滝	waterfall
さばく	砂漠	desert
たんぼ	田んぼ	rice paddy
た	田	rice paddy
はやし	林	woods
はたけ	畑	agricultural field
かいがん	海岸	seashore

Paragraph Writing

トピックセンテンス		topic sentence
サポートセンテンス		supporting sentence
れい	例	example
ひょうか	評価	evaluation
きじゅん	基準	criterion, standard
フィードバック		feedback
ろんりてきに	論理的に	logically
せいかくに	正確に	accurately
てきせつに	適切に	appropriately
くわしく	詳しく	in detail
おもしろく	面白く	in an interesting-manner

People

おとこのひと	男の人	man, male
おんなのひと	女の人	woman, female
わかもの	若者	young people
ともだち	友達	friend
わたしたち	私達	we (pronoun)
コーチ		coach
ボランティア		volunteer

Positional Words

うえ	上	up, upward, above
した	下	below, underneath
なか	中	inside
そと	外	outside, outdoor
ひだり	左	left
みぎ	右	right
まえ	前	front
うしろ	後ろ	rear, back, behind

ちかく	近く	near
まんなか	真ん中	center
そば	側	beside, near
よこ	横	side
となり	隣	next-door, adjoining
まわり	回り	around, surrounding
いち	位置	position, location

Stores and Shopping

みせ	店	store
かいもの	買い物	shopping
しょうてんがい	商店街	shopping arcade
はなや	花屋	flower shop
くだものや	果物屋	fruits store
さかなや	魚屋	fish market
にくや	肉屋	butcher
パンや	パン屋	bakery
やおや	八百屋	vegetable store
ケーキや	ケーキ屋	cake shop
ほんや	本屋	bookstore
おもちゃや	おもちゃ屋	toy store
くすりや	薬屋	pharmacy
レンタルビデオや	レンタルビデオ屋	video rental store
レストラン		restaurant
コーヒーショップ		coffee shop
デパート		department store
スーパー		supermarket
コンビニ		convenience store
ドラッグストア		drugstore

Verbs

つくる	作る	make
できる	出来る	can do
れんしゅうする	練習する	practice
くばる	配る	distribute
えらぶ	選ぶ	choose
かこむ	囲む	surround, enclose
さく	咲く	bloom
あそぶ	遊ぶ	play (for fun)
しょうかいする	紹介する	introduce
かくにんする	確認する	confirm
およぐ	泳ぐ	swim
つかう	使う	use
かりる	借りる	borrow
なる	成る	become

ちがう	違う	differ
わかる	分る	understand
ひかくする	比較する	compare
おしえる	教える	teach
ふる	降る	drop (rain, etc.) fall
やむ	止む	(sound, rain, etc.) stop

Weather and Natural Disaster

てんき	天気	weather
はれ	晴れ	sunny
くもり	曇り	cloudy
あめ	雨	rain
ゆき	雪	snow
はれのひ	晴れの日	sunny day
かぜ	風	wind
かみなり	雷	thunder
らいう	雷雨	thunder storm
たいふう	台風	typhoon
きおん	気温	(air) temperature
しつど	湿度	humidity
せっし／セし	摂氏／セ氏	centigrade, Celsius
かし／カし	華氏／カ氏	Fahrenheit
～ど	～度	- degree
こうすいりょう	降水量	amount of precipitation
せきせつりょう	積雪量	amount of snow accumulation
マイナス		minus
かぜがつよい	風が強い	windy
かぜがふく	風が吹く	wind blows
じしん	地震	earthquake
つなみ	津波	*tsunami*
ふぶき	吹雪	snowstorm
こおる	凍る	freeze
つゆ	梅雨	rainy season
あつい	暑い	hot
むしあつい	蒸し暑い	hot and humid
さむい	寒い	cold
あたたかい	暖かい	(comfortably) warm
すずしい	涼しい	(comfortably) cool
きびしい	厳しい	severe, strict
きもちがいい	気持ちがいい	pleasant
つきべつ	月別	monthly
へいきん	平均	average
せきせつ	積雪	snowfall
あらし	嵐	storm

399

3.8 Virtual Reality 実践
Writing About Your Town
町について書く

Overview

In the Mechanics sections, you have learned about basic paragraph writing step by step. Starting with the creation of a topic sentence, you have practiced developing your paragraph by adding supporting sentences and examples. You have also learned to make a "sum-up" paragraph in which you reiterate your main point. In Virtual Reality you will write both the main and the sum-up paragraphs entirely on your own. You may write about anything you like as long as it is related to your town. You may compile everyone's creation at the end and make a booklet about your town.

Preliminary Activities
前作業

9	Decide upon a topic	トピックを決める
10	Learn vocabulary	語彙を学ぶ
11	Confirm the structure	構造の確認をする

Main Activity
本作業

| 12 | Create your work | 作品を書く |

| 13 | Evaluate and reflect | 評価と振り返りをする |

Wrap-up Activities
後作業

| 14 | Make a hand-written version | 原稿用紙に書く |

Optional

| 15 | Make a booklet | 小冊子を作る |

9 | **Decide upon a topic**   トピックを決^きめる

Decide what you will write about. Any town-related topic will be fine, but you must make sure that it will be something about which you can collect enough information and that you can describe without using too many new words and expressions.

10 | **Learn vocabulary**   語彙^{ごい}を学^{まな}ぶ

Make a list of any new words and expressions you will need in your writing. Then find out their Japanese equivalent by using dictionaries, checking the vocabulary sections and glossaries of this book, and by asking your teachers and classmates.

11 | **Confirm the structure**   構造^{こうぞう}の確認^{かくにん}をする

You will follow the same structure as you did when you wrote about your town's winter weather in the previous section.   In fact you may turn to that section for a step-by-step guidance of your work.

TOPIC SENTENCE	
SUPPORTING SENTENCE 1	
EXAMPLE 1 EXAMPLE 2 EXAMPLE 3	
SUPPORTING SENTENCE 2	
EXAMPLE 1 EXAMPLE 2 EXAMPLE 3	
"SUM-UP" PARAGRAPH	

12 Create your work　　さくひん
作品を書く

Now it's time to start writing. Good luck.

13 Evaluate and reflect　　ひょうか　ふ　かえ
評価と振り返りをする

You may conduct self-and peer-evaluations in the same manner as you did in the previous section. After exchanging feedback with your classmates, reflect on your experience by using the "Checklist for Reflection."

	はい、たいへん	はい、だいたい	はい、まあまあ	いいえ、あまり
Logical sequence ろんりてき 論理的に書きましたか。	The information sequence is always logical, coherent, and easy to follow.	The information sequence is mostly logical, coherent, and easy to follow.	The information sequence is not always logical, coherent, and easy to follow.	The information sequence is problematic and not easy to follow.
Details くわ 詳しく書きましたか。	All examples are very appropriate and they effectively add details to the topic and supporting sentences.	Most examples are appropriate and they effectively add details to the topic and supporting sentences.	Examples are adequate and they add details to the topic and supporting sentences.	Examples are not very adequate and do not always match well with the topic and supporting sentences.
Accuracy せいかく 正確に書きましたか。	The text has little or no grammatical, spelling and usage errors.	The text has grammatical, spelling, and usage errors, for the most part.	The text has more than a few grammatical, spelling,and usage errors.	The text has many grammatical, spelling, and usage errors.
Content おもしろ 面白く書きましたか。	The content is very interesting and masterfully elaborated. It also has no factual errors.	The content is interesting and well-elaborated, for the most part. It also has no factual errors.	The content is modestly interesting and adequately elaborated. It also may contain a few factual errors.	The content is not very interesting and not well-elaborated. It also may contain many factual errors.

Checklist for Reflection

	Yes, absolutely positive			Don't think so

1. I made a good choice for my topic.

2. I was able to find and learn all the words and expressions needed to complete my work.

3. I organized my ideas before I started writing.

4. I was able to make a good topic sentence.

5. I was able to make good supporting sentences.

6. My examples were all effective and appropriate.

7. I was able to make a good sum-up paragraph.

8. I was able to create a logical and coherent work.

9. I used kanji whenever I could.

10. My work was grammatically accurate.

11. My work had no spelling and kanji errors.

12. My work had no factual discrepancies.

13. My classmates found my work interesting.

14. I found feedbacks from my classmates very helpful .

15. The quality of my writing was reflective of the quality of my preparation.

16. CREATE YOUR OWN STATEMENT.

Your Comments

14 Make a hand-written version 原稿用紙に書きます

You have already become quite accustomed to using げんこうようし (Japanese style writing pads), haven't you?

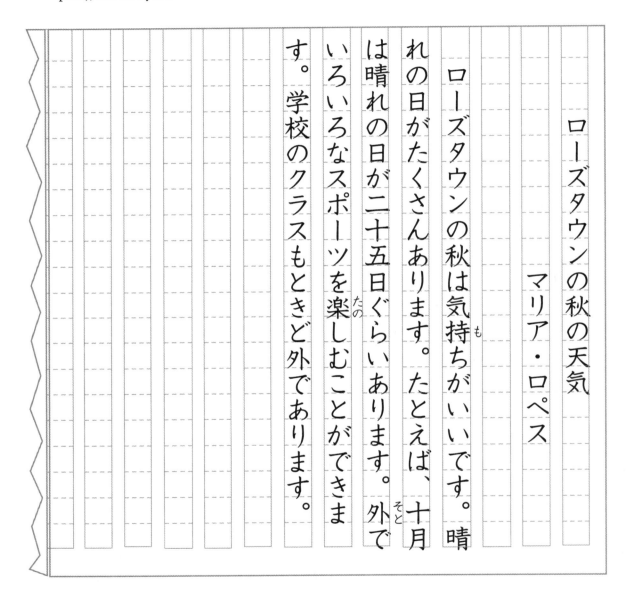

ローズタウンの秋の天気

マリア・ロペス

ローズタウンの秋は気持ちがいいです。晴れの日がたくさんあります。たとえば、十月は晴れの日が二十五日ぐらいあります。外でいろいろなスポーツを楽しむことができます。学校のクラスもときどき外であります。

14 Make a booklet (Optional) 小冊子を作る

Since everyone has written something about their towns, why not put them together and make a little Japanese booklet!

SUM-UP

1. **What differences do you find between your town and a Japanese town?**

2. **Writing about your environment in Japanese is: (circle one)**

    a. very difficult

    b. difficult

    c. easy

    d. very easy

3. **What do you think about the structure of expository writing?**

4. **How did you compare your town with a Japanese town during your writing?**

5. **Did you make any progress in your paragraph writing ability? Please rate your progress on a scale of 0 to 5. (0 = no progress, 5 = excellent progress)**

0	1	2	3	4	5

6. **Were you able to use the paragraph-writing analogical and /or attributional strategies? Please rate your progress on a scale of 0 to 5. (0 = no progress, 5 = excellent progress)**

0	1	2	3	4	5

ADDITIONAL VOCABULARY

Notional Vocabulary

Administrative Units

ぐん	郡	county
しゅう	州	state
とし	都市	city, urban area
けん	県	prefecture
く	区	ward

Bingo Games

かち	勝ち	win (noun)
まけ	負け	loss
けっか	結果	result
はんそく	反則	violation of rules
じゅんばん	順番	turn, order

Categories for Describing Towns

ふくし	福祉	welfare
きこう	気候	climate
ぎょうじ	行事	event
たてもの	建物	building
めいさん	名産	speciality (product)
めいしょ	名所	place of interest
かんこう	観光	tourism, sightseeing
ぎょうせい	行政	administration
ざいせい	財政	finance

Counters

しゅうかん	週間	weeks
かげつ	ヵ月	months

Descriptive Words

はやい	早い	early
さわやか(な)	爽やか(な)	refreshing, delightful
かいてき(な)	快適(な)	comfortable, pleasant
にぎやか(な)	賑やか(な)	lively, bustling
てきせつ(な)	適切(な)	appropriate
へん(な)	変(な)	strange
きけん(な)	危険(な)	dangerous
あんぜん(な)	安全(な)	safe
じゆう(な)	自由(な)	free
ユニーク(な)	ユニーク(な)	unique
きんだいてき(な)	近代的(な)	modern
でんとうてき(な)	伝統的(な)	traditional
しんぽてき(な)	進歩的(な)	progressive
ほしゅてき(な)	保守的(な)	conservative
しゅうきょうてき(な)	宗教的(な)	religious
みりょくてき(な)	魅力的(な)	appealing, charming

かつどうてき(な)	活動的(な)	active

Dining and Restaurants

しょくどう	食堂	dining room, restaurant
いっぱんしょくどう	一般食堂	general restaurant
にほんりょうりてん	日本料理店	Japanese restaurant
せいようりょうりてん	西洋料理店	Western restaurant
ちゅうかりょうりてん	中華料理店	Chinese restaurant
アジアりょうりてん	アジア料理店	Asian restaurant
タイりょうりてん	タイ料理店	Thai restaurant
そばや	蕎麦屋	*soba* noodle shop
うどんや	うどん屋	*udon* noodle shop
ラーメンや	ラーメン屋	*ramen* noodle shop
すしや	鮨屋、寿司屋	sushi restaurant
カフェ		cafe
きっさてん	喫茶店	coffee shop
がいしょく	外食	eating out
りょうり	料理	food, cooking
ファストフード		fast food
フードコート		food court
ねだん	値段	price
サービス		service
ちゅうもん(する)	注文(する)	(to) order
でまえ(する)	出前(する)	(to) deliver

Events and Gatherings

スポーツたいかい	スポーツ大会	athletic tournament
こくさいこうりゅう	国際交流	international exchange
しあい	試合	game, match
フェア		fair
バザー		bazaar
フリーマーケット		flea market
ガレージセール		garage sale
ベークセール		bake sale
てんらんかい	展覧会	exhibit
べんきょうかい	勉強会	study group
ワークショップ		workshop
オークション		auction
どくしょクラブ	読書クラブ	book club
スクエアダンス		square dance
せいじしゅうかい	政治集会	political rally
どうそうかい	同窓会	(school) reunion

Facilities

ふくししせつ	福祉施設	welfare facilities
かいごしせつ	介護施設	nursing care facilities

きょういくしせつ	教育施設	educational facilities
やくしょ	役所	government office
しやくしょ	市役所	city hall
まちやくば	町役場	town hall
しゅうちょうしゃ	州庁舎	state office building
ぎじどう	議事堂	assembly-hall
さいばんしょ	裁判所	courthouse
けいむしょ	刑務所	prison, jail
たいしかん	大使館	embassy
りょうじかん	領事館	consulate
はくぶつかん	博物館	museum
すいぞくかん	水族館	aquarium
しょくぶつえん	植物園	botanical garden
いいん	医院	clinic
ようろういん	養老院	nursing home
しんりょうじょ	診療所	clinic
けんきゅうじょ	研究所	research institute
あんないじょ	案内所	information center
はつでんしょ	発電所	power plant
げんしりょくはつでんしょ	原子力発電所	nuclear power plant
テレビきょく	テレビ局	TV station
ラジオきょく	ラジオ局	radio station
プラネタリウム		planetarium
ショッピングセンター		shopping center
コンベンションセンター		convention center
おてあらい	お手洗い	bathroom, toilet
はし	橋	bridge
みなと	港	sea port
ダム		dam
ていぼう	堤防	bank, embankment
ぼくじょう	牧場	ranch
のうじょう	農場	farm
どうろ	道路	road
きょうかい	教会	church
モスク		mosque
シナゴーグ		synagogue
ヘルスクラブ		health club
スタジアム		stadium
げきじょう	劇場	theater
ボウリングじょう	ボウリング場	bowling alley
ゴルフじょう	ゴルフ場	golf course
サッカーじょう	サッカー場	soccer field
やきゅうじょう	野球場	baseball field
うんどうじょう	運動場	ground, playground
おくないプール	屋内プール	indoor swimming pool
キャンプじょう	キャンプ場	campground
スキーじょう	スキー場	ski slope/resort
スケートリンク		skating rink

ホテル		hotel
ガソリンスタンド		gas station
サービスステーション		gas station
じどうしゃしゅうりこうじょう	自動車修理工場	(auto repair) garage
そうごうたいいくかん	総合体育館	composite gymnasium
アパート		apartment
だんち	団地	a housing complex
じゅうたく	住宅	residence, housing
じゅうたくち	住宅地	residential area
りょかん	旅館	Japanese inn
ちゅうしゃじょう	駐車場	parking lot
ちゅうりんじょう	駐輪場	bicycle parking lot
じてんしゃおきば	自転車置き場	bicycle parking lot
やたい	屋台	a street stall
ターミナル		terminal
きち	基地	base

Government

しちょう	市長	mayor
ちょうちょう	町長	town manager, mayor
そんちょう	村長	village chief, mayor
ちじ	知事	governor
ほあんかん	保安官	sheriff
せんきょ	選挙	election
にんき	任期	one's term of office
ぎかい	議会	council, assembly
ぎいん	議員	representative
とうひょう(する)	投票(する)	(to) vote
しまいとし	姉妹都市	sister city

Industry

さんぎょう	産業	industry
だいいちじさんぎょう	第一次産業	primary industry
だいにじさんぎょう	第二次産業	secondary industry
だいさんじさんぎょう	第三次産業	tertiary industry
のうぎょう	農業	agriculture
ぎょぎょう	漁業	fishery
りんぎょう	林業	forestry
ぼくちくぎょう	牧畜業	stock farming
せいぞうぎょう	製造業	manufacturing industry
きんゆうぎょう	金融業	financial industry
サービスぎょう	サービス業	service industry
しょうぎょう	商業	commerce
かんこうぎょう	観光業	tourism
じょうほうぎじゅつさんぎょう	情報技術産業	IT industry
ぼうえき	貿易	trade

Measurement

どりょうこう	度量衡	unit of measurement
ながさ	長さ	length
おおきさ	大きさ	size
ひろさ	広さ	(floor) size
おもさ	重さ	weight, heaviness
たかさ	高さ	height
ふかさ	深さ	depth
めんせき	面積	area
きょり	距離	distance
やく〜	約〜	approximately -
キロ（メートル）		kilometer
ヤード		yard
マイル		mile
へいほう〜	平方〜	square -
エーカー		acre

Nature and Environment

けしき	景色	scenery
へいげん	平原	prairie, plain
へいや	平野	plain
そうげん	草原	grassland
ぼんち	盆地	basin
しっちたい	湿地帯	wetland
わん	湾	bay, gulf
たに	谷	valley
しま	島	island
はんとう	半島	peninsula
かいきょう	海峡	strait
すなはま	砂浜	sand beach
しんりん	森林	woods and forest
ぬま	沼	swamp, marsh
やぶ	薮	bush, thicket
さんみゃく	山脈	mountain chain
おか	丘	hill
さか	坂	slope
がけ	崖	cliff
かざん	火山	volcano
いし	石	stone
いわ	岩	rock
こくりつこうえん	国立公園	national park
しょくぶつ	植物	plant
こうよう	紅葉	autumn foliage
かじゅえん	果樹園	orchard
すいでん	水田	paddy field
とうもろこしばたけ	玉蜀黍畑	cornfield
たいきおせん	大気汚染	air pollution

Population

こくじん	黒人	black people
アフリカけいアメリカじん		
	アフリカ系アメリカ人	African-American
はくじん	白人	white people
ラテンけい	ラテン系	Latino
アジアけい	アジア系	Asian
アジアじん	アジア人	Asian
ネイティブアメリカン		Native American
イヌイット		Inuit
いみん	移民	immigrant

Positional Words

むこうがわ	向こう側	the other side
はんたいがわ	反対側	the opposite side/end
りょうがわ	両側	both sides
ひがしがわ	東側	eastern side/end
にしがわ	西側	western side/end
きたがわ	北側	northern side/end
みなみがわ	南側	southern side/end
とうぶ	東部	eastern part
せいぶ	西部	western part
ほくぶ	北部	northern part
なんぶ	南部	southern part
はし	端	end, edge

Stores and Shopping

ショッピングセンター		shopping center
くすりや	薬屋	pharmacy
ぶんぼうぐや	文房具屋	stationery store
カメラや	カメラ屋	camera shop
おかしや	お菓子屋	confectionery store
ビデオや	ビデオ屋	video (rental) shop
おみやげや	お土産屋	souvenir shop
じてんしゃや	自転車屋	bicycle shop
りょこうだいりてん	旅行代理店	travel agency
かなものや	金物屋	hardware store
じどうしゃはんばいてん		
	自動車販売店	automobile dealer
ちゅうこしゃはんばいてん		
	中古車販売店	used car dealer
ひゃくえんショップ	百円ショップ	dollar store
ピザや	ピザ屋	pizza shop
ようふくや	洋服屋	tailor shop
ようひんてん	洋品店	clothing store
ブティック		boutique
くつや	靴屋	shoe store
めがねや	眼鏡屋	optician
かぐや	家具屋	furniture store
とこや	床屋	barbershop

びょういん	美容院	beauty shop
クリーニングや	クリーニング屋	(dry) cleaner
さかや	酒屋	liquor store
サービスステーション		gas station
コインランドリー		laundromat
オーディオショップ		audio equipment store
パソコンショップ		computer store
スポーツショップ		sporting goods store
ペットショップ		pet shop
ディスカウントショップ		discount shop
アウトレットストア		outlet store
ホームセンター		home decor store
かでんりょうはんてん	家電量販店	(large, department-like) electric appliances store

Verbs

しらべる	調べる	investigate, search
かいとうする	解答する	answer
すむ	住む	reside, live
おもう	思う	think
あつめる	集める	assemble, collect
しあいする	試合する	play a match
たのしむ	楽しむ	enjoy, get pleasure
えんそうする	演奏する	perform
えんぎする	演技する	act
かんがえる	考える	consider, think
みえる	見える	be visible
はれる	晴れる	become clear/sunny
くもる	曇る	become cloudy
ふえる	増える	increase (intransitive)
へる	減る	decrease (intransitive)
かよう	通う	commute
りようする	利用する	make use of
ひかくする	比較する	compare
はたらく	働く	work
はってんする	発展する	grow, develop
はんえいする	繁栄する	prosper, thrive
すいたいする	衰退する	decline
けんせつする	建設する	build, construct
かいちくする	改築する	renovate

Weather and Natural Disaster

きこう	気候	climate
おんど	温度	(general) temperature
しっけ	湿気	moisture, humidity
はだざむい	肌寒い	chilly
さわやか(な)	爽やか(な)	refreshing, delightful
おだやか(な)	穏やか(な)	calm, mild, tranquil
おんだん(な)	温暖(な)	mild
そら	空	sky
あおぞら	青空	blue sky
くも	雲	cloud
にじ	虹	rainbow
にじがでる	虹が出る	rainbow appears
うりょう	雨量	amount of rain
こさめ	小雨	light rain
おおあめ	大雨	heavy rain
はるさめ	春雨	spring rain
こゆき	小雪	light snow
おおゆき	大雪	heavy snow
みぞれ	霙	sleet
ひょう	雹	hail
こおり	氷	ice
こおりがはる	氷が張る	be frozen over
しも	霜	frost
しもがおりる	霜が降りる	have frost
こがらし	木枯らし	bitter cold wind
はるいちばん	春一番	first spring wind
もうしょ	猛暑	heat wave
ハリケーン		hurricane
たつまき	竜巻	tornado
ゆきかき	雪掻き	shoveling of snow
さいがい	災害	calamity, disaster
こうずい	洪水	flood
かんばつ	旱魃	drought
なだれ	雪崩	avalanche
じしん	地震	earthquake
やまかじ	山火事	forest fire

Sightseeing at New York

かんこうあんない	観光案内	sightseeing guide
ばしょ	場所	place
ぜひ	是非	by all means
できるだけ		as possible as
グリニッチ・ビレッジ		Greenwich Village
ワシントン・スクエアー・パーク		Washington Square Park
ベーグル		bagel
ウィンドーショッピング		window shopping
ユニオン・スクエアー・パーク		Union Square Park
グリーン・マーケット		green market
ハイライン		High Line
とおる	通る	pass
いくまえ	行く前	before going
けんがく	見学	visit
えんそう	演奏	performance
きける	聞ける	can listen
そう	沿う	along
ほそながい	細長い	long and narrow
むかし	昔	old, long ago
こうかてつどう	高架鉄道	elevated railway
つくられた	作られた	was made
おすすめ	お勧め	recommendation
いちにちじゅう	一日中	all day along

あそぶ	遊ぶ	play
やがい	野外	outside
どうぶつえん	動物園	zoo

Sightseeing at Yokohama

よこはま	横浜	place name
みなとみらい２１ちく	港未来２１地区	Minato Mirai 21 district
ビル		building
ちゅうかがい	中華街	Chinatown
ならぶ	並ぶ	stand in line
ベイブリッジ		name of bridge
みえる	見える	can see
げんだいてき	現代的	contemporary
こくれんかんけい	国連関係	United Nations related
こくさいてき	国際的	international
はってん	発展	development
やましたこうえん	山下公園	name of park
まわり	回り	around
めいじじだい	明治時代	Meiji era (1868 -1912)
しょうわのはじめころ	昭和の始め頃	early part of the Showa era
たてもの	建物	building
のこる	残る	leave
はくぶつかん	博物館	museum
しりょうかん	資料館	museum for material
など	等	etc.
しる	知る	know
ちゅうごくりょうり	中国料理	Chinese food
ざいりょう	材料	ingredients
けいえい	経営	manage
しょうてんがい	商店街	shopping arcade
ちゅうしん	中心	center
こくさいがっこう	国際学校	international school
かんじがする	感じがする	feeling

Weather in Yokohama

あたり	辺り	vicinity
さくら	桜	cherry blossom
あちらこちら		everywhere
さく	咲く	bloom
どて	土手	riverbank
きせつ	季節	seasons
うめ	梅	plum
もも	桃	peach
チュウリップ		tulip
ちがう	違う	different
へいきんさいこうきおん	平均最高気温	average highest temperature
ゆかた	浴衣	kimono for summer

てんこう	天候	climate
てんたかく	天高く	clear air
うまこゆる	馬肥ゆる	horse gets fat
ひかくてき	比較的	comparatively
しんぱい	心配	worry
だんぼう	暖房	heater
だけ		only, just
ちこく	遅刻	late
たいいくさい	体育祭	field day, sport event
じき	時期	forest fire
きをつける	気を付ける	take care
エアコン		air conditioning
でかける	出掛ける	go out
はつとこうび	初登校日	first day for school
けど		although
いわれる	言われる	be called
いみがちがうそうです	意味が違うそうです	I heard it's a different meaning

Trip to Japan

せつめいするから	説明するから	because I will explain
おぼえる	覚える	memorize
おりる	降りる	get off
せいなんせん	西南線	Seinan line
のぼりでんしゃ	上り電車	upward bound train
よっつめのえき	四つ目の駅	fourth station
まもなく		soon
ぶんかこうえんいき	文化公園行き	bound for cultural park
かいそくでんしゃ	快速電車	intercity rapid train
まいります	参ります	come
きいろいせん	黄色い線	yellow line
おまちください	お待ち下さい	please wait
ごちゅうい	御注意	pay attention
かくえき	各駅	local train
きたぐち	北口	north exit
みなみぐち	南口	south exit
かど	角	corner
しんごう	信号	signal
わたる	渡る	pass
うら	裏	back
かかる		take (time)
こくさいかいかん	国際会館	international hall
しぜんかんきょうびょういん	自然環境病院	hospital name
じゆうとしだいがく	自由都市大学	college name
ぎんがこうこう	銀河高校	high school name
へいわびょういんいき	平和病院行き	bound for Heiwa hospital
みどりきねんえき	みどり記念駅	station name

Mini Conversation 3:
ミニ会話 3

Travel to Japan: 日本へ旅行

会話 1 （初登校日）

マイク： 　　　　行ってきます。

ホストマザー： 　学校の<u>行き方(1)</u>は大丈夫ですか。

マイク： 　　　　うーん、ちょっと心配なんですけど。

ホストマザー： 　じゃあ、説明するから覚えてください(ね)。まず家の前で平和病院
　　　　　　　　行きのバスに乗って、みどり記念駅で降ります。それから西南線の
　　　　　　　　上り電車に乗って、4つ目の駅です。学校は駅のすぐそばですよ。

マイク： 　　　　わかりました。ありがとうございます。では、行ってきます。

ホストマザー： 　行ってらっしゃい。

会話 2 （みどり記念駅）

アナウンス： 　まもなく文化公園行きの快速電車がまいります。黄色い線まで下が
　　　　　　　ってお待ちください。この電車は、次は国際会館に停まります。
　　　　　　　自由都市大学と銀河高校駅には停まりません<u>ので(2)</u>ご注意ください。

マイク： 　　　（駅にいる女性に）あのー、すみません。次の電車は銀河高校駅に
　　　　　　　停まりますか。

女性： 　　　　いいえ、停まりませんよ。次の各駅の電車まで待ってください。

マイク： 　　　わかりました。どうもありがとうございます。

会話3 （銀河高校駅から出て）

マイク： (歩いている男性に)すみません、銀河高校はどこですか。

男性： え、（→ええと）銀河高校は北口ですよ。ここは南口ですよ。

マイク： あ、しまった。間違えた。

男性： 大丈夫ですよ。ここからも行く<u>ことができます</u>。<u>(3)</u>あの本屋さんの角を右に曲がって、二つ信号を渡ってください。左側に自然環境病院があります。銀河高校はその病院の裏ですよ。

マイク： ここから何分ぐらいかかりますか。

男性： そうですねえ、5、6分かな。

マイク： そうですか。どうもありがとうございます。

Dialogue 1 (The first day of school Mike attends)

Mike: I am going to school.
Host mother: Do you know how to get to school?
Mike: Uhhh, I'm a bit worried.
Host mother: I'll explain it. So, please memorize it. At first, get on the bus in front of our house bound for The Peace Hospital, and get off at Midori Memorial Station. Then, ride the Seinan line upward bound train, and get off at the fourth station. Your school is near the station.
Mike: I understand. Thank you very much. Well, I am going.
Host mother: Take care.

Dialogue 2 (at Midori Memorial Station)

Announcement: Shortly, the intercity rapid train going to Cultural Park will be coming. Please step back behind the yellow line and wait for it. The next stop will be the International Hall. Please note that the train will not stop at the Freedom City College station and Ginga High School station.
Mike: (to a lady at the station) Excuse me, will the next train stop at the Ginga High School?
Lady: No, the train will not stop at the station. Please wait for the next local train.
Mike: I understand. Thank you very much.

Dialogue 3 (Going out from the Ginga High School station

Mike: (To a man walking) Excuse me. Where is Ginga High School?
Man: Well, the Ginga High School is located at the north exit of the station. This is the south exit of the station.
Mike: Oh my god. I made a mistake.
Man: It is all right. You can still go to the school from here. Make a right at the corner of that bookstore and pass two light signals. There will be the Natural Environmental Hospital on the left side. The Ginga High School is behind the hospital.
Mike: From here to there how many minutes does it take?
Man: Well, I believe 5 or 6 minutes.
Mike: I got it. Thank you very much.

Dialogue 1 Notes

- 初登校日：The first day of school
- いってきます：I will go.
- 学校の行き方：how to get to the school
- 大丈夫ですか：Are you al right?
- うーん：yes
- ちょっと：a little
- 心配なんですけど：I'm worried
- けど：although
- じゃあ：then
- 説明するから：I will explain so
- から：because
- 覚えてください（ね）：please memorize
- まず：at first
- 家の前で：in front of my house
- 平和病院行きのバスに：bus going to Heiwa Peace Hospital
- 乗って：ride on
- みどり記念駅で：at the Midori Memorial Station
- 降ります：get off
- それから：and then
- 西南線：Seinan line
- 上り電車：train going to Central Station/ upward bound train
- ４つ目の駅：fourth station
- 駅のすぐそばですよ：it is near the station
- わかりました：I get it
- ありがとうございます：thank you
- では、行ってきます：then, I am going
- 行ってらっしゃい：safe trip

Dialogue 2 Notes

- みどり記念駅：Midori Memorial station
- アナウンス：announcement
- まもなく：soon
- 文化公園行きの：train going to Cultural Park
- 快速電車が：intercity rapid train
- まいります：きます：humble form of "to come"
- 黄色い線まで：behind the yellow line
- 下がって：step back
- お待ちください：wait please
- 次は：next (station)
- 国際会館に：International Hall
- 停まります：stop
- 自由都市大学：Freedom City College
- 銀河高校駅：Ginga High School Station
- 停まりませんので：because it will not be stopping
- ご注意ください：pay attention
- 女性：woman
- 各駅の電車：local train

Dialogue 3 Notes

- 出て：go out
- 男性：man
- 北口：north exit
- 南口：south exit
- あ、しまった：Oh my god.
- 間違えた：made a mistake
- 大丈夫ですよ：It is OK.
- 角：corner
- 右に曲がって：turn right
- 二つ信号：second signal
- 渡ってください：please pass
- 左側に：left side
- 自然環境病院：Natural Environment Hospital
- 裏：behind
- 何分ぐらいかかりますか：How many minutes does it take?

Grammar Keys and Practice

(1) ～かた

The stem of the masu form + kata means "how to ~" in English.

Speak a sentence in Japanese using the following example. 例にならって、日本語で言いましょう。

EX. Teach me how to drink. ⇒ 飲み方を教えてください。

1. How to eat
2. How to get
3. How to study

413

(2) ～ので

～ので means "because," or "since."

Make a single sentence using the following example. 例にならって、一つの文にしましょう。

EX. シャワーをあびます。寝ます。⇒シャワーをあびたので寝ます。

1. メールをチェックします。でかけます。⇒
2. 歯をみがきます。学校に行きます。⇒
3. くつをぬぎます。うちに入ります。⇒

(3) ～こともできます

～こともできます means "be able to ～"; if indicates a possibility.

Make a single sentence using the following example. 例にならって、一つの文にしましょう。.

EX. シャワーをあびます。⇒ 暑いので、シャワーをあびることもできます。

1. 学校に行きます。⇒
2. うちに入ります。⇒
3. でかけます。⇒
4. メールをチェックします。⇒
5. 歯をみがきます。⇒

Travel Practice 1

When you arrive at your host family, you will ask your host mother how to do certain things, using ～かた.

Travel Practice 2

When you arrive at your host family, you will ask your host mother if you are able to do certain things , using ～こともできますか.

Travel Practice 3

Form pairs. One person will be the host mother in Japan. The other is an exchange student from outside of Japan. The exchange student will try to communicate with his host mother in Japanese and ask about possible issues on reasonable matters.

Travel Practice 4

Form pairs. One person will be a host for a Japanese exchange student. The other is an exchange student from Japan. You will try to communicate with your exchange student in Japanese and discuss a possible transportation route from your house to the location where your exchange student wishes to go.

Travel Practice 5

Create another activity describing host family life. Be sure that the activity is interesting and integrates cultural issues.

New Kanji 6: 新出漢字 6

社

ON: シャ　　　　　**KUN**: やしろ
社会: しゃかい society　　会社: かいしゃ company

、ラ ネ ネ ネ ー社 社

夜

ON: ヤ　　　　　**KUN**: よる、よ
夜: よる night　　　今夜: こんや tonight

、亠 广 疒 疒 夜 夜 夜

買

ON: バイ　　　　**KUN**: か(う)
買う: かう buy　　　買い物: かいもの shopping

、罒 罒 罒 罒 罒 罒 買 買 買 買 買

家

ON: カ、ケ　　　**KUN**: いえ、や、うち
家: いえ house　　　家族: かぞく family

、宀 宀 宀 宁 宁 宵 家 家 家

京

ON: キョウ、ケイ　**KUN**: ―
京: きょう capital city　　東京: とうきょう Tokyo

、亠 亠 古 古 亩 京 京

駅

ON: ―　　　　　**KUN**: えき
駅: えき station　　　東京駅: とうきょうえき Tokyo station

ー 厂 厂 厂 厍 馬 馬 馬 馬 馬 馬 馹 駅 駅

園

ON: エン　　　　**KUN**: その
公園: こうえん park　　花園: はなぞの flower garden

一 冂 冂 园 周 周 周 周 園 園 園 園 園

地

ON: チ、ジ　　　**KUN**: つち
土地: とち land　　　地下: ちか underground

ー 十 土 圫 地 地

415

Additional Kanji 8: 追加漢字 8

明治	めいじ、Meiji 明:**ON:**メイ **KUN:**あかる(い)、あ(く) 治:**ON:**ジ **KUN:**おさ(める) 明治時代は新しい時代を作りました。 Meiji era made a new era.
昭和	しょうわ、Showa 昭:**ON:**ショウ **KUN:**ー 和:**ON:**ワ **KUN:**やわ(らぐ)、なご(む) 昭和時代に戦争がありました。 There was a war in the Showa era.
建物	たてもの、building 建:**ON:**ケン **KUN:**たて(る) 物:**ON:**ブツ **KUN:**もの 現代的な建物を作ります。 I am making a modern building.
現代的	げんだいてき、modern 現:**ON:**ゲン **KUN:**あらわ(れる) 代:**ON:**ダイ **KUN:**かわ(り) 的:**ON:**テキ **KUN:**まと 現代的な建物を作ります。 I am making a modern building.
国連	こくれん、United Nations 国:**ON:**コク **KUN:**くに 連:**ON:**レン **KUN:**つら(なる)、つれ(る) 国連で話します。 I talk at the United Nations.
関係	かんけい、relation 関:**ON:**カン **KUN:**せき、かか(わる) 係:**ON:**ケイ **KUN:**かかり、かか(る) 国連関係の計画を作ります。 I am making a plan of UN relations.
船	ふね、ship 船:**ON:**セン **KUN:**ふね 新しい船に乗ります。 I am riding on a new ship.
博物館	はくぶつかん、museum 博:**ON:**ハク **KUN:**ひろ(い) 物:**ON:**ブツ **KUN:**もの 館:**ON:**カン **KUN:**やかた、たち 博物館に行きます。 I am going to the museum.
中華街	ちゅうかがい、Chinatown 中:**ON:**チュウ **KUN:**なか、うち 華:**ON:**カ **KUN:**はな 街:**ON:**ガイ **KUN:**まち 横浜の中華街は有名です。 Chinatown in Yokohama is famous.

Chapter 4
Let's Present
Your School!

Photo: Tsukasa Yokozawa ¨Parallel Lives #C1¨ 2009

Chapter 4: Let's Present Your School!

<ruby>学校<rt>がっこう</rt></ruby>を<ruby>紹介<rt>しょうかい</rt></ruby>しましょう

4.1 Introduction 序論<ruby>じょろん</ruby>

CHAPTER OBJECTIVES

AT THE END OF THIS SECTION, YOU WILL BE ABLE TO:

- plan and run student-led review sessions from start to finish

- choose a leader and select a topic for student-led review sessions

- check the progress of various tasks

- prepare several types of questions and exercises for the review sessions

- give instructions and lead language exercises

- prepare and conduct several types of warm-up exercises

- give directions for a simple physical workout

- greet the participants and introduce the topic in the review sessions

- deal with basic problems regarding class management

- conduct a question and answer session as a wrap-up

- conduct a purposeful evaluation of the review sessions

- make a list of things to do using the dictionary form of a verb

- tell someone not to do something

- recognize about 80 kanji and their basic compounds

- read and write 32 kanji and their basic compounds.

YOU WILL ALSO LEARN:

- about various types of questions and exercises

- basic instructional vocabulary

- about the dictionary form and the ない form of a verb

- how to make suggestions for consideration

- how to indicate an action in progress

- about the こそあど demonstrative words.

KISETSU THEATER 季節劇 <ruby>季<rt>き</rt></ruby><ruby>節<rt>せつ</rt></ruby><ruby>劇<rt>げき</rt></ruby>

Let's Present Your School!

学校を紹介しましょう
<ruby>学校<rt>がっこう</rt></ruby>を<ruby>紹介<rt>しょうかい</rt></ruby>しましょう

Making a booklet about your school

In this chapter you will be teaming up with some of your classmates to create a booklet in which you will introduce your school to Japanese high school students. You will write about various aspects of your school and create accompanying visuals such as photos and maps. During the course of study you will learn a substantial amount of useful vocabulary as well as sentence structure. Furthermore, you will be introduced to three writing style models that will surely improve and refine your writing skills. So let's get ready to showcase your talent as a writer, an artist, and an editor of the booklet!

Three writing style models for the school booklet

Your school booklet will be made based on three writing style models. We call the first one きそ じょうほうがた or the basic information style. A typical basic information writing style consists of sentences representing some fundamental information about school or any other theme of description. The second writing style model is called せつめいぶんがた or the expository style. You are already familiar with this style as the essay you wrote about winter weather in chapter 3 was based on this model. You may recall that your weather essay consisted of a topic sentence, supporting sentences and their examples, and sum-up sentences. The third writing style model, かんそうぶんがた, represents a kind of writing popular in Japan and therefore we will keep the name as it is. A *kansoubun* writing style consists of a leading sentence, a descriptive part, and a comment part that will include both direct comment and indirect comment sentences. The *kansoubun* style is flexible and, unlike in the expository style, you may express your feelings, opinions, and suggestions in the comment part. Take a look at the examples on the right and see which writing style you may want to use to write about certain aspects of your school.

Linking system and strategies

In this chapter you will learn various ways to join sentences. You will learn more about useful conjunctions and will be guided how to join two or more sentences by changing the ending of a connecting part. You will also learn how to use language strategies to make your writing easier to follow for your readers, and how to create complex sentences in your paragraph development. In complex sentences, the style (informal or formal) used in the main clause, determines the style of the entire sentence. Both the linking skills and the writing strategies in this chapter will help you become a competent and skillful user of the language as a whole, and not just limited to writing.

Kisetsu High School

Product

学校のパンフレット

BASIC INFORMATION STYLE
基礎情報型（きそじょうほうがた）

BASIC INFORMATION
:   :
BASIC INFORMATION
:   :
BASIC INFORMATION

私達（たち）の学校は公立（こうりつ）の共学校（きょうがくこう）です。3学期制（がっきせい）で、学年（がくねん）は9年生から12年生までです。生徒数（せいとすう）は1,300人です。女子（じょし）が700人いて、男子（だんし）が600人います。教員（きょういん）は80人います。

EXPOSITORY STYLE
説明文型（せつめいぶんがた）

TOPIC SENTENCE
SUPPORTING SENTENCE
EXAMPLES
SUPPORTING SENTENCE
EXAMPLES
SUM UP

私達（たち）の学校は規則（きそく）が厳（きび）しい。服装（ふくそう）の規則がかなりある。例（たと）えば、シャツは白（しろ）じゃなければならないし、ブレザーとネクタイも必要（ひつよう）だ。それから、持ち物（もちもの）の規則もけっこううるさい。例えば、学校で携帯電話（けいたいでんわ）を使ってはいけない。この学校の規則は日本の学校と同（おな）じぐらい厳しいだろう。

"KANSOUBUN" STYLE
感想文型（かんそうぶんがた）

LEADING SENTENCE

DESCRIPTIVE SENTENCES

COMMENT SENTENCES

この学校のキャンパスは公園（こうえん）のようだ。花や木や池（いけ）があってきれいだし、ベンチもたくさんある。そして、昼休（ひるやす）みにはベンチでお弁当（べんとう）を食べる人が多（おお）い。学校はとても忙（いそが）しく、授業（じゅぎょう）も難（むずか）しい。しかし、公園のようなキャンパスがあるから、生徒（せいと）はリラックスしやすいと思（おも）う。

Process フローチャート

Mechanics	4.2	**Linking expressions**	**1** **Learn linking expressions** せつぞくひょうげん　まな 接続表現を学ぶ
	4.3 4.4	**Basic information style**	**2** **Collect and organize basic information** き そ じょうほうしゅうしゅう びょうしゃ 基礎情報の収集と描写
	4.5	**Expository style**	**3** **Expository style** せつめいぶんがた 説明文型
	4.6	*Kansoubun* style	**4** ***Kansoubun* style writing** かんそうぶんがた 感想文型
	4.7		**5** **"Japanese style" comment sentences** しき　　　　　　　ぶん 「日本式」コメント文
			6 **Read a letter from Japan** て がみ 日本からの手紙を読む
	4.8	**Editorial meeting**	**7** **Hold an editorial meeting** へんしゅうかいぎ 編集会議をする
			8 **Create main texts and visuals** ほんぶん 本文とビジュアルを作る
Virtual Reality	4.9	**Booklet editing**	**9** **Edit a booklet** へんしゅう パンフレットを編集する
		Presenting	**10** **Conduct presentations** はっぴょう 発表をする

Link qualities or actions
Link paradoxical qualities or actions

Type of school, students, campus
Academic divisions and subjects
Athletic teams and clubs
School events in Japan
Strategies to make something easy to understand

Combined or compound topic sentence
Supporting sentences and examples
Sum-up sentences and conjunctions

Describing school friends
Developing descriptive sentences
Simple comment sentences

Direct comment sentences
Indirect comment sentences
Multiple comment sentences

Choose the editor-in-chief
Choose topics
Set basic structure of the booklet

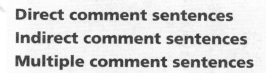

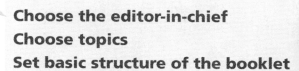

423

BASIC VOCABULARY 基礎語彙

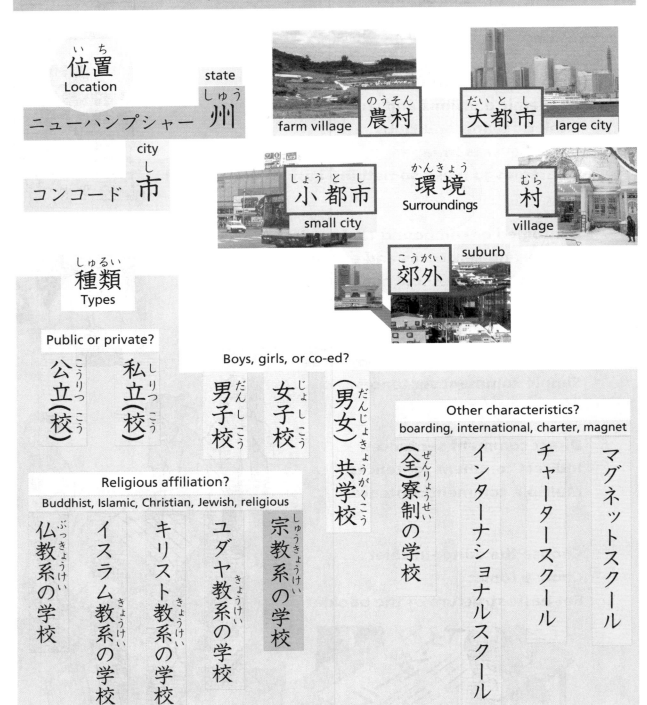

学校の基礎情報

位置
Location

ニューハンプシャー 州
state

コンコード 市
city

農村
farm village

大都市
large city

小都市
small city

環境
Surroundings

村
village

郊外
suburb

種類
Types

Public or private?

公立（校）

私立（校）

Boys, girls, or co-ed?

男子校

女子校

（男女）共学校

Other characteristics?
boarding, international, charter, magnet

（全）寮制の学校

インターナショナルスクール

チャータースクール

マグネットスクール

Religious affiliation?
Buddhist, Islamic, Christian, Jewish, religious

仏教系の学校

イスラム教系の学校

キリスト教系の学校

ユダヤ教系の学校

宗教系の学校

がくねん 学年	がっき 学期	きょういん 教員	せいと 生徒	だんし 男子	じょし 女子
grade level	academic term	teacher faculty	student	boys	girls

がっか かもく
学科と科目

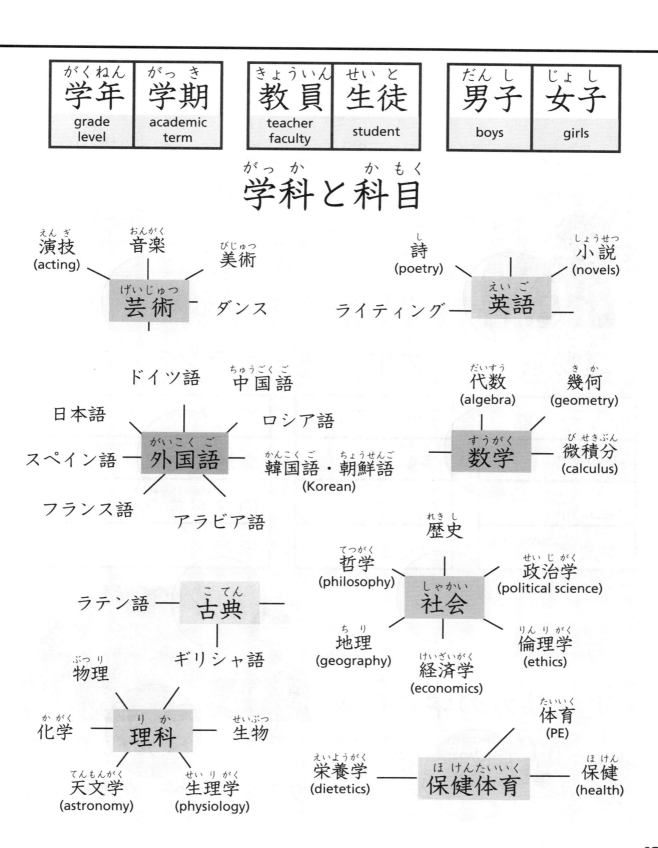

演技 (acting) ・ おんがく 音楽 ・ びじゅつ 美術
げいじゅつ 芸術
ダンス

し 詩 (poetry) ・ しょうせつ 小説 (novels)
ライティング ― えいご 英語

ドイツ語 ・ ちゅうごくご 中国語
日本語 ・ ロシア語
スペイン語 ― がいこくご 外国語 ・ かんこくご ちょうせんご 韓国語・朝鮮語 (Korean)
フランス語 ・ アラビア語

だいすう 代数 (algebra) ・ きか 幾何 (geometry)
すうがく 数学 ・ びせきぶん 微積分 (calculus)

ラテン語 ― こてん 古典 ― ギリシャ語

れきし 歴史
てつがく 哲学 (philosophy) ・ しゃかい 社会 ・ せいじがく 政治学 (political science)
ちり 地理 (geography) ・ けいざいがく 経済学 (economics) ・ りんりがく 倫理学 (ethics)

ぶつり 物理
かがく 化学 ― りか 理科 ― せいぶつ 生物
てんもんがく 天文学 (astronomy) ・ せいりがく 生理学 (physiology)

たいいく 体育 (PE)
えいようがく 栄養学 (dietetics) ― ほけんたいいく 保健体育 ― ほけん 保健 (health)

学校生活：
せいかつ

school life

部活 (部活動・クラブ活動)
ぶ かつ　　ぶ かつどう　　　　　かつどう

club activities

In most Japanese schools, athletics are a part of ぶかつ. Since all the club activities take place concurrently, students usually join only one team or club and devote their time to it throughout the year.

うんどうけい
運動系

ぶん か けい
文化系

けい
ボランティア系

サッカー部 ぶ	オーケストラ	アムネスティ
すいえい ぶ (swimming) 水泳部	えんげき ぶ (theater) 演劇部	こうつうあんぜん (traffic safety) 交通安全クラブ
りくじょうぶ (track & field) 陸上部	びじゅつぶ 美術部	こくさいしんぜん (international exchange) 国際親善クラブ
たいそう ぶ (gymnastics) 体操部	がっしょうぶ (chorus) 合唱部	も ぎ こくれん (Model UN) 模擬国連

ぎょうじ
アメリカの学校行事

Dance

How do you explain your school activity to a Japanese friend?

プロム　　ホームカミング　　ベークセール

ペップラリー

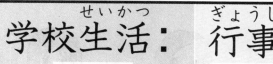

学校生活<ruby>せいかつ</ruby>：行事<ruby>ぎょうじ</ruby>

school life　**events**

入学式<ruby>にゅうがくしき</ruby>
school entrance ceremony
— ○○式<ruby>しき</ruby> **Ceremonies** — 卒業式<ruby>そつぎょうしき</ruby> graduation

中間試験<ruby>ちゅうかんしけん</ruby>
midterm exams

|

○○試験<ruby>しけん</ruby>
Examinations

|

期末試験<ruby>きまつしけん</ruby>
final exams

スピーチコンテスト

|

○○大会<ruby>たいかい</ruby>
Competitions
コンテスト
コンクール

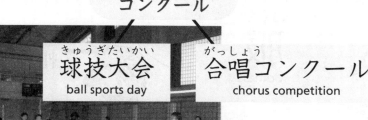

球技大会<ruby>きゅうぎたいかい</ruby>
ball sports day　合唱<ruby>がっしょう</ruby>コンクール
chorus competition

合宿<ruby>がっしゅく</ruby>
camp

修学旅行<ruby>しゅうがくりょこう</ruby>
(senior) trip

○○祭<ruby>さい</ruby>
Festivals

体育祭<ruby>たいいくさい</ruby>
athletic festival　文化祭<ruby>ぶんかさい</ruby>
cultural festival

427

BASIC VOCABULARY

学校生活: 服装
せいかつ　　　ふくそう

school life　　　dress

制服
せいふく

私服
しふく

洋服
ようふく

和服
わふく

服
ふく
clothes

上着
うわぎ

下着
したぎ

帽子
ぼうし

シャツ

靴下
くつした

眼鏡
めがね

ネクタイ

ベルト

パンツ or ズボン

スカート

靴
くつ

wear; put on

⇅

remove; take off

着<ruby>き</ruby>る

⇅

脱<ruby>ぬ</ruby>ぐ

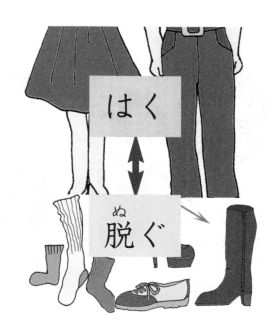

はく

⇅

脱<ruby>ぬ</ruby>ぐ

かぶる

⇅

取<ruby>と</ruby>る / 脱<ruby>ぬ</ruby>ぐ

かける

⇅

取<ruby>と</ruby>る / はずす

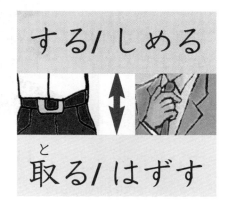

する / しめる

⇅

取<ruby>と</ruby>る / はずす

429

学校生活： 規則 (校則)

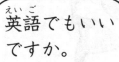
せいかつ
きそく こうそく

school life   rules

英語でもいい
ですか。
えいご

はい、英語でも
いいですよ。
えいご

-てもいいです
(permission: permitted)

スカートが短く
てはだめです。
みじか

教室で携帯電話
を使ってはいけ
ません。
きょうしつ けいたいでんわ

-てはだめです
-てはいけません
(prohibition: not permitted)

制服を着なければ
なりません。
せいふく き

mandatory

optional

制服を着なくても
いいです。

-なければなりません
(mandatory: must)

-なくてもいいです
(optional: don't have to)

学校生活：　生徒
せいかつ　　　　　　せいと

school life　　　students

生徒会・生徒会長
せいとかい　せいとかいちょう

student council,　student council president

クラブ・部長
ぶちょう

club,　　club head

信頼できる
しんらい

reliable

頭がいい
あたま

bright

指導力がある
しどうりょく

has leadership skills

チーム・キャプテン/主将
しゅしょう

team, captain

委員会・委員長
いいんかい　いいんちょう

committee,　committee chair

責任感がある
せきにんかん

has sense of responsibility

-が 好き/嫌い
す　きら

(like/dislike)

旅行が好き
りょこう

travel

詩を作るのが嫌い
し　つく　　　きら

poems

-が 得意/苦手
とくい　にがて

(good, strong/poor, weak)

ディベートが得意
とくい

debate

踊るのが苦手
おど　　　にがて

dancing

-が 上手/下手
じょうず　へた

(skillful/unskillful)

料理が上手
りょうり

cooking

歌を歌うのが下手
うた

singing a song

-が ある

(possesses a certain ability or sense)

実行力がある
じっこうりょく

(ability to get things done)

思いやりがある
おも

(consideration for others)

431

BASIC VOCABULARY

学校生活：授業と先生

せいかつ　　　　　じゅぎょう　　せんせい

school life　　　classes and teachers

難しすぎる
むずか
too hard

試験
しけん
examination

授業
じゅぎょう

宿題
しゅくだい
homework

多すぎる
おお
too much

易しすぎる
やさ
too easy

少なすぎる
すく
too little

内容
ないよう
content

教材
きょうざい
teaching
materials

使いにくい
hard to use

分かりやすい
わ
easy to understand

分かりにくい
わ
hard to understand

使いやすい
easy to use

-すぎる
(Indicating excess)

-やすい
(easy to do-)

-にくい
(hard to do-)

上手
じょうず
skillful

ユニーク
unique

教え方
おし　かた
how to teach

先生

説明
せつめい
explanation

役に立つ
やく　た
useful

少なすぎる
すく
not enough explanations

分かりやすい
わ
easy to understand

指導力がある
しどうりょく

優しい
やさ

元気
げんき

思いやりがある
おも

いろいろな接続

ジル

1. 17才です。 +
   11年生です。 =

2. ピアノが上手です。 +
   ジャズバンドのメンバーです。 =

3. 優しいです。 +
   頭がいいです。 +
   真面目です。 =

4. 指導力があります。 +
   信頼できます。 =

-で -で... nouns　な-adjectives　conversational　literary/written

1. ジルさんは17才で、11年生です。

2. ジルさんはピアノが上手で、ジャズバンドのメンバーだ。

-くて -くて... い-adjectives　conversational

3. ジルさんは優しくて、頭がよくて、真面目です。

-く -く... い-adjectives　literary/written

3. ジルさんは優しく、頭がよく、真面目だ。

-て -て... verbs　conversational

4. ジルさんは指導力があって、信頼できます。

Stem、Stem... verbs　literary/written

"Stem" (of a verb) is the part preceding ます in the ます form.

4. ジルさんは指導力があり、信頼できる。

せつぞくひょうげん
いろいろな接続表現 various linking expression

Unfavorable qualities

むずか
A. 難しい

しゅくだい　おお
B. 宿題が多すぎる

し　けん　　なが
C. 試験が長すぎる

きび
D. 先生が厳しすぎる

じゅぎょう
授業

Favorable qualities

おもしろ
E. 面白い

たの
F. 楽しい

やく　た
G. 役に立つ (useful)

ないよう　　わ
H. 内容が分かりやすい

S1が、S2　conversational　literary/written

せいぶつ　じゅぎょう　むずか　　　　　　　　やく　た
A but G　生物の授業は難しいですが、役に立ちます。

し　けん　なが　　　　　　　　ないよう　わ
C but H　生物の授業は試験が長すぎるが、内容が分かりやすい。

S1けれど、S2　conversational

せいぶつ　じゅぎょう　しゅくだい　おお　　　　　　たの
B but F　生物の授業は宿題が多すぎるけれど、楽しいです。

きび　　　　　　　　おもしろ
D but E　生物の授業は先生が厳しすぎるけれど、面白い。

S1。だから、S2。

S1. Therefore, S2 (introduce a logical outcome of S1) "so, that's why..."

だい　す　　　　　　　まいにち
私はオレンジジュースが大好きです。だから、毎日飲みます。

S1。でも、しかし、S2。

S1. However, S2 (introduce something paradoxical or contrasting to S1).
しかし is primarily used in writing and formal speech while でも is used in conversation and casual writing.

だいきら　　　　　　　まいにち
私はオレンジジュースが大嫌いです。でも、毎日飲みます。

せいぶつ　じゅぎょう　しゅくだい　おお　　　　　　たの　　　やく
生物の授業は宿題が多すぎる。しかし、楽しくて役に立つ。

それから、
S1。そして、S2。
また、

S1. And (then), S2 (introduce something enumerative, additional, or sequential to S1). Both それから and そして may indicate chronological development and the latter is especially useful in introducing the final item of a sequence ("...And finally..."). また does not have chronological implications and what follows it tends to be supplementary to S1. それから may be the most colloquial among the three, while また tends to be used in writing.

S1。それに、
そのうえ、 S2。

S1. And (on top of that) S2 (introduce something to be mentioned on top of S1). Compared with それから and そして, this group of conjunctions sounds as if information is being accumulated vertically rather than being listed one by one.

このオレンジジュースはおいしい。それに、安い。

生物の授業は難しい。その上、宿題も多い。それに、テストも毎週ある。

S1。たとえば、
とくに、 S2。

たとえば
S1. For example, S2 (introduce examples of S1).

とくに
S1. Especially, S2 (introduce noteworthy examples or aspects of S1).

トムはスポーツが好きです。とくに、サッカーが大好きです。

まず、S1。つぎに、S2。さらに、S3。

First of all, S1. Next, S2. Furthermore, S3 (introduce something enumerative, or sequential to S1). まず and つぎに mean "first of all" and "next," respectively and they are useful in indicating the order of actions to be taken or a procedure for something. You already know that both はじめに and さいしょに also mean "first of all" and they are interchangeable with まず for the most part. さらに means "moreover" and it is useful in indicating an additional step to be followed. You already know that both おわりに and さいごに mean "finally" or "lastly" and they may be used to indicate a final step in the procedure.

まず、単語を勉強します。つぎに、漢字を勉強します。

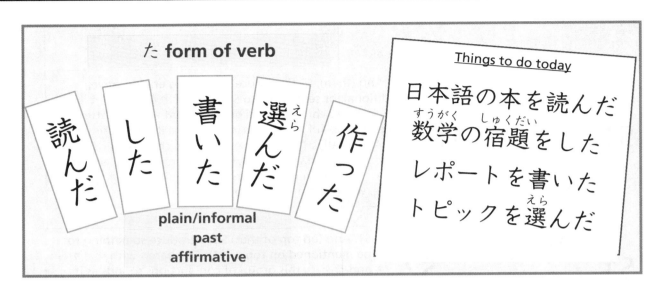

た **form of verb**

読んだ　した　書いた　選んだ　作った

plain/informal
past
affirmative

Things to do today

日本語の本を読んだ
数学の宿題をした
レポートを書いた
トピックを選んだ

Indicating a reason

-(だ)から ｜ -(な)ので

日本は今夏だから、暑いです。
暑いので、海に行きたいです。

Expressing opinions: I think that-

-(だ)と思います

Turning a verb into a noun by nominalizer の or こと

Plain form of a verb + の/こと

日本語を話すのは楽しいです。

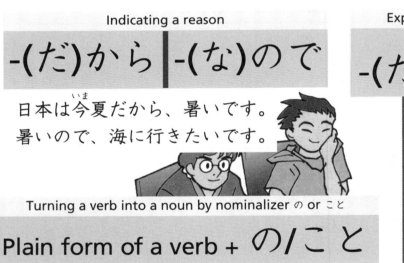

Easy to do -

Verb stem + やすい

読みやすい

れきし

れきし

Hard to do -

Verb stem + にくい

読みにくい

Strategies

for making something easier to understand

Paraphrasing
(言い換え)

Classifying
(分類)

Indicating resemblance
(類似点の指摘)

XとはYのことです

部活とはクラブ活動のことです。

Bukatsu is synonymous with club activities.

XというY Y called X

エコフェストという行事

An event called Eco Fest

XのようなY

プロムのような行事

An event like a prom

Adverbial usage of adjectives

い-Adj.く ┐┌ なる
な-Adj.に ┘└ する

授業が難しくなる。
Classes become hard(er).

授業を難しくする。
(Someone) makes classes hard(er).

Assertive direct comment marker

-(な)のだ

制服は必要なのだ。
Uniforms are indeed necessary.

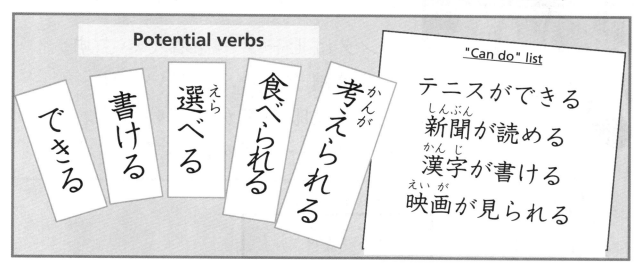

Potential verbs

できる
書ける
選べる
食べられる
考えられる

"Can do" list

テニスができる
新聞が読める
漢字が書ける
映画が見られる

437

BASIC VOCABULARY

背が高い
せ たか

背が低い
せ ひく

状態表現
じょうたいひょうげん

やせている

太っている
ふと

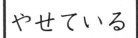

Xは-ている

good-looking

かっこいい

リンダ　　　ジム　　　マーク　　　トム

リンダはセーターを着ています。
き

ジムは帽子をかぶっています。
ぼうし

マークは眼鏡をかけています。
めがね

トムはジーンズをはいています。

awkward-looking

かっこわるい

せつめいぶん	かんそうぶん
説明文	**感想文**
Expository writing	***Kansoubun* writing**

トピックセンテンス	リードセンテンス
Topic Sentence	**Leading Sentence**
サポートセンテンス	
Supporting Sentence	
れいぶん	びょうしゃぶん
例文	**描写文**
Example Sentences	
サポートセンテンス	
Supporting Sentence	
れいぶん	**Descriptive Sentences**
例文	
Example Sentences	コメント文
サポートセンテンス	ちょくせつ
Supporting Sentence	直接コメント文
れいぶん	かんせつ
例文	間接コメント文
Example Sentences	
まとめ	**Comment Sentences**
Sum-up Sentences	**(Direct Comment Sentences)**
	(Indirect Comment Sentences)

きそじょうほう	
基礎情報	**Basic information**

439

4.2 Mechanics 組立て
くみ た

Linking Expressions
接続表現
せつぞくひょうげん

Objectives

Learn how to link two or more qualities and actions in a single statement.

Overview

First you will learn how to link two or more qualities and actions in a single statement.   This will allow you to write something in one sentence that previously required multiple sentences, and it will also help you effectively organize and present information about your school.

1 Learn linking expressions　　接続表現を学ぶ
せつぞくひょうげん　まな

　1 Link qualities or states　　性質・状態の接続
せいしつ　じょうたい　せつぞく

　2 Link actions　　動作の接続
どうさ　せつぞく

　3 Link paradoxical qualities or actions　　逆接
ぎゃくせつ

1 Learn linking expressions

接続表現を学ぶ

1 Link qualities or states

性質・状態の接続

A. Read and compare the descriptions below. How do they differ from each other? Which description flows best and why? Share your thoughts with your classmates.

次の四つの文章を比べてみましょう。どれが読みやすいですか。

1. 私の妹は13才です。中学1年生です。得意な科目は日本語です。苦手な科目は歴史です。それから、好きな食べ物はパスタです。好きな飲み物はアイスコーヒーです。趣味はダンスです。妹はとても元気です。かわいいです。

2. 私の妹は13才で、中学1年生です。得意な科目は日本語で、苦手な科目は歴史です。それから、好きな食べ物はパスタで、好きな飲み物はアイスコーヒーです。趣味はダンスです。妹はとても元気で、かわいいです。

3. 私の妹は13才です。中学1年生です。得意な科目は日本語です。それから、好きな食べ物はパスタです。妹はとても元気です。苦手な科目は歴史です。趣味はダンスです。好きな飲み物はアイスコーヒーです。妹はかわいいです。

4. 私の妹は13才で、中学1年生です。得意な科目は日本語で、好きな食べ物はパスタです。それから、妹はとても元気で、苦手な科目は歴史です。趣味はダンスで、好きな飲み物はアイスコーヒーです。妹はかわいいです。

B. Why do you think knowing how to link two or more qualities or ideas effectively will make you a better writer and presenter? Come up with at least two reasons based on your experience in the previous section. After that, read the following notes.

接続が重要な理由を二つ考えて下さい。

Effects of linking (接続の効果)

1. No more "choppy" writing

   Conjunctions such as それから and そして are useful in presenting your thoughts and ideas in a clear and coherent fashion. These conjunctions, however, cannot link two or more qualities in one sentence because they have to be placed in the beginning of a sentence. As a result, your writing will still have to consist of short sentences with each representing a single quality or idea. Knowing how to link two or more qualities in one sentence, therefore, will provide a solution to "choppy" writing.

2. Achieve both clarity and brevity in your writing

   Descriptions 1 and 3 in the preceding exercise convey the same message, but the latter is shorter and flows better thanks to the effective linking of two qualities in the same sentence. Note that それから is still present in description 3 and provides a smooth transition from one "linked" sentence to the other.

3. Organize your ideas better

   Awareness of effective linking will also help you organize your ideas better in your writing. Descriptions 2 and 4 in the preceding exercise do not flow as smoothly as 1 and 3, as the information in the former pair is arranged in a rather arbitrary manner. This problem is more easily noticeable in description 4 than in 2, as qualities that differ in categories or that are unrelated to each other have been linked and presented in the same sentence.

ノート: Connecting nouns and な adjectives (名詞・な形容詞の接続)

| (Noun or な-adjective) 〜で〜で... | Attaching で to a noun or な adjective will enable you to continue to add more information without ending your sentence. For な adjectives, make sure to remove な before attaching で. |

今日の天気は雨で、寒いです。

Today's weather is rainy and it is cold.

町の図書館は便利で、静かで、広いです。

The town library is convenient, quiet, and spacious.

好きな食べ物はパスタで、好きな飲み物はコーヒーです。

My favorite food is pasta and my favorite beverage is coffee.

C. Read the example below and do the following "additions."

ノートを読んで、次の「足<ruby>し<rt>た</rt></ruby>算<ruby><rt>ざん</rt></ruby>」をしましょう。

EX. ジルさんは17才<ruby><rt>さい</rt></ruby>です。　+　ジルさんは11年生<ruby><rt>ねんせい</rt></ruby>です。　=

ジルさんは17才で、11年生です。

1. 出身<ruby><rt>しゅっしん</rt></ruby>はトロントです。　+
カナダ人です。　=

ジル

2. ジルさんは元気<ruby><rt>げんき</rt></ruby>です。　+
ジルさんは優<ruby><rt>やさ</rt></ruby>しいです。　=

3. 得意<ruby><rt>とくい</rt></ruby>な科目<ruby><rt>かもく</rt></ruby>は数学<ruby><rt>すうがく</rt></ruby>です。　+
苦手<ruby><rt>にがて</rt></ruby>な科目<ruby><rt>かもく</rt></ruby>は音楽<ruby><rt>おんがく</rt></ruby>です。　=

4. 趣味<ruby><rt>しゅみ</rt></ruby>は映画<ruby><rt>えいが</rt></ruby>です。　+
クラブは映画部<ruby><rt>えいがぶ</rt></ruby>です。　=

5. 秋<ruby><rt>あき</rt></ruby>のスポーツはサッカーです。　+
春<ruby><rt>はる</rt></ruby>のスポーツはソフトボールです。　=

ノート: Linking two or more qualities 2 (性質<ruby><rt>せいしつ</rt></ruby>・状態<ruby><rt>じょうたい</rt></ruby>の接続<ruby><rt>せつぞく</rt></ruby>　その二)

い Adj. Root + くて

〜くて〜くて

Attaching くて to an い adjective root will enable you to continue to add more information without ending your sentence. "Adjective root" indicates the part preceding い in い adjectives.

このケーキは安<ruby><rt>やす</rt></ruby>くて、おいしいです。(安い + おいしい)

This cake is inexpensive and delicious.

学校のプールは新<ruby><rt>あたら</rt></ruby>しくて、大きいです。(新しい + 大きい)

The swimming pool at the school is new and large.

今日<ruby><rt>きょう</rt></ruby>は天気がよくて、気持<ruby><rt>きも</rt></ruby>ちがいいです。

Note that いい becomes よくて。

The weather is good and (we feel) pleasant today.

(天気がいい + 気持ちがいい)

D. Let's try い adjective additions this time.

今度は「い形容詞」の「足し算」です。

EX. 古い ＋ 大きい ＝ 古くて、大きいです。

1. 長い ＋ つまらない ＝

2. 新しい ＋ いい ＝

3. 明るい ＋ 広い ＝

4. 涼しい ＋ 気持ちがいい ＋ 静か ＝

E. Suppose your school has facilities or people with the characteristics given below. Describe them as shown in the example.

学校の施設や人について話しましょう。

会話の例 (Sample Dialogue)

A: メディアルームはきれいですか。

B: はい、きれいで、新しくて、涼しいです。

EX.
きれい
あたらしい
すずしい

1.
ひろい
おおきい
べんり

まじめ
やさしい
すてき

3.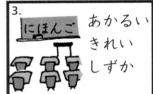
あかるい
きれい
しずか

4.
やすい
おいしい
ヘルシー

ノート: Connecting verbs 1 (動詞の接続)

(Verb)

〜て〜て

The て form of a verb will enable you to continue to add some relevant information without ending your sentence. For example, みせがたくさんあって、べんりです means "There are many stores and (therefore) it is convenient" and ともだちがたくさんいて、たのしいです means "I have many friends and (therefore) it is fun."

私の学校には先生が20人いて、生徒が250人います。

There are 20 teachers and 250 students in my school.

家の近くは大きい湖があって、きれいです。

My neighborhood has a large lake and it is beautiful.

F. Appropriately combine the statements on the left with those on the right using ～て.

「～て」を使って左（ぶん）の文と右（ぶ）の文をつなげましょう。

> 例 (Example)
>
> 晴（は）れの日がたくさんあって、気持（き も）ちがいいです。

EX. 晴（は）れの日がたくさんあります。 ●————● 気持（き も）ちがいいです。

1. 金曜日にコンサートがあります。 ●　　　● 土曜日にダンスがあります。
2. 数学（すう がく）の先生が7人います。 ●　　　● 科学（か がく）の先生が6人います。
3. 学校の東（ひがし）に山があります。 ●　　　● うるさいです。
4. コンビニがたくさんあります。 ●　　　● 学校の西（にし）に森（もり）があります。
5. 弟が2人と妹が3人います。 ●　　　● 便利（べん り）です。

2 Link actions 動作（どう さ）の接続（せつ ぞく）

ノート: Connecting verbs 2 (動詞（どう し）の接続（せつ ぞく）)

（Verb）

～て～て

The て form of a verb may be used to connect two or more actions to be performed in sequence. For example、にほんへいって、すもうをみます means "I will go to Japan and watch sumo wrestling," and おんがくをきいて、ねました means "I listened to the music and then went to bed."

6時に起（お）きて、6時半（はん）に朝（あさ）ごはんを食べます。

I wake up at 6 o'clock and eat breakfast at 6:30.

リーダーを選（えら）んで、トピックを決（き）めて、準備（じゅん び）を始（はじ）めました。

We chose a leader, decided upon the topic, and started our preparation.

445

A. Describe the following sequence of actions using ～て.

「～て」を使ってつなげましょう。

会話の例 **A** (Sample Dialogue A: Formal)	会話の例 **B** (Sample Dialogue B: Informal)
A: これから何をしますか。	A: これから何する。
B: ええと、<u>コーヒーを飲んで、音楽を聞きます</u>。	B: ええと、<u>コーヒー飲んで、音楽聞く</u>。

EX.

1.

2.

3.
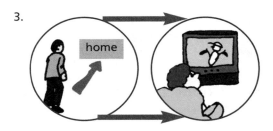

例 (Example)

<u>サッカーをして柔道をしてジョギングをしました。</u>

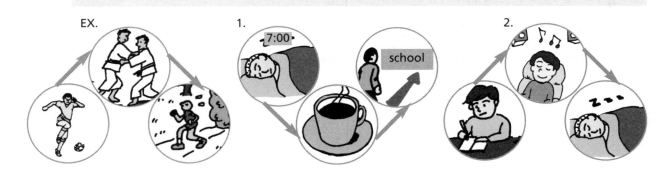

EX.　　　　1.　　　　2.

ノート：Linking with 〜て vs. それから (「〜て〜て」と「それから」)

昼ご飯を食べて、数学のクラスに行きました。

昼ご飯を食べました。それから、数学のクラスに行きました。

Both sentences above describe the two sequential actions of eating lunch and going to math class. What do you think then is the difference between these two descriptions? それから usually marks the beginning of a new sentence, so the distinction between the connecting actions is more distinct than that in the て form description. Because of this, それから is especially useful in connecting actions while signaling a new development or a change of scene at the same time. Let's look at an example in which both それから and 〜て can be used effectively.

(1) woke up at 7 o'clock
(2) ate breakfast
(3) went to the library
(4) read science books

The four activities mentioned above happened in sequence and they may be divided into two chunks: the ones before leaving home and the others after. Linking two activities within each chunk with the て form, and starting the second chunk with それから, will make the transition smooth and the entire description easy to follow as a result.

7時に起きて、朝ご飯を食べました。それから、図書館へ行って、科学の本を読みました。

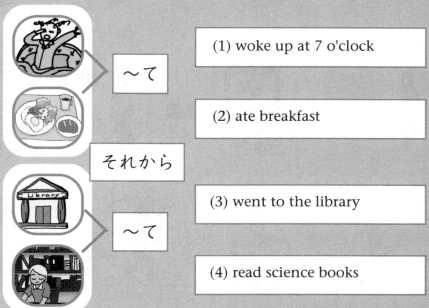

(1) woke up at 7 o'clock

(2) ate breakfast

(3) went to the library

(4) read science books

447

B. Describe the following sequence of actions using ～て and それから.

「～て」と「それから」を使って、練習しましょう。

> 会話の例 A (Sample Dialogue A: Formal)
>
> A: きのう、何をしましたか。
>
> B: ええと、<u>ハンバーガーを食べて、コーラを飲みました</u>。
> それから、<u>図書館へ行って、本を読みました</u>。

> 会話の例 B (Sample Dialogue B: Informal)
>
> A: きのう、何した。
>
> B: ええと、<u>ハンバーガー食べて、コーラ飲んだ</u>。
> それから、<u>図書館行って、本読んだ</u>。

3 Link paradoxical qualities or actions　　逆接<small>ぎゃくせつ</small>

A. One of the sentences in each pair sounds awkward.　Can you tell which one and why it may sound so?　Share your answers with your classmates.

適切<small>てきせつ</small>じゃない文<small>ぶん</small>はどちらですか。その理由<small>りゆう</small>は何<small>なん</small>ですか。

1. a. 歴史<small>れきし</small>の宿題<small>しゅくだい</small>は難<small>むずか</small>しくて、長<small>なが</small>いです。
   b. 歴史<small>れきし</small>の宿題<small>しゅくだい</small>は難<small>むずか</small>しくて、短<small>みじか</small>いです。

2. a. このピザは高<small>たか</small>くて、おいしいです。
   b. このピザは安<small>やす</small>くて、おいしいです。

3. a. このタオルは新<small>あたら</small>しくて、きれいです。
   b. このタオルは古<small>ふる</small>くて、きれいです。

4. a. 私<small>わたし</small>の家<small>いえ</small>の回<small>まわ</small>りはうるさくて、便利<small>べんり</small>です。
   b. 私<small>わたし</small>の家<small>いえ</small>の回<small>まわ</small>りはうるさくて、不便<small>ふべん</small>です。

ノート: Combining contrasting or contradicting qualities
(相反<small>あいはん</small>する性質<small>せいしつ</small>・状態<small>じょうたい</small>の接続<small>せつぞく</small>)

けれど/けれども/けど

One of the paired sentences in the preceding exercise sounds awkward because the two linked qualities contrast each other.　For example, 1-b (れきしのしゅくだいはむずかしくてみじかいです) sounds awkward as むずかしい (difficult) and みじかい (short) are qualities that may make the homework more challenging and less challenging, respectively.　The conjunctions けれど, けれども and their more colloquial equivalent けど are used to connect contrasting or contradicting qualities like these.　These conjunctions are placed at the end of the statement being qualified.　They follow either a plain or a polite style, though the latter case is limited to very polite speech.　Note that だ and だった must be added to a *na* adjective and a noun in the plain affirmative nonpast and to the plain affirmative past statement, respectively.

このケーキは高<small>たか</small>い(です)けれど、おいしいです。

Although this cake is expensive, it is delicious.

continued to the next page

学校のプールは新しい(です)けれども、小さいです。

Although the swimming pool at the school is new, it is small.

図書館は静かだ(or 静かです)けど、不便です。

Although the library is quiet, it is inconvenient.

近くに映画館がある(or あります)けど、あまり行きません。

Although there is a movie theater nearby, I don't go there much.

Note that けれど, けれども, and けど can be used only once in a sentence.　See the following in which the first sentence is UNGRAMMATICAL.

× 図書館は新しいけど、静かだけど、不便です。

○ 図書館は新しくて、静かだけど、不便です。

○ 図書館は新しくて、静かですけど、不便です。

Although the library is new and quiet, it is inconvenient.

B. Which one should you use?　適切な文はどちらですか。

1.　a.　漢字の勉強は難しくて、楽しいです。
　　b.　漢字の勉強は難しいけど、楽しいです。

2.　a.　トムさんはやさしくて、まじめです。

　　b.　トムさんはやさしいけれど、まじめです。

3.　a.　私の家の回りは店や工場が多くて、静かです。
　　b.　私の家の回りは店や工場が多いけれども、静かです。

4.　a.　花屋に行って、花を買いません。

　　b.　花屋に行くけど、花を買いません。

5.　a.　今日は雨で、野球をします。

　　b.　今日は雨ですけれど、野球をします。

6.　a.　図書館は静かで便利で、よく行きます。
　　b.　図書館は静かで便利ですけれども、よく行きます。

C. Describe the following using 〜(だ)けど.

「〜(だ)けど」を使って答えましょう。

会話の例 (Sample Dialogue)

A: 学校は忙しいですか。

B: はい、忙しいけど、楽しいです。

EX.

いそがしい
たのしい

1.

あたらしい
ふべん

2.

きびしい
おもしろい

3.

げんき
うるさい

4.

cafeteria

たかい、おいしい
ヘルシー

D. Let's talk about your former school.   前の学校について話しましょう。

Preparation

Choose 2 - 3 adjectives most suitable to describe each of the following.

history

1.

science

2.

げんき(な)、やさしい、こわい (scary)、
すてき(な)、まじめ(な)、きびしい、
がまんづよい (patient)、おもしろい、
クリエイティブ(な)、こせいてき(な)
がんこ(な) (stubborn)、いじわる(な)
(mean)、れいせい(な) (calm and cool)、

3. home-work   4. home-work

やさしい、おもしろい、むずかしい、
たのしい、つまらない、みじかい
じゅうよう(な)、ながい、おおい、
すくない

6.

5.

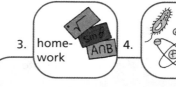

cafeteria food

おいしい、まずい、
たかい、やすい、おおい、すくない、
ヘルシー(な)、あぶらっこい (greasy)

ちいさい、おおきい、あたらしい、
ふるい、きれい(な)、すずしい、
せまい、ひろい、あかるい、くらい、
べんり(な)、ふべん(な)

Conversation

Go around the class and conduct a conversation like the one below with your classmates. You may combine two or more characteristics using the て form or 〜(だ)けど. You may also describe them in multiple sentences using それから, そして, or でも.

> **会話の例 (Sample Dialogue)**
>
> A: 前の学校の歴史の先生はどんな先生ですか。
>
> B: あのう、やさしくて、元気な先生です。それから、個性的な先生です。
>
> A: へえ。じゃ、科学の先生は？
>
> B: 科学の先生は厳しいけれど、面白いです。
>
> A: あ、そうですか。(continued)

E. Make a "Top Three List."　　トップ3のリストを作りましょう。

Think about three personal character adjectives that you feel would be ideal for each of the following subjects. After that, share your thoughts with your classmates using the て form or 〜(だ)けど.

1. チームメート　teammate
2. プロジェクトの相手　project partner
3. ルームメート　roommate
4. 結婚の相手　marriage partner
5. ボーイフレンド / ガールフレンド　boy/girl friend

> **会話の例 (Sample Dialogue)**
>
> A: 私はまじめでがまんづよいチームメートがいいです。
> Bさんはどんなチームメートがいいですか。
>
> B: ええと、面白いけど、冷静なチームメートがいいです。

ノート: Combining contrasting conditions (相反_{あいはん}する性質_{せいしつ}・状態_{じょうたい}の接続_{せつぞく})

〜が

The conjunction particle が is used to connect two qualities that contrast or contradict one another. Like 〜けれど, 〜けれども, and 〜けど, が is placed at the end of the preceding statement and it can mark either a plain or a polite form.

Unlike 〜けれど, 〜けれども, and 〜けど, however, が usually marks a polite form when the combined sentence is in the polite style. Compare the following four sentences. Only the second sentence is awkward.

◯ このケーキは高_{たか}いですが、おいしいです。

✕ このケーキは高_{たか}いが、おいしいです。

◯ このケーキは高いが、おいしい。

◯ このケーキは高いけれど、おいしいです。

◯ このケーキは高いですけれど、おいしいです。

Although this cake is expensive, it is delicious.

Note that the conjunction particle が can be used only once in a sentence. See the following in which the first sentence is UNGRAMMATICAL.

✕ 図書館_{としょかん}は新_{あたら}しいですが、静_{しず}かですが、不便_{ふべん}です。

◯ 図書館_{としょかん}は新_{あたら}しくて、静_{しず}かですが、不便_{ふべん}です。

Although the library is new and quiet, it is inconvenient.

F. Appropriately combine the statements on the left with those on the right using 〜が.

「〜が」を使って左の文_{ぶん}と右の文をつなぎましょう。

1. テストは短_{みじか}いです ・ ・あまり寒_{さむ}くありません
2. 映画_{えいが}は長_{なが}いです ・ ・うるさいです
3. 今日_{きょう}は風_{かぜ}が強_{つよ}いです ・ ・本を読みませんでした
4. 明日_{あした}は日曜日_{にちようび}です ・ ・難_{むずか}しいです
5. 妹_{いもうと}はかわいいです ・ ・暗_{くら}いです
6. 朝_{あさ}の七時です ・ ・忙_{いそが}しいです
7. 図書館_{としょかん}に行きました ・ ・面白_{おもしろ}いです

G. *Rewrite the following by combining two or more characteristics using the* て *form,* ～(だ)けれど(も) *and/or. Make sure to think about the appropriate length of your sentences and avoid cramming too much information into one sentence. After all, your rewrite should be making your readers' job easier, not harder.*

適当に文を接続して、書き直してください。

私の家の近くは自然が多いです。それから、静かです。家の東は林です。家が少ないです。西は畑です。あまり人がいません。南は商店街です。でも、店が少ないです。そして、北は湖です。あまり車が来ません。駅やデパートは遠いです。だから、不便です。でも、私の家の近くは静かです。本当にいいところです。

私の町の公民館は楽しいです。若者のための催しがたくさんあります。たとえば、先月、ファッションショーがありました。今月はダンスパーティーがあります。それに、毎週、有名な映画を見ることができます。今週は「ゴジラ」を見ます。来週は「七人の侍」を見ます。それから、面白いクラスもたくさんあります。たとえば、木曜日にヨガのクラスがあります。金曜日に折り紙のクラスがあります。私は妹とよく公民館に行きます。公民館は古いです。でも、とても楽しい場所です。

Recognition Kanji 1: 認識漢字 1

きょうしつ
教室
classroom

しゅくだい
宿題
homework

ぎょうじ
行事
event/occasion

そつぎょうせい
卒業生 ⟶
graduate

かつどう
活動
activity

せいとすう
生徒数
number of students

きょういんすう
教員数
number of teachers

かもく
科目
subject

Culture Note 3

High School in Japan:
日本の高校

Mary Ellen Jebbia

My life at Seikei High School in Tokyo, Japan was quite different than my life at my high school in the United States. There were many similarities, like the subjects I studied, and the buildings and facilities in Japan were typical of those in the United States. There were many differences, however, in the daily schedule, the class size and how classes operated, and in the management of after school activities.

At Seikei, I studied trigonometry, English, Japanese, and history. At my high school in the United States, I studied very similar subjects, though the class sizes in the United States were much smaller. For example, in my Japanese class in the United States, there were four students, and at Seikei, there were about forty students to a class. Another big difference was that, in the United States, I moved from class to class according to which subjects I was studying. In Japan, it is normal for students to stay in the same classroom almost the entire day (they might only move for electives), and the teachers are the ones to move to different classrooms after each period. At Seikei, the teachers usually lectured and asked for questions at the end of class, whereas in the United States, I participated throughout class with comments and ideas. I also studied calligraphy, cooking, physical education, and art in Japan. Calligraphy was interesting because it required so much concentration and practice. In cooking, we received directions at the start of class and were expected to make a full meal with little assistance from the teacher. This helped me to learn some very useful vocabulary and new kanji. In physical education, the girls studied dance, while the boys studied judo. Because there were so many subjects, the schedule differed a little from that of an American high school.

In Tokyo I had to wake up very early to get to school on time (usually around five thirty). I showered, ate breakfast with my host sister, and walked about seven minutes to the subway station. The train always arrived on the time. I took the Sobu sen, or Sobu line train for about ten stops until I arrived at Kichijoji station. The ride took about forty minutes. During the first couple of weeks, I didn't recognize anyone at the station, and I was constantly worried about getting lost. As time went by, I started to recognize Seikei students and would walk with them. It took about half an hour to walk to the Seikei campus, but it was well worth it. I always tried to practice casual conversation with friends during the walks and learned many colloquial phrases I wouldn't have learned in class. Many of the students stopped at a *conbini*, a convenience store, to buy snacks or a sandwich for lunch. Before we entered the actual classrooms, we took off our shoes and put on our indoor slippers in the *genkan*, a room set aside specifically for changing shoes. Homeroom usually started at about eight thirty. When our homeroom teacher walked in, one student in the class cued everyone to stand, bow, and say good morning. Our homeroom teacher would give announcements, and then class would start. Classes weren't too long, usually fifty minutes. At lunchtime, students would sit in the classroom and eat their obento, or lunches packed in little boxes. Some typical foods in a *bento* box included rice and seaweed, little sandwiches, small fruits, or little hotdogs. Some of the students would eat at the cafeteria, and others would play basketball or soccer. After lunch, classes would start again and would end about three o'clock. Then it was time for club activities.

While not all students participated in club activities, an overwhelming number of students stayed at school well after classes ended. There were sports clubs, such as basketball, baseball, soccer, rugby, or traditional Japanese sports like *judo* and *kendo*. There were also art and craft clubs, like calligraphy, photography, or ceramics. I decided to join the basketball team because I had previously played basketball at my high school in America. The basketball club at Seikei practiced for at least two hours every afternoon, and sometimes even in the early morning. The practices were very disciplined and were run by the members of the club instead of a coach. Each sports club had two team managers who were also students. In Japan, students usually devote all their free time to one club, whereas in the United States many students may be involved in a sports team, an academic club, and a community service project at the same time. While I didn't meet as many students through the basketball club, I felt very close to my teammates by the end of my time at Seikei. Sometimes after practice, the basketball club would have dinner at a fast food restaurant. When it was finally time to go home, we would walk back to the subway station together. In Japan I didn't have too much homework, so I would watch television with my host sister and try to understand the Japanese as much as possible. Finally, I would go to bed and start again the next day.

4.3 Mechanics 組立て
<ruby>くみ た</ruby>

Basic Information Style I
基礎情報型　その１
<ruby>きそじょうほうがた</ruby>

Objectives

Collect and organize basic information about your school with respect to its location, environment, enrollment, campus, academic subjects, and athletic teams/clubs.
Make a list of selected information to be included in your description.
Create descriptions based on the list according to a "primary source" writing style model.

Overview

You will now create descriptions in which you give some basic information about your school. We will follow three steps to do this. First you will sort relevant information. Second you will make a list of selected information. Third you will create descriptions based on the list. These simple descriptions fall into the category of a "primary source" or basic information style of writing, one of the three writing styles featured in this chapter. The topics in this section include your school's location, environment, enrollment, campus, academic subjects, and athletic teams/clubs.

2 Collect and organize basic information　　基礎情報の収集と整理

1 School location and its surroundings　　位置と環境

2 Type of school, students, campus　　種類、生徒、キャンパス

3 Academic divisions and subjects　　教科と科目

4 Athletic teams and clubs　　スポーツチームとクラブ

1 **School location and its surroundings**　位置と環境
い ち かんきょう

A. Match the images with the words.

写真と単語をマッチさせてください。
しゃしん たんご

1. (　　　　　)

2. (　　　　　)

3. (　　　　　)

大都市、農村、村、町、郊外、小都市
だいとし のうそん むら まち こうがい しょうとし

4. (　　　　　)

5. (　　　　　)

MY TOWN

6. (　　　　　)

B. Circle the appropriate word in each parenthesis.

適切なことばを◯で囲んでください。
てきせつ まる かこ

1. シカゴやアトランタは(大都市、小都市、郊外、農村、国)です。
2. その学校は人口30,000人の(大都市、小都市)にあります。
3. 私達の町はシカゴの(小都市、郊外、農村)にあります。
4. (大都市、農村)には田や畑がたくさんあります。
5. 出身はアリゾナ(村、市、州、町)のフェニックスです。
6. インドやフランスは(村、市、州、国)です。
7. ニューイングランド(地方、市)の秋はとてもきれいです。
8. その学校は人口1,000人の(大都市、小都市、村)にあります。

C. Match the words on the left with their English counterparts on the right.

日本語と英語をマッチさせてください。

1. 東部（　　）
2. 北東部（　　）
3. 中西部（　　）
4. 西部（　　）
5. 南部（　　）
6. 南東部（　　）
7. 北西部（　　）
8. 北部（　　）
9. 南西部（　　）
10. 中部（　　）

a. northwestern section/part

b. southwestern section/part

c. midwestern section/part

d. northern section/part

e. midland/middle section/part

f. eastern section/part

g. northeastern section/part

h. southern section/part

i. western section/part

j. southeastern section/part

ノート; Primary Source/Basic Information Style (基礎情報型)

Descriptions you will be making in this section are intended to provide some basic information about your school and not to analyze and evaluate specific aspects or issues as you did in the previous chapter. We will call them "primary source" or the basic information style of writing and you will follow the three steps as shown below.

Gather information

情報の収集

Make a list

情報のリスト化

Make a description

情報の文章化

ウエスト高校は：

シカゴの西部にある。
男女共学の公立高校。
生徒は2,200人いる。
教員は150人いる。

ウエスト高校はシカゴの西部にあって、男女共学の公立高校です。生徒は2,200人いて、教員は150人います。

D. Check the location of your school and create a sentence.

皆(みな)さんの学校の位置(いち)を確認(かくにん)して書(か)きましょう。

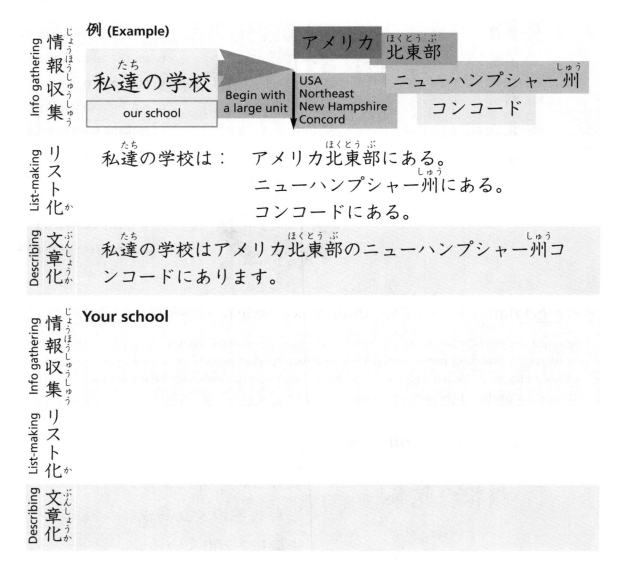

例 (Example)

Info gathering 情報(じょうほう)収集(しゅうしゅう)

私達(たち)の学校 / our school → Begin with a large unit → USA Northeast New Hampshire Concord / アメリカ 北東部(ほくとうぶ) ニューハンプシャー州(しゅう) コンコード

List-making リスト化(か)

私達(たち)の学校は： アメリカ北東部(ほくとうぶ)にある。
ニューハンプシャー州(しゅう)にある。
コンコードにある。

Describing 文章(ぶんしょう)化(か)

私達(たち)の学校はアメリカ北東部(ほくとうぶ)のニューハンプシャー州(しゅう)コンコードにあります。

Info gathering 情報(じょうほうしゅうしゅう)収集 **Your school**

List-making リスト化(か)

Describing 文章(ぶんしょう)化(か)

E. Give a short description of the following places as shown in the example according to the given information.

例(れい)に従(したが)って、次(つぎ)の場所(ばしょ)について文を作(つく)りましょう。

例 (Example)

A市(し)は人口約(じんこうやく)50,000人(にん)の小都市(しょうとし)で、アメリカの中西部(ちゅうせいぶ)にあります。
(approximately 50,000)

地名（ちめい）	人口（じんこう）	分類（ぶんるい）		国（くに）	位置（いち）
EX. A市（し）	50,000人	small city		アメリカ	midwestern part
1. B市（し）	18,400,000人	large city		インド	western part
2. C町（まち）	14,000人	town		フィリピン	southern part
3. D村（むら）	3,000人	village		日本	northeastern part
4. E市（し）	72,000人	small city		オーストラリア	northern part

F. Give a short description of the place in which your school is located.

皆（みな）さんの学校がある場所（ばしょ）について書きましょう。

Info gathering 情報収集（じょうほうしゅうしゅう）

例 (Example)

| コンコード
Concord, NH | 43,000人 | 小都市（しょうとし） | 州の中南部（しゅうちゅうなんぶ） |

List-making リスト化（か）

コンコードは： 人口（じんこう）43,000人。
小都市（しょうとし）。
州の中南部（しゅうちゅうなんぶ）にある。

Describing 文章化（ぶんしょうか）

コンコードは人口約（じんこうやく）43,000人の小都市（しょうとし）で、州の中南部（しゅうちゅうなんぶ）にあります。

Info gathering 情報収集（じょうほうしゅうしゅう）

Your town

List-making リスト化（か）

Describing 文章化（ぶんしょうか）

G. In small groups, gather information about your school's neighborhood, make a list of noteworthy natural and man-made features, and create a description based on the list.

グループで学校の近くにある物や風景について話し合ってください。そして、その結果をリスト化、文章化してください。

例 (Example)

Information gathering
情報収集

学校の近くに何がある?

川がある。
林もある。

店も小さいけど、たくさんある。

公共施設がたくさんある。

List-making
リスト化

学校の近くには: 　川がある。

林がある。

公共施設がたくさんある。

小さい店がたくさんある。

Describing
文章化

学校の近くには川や林があります。それから、公共施設がたくさんあります。店も小さいけど、たくさんあります。

Info gathering
情報収集

Your town

List-making
リスト化

Describing
文章化

H. Put together all the sentences you have made so far.

これまでに作成した文を一つにまとめましょう。

例 (Example)

Describing 文章化

私達の学校はアメリカ北東部のニューハンプシャー州コンコードにあります。コンコードは人口約43,000人の小都市で、州の中南部にあります。学校の近くには川や林があります。それから、公共施設がたくさんあります。

Your school

Describing 文章化

I. Practice talking about the location and the surroundings of a school through role plays.

学校の位置と環境について話しましょう。

Role A

You are a Japanese high school student and classmate of an exchange student from abroad. Go talk to him or her and find out about the location of his or her school so that you have a good idea about where it is even if you may not be familiar with the town/city where it is located. After that, find out about the surroundings of the school as much as possible. You may begin by asking a question such as Xはどんなところですか (What kind of place is X?), がっこうのまわりはどうですか (How about the surroundings of your school?), and かんきょうはいいですか (Is the environment good?). Make sure to ask some follow-up questions as well.

Role B

You are an exchange student studying at a high school in Japan. A classmate will approach you and ask you questions about the location and surroundings of your home school. Answer his or her questions and carry out the conversation as much as possible. Keep in mind that he or she may not be familiar with the town/city in which your school is located. Give information such as "the northern part of California" or "the suburbs of Boston." You may talk about your current (home) school or one of your previous schools.

J. **Look at a map of Japan and check your geographical knowledge. This is to prepare for the following reading exercises.**

日本の地図を見て、地理の知識を確認しましょう。

K. **Read the descriptions and fill in the blanks with the appropriate number on the map.**

説明を読んで、地図で学校の位置を確認しましょう。

Aさんの学校は北海道南東部の町にあります。広い町ですが、人口は約9000人です。学校の回りは自然が豊かで、スポーツ施設もたくさんあります。

Aさんの学校 ＿＿＿＿

Bさんの学校 ＿＿＿＿

Cさんの学校 ＿＿＿＿

Dさんの学校 ＿＿＿＿

1.

2.

3.

7.

8.

4.

5.

6.

9.

10.

Bさんの学校は東京都の東部にあります。学校の近くには大きい大学があって、若者がたくさんいます。店や会社もたくさんあって、にぎやかです。

Cさんの学校は神奈川県横浜市の東部にあります。学校の近くに公園があります。回りには家がたくさんあって、けっこう静かです。

Dさんの学校は山口県の西部にあります。山口県は九州のとなりです。学校の近くに広い海岸があります。博物館や公園もあって、すばらしいです。

2 Type of school, students, campus　種類、生徒、キャンパス

A. Circle those words that are applicable to your school.

皆さんの学校に当てはまる言葉をまるで囲みましょう。

Public or private?

公立(校)　私立(校)

Boys, girls, or co-ed?

男子校　女子校　(男女) 共学校

Other characteristics?

ボーディングスクール　インターナショナルスクール　チャータースクール (特別認可校)　マグネットスクール (特別カリキュラムの学校)

Information gathering　情報収集

Religion?

仏教系の学校　イスラム教系の学校　キリスト教系の学校　ユダヤ教系の学校　宗教系の学校

B. Describe your school by using the words you have circled above. Add or replace some words if necessary.

まるで囲んだ言葉を使って学校について書いてください。

List-making　リスト化

例 (Example)

学校は：　公立の男女共学校。

マグネットスクール(特別カリキュラムの学校)。

Describing　文章化

学校は公立の共学校で、マグネットスクール(特別カリキュラムの学校)です。

The school is a public coeducational school and it is a magnet school (a school with a special curriculum.)

リスト化（か）List-making **Your School**

文章化（ぶんしょうか）Describing

C. Indicate the number of academic terms per year in your school as well as the grade levels.

学期（がっき）の数（かず）と学年（がくねん）を書（か）いてください。

情報収集（じょうほうしゅうしゅう）Info gathering

例（Example）

学期数（がっきすう）	3
学年（がくねん）	9-12

リスト化（か）List-making

学校（がっこう）は：3学期制（がっきせい）。
9年生（ねんせい）から12年生（ねんせい）まで。

文章化（ぶんしょうか）Describing

学校（がっこう）は3学期制（がっきせい）で、学年（がくねん）は9年生（ねんせい）から12年生（ねんせい）までです。

文章化（ぶんしょうか）Describing **Your school**

D. Check the number of students and faculty at your school and make sentences.

生徒数（せいとすう）や教員数（きょういんすう）を調（しら）べて書（か）きましょう。

情報収集（じょうほうしゅうしゅう）Info gathering

例（Example）

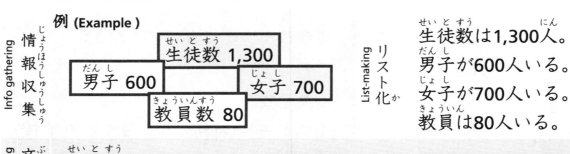

生徒数（せいとすう）1,300
男子（だんし）600
女子（じょし）700
教員数（きょういんすう）80

リスト化（か）List-making

生徒数（せいとすう）は1,300人（にん）。
男子（だんし）が600人いる。
女子（じょし）が700人いる。
教員（きょういん）は80人いる。

文章化（ぶんしょうか）Describing

生徒数（せいとすう）は1,300人です。男子（だんし）が600人いて、女子（じょし）が700人います。それから、教員（きょういん）は80人います。

文章化（ぶんしょうか）Describing **Your school**

E. What kind of campus does your school have? Have a small group discussion and write your description.

皆<ruby>みな</ruby>さんの学校のキャンパスはどんなキャンパスですか。

例 (Example)

Information gathering
情報収集<ruby>じょうほうしゅうしゅう</ruby>

ひろい —— 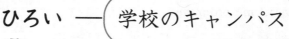学校のキャンパス きれい

しぜんがおおい
しずか

List-making
リスト化<ruby>か</ruby>

キャンパスは：
広<ruby>ひろ</ruby>くてきれい。
自然<ruby>しぜん</ruby>が多<ruby>おお</ruby>くて静<ruby>しず</ruby>か。

Describing
文章化<ruby>ぶんしょうか</ruby>

キャンパスは広<ruby>ひろ</ruby>くてきれいです。
それから、自然<ruby>しぜん</ruby>が多<ruby>おお</ruby>くて静<ruby>しず</ruby>かです。

List-making
リスト化<ruby>か</ruby>

Your school

Describing
文章化<ruby>ぶんしょうか</ruby>

F. Put together all the sentences you have made so far.

これまでに作成<ruby>さくせい</ruby>した文を一つにまとめましょう。

例 (Example)

Describing
文章化<ruby>ぶんしょうか</ruby>

私達<ruby>たち</ruby>の学校は公立<ruby>こうりつ</ruby>の共学校<ruby>きょうがくこう</ruby>で、マグネットスクール(特別<ruby>とくべつ</ruby>カリキュラムの学校<ruby>がっこう</ruby>)です。3学期制<ruby>がっきせい</ruby>で、学年は9年生から12年生までです。生徒数<ruby>せいとすう</ruby>は1,300人です。女子が700人いて、男子が600人います。それから、教員<ruby>きょういん</ruby>は80人います。キャンパスは広<ruby>ひろ</ruby>くてきれいです。それから、自然<ruby>しぜん</ruby>が多<ruby>おお</ruby>くて静<ruby>しず</ruby>かです。

Your school

Describing
文章化<ruby>ぶんしょうか</ruby>

469

3 Academic divisions and subjects　教科と科目
<small>きょうか　かもく</small>

A. Review academic subject vocabulary with your classmates.

クラスメートと教科と科目の語彙を復習しましょう。
<small>きょうか　かもく　ごい　ふくしゅう</small>

B. List and describe your academic programs.

皆さんの学校の教科についてリスト化、文章化しましょう。
<small>みな　きょうか　か　ぶんしょうか</small>

例 (Example)

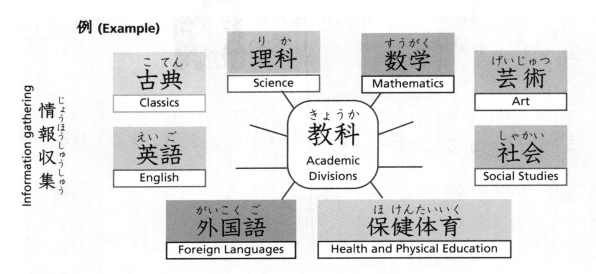

Information gathering　情報収集
<small>じょうほうしゅうしゅう</small>

古典　Classics <small>こてん</small>
理科　Science <small>りか</small>
数学　Mathematics <small>すうがく</small>
芸術　Art <small>げいじゅつ</small>
英語　English <small>えいご</small>
教科　Academic Divisions <small>きょうか</small>
社会　Social Studies <small>しゃかい</small>
外国語　Foreign Languages <small>がいこくご</small>
保健体育　Health and Physical Education <small>ほけんたいいく</small>

List-making　リスト化 <small>か</small>

教科：8つある。
<small>きょうか</small>

英語、外国語、古典、理科、数学、芸術、社会、保健体育
<small>えいご　がいこくご　こてん　りか　すうがく　げいじゅつ　しゃかい　ほけんたいいく</small>

Describing　文章化 <small>ぶんしょうか</small>

私達の学校には教科が8つあります。英語、外国語、古典、
<small>たち　きょうか　えいご　がいこくご　こてん</small>
理科、数学、芸術、社会、そして、保健体育です。
<small>りか　すうがく　げいじゅつ　しゃかい　ほけんたいいく</small>

List-making　リスト化 <small>か</small>

Your school

Describing　文章化 <small>ぶんしょうか</small>

ノート: Providing a list of examples (例をあげる)

X(に)は次のようなものがあります

The sentence above may be placed before a list of examples you provide about category X. つぎ means "next" or "the following" and つぎのようなもの means "things such as the following." This expression is useful, especially when you have rather a long list of examples.

学校のスポーツチームには次のようなものがあります。
サッカー、野球、ソフトボール、テニス、バレーボール、バスケットボール、レスリング、アイスホッケー、陸上

We have athletic teams in our school such as the following: soccer, baseball, softball, tennis, volleyball, basketball, wrestling, ice hockey, and track and field.

C. Study the note above and practice providing a list of examples.

上のノートを読んで、練習をしましょう。

例 (Example)

学校の近くの公共施設には次のようなものがあります。

図書館、病院、郵便局、駅、博物館、動物園、プール

	category	examples
EX.	学校の近くの公共施設	library, hospital, PO, train station, museum, zoo, swimming pool
1.	カフェテリアの食べ物	
2.	去年見た映画	Create
3.	去年読んだ本	Your Own.
4.	Create your own.	

471

D. Name subjects or courses available in each academic division and make a list.

各学科の科目の名前をあげて、リスト化してください。

例 (Example)

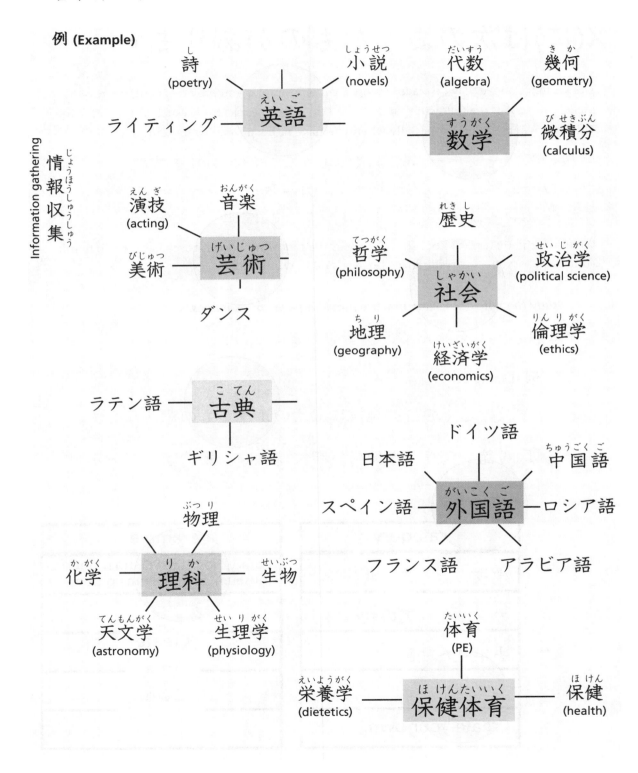

詩
(poetry)

小説
(novels)

代数
(algebra)

幾何
(geometry)

ライティング ― 英語

数学 ― 微積分
(calculus)

Information gathering

情報収集

演技
(acting)

音楽

美術 ― 芸術

ダンス

歴史

哲学
(philosophy)

政治学
(political science)

社会

地理
(geography)

経済学
(economics)

倫理学
(ethics)

ラテン語 ― 古典

ギリシャ語

ドイツ語

日本語

中国語

スペイン語 ― 外国語 ― ロシア語

物理

化学 ― 理科 ― 生物

フランス語

アラビア語

天文学
(astronomy)

生理学
(physiology)

体育
(PE)

栄養学
(dietetics)

保健体育

保健
(health)

List-making

教科と科目：

英語—小説、詩、ライティング

外国語—日本語、フランス語、ドイツ語、中国語、ロシア語

古典—ラテン語、ギリシャ語

理科—物理、化学、生物、天文学、生理学

数学—代数、幾何、微積分

芸術—音楽、美術、演技、ダンス

社会—歴史、地理、哲学、政治学、倫理学、経済学

保健体育—体育、保健、栄養学

E. You may include a whole list of subjects or just a few examples in your description. For the former you will begin by saying "Subjects and courses in each division are as follows" and simply attach the list.

科目の名前を全部あげる場合について、練習しましょう。

Describing 文章化

教科と科目には次のようなものがあります。

Attach the list here.

ノート: Giving examples 2 (例をあげる)

XはY1、Y2、Y3 などがあります/などです

XはY1、Y2、Y3など、いろいろ(or たくさん)あります

The constructions above are useful in giving examples. You may give any number of examples, though 2-6 seem appropriate. Yなど means Y, etc. たくさん and いろいろ(な) mean "various" and "many," respectively.

果物はバナナ、メロン、いちごなどがあります。

As for the fruits we have bananas, melons, strawberries, etc.

科目は物理、天文学、歴史、演技、音楽など、いろいろあります。

We have a variety of subjects such as physics, astronomy, history, acting, and music.

continued to the next page

XはY1やY2やY3など・・・

The particle や may be used to mark an example, except for the final one in the previous constructions. Although や is very effective and frequently used in giving examples, it sounds redundant when the number of examples is more than a few.

科目(かもく)は物理(ぶつり)や天文学(てんもんがく)や歴史(れきし)など、いろいろあります。

We have a variety of subjects, such as physics, astronomy, and history.

F. Practice making sentences using the constructions introduced in the previous note.

たくさん(いろいろ)あるものの例(れい)をあげる練習(れんしゅう)をしましょう。

> **例 (Example)**
>
> デザート
>
> →アイスクリーム、チーズケーキ、パンプキンパイ・・・
>
> デザートはアイスクリーム、チーズケーキ、パンプキンパイ などたくさんあります。

G. You may include a whole list of subjects or just a few examples in your description. For the former you will begin by saying "Subjects and courses in each division are as follows" and simply attach the list.

科目(かもく)の名前(なまえ)を全部(ぜんぶ)あげる場合(ばあい)について、練習(れんしゅう)しましょう。

> **例 (Example)**
>
> 英語(えいご)の科目(かもく)は小説(しょうせつ)、詩(し)、ライティングなどです。外国語(がいこくご)は日本語(にほんご)やドイツ語やギリシャ語(ちゅうごくご)など、たくさんあります。古典(こてん)はラテン語とギリシャ語です。理科(りか)は物理(ぶつり)、化学(かがく)、天文学(てんもんがく)など、いろいろあります。数学(すうがく)は代数(だいすう)、幾何(きか)などがあります。芸術(げいじゅつ)は音楽(おんがく)や美術(びじゅつ)や演技(えんぎ)などです。それから、社会(しゃかい)は歴史(れきし)や政治(せいじ)学(がく)など、たくさんあります。そして、保健体育(ほけんたいいく)は体育(たいいく)と保健(ほけん)と栄養学(えいようがく)です。
>
> Describing 文章化(ぶんしょうか)

Describing 文章化(ぶんしょうか)

Your School

list or examples.

4 Athletic teams and clubs

スポーツチームとクラブ

A. Which athletic teams do you have in your school? Place a checkmark in the appropriate boxes in the ある column. Which teams do you think have been doing especially well lately? Place a checkmark in the appropriate boxes in the つよい column. Use the blank spaces at the bottom of the list to indicate any other athletic teams your school may have.

皆さんの学校にはどんなスポーツチームがありますか。下のリストの「ある」の欄に印をつけてください。また、最近特に強いチームはどれですか。「つよい」の欄に印をつけてください。リストにないスポーツチームがあったら、空欄に書きましょう。

情報収集・整理
information gathering/sorting

ある	つよい	
		フットボール
		サッカー
		フィールドホッケー
		クロスカントリー
		バレーボール
		バスケットボール
		野球 (baseball)
		ソフトボール
		陸上競技 (track)
		体操 (gymnastics)
		水泳 (swimming)
		水球 (water polo)

ある	つよい	
		アイスホッケー
		ゴルフ
		ボウリング
		レスリング
		スキー
		ラクロス
		ラケットボール
		スカッシュ
		バドミントン
		テニス
		ラグビー
		ボート

475

とくに

とくに is an adverb and it corresponds to "especially" in English. It is useful when you want to indicate something particularly noteworthy in connection with the information you have provided.

好きな音楽はジャズ、クラシック、ロックなどいろいろあるけど、特に、ジャズをよく聞きます。

As for the music I like, there is a variety such as jazz, classical, and rock, but I especially like to listen to jazz often.

B. Create a list of athletic teams in your school, and name a few among them that are particularly strong.

皆さんの学校のスポーツチームのリストを作って、その中で特に強いチームも書いてください。

List-making リスト化か

Your school

スポーツチーム：　　　　　　　　　　特に強いチーム：

C. You may include a whole list of teams or several examples in your description. Proceed in the same manner as the academic subjects except that you will add information about those teams that are especially successful.

科目の時と同じようにスポーツチームについて文章化しましょう。特に強いチームをあげてください。

Describing 文章化か

例 (Example)

学校のスポーツチームはサッカー、バレーボール、野球、ソフトボール、レスリング、アイスホッケーなど、いろいろありますが、特にアイスホッケーチームが強いです。

Describing 文章化か

Your school

D. What sort of clubs do you have in your school? Place a checkmark in the appropriate boxes in the ある *column. Which ones do you think have been especially active lately? Place a checkmark in the appropriate boxes in the* さかん *column.* さかん *means "popular' or "prosperous." Use the blank spaces at the bottom of the list to indicate any other clubs in your school.*

皆さんの学校にはどんなクラブがありますか。下のリストの「ある」の欄に印をつけてください。その中で特に盛んなクラブがあったら、「さかん」の欄に印をつけてください。

Information gathering/sorting

ある	さかん	文化系（ぶんかけい）	ある	さかん	ボランティア系（けい）
		オーケストラ			スープ＆キッチン
		ジャズバンド			アムネスティ (Amnesty International)
		アニメクラブ			老人（ろうじん）のためのクラブ (helping the elderly)
		ロボット部（ぶ）			障害者（しょうがいしゃ）のためのクラブ (helping people with disabilities)
		英語部（えいごぶ） (English)			子供（こども）のためのクラブ (helping children)
		写真部（しゃしんぶ） (photo)			ホームレスのためのクラブ (traffic safety)
		美術部（びじゅつぶ） (arts & crafts)			交通安全（こうつうあんぜん）のためのクラブ
		音楽部（おんがくぶ） (music)			国際親善（こくさいしんぜん）のためのクラブ (international exchange)
		数学部（すうがくぶ） (math)			緑化（りょっか）のためのクラブ (protesting deforestation)
		演劇部（えんげきぶ） (drama)			環境（かんきょう）のためのクラブ (the environment)
		科学部（かがくぶ） (science)			日本語のためのクラブ
		茶道部（さどうぶ） (tea ceremony)			模擬国連（もぎこくれん） [モデルUN]

ノート：Y (Noun 2) for the benefit/sake of X (Noun 1)

Xのための Y

This construction is useful when you want to indicate the benefit or purpose of something.

子供のためのクラブ　Clubs that are intended to help children

E. *Create a list of clubs in your school and name a few among them that are particularly active.*

皆さんの学校のクラブのリストを作って、その中で特に盛んなクラブも書いてください。

List-making リスト化

Your school

クラブ：　　　　　　　　　　　　　　特に盛んなクラブ：

F. *You may include a whole list of clubs or several examples in your description. Proceed in the same manner as the athletic teams except that you will add information about those clubs that are especially successful.*

スポーツチームの時と同じようにクラブについて文章化しましょう。特に盛んなクラブも挙げてください。

Describing 文章化

例 (Example)

学校の文化系クラブは写真部、演劇部、科学部、オーケストラなど、たくさんあります。ボランティア系クラブも子供のためのクラブや環境のためのクラブなど、いろいろあります。特に、写真部と環境のためのクラブが盛んです。

Describing 文章化

Your school

G. Put together all the sentences you have made with respect to academic programs, athletic teams, and clubs.

これまでに作成した教科と科目、スポーツチーム、クラブについての文章を一つにまとめましょう。

例 (Example)

私達の学校には教科が8つあります。英語、外国語、古典、理科、数学、芸術、社会、そして、保健体育です。英語の科目は小説、詩、ライティングなどです。外国語は日本語やドイツ語や中国語など、たくさんあります。古典はラテン語とギリシャ語です。理科は物理、化学、天文学など、いろいろあります。数学は代数、幾何などがあります。芸術は音楽や美術や演技などです。それから、社会は歴史や政治学など、たくさんあります。そして、保健体育は体育と保健と栄養学です。

学校のスポーツチームはサッカー、バレーボール、野球、ソフトボール、レスリング、アイスホッケーなど、いろいろありますが、特にアイスホッケーチームが強いです。

学校の文化系クラブは写真部、演劇部、科学部、オーケストラなど、たくさんあります。ボランティア系クラブも子供のためのクラブや環境のためのクラブなど、いろいろあります。特に、写真部と環境のためのクラブが盛んです。

Your school

Describing 文章化

Recognition Kanji 2: 認識漢字 2
にんしきかんじ

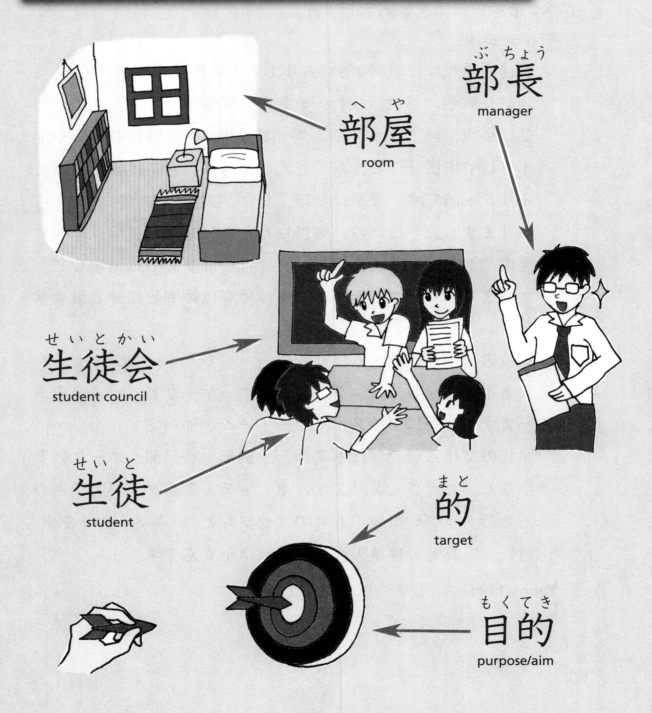

部屋
へや
room

部長
ぶちょう
manager

生徒会
せいとかい
student council

生徒
せいと
student

的
まと
target

目的
もくてき
purpose/aim

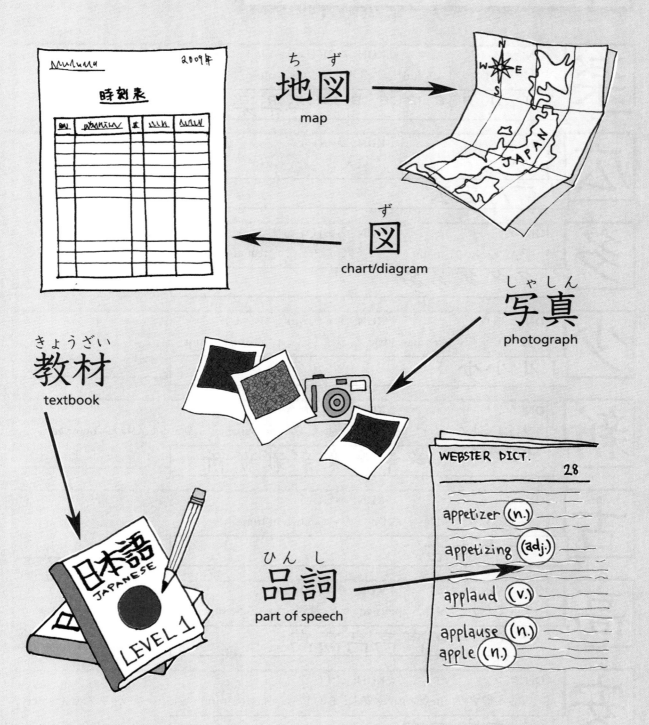

ち ず
地図
map

ず
図
chart/diagram

しゃしん
写真
photograph

きょうざい
教材
textbook

ひん し
品詞
part of speech

New Kanji 1: 新出漢字 1

しんしゅつかんじ

楽

ON: ラク、ガク　　　　**KUN**: たの(しい)

楽しい: たのしい　fun　　　音楽: おんがく　music　　　楽: らく　comfortable

`ノ イ 白 白 白 泊 泊 泊 泊 楽 楽 楽`

広

ON: コウ　　　　**KUN**: ひろ(い)

広い: ひろい　spacious　　　広大: こうだい　vast

`ノ 亠 广 広 広`

多

ON: タ　　　　**KUN**: おお(い)

多い: おおい　many　　　多大: ただい　a great amount

`ノ ク タ タ 多 多`

少

ON: ショウ　　　　**KUN**: すく(ない)、すこ(し)

少ない: すくない　few, little　　　少し: すこし　a little amount

`ノ 丨 小 少`

新

ON: シン　　　　**KUN**: あたら(しい)

新しい: あたらしい　new　　新聞: しんぶん　newspaper　　新年: しんねん　new year

`ノ 亠 ヤ ウ 立 立 辛 辛 亲 新 新 新 新`

古

ON: コ　　　　**KUN**: ふる(い)

古い: ふるい　old　　　古代: こだい　ancient times

`一 十 古 古 古`

高

ON: コウ　　　　**KUN**: たか(い)

高い: たかい　high, expensive　　　最高: さいこう　superb, best

`ノ 亠 亠 古 古 产 高 高 高 高`

安

ON: アン　　　　**KUN**: やす(い)

安い: やすい　inexpensive　　安心: あんしん　peace of mind, security　　安全: あんぜん　safety

`ノ ノ 宀 宀 安 安`

Language Note 4

Kamishibai Presentation

絵草子
浮世絵

What is kamishibai?

Kamishibai can be literally translated as "paper play." Instead of a play that is acted out by a number of people or dolls, one person brings the *kamishibai* to life using picture cards.

Origin of kamishibai

Kamishibai's origins are rooted in Japan, but it is a part of a long-standing Asian picture storytelling tradition. Popular throughout Japan from the 1920s and continuing into the 1950s, *Kamishibai* began as the art of street storytelling.

It's a children's favorite

The storyteller traveled through villages and neighborhoods on a bicycle equipped with a small stage for showing the picture cards. The sound of the two wooden clappers, which the storyteller would loudly strike together upon dismounting from his bicycle, brought the children running from their homes. The storyteller also sold candy and those who bought candy were given the privilege of standing nearest the stage.

The art of kamishibai storytelling

The story was always told in a dramatic manner to accompany the vivid images on each of the picture cards. Oftentimes, the whole story was not told. Instead the *kamishibai* stories were told in serial form. The storyteller would stop at an exciting moment, leaving the children impatient for the next visit. At that time, the picture cards were drawn by hand and on the back of each card was only a pointer about the story line. The storyteller had to be able to improvise. In most cases, modern day *kamishibai* have the entire story printed on the back of each picture card so that the storyteller is able to hold the card and read from the back, while displaying the printed picture to his or her audience.

Kamishibai today

Although the advent of television in 1953 gradually brought about the decline of the itinerant storytellers and their *kamishibai,* it is used today by some teachers to read to large groups of children. In some ways, the *kamishibai* picture cards are not much different from today's presentation aids, such as PowerPoint™. One could say that PowerPoint™ is a modern day version of *kamishibai*. If you do not have access to such programs, *kamishibai* could be used in an equally effective presentation.

4.4 Mechanics 組立て
<ruby>組<rt>く</rt></ruby><ruby>立<rt>み た</rt></ruby>て

Basic Information Style II
基礎情報型 その２
<ruby>基礎情報型<rt>きそじょうほうがた</rt></ruby>

Objectives

Collect and organize basic information about your school events.

Learn strategies to make your writing easy to understand for your intended readers and create appropriate descriptions using these strategies.

Confirm your understanding about the "primary source" or basic information style of writing.

Overview

In this section you will deal with basic information about your school events. The three-step approach from the previous section is in effect here and you will learn to use various strategies such as paraphrasing and simile in your descriptions as well. These strategies are quite useful since your potential readers are Japanese and they may not be familiar with the events in your school or the terms you may use. You will also learn about some popular school events in Japan and this will help you present your information in a manner that is easy to understand for your Japanese readers.

2	Collect and describe basic information	基礎情報の収集と描写
5	School events in Japan	日本の学校行事
6	Strategies to make something easy to understand	わかりやすくする工夫
7	Describing contents	内容の描写
8	Basic information style writing: A wrap-up	基礎情報型のまとめ
9	Events in your school	皆さんの学校の行事

5 School events in Japan　　　　　　　　　日本の学校行事

A. Let's first learn about some popular Japanese school events. Take a look at the sample calendar of events of a school with a trimester system.

まず日本の学校行事について学びましょう。

1学期	4月	入学式 (entrance ceremony)、始業式 (term opening ceremony)
		対面式 (ceremonial meeting between old and new students)
	5月	遠足 (school excursion)
		体育祭 (sports day)
	6月	中間試験 (midterm examinations)
		保護者会 (parent/guardian teacher meeting)
	7月	期末試験 (final examinations)、球技大会 (ball sports day)
		終業式 (term closing ceremony)
夏休み	8月	夏期講習 (summer sessions)、部活動合宿 (club/team camps)
2学期	9月	始業式、水泳大会 (swimming competition)
	10月	文化祭 (cultural festival)、中間試験
		修学旅行 (school trip)
	11月	創立記念日 (anniversary)、芸術鑑賞 (art appreciation)
		合唱コンクール (chorus competition)
	12月	期末試験、終業式
冬休み	1月	始業式
3学期	2月	中間試験
		演劇コンクール (drama competition)
	3月	学年末試験 (final examinations for the year)
		卒業式 (graduation)、終業式 (term ending ceremony)
春休み		

日本の学校行事(ぎょうじ): Japanese School Events

Ceremonies (式(しき))

The sample school calendar includes quite a few events in which the name ends with しき (ceremony). There are ceremonies for both incoming and outgoing students (にゅうがくしき and そつぎょうしき) and each academic term begins and ends with a ceremony (しぎょうしき and しゅうぎょうしき). Some schools may also have たいめんしき, in which new and returning students officially meet with one another for the first time.

Festivals (祭(まつ)り)

ぶんかさい (cultural festival) and たいいくさい (athletic festival) are popular "festivals" in Japanese schools. ぶんかさい is often the biggest and most anticipated school event. At ぶんかさい, students display their talents and achievements though various activities ranging from rock concerts to academic presentations. Schools are open to outside visitors during ぶんかさい and the atmosphere is indeed lively and festive. At たいいくさい, students representing their homeroom classes show off their athletic talents and compete in various events. The winning homeroom class is announced at the end.

Camp (合宿(がっしゅく))

がっしゅく literally means "lodge together," and it is used to refer to an activity in which a group of students and their adult supervisors go to some place for a few days or longer for a common purpose. Some athletic clubs may have a mandatory summer training camp and some schools may hold an optional ski camp for their students.

Competitions (コンクール、コンテスト、大会(たいかい))

Some of the events facilitate friendly competition among individuals as well as groups. Both コンクール (from French "concour") and コンテスト (contest) may be used to indicate these events, though the former tends to be preferred especially in art and music-related competitions. たいかい literally means "big meeting" and it is often used to indicate athletic tournaments, such as きゅうぎたいかい (ball sports day) and すいえいたいかい (swimming competition).

Examinations (試験(しけん))

Many schools have both midterms (ちゅうかんしけん) and final exams (きまつしけん). The word しけん may be used interchangeably with テスト (test), though the former tends to represent more formal kinds than the latter. There is a Japanese word クイズ, which comes from "quiz" in English, but it is NOT used to indicate a short test given in schools. クイズ usually refers to quiz shows on television or the questions given in those shows.

Excursions and Trips (遠足(えんそく)、修学旅行(しゅうがくりょこう))

えんそく is a day trip held mainly for social and relaxation purposes. しゅうがくりょこう, on the other hand, is up to about a week long and its itinerary usually includes visits to historical sites and famous landmarks.

B. What school event do the following pictures depict?

学校行事の絵や写真です。行事の名前は何でしょう。

1.

2.

3.

4.

C. Match the school events on the left with the relevant descriptions on the right.

学校行事の単語について適切な文を選んでください。

1.	終業式	( )	a.	学期の最初の日にあります。
2.	保護者会	( )	b.	みんなで歌を歌います。
3.	文化祭	( )	c.	サッカーやバレーボールをします。
4.	期末試験	( )	d.	みんなで遠い所に行きます。
5.	合唱コンクール	( )	e.	学期の最後のテストです。
6.	始業式	( )	f.	父や母が学校で先生と話します。
7.	卒業式	( )	g.	学期の最後の日にあります。
8.	球技大会	( )	h.	発表やコンサートやダンスがあります。
9.	創立記念日	( )	i.	明日から高校生じゃありません。
10.	入学式	( )	j.	いろいろなスポーツをします。
11.	修学旅行	( )	k.	学校の誕生日です。
12.	体育祭	( )	l.	今日から高校生です。

6 Strategies to make something easy to understand

わかりやすくする工夫(くふう)

A. *As you know by now, there are quite a few school events in Japan and they are also different from typical school events in the United States. While Japanese schools may have final exams, a graduation ceremony, and vacations, they have neither a homecoming nor a prom. First, discuss how you may be able to successfully introduce these unfamiliar events to your contemporaries in Japan. After that, go over the following note.*

学校行事(ぎょうじ)の紹介(しょうかい)の仕方(しかた)について話(はな)し合(あ)いましょう。

ノート: Making something easier to understand (分(わ)かりやすくする工夫(くふう))

When you use a term that is unfamiliar to your potential readers, you will need to provide some information or explanation about it to make it easier to understand. Here are some effective ways to do that.

1. Paraphrasing (言(い)い換(か)え)

9月1日に始業式(しぎょうしき)があります。始業式(しぎょうしき)とは学期(がっき)の最初(さいしょ)の日(ひ)にある式(しき)のことです。

Shigyooshiki happens on September 1. *Shigyooshiki* is a ceremony held on the first day of a term.

2. Classifying (分類(ぶんるい))

私(わたし)の町(まち)では10月に「パンプキンフェスト」という行事(ぎょうじ)があります。

An event called "Pumpkin Fest" takes place in October in my town.

3. Indicating resemblance (類似点(るいじてん)の指摘(してき))

シニアトリップは修学旅行(しゅうがくりょこう)のようなものです。

A senior trip is something like *shuugakuryokoo*.

シニアトリップは修学旅行(しゅうがくりょこう)に似(に)ています。

A senior trip resembles *shuugakuryokoo*.

489

ノート：Paraphrasing（言い換え）

X(と)はYのことです

In this construction, X represents an original word and Y represents its paraphrased counterpart.

シニア(と)は高校3年生のことです。

Seniors are synonymous with third year high school students.

コンビニ(と)はコンビニエンスストアのことです。

Konbini refers to convenience stores.

終業式(と)は学期の最後にある式のことだ。

Shuugyooshiki is a ceremony held on the last day of a term.

B. Paraphrasing exercise - Complete the following sentences using X とは Y のことです。

「X(と)はYのことです」を使って文を完成してください。

EX1. 7年生は中学1年生のことです。

EX2. 始業式とは学期の最初の日にある式のことだ。

1. 8年生は＿＿＿＿＿＿＿＿＿＿＿＿＿＿＿＿＿＿＿＿＿＿。

2. 9年生は＿＿＿＿＿＿＿＿＿＿＿＿＿＿＿＿＿＿＿＿＿＿。

3. 10年生は＿＿＿＿＿＿＿＿＿＿＿＿＿＿＿＿＿＿＿＿＿。

4. 11年生は＿＿＿＿＿＿＿＿＿＿＿＿＿＿＿＿＿＿＿＿＿。

5. 12年生は＿＿＿＿＿＿＿＿＿＿＿＿＿＿＿＿＿＿＿＿＿。

6. 終業式とは＿＿＿＿＿＿＿＿＿＿＿＿＿＿＿＿＿＿＿＿。

7. 中間試験とは＿＿＿＿＿＿＿＿＿＿＿＿＿＿＿＿＿＿＿。

8. 期末試験とは＿＿＿＿＿＿＿＿＿＿＿＿＿＿＿＿＿＿＿。

C. *Match the abbreviated and contracted loanwords on the left with their non-abbreviated and non-contracted counterparts on the right.*

短縮された言葉とその元の言葉をマッチさせてください。

1. ファミレス　　（　　）
2. パソコン　　　（　　）
3. アメフト　　　（　　）
4. アイス　　　　（　　）
5. デジカメ　　　（　　）
6. エアコン　　　（　　）
7. チョコ　　　　（　　）
8. パンフ　　　　（　　）
9. アパート　　　（　　）
10. リモコン　　　（　　）

a. アパートメント
b. アイスクリーム
c. チョコレート
d. パーソナルコンピューター
e. デジタルカメラ
f. パンフレット
g. ファミリーレストラン
h. リモートコントローラー
i. エアーコンディショナー
j. アメリカンフットボール

D. *Practice the following conversation in which speaker A uses a "paraphrasing strategy" for a successful communication with speaker B. Continue to practice by rewriting the underlined parts below using the words that appeared in the previous exercise and practice.*

「言い換えのストラテジー」を使って会話を練習しましょう。

> **会話の例 (Sample Dialogue)**
>
> A: 昨日、新しいコンビニに行きました。
>
> B: コンビニ?
>
> A: コンビニエンスストアのことですよ。
>
> B: あ、コンビニエンスストアですか。

XというY

XというY is the Japanese equivalent of "Y called X," and it is useful when you introduce something or someone for the first time. If you have a dog whose name is Miro, you may say ミロといういぬがいます (I have a dog called Miro). と in という is a particle used to mark quotations.

私の学校では5月に「スプリングフリング」という行事があります。

An event called "Spring Fling" takes place in my school in May.

昨日「ラフテー」という沖縄の食べ物を食べました。

I ate an Okinawan food called *rafutee*.

E. Practice making X という Y according to the following information. Also create additional X という Y by replacing X with applicable words other than the ones given below.

「分類のストラテジー」を使って会話を練習しましょう。

例 (Example)　　ツバルという国 (a country called Tuvalu)

Y / X	1. 国 / ツバル	2. 人 / 森さん	3. 町 / 酒田	4. 映画 / ゴジラ	5. 湖 / 琵琶湖	6. 行事 / 対面式

F. Read the following paragraphs and underline X という Y as you go along. Also guess what のぼります in the first paragraph and ゆうしょうします in the second paragraph may mean. Finally fill in the blanks with the appropriate word from the paragraphs.

文章を読んで、「XというY」部分に下線を引いて下さい。それから、「登ります」と「優勝します」の意味も考えましょう。そして、下の文の空欄に文章の中から適当な言葉を選んで入れてください。

1.
> 　　私達の学校に「マンスリーウォーカーズ」というクラブがあります。このクラブでは毎月いろいろな場所を歩きます。先月は学校の前から「リバーライド」という遊園地まで歩きました。今月は「ウエストゲート」という公園に行きました。そして、来月は「パッツピーク」という山に登ります。

2.

私達（たち）の学校では、秋（あき）にコンテストがいろいろある。10月には「ヒューキャンプカップ」というスピーチコンテストがある。去年（きょねん）のコンテストは「クールな日本語」というスピーチをした人が優勝（ゆうしょう）した。11月には「フィスクカップ」というドラマコンテストや「オータムリズム」というダンスコンテストもある。

3.

私達（たち）の学校にはボランティア系（けい）のクラブがたくさんあります。例（たと）えば、「キッズフォーラム」という子供（こども）のためのクラブ、「サッド」という交通安全（こうつうあんぜん）のためのクラブ、「エコアクション」という環境（かんきょう）のためのクラブがあります。

EX. 「マンスリーウォーカーズ」は<u>クラブ</u>です。

1. 「ウエストゲート」は＿＿＿＿＿＿＿です。

2. 「パッツピーク」は＿＿＿＿＿＿＿です。

3. 「リバーライド」は＿＿＿＿＿＿＿です。

4. 「フィスクカップ」は＿＿＿＿＿＿＿です。

5. 「クールな日本語」は＿＿＿＿＿＿＿です。

6. 「ヒューキャンプカップ」は＿＿＿＿＿＿＿です。

7. 「エコアクション」は＿＿＿＿＿＿のためのクラブです。

8. 「キッズフォーラム」は＿＿＿＿＿＿のためのクラブです。

ノート: Indicating resemblance 1 (Simile) (類似点の指摘1 直喩)

XはYのようです　　XはYのようなZです

X はYのようです("X is like Y") simply indicates X's similarity to Y.　X はYのようなZです ("X is Z similar to Y") enables you to identify a category (Y) to which X belongs as well.

そばはスパゲティーのようです。

Soba is like spaghetti.

そばはスパゲティーのような食べ物です。

Soba is a food like spaghetti.

私達の学校のファミリーデーは日本の学校の保護者会のようです。

Family Day in our school is like *hogoshakai* in Japanese schools.

私達の学校のファミリーデーは保護者会のような行事です。

Family Day in our school is an event like *hogoshakai*.

G. Circle the appropriate choice in the parentheses.　正しい方を選んでください。

1. この猫は大きくて黄色で虎の (よう、ような) です。

2. 今日は暑くて夏の (よう、ような) 天気です。

3. 私のアパートのロビーはホテルのロビーの (よう、ような) です。

4. 「スプリングフリング」はプロムの (よう、ような) 行事です。

5. A: 家には本が3,000冊あります。
   B: 3,000冊ですか。じゃ、本屋さんの (よう、ような) ですね。

6. A: 今日は暖かいですね。B: ええ、春の (よう、ような) ですね。

7. 学校のメディアルームはテレビスタジオの (よう、ような) だ。

8. この町はニューヨークの (よう、ような) 町だ。

9. 音楽の先生はロックスターの (よう、ような) だ。

10. 日本語の教室は暑くて日本の町の (よう、ような) 部屋です。

H. Four sets of dialogue will be read to you. Listen carefully and fill in the blanks according to the contents of the dialogue.

四つの会話を聞いて、次の文を完成させましょう。

D1. 学校の店は＿＿＿＿＿＿＿＿＿＿のようです。

D2. サラさんの町の6月の天気は＿＿＿＿＿＿＿＿＿のようです。

D3. 「フィールドデー」は＿＿＿＿＿＿＿＿のような行事です。

D4. 学校のカフェテリアは＿＿＿＿＿＿＿＿のようです。

I. Here are scripts of the dialogues you just listened to. Pair up and practice them with your partner. After that create a short dialogue similar to these four.

最初にペアで四つの会話を練習しましょう。次にこれらの会話に似た会話を作ってください。

1.
> A: 学校の中に店がありますか。
> B: あります。本や雑誌やペンなどを買うことができます。それから、食べ物や飲み物もあります。
> A: じゃ、コンビニのようですね。
> B: ええ、とても便利ですよ。

2.
> A: サラさんの町の天気はどうですか。
> B: 春は暖かくて、気持ちがいいです。でも、6月と7月は雨の日が多くて、少し蒸し暑いですよ。
> A: じゃ、日本の梅雨のようですね。
> B: あ、そうですね。

3.
> A: 明日はフィールドデーです。
> B: フィールドデー?
> A: ええ、外でいろいろなスポーツやゲームをします。ちょっと、日本の学校の運動会のようです。
> B: あ、そうですか。じゃ、楽しいですね。

495

4.

> A: 学校のカフェテリアはどうですか。
>
> B: ラーメン、ピザ、すし、サンドイッチなど、いろいろあります。それから、飲み物やデザートもたくさんあります。値段も安いですよ。
>
> A: じゃ、ファミリーレストランのようですね。
>
> B: ええ。

ノート: Indicating resemblance 2 (類似点の指摘2)

XはYに似ています

XはYににている corresponds to "X resembles Y" in English, and it is useful in indicating X's resemblance to Y.

私達の町の天気は東京の天気に似ています。
The weather in our town resembles the weather in Tokyo.

J. *Pair up and fill in the blanks with an appropriate word you come up with after consulting with your partner. Share the results with the class.*

ペアで相談して文を完成させてください。

1. 私達の町は＿＿＿＿＿＿＿に似ています。

2. 私達の町の天気は＿＿＿＿＿＿＿の天気に似ている。

3. 私達の町の自然は＿＿＿＿＿＿＿の自然に似ている。

4. 私達の学校の校長先生は＿＿＿＿＿＿＿に似ています。

5. 私達の日本語の先生は＿＿＿＿＿＿＿に似ています。

K. Which of the three strategies that you just learned appears in the following?

文を読んで、その中の「分かりやすくする工夫」を選びましょう。

EX. [a]
9月15日にペップラリーがあります。ペップラリーとはスポーツチームを応援する集会のことです。

a. Paraphrasing (言い換え)
b. Providing definition (定義)
c. Indicating resemblance
(類似点の指摘)

1. [   ]
11月に剣道大会があります。剣道はフェンシングに似ています。

2. [   ]
10月にペアレンツデーがあります。ペアレンツデーは保護者会のような行事です。

3. [   ]
私達の学校には「ハピネス」というロックのバンドや「マジック」というジャズのバンドがあります。

4. [   ]
私達の学校はマグネットスクールです。マグネットスクールとは特別なカリキュラムの学校のことです。

7 Describing contents　　内容の描写

ノート: Describing contents (内容の描写)

In some cases you may need to briefly explain an event unfamiliar to your readers. For example, there are no events similar to Homecoming in Japanese schools, and attaching a brief description about it seems necessary and appropriate. We will consider such an attachment as part of the "primary source" or basic information style of writing at this time.

10月に「ホームカミング」という行事があります。卒業生がたくさん学校に来ます。パレードやフットボールの試合もあります。

An event called Homecoming takes place in October. Many alumni/alumnae come back to the school. A parade and a football game also take place.

A. Practice introducing the following events based on the given information.

次の行事を紹介し、その内容を簡単に説明しましょう。

EX.

行事 event	カラーデー (color day)
内容 contents	同じ学年が同じ色の服を着ます。 1年生の色は赤です。 2年生の色は青です。 3年生は黒い服を着ます。

> 10月1日はカラーデーです。この日は同じ学年が同じ色の服を着ます。1年生の色は赤で、2年生の色は青です。3年生は黒い服を着ます。

1.

行事 event	ベークセール (bake sale)
内容 contents	ケーキやクッキーを作ります。 ケーキやクッキーを売ります。 目的はファンドレイジングです。

---

8 **Basic information style writing: A wrap-up**　　基礎情報型のまとめ

A. Go over the following basic information writing, and match the following examples with their most appropriate description.

次の基礎情報型の文章を読んで、その特徴を示す文とマッチさせてください。

1. [　　]

　私達の学校は3学期制で、学年は9年生から12年生までです。生徒数は900人です。女子が500人いて、男子が400人います。それから、教員は60人います。キャンパスは広くてきれいです。

2. [　　]

　私達の学校はオレゴン州ポートランドにあります。学年は9年生から12年生までです。生徒数は1,300人です。学校の近くには池や林があります。公園もたくさんあります。

3. [　　]

　教科には次のようなものがあります。
英語(小説、詩など)
外国語(日本語、ドイツ語など)
理科(物理、天文学など)
数学(代数、微積分など)
芸術(音楽、美術など)
社会(歴史、哲学など)
保健体育(体育、栄養学など)

4. [　　]

　10月に「ホームカミング」という行事があります。卒業生がたくさん学校に来ます。パレードやフットボールの試合もあります。

5. [　　]

　9月にペップラリーがあります。ペップラリーとはスポーツチームを応援する集会のことです。10月にペアレンツデーがあります。ペアレンツデーは保護者会のような行事です。

a. Use of strategies such as paraphrasing (言い換え等ストラテジーを使用)
b. Incorporation of a list (リストを編入)
c. Accumulation of simple sentences (単文のみを使用)
d. Use of linked sentences (結合された文を使用)
e. Describing contents (内容を描写)

A. In small groups discuss what sort of school events your school has and make a calendar of events based on your discussion.

<ruby>小<rt>しょう</rt></ruby>グループで<ruby>皆<rt>みな</rt></ruby>さんの学校の<ruby>行事<rt>ぎょうじ</rt></ruby>について話し<ruby>合<rt>あ</rt></ruby>って、<ruby>行事表<rt>ぎょうじひょう</rt></ruby>を作ってください。

<ruby>例<rt></rt></ruby> (Example)

Information gathering <ruby>情報収集<rt>じょうほうしゅうしゅう</rt></ruby>

どんな学校<ruby>行事<rt>ぎょう じ</rt></ruby>がある？

カラーデーやベークセール

ペアレンツデーやホームカミング

<ruby>中間試験<rt>ちゅうかんしけん</rt></ruby>と<ruby>期末試験<rt>きまつ しけん</rt></ruby>。

List-making リスト<ruby>化<rt>か</rt></ruby>

<ruby>秋学期<rt>あきがっき</rt></ruby>

9月	オリエンテーション
10月	カラーデー
	ヒューキャンプカップ
	ホームカミング
	ハロウィンパーティー
11月	<ruby>中間試験<rt>ちゅうかんしけん</rt></ruby>
	ペアレンツデー
12月	ホリデーベークセール

Your school

List-making リスト<ruby>化<rt>か</rt></ruby>

9月
10月
11月
12月

B. *Now you will decide which events you can introduce as they are, and which events you may need to elaborate on by using strategies such as paraphrasing and/or by describing their contents. Classify all the events into the following categories.*

そのまま紹介できる行事と補足が必要な行事について考えて、次のうちどれかに分類しましょう。

例 (Example)

Present as it is [そのまま提示] オリエンテーション ハロウィンパーティー 中間試験	Use strategies [ストラテジーを使用] ヒューキャンプカップ ペアレンツデー
Describe contents [内容を描写] ホリデーベークセール	Use strategies and describe contents [ストラテジー使用と内容描写] ホームカミング カラーデー

Your school

Present as it is [そのまま提示]	Use strategies [ストラテジーを使用]
Describe contents [内容を描写]	Use strategies and describe contents [ストラテジー使用と内容描写]

C. Create your descriptions introducing your school events, keeping in mind the classifications you just made.

今作った分類に基づいて基礎情報の文を作ってください。

例 (Example)

Describing 文章化

9月の始めにオリエンテーションがあります。10月にはカラー・デー、ヒューキャンプ・カップというスピーチ大会、ホームカミング、ハロウィンパーティーがあります。カラー・デーの日は同じ学年が同じ色の服を着ます。1年生は赤で、2年生は青で、3年生は黒です。ホームカミングの週末には卒業生がたくさん学校に来ます。パレードやフットボールの試合もあります。11月には中間試験とペアレンツデーがあります。ペアレンツデーは保護者会のような行事です。

Your school

Describing 文章化

Recognition Kanji 3: 認識漢字 3

練習
practice

3回
three times

最後
last

最初
first

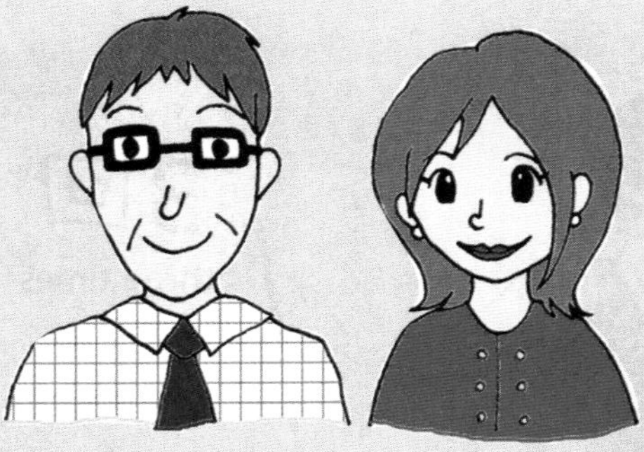

かぞく
家族
family

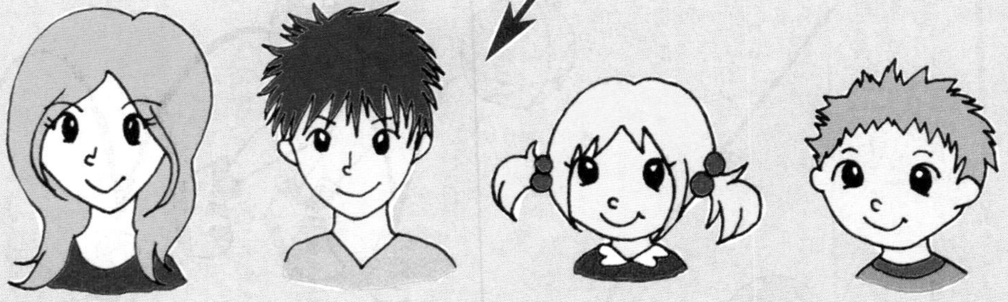

ま
曲げる
to bend

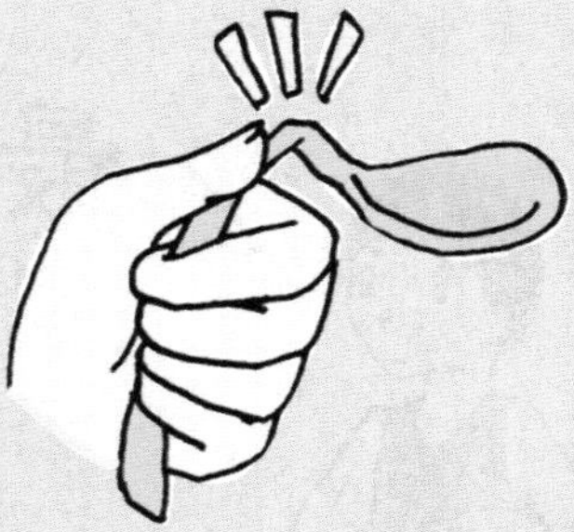

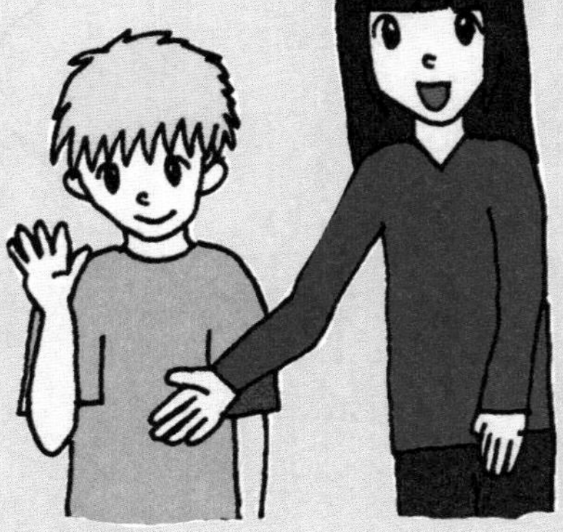

しょうかい
紹介
introduction

New Kanji 2: 新出漢字 2
<small>しんしゅつかんじ</small>

朝 **ON**: チョウ　　　**KUN**: あさ
朝: あさ morning　　朝食: ちょうしょく breakfast　朝ご飯: あさごはん breakfast
一 十 ｢ 古 吉 直 卓 龺 朝 朝 朝

数 **ON**: スウ　　　**KUN**: かず
数: かず number　　数学: すうがく mathematics　数字: すうじ number, digit
` ` ` 半 米 米 半 娄 娄 娄 数 数

科 **ON**: カ　　　**KUN**:ー
理科: りか science　　科学: かがく natural science
一 二 千 千 禾 利 和 科 科

昼 **ON**: ちゅう　　　**KUN**: ひる
昼: ひる noon　　昼食: ちゅうしょく lunch　昼ご飯:ひるごはん lunch
一 コ コ 尸 尺 尺 尽 昼 昼

半 **ON**: ハン　　　**KUN**: なか(ば)
半: はん 30 minutes　　半分: はんぶん half
丶 丷 ソ 兰 半

外 **ON**: ガイ　　　**KUN**: そと
外: そと outside　　外国: がいこく foreign country　外国語: がいこくご
　　　　　　　　　　　　　　　　　　　　　　　　　　foreign language
丿 ク タ 列 外

親 **ON**: シン　　　**KUN**: おや
親: おや parents　　母親: ははおや mother　両親: りょうしん both parents
丶 二 ナ 立 立 辛 辛 亲 новый 新 新 親 親 親

英 **ON**: エイ　　　**KUN**:ー
英語: えいご English　　英国: えいこく England
一 十 艹 艹 苎 苎 英 英

Choosing Strategy Part I: Using Speed Reading

A. The most effective speed reading is decreasing reading volume using kanji reading. Compare three sentences below and find the most effective speed reading.

らいしゅうのもくようびのさんじからにほんごのきょうしつでたなかせんせいの
にじゅうろくさいのたんじょうかいをします。

来週　木曜日　三時　日本語　教室　田中先生　二十六才　誕生会

来週の木曜日の三時から日本語の教室で田中先生の二十六才の誕生会をします

Choosing Strategy Part II: Using Kanji

You can pick up the important information from Kanji which was wrote in the sentences.

わたしの町は便利です。バスや地下鉄があります。ショッピングセンターも多いです。
それから、郵便局もたくさんあります。

B. Find the same content of Kanji in red.

1. 郵便局：手紙、投手、足　　2. 地下鉄：泳ぐ、休む、動く
3. 町：市、山、国

リック・チョーさんは毎日朝ご飯を食べます。ホットケーキとコーヒーがすきです。
果物も食べます。バナマとりんごとオレシジとぶどうが好きです。メロンもときどき
食べます。

C. Find the similar Kanji in red.

1. ご飯：動物、毎日、食物　　2. 果物：朝、好、食物、動物

Choosing Strategy Part III: Using the Beginning of the Sentence

You should try to use the beginning of the sentences to understand the summary.

わたしのまちの冬(ふゆ)は寒(さむ)いです。1月の気温(きおん)は35度(ど)です。2月の気温(きおん)は38度(ど)です。それから、雪(ゆき)もたくさんふります。

D. Find the same category of Kanji in red.

1. 冬：度、気温、雪、雨   2. 気温：雪、冬、夏、度

Fill the line and complete the sentence choosing the appropriate word in the parenthesis below.

The first sentence:_____

私達の町は（暑い、むしあつい、きれい、さむい）です。

Choosing Strategy Part IV: Using the Demonstrative Words and Conjunctions

You can grasp the network of topic and the development of the sentences from the demonstrative words and conjunctions.

私の学校ではだいたい同じ教室(きょうしつ)で勉強(べんきょう)しています。一時間目のクラスは朝いつも8時半から始ります。この教室では、国語や社会や英語や数学の授業(じゅぎょう)が行われます。理科や音楽や芸術(げいじゅつ)の授業はこの場所から移動(いどう)して、ほかの教室にいきます。このクラスには40人くらいて、とても移動がたいへんです。でも、移動時間が10分あるので、この間に遊びます。

教室(きょうしつ): class room   授業(じゅぎょう): class   芸術(げいじゅつ): art   移動(いどう)する: move

E. Choose the appropriate phrase in the parenthesis for the underlined demonstrative word.

1. この教室　（同じ学校、8時半の教室、理科の学校）
2. この場所　（音楽の学校、国語の学校、移動の学校）
3. このクラス　（一時間目のリーダー、移動時間、遊ぶ）
4. この間　（歯を磨いた、6時半に起きた、顔を洗った）

F. Choose the appropriate word in the parenthesis and complete the sentence.

私たちの学校は同じ教室で（おしゃべり、スポーツ、宿題(しゅくだい)、勉強）していることがおおいけれど、（理科、国語、数学）の授業は移動します。

We recommend that you might use the following reading choosing strategy part V, after studying Mechanics 4.6 on this textbook and use the following reading choosing strategy part VI, after studying Mechanics 4.7 on this textbook."

Choosing Strategy Part V: Using the End of the Comment Sentence

Check the end of the sentence. If the writer has some opinions, you will find "to omou," "kamoshirenai," "darootoomou," and "ta-hoogaii."

私たちの学校はスポーツをする生徒がたくさんいる。秋はマラソン大会があって、春は野球大会がある。夏もサマーキャンプをしている。この学校は毎日スポーツする人が300人くらいいるだろうと思う。

私たちの学校の中にはコンビニがあります。本やざっしやペンを買うことができます。それから、食べ物や飲み物もあります。ちょっと高いけど、毎日生徒がたくさん来ます。だから、とても便利だと思います。

G. *The end of the sentences such a "darootoomou"and "to omou" represent the writer's opinion (indirect comment). Fill the lines and complete the sentence choosing the appropriate word in the parenthesis below.*

1. と思うsentence_____

  私達の学校はよく（おしゃべり、勉強、スポーツ）している。

2. と思うsentence_____

  私達の学校はコンビニがあって（不便、便利、きれい）です。

Choosing Strategy Part VI: Using the "No-da" Sentence

私たちの学校の中にはコンビニがある。本やざっしやペンを買うことができる。それから、食べ物や飲み物もある。ちょっと高いけど、毎日生徒がたくさん来る。だから、とても便利なのだ。

F. *The end of the sentences such a "noda"and "nodearu" represent the writer's opinions (direct comment). Fill the line and complete the sentence choosing the appropriate word in the parenthesis below.*

1. のだsentence_____

  学校は（パン、飲み物、宿題、コンビニ）があって、便利だ。

4.5 Mechanics 組立て
くみ た

Expository Style: School Uniforms and Rules
せつめいぶんがた　　せいふく　　こうそく
説明文型：制服と校則

Objectives

Learn useful school terms and describe various school dress codes and regulations.
Create expository style writings with a compound or complex topic sentence.
Learn additional conjunctions.

Overview

This section will deal with the rules and expectations in your school including dress code. In terms of writing, we will shift from the basic information style to the expository style. You will first learn useful words and expressions. Then you and your classmates will sort information and create a paragraph consisting of a topic sentence, four supporting sentences, and accompanying examples as well as sum-up sentences. You may recall your writing about winter weather in Chapter 3 had a simple topic sentence that included only one descriptive word for expressing the severity of winter. This time your topic sentence will include two such words that will be joined by a coordinate conjunction.

2	**Collect and describe basic information**	き そ じょうほうしゅうしゅう びょうしゃ 基礎情報の収集と描写
10	**School uniforms and clothes**	せいふく ふくそう 学校の制服と服装
11	**School rules**	こうそく 校則
3	**Expository style**	せつめいぶんがた 説明文型
1	**Combined or compound topic sentence**	じょうほう つな ぶん 二つの情報を繋げたトッピク文
2	**Supporting sentences and examples**	れい サポートセンテンスと例
3	**Sum-up sentences and conjunctions**	せつぞく ご まとめの文と接続語

10 | School uniforms and clothes

学校の制服と服装

A *Do you have some preferences in your clothing? If you have the following items, place a checkmark in the appropriate boxes in the* もっている *column. And mark the* よくきる *column if you tend to wear them often. Use the blank spaces at the bottom of the list to indicate any other clothing item you may have.*

皆さんはどんな洋服を着ていますか。下のリストの「もっている」の欄に印をつけてください。また、最近特によく着る洋服はどれですか。「よくきる」の欄に印をつけてください。リストにない洋服があったら、空欄に書きましょう。

情報収集・整理

Information gathering/sorting

もっている	よくきる	
		コート
		Ｔーシャツ
		ジャケット
		オーバー
		セーター
		ワイシャツ
		スーツ
		タキシード
		ドレス
		制服 (uniform)
		タンクトップ
		キャミソール

もっている	よくきる	
		パンツ
		スカート
		くつ (shoes)
		くつした (socks)
		ショーツ
		ストッキング
		ネクタイ
		ネックレス
		下着 (underwear)
		制帽 (uniform hat)
		野球帽 (baseball cap)
		帽子 (hat)

Additional useful words and expressions

着_きる

wear
洋服_{ようふく}を着_きる。

セーター、シャツ
上着_{うわぎ}、下着_{したぎ}
着物_{きもの}、制服_{せいふく}
コート
ジャケット
オーバー

はく

wear
パンツをはく。

ズボン
スカート
ジーンズ
靴_{くつ}、靴下_{くつした}
ショーツ

脱_ぬぐ

take off
洋服_{ようふく}を脱_ぬぐ。

かぶる

wear
帽子_{ぼうし}をかぶる。

ヘルメット

しめる

wear
ネクタイをしめる。

帯_{おび}、ベルト

取_とる、外_{はず}す

take off
ネクタイを取_とる。

脱_ぬぐ、取_とる

take off
帽子_{ぼうし}を脱_ぬぐ。

生_はやす

grow
髭_{ひげ}を生_はやす

剃_そる

shave
髭_{ひげ}を剃_そる

付_つける

wear
指輪_{ゆびわ}をつける。

ブレスレット
ベルト

かける

wear
眼鏡_{めがね}をかける。

サングラス

切_きる

cut
髪_{かみ}を切_きる

伸_のばす

grow
髪_{かみ}を伸_のばす

染_そめる

dye
髪_{かみ}を染_そめる

する

wear
時計_{とけい}をする。

イヤリング
ネクタイ
ブラジャー

着_つける

tie, put on
リボンを着_つける。

かつら(wig)

アクセサリー

化粧_{けしょう}(を)する

wear makeup
化粧_{けしょう}をする。

B. Fill in the parentheses with an appropriate word from below.

正しいことばを下のリストから選んでください。

1. (　　　　　　　)

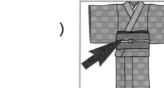
2. (　　　　　　　)

3. (　　　　　　　)

衣服
clothing

4. (　　　　　　　)

5. (　　　　　　　)

6. (　　　　　　　)

はく、きる、つける、ぬぐ、しめる

C. Fill in the parentheses with an appropriate word from below.

関係のあることばを下のリストから選んでください。

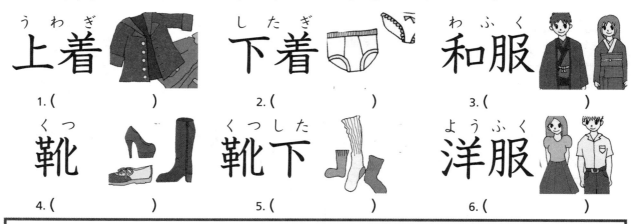

上着
1. (　　　　　　　)

下着
2. (　　　　　　　)

和服
3. (　　　　　　　)

靴
4. (　　　　　　　)

靴下
5. (　　　　　　　)

洋服
6. (　　　　　　　)

jacket, underwear, socks, shoes, Japanese style outfit, Western style outfit

ノート: Describing situation (状態を表す)

(〜を)着ています
(〜を)はいています

Here are two major verbs you need when describing your outfit. Both きています and はいています indicate the fact that someone has a piece of clothing on their body. Use きています when referring to items put on the upper body and はいています when referring to the items for the lower body, including shoes. The particle を is used to mark direct object.

私は青いシャツを着ています。　　　　(I have a blue shirt on.)

トムさんはジーンズをはいています。　(Tom wears jeans.)

ノート: The progressive/stative form

～ている

て form of a verb + いる is known as the progressive/stative form and it is used to express the following.

A. Actions in progress

食べている (someone) is eating　話している (someone) is speaking

B. A state resulting from an already completed action

着ている (someone put something on and, as a result, he or she) <u>has it on</u>

起きている (someone woke up and, as a result, he or she) <u>is awake</u>

C. Habitual and repeated actions

教えている (someone) teaches (on a regular basis)

D. Match the sentences on the left with the appropriate English words on the right.

単語と英語をマッチさせてください。

1. ワイシャツを着ている　　　(　　　)
2. イヤリングをしている　　　(　　　)
3. ネクタイをしめている　　　(　　　)
4. 制服を着きている　　　　　(　　　)
5. パンツをはいている　　　　(　　　)
6. 帽子をかぶっている　　　　(　　　)
7. ベルトをしめている　　　　(　　　)
8. 靴を脱いでいる　　　　　　(　　　)
9. 髪を染めている　　　　　　(　　　)
10. ネクタイを取っている　　　(　　　)
11. 携帯電話を持ってきている　(　　　)

a.	bring a cellular phone
b.	wearing a dress shirt
c.	wearing a tie
d.	taking off a tie
e.	dyed hair
f.	wearing a hat
g.	has shoes removed
h.	wearing pants
i.	wearing a uniform
j.	wearing earrings
k.	has a belt fastened

513

E. Match the images with the words by filling each parenthesis with the appropriate letter from the blue box. Match the images with the verbs by filling the second parenthesis with the appropriate number from the yellow box.

絵と単語をマッチさせてください。

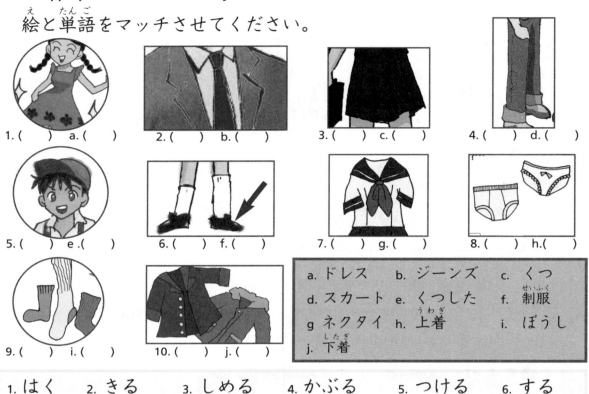

1. (　　) a. (　　)　　2. (　　) b. (　　)　　3. (　　) c. (　　)　　4. (　　) d. (　　)

5. (　　) e. (　　)　　6. (　　) f. (　　)　　7. (　　) g. (　　)　　8. (　　) h. (　　)

9. (　　) i. (　　)　　10. (　　) j. (　　)

a. ドレス	b. ジーンズ	c. くつ
d. スカート	e. くつした	f. 制服
g ネクタイ	h. 上着	i. ぼうし
j. 下着		

| 1. はく | 2. きる | 3. しめる | 4. かぶる | 5. つける | 6. する |

F. Answer the questions. Go ask your classmates and find out.

質問に答えましょう。クラスメートに聞いてみましょう。

1. 赤い洋服を着ている人は何人いますか。　　　　　　(　　人)

2. ピアスをしている人は何人いますか。　　　　　　　(　　人)

3. 青いジーンズをはいている人は何人いますか。　　　(　　人)

4. 眼鏡をかけている人は何人いますか。　　　　　　　(　　人)

5. ネクタイをしめている先生は何人いますか。　　　　(　　人)

6. 白い靴下をはいている人は何人いますか。　　　　　(　　人)

7. 指輪をはめている人は何人いますか。　　　　　　　(　　人)

8. 黒いオーバーを持っている人は何人いますか。　　　(　　人)

G. Circle the appropriate word in the parentheses.

適切なことばを○で囲んでください。

1. 私たちの学校はいつも (制服、私服、着物) を着ます。

2. 私たちの学校は卒業式に (制服、私服、着物、ガウン) を着ます。

3. 私たちの学校は体操の時 (制服、体操着、私服) を着ます。

4. 私服は (週末、いつも、昼) 着ます。

5. 学校ではジーンズを (毎日はきます、毎日はきません)。

私服: personal/own outfits

H. In small groups, discuss what adjectives will be suitable to describe either your school uniforms or your school fashion by season.

学校の制服や服装はどうですか。適切な形容詞を探しましょう。

> **例 (Examples)**
>
> 夏に着ている学校の制服は冬の制服より経済的でかっこいいです。
>
> 冬に着ている服はかっこ悪くてみすぼらしいです。
>
> 春と秋に着ている学校の制服は冬のよりオシャレでかわいいです。

経済的な
economical

軍隊のような
militaristic

オシャレな
fashionable

ダサイ
senseless

夏

学校の
制服/服装

着やすい
easy to wear

春と秋

かっこ悪い
bad looking

みすぼらしい
shabby

カラフルな
colorful

冬

515

ノート: Conjunction; enumerative states or actions (接続の言葉: 〜し、〜し)

〜し、〜し

し in this construction is a conjunction particle and follows a plain form of a verb or an *i* adjective as well as a *na* adjective or a noun + だ (だった in past tense).

兄の制服は経済的だし、かっこいいし、かわいいです。

My older brother's uniform is economical, good looking, and (what is more, it's) cute.

私の学校には山があるし、池もあります。

My school has not only mountains, but also ponds.

Like the て form, し connects states or actions. While the former offers a mere listing of states or actions, the latter sounds more like stacking them up. Compare the following.

私の学校の科目はたくさんあって、おもしろい。

Academic subjects in my school are many and interesting.

私の学校の科目はたくさんあるし、おもしろい。

Academic subjects in my school are many and, what is more, they are interesting.

I. **Describe the following actions in Japanese by using the て form or the 〜し、〜し construction.**

て形 か「〜し、〜し」を使って次の文を接続してください。

1. 学校の制服は新しいです。そしてきれいです。
2. ヤンキースのユニフォームはいつも同じです。ストライプがあります。
3. この音楽は個性的です。音楽のタイトルも面白いです。
4. 明日は日本語の宿題をします。ともだちと映画を見ます。

J. **Describe the following in Japanese using 〜し、〜し.**

「〜し、〜し」を使って次の文を表現してください。

1. Sara is pretty and bright.
2. Our uniforms are economical, colorful, and easy to wear.
3. Sara's mother wears not only western clothes, but also Japanese clothes.
4. I read manga, watch television, and play video games.
5. Many students come to school by bicycle and on foot.

K. Ask your classmates about clothes (jewelry and accessories included) that they usually wear when they go shopping. Also respond to this question when asked by your classmates. Use the appropriate linking devices including 〜し、〜し.

買い物に行く時の服装についてクラスメートに聞きましょう。
「〜し、〜し」等の接続表現も使いましょう。

会話の例 (Sample Dialogue)

A: あなたの学校は制服があります (or ありません) けれど、買い物の時、どんなファッション (or 服装) で行きますか。

B: そうですね。ジーンズをはいて、Tシャツを着て行きます。それから、黒いスニーカーをはくし、ネックレスをつけてちょっとオシャレもします。

L. Let's talk about fashion and school uniforms.

ファッションと学校の制服について話しましょう。

Set initial questions

Be prepared to ask your classmates questions #1 and #2 below. You may also ask either #3 and #4 or create two questions of your own.

1. 毎日の生活でどんな服を着ていますか。
2. この学校には制服が必要ですか。
3. どんなファッションが好きですか。
4. どんなアクセサリーを持っていますか。
5. ＿＿＿＿＿＿＿＿＿＿＿＿＿＿＿＿＿＿＿＿＿か。
6. ＿＿＿＿＿＿＿＿＿＿＿＿＿＿＿＿＿＿＿＿＿か。

Think about follow-up questions

When you ask the set of questions above, you may initially get a brief response. Therefore, be prepared to ask some follow-up questions to obtain more detailed information from your classmates. See the examples below and create your own follow-up questions for questions #3 and #4.

EX1. Possible follow-up questions for Question 1.

毎日の生活でどんな服を着ていますか。
どこの店で買いますか。　　　　　Where (which store)?

いくらぐらいですか。 How much?

どんな色やデザインですか。 What color and design?

いつオシャレな服を着ますか。 When?

他にどんな服が好きですか。 What else?

今を何を買いたいですか。 What do you want to buy?

EX2. Possible follow-up questions for Question 2.

この学校には制服が必要ですか。

どうして必要ですか。 Why?

どうしてですか。 Why?

制服のほうが経済的ですか。 Comparing

制服のほうがかっこ悪いですか。 Comparing

必要な理由をもう一つ教えてください。 Tell me more

必要なじゃない理由をもう一つ教えてください。 Tell me more

Practice developing conversation using じゃ

As you have learned in *Haruichiban*, じゃ is useful in developing conversation. You may use じゃ when you want to say something that would logically follow what your conversation partner has just said, or when you want to indicate a shift of topic or focus in conversation. With this in mind, practice the following dialogue by paying attention to the use of じゃ.

会話の例A (Sample Dialogue A)

A: 制服が必要ですか。

B: はい、必要です。

A: じゃ、どうして必要ですか。

B: 制服はかわいいからですよ。

A: そうですか。じゃ、必要な理由をもう一つ教えてくだ さい。 continued.

会話の例B (Sample Dialogue B)

A: 制服が必要ですか。

B: いいえ、必要じゃありません。

A: じゃ、どうしてですか。

B: 制服はかっこ悪いからですよ。

A: そうですか。じゃ、必要じゃない理由をもう一つ教えてく ださい。 continued.

Activities

1. Interview
   Pair up and ask your partner the questions you have prepared. Make sure to ask follow-up questions and use じゃ effectively.

2. Report
   Report the results of your interview to the class.

報告の例 (Sample Report)

Q1
Aさんは毎日の生活で経済的で、着やすい服を着ています。たいてい、家の近くのモールの中の店で買います。色は白や紫が多いです。週末のデートの時、化粧をしてリボンをつけてちょっとオシャレをします。

Q2
この学校では制服が必要じゃありません。制服はかっこ悪いし、色もよくないからです。私服のほうがかっこいいです。そのうえ、好きな服を選ぶことができるし、楽しいです。でも、Aさんは服のためにお金をあまり使いません。たいてい、同じ洋服を着て、学校に行きます。

M. Match the descriptions about school clothes with their English equivalents on the next page. たいへん **means "very hard" and** かわり **means "substitute."**

制服についての記述とその英語の要点をマッチさせてください。

1.
この学校では制服が必要です。特に、この学校の制服は有名なデザイナーが作った制服だし、いい服です。だから、この制服は少し高いそうです。

2.
この学校では制服が必要じゃありません。だから、みんな毎日違う洋服を着て学校に行きます。特に、女子の洋服は毎日カラフルでおしゃれです。

3.
この学校では制服が必要じゃ
ない。しかし、みんな、Tーシ
ャツを着てジーンズをはいてい
るし、同じモールで買う。だか
ら、Tーシャツとジーンズが制
服のようだ。

4.
この学校では制服が必要だ。
学校は厳しくて、大変だ。だ
から、特に、女子は制服の代
わりの洋服を持っていて、学
校の帰りにはその洋服を着て
帰る。

a. This school's uniforms are uniquely designed and expensive.

b. This school has uniforms, but many girls change their uniforms into regular clothes on their way home from school.

c. This school does not have uniforms, but many students wear T-shirts and jeans.

d. This school does not have uniforms and many students are fashion-conscious.

N. Choose a description that is most applicable to your school clothes from section A and create a brief description about clothes in your school.

皆さんの学校の服装について簡単に紹介しましょう。

例 (Example)

Describing 文章化

この学校には制服がありません。だから、生徒たちは好きな
服を着ることができて、教室はカラフルです。でも、オシャ
レな人はあまりいません。皆、経済的で着やすい服を着てい
ます。化粧をする人や髪を染める人も少ないです。

Your school

Describing 文章化

11 School rules　　　　　　　　校則<ruby>こうそく</ruby>

Do you go to a school with lots of rules and regulations including dress code? In this section you will write about these rules in Japanese after learning some constructions and expressions useful in such occasions.

ノート: Asking for permission to do something (許可と禁止)

Q: 〜てもいいですか

A1: はい、〜てもいいです
A2: いいえ、〜てはいけません

The て form of a verb + も + いいですか is used to ask someone his or her permission to do something. You may grant permission by saying はい、〜てもいいです or you may deny it by saying いいえ、〜てはいけません.

ひらがなで書いてもいいですか。　　　May I write in *hiragana*?

はい、ひらがなで書いてもいいです。　　Yes, you may write in *hiragana*.

髪をそめてもいいですか。　　　　　May I dye my hair?

いいえ、髪をそめてはいけません。　　No, you may not dye your hair.

A. Practice asking and granting/denying permission as in the example.

例のように許可を求めたり、与えたりする練習をしましょう。

EX. go to the dance

Q: ダンスに行ってもいいですか。

A1: はい、ダンスに行ってもいいです。or はい、いいです。

A2: いいえ、ダンスに行ってはいけません。or いいえ、いけません。

1. go home	2. use the computer	3. play video games
4. read manga	5. eat in the classroom	6. wear blue jeans
7. wear a hat	8. wear makeup	9. wear sunglasses

B. Practice telling someone he or she may or may not do the following.

許可と禁止の表現を練習しましょう。

You are a school dormitory supervisor. Tell your students that they:

1. may go home on the weekends	2. may not watch TV
3. may not dye their hair	4. may not listen to loud music
5. may wear clothes they like	6. may not CREATE YOUR OWN

521

ノート: "Must do-" (必要)

〜なければなりません

The pre ない form of a verb +なければなりません forms the English equivalent of "must do-." For example, 食べなければなりません and 読まなければなりません mean "must eat" and "must read" respectively. The pre ない form refers to the part that precedes ない in the ない form (はなさない, あわない, きかない, みない, etc.).

5時に起きなければなりません。　I must wake up at 5 o'clock.

リーダーを選ばなければなりません。　We must choose a leader.

C. Practice telling someone he or she must do the following.

「〜なければなりません」を練習しましょう。

You are a school dormitory supervisor. Tell your students that they MUST:

1. wake up at 5:00
2. eat breakfast at 6:00
3. read newspapers everyday
4. speak with their advisors everyday
5. do the cleaning (そうじ) everyday
6. wear clean clothes
7. go to school at 7:30
8. go to bed at 10:00
9. CREATE YOUR OWN
10. CREATE YOUR OWN

ノート: "Don't have to do-" (不必要)

〜なくてもいいです

The pre ない form of a verb + なくてもいいです forms the English equivalent of "don't have to do." For example, 食べなくてもいいです and 読まなくてもいいです mean "don't have to eat" and "don't have to read," respectively.

5時に起きなくてもいいです。　You don't have to wake up at 5 o'clock.

リーダーを選ばなくてもいいです。　We don't have to choose a leader.

D. Practice telling someone he or she doesn't have to do the following.

「～なくてもいいです」を練習しましょう。

You are a school dormitory supervisor. Tell your students that they DON'T HAVE TO:

1. wake up at 5:00
2. read newspapers everyday
3. go to school tomorrow
4. wear the uniform
5. wear a tie
6. take off their shoes
7. write in kanji
8. go to bed at 10:00
9. CREATE YOUR OWN
10. CREATE YOUR OWN

E. Match the sentences with the appropriate English words from the box below.

日本語と英語をマッチさせてください。

1. 学校でYシャツを着なければなりません。（　　）

2. 学校でイヤリングをしてはいけません。（　　）

3. 学校ではネクタイを締めなければなりません。（　　）

4. 学校では制服を着なくてもいいです。（　　）

5. 冬にはパンツをはいてもいいです。（　　）

6. 夏には帽子をかぶらなければなりません。（　　）

7. 学校では化粧をしていもいいです。（　　）

8. 日本の学校では靴を脱がなければなりません。（　　）

9. 日本の学校では髪を染めてもいいです。（　　）

10. 日本の学校ではネクタイを締めてもいいです。（　　）

11. 学校には携帯電話を持ってきてもいいけれど、ロビーだけで使わなければいけません。（　　）

もってくる bring

---

a   must wear a dress shirt

b   must wear a tie

c   must wear a hat in the summer

d   may not wear earrings

e   may wear make up in the school

f   may not wear uniforms

g   may wear pants in the winter

h   may bring cellular phones but use them only in the lobby

i   may wear a tie in Japanese schools

j   may dye your hair in Japanese schools

k   must take off shoes in Japanese schools

F. In small groups, discuss what you are allowed or not allowed to do, as well as what you must do or don't have to do in your school, and make a list.

小グループで話し合って、リストを作りましょう。

Information gathering　情報収集

例 (Example)

携帯電話を持って来てはいけません。

制服を着なければなりません。

List-making　リスト化

・制服を着なければならない。
・化粧をしてもいい。
・携帯電話を持ってきてもいい。
・スポーツをしなければならない。

Your school

List-making　リスト化

・
・
・

G. Create descriptions such as the one below based on the list you just made.

作成したリストを次の例のように文章化してください。

Describing　文章化

例 (Example)

この学校では制服を着なければなりません。でも、化粧をしてもいいし、アクセサリーをつけてもいいです。それから、携帯電話を持って来てもいいです。でも、教室で携帯電話を使ってはいけません。そして、毎日スポーツをしなければなりませんが、好きなスポーツを選ぶことができます。

Your school

Describing　文章化

3 Expository style 説明文型<ruby>説明文型<rt>せつめいぶんがた</rt></ruby>

1 Combined or compound topic sentence 二つの<ruby>情報<rt>じょうほう</rt></ruby>を<ruby>繋<rt>つな</rt></ruby>げたトピク文

We will now start creating an expository paragraph about schools. Your paragraphs will consist of a topic sentence, supporting sentences, and examples. As mentioned earlier, your topic sentence will include two such descriptive words joined by a coordinate conjunction. In the following exercises your topic sentence will concern how strict rules at your school are and how interesting or fun your school is in general. You may do the exercises individually or in small groups, and write about any school as long as you are familiar with it.

A. Here are the questions that will help you form your topic sentence. Choose the most suitable response based on your own experience and knowledge.

<ruby>質問<rt>しつもん</rt></ruby>を読んで、<ruby>一番適切<rt>いちばんてきせつ</rt></ruby>な<ruby>答<rt>こた</rt></ruby>えを<ruby>選<rt>えら</rt></ruby>んでください。

1. **First Topic:** <ruby>学校<rt>がっこう</rt></ruby>は<ruby>規則<rt>きそく</rt></ruby>が<ruby>厳<rt>きび</rt></ruby>しいですか。

   □ X1　はい、<ruby>大変<rt>たいへん</rt></ruby><ruby>厳<rt>きび</rt></ruby>しいです。

   □ X2　はい、<ruby>厳<rt>きび</rt></ruby>しいです。

   □ X3　いいえ、あまり<ruby>厳<rt>きび</rt></ruby>しくありません。

   □ X4　いいえ、ぜんぜん<ruby>厳<rt>きび</rt></ruby>しくありません。

2. **Second Topic:** <ruby>学校<rt>がっこう</rt></ruby>は<ruby>面白<rt>おもしろ</rt></ruby>いですか。

   □ Y1　はい、とても<ruby>面白<rt>おもしろ</rt></ruby>いです。

   □ Y2　はい、<ruby>面白<rt>おもしろ</rt></ruby>いです。

   □ Y3　いいえ、あまり<ruby>面白<rt>おもしろ</rt></ruby>くありません。

   □ Y4　いいえ、ぜんぜん<ruby>面白<rt>おもしろ</rt></ruby>くありません。

<ruby>大変<rt>たいへん</rt></ruby>　very (a bit more formal than とても)

B. How do you connect your two choices above? See the chart on the next page and choose the one most appropriate as your topic sentence.

<ruby>表<rt>ひょう</rt></ruby>を見て<ruby>自分<rt>じぶん</rt></ruby>のトピックセンテンスを<ruby>決<rt>き</rt></ruby>めましょう。

525

TOPIC X (Sub-Topic)		TOPIC Y (Main Topic)
☐ X4 and Y1	学校は規則がぜんぜん厳しくないし、とても面白い。	
☐ X3 and Y1	学校は規則があまり厳しくないし、とても面白い。	
☐ X2 but Y1	学校は規則が厳しいが、とても面白い。	
☐ X1 but Y1	学校は規則が大変厳しいが、とても面白い。	
☐ X4 and Y2	学校は規則がぜんぜん厳しくないし、面白い。	
☐ X3 and Y2	学校は規則があまり厳しくないし、面白い。	
☐ X2 but Y2	学校は規則が厳しいが、面白い。	
☐ X1 but Y2	学校は規則が大変厳しいが、面白い。	
☐ X4 but Y3	学校は規則がぜんぜん厳しくないが、あまり面白くない。	
☐ X3 but Y3	学校は規則があまり厳しくないが、あまり面白くない。	
☐ X2 and Y3	学校は規則が厳しいし、あまり面白くない。	
☐ X1 and Y3	学校は規則が大変厳しいし、あまり面白くない。	
☐ X4 but Y4	学校は規則がぜんぜん厳しくないが、ぜんぜん面白くない。	
☐ X3 but Y4	学校は規則があまり厳しくないが、ぜんぜん面白くない。	
☐ X2 and Y4	学校は規則が厳しいし、ぜんぜん面白くない。	
☐ X1 and Y4	学校は規則が大変厳しいし、ぜんぜん面白くない。	

Your topic sentence:

Your topic sentence includes two different (positive and/or negative) descriptive words which are joined by either a positive and/or negative coordinate conjunctions, such as X and Y, X and Y: 〜し、〜/X but Y, X but Y: 〜が、〜. These coordinate conjunctions are related with the transition connectors that you will study in the next section.

2 Supporting sentences and examples　　サポートセンテンスと例

A. Your next step is to prepare supporting sentences. You will make four sentences at this time. The first two should support topic X (how strict the school rules are), while the last two should support topic Y (how much fun school is as a whole). Keep in mind that you will be adding examples to each supporting sentence later.

トピックセンテンスのXとYの部分にそれぞれサポートセンテンスを二つずつ作りましょう。

Choose the most applicable one or create your own predicate.

TOPIC X

規則(きそく) ──

服装(ふくそう)の規則(きそく)

- □ たくさんある。
- □ けっこうある。
- □ 少(すく)ない。
- □ ない。
- □ _____

In this example, supporting sentences will be based on two specific groups of rules: dress code and personal belongings (what may or may not be allowed to be brought to school or used there).

持(も)ち物(もの)の規則(きそく)

- □ かなりうるさい。
- □ けっこううるさい。
- □ あまりうるさくない。
- □ ぜんぜんうるさくない。
- □ _____

| Transition connector 接続(せつぞく) | X and Y, X and Y : そして、それから、(し) *Topic sentence |
| | X but Y, X but Y : でも、けれども、(が) *Topic sentence |

TOPIC Y

学校(がっこう) ──

クラブ活動(かつどう)

- □ 非常(ひじょう)に盛(さか)んだ。　ひじょうに extremely, very
- □ けっこう盛(さか)んだ。
- □ あまり盛(さか)んじゃない。
- □ 盛(さか)んじゃない。
- □ _____

In this example, supporting sentences will be made based two criteria: how prosperous club activities are and how many enjoyable school events there are.

楽(たの)しい行事(ぎょうじ)

- □ とても多(おお)い。
- □ 多(おお)い。
- □ 少(すく)ない。
- □ ない。
- □ _____

Your supporting sentences:

規則(きそく)
1. 服装(ふくそう)の規則(きそく)が_____。
2. 持(も)ち物(もの)の規則(きそく)が_____。

接続(せつぞく)
そして、それから、or でも、けれども

学校(がっこう)
1. クラブ活動(かつどう)が_____。
2. 楽(たの)しい行事(ぎょうじ)が_____。

527

B. Read the following expository style essay (setsumeibun) and cross out any examples that are irrelevant or ineffective. Remember that examples not only add details to each supporting sentence, but also uphold and reinforce the topic sentence.

適切でない例を線で消してください。

TOPIC (X, Y)　学校は規則が大変厳しいが、とても面白い。

SUPPORT X-1　服装の規則がたくさんある。

EXAMPLES　シャツは白じゃなければならない。

ジーンズをはいてはいけない。

ブレザーとネクタイが必要だ。

~~好きな服を着ることができる。~~

SUPPORT X-2　それから、持ち物の規則もけっこううるさい。

EXAMPLES　音楽プレーヤーを持って来てはいけない。

町で昼ごはんを食べてもいい。

教室で携帯電話を使ってはだめだ。

空港のような持ち物検査がある。

SUPPORT Y-1　でも、クラブ活動が非常に盛んだ。

EXAMPLES　クラブが全部で60ある。　　　　　ぜんぶで in all

クラブ活動をしない生徒がたくさんいる。

ボランティア系のクラブが特に多い。

学校の近くに店がたくさんある。

SUPPORT Y-2　それに、楽しい行事も多い。

EXAMPLES　私はダンスやうるさい音楽が苦手だ。

秋にはホームカミングやハロウィンダンスがある。

毎週、講堂で映画やコンサートやダンスがある。

長くて難しい試験がたくさんある。

SUM-UP　この学校の規則は日本の学校と同じくらい厳しいだろう。でも、クラブ活動が盛んだし、楽しい行事もたくさんある。だから、学校が好きな人が多い。　　　　　～だろう plain counterpart of ～でしょう

C. Create 2-3 examples for each supporting sentence below.

各サポート文に2つか3つの例を作りましょう。

TOPIC SENTENCE	学校は規則がぜんぜん厳しくないが、あまり面白くない。
SUPPORTING SENTENCE X-1	服装の規則が少ない。
EXAMPLE 1 **EXAMPLE 2** **EXAMPLE 3**	
SUPPORTING SENTENCE X-2	持ち物の規則もあまりうるさくない。
EXAMPLE 1 **EXAMPLE 2** **EXAMPLE 3**	
SUPPORTING SENTENCE Y-1	でも、クラブ活動が盛んじゃない。
EXAMPLE 1 **EXAMPLE 2** **EXAMPLE 3**	
SUPPORTING SENTENCE Y-2	それに、楽しい行事も少ない。
EXAMPLE 1 **EXAMPLE 2** **EXAMPLE 3**	
SUM-UP SENTENCES	この学校は日本の学校より自由だ。でも、クラブ活動が盛んじゃないし、楽しい行事も少ない。だから、あまり面白くない。

529

3 Sum-up sentences and conjunctions

まとめの文と接続語

You may recall that your expository essay about winter weather in your town in chapter 3 ended with a sum-up paragraph in which you compared your town with some well known Japanese towns. By doing so, you not only helped your intended readers better understand your points, but also reinforced the message in your topic sentence. Let's try and develop your sum-up paragraph in a similar fashion this time as well.

A. First, read the sum-up paragraphs in the two preceding exercises and see how they reinforce the topic sentence and conclude the essay. Then, share your ideas with your class.

前ページの二つの説明文のまとめの部分を読んで、その部分がトピック文をいかに効果的に補強し、説明文を終わらせているかを考えてください。そして、クラスで意見交換しましょう。

ノート: A sample sum-up paragraph development

TOPIC SENTENCE

学校は規則が大変厳しいが、とても面白い。

SUPPORTING SENTENCES (EXAMPLES OMITTED)

服装の規則がたくさんある。それから、持ち物の規則も結構うるさい。でも、クラブ活動が非常に盛んだ。それに、楽しい行事も多い。

SUM-UP PARAGRAPH

この学校の規則は日本の学校と同じくらい厳しいだろう。でも、クラブ活動が盛んだし、楽しい行事もたくさんある。だから、学校が好きな人が多い。 だろう: plain counterpart of でしょう

As you can see, the sum-up paragraph above reinforces the points made in the topic sentence by:

incorporating a comparative perspective (1st sentence)

reiterating arguments in the supporting sentences (2nd sentence)

closing with a wrap-up statement that corresponds with the main point in the topic sentence (3rd sentence)

B. Create a suitable sum-up paragraph for the following.

次の説明文に適切なまとめのパラグラフを作ってください。

TOPIC SENTENCE

学校は規則がぜんぜん厳しくないし、とても面白い。

SUPPORTING SENTENCES (EXAMPLES OMITTED)

服装の規則がない。そのうえ、持ち物の規則もぜんぜんうるさくない。それから、クラブ活動が非常に盛んだ。それに、楽しい行事も多い。

SUM-UP PARAGRAPH

TOPIC SENTENCE

学校は規則が厳しいし、あまり面白くない。

SUPPORTING SENTENCES (EXAMPLES OMITTED)

服装の規則が結構ある。そのうえ、持ち物の規則もかなりうるさい。それから、クラブ活動があまり盛んじゃない。それに、楽しい行事も少ない。

SUM-UP PARAGRAPH

C. Go over the expository writing samples in the preceding pages again and see how various conjunctions are used there. Then, in small groups, read the following descriptions and circle the conjunction that is more appropriate in the parentheses.

これまでの説明文の例をもう一度読み、使われている接続語について考えましょう。それから、下の練習問題をしましょう。

1.

　私達の学校は服装の規則がたくさんあって厳しいです。(まず、また)制服を着なければなりません。(たとえば、それから)化粧をしてはいけません。髪を染めるのもだめです。(さらに、だから)バックの色は黒じゃなければなりません。

2.

　私達の学校は規則が厳しいですが、楽しいです。毎朝服装のチェックがあります。服の色はグレーか白じゃなければなりません。(とくに、それに)、持ち物の規則もかなり多いです。(でも、それから)部活が盛んだし、楽しい行事もたくさんあります。

3.

　私達の学校の回りは自然が多い。東には山があって、西には森がある。(たとえば、そして)南と北には田んぼや畑がある。いろいろな所に池もある。(また、まず)駅も遠いし、車も少ないから静かだ。

4.

　私達の学校の回りは自然が多くて静かだ。東には山があって、西には森がある。南と北には田んぼや畑がある。(しかし、そのうえ)いろいろな所に池もある。(そして、だから)駅も遠いし、車も少ない。

5.

　私達の家の回りはうるさいが、便利だ。家の前には駅があって、後ろには大きい工場がある。公園や自然も少ない。(でも、しかし)スーパーやコンビニが多いし、近くに図書館や公民館もある。

6.

> 私達の学校はクラブ活動が盛んだ。(また、とくに)、運動系のクラブが有名だ。(たとえば、だから)、サッカー部と柔道部は去年リーグのチャンピオンになったし、野球部やソフトボール部も強い。(でも、さらに)、テニス部や剣道部には有名なコーチがいる。(だから、しかし)、運動系のクラブはいつも人気があって、人数も多い。

D. See the conjunctions section of Basic Vocabulary and confirm your understanding of the conjunctions which appeared in the preceding exercise. Then read the note below.

基礎語彙の接続の部分を見て、接続語についての理解を確認してください。それから、下のノートを読んでください。

も ノート：Particle も in paragraph development（累加の助詞「も」）

Particle も often replaces を, が or は in paragraph writing, as it may add an effect similar to that of conjunctions such as それに and そのうえ (furthermore, additionally). Effective use of these "accumulation" conjunctions and the particle も will help you make your writing cohesive, coherent, and easy to follow. Furthermore effective use of も in particular will prevent you from overusing the conjunctions, though two can appear in the same sentence and reinforce each other. Go over the following and see how individual sentences can be made into a cohesive unit under the same topic sentence.

> 私の春休みは最高でした。
>
> | ハワイに行って、毎日海で泳ぎました。
面白い映画をたくさん見ました。
おいしい食べ物をたくさん食べました。
宿題はありませんでした。 | → | ハワイに行って、毎日海で泳ぎました。面白い映画もたくさん見ました。おいしい食べ物もたくさん食べました。それに、宿題もありませんでした。 |
>
> だから、とても楽しい春休みでした。

E. Create 2-3 expository essays about some aspects of your school. Pay careful attention to their organization (topic sentence, supporting sentences, examples, wrap-up) as well as conjunctions.

構造や接続にも注意して学校についての説明文を作りましょう。

533

Recognition Kanji 4: 認識漢字 4

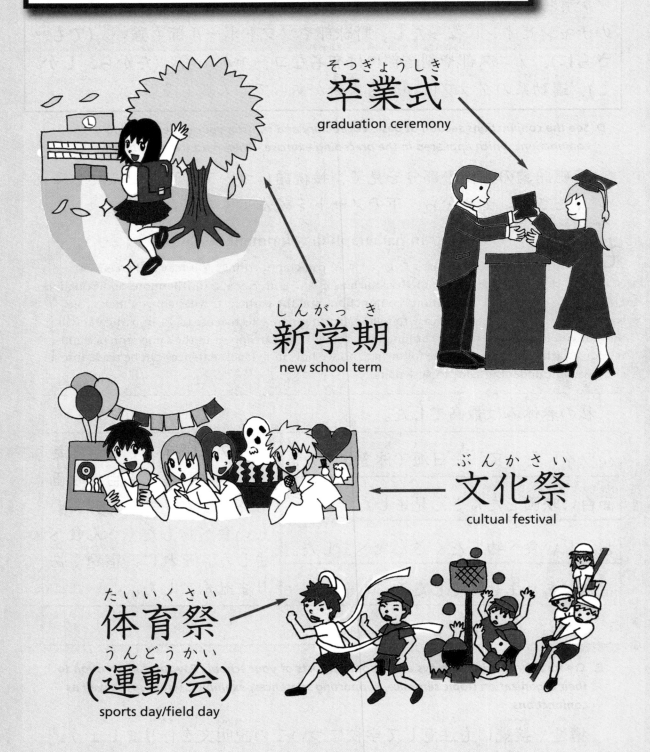

そつぎょうしき
卒業式
graduation ceremony

しんがっき
新学期
new school term

ぶんかさい
文化祭
cultual festival

たいいくさい
体育祭
うんどうかい
(運動会)
sports day/field day

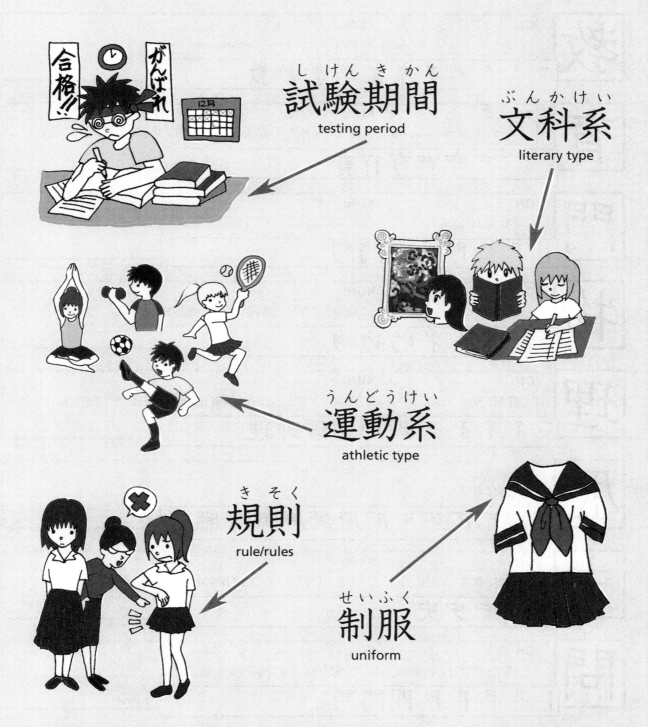

しけんきかん
試験期間
testing period

ぶんかけい
文科系
literary type

うんどうけい
運動系
athletic type

きそく
規則
rule/rules

せいふく
制服
uniform

New Kanji 3: 新出漢字 3

教	**ON**: キョウ　　　　　**KUN**: おし(える)
	教える: おしえる teach　　教育: きょういく education
	一 十 土 耂 耂 孝 孝 孝 孝 教 教

育	**ON**: イク　　　　　**KUN**: そだ(つ)、そだ(てる)
	育つ: そだつ grow up　　育てる: そだてる raise　　教育: きょういく education
	亠 亠 产 产 育 育 育

門	**ON**: モン　　　　　**KUN**: かど
	門: もん gate
	丨 冂 冂 冂 門 門 門 門

物	**ON**: ブツ　　　　　**KUN**: もの
	物: もの thing　　物理: ぶつり physics　　食べ物: たべもの food
	丿 牛 牛 牛 牜 物 物 物

理	**ON**: リ　　　　　**KUN**: ―
	理科: りか science　　理数: りすう science and math　物理: ぶつり physics
	一 丁 王 王 玕 玾 珅 理 理 理 理

歴	**ON**: レキ　　　　　**KUN**: ―
	歴史: れきし history
	一 厂 厂 厈 厈 厈 厞 厤 麻 厤 厤 歴 歴 歴

史	**ON**: シ　　　　　**KUN**: ―
	歴史: れきし history　　史学: しがく study of history
	丨 口 口 史 史

問	**ON**: モン　　　　　**KUN**: と (う)、と (い)、とん
	問う: とう question　　問題: もんだい question, problem
	丨 冂 冂 冂 冂 門 門 門

Reading 9:
読み物 9

School Morning:
学校の朝

1. 私は中田雅子です。高校3年生で、いつも朝は忙しいです。6時半に起きます。まず、歯を磨きます。それから、ちょっとにきびに気をつけて顔を洗います。7時半ごろ学校に着きます。学校に入る時に、靴を脱いで、うわばきにします。でも、まだちょっと早いので、教室にはだれもいません。だから、その間、好きな雑誌や本を読みます。先生がホームルームに来る前に、みんなでおしゃべりをします。その時の色々なことについて話すので、とっても楽しいんです。

2. 私の学校は、滋賀県の長浜にあってとても楽しいけれど、朝は忙しいです。毎朝私は好きな制服を着ながら、色々考えます。制服は3種類あります。夏の制服と冬の制服と春/秋の制服です。高校の制服はかなりシンプルなデザインで人気があるのです。それに、私はこの学校のアメフトのチアリーダーをしています。このチームはとても強くて、試合も多いです。だから、いつも家を出る前にクラブ活動のプランを作ります。

A. Write the title and the first sentence of each story. Then complete the following sentences choosing the appropriate word in the parenthesis.

Title:_____

1. First sentence:_____

　この最初の言葉は「中田さんの（朝、昼、夜）は（静か、忙しい、楽しい）。」です。

2. First sentence:_____

　この最初の言葉は「中田さんの学校の（朝、昼、夜）は（静か、忙しい、楽しい）。」です

B. Find the high frequency words which refer to school life.

1. おしゃべり、顔、歯、朝、春、教室

2. うわばき、京都、制服、くるま、クラブ

C. Skim through the stories and circle the Kanji that matches with the Hiragana given below.

にんき(popular):　人木、入気、人着、人気、入来

せいふく(uniform):　生腹、制福、製服、征服、制服

D. Choose the appropriate words by using your prior knowledge and experience to complete the sentences.

1. 雅子さんは学校に7時半に着き、（おしゃべりをする、ほんをよむ、べんきょうする）。

2. 雅子さんの朝は（制服を着る、ほんをよむ、べんきょうする）ので忙しい。

E. Choose the appropriate phrases for the underlined demonstrative words.

この学校：雅子の学校、18の学校、制服の学校

このチーム：雅子のチアリーダー、強いクラブの、私のアメフトクラブ

そのあと：歯を磨いた、6時半に起きた、顔を洗った

G. The end of sentence such a "noda" represents the writer's opinion. Fill the lines and complete the sentences choosing the appropriate word in the parenthesis below

1. のださsentence:＿＿＿＿＿＿＿＿＿＿＿＿＿＿＿＿＿＿＿＿
雅子さんは（おしゃべり、ジョッキング、宿題、水泳）している。

2. のださsentence:＿＿＿＿＿＿＿＿＿＿＿＿＿＿＿＿＿＿＿＿
雅子さんの（勉強、アメフト、制服、チアーリーダー）はいいのです。

H. Read the following sentences and choose the best summary of each story.

1. a. 雅子さんの新しい学校についてです。
   b. 雅子さんは朝はいろいろありますが、楽しいおしゃべりができます。
   c. 雅子さんはいろいろなスポーツができます。
   d. 雅子さんの古い学校についてです。

2. a. 雅子さんにはお金が必要です。
   b. 雅子さんには朝忙しいですが楽しいです。
   c. 雅子さんは学校に行くのはたいへんです。
   d. 雅子さんは朝早いです。

I. Link three items in the vocabulary list below.

単語 たんご	読み よ	意味 いみ
Ex. 同じ ⟷	おなじ ⟷	same
1. 強い	にんき	ride
2. 入る	つよい	take care
3. 人気	きをつける	strong
4. 気をつける	つく	popular
5. 着る	せいふく	uniform
6. 制服	つくる	wear
7. 作る	はいる	arrive
8. 乗る	いれる	enter
9. 着く	きる	put in
10. 入れる	のる	make

J. Check whether the following information is true or false.

1. この人はアメフトをしている。　　　　　　　　（本当、嘘）

2. この人の制服は人気がある。　　　　　　　　　（本当、嘘）

3. この高校は入る時に靴を脱ぐ。　　　　　　　　（本当、嘘）

K. Form a group and answer these guided questions in Japanese.

1. この学校はどこにありますか。

2. この学校の制服は何種類ありますか。それは何ですか。

3. この人は朝のホームルームで何をしますか。

4. あなたの高校とこの高校を比べてみて、どう思いますか。

私は中田雅子です。高校3年生で朝いつも忙しいです。6時半に起きます。まず、歯を磨きます。それから、ちょっとにきびに気をつけて顔を洗います。いつも7時半ごろ学校に着きます。学校に入る時に、靴を脱いで、うわばきにしなければなりません。でも、まだちょっと早いので、教室にはだれもいません。だから、その間、好きな雑誌や本を読みます。友達や先生がホームルームに来ると、みんなでおしゃべりをします。その時の色々な話題について話すので、とっても楽しいです。

高校3年生：twelfth grade　朝：morning　起きる：wake up　歯：teeth　磨く：brush　にきび：pimple
気をつける：take care　顔：face　洗う：wash　ごろ：around　着く：arrive　入る：enter
靴：shoes　脱ぐ：take off　うわばき：shoes for inside　しなければなりません：must do
ちょっと：a little　早い：early　教室：classroom　だれも：no one　その間：during that time
雑誌：magazine　おしゃべり：chatter　その時：that time　色々な：various　話す：speak

私の学校は、滋賀県の長浜にあってとても楽しいけれど、朝は忙しいです。制服を着ます。制服は3種類あります。夏の制服と冬の制服と春/秋の制服です。高校の制服はかなりシンプルなデザインで人気があるのです。私はこのアメフトのチアリーダーをしています。この学校のアメリカンフットボールはとても強くて、試合も多いです。だから、いつも家を出る前にクラブ活動のプランを作ります。

滋賀県：prefecture name　長浜：city name　制服：uniform　着る：wear　種類：kinds　夏：summer
冬：winter　春/秋：spring/fall　人気：popular　とても：very　アメフト：American football
チアリーダー：cheerleader　強い：strong　試合：game　前に：before　活動：activity

539

4.6 Mechanics 組立て
くみ た

Kansoubun Style: Descriptions and Comments
かんそうぶんがた　　　びょうしゃ
感想文型：描写とコメント

Objectives

Learn about and make *kansoubun* (essay) style writing.
Make descriptive sentences about school friends and teachers.
Learn about verb classification and plain forms.
Make simple comment sentences.

Overview

In the previous section, you wrote a paragraph in the expository style in which you presented your argument in a logical, consistent, and rather objective fashion. While this style of writing enables you to convey a clear message, it provides little room for inserting your own feelings and opinions along the way. It's certainly appropriate for a school booklet to feature its creators' thoughts on certain issues therefore, in this section, we will turn our attention to another style of writing suitable for such a purpose. We call it essay or *kansoubun* style. This style accommodates both factual descriptions and personal comments and it's more flexible and creative than expository writing. A typical *kansoubun* style paragraph consists of a leading sentence, several descriptive sentences, and comment sentences. A successful mastery of *kansoubun* style will allow you to write about school rules, facilities, activities, classes, friends, teachers, and so on, in a personal, vivid, and reflective fashion. Let's add a new dimension to your Japanese writing inventory!

4	*Kansoubun* style writing	かんそうぶんがた 感想文型
1	*Kansoubun* style overview	かんそうぶん　　　　がいよう 感想文スタイルの概要
2	Describing school friends	だち　びょうしゃ 学校の友達の描写
3	Developing descriptive sentences	びょうしゃ　　　はってん 描写の文の発展
4	Verb forms and classification	どうし　かたち　ぶんるい 動詞の形と分類
5	Simple comment sentences	かんたん 簡単なコメント文

4 Kansoubun style writing
かんそうぶんがた
感想文型

1 Kansoubun style overview
かんそうぶん　　　　　がいよう
感想文スタイルの概要

A. Read and compare the four paragraphs below with your classmates. Two of them are considered to be the kansoubun (essay) style writing while the rest demonstrate the expository style writing. Can you distinguish one style from the other?

か き　　　よっ　ぶんしょう　　よ　　　ひかく　　　　　　　　　　　か き
下記の四つの文章を読んで比較してください。下記の文章のスタ
せつめいぶんがた　かんそうぶんがた　わ
イルは説明文型と感想文型に分けられます。

---

1. この学校の生徒の太郎さんは
人気がある。太郎さんは高校3
年生で、背が高くて明るい。太
郎さんは生徒会と各種の委員会
の委員で活動をしている。明る
くて面白くて個性的で、私はと
てもいい人だと思う。

にんき
人気 popularity　　背が高い tall
かくしゅ
各種 all kinds　　～(だ)と思う I think -

---

2. 私の学校の行事は色々ありま
す。たとえば、5月にスピーチ
コンテストとマラソン大会があ
って、7月に学校祭があります。
それから、10月に体育大会や
修学旅行があります。12月には
研究発表大会もあります。
試験は年に4回あります。

---

3. この学校では生徒の活動が盛
んだ。クラブ活動も盛んだ。特
に、野球部やサッカー部は強く、
有名だ。また、生徒会と各種の
委員会の生徒の活動も盛んだ。
生徒会の行事もたくさんある。
委員会も色々な活動をしている。

さか
盛ん prosperous, popular

---

4. この学校では生徒の活動が盛
んだ。特に、クラブ活動はいく
つもある。そして、だれでもク
ラブに入ることができる。その
上、クラブ活動が面白いから、
皆 一生懸命だと思う。

いくつも numerous, many
クラブに入る join a club

B. See the note below and check how the paragraphs you identified as the kansoubun (essay) style writing in the previous section may be structured.

下のノートを読み、前の練習問題で感想文型に分類したパラグラフの構造をチェックしましょう。

ノート

On the left is the basic structure of the expository style (せつめいぶん) and on the right is the basic structure of the kansoubun or essay style (かんそうぶん).

EXPOSITORY PARAGRAPH DEVELOPMENT	KANSOUBUN WRITING DEVELOPMENT	
TOPIC SENTENCE	**LEADING SENTENCE**	
SUPPORT SENTENCE	**DESCRIPTIVE PART**	**DESCRIPTIVE SENTENCES**
EXAMPLE SENTENCES		
SUPPORT SENTENCE		
EXAMPLE SENTENCES	**COMMENT PART**	**COMMENT SENTENCES**
SUM-UP SENTENCES		

As you can see, a *kansoubun* or essay style paragraph consists of a leading sentence, the descriptive part, and the comment part. In the descriptive part, you may describe and explain about a variety of topics in a flexible, creative, and somewhat casual manner. In the comment part, you may offer your feelings, opinions, and any other comments about the topics. In this section, you will practice creating kansoubun style paragraphs.

感想文スタイルはリードセンテンス、描写部分及びコメント部分によって成り立っています。描写部分では説明文に比べて自由な発想で各種トピックについて描写でき、コメント部分ではあなたの意見、感想、その他のコメントを述べることが出来ます。このセクションでは感想文スタイル、特に描写部分とコメント部分の作り方を練習してみたいと思います。

The leading sentence in *kansoubun* style writing is different from the topic sentence in expository style writing. While the topic sentence controls both the supporting sentences and the examples, the leading sentence is more like an introductory sentence that prepares the readers for your descriptions and comments. Your first descriptive sentence is usually based on your observation, while the second descriptive sentence is based on your research. See the following examples and pay particular attention to how the first and second descriptive sentences are constructed.

LEADING SENTENCE → この学校の生徒の太郎さんは人気がある。

LEAD!

Taro, a student at this school, is very popular.

DESCRIPTIVE SENTENCE 1 → 太郎さんは高校3年生で、背が高くて明るい。

OBSERVED/Describe

Taro is a senior and he is tall and cheerful.

DESCRIPTIVE SENTENCE 2 → 太郎さんは生徒会と各種の委員会の委員で活動をしている。

RESEARCHED/Explain

He is so active in the student council and many student committees.

COMMENT SENTENCE 1 → 明るくて面白くて個性的で、私はとてもいいと思う。

He has a bright, fun, and unique personality, which I think is great.

LEADING SENTENCE → この学校では生徒の活動が盛んだ。

LEAD!

Student activities are very prosperous at this school.

DESCRIPTIVE SENTENCE 1 → 特に、クラブ活動はいくつもある。

OBSERVED/Describe

Especially, there are a lot of clubs.

DESCRIPTIVE SENTENCE 2 → そして、だれでもクラブに入ることができる。

RESEARCHED/Explain

And everybody is able to join the clubs.

COMMENT SENTENCE 1 → その上、クラブ活動が面白いから、皆 一生懸命だと思う。

Moreover, I think that everybody works hard, because their activities are fun.

Now compare how the paragraphs below, in which one is the *kansoubun* style and the other is expository style. Note that the leading sentence and the topic sentence happen to be the same.

KANSOUBUN STYLE WRITING DEVELOPMENT

LEADING SENTENCE → この学校では生徒の活動が盛んだ。

Student activities are very prosperous at this school.

DESCRIPTIVE SENTENCE 1 → 特に、クラブ活動はいくつもある。

Especially, there are a lot of clubs.

DESCRIPTIVE SENTENCE 2 → そして、だれでもクラブに入ることができる。

And everybody is able to join the clubs.

COMMENT SENTENCE 1 → その上、クラブ活動が面白いから、皆 一生懸命だと思う。

Moreover, I think that everybody works hard, because the activities are fun.

EXPOSITORY PARAGRAPH WRITING DEVELOPMENT

TOPIC SENTENCE → この学校では生徒の活動が盛んだ。

Student activities are very prosperous at this school.

SUPPORTING SENTENCE 1 → 生徒会と各種の委員会の生徒の活動が盛んだ。

The student council and various committees are very popular.

SUPPORTING SENTENCE 2 → クラブ活動も盛んだ。

Club activities are also very popular.

SUPPORTING SENTENCE 3 → 特に、野球部やサッカー部は強く、有名だ。

Especially, the baseball club and soccer club are strong and famous.

C. Classify the following paragraphs into two groups based on how they have been developed. Fill in the brackets with numbers representing the appropriate paragraphs.

パラグラフを次の二つのタイプに分類してください。

1. Made by kansoubun style writing   [   ]
2. Made by expository paragraph writing   [   ]

1. 日本語の勉強は面白いです。会話の練習は楽しいです。漢字の勉強も大好きです。そして、単語のゲームも楽しいです。

2. トムさんの寮は静かです。テレビやステレオがありません。便利な図書室があります。だから、好きな時間に勉強することができると思います。

3. スミスさんは忙しいです。朝と昼は会社にいます。夜は学校に行きます。いつも疲れているから、危険 (dangerous) だと思います。

4. 学校の回りは不便です。公共施設がありません。商店街やコンビニもありません。そして、駅も遠いです。

5. サラの家の回りはうるさい。家の前にはクラブがあって、後ろには工場がある。いつも うるさいから、寝ることができなくて大変 (hard) だと思う。

6. 学校は楽しい。毎日友達と会うことができる。日本語を勉強することもできる。その上、面白いクラブもたくさんある。

7. 去年の夏休みは最高だった。6月はサッカーのキャンプに行った。7月は日本に行った。そして、8月は好きなアニメをたくさん見た。

8. 去年の夏休みは最高だった。毎日、海やプールで泳いだ。おいしい食べ物もたくさん食べた。今年の夏休みも楽しいことをたくさんしたいと思う。

<ruby>学<rt></rt></ruby>校の<ruby>友<rt>だち</rt></ruby>達の<ruby>描写<rt>びょうしゃ</rt></ruby>

Students, teachers, administrators, staff members, parents, alumni—they all make significant contributions to the well-being of your school. Above all, the students represent a great majority in their daily presence on campus, and your school booklet should certainly feature these young talents. As you have already seen in some of the examples in this section, the *kansoubun* style of writing is well suited for student profiles. In this segment you will first learn some useful constructions in describing a person and then learn how to link two or more descriptive words and sentences.

ノート: Turning a verb into a noun by the nominalizer の and こと

Plain form of a Verb + の/こと

You can turn a verb into a noun by attaching either の or こと to a plain form of a verb. For example, both 食べるの and 食べること mean "(the act of) eating" and you can make sentences such as 食べるのはたのしいです (Eating is fun) and かんじをかくことはよむことよりむずかしいです (Writing *kanji* is more difficult than reading *kanji*).

A. Combine the two sentences into one using の or こと **as shown in the example.**

<ruby>例<rt>れい</rt></ruby>のように二つの文を一つにしましょう。

EX. <ruby>友<rt>だち</rt></ruby>達と話します。それは<ruby>楽<rt>たの</rt></ruby>しいです。　　I talk with friends. That's fun.

<u><ruby>友<rt>だち</rt></ruby>達と話すのは楽しいです。</u> or <u><ruby>友<rt>だち</rt></ruby>達と話すことは楽しいです。</u>

1. 学校に行きます。それは楽しいです。
2. <ruby>映画<rt>えいが</rt></ruby>を見ます。それは楽しいです。
3. <ruby>友<rt>だち</rt></ruby>達とあそびます。それは楽しいです。
4. <ruby>朝<rt>あさ</rt></ruby>五時に<ruby>起<rt>お</rt></ruby>きます。それは<ruby>大変<rt>たいへん</rt></ruby>です。　　<ruby>大変<rt>たいへん</rt></ruby>(な) hard
5. スピーチを<ruby>練習<rt>れんしゅう</rt></ruby>します。それは<ruby>大変<rt>たいへん</rt></ruby>です。
6. <ruby>漢字<rt>かんじ</rt></ruby>を書きます。それは<ruby>大変<rt>たいへん</rt></ruby>だけど、楽しいです。

B. Ask your classmates the following questions and share your findings with the class.

クラスメートに次の<ruby>質問<rt>しつもん</rt></ruby>をして、クラスに<ruby>報告<rt>ほうこく</rt></ruby>してください。

質問 (Questions)
1. <ruby>週末<rt>しゅうまつ</rt></ruby>、<ruby>何<rt>なに</rt></ruby>をするのが<ruby>一番楽<rt>いちばんたの</rt></ruby>しいですか。
2. 学校で何をするのが<ruby>一番大変<rt>いちばんたいへん</rt></ruby>ですか。

ノート：Describing someone's preferences, strength, or skills

$$
\text{Xは Vの/こと が} \begin{bmatrix} \text{すき/きらい です。} \\ \text{とくい/にがて です。} \\ \text{じょうず/へた です。} \end{bmatrix}
$$

The construction above will enable you to describe what a person likes or dislikes to do, what he or she is good/poor at doing, as well as what he or she is skillful in doing. Use の if you want to sound rather casual and personal, and こと if you want to sound a bit formal and firm.

一郎さんは映画を見るのが好きです。　Ichiro likes watching movies.

香菜さんは泳ぐことが得意です。　Kana is good at swimming.

洋さんはケーキを作るのが上手です。　Hiroshi is skillful in making cakes.

C. Practice making a short description about the following people according to the information provided below using the construction introduced above.

次の人物について下の情報に基づいて描写してください。

例 (Example)

シャンタルさんは映画を見るのが好きです。それから、漢字を読むのが得意で、スピーチをするのが上手です。

	シャンタル	しげる	ジル	マイケル
好き	watching movies	going shopping	listening to jazz	talking with friends
とくい	reading *kanji*	making home pages	speaking French	swimming
じょうず	making a speech	playing tennis	wearing *kimono*	making presentations

547

D. Are any of the following descriptions applicable to any of your schoolmates? Go over the descriptions and write down the names of your schoolmates that may fit. Also create additional descriptions as needed.

次の描写を読んで当てはまる学校の友達がいたら、名前を書いてください。必要に応じて描写を追加してください。

Description　　～が 好き	Name(s)
1. 部活が好き	
2. 旅行が好き　　　　　　　　(travel)	
3. 買い物が好き　　　　　　　(shopping)	
4. ボランティア活動が好き	
5. 詩を作るのが好き　　　　　(making poems)	
6. 小説を書くのが好き　　　　(writing novels)	
7. 科学の実験をするのが好き　(doing science experiments)	
8. 日本文化を勉強するのが好き	
9. 哲学の本を読むのが好き　　(reading philosophy books)	
10. 赤い服を着るのが好き	
11. 髪を伸ばすのが好き　　　(growing hair long)	
12. ＿＿＿＿＿＿＿＿＿＿＿が好き	

Description　　～が 得意	Name(s)
1. ディベートが得意	
2. 料理をするのが得意　　　(doing cooking)	
3. 泳ぐのが得意　　　　　　(swimming)	
4. 単語を覚えるのが得意　　(memorizing words)	
5. ＿＿＿＿＿＿＿＿＿＿＿が得意	

	Description ～が 上手<ruby>じょうず</ruby>	Name(s)
1.	ギターが上手<ruby>じょうず</ruby>	
2.	演技<ruby>えんぎ</ruby>が上手　　　　　　(acting)	
3.	司会<ruby>しかい</ruby>が上手　　　　　(acting as MC)	
4.	踊<ruby>おど</ruby>るのが上手　　　　　(dancing)	
5.	歌<ruby>うた</ruby>を歌<ruby>うた</ruby>うのが上手　　(singing songs)	
6.	絵<ruby>え</ruby>を描<ruby>か</ruby>くのが上手　　(drawing pictures)	
7.	車<ruby>くるま</ruby>を運転<ruby>うんてん</ruby>するのが上手　(driving a car)	
8.	＿＿＿＿＿＿＿＿＿が上手	

	Description ～が ある possesses a certain ability or sense	Name(s)
1.	指導力<ruby>しどうりょく</ruby>がある　　　(leadership skills)	
2.	実行力<ruby>じっこうりょく</ruby>がある　(ability to get things done)	
3.	責任感<ruby>せきにんかん</ruby>がある　(sense of responsibility)	
4.	思<ruby>おも</ruby>いやりがある　(consideration for others)	
5.	ファッションのセンスがある (good taste in fashion)	
6.	＿＿＿＿＿＿＿＿＿がある	

	Description additional useful descriptive words I		Name(s)
1.	まじめ	6. 優<ruby>やさ</ruby>しい	
2.	個性的<ruby>こせいてき</ruby>	7. 頭<ruby>あたま</ruby>がいい	
3.	かっこいい (good looking)		
4.	かっこ悪<ruby>わる</ruby>い (awkward looking)		
5.	信頼<ruby>しんらい</ruby>できる (reliable, trustworthy)		

549

	Description	additional useful descriptive words II	Name(s)
1.	背が高い	(tall)	
2.	背が低い	(short)	
3.	やせている	(thin, skinny)	
4.	太っている	(stout, fat)	
5.	体格がいい	(has a fine physique)	
6.			

E. In the beginning of this chapter, you learned how to link two or more qualities or actions that have enabled you to present your ideas more coherently and effectively than before. Review what you learned, and also see whether or not the linking methods and techniques you use in writing differ from those you use in speaking in your native language. After that, compare the following paired descriptions, underline any differences you may find between the two, and share your thoughts about the differences with your classmates.

このチャプターの始めに接続とその効果について学びました。その時のことを確認してください。また、書き言葉の中の接続と話し言葉の中の接続のし方に違いがあるかも考えてください。その後、次のペアになった文章を比べ、違う部分に下線を引いてください。そして、違いについての皆さんの考えを話し合いましょう。

1-A
私の友達のリサさんは詩を作るのが好きで、絵を描くのが上手です。リサさんは今17才で、頭がよくて、優しくて、思いやりがあって、とてもいい人です。私はよくリサさんと公民館に行って、ボランティア活動をします。

1-B
私の友達のリサさんは詩を作るのが好きで、絵を描くのが上手です。リサさんは今17才で、頭がよく、優しく、思いやりがあり、とてもいい人です。私はよくリサさんと公民館に行き、ボランティア活動をします。

2-A

　　去年の夏休みは最高だった。天気がいい日が多くて、雨はあまり降らなかった。よく、プールで泳いで、おいしい食べ物をたくさん食べて、面白い映画を見た。問題もなくて、本当にいい夏休みだった。

2-B

　　去年の夏休みは最高だった。天気がいい日が多く、雨はあまり降らなかった。よく、プールで泳ぎ、おいしい食べ物をたくさん食べ、面白い映画を見た。問題もなく、本当にいい夏休みだった。

ノート: Linking two or more qualities and actions in written style 1
(書き言葉における接続1)

As you can see, two or more qualities and actions in 1-B and 2-B in the preceding exercise are linked a bit differently from those in 1-A and 2-A. Instead of the て form, the く form (or the adverbial form) and the pre-ます form (or the stem) are used for the い adjectives and the verbs respectively, while the linking of the な adjectives and the nouns remain unchanged. 1-B and 2-B are the less colloquial and more written-leaning equivalents of 1-A and 2-A, and represent a style popular in writing as well as in rather formal speaking occasions.

Nouns/な-adjectives

～で、　～で...

い-adjectives

～く、　～く...

Take out い and add く.

Verbs

stem、stem...

"Stem" (of a verb) refers to the part preceding ます in the ます form.

今日は土曜日で、ダンスがあります。
Today is Saturday, and there is a dance.

町の図書館は便利で、静かで、広い。
The town library is convenient, quiet, and spacious.

学校の寮は新しく、部屋がきれいです。
Dormitories in my school are new and have beautiful rooms.

トムさんは頭がよく、優しく、まじめだ。
Tom is bright, kind, and sincere.

サラさんは思いやりがあり、信頼でき、とてもいい人です。
Sara is considerate, trustworthy, and a real nice person.

五時にうちに帰り、音楽を聞き、晩ご飯を食べた。
I returned home at 5:00, listened to music, and ate supper.

F *Connect the following two or more adjectives or nouns using the linking patterns introduced in the preceding note.*

前のページのノートにある方法で二つの描写をつなげましょう。

EX1. 古い   ＋ 静か   ＝ 古く、静かだ。
EX2. 自然が多い   ＋ 大きい   ＝ 自然が多く、大きい。
EX3. まじめ   ＋ 優しい   ＝ まじめで、優しい。
EX4. 高校2年生   ＋ 16才   ＝ 高校2年生で、16才だ。
1. 涼しい   ＋ 気持ちがいい   ＝
2. 頭がいい   ＋ かっこいい   ＝
3. 店が少ない   ＋ 不便   ＝
4. 背が高い   ＋ 泳ぐのが得意   ＝
5. 演技が上手   ＋ 面白い   ＝
6. スポーツが得意   ＋ 元気   ＝
7. 音楽が好き   ＋ 歌を歌うのが上手 ＝
8. 中学1年生   ＋ 13才   ＝

G. *State the following actions in sequence using the linking patterns introduced in the preceding note.*

前のページのノートにある方法で次の動作をつなげましょう。

例 (Example)

EX. <u>サッカーをし</u>、<u>柔道をし</u>、<u>ジョギングをした</u>。

EX.   1.   2.

H. Practice describing the following as in the example.

例のように描写の練習をしてください。

EX. 生徒会長のジルさん→指導力がある、信頼できる、頭がいい、スピーチが上手

生徒会長のジルさんは<u>指導力があり</u>、<u>信頼でき</u>、<u>頭がよく</u>、<u>スピーチが上手</u>です。

Jill, who is the president of our student council, has leadership skills, and she is reliable, smart, and skillful in giving speeches.

1. クラブの友達→部活が好き、かっこいい、実行力がある

2. 日本語のクラスメート→毎日漢字を書く、日本語の詩を作る、単語を覚える、日本文化の勉強をする

3. 学校の友人→背が高い、頭がいい、料理が得意、演技が上手

4. サッカー部のキャプテン→体格がいい、面白い、人気がある

5. 学校の委員会の友人→信頼できる、司会が上手、いつも忙しい

6. 生物の先生→小さい、かっこわるい、洋服のセンスがない

7. 英語の先生→劇を教えるのが好き、厳しい、背が低い

8. 音楽の先生→音楽を聞くのがとても好き、声がきれい、優しい

9. 隣に座っている人→まじめ、授業をよく聞く、質問をよくする

10. 日本語の教室→教科書がたくさんある、日本の物がたくさんある、日本の映画を見ることができる、ちょっと狭い

11. 私達の学校→歴史が古い、キャンパスがきれい、個性的な先生が多い、クラブ活動が盛ん

12. カフェテリアの食べ物→おいしい、ヘルシー、値段もまあまあ

3 Developing descriptive sentences 描写の文の発展

You have learned that typical kansoubun or essay style writing consists of a leading sentence, several descriptive sentences, and comment sentences. Here we will focus on the descriptive sentences and their relationship to the leading sentence. Although kansoubun style writing affords a good deal of flexibility, you need to keep in mind three key words—observation, research, and comparison—when making your descriptive sentences. Let's assume you will be making three descriptive sentences. You may make one sentence based primarily on your observation, one sentence based primarily on your research, and one sentence from a comparative viewpoint. These sentences should provide your readers with further information and evidence of what you have stated in your leading sentence. See the following example.

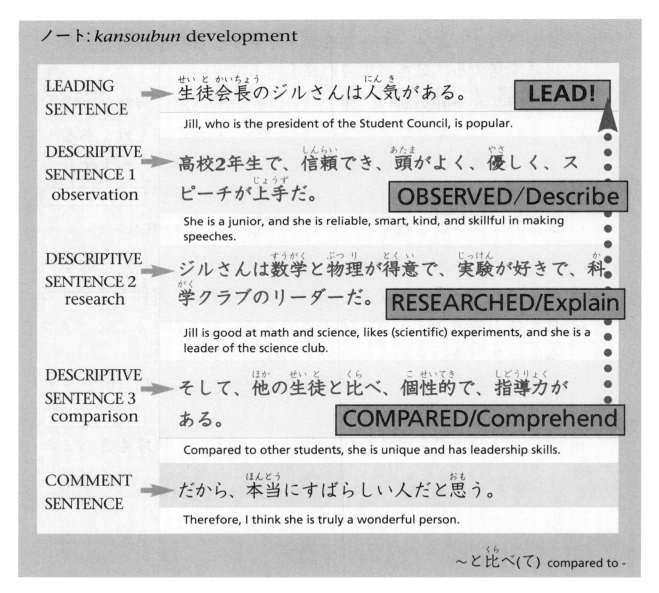

ノート：*kansoubun* development

LEADING SENTENCE
生徒会長のジルさんは人気がある。 **LEAD!**
Jill, who is the president of the Student Council, is popular.

DESCRIPTIVE SENTENCE 1 observation
高校2年生で、信頼でき、頭がよく、優しく、スピーチが上手だ。 **OBSERVED/Describe**
She is a junior, and she is reliable, smart, kind, and skillful in making speeches.

DESCRIPTIVE SENTENCE 2 research
ジルさんは数学と物理が得意で、実験が好きで、科学クラブのリーダーだ。 **RESEARCHED/Explain**
Jill is good at math and science, likes (scientific) experiments, and she is a leader of the science club.

DESCRIPTIVE SENTENCE 3 comparison
そして、他の生徒と比べ、個性的で、指導力がある。 **COMPARED/Comprehend**
Compared to other students, she is unique and has leadership skills.

COMMENT SENTENCE
だから、本当にすばらしい人だと思う。
Therefore, I think she is truly a wonderful person.

〜と比べ(て) compared to -

A. Rearrange the descriptive sentences on the right according to the order given on the left and place them on the middle column. After that, study the entire paragraph.

右にある描写文を左の順番で配置し、パラグラフ全体を読みましょう。

Leading sentence	この学校では生徒の活動が盛んだ。	a. 特に、生徒会とスポーツクラブの活動が盛んだ。
Observed descriptive sentence ➡	_____	b. 他の学校に比べ、クラブの数も多い。
Researched descriptive sentence ➡	_____	
Compared descriptive sentence ➡	_____	c. そして、野球部やサッカー部は強く、有名だ。
Comment sentence	だから、いい学校だと思う。	

Leading sentence	カフェテリアの食べ物は人気がある。	a. そして、他の学校に比べ、デザートもたくさんある。
Observed descriptive sentence ➡	_____	b. 特に、魚とパスタがおいしい。
Researched descriptive sentence ➡	_____	c. その上、カロリーが低いものが多く、材料もオーガニックのものを使う。
Compared descriptive sentence ➡	_____	
Comment sentence	おいしい食べ物がたくさんあって、幸せだと思う。	幸せ(な) fortunate 材料 ingredients

Leading sentence	この学校の授業はユニークだ。	a. 特に、英語の授業が有名で、町のディベートコンテストでよく優勝する。
Observed descriptive sentence ➡	_____	b. そして、他の学校の授業と比べ、プロジェクトやディスカッションが多い。
Researched descriptive sentence ➡	_____	
Compared descriptive sentence ➡	_____	c. 英語のクラスのディベートや化学のクラスの実験は難しいけど、面白い。
Comment sentence	授業が面白いから、皆 一生懸命だと思う。	

555

B. Create three descriptive sentences to complete the following kansoubun.

描写の文を三つ作り、次の感想文を完成させてください。

1.

LEADING SENTENCE	スミス先生は人気があります。
	Mr. Smith is popular.
DESCRIPTIVE SENTENCE 1	
DESCRIPTIVE SENTENCE 2	
DESCRIPTIVE SENTENCE 3	
COMMENT SENTENCE	スミス先生はとてもいい先生だと思います。

2.

LEADING SENTENCE	私の友達はとても面白いです。
	My friend is very funny.
DESCRIPTIVE SENTENCE 1	
DESCRIPTIVE SENTENCE 2	
DESCRIPTIVE SENTENCE 3	
COMMENT SENTENCE	いい友達がいて、幸せだと思います。

C. Let's describe your fellow classmates! Choose three people and create a leading sentence and at least three descriptive sentences for each of them. As for the comment sentences, you may create them now or later when we study them in depth.

仲間の生徒について書こう。三人選んで、それぞれリード文一つと描写文を少なくとも三つ作ってください。コメント文は今でも、後で詳しく学習する時でもいいです。

4 **Verb forms and classification**　　動詞の形と分類
<ruby>動<rt>どう</rt></ruby><ruby>詞<rt>し</rt></ruby>の<ruby>形<rt>かたち</rt></ruby>と<ruby>分類<rt>ぶんるい</rt></ruby>

ノート: Verb forms and classification

Japanese verbs change form according to style (plain/polite), tense (nonpast/past), and affirmativeness/negativeness. You may recall you first learned verbs in the ます form such as たべます, かきます, あります, はなします, and いきます. The ます form is a polite, nonpast and affirmative form, and you stayed in the polite side for a while as you learned the negative ません, the past ました, and the negative past ませんでした. After that, you learned the plain counterpart of the ます form called the dictionary form. It is by this form that verbs are listed in dictionaries. Even though the dictionary form is a plain style form by itself, it is frequently used in a polite sentence, since this form, along with other plain forms, appears in many sentence patterns, such as "the dictionary form of a verb + ことができます" which indicates ability or possibility. (かんじをよむことができます means "can read kanji.") We suggest that you remember both the ます form and the dictionary form of a verb since this will enable you to easily classify verbs and make other forms.

Verbs (どうし) can be classified into two groups: ごだんどうし (*U*-verbs) and いちだんどうし (*Ru*-verbs). There are a few verbs which cannot be classified into either. They are called ふきそくどうし (irregular verbs). You will learn more about verb classification in the next segment.

A. Do you remember learning about the so-called dictionary form and the ない form of verb in chapter 2? 食べる, 食べない *and* 話す, 話さない *are the dictionary forms and the ない forms of* 食べます *and* 話します *respectively. Circle any words that appropriately describe each of the forms.*

<ruby>動詞<rt>どうし</rt></ruby>の<ruby>辞書形<rt>じしょけい</rt></ruby>と<ruby>ない<rt></rt></ruby>形に<ruby>当<rt>あ</rt></ruby>てはまる<ruby>言葉<rt>ことば</rt></ruby>を○で<ruby>囲<rt>かこ</rt></ruby>みましょう。

1. <ruby>辞書形<rt>じしょけい</rt></ruby> (dictionary form): plain, polite, past, nonpast, affirmative, negative

2. ない<ruby>形<rt>けい</rt></ruby> (-nai form): plain, polite, past, nonpast, affirmative, negative

ノート: Plain past forms

Both the dictionary form and the ない form are in the nonpast tense. This time you will learn their past tense counterparts: the た form and the なかった form. These forms will allow you to not only carry on casual conversations with your friends and family members, but also to write sentences in plain style and they will be useful in making your booklet. The plain forms are also used in various sentence constructions as well, including ～(だ)とおもいます (I think -), which is especially useful in writing comment sentences.

continued to the next page

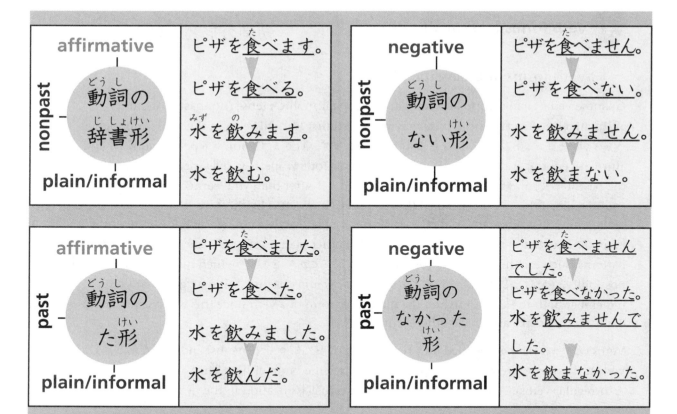

The た form can be obtained by replacing て/で in the て form with た/だ while the なかった form can be obtained by replacing ない in the ない form with なかった.

Dictionary form **Nonpast affirmative**	た form **Past affirmative**	ない form **Nonpast negative**	なかった form **Past negative**
GROUP 1. U-verbs / 五段動詞（ごだんどうし）			
きく (listen, hear)	きいた	きかない	きかなかった
いく (go)	いった*	いかない	いかなかった
かく (write)	かいた	かかない	かかなかった
よむ (read)	よんだ	よまない	よまなかった
のむ (drink)	のんだ	のまない	のまなかった
あそぶ (play)	あそんだ	あそばない	あそばなかった
はなす (speak)	はなした	はなさない	はなさなかった
かえる (return)	かえった	かえらない	かえらなかった
つくる (make)	つくった	つくらない	つくらなかった
たつ (stand up)	たった	たたない	たたなかった
かう (buy)	かった	かわない	かわなかった
あう (meet)	あった	あわない	あわなかった
つかう (use)	つかった	つかわない	つかわなかった
ある (exist)	あった	ない**	なかった**

		Affirmative zone	Negative zone	

Dictionary form	た form	ない form	なかった form
Nonpast affirmative	**Past affirmative**	**Nonpast negative**	**Past negative**

GROUP 2. RU-verbs / 一段動詞（いちだんどうし）

おきる (wake up)	おきた	おきない	おきなかった
みる (look, watch, see)	みた	みない	みなかった
ねる (sleep, go to bed)	ねた	ねない	ねなかった
たべる (eat)	たべた	たべない	たべなかった

GROUP 3. Irregular verbs / 不規則動詞（ふきそくどうし）

する (do)	した	しない	しなかった
くる (come)	きた	こない	こなかった

Note that the ない form and the なかった form of あります/ある is ない and なかった respectively, and that the た form of いきます/いく is いった.

B. To which of the four "zones" below do each of the following sentences belong? The zones are based on the horizontal line serving as the "Time" axis and the vertical line serving as the "Affirmative/negative" axis.

（　　）にゾーンのイニシャルを入れてください。

辞書形 じしょけい	Nonpast zone	**Affirmative zone** **NA**ゾーン (Nonpast affirmative)	**Negative zone** **NN**ゾーン (Nonpast negative)	ない形 けい
た形 けい	Past zone	**PA**ゾーン (Past affirmative)	**PN**ゾーン (Past negative)	なかった形 けい

1. 六時にうちへ帰る。　　　　　　　　（　　　）ゾーン
2. 数学の宿題がなかった。　　　　　　（　　　）ゾーン
3. 図書館で漢字を練習した。　　　　　（　　　）ゾーン
4. 水曜日に友達とサッカーをする。　　（　　　）ゾーン
5. 今日は朝ごはんを食べなかった。　　（　　　）ゾーン
6. 兄はガールフレンドがいない。　　　（　　　）ゾーン
7. 水曜日に友達とサッカーをしなかった。（　　　）ゾーン
8. 今日は朝ごはんを食べた。　　　　　（　　　）ゾーン
9. 兄はガールフレンドがいた。　　　　（　　　）ゾーン

559

ノート：Verb classification

As indicated earlier, verbs (どうし) can be classified into ごだんどうし (U-verbs), いちだんどうし (Ru-verbs), and ふきそくどうし (irregular verbs). See the information below and also go over the Form section of this chapter for a detailed discussion of this topic.

Verbs どうし 動詞	Group 1　ごだんどうし 五段動詞 (U-verbs)	The dictionary form of verbs in this group ends with く, ぐ, す, う, つ, る, ぶ, む, and ぬ.
	Group 2　いちだんどうし 一段動詞 (RU-verbs)	The dictionary form of verbs in this group ends with either -e ru or -i ru. 食べる(ta be ru) and 見る(mi ru).
	Group 3　ふきそくどうし 不規則動詞 (Irregular verbs)	する and 来る

ます form	Dictionary form	ない form	なかった form	て form	た form	
GROUP 1. U-verbs / 五段動詞（ごだんどうし）						
ききます	きく	きかない	きかなかった	きいて	きいた	(listen, hear)
いきます	いく	いかない	いかなかった	いって**	いった	(go)
かきます	かく	かかない	かかなかった	かいて	かいた	(write)
よみます	よむ	よまない	よまなかった	よんで	よんだ	(read)
のみます	のむ	のまない	のまなかった	のんで	のんだ	(drink)
あそびます	あそぶ	あそばない	あそばなかった	あそんで	あそんだ	(play)
はなします	はなす	はなさない	はなさなかった	はなして	はなした	(speak)
かえります	かえる	かえらない	かえらなかった	かえって	かえった	(return)
つくります	つくる	つくらない	つくらなかった	つくって	つくった	(make)
たちます	たつ	たたない	たたなかった	たって	たった	(stand up)
かいます	かう	かわない	かわなかった	かって	かった	(buy)
あいます	あう	あわない	あわなかった	あって	あった	(meet)
つかいます	つかう	つかわない	つかわなかった	つかって	つかった	(use)
あります	ある	ない**	なかった**	あって	あった	(exist)
GROUP 2. RU-Verbs/ 一段動詞（いちだんどうし）						
おきます	おきる	おきない	おきなかった	おきて	おきた	(wake up)
みます	みる	みない	みなかった	みて	みた	(look, watch, see)
ねます	ねる	ねない	ねなかった	ねて	ねた	(sleep, go to bed)
たべます	たべる	たべない	たべなかった	たべて	たべた	(eat)
GROUP 3. Irregular verbs/ 不規則動詞（ふきそくどうし）						
します	する	しない	しなかった	して	した	(do)
きます	くる	こない	こなかった	きて	きた	(come)

5 **Simple comment sentences**　簡単なコメント文の作成

ノート: Giving comments and feedback as an opinion

(Xは)Yと思う

(Xは) Yと おもう corresponds to "(I/you/she/he) think that (X is) Y" in English. Consider using this construction when you want to make simple comment sentences in your *kansoubun* writing. By ending with と おもう, you can stress the fact that your statement is a subjective one based on your own observation and feelings, and therefore can effectively distinguish your comment sentence from your descriptive sentences.

ちょっと面白いと思います。	I think it is a bit interesting.
たいへん個性的だと思います。	I think he is very unique.
教えるのが上手な先生だと思います。	I think she is a skillful teacher.
指導力があると思います。	I think she has leadership skills.
ちょっと面白かったと思います。	I think it was a bit interesting.
たいへん個性的だったと思います。	I think he was very unique.
教えるのが上手な先生だったと思います。	I think she was a skillful teacher.
指導力があったと思います。	I think she had leadership skills.

As you can see from the examples above, whatever immediately precedes と おもう has to be in plain style. Note that for nouns and な adjectives, だ (nonpast) and だった (past) precede と おもう.

verbs (動詞)	書くと思います。書いたと思います。
i-adjectives (い形容詞)	大きいと思います。大きかったと思います。
na-adjectives (な形容詞)	元気だと思います。元気だったと思います。
nouns (名詞)	先生だと思います。先生だったと思います。

A. Circle the correct one.

「〜と思います or 〜だと思います。」のうち、どれが正しいですか。

1. 七月の日本の学校は蒸し暑い（と、だと）思います。
2. ダンスの場所はジム（と、だと）思います。
3. キムの発表は面白い（と、だと）思います。
4. ジェニーはとてもクリエイティブ（と、だと）思います。
5. 図書館は静かで、便利（と、だと）思います。
6. デービス先生は厳しいけど、思いやりがある（と、だと）思います。
7. ひろしは1992年生まれ（と、だと）思います。
8. リナは数学が好き（と、だと）思います。

B. How do you describe the following people?

皆さんの先生やコーチについて話しましょう。

例 (Examples)
私の<u>日本語の先生</u>は<u>まじめだ</u>と思います。 私の<u>日本語の先生</u>は<u>やさしい</u>と思います。 私の<u>日本語の先生</u>は<u>冷静で、頼もしくて、素敵だ</u>と思います。

わたしの・・・

EX. にほんごのせんせい

1. カウンセラー

2. すうがくのせんせい

3. コーチ

元気(な)、優しい
厳しい、素敵(な)
個性的(な)、面白い
真面目(な)、クール(な)
我慢強い (patient)
冷静(な) (calm)
心が広い (open-minded)
頼もしい
思いやりがある

ノート: Asking for someone's comments, feedback, and opinions
(コメントをもとめる)

Xを/Xについて　どう思いますか。

Both Xをどうおもいますか (What do you think of X?) and Xについてどうおもいますか (What do you think about X?) are used to ask someone for his or her comments, feedback, or opinion about something. While the former sounds a bit spontaneous, the latter, Xについてどうおもいますか, sounds like asking for some thoughtful analysis of an issue.

Q: 制服をどう思いますか。
What do you think of your uniform?

A: デザインや色がよくて、好きです。
It has a good design and color, and I like it.

> Note that a highly personal word like すき is not usually used with おもいます.

Q: 制服についてどう思いますか。　A: 経済的で、必要だと思います。
What do you think about the school uniform?　It is economical and I think it is necessary.

C. Practice asking and giving comments about things or persons listed below or about any other things or persons relevant to your school.

コメントを求める練習とコメントを言う練習をしましょう。

会話の例 (Sample dialogues)

EX1. Q: サッカー部のキャプテンをどう思いますか。

What do you think of the captain of the soccer club?

A: 信頼できて、面白くて、人気があると思います。or好きです。
I think she is reliable, interesting, and popular.　　　　　(and) I like her.

EX2. Q: 学校のまわりについてどう思いますか。

What do you think about the area surrounding your school?

A: 店が多くて、駅が近くて、便利だと思います。
でも、車が多くて、ちょっと危険だと思います。
There are many stores and the station is nearby and I think it's very convenient.
However, there are many cars and I think it's a bit dangerous.

1.	生徒会長 (SC president)	2.	校長先生 (principal)
3.	クラスメート	4.	科学の先生
5.	学校の食べ物	6.	学校の規則
7.	学校の制服	8.	学校のクラブ
9.	学校の授業	10.	生徒のファッション

ノート: Stating a reason (理由を述べる)

(な)ので

X (な)ので、Yだ corresponds to "It is Y because (of) X" in English and it is useful in indicating a reason for your forthcoming statement. ので follows a plain style word or sentence and requires な when it connects with a noun or な adjective (しずかなので..., because it's quiet..., and どようびなので..., because it's Saturday...).

私達の町の夏の天気は蒸し暑いので、東京の天気に似ている。

As summer weather in our town is hot and humid, it resembles the weather in Tokyo.

制服は便利で、経済的なので、必要だと思う。

As uniforms are convenient and economical, I think they are necessary.

リサは優しくて、信頼できるので、人気があると思う。

I think Lisa is popular as she is kind and reliable.

D. Complete the following sentences by providing your thoughts ([だ]と おもう) and the reason for your thoughts ([な]ので).

次の文をあなたの考え「(だ)と 思う」とその理由「(な) ので」を入れて完成させてください。

EX. 私達の学校の回りは車が多いので、ちょっと危険だと思う。

1. 私達の校長先生は＿＿＿＿＿＿ので、＿＿＿＿＿と思う。

2. 私達の日本語の先生は＿＿＿＿＿ので、＿＿＿＿＿と思う。

3. 私達の日本語の教室は＿＿＿＿＿ので、＿＿＿＿＿と思う。

4. 私達の学校の規則は＿＿＿＿＿ので、＿＿＿＿＿と思う。

5. 私達の町の冬の天気は＿＿＿＿＿ので、＿＿＿＿＿と思う。

E. Create the descriptive part and the comment part to complete the following kansoubun style paragraphs. Make use of "(な)ので～(だ)とおもう" construction in your comment part.

描写の部分と、コメントの部分を作り、次の感想文を完成させてください。コメントの部分では「～(な)ので～(だ)と 思う」も使ってください。

1.

LEADING SENTENCE	私達の学校の授業はユニークだ。
	Classes in our school are unique.
DESCRIPTIVE PART (SENTENCES)	
COMMENT PART (SENTENCES)	

2.

LEADING SENTENCE	私のペンパルの洋子さんは最高のペンパルです。
	My pen pal Yoko is an outstanding pen pal.
DESCRIPTIVE PART (SENTENCES)	
COMMENT PART (SENTENCES)	

F. Create several kansoubun style paragraphs about the following;

1. one or a group of your fellow classmates

2. one or a group of teachers in your school

3. any other things you want to write about

次のことについて感想文を書いてください。

1.生徒個人又は団体

2.先生個人又は団体

3.上の二つ以外に書きたいこと

Recognition Kanji 5: 認識漢字 5

うわぎ
上着
outerwear

したぎ
下着
underwear

くつした
靴下
socks

ようふく
洋服
(western)

くつ
靴
shoes

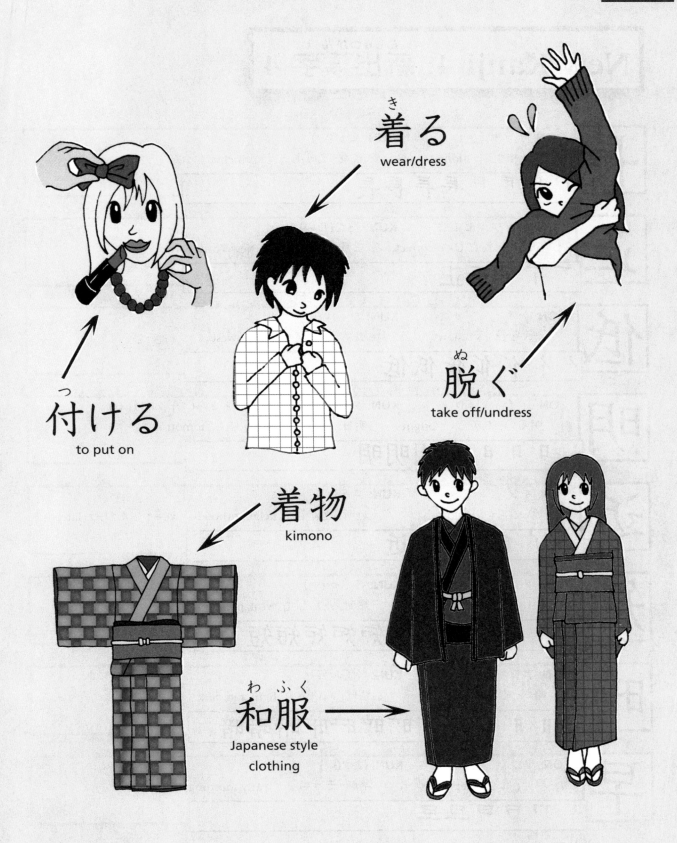

着る
wear/dress

付ける
to put on

脱ぐ
take off/undress

着物
kimono

和服
Japanese style clothing

567

New Kanji 4: 新出漢字 4
しんしゅつかんじ

長
ON: チョウ　　　　KUN: なが(い)
長い: ながい long　　　　校長: こうちょう principal
｜ 厂 厂 厃 巨 長 長 長

正
ON: ショウ、セイ　　　　KUN: ただ(しい)
正しい: だだしい correct　　　正月: しょうがつ New Year's Day
一 丁 下 正 正

低
ON: テイ　　　　KUN: ひく(い)
低い: ひくい low　　　　最低: さいてい the lowest
ノ 亻 亻 仁 仟 低 低

明
ON: メイ、ミョウ　　　KUN: あか(るい)、あかり、あきら(か)、あけ(る)
明るい: あかるい bright　　　明日: あした、みょうにち tomorrow
｜ 冂 月 日 町 明 明 明

近
ON: キン　　　　KUN: ちか(い)
近い: ちかい close　　　近所: きんじょ neighborhood　　　近年: きんねん lately
ノ 亇 斤 斤 沂 近 近 近

短
ON: タン　　　　KUN: みじか(い)
短い: みじかい short　　　短所: たんしょ weak point
ノ 亼 上 ヶ 失 矢 知 知 知 知 短 短

暗
ON: アン　　　　KUN: くら(い)
暗い: くらい dark　　　明暗: めいあん light and dark
｜ 冂 月 日 日' 旷 旷 旷 晬 晬 暗 暗 暗

早
ON: ソウ　　　　KUN: はや(い)
早い: はやい early　　　早朝: そうちょう early morning
｜ 冂 日 日 旦 早

Reading 10:
読み物 10

School Facilities:
学校の施設

1. 私達の学校には色々な施設があります。その施設を紹介します。それは、体育館と食堂と劇場と図書館です。学校はとても広いので、自転車を使うこともあります。
劇場: theater

2. まず、食堂は学校のほぼ真ん中にあります。この食堂には500人入れます。食べ物も色々あって、とても楽しい所です。主食のカウンターの他にデザートカウンターやサラダバーやアイスクリームの機械があります。とくに、デザートがとてもおいしいです。
主食: main dish　機械: machine

3. 次に、最も新しい施設が、体育館です。体育館は学校の一番北の森の中にあります。この体育館にはテニスコート、プール、バスケットボールのコート、トラックやサッカーの室内競技場があります。とても大きくて新しいので、気持ちがいいです。
室内競技場: indoor gym

4. それから、劇場は、教室のある建物の西の方にあって、ギリシャの劇場のようになっています。そこで、色々な劇が行われています。先月もシェークスピアのマクベスを見ました。

5. そして、南にある湖の前に図書館があります。ですから、図書館から湖を見ることができます。とても静かな図書館からゆっくり湖を見ることができます。静かなので、勉強もよくできます。また、ここではコンピュータによって本を探すことができます。
探す: search

A. Answer the following questions about each description using the choosing strategy.

1-1 Find the similar Kanji in red.

    a. 体育館：図書館、自転車、紹介　　**b.** 施設：図書館、川、広い

1-2 Finding the same radical of Kanji in red.

    a. 館：自転車、食堂、図書館　　　**b.** 転：校、時、車

1-3 Fill the line and complete the sum up sentence choosing the appropriate word from the parenthesis below.

beginning of the sentence: _____

私達の学校の施設は（大きい、便利、広い、多い）です。

2-1 Find the similar Kanji in red.

    a. 食堂：図書館、食事、施設   b. 主食：図書館、所、食堂

2-2 Fill the line and complete the sum up sentence choosing the appropriate words in the parenthesis below.

    Frist sentence: _____

    食堂は学校の（南、真ん中、北、西、東）にあって、（暑い、楽しい、きれい、おいしい）です。

3-1 Find the same radical of Kanji in red.

    a. 体育：森、食べる、休む   b. 森：林、時、地

3-2 Fill the line and complete the sum up sentence choosing the appropriate words in the parenthesis below.

    First sentence: _____

    体育館は学校の（南、真ん中、北、西、東）にあって、（暑い、小さい、きれい、新しい）です。

4-1 Find the similar Kanji in red.

    a. 劇場：建物、施設、場所   b. 飲み物：建物、食べ物、動物

4-2 Fill the line and complete the sum up sentence choosing the appropriate words in the parenthesis below.

    First sentence: _____

    劇場は学校の（南、北、西、東）にあって、色々な劇を（聞く、見る、食べる、さむい）ことができます。

5-1 Find the category of Kanji in red.

    a. 図書館：湖、施設、学性、森   b. 施設：道、川、体育、食堂

5-2 Fill the line and complete the sum up sentence choosing the appropriate words in the parenthesis below.

    First sentence: _____

    図書館は学校の（南、真ん中、北、西、東）にあって、色々（飲む、見る、食べる、調べる）ことができます。

B. Link three items in the vocabulary list below.

	単語 (たんご)	読み (よ)	意味 (いみ)
Ex.	同じ ⟷	おなじ ⟷	same
1.	自転車	としょかん	gym
2.	体育館	にし	cafeteria
3.	所	きた	library
4.	新しい	しょくどう	place
5.	食堂	じてんしゃ	west
6.	湖	あたらしい	front
7.	北	たいいくかん	north
8.	西	ところ	bicycle
9.	南	みなみ	lake
10.	図書館	まえ	new
11.	前	みずうみ	south

C. *Check whether the following statements are true or false.*

a. この高校の体育館は新しくて大きい。 (本当、嘘)

b. この高校の食堂は問題がある。 (本当、嘘)

c. この高校の劇場はギリシャの劇場と似ている。 (本当、嘘)

d. この高校の図書館は中学と同じである。 (本当、嘘)

e. この高校は放課後スナックを食べる事ができる。 (本当、嘘)

f. この高校は放課後勉強をすることができる。 (本当、嘘)

D. *Form groups and answer the guided questions in Japanese.*

a. この学校の広さはみなさんの学校より広いですか。

b. この学校の広告(ad)を作りたいです。どんな物ができますか。

c. この学校の環境はどんな環境だと思いますか。

d. この学校はどんな勉強ができると思いますか。

e. あなたの高校とこの高校を比べてみて、どう思いますか。

私達の学校には色々な施設があります。その施設を紹介します。それは、体育館と食堂と劇場と図書館です。学校はとても広いので、自転車を使って行くこともあります。

私達：we　　紹介：introduce　色々な：various　施設：facility　　体育館：gym　　食堂：cafeteria
劇場：theater　図書館：library　広い：wide　　自転車：bicycle　　使う：use

まず、食堂は学校のほぼ真ん中にあります。この食堂には500人入れます。食べ物もいろいろあって、とても楽しい所です。主食のカウンターの他にデザートカウンターやサラダバーやアイスクリームの機械があります。デザートがとてもおいしいです。

食堂：cafeteria　　ほぼ：almost　　真ん中：center　入れる：can fit　　主食：main dish
他に：besides　　機械：machine

次に学校で最も新しい施設が、体育館です。体育館は学校の一番北の森の中にあります。この体育館にはテニスコート、プール、バスケットボールのコート、トラックやサッカーの室内競技場があります。とても大きくて新しいので、気持ちがいいです。

最も：most　新しい：new　　施設：facility　　北：north　　森：forest　　室内競技場：indoor gym
気持ちがいい：comfortable

それから、劇場は、教室のある建物の西の方にあって、ギリシャの劇場のようになっています。そこで、色々な劇が行われています。先月もシェークスピアのマクベスを見ました。

劇場：theater　　教室：classroom　　西：west　方：direction　ギリシャ：Greek　ような：like
劇：drama　　行われる：is performed　　先月：last month　　シェークスピア：Shakespeare

そして、南にある湖の前に図書館があります。ですから、図書館から湖を見ることができます。とても静かな図書館からゆっくり湖をみることができます。静かなので、勉強もよくできます。また、ここではコンピュータによって本を探すことができます。

図書館：library　　南：south　　湖：lake　　前：front　　静か：quiet　　探す：search

4.7   Mechanics 組立て
くみ た

Kansoubun Style: Direct and Indirect Comments
かんそうぶんがた　　ちょくせつてき　　かんせつてき
感想文型：直接的・間接的コメント文

Objectives

Enhance comment sentence writing skills.
Make a variety of direct and indirect sentences and use them effectively in one's writing.
Learn how to give a reason.
Learn potential verbs.

Overview

This section is primarily about comment sentences in *kansoubun* (essay) style writings. Japanese elementary and secondary schools spend a good deal of time teaching their students how to write good *kansoubun* and this is in tune with Japanese rhetorical traditions and promotes the practice of sharing your thoughts with others through reflective essay writing. Skills and ability to write effective comment sentences are critically important in *kansoubun* style writings and you will practice making two types of comment sentences: direct and indirect.

5 "Japanese style" comment sentences	しき 「日本式」コメント文
1 Comment sentence development	くわ さくせい 詳しいコメント文の作成
2 Direct comment sentences	ちょくせつてき 直接的コメント文
3 Indirect comment sentences	かんせつてき 間接的コメント文
4 Multiple comment sentences	ふくすう くみあわ 複数のコメント文の組合せ

5 "Japanese style" comment sentences 「日本式」コメント文

1 Comment sentence development 詳しいコメント文の作成

The comment part of your *kansoubun* style writing will be greatly enhanced if you can offer both general and specific comments. Commenting on your math class, for example, you may say something general like "I think our math class is hard." You may say something more specific such as "I think our tests are hard though our homework is easy," "I think we get too much homework," or "Our teacher's explanation is easy to understand." At this time you will learn those sentence structures that are especially useful in making specific comments.

ノート: Indicating excess

Adj. Root + すぎる

"Adjective root" is a term used to indicate the part preceding い in い- adjectives. For example, in おおきい and やさしい, the roots are おおき and やさし respectively. When adjective roots like these are immediately followed by すぎます/すぎる, an *ichidan* verb meaning "exceed," the combination indicates the state of being in excess. おおきすぎます means "too large" and いそがしすぎます means "too busy." Note that "too good" is よすぎます. いすぎます does not occur. Also ない becomes なさすぎます. なすぎます does not occur. For な adjectives, just take out な before connecting to すぎます.

この本は難しすぎます。 This book is too difficult.

私の家の近くは静かすぎます。 It is too quiet around my house.

Verb Stem + すぎる

When すぎます is attached to the stem of a verb, the combination indicates an action being excessively done. For example, 話しすぎます means "talk too much."

ベンはチョコレートを食べすぎます。 Ben eats too much chocolate.

A. Circle the one you think is correct. 正しいものを○で囲んでください。

1. このテストは (やさし、やさ、やさしい) すぎると思います。

2. ジルは (まじめな、まじめだ、まじめ) すぎると思います。

3. このクラブは(魅力がある、魅力があ、魅力があり)すぎると思う。

4. この科目は (魅力がなさ、魅力がな、魅力がない) すぎると思う。

5. マイクはテレビを (見、見る、見て、見た) すぎると思う。

B. Make comment sentences using 〜すぎます as in the example and share them with the class.

「〜すぎます」を使ってコメント文を作りましょう。

> ### 例 (Example)
>
> EX. 東京の夏は蒸し暑すぎると思います。
> I think that summers in Tokyo are too hot and humid.

EX. 蒸し暑い　　　　　1. 難しい　　　　　　2. 遠い

3. 長い　　　　　　　4. 頭がいい　　　　　5. 早い

6. 不便(な)　　　　　7. ひま(な)　　　　　8. 静か(な)

9. (-を)する　　　　　10. 魅力がある　　　　11. 魅力がない

ノート: Indicating how easy or difficult something is to do

Verb Stem + やすい
Verb Stem + にくい

When the stem of a verb (the part preceding ます) is immediately followed by やすい or にくい, it forms a pattern indicating that something is "easy to do -" (-やすい) or "difficult to do-" (-にくい). よみやすい means "easy to read" and よみにくい means "difficult to read." They are a kind of い adjective and conjugate accordingly.

リサは優しくて、話しやすいと思います。　　I think Lisa is kind and easy to talk to.

この漢字は書きにくいと思います。　　This *kanji* is hard to write.

C. Practice 〜やすい and 〜にくい by substituting the underlined parts of the sample dialogue.

次の会話を使い「〜やすい/にくい」を練習してください。

> ### 会話の例 (Sample Dialogue)
>
> A: 読みにくいですか。
>
> B: いいえ、読みにくくありません。読みやすいです。

EX. 読みます

1. 見ます　　　　　　2. わかります　　　　3. 持ちます

4. 使います　　　　　5. 選びます　　　　　6. 歩きます

7. 発音します　　　　8. 着ます(wear)

D. Activity. 「〜やすい/にくい」を使ったアクティビティーです。

Preparation:

Complete the following list based on your own experience and judgment.

1-A 一番書きやすいカタカナ　　　　_____

Katakana, which is easiest to write

1-B 一番書きにくいカタカナ　　　　_____

Katakana, which is hardest to write

2-A 一番書きやすいひらがな　　　　_____

2-B 一番書きにくいひらがな　　　　_____

3-A 一番書きやすい漢字　　　　_____

3-B 一番書きにくい漢字　　　　_____

Interview:

Go ask your classmates six questions based on the items on the list above and record their answers.

> 会話の例 (Sample Dialogue)
>
> A: あのう、すみません。
>
> B: はい、何でしょう。
>
> A: 一番書きやすいカタカナは、どれですか。
>
> B: ええと、「ノ」です。
>
> A: じゃ、一番書きにくいカタカナは？
>
> B: 「ツ」が一番書きにくいです。
>
> A: ああ、そうですか。じゃ・・・。continued.

Sharing:

Share the results of your survey with your class.

> 例 (Example)
>
> スミスさんの一番書きにくいカタカナは「ツ」です。

E. Are the following subjects or similar ones available in your school? If so, place a checkmark in the box representing the most appropriate category. Note that the categories for the list on the left and those for the list on the right are different. As an alternative, you may create a list of subjects offered in your school and use it instead. Compare your checkmarks with those of your classmates' and exchange comments in Japanese.

科目ごとに該当する空欄に印をつけてください。皆さんで科目の
リストを作り、それを使ってもかまいません。

やさしすぎる	むずかしすぎる	どちらでもない	too easy / too difficult / neither (of the above)
			ジャーナリズム
			シェークスピア
			アフリカ文学 African literature
			アメリカ文学
			世界のドラマ world drama
			世界の詩 world poetry
			世界史 world history
			アメリカ史 U.S. history
			政府 government
			体育 PE
			保健 health
			外国語 foreign languages
			古典 classics

わかりやすい	わかりにくい	どちらでもない	easy to understand / difficult to understand / neither (of the above)
			生物 biology
			天文学 astronomy
			化学 chemistry
			応用化学 applied chemistry
			物理 physics
			地学 earth science
			代数 algebra
			幾何 geometry
			微分・積分 calculus
			音楽
			演技 acting
			美術
			コンピュータ

ノート: Class, lesson, or teaching

The word じゅぎょう is often used as the English equivalent of "class," "lesson," or "teaching." じゅぎょう indicates a structured period of learning in which a teacher teaches his or her students a particular subject and it is a popular word used in school when someone refers to his or her specific classes, such as English and math.

F. Match the comments about classes (じゅぎょう) on the left with their English keywords on the right.

授業に関する左のコメントと右の英語をマッチさせてください。

1. 教え方がユニークだ　　（　　）
2. テストが多すぎる　　　（　　）
3. 説明が少なすぎる　　　（　　）
4. 内容が分かりにくい　　（　　）
5. 生徒の発表が少なすぎる（　　）
6. 教材が使いにくい　　　（　　）
7. 教え方が上手だ　　　　（　　）
8. 内容がいい　　　　　　（　　）
9. 発言しやすい　　　　　（　　）
10. (ペースが)速すぎる　　（　　）
11. 役に立つ　　　　　　　（　　）
12. 宿題がやりにくい　　　（　　）

a. too many tests

b. hard-to-use materials

c. skillful teaching (method)

d. hard-to-do homework

e. good content

f. unique teaching (method)

g. goes too fast

h. useful

i. content not easy to understand

j. easy to speak up/offer opinions

k. not enough explanations

l. not enough student presentations

G. Study the following example and create comment sentences about some of your classes (じゅぎょう). Make use of the expressions that appeared in the previous exercises.

授業に関するコメントの例を見てから、皆さんの授業に関するコメントを作りましょう。前の練習で出て来た表現も活用してください。

EX.

COMMENT PART (SENTENCES)

私の世界史の授業は面白くて、役に立つと思います。それから、教え方がユニークで、内容が分かりやすいと思います。テストと宿題が多すぎるので、大変です。でも、とてもいい授業だと思います。

I think my world history class is interesting and useful. And I think the teaching method is unique and the contents are easy to understand. The class is demanding, as we have too many tests and too much homework. However, I think it is a great class.

YOUR OWN COMMENT PART (SENTENCES)

2 | Direct comment sentences 直接的コメント文

The tone of your *kansoubun* will vary depending on how you present your comments. So far you have learned to present them using the ～とおもう construction. While this construction is appropriate in most situations, you may consider offering your comment in a more direct and assertive fashion. So now we turn our attention to direct comment sentences and learn to make them using the ～のだ construction.

ノート：～のだ as an assertive direct comment marker
(断定的直接コメント文としての「～のだ」)

～のだ/のです

～のだ/のです and its conversational equivalent ～んだ/んです are used fairly often in Japanese when people try to explain or comment on something of which both the writer/speaker and the reader/listener have some shared knowledge or familiarity. At this time we will focus on ～のだ and its polite counterpart ～のです and practice writing direct comment sentences using this construction. The use of ～のだ/のです will allow you to offer your comment in a direct and assertive manner. At the same time ～のだ/のです will prevent your comment from sounding overconfident or aggressive as it assumes that the writer and the reader have some shared knowledge about the topic. ～のだ/のです and ～んだ/んです as a grammatical unit will be referred to as the extended explanation form.

ノート: The extended explanation form 1

Verb (Plain form) い Adjective な Adjective(with な) Noun + な	**+**	〜のです 〜のだ 〜んです 〜んだ

Both 〜のだ and its polite equivalent 〜のです are attached to a plain form of a verb or an *i* adjective. You need to have な for both *na* adjectives and nouns in the nonpast tense. 〜んです/んだ are more conversational equivalents of 〜のです/のだ.

学校に行く＋のです/だ。
(It is the case that) I go/will go to school.

学校に行った＋のです/だ。
(It is the case that) I went to school.

学校に行かない＋のです/だ。
(It is the case that) I don't go to school.

学校に行かなった＋のです/だ。
(It is the case that) I didn't go to school.

本当に安くておいしい＋のです/だ。
(It is the case that) truly it was cheap and delicious.

本当に全然おもしろくなかった＋のです/だ。
(It is the case that) truly it was not interesting at all.

制服は必要な＋のです/だ。
(It is the case that) uniforms are necessary.

昨日は始業式だったのです/だ。
(It is the case that) *Shigyooshiki* happened yesterday.

A. Convert the following into the (な)のです ending.

「〜(な)のだ」「〜(な)のです」を使って文を書き換えましょう。

1. 明日重要な試験がある。
2. 明日トムに会います。
3. 昨日アラスカに行った。
4. 新しい服を買いました。
5. 全然勉強しない。
6. 日本語が上手です。
7. 昨日寝なかった。
8. ここは学校だ。
9. 夏は暑い。
10. 食べ物がおいしい。
11. 数学が苦手だ。
12. 料理が上手です。
13. 今日は卒業式だ。
14. 試験は木曜日です。
15. ここは学校じゃない。
16. 明日は休みじゃありません。
17. 昨日は雨だった。
18. 昨日は晴れでした。
19. 内容がよかった。
20. 映画が面白かった。

ノート: Stating a reason (理由)

Verb (Plain form)
い Adjective
な Adjective +だ
Noun +だ
＞から

Xから、Yだ corresponds to "It is Y because of X" in English and it is useful in indicating a reason. You have learned that ので is also used to state a reason. ので represents a more personal reason than から and, therefore, it is more effective in indirect comment sentences. Now that we have started learning to make direct comment sentences, we need to know から and use it effectively in direct comment sentences. Also から sounds firmer and more exclusive than ので.

指導力があるから、彼女をキャプテンに選んだのだ。
It is because of her leadership skills that we chose her as a captain.

東京は夏暑すぎるから、東京では夏にネクタイをしめないのだ。
It is because summers in Tokyo are so hot that people there do not wear ties during summer.

私達の学校の数学の授業は教え方がユニークだから、有名なのだ。
It is because the math classes in our school employ unique teaching methods that they are famous.

B. *Complete the sentences by filling in the blanks with the appropriate letter. You may consult with your partner. Share the results with the class.*

ペアで相談して文を完成させてください。

1. 私達の町は人口が多いから、＿＿＿＿＿＿＿＿。
2. 私達の町の天気は冬が厳しいから、＿＿＿＿＿＿＿。
3. 私達の町の自然は環境問題が流行っているから、＿＿＿＿＿＿。
4. 私達の学校の校長先生は指導力があるから、＿＿＿＿＿＿＿。
5. 私達の日本語の先生は優しいから、＿＿＿＿＿＿＿。

> a. いい先生がたくさんいるのだ。
> b. 皆でそれを守っている(protect)のだ。
> c. 東京に似ているのだ。
> d. 外を歩くのが大変なのだ。
> e. たくさん生徒が来るのだ。

C. Choose the most appropriate direct comment sentence for the following descriptive sentences.

次の描写文に最も適切な直接的コメント文を選びましょう。

1. 音楽の授業は、卒業式の音楽を決め、皆でその音楽を練習し、卒業式で皆で演奏をする。＿＿＿＿＿＿＿

2. プロムは、ダンスの相手(partner)を決め、大きな車でダンスの場所まで行き、卒業式の前に皆でダンスをする。＿＿＿＿＿＿＿

3. 私達の学校の校長先生はすばらしい先生です。問題のある生徒の話し相手(conversation partner)になり、講堂で生徒達にいろいろなことを話し、卒業式には皆を誉める(praise)。＿＿＿＿＿＿＿

4. ペップラリーは、ジムに皆が集り、チアリーダーとスポーツチームの応援をし、マーチングバンドの音楽もある。＿＿＿＿＿＿＿

---

a. 学校の最後に皆がお祝(celebrate)をするのだ。

b. 生徒の計画性(planning)や協力は必要なのだ。

c. 学校の応援に皆が協力するのだ。

d. 先生の指導力(leadership skills)は必要なのだ。

D. Working in pairs, complete the following direct comment sentences.

ペアで相談して次の直接的コメント文を完成させてください。

1. ＿＿＿＿＿＿＿＿＿から、私達の町は人口が少ないのだ。

2. ＿＿＿＿＿＿＿＿＿から、私達の町の天気は冬が厳しいのだ。

3. 環境問題が重要だから、＿＿＿＿＿＿＿のだ。

4. ジルさんは旅行が好きだから、＿＿＿＿＿＿＿のだ。

5. 私達の先生は指導力があるから、＿＿＿＿＿＿＿のだ。

6. 制服は経済的だから、＿＿＿＿＿＿＿のだ。

E. Create an appropriate direct comment sentence that will follow the descriptive sentences below .

次の描写文に続く直接的コメント文を作りましょう。

リード
leading
(sentence)

描写
description

コメント
comment

EX1. この学校の生徒の太郎さんは人気がある。太郎さんは高校3年生で、背が高くて明るい。太郎さんは生徒会と各種の委員会の委員で活動をしている。明るくて面白くて個性的で、とてもいい人なのだ。

リード
leading
(sentence)

描写
description

コメント
comment

EX2. この学校では生徒の活動が盛んだ。特に、クラブ活動はいくつもある。そして、だれでもクラブに入ることができる。その上、クラブ活動が面白いから、皆一生懸命なのだ。

リード
leading
(sentence)

描写
description

コメント
comment

1. 私達の学校の制服は人気がある。上着は青いブレザーで、デザインがいい。男子はグレーのズボン、女子はグレーのスカートをはく。シャツは何色でもいい。＿＿＿＿＿＿＿＿＿＿＿のだ。

リード
leading
(sentence)

描写
description

コメント
comment

2. カフェテリアは私が一番好きな場所だ。特に、お昼のメニューはヘルシーで、人気がある。私はよく野菜のサンドイッチを食べる。コーヒーもおいしく、デザートもたくさんある。＿＿＿＿＿＿＿＿＿＿のだ。

リード
leading
(sentence)

描写
description

コメント
comment

3.

**CREATE THE ENTIRE *KANSOUBUN* WITH
DIRECT COMMENT SENTENCE(S)**

3 **Indirect comment sentences** 間接的コメント文

You just learned to write direct comment sentences using 〜のだ. We will call the comment sentences you studied earlier that ended with 〜とおもう indirect comment sentences. However, indirect comment sentences in *kansoubun* are not limited to 〜とおもう and we now turn our attention back to indirect comment sentences to learn more about them.

A. Compare the following kansoubun and divide them into those with direct comment sentences and those with indirect comment sentences.

下記の四つの文章を読んで比較してください。そして、直接的コメント文のある感想文と間接的コメント文のある感想文の違いを確認してください。

---

1. 私の学校の行事はいろいろある。例えば、5月にマラソン大会があって、7月に学校祭がある。それから、10月には体育大会や修学旅行、2月には研究発表大会もある。楽しい行事が多い。でも、試験も年に4回あるので、けっこう厳しいと思う。

---

2. 学校のカフェテリアのお昼のメニューはユニークです。毎日違う国の料理があります。例えば、水曜日は日本で、カレーライスやうどんがあります。時々、すしもあります。とてもいいアイディアだと思います。

---

3. 私の学校では写真部の活動が盛んだ。メンバーが50人いて、毎週いろいろな場所で写真を撮っている。よく町の写真コンテストで優勝するし、卒業してプロになった人もいる。皆、一生懸命で、感動的なのだ。

感動的 impressive

---

4. この学校ではボランティア活動が盛んです。老人のためのクラブや障害者のためのクラブや子供のためのクラブがあります。そして、いろいろな場所で活動しています。皆、人の役に立ちたいのです。

Indirect Comment Sentences at a Glance
いろいろな間接的コメント文の使い分け

---

1. Expressing the writer's feelings, thoughts, opinions
(書き手の感情、思想、意見を示す文末表現を使う)

XはYと思う

制服は便利だと思う。
I think uniforms are convenient.

私達の学校の試験は他の学校の試験より難しいと思う。
I think exams in our school are harder than exams in other schools.

皆は個性的な人を生徒会長に選ぶと思う。
I think everyone will choose someone unique as their student council president.

---

2. Expressing the writer's modest and inferential attitude
(書き手の控え目で推量的態度を示す文末表現を使う)

XはYではないだろうか
(XはYじゃないでしょうか)

制服は便利ではないだろうか。
Wouldn't it be convenient to have uniforms?

私達の学校の試験は他の学校の試験より難しいのではないだろうか。
Wouldn't exams in our school be harder than exams in other schools?

皆は個性的な人を生徒会長に選ぶのではないだろうか。
Wouldn't everyone choose someone unique as their student council president?

---

3. Expressing the writer's guesses and assumptions

(書き手の推理・推測を示す文末表現を使う)

XはYだろうと思う

制服は便利だろうと思う。
I think uniforms will probably be convenient.

私達の学校の試験は他の学校の試験より難しいだろうと思う。
I think exams in our school are probably harder than exams in other schools.

皆は個性的な人を生徒会長に選ぶだろうと思う。
I think everyone will probably choose someone unique as their student council president.

XはYかも知れない

制服は便利かも知れない。
Uniforms may be convenient.

私達の学校の試験は他の学校の試験より難しいかも知れない。
Exams in our school may be harder than exams in other schools.

皆は個性的な人を生徒会長に選ぶかも知れない。
I think everyone may choose someone unique as their student council president.

4. Expressing the writer's suggestions or preferences

(書き手の提案や好みを示す文末表現を使う)

XはY(た)ほうがいい(と思う)

制服は便利な方がいいと思う。
I think it is better to have uniforms that are convenient.

私達の学校の試験は他の学校の試験より難しい方がいいと思う。
I think exams in our school should be harder than exams in other schools.

皆は個性的な人を生徒会長に選んだ方がいいと思う。
I think everyone should choose someone unique as their student council president.

B. In which of the four types of indirect comment sentences do the following kansoubun belong?

次の文章に使われている間接的コメント文のタイプを選びましょう。

1.[ ] この学校には制服がありません。皆が好きな服を着ていて、カラフルです。でも、高すぎる服や、大きすぎる服を着ている人がけっこういます。パジャマのような服を着ている人もいます。だから、制服が必要かも知れません。

2.[ ] この学校のキャンパスは公園のようだ。花や木や池があってきれいだし、ベンチもたくさんある。そして、昼休みにはベンチでお弁当を食べる人が多い。学校はとても忙しく、授業も難しい。でも、公園のようなキャンパスがあるので、生徒はリラックスしやすいと思う。

3.[ ] この学校では生徒の活動があまり盛んじゃありません。でも、活動の数は多いです。生徒会と学級会と各種の委員会などがあります。クラブもいろいろありますが、あまり活動しません。これからはもっと盛んになった方がいいです。

4.[ ] この学校の規則は大変厳しい。制服を着なければならないし、化粧をすることもできない。それから、携帯電話を持って来てはいけない。日本の学校の規則より厳しいだろうと思う。

5.[ ] この学校ではスポーツが盛んだ。秋にはマラソン大会があり、春には野球大会やソフトボール大会がある。スポーツ系の部活もたくさんある。特に、サッカー部や柔道部は強くて有名だ。生徒の数は330人だが、毎日スポーツをする人が300人ぐらいいるのではないだろうか。

a. Expressing the writer's feelings, thoughts, opinions
(書き手の感情、思想、意見を示す文末表現を使う)

b. Expressing the writer's modest and inferential attitude
(書き手の控え目で推量的態度を示す文末表現を使う)

c. Expressing the writer's guesses and assumption (書き手の推理・推測を示す文末表現を使う)

d. Expressing the writer's suggestions or preferences (書き手の提案や好みを示す文末表現を使う)

C. Practice making indirect comment sentences using ではないだろうか.

「ではないだろうか」を使ってコメント文を作る練習です。

EX1. 私達の町の人口は<u>約7万人</u>だ。

→私達の町の人口は<u>約7万人</u>ではないだろうか。

1. 校長先生の誕生日は<u>来週の木曜日</u>だ。

→校長先生の誕生日は＿＿＿＿＿＿＿＿＿＿＿＿。

EX2. リサの家の回りは<u>自然が多くて静か</u>だ。

→リサの家の回りは<u>自然が多くて静か</u>ではないだろうか。

2. トムの家の回りは<u>店が多くて便利</u>だ。

→トムの家の回りは＿＿＿＿＿＿＿＿＿＿＿＿。

EX3. 次の数学の試験は<u>難しい</u>。

→次の数学の試験は<u>難しい</u>のではないだろうか。

3. 東京の春は<u>私達の町の春より暖かい</u>。

→東京の春は＿＿＿＿＿＿＿＿＿＿＿＿。

EX4. ジルは<u>来年日本に行く</u>。

→ジルは<u>来年日本に行く</u>のではないだろうか。

4. 私達の学校には<u>スポーツが好きな人がたくさんいる</u>。

→私達の学校には＿＿＿＿＿＿＿＿＿＿＿＿。

D. Practice making indirect comment sentences using だろうとおもう.

「だろうと思う」を使ってコメント文を作る練習です。

EX1.　トムの趣味は料理だ。→トムの趣味は料理だろうと思う。

1.　リサの好きな色は緑だ。→リサの好きな色は＿＿＿＿＿＿＿＿＿＿。

EX2.　トムは泳ぐのが得意だ。→トムは泳ぐのが得意だろうと思う。

2.　リサはピアノが上手だ。→リサは＿＿＿＿＿＿＿＿＿＿。

EX3.　札幌の冬は寒い。→札幌の冬は寒いだろうと思う。

3.　東京の夏は蒸し暑い。→東京の夏は＿＿＿＿＿＿＿＿＿＿＿。

EX4.　ジョンは制服を着る。→ジョンは制服を着るだろうと思う。

4.　ジルは生徒会長になる。→ジルは＿＿＿＿＿＿＿＿＿＿＿。

E. Practice making indirect comment sentences with かもしれない.

「かも知れない」を使って文を作る練習をしましょう。

EX1.　Sara may be skillful in tennis.→サラはテニスが上手かも知れない。

1.　John may be good at physics.→＿＿＿＿＿＿＿＿＿＿＿＿＿＿＿＿。

EX2.　Linda may be busy.→リンダは忙しいかも知れない。

2.　The science exam may be easy.→＿＿＿＿＿＿＿＿＿＿＿＿＿＿＿。

EX3.　Sara may speak French.→サラはフランス語を話すかも知れない。

3.　John may have leadership skills.→＿＿＿＿＿＿＿＿＿＿＿＿＿＿。

EX4.　Tom may not come.→トムは来ないかも知れない。

4.　Linda may not buy a car.→＿＿＿＿＿＿＿＿＿＿＿＿＿＿＿。

F. Circle the one that reflect your opinion and practice (た)ほうがいい.

望ましいものに○をつけて「(た)ほうがいい」を練習しましょう。

1. 説明は (分かりやすい、分かりにくい) 方がいいと思う。

2. 校則は (厳しい、厳しくない) 方がいいと思う。

3. 宿題は (難しいけど短い、易しいけど長い) 方がいいと思う。

4. カフェテリアの食べ物は(野菜が多い、肉が多い)方がいいと思う。

5. 家の回りは (便利だけどうるさい、不便だけど静かな) 方がいい。

6. 制服は (あった、ない) 方がいい。

7. 日本語のクラスで英語を (使った、使わない) 方がいいと思う。

8. 日本語のクラスでもっと日本語を (話した、書いた、読んだ、聞いた) 方がいいと思う。

9. 週末は (外でスポーツをした、うちでテレビを見た) 方がいい。

G. Create an indirect comment sentence for the following kansoubun and share it with your classmates.

間接的コメント文を作って、クラスメートのものと比べましょう。

リード
leading
(sentence)

描写
description

コメント
comment

1. 私達の学校の中にコンビニのような店がある。本や雑誌やペンなどを買うことができる。それから、食べ物や飲み物もある。値段はちょっと高いけど、毎日たくさんの人が来る。＿＿＿＿＿＿＿＿＿＿。

リード
leading
(sentence)

描写
description

コメント
comment

2. 私達の日本語のクラスはよくフィールドトリップに行く。美術館で日本の美術を見たり、お花やお茶の先生の家に行ったりする。とても面白い。でも、日本のレストランには行かない。＿＿＿＿＿＿＿＿＿。

ノート：Potential Verds

書ける

You already know that 書くことができる (the dictionary form of a verb ＋ことができる) makes an English equivalent of "one can write such and such" or "it is possible to write such and such…" There is a shorter equivalent to this expression known as the potential verb. For example, 書ける(can write) is a potential verb and, as you see, it is much shorter than 書くことができる. Potential verbs can be obtained from their "non-potential" equivalents as shown in the following.

五段動詞 (U-verbs)　　Replace the final-*u* with *-eru*

書く→書ける、会う→会える、遊ぶ→遊べる、話す→話せる

一段動詞 (RU-verbs)　　Replace the final-*ru* with *-rareru* alternative way *-reru*

食べる→食べられる (食べれる)、寝る→寝られる (寝れる)

不規則動詞 (irregular verbs)

する→できる、来る→来られる (来れる)

It should be noted that all the potential verbs belong to いちだん/RU verb.

A. Complete the list below. リストを完成させてください。

会う		can meet	決める		can decide
遊ぶ	あそべる	can play	聞く		can listen/ask
洗う		can wash	来る		can come
教える	おしえられる	can teach	答る		can answer
言う		can say	する	できる	can do
行く		can go	食べる		can eat
いる	いられる	can exist/stay	作る		can make
選ぶ		can choose	寝る	ねられる	can sleep
起きる		can wake up	飲む		can drink
終わる	おえる	can end	始める		can begin
買う		can buy	話す	はなせる	can speak
帰る	かえれる	can go home	見る		can watch/see
書く		can write	読む		can read

B. Replace the underlined part with the potential form of the verb.

下線部分を可能動詞を使って書き換えてください。

EX1. 私の学校では世界の国々の人達とテレビで<u>話すことができます</u>。

→私の学校では世界の国々の人達とテレビで<u>話せます</u>。

EX2. その店では日本の食べ物を<u>買うことができます</u>。

→その店では日本の食べ物を (or が) <u>買えます</u>。

> Note that potential verbs can take either を or が when marking their direct object. So you can say, for example, either たべもの<u>を</u>かえる or たべもの<u>が</u>かえる (can buy food) and either えいが<u>を</u>見られる or えいが<u>が</u>見られる (can watch a movie).

1. いろいろな人のスピーチを<u>聞くことができる</u>。

2. ひろしは四年生の漢字を<u>書くことができます</u>。

3. ジェニーは上手に日本語を<u>読むことができる</u>と思います。

4. デービス先生は日本語と数学を<u>教えることができる</u>と思います。

5. 私達の町は映画館が多く、いろいろな映画を<u>見ることができます</u>。

6. 今、パーティーの場所を<u>決めることができます</u>か。

7. 宿題がたくさんあるので、10時に<u>寝ることができません</u>。

8. 田中さんの家に行きましたが、<u>会うことができませんでした</u>。

C. Indicate what you can do and cannot do in the following places in your school using potential verbs.

可能動詞を使って、学校の次の場所でできることとできないことを言いましょう。

> **例 (Example)**
>
> 図書館　私の学校の図書館では日本の新聞が読めますが、漫画は読めません。

1. 体育館　　2. 日本語の教室　　3. 講堂　　4. カフェテリア

5. 校庭 (school yard)　6. 寮 (dormitory)

D. Read the following kansoubun and compare its three comment parts. Do they sound different from each other? Discuss in class and choose the appropriate comment type and impression for each of them from below.

次の感想文の三つのコメント部分を読んで比べてください。そして、コメント文の種類と印象を下から選びましょう。

リード
Leading
(sentence)

| 私達の学校では毎朝7時から講堂で朝礼がある。 |

描写
Description

| まず、校長先生が話し、次に、生徒会長が話す。それから、クラブの発表や生徒のスキットなどがある。朝礼では皆と会えるし、校長先生の面白い話も聞けるし、色々な発表やスキットも見られる。それに、朝礼があるから、皆は授業に遅刻しない。 |

コメント
Comment

| 朝早くて大変だが、朝礼はあった方がいいと思う。実際、朝礼が好きな生徒が多いのではないだろうか。 | 朝早くて大変だが、朝礼は必要だ。実際、朝礼が好きな生徒が多いのだ。 | 朝早くて大変だが、朝礼は必要だと思う。実際、朝礼が好きな生徒が多いのだ。 |

Comment sentences	Impression
A. indirect + indirect	E. humble
B. indirect + direct	F. humble/assertive
C. direct + indirect	G. assertive/humble
D. direct + direct	H. assertive

Vocabulary

ちょうれい
朝礼
morning assembly

たいへん
大変(な)
tough, demanding

じっさい
実際
in fact, actually

ノート: Options for direct comment sentences

<ruby>朝<rt>ちょう</rt></ruby><ruby>礼<rt>れい</rt></ruby>は<ruby>必<rt>ひつ</rt></ruby><ruby>要<rt>よう</rt></ruby>だ vs <ruby>朝<rt>ちょう</rt></ruby><ruby>礼<rt>れい</rt></ruby>は<ruby>必<rt>ひつ</rt></ruby><ruby>要<rt>よう</rt></ruby>なのだ

You may have noticed that the first comment sentence in the middle example in the preceding exercise ends with neither (な)のだ nor any of the indirect comment constructions such as (だ)とおもう. It is an ordinary plain style sentence and it is considered a direct comment sentence. Since (な)のだ may sound repetitive and too strong when used in succession, you may use the regular plain style in some of your direct comment sentences instead.

ノート: Three approaches in *kansoubun* writing development

You may follow one of the three approaches shown below when creating *kansoubun* style writing. Your decision will depend upon how assertive, strong, and/or confident, or how humble, modest, and/or unsure you may want to sound in your writing.

KANSOUBUN WRITING DEVELOPMENT

Direct Approach	Hybrid Approach	Indirect Approach
LEADING SENTENCE	LEADING SENTENCE	LEADING SENTENCE
DESCRIPTIVE PART — DESCRIPTIVE SENTENCES	DESCRIPTIVE PART — DESCRIPTIVE SENTENCES	DESCRIPTIVE PART — DESCRIPTIVE SENTENCES
COMMENT PART — DIRECT COMMENT SENTENCES	COMMENT PART — DIRECT AND INDIRECT COMMENT SENTENCES	COMMENT PART — INDIRECT COMMENT SENTENCES

assertive strong sure ⟵⟶ humble modest unsure

593

E. Which approach do the comment parts of the following kansoubun reflect?

次の感想文のコメント部分のアプローチはどれですか。

リード
leading
(sentence)

> 私達の学校では外国に行けるプログラムが人気がある。

描写
description

> 特に、外国でボランティア活動をするプログラムの人気が高い。いろいろな国で英語を教えたり、子どもと遊んだりする。

コメント
comment

1.
> 学校で勉強している外国語が使えるし、人の役に立てるので、とてもいいプログラムだと思う。だから、このようなプログラムがもっと必要かも知れない。

2.
> 学校で勉強している外国語が使えるし、人の役に立てるので、とてもいいプログラムだ。だから、このようなプログラムがもっと必要なのだ。

3.
> 学校で勉強している外国語が使えるし、人の役に立てるので、とてもいいプログラムだと思う。だから、このようなプログラムがもっと必要なのだ。

4.
> 学校で勉強している外国語が使えるし、人の役に立てるので、とてもいいプログラムではないだろうか。だから、このようなプログラムがもっと必要かも知れない。

5.
> 学校で勉強している外国語が使えるし、人の役に立てるので、とてもいいプログラムなのだ。だから、このようなプログラムがもっと必要なのだ。

6.
> 学校で勉強している外国語が使えるし、人の役に立てるので、とてもいいプログラムだと思う。だから、このようなプログラムがもっとあった方がいい。

Direct Approach   **Hybrid Approach**   **Indirect Approach**

F. Further examine comments 1-6 in the preceding exercise and place them in the following scale in which the one that sounds most assertive and strong will occupy the left end.

前の練習問題のコメント部分をもう一度読み、断定の度合いの順に並べましょう。

[   ]   [   ]   [   ]   [   ]   [   ]   [   ]

| assertive strong, sure | 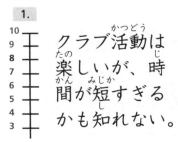 | humble modest, unsure |

ノート: Relative degree of assertiveness among comment sentences
(コメント文との相対的断定度)

Comment sentences may be ranked as shown below in terms of their relative degree of assertiveness. Obviously indirect comment sentences sound less assertive than their direct counterparts, and you can further adjust your assertiveness level by knowing how they may be compared to each other in this respect.

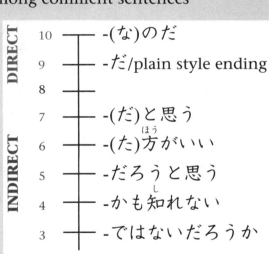

DIRECT
- 10 ── -(な)のだ
- 9 ── -だ/plain style ending
- 8 ──
- 7 ── -(だ)と思う

INDIRECT
- 6 ── -(た)方がいい
- 5 ── -だろうと思う
- 4 ── -かも知れない
- 3 ── -ではないだろうか

G. Read the following comment sentences and circle the appropriate number according to the assertiveness scale just introduced.

次のコメント文の断定度を表す適切な数字を○で囲みましょう。

EX.
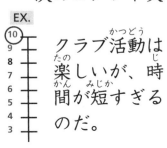
⑩ 9 8 7 6 5 4 3
クラブ活動は楽しいが、時間が短すぎるのだ。

1.
10 9 8 7 6 5 4 3
クラブ活動は楽しいが、時間が短すぎるかも知れない。

2.
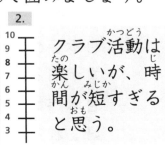
10 9 8 7 6 5 4 3
クラブ活動は楽しいが、時間が短すぎると思う。

595

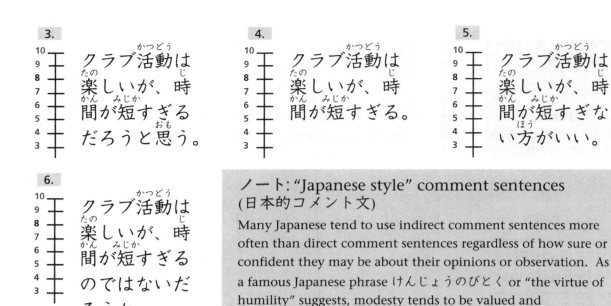

3.

クラブ活動（かつどう）は楽（たの）しいが、時間（じかん）が短（みじか）すぎるだろうと思（おも）う。

4.

クラブ活動（かつどう）は楽（たの）しいが、時間（じかん）が短（みじか）すぎる。

5.

クラブ活動（かつどう）は楽（たの）しいが、時間（じかん）が短（みじか）すぎない方（ほう）がいい。

6.

クラブ活動（かつどう）は楽（たの）しいが、時間（じかん）が短（みじか）すぎるのではないだろうか。

ノート: "Japanese style" comment sentences
(日本的コメント文)

Many Japanese tend to use indirect comment sentences more often than direct comment sentences regardless of how sure or confident they may be about their opinions or observation. As a famous Japanese phrase けんじょうのびとく or "the virtue of humility" suggests, modesty tends to be valued and appreciated in Japanese society more than outright assertion, and this certainly affects the way people communicate.

H. Read the explanation below and indicate whether the following sentences are true (ほんとう) or false (うそ).

次（つぎ）の説明（せつめい）を読（よ）んで、それに続（つづ）く文（ぶん）が本当（ほんとう）か嘘（うそ）か判断（はんだん）しましょう。

日本語（にほんご）のコメント文や判断文（はんだんぶん）では、書（か）き言葉（ことば）文（ぶん）の中（なか）の「のだ」のような直接的（ちょくせつてき）な表現（ひょうげん）より、柔（やわら）かい間接的（かんせつてき）な表現（ひょうげん）の方（ほう）がよく使（つか）われます。日本語（にほんご）の世界（せかい）ではこのような間接的（かんせつてき）な表現（ひょうげん）でコメントすることが好（この）まれています。すなわち、読者（どくしゃ）に対（たい）して直接的（ちょくせつてき）に対決（たいけつ）するよりも間接的（かんせつてき）にコメントすることが好（この）まれているのです。

判断文（はんだんぶん）: judgment sentences　書（か）き言葉（ことば）: writing words　直接的（ちょくせつてき）な: direct
間接的（かんせつてき）な: indirect　柔（やわら）かい: soft　対決（たいけつ）する: confront　好（この）まれている: be favored
すなわち: that is to say　読者（どくしゃ）: audience　対（たい）して: at, toward

1. 日本語（にほんご）のコメント文には直接的（ちょくせつてき）なコメント文と間接的（かんせつてき）コメント文がある。(本当（ほんとう）、嘘（うそ）)

2. 日本語（にほんご）では直接的（ちょくせつてき）なコメント文のほうが間接的（かんせつてき）コメント文より好（この）まれる。(本当（ほんとう）、嘘（うそ）)

I. Complete the following paragraphs by creating a couple of descriptive sentences and comment sentences for each leading sentence.

描写文とコメント文を作って感想文を完成させてください。

1.

LEADING SENTENCE	数学のスミス先生は人気があります。
	Ms. Smith, a math teacher, is popular.
DESCRIPTIVE SENTENCES	
COMMENT SENTENCES **DIRECT** AND/OR **INDIRECT**	

2.

LEADING SENTENCE	私は授業の後でよく学校の図書館に行く。
	I often go to the school library after my classes.
DESCRIPTIVE SENTENCES	
COMMENT SENTENCES **DIRECT** AND/OR **INDIRECT**	

J. Choose two specific topics about your school that you want to include in your booklet and write a kansoubun for each of them.

学校のパンフレットに入れたい話題を二つ選び、感想文を作りましょう。

Recognition Kanji 6: 認識漢字 6
<ruby>認識漢字<rt>にんしきかんじ</rt></ruby>

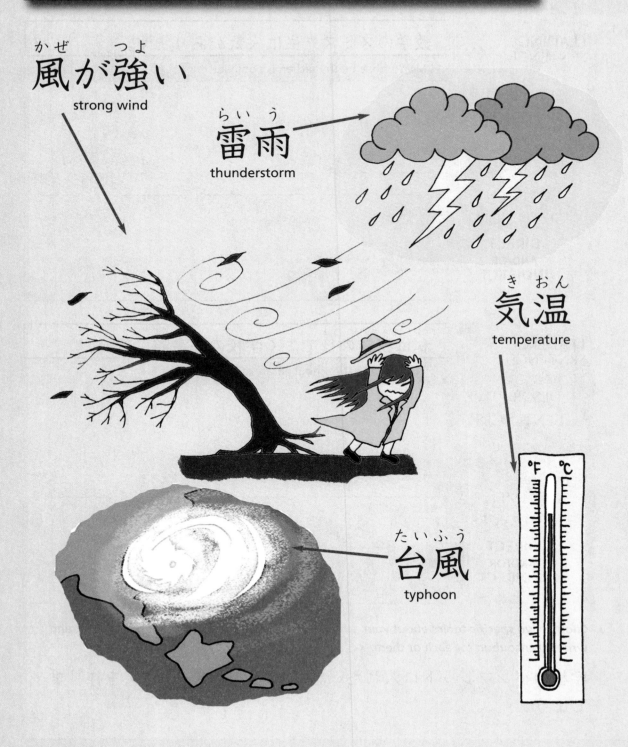

<ruby>風<rt>かぜ</rt></ruby>が<ruby>強<rt>つよ</rt></ruby>い
strong wind

<ruby>雷雨<rt>らいう</rt></ruby>
thunderstorm

<ruby>気温<rt>きおん</rt></ruby>
temperature

<ruby>台風<rt>たいふう</rt></ruby>
typhoon

<ruby>涼<rt>すず</rt></ruby>しい

cool

<ruby>暖<rt>あたた</rt></ruby>かい

warm

<ruby>気<rt>き</rt>持<rt>も</rt></ruby>ちがいい

feel good/comfortable

<ruby>方<rt>ほう</rt>角<rt>がく</rt></ruby>

direction

New Kanji 5: 新出漢字 5

速

ON: ソク   **KUN:** はや(い)

速い: はやい fast   速度: そくど rate of speed

一 ア 戸 戸 申 東 東 凍 涑 速

美

ON: ビ   **KUN:** うつく(しい)

美しい: うつくしい beautiful   美人: びじん beautiful lady

丶 丷 亠 亼 羊 兰 美 美

青

ON: セイ   **KUN:** あお(い)

青い: あおい blue   青: あお blue

一 十 キ 主 キ 青 青 青

赤

ON: セキ   **KUN:** あか(い)

赤い: あかい red   赤: あか red

一 十 土 ナ 方 赤 赤

白

ON: ハク、ビャク   **KUN:** しろ(い)

白い: しろい white   白: しろ white   白人: はくじん white people

ノ イ 白 白 白

黒

ON: コク   **KUN:** くろ(い)

黒い: くろい black   黒: くろ black   黒人: こくじん black people

丶 口 日 日 甲 甲 里 里 黒 黒 黒

遠

ON: エン   **KUN:** とお(い)

遠い: とおい far   遠足: えんそく field trip

一 十 土 卡 吉 吉 声 亨 亨 袁 袁 遠 遠

静

ON: セイ   **KUN:** しず(か)

静か: しずか quiet

一 十 キ 主 キ 青 青 青 青 靑 静 静 静 静

Additional Kanji 9: 追加漢字 9

料理店	りょうりてん　　　　　料：**ON:**リョウ　　　**KUN:**一 　restaurant　　　　　理：**ON:**リ　　　　　**KUN:**ことわり 　　　　　　　　　　　店：**ON:**テン　　　　**KUN:**みせ 新しい料理店があります。　There is a new restaurant.
中心	ちゅうしん、center　　中：**ON:**チュウ　　　**KUN:**なか 　　　　　　　　　　　心：**ON:**シン　　　　**KUN:**こころ 劇場は町の中心にあります。 　　　　　　　　The theater is in the center of the town.
感じ	かんじ、feeling　　　　感：**ON:**カン　　　　**KUN:** 一 新しい料理店は感じの良いイメージがあります。 　　　　　　　New restaurant has an affable image.
地下鉄	ちかてつ、subway　　地：**ON:**チ、ジ　　　**KUN:**つち 　　　　　　　　　　　下：**ON:**カ　　　　　**KUN:**した、さ(がる) 　　　　　　　　　　　鉄：**ON:**テツ　　　　**KUN:**くろがね 新しい地下鉄があります。　There is a new subway.
郵便局	ゆうびんきょうく　　　郵：**ON:**ユウ　　　　**KUN:** 一 　post office　　　　　便：**ON:**ビン、ベン　**KUN:**たよ(り) 　　　　　　　　　　　局：**ON:**キョク　　　**KUN:**つぼね 新しい郵便局があります。　There is a new post office.
果物	くだもの、fruit　　　果：**ON:**カ　　　　　**KUN:**は(たす) 　　　　　　　　　　　物：**ON:**ブツ　　　　**KUN:**もの どんな果物がありますか。　What kind of fruits do you have?
授業	じゅぎょう、class　　授：**ON:**ジュ　　　　**KUN:**さず(かる) 　　　　　　　　　　　業：**ON:**ギョウ、ゴウ **KUN:**わざ 新しい授業を作ります。　I am making a new lesson.
芸術	げいじゅつ、art　　　芸：**ON:**ゲイ　　　　**KUN:**一 　　　　　　　　　　　術：**ON:**ジュツ　　　**KUN:**わざ 新しい芸術を作ります。　I am making a new art.
忙しい	いそがしい、busy　　忙：**ON:**ボウ　　　　**KUN:** いそが(しい) とてもいそがしいです。　I am so busy.

601

Reading 11:
読み物 11

Story of Mr. Hotta:
堀田君のこと

This further reading will be much advanced. However, You will see this narrative style writing such as biography on next volume "Kisetsu 3: Akimaturi."

---

1. 堀田　大介さんは、横浜の近くの湘南海岸に住んでいました。ニューヨークに来たのは、高校の時でした。学校に入った後すぐに野球部に入りました。また、ニューヨーク・メッツの学生のリーグに入りました。そこで活躍しました。活躍: success

---

2. アメリカでは、英語の勉強もたくさんしましたが、宮沢賢治等を勉強しながら日本語にも興味を持ち始めました。日本で勉強している時には覚えることだけで自分で考えることはありませんでした。けれども、英語を勉強しなくてはならなくなって、自分の言葉である日本語で自分で考え始めました。自分で表現することを習って、自分の意味を考え始めました。

興味: interest　表現: express　覚える: memorize　考える: think

---

3. 大学では教育学部で人間の勉強をしたいと思い、一方、アメリカンフットボール部にも入りました。その大学でランニングバックで活躍して、有名になりました。

教育学部: Education Dept.

人間: human being

---

4. 大学を卒業した後、日本の会社に勤めたが、環境を勉強したいと思い、大学院で環境問題を専攻しました。そして、自分とは色々な環境の中でどのように生きてきたかと考えて、小説を書きたくなりました。残念ながら、堀田さんは、環境問題と小説を書く前に、京都の大学から湘南の家にバイクで帰る時、高速道路で交通事故で死にました。環境: environment　専攻: major　小説: novel

---

A. Answer the following questions about each paragraph using the choosing strategy.

1-1 Find the same category of Kanji in red.

a. 野球部：活躍、学校、林、部活　　b. 学生：生徒、学校、食堂、高校

1-2 Fill the line and complete the sum up sentence choosing the appropriate words in the parenthesis below.

First sentence: _____

堀田君は（日本、中国、アメリカ）の（高校、メッツ、大学院）で（アメフト、野球、柔道）をしていた。

2-1 Find the similar Kanji in red.

    a. 英語：勉強、日本語、図書館   b. 考え：興味、意味、思う、表現

2-2 Fill the line and complete the sum up sentence choosing the appropriate words in the parenthesis below.

First sentence: _____

英語を勉強しながら、自分で考え、自分で（表現、専攻、活躍）し、意味を考え始めました。

3-1 Find the same category of Kanji in red.

    a. 教育：生徒、活躍、学校、人間   b. 活動：野球、学校、有名、高校

3-2 Fill the line and complete the sum up sentence choosing the appropriate words in the parenthesis below.

First sentence: _____

大学時代に（政治学、工学、教育学）を勉強し、（アメフト、音楽、ダンス）のクラブ部に入って、（ランニングバック、クォーターバック、チアーリーダー）をした。

4-1 Find the same radical of Kanji in red.

    a. 説：悦、言、語   b. 速：題、遠、足

4-2 Fill the line and complete the sum up sentence choosing the appropriate words in the parenthesis below.

First sentence: _____

（大学、高校、中学）を卒業したあと、（環境問題、経済問題、国際問題）を勉強していたが、（交通事故、病気、事件）で死んだ。

B. Link three items in the vocabulary list below.

	単語 たんご	読み よ	意味 いみ
Ex.	同じ ⟷	おなじ ⟷	same
1.	入学後	もんだい	novel
2.	野球部	しょうせつ	education
3.	季節	じぶん	baseball club
4.	自分	にゅうがくご	word
5.	言葉	きせつ	self
6.	表現	ゆうめい	expression
7.	教育	やきゅうぶ	environment
8.	有名	きょういく	after entering
9.	環境	ことば	famous
10.	問題	ひょうげん	season
11.	小説	かんきょう	problem

603

C. Check whether the following information is true or false.

1. この人は野球が上手でした。 （本当、嘘）
2. この高校の日本語の勉強は暗記をしていた。 （本当、嘘）
3. 大学で有名な選手だった。 （本当、嘘）
4. 大学院で環境問題を勉強していた。 （本当、嘘）

D. Form groups and answer the guided questions in Japanese.

1. 高校の時、メッツの下部組織に入ったのはどうしてですか。
2. どうして高校で日本語に興味を持ちましたか。
3. 環境問題と自分についてどんな勉強ができると思いますか。
4. 交通事故を起さないようにするにはどうしたらいいですか。

　堀田　大介さんは、横浜の近くの湘南海岸に住んでいました。ニューヨークに来たのは高校の時でした。学校に入った後、すぐに野球部に入りました。また、ニューヨーク・メッツの学生のリーグに入りました。そこで活躍しました。

近く：near	湘南海岸：place	時：time	入学後：after entering	野球部：baseball club
季節：season	変わる：change	学生：student	入る：enter	活躍：(play) actively

　英語の勉強もたくさんしましたが、宮沢賢治等を勉強しながら日本語にも興味を持ちました。日本で勉強している時には、覚えることだけで自分で考えることはありませんでした。けれども、英語を勉強しなくてはならなくて、自分の言葉である日本語で自分で考えました。自分で表現することを習って、自分の意味を考え始めました。

宮沢賢治：author	等：etc.	興味：interest	持つ：hold	覚える：memorize　だけ：only
自分：self	考える：think	しなくてはならい：must	状況：situation	言葉：word
表現：expression	習う：learn	意味：mean	始め：start	

　大学時代は教育学部で人間の勉強をしたいと思い、一方、アメリカンフットボール部にも入りました。その大学でもランニングバックで活躍して、有名になりました。

大学：college	時代：days, period	教育学部：Education Department/major	人間：human
一方：on the other hand	部：club	入る：enter	ランニングバック：running back
活躍：actively	有名：famous		

　大学を卒業した後、日本の会社に勤めましたが、環境を勉強したいと思い、大学院で環境問題を専攻しました。でも、自分とはいろいろな環境の中でどのように生きてきたかと考えて、小説を書きたいとも思っていました。残念ながら、堀田さんは、環境問題と小説を書く前に、京都の大学院から湘南の自宅にバイクで帰る時高速道路で交通事故で死にました。

卒業：graduation	後：after	会社：company	勤める：be employed	環境：environment
思う：think	大学院：graduate school	問題：problem	専攻：major	自分：self
考える：consider	小説：novel	残念ながら：unfortunately	本格的に：seriously	
追究：pursuit	前：before	京都：place	自宅：residence	帰る：return
東名高速道路：Tomei highway	交通事故：traffic accident	死：die		

4.8 Mechanics 組立て
<small>くみたて</small>

Editorial Meeting
編集会議
<small>へんしゅうかいぎ</small>

Objectives

Read a letter from Japan and become familiar with its format.

Form an editorial team for booklet production and choose an editor-in-chief.

Sort through the existing basic information writings and create additional ones if necessary.

Choose topics to be covered in the booklet and create texts and visuals on assigned topics.

Overview

It's time to start planning your booklet. First you will form an editorial team and choose the editor-in-chief. Then you will have an editorial meeting in which you sort through the existing basic information writings and choose additional topics to be covered in the booklet. After that, you will check the structure of the booklet, you will write your articles, and prepare your visuals.

6	Read a letter from Japan	日本からの手紙を読む
7	Hold an editorial meeting	編集会議をする
1	Choose the editor-in-chief	編集長を選ぶ
2	Check and organize basic information about your school	基礎情報の確認と整理
3	Choose visuals	ビジュアルを選ぶ
4	Include writings about school rules	学校の規則についての文章
5	Choose topics	トピックを選ぶ
6	Set the basic structure of the booklet	基本構成を決める
8	Create main texts and visuals	本文とビジュアルを作る

Your booklet production will proceed more purposefully if you always keep the intended users in mind. For this reason we will provide a context in which you will be making your booklet. Let's assume that a letter has arrived from a Japanese friend who will be coming to America on a school trip in the near future and who wants to visit your school then. Her school has a sister school relationship with yours and she asks for more information about your school. The letter came with a booklet about her school that she and her schoolmates had produced. Upon reading the letter and the booklet, you have decided to create a booklet about your own school with your classmates and to send copies to her school. We begin with the reading of a sample letter in which a Japanese student (はやしゆうき) writes to her American friend (アンドレ).

A. Read the sample letter from Japan and do the following exercises.

次の日本からのメッセージを読みましょう。

こんにちは。

アンドレさん。お元気ですか。私も元気です。こちらは桜もさいて暖かいです。そちらの天気はどうですか。

さて、私達の学校の修学旅行でアメリカに行くことが決まりました。その時、一日自由時間があるので、アンドレさんの学校に行きたいと考えています。それで、すみませんが、アンドレさんの学校の紹介を送っていただけますか。

それでは、アンドレさんの学校で会えるのを楽しみにしています。みなさんによろしく。それから、参考に私の学校紹介のパンフレットをお送りします。

さようなら

二千XY年四月五日

林 有紀

アンドレさん

B. Link three items in the vocabulary list using the hint below.

線を結んで、漢字／語彙のリストを完成させてください。

単語	読み	意味
Ex. 桜 ←——→	さくら ←——→	cherry blossoms/trees
1. 元気	さんこう	healthy
2. 暖かい	がっこうしょうかい	send
3. 私達の学校	おくって	our school
4. 修学旅行	しゅうがくりょこう	reference
5. 参考	わたしたちのがっこう	free time
6. 自由時間	げんき	warm
7. 送って	じゆうじかん	introducing a school
8. 学校紹介	あたたかい	senior school trip

C. Write the meaning of the following words in English.

例のように下の語彙のリストを完成させてください。

単語	知っている漢字	その意味	英語
EX. 自由時間	自由、時間 —→	freedom, time —→	free time
1. 私達の学校	学校、私	_____	_____
2. 修学旅行	学生、行く	_____	_____
3. 学校 紹介	学校、紹介	_____	_____
4. 送る	送る	_____	_____

D. Read the note below. After that, take a closer look at the sample letter and learn how to write a simple letter in Japanese.

始めにノートを読んでください。次に手紙の例をもう一度詳しくチェックし、簡単な手紙の書き方を学びましょう。

ノート: Writing letters in Japanese (手紙について)

Thanks to the proliferation of electronic communication, letter-writing may be on the verge of becoming an "endangered species." Nevertheless, hand-written letters are still considered more appropriate in some personal communications such as asking for a favor, making a request, or for an apology, and you may need to know the basics of letter-writing. Formal letters in Japanese require some set words in both the beginning and the end. However, as you can see from the preceding example, letters exchanged between school age friends can forgo this ritual. You may learn more about formal letter-writing in the forthcoming volumes.

Start with a simple greeting such as こんにちは. ▶

こんにちは。

After the greeting you may ask about your addressee's well being and refer to the weather and/or other seasonal topics. ▶

アンドレさん。お元気ですか。私も元気です。こちらは桜もさいて暖かいです。そちらはみなさんいかがですか。そちらの天気はどうですか。

さて effectively sends a signal to the reader that the main part of your letter will begin. ▶

さて、私達の学校の修学旅行でアメリカに行くことが決まりました。その時、一日自由時間があるので、アンドレさんの学校に行きたいと考えています。

Before you make your request, write something like それで、すみませんが (And I am sorry to bother you but....). ▶

それで、すみませんが、アンドレさんの学校の紹介を送っていただけますか。

Before closing, you may want to express your excitement and anticipation for the future. ▶

それでは、アンドレさんの学校で会えるのを楽しみにしています。みなさんによろしく。それから、参考に私の学校紹介のパンフレットをお送りします。

End with a simple greeting such as さようなら. ▶

さようなら

Write the date and your (addresser's) name on the right side as shown ▶

20XY年4月5日

林　有紀

Write the addressee's name on the left side as shown ▶

アンドレさん

E. Read the instructions below about your booklet-making project and fill in the parentheses with either T (true, ほんとう) or F (false, うそ), according to the instructions.

パンフレット作成プロジェクトの指示を読んで、英文が本当か嘘か判断してください。

日本の姉妹校から生徒が来ます。その前に私達の学校紹介のパンフレットを作って、姉妹校に送りたいと思います。どんなトピックがいいですか。各グループで10個のトピックを選んで、パンフレットを作りたいと思います。今月の終わりか来月の始めにはパンフレットができればいいと思います。まず最初に、先生の指示でグループになってください。それから、編集長と副編集長を選んで下さい。次に、グループの日本語の名前を決め、メンバーのリストを作って下さい。それから、10個のトピックを選んで下さい。そして、各トピックの文章を作ってください。文章は基礎情報型、説明文型、感想文型のどのスタイルで書くか決めてください。また、各トピックのための写真を撮って、その写真についての説明も考えてください。他のビジュアルも用意してください。それでは、始めましょう。

---

1. You will be making a booklet about your school and give it to the students at your sister school when they visit your school later this month. (   )

2. Your teacher may assign you to a group. (   )

3. You need to make a membership list of your group before choosing a leader. (   )

4. You must take pictures of yourself and put them in the booklet. (   )

5. Your group will choose 10 topics to be included in the booklet. (   )

6. Your writing must be written either in the basic information style or in the expository style. (   )

7. You will decide upon the name of your group after choosing a leader. (   )

8. The photos you will be taking must be relevant to your chosen topics. (   )

9. Photographs will be the only visuals that may be used in your booklet. (   )

10. You must make your booklet by the end of this month. (   )

Finally it's time to start making your booklet. You will have a series of editorial meetings in Japanese in which you will make some important decisions about your booklet. But first, you will learn about the adverbial usage of adjectives since it will be useful in the editorial meetings.

ノート：Adverbial usage of adjectives 形容詞の副詞的使用

い-Adj. く
な-Adj. に ⎤ なる

い-Adj. く
な-Adj. に ⎤ する

Both い adjectives and な adjectives can be used adverbially. For い adjectives you must drop い and add く and for な adjectives you must drop な and add に to make them adverbial. At this time you will learn two constructions that involve the adverbial use of an adjective and they are useful in indicating changes. You should be somewhat familiar with both constructions as you already know expressions like はつおんがもっとじょうずになりたいです (I want to become better at pronunciation) and しずかにしてください (Please be quiet).

くなる and になる are used to indicate a change of state from an observe"s standpoint. For example, やすくなる and しずかになる mean "become cheap(er)" and "become quiet" respectively.

くする and -にする on the other hand are used to indicate a change of state from the standpoint of someone causing the change. For example, やすくする and しずかにする mean "make (something) cheap(er)" and "make (oneself) quiet" respectively.

Note that the adverbial form of いい is よく. Thus "become better" and "make (it} better" are よくなる and よくする respectively. いくなる and いくする do not occur.

F. Circle the correct one. 正しいものを○で囲みましょう。

1. 数学の試験が (難しく、難しいに、難しいく) なりました。

2. 図書館が (便利なに、便利く、便利に) なりました。

3. ジョンさんは物理が (好きいに、好きに、好きく) なりました。

4. 明日は (寒いく、寒く、寒いに) なるかも知れません。

5. クラブの部屋が (新しく、新しいなに、新しいく) なりました。

6. もっと (まじめで、まじめに、まじめく) なってください。

7. クラブの練習時間が (短く、短いに、短に) なりました。

8. 明日は天気が (いく、よく、よいく) なるでしょう。

G. Circle whichever is applicable to your situation and also state a reason for the change. After that, ask your classmates the questions and share information about each other.

自分に当てはまる方を〇で囲み、その理由も書いてください。そして、クラスメートに聞いて、お互いの情報を交換しましょう。

EX. 私は前の学期より学校が (面白く、⌾つまらなく⌾) なりました。
理由は<u>面白い行事が少ない</u>からです。

School has became more boring than the previous term/semester. The reason is because there are fewer interesting school events (this term).

1. 私は前の学期より学校が (面白く、つまらなく) なりました。
理由は＿＿＿＿＿＿＿＿＿＿からです。

2. 私は前の学期より (忙しく、ひまに) なりました。
理由は＿＿＿＿＿＿＿＿＿＿からです。

3. 私は前の学期より図書館に行くことが (多く、少なく)なりました。
理由は＿＿＿＿＿＿＿＿＿＿からです。

4. 私の部屋は前の学期より (きれいに、汚く) なりました。
理由は＿＿＿＿＿＿＿＿＿＿からです。

H. Fill in the blank with an appropriate くする construction, as shown in the example.

空欄に適当な「〜くする」の形を入れてください。

EX. 試験が難しすぎるから、<u>易しくして</u>ください。

Please make the exams easy/easier as they are too difficult.

1. 試験が長すぎるから、＿＿＿＿＿＿＿ください。
2. うるさいから、＿＿＿＿＿＿＿ください。
3. 値段が高すぎるから、＿＿＿＿＿＿＿ください。
4. 部屋が汚いから、＿＿＿＿＿＿＿ください。
5. 宿題が少なすぎるから、＿＿＿＿＿＿＿ください。
6. 部屋が暗いから、＿＿＿＿＿＿＿ください。
7. カフェテリアは不便だから、＿＿＿＿＿＿＿ください。

1 Choose the editor-in-chief　　編集長を選ぶ

A. Choose the editor-in-chief.　編集長を選びましょう

Have a group meeting and choose the editor-in-chief of your booklet. A volunteer from each group will chair the meeting. Your experience in the review sessions in chapter 2 should help you conduct the meeting entirely in Japanese.

B. Choose the assistant editor-in-chief.　副編集長を選びましょう

The newly chosen editor-in-chief will take over the chair's role and lead a discussion for choosing the assistant editor-in-chief who will also serve as a board writer in editorial meetings.

2 Check and organize basic information about your school　　学校の基礎情報の確認と整理

A. In 4.3 and 4.4 you collected some basic information about your school and made simple descriptions in the following areas. Do you still have them? Call an editorial meeting and find out. If you don't have all of them, decide who will create the missing pieces.

この課の4.3と4.4で皆さんの学校の基礎情報を集め、次の分野ごとに文章にしました。文章はまだありますか。編集会議を開き、確認してください。文章がない場合は、書く人を決めてください。

	基礎情報	Basic Information	文章	書く人
4.3	位置と環境	Location and surroundings	(ある、 ない)	
4.3	種類や生徒やキャンパス	School type, students, campus (and terms, grade levels, and teachers)	(ある、 ない)	サム
4.3	教科と科目	Academic divisions and subjects	(ある、 ない)	
4.3	チームとクラブ	Teams and clubs	(ある、 ない)	
4.4	学校行事	School events	(ある、 ない)	

会議の例 (Sample Meeting)

編集長：　これから、編集会議を始めます。議題は学校の基礎情報です。まず、「位置と環境」です。文章がありますか。

メンバーA：　はい、あります。

編集長：　次は、「種類や生徒やキャンパス」です。文章がありますか。

メンバーB：　あのう、ありません。

編集長：　じゃ、誰が書きますか。

メンバーC：　私が書きます。

編集長：　じゃ、サムさんお願いします。次は、「教科と科目」です。文章がありますか。continued.

Instructions to the Editor-in-Chief
編集長への指示

Assign all the existing descriptions evenly to your group members and ask them to individually do the following exercise.

B. Examine the descriptions assigned to you one at a time and check any applicable boxes below. Then write down your opinions and suggestions as shown in the examples.

質問を読んで、一番適切な答えを選んでください。それから、例のようにあなたの意見と提案を書いてください。

意見: Opinions

□ 長すぎる

□ 短すぎる

□ 分かりにくい

□ 分かりやすい

□ 内容に問題がある

□ 日本語に問題がある

□ 問題はない

提案: Suggestions

□ 長くした方がいい

□ 短くした方がいい

□ 分かりやすくした方がいい

□ 書き直した方がいい

□ 内容をチェックした方がいい

□ 日本語をチェックした方がいい

□ このままでいい

613

例1 (Example 1)

「位置と環境」の文章は分かりやすいです。でも、内容に問題があります。町の人口が正しくありません。だから、書き直した方がいいと思います。日本語には問題がありません。

例2 (Example 2)

「教科と科目」の文章は長すぎて、ちょっと分かりにくいです。だから、短くして、科目の表を作った方がいいと思います。それから、日本語もチェックした方がいいと思います。でも、内容には問題がありません。

C. Resume the editorial meeting and share your opinions and suggestions with your group.

編集会議を再開して、それぞれの意見と提案を話し合いましょう。

会議の例 (Sample Meeting)

編集長： 「位置と環境」の文章はどうですか。

メンバーA： 分かりやすいです。でも、内容に問題があります。

編集長： そうですか。どんな問題ですか。

メンバーA： 町の人口が正しくありません。だから、書き直した方がいいと思います。

編集長： わかりました。日本語に問題がありますか。

メンバーA： いいえ、ありません。

編集長： 次は「種類や生徒やキャンパス」です。文章はどうですか。

メンバーB： あのう、continued.

Instructions to the Editor-in-Chief
編集長への指示

Decide if the suggested revisions are necessary and assign the revision work evenly to your group members. You may consult your teacher at any point during this process and finalize all the basic information texts.

3 **Choose visuals**　　　　　　　　ビジュアルを選ぶ

Photos, illustrations, charts, maps, and any other carefully selected visuals will greatly enhance the quality of your booklet. At this time you will decide which visuals should accompany which sections of your basic information texts. First, individually go over the list below and check any items you think will be necessary. Then have a meeting and make decisions as a group.

ビジュアルはパンフレットを作るために必要です。まず、各自下のリストを見て、必要と思うビジュアルをチェックしてください。それから、みんなで使用するビジュアルを決めてください。

	基礎情報	Basic Information	写真	イラスト	表	地図	その他
4.3	位置と環境	*Location and surroundings*	✓			✓	
4.3	種類や生徒やキャンパス	*School type, students, campus (and terms, grade levels, and teachers)*					
4.3	教科と科目	*Academic divisions and subjects*					
4.3	チームとクラブ	*Teams and clubs*					
4.4	学校行事	*School events*					

会議の例 (Sample Meeting)

編集長：　「位置と環境」の文章にはどんなビジュアルが必要ですか。

メンバーA: 写真が必要です。

編集長：　Bさん。

メンバーB: 地図もあった方がいいと思います。

メンバーC: 私も写真と地図が必要だと思います。

編集長：　じゃ、写真と地図にしましょう。continued.

Instructions to the Editor-in-Chief

編集長への指示

Assign visual production tasks evenly to group members based on your discussions and decisions. Make sure to sort the visuals by theme and keep them in order, along with the text files.

4 Include writings about school rules

学校の規則についての文章

In section 4.5 of this chapter you first wrote some basic information about the rules of your school and then proceeded to write more about them in expository style. It is also possible to write *kansoubun* on this topic and you will need to make some decisions in your group on how and to what extent you want to cover this topic in your booklet. You may certainly choose to include more than one style of writings. For example, you may include an article in the basic information style for an overview, and several *kansoubun* pieces in which students offer their comments on the rules of their school. And this certainly applies to any other topics you may choose to cover in your booklet and, therefore, it is important for you to be fully aware of the characteristics of each writing style. As you see, the sample articles on the right are written in plain style. You may decide whether your booklet will primarily be written in polite style (*-desu*, *-masu*) or in plain style.

BASIC INFORMATION STYLE

基礎情報型

BASIC INFORMATION
:   :
BASIC INFORMATION
:   :
BASIC INFORMATION

この学校では制服を着なければならない。化粧をしたり、アクセサリーをつけたりしてはいけない。髪を染めることもできない。それから、携帯電話を持ってきてはいけない。お昼も学校のカフェテリアで食べなければならない。

- presents basic information in a matter-of-fact fashion
- can be accompanied or replaced by a list or a chart

Key question to consider:

基礎情報が必要ですか。

A. Read the three sample articles on the right. Then meet with your group and decide how you want to cover the school rules in your booklet. After that, choose the types of visuals that may accompany your articles.

学校の規則についての三つの文章を読んでください。それから、編集会議をしてこのトピックの扱い方を決めてください。最後にビジュアルについても決めてください。

EXPOSITORY STYLE 説明文型（せつめいぶんがた）		KANSOUBUN STYLE 感想文型（かんそうぶんがた）	
	TOPIC SENTENCE		LEADING SENTENCE
	SUPPORTING SENTENCE		DESCRIPTIVE SENTENCES
	EXAMPLES		
	SUPPORTING SENTENCE		COMMENT SENTENCES
	EXAMPLES		
	SUM UP		

この学校の規則（きそく）は大変（たいへん）厳（きび）しい。服装（ふくそう）の規則がたくさんある。例（たと）えば、制服（せいふく）を着（き）なければなりません。化粧（けしょう）をしたり、アクセサリーをつけたりしてはいけない。髪（かみ）を染（そ）めることもできない。他（ほか）の規則（きそく）もかなりある。携帯（けいたい）電話（でんわ）を持（も）ってきてはだめだ。そして、お昼（ひる）も学校のカフェテリアで食べなければならない。この学校の規則（きそく）は日本の学校と同（おな）じくらい厳（きび）しいだろう。

この学校には規則（きそく）がたくさんある。まず、制服（せいふく）を着（き）なければならない。それから、化粧（けしょう）もアクセサリーもだめだ。髪（かみ）を染（そ）めることや携帯電話（けいたいでんわ）を持（も）ってくることもできない。よく、服装（ふくそう）や持（も）ち物（もの）の検査（けんさ）がある。そして、お昼（ひる）も学校のカフェテリアで食べなければならない。この学校の規則（きそく）は厳（きび）しすぎると思う。でも、授業（じゅぎょう）や部活（ぶかつ）が面白（おもしろ）いから、みんな我慢（がまん）できる(can tolerate)のだ。

- explains something in a clear, logical, and unemotional fashion
- presents information in a persuasive manner
- contents tightly bound by the topic sentence with no room for sidetracking or inserting personal feelings

- describes something and offers personal comments about it
- presents information in a reflective manner
- contents only loosely bound by the leading sentence with a section set aside for personal comments

▼

Key question to consider:

説明（せつめい）したいですか。

▼

Key question to consider:

コメントしたいですか。

会議の例 (Sample Meeting)

編集長（へんしゅうちょう）:	この学校の規則（きそく）についての基礎情報（きそじょうほう）が必要（ひつよう）ですか。
メンバーA:	はい、必要だと思います。
メンバーB:	私も、必要だと思います。
編集長（へんしゅうちょう）:	じゃ、説明（せつめい）したいですか。
メンバーA:	いいえ。でも、コメントしたいです。
編集長（へんしゅうちょう）:	Cさんは。
メンバーC:	私も、コメントしたいです。
編集長（へんしゅうちょう）:	わかりました。じゃ、基礎情報文（きそじょうほうぶん）と感想文（かんそうぶん）を作（つく）りましょう。みなさん、いいですか。
メンバー:	はい、いいです。
編集長（へんしゅうちょう）:	じゃ、誰（だれ）が基礎情報文（きそじょうほうぶん）を作りますか。
メンバーA:	私が作ります。
編集長（へんしゅうちょう）:	じゃ、Aさんお願（ねが）いします。それから、BさんとCさんは感想文（かんそうぶん）をお願いします。
メンバーB, C:	はい。
編集長（へんしゅうちょう）:	どんなビジュアルが必要ですか。continued.

Instructions to the Editor-in-Chief
編集長（へんしゅうちょう）への指示（しじ）

Decide whether the articles will be written in the plain style or in the polite style. After that, assign writing and visual production tasks evenly to group members based on your discussions and decisions. Make sure to proofread each other's work and revise if necessary.

ノート: Note on style

Polite vs Plain Style

You have learned that the polite (です/ます) style and the plain style are used in formal occasions and informal occasions respectively. While this is a good yardstick to use, how one may choose the style in their speech or writing involves more than just the formal/informal dichotomy. For example, use of the plain form is effective in some reflective writings and may narrow the social or interpersonal distance between the writer and the reader. So you may consider writing your *kansoubun* in the plain style regardless of how the rest of the articles in your booklet may be styled.

5 Choose topics　　　　　　　　トピックを選ぶ

So far you have prepared some basic information about your school in terms of its location and surroundings, enrollment, academic subjects, clubs and teams, school events, and a few other areas. You have also written about the rules of your school. This time you will choose topics you would like to cover or elaborate upon in your booklet. Your topic may be broad, such as "facilities" and "popular school events," or more specific such as "our gymnasium" and "graduation." You have written two *kansoubun* at the end of section 4.7 and they can certainly be a part of your contribution in this respect. Although the number of topics you choose may depend upon the size of your editorial team as well as the amount of production time you may have, we will proceed with an assumption that you may be choosing 10 topics.

A. Brainstorming　　ブレインストーミングから始めましょう。

Start with a brainstorming session, just like when you chose the topic of your review session in chapter 2.

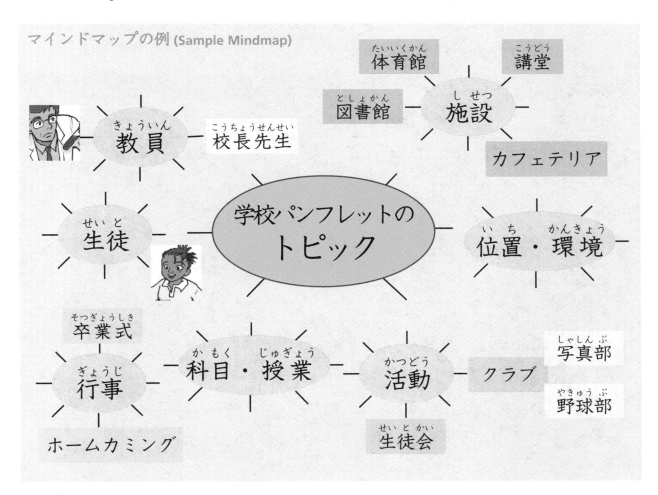

マインドマップの例 (Sample Mindmap)

B. Procedure for deciding on topics in the booklet トピック決定の手順

Topics in your booklet have to be relevant to the objectives of the booklet and appealing to its intended readers. Follow the procedure below to decide on the topics.

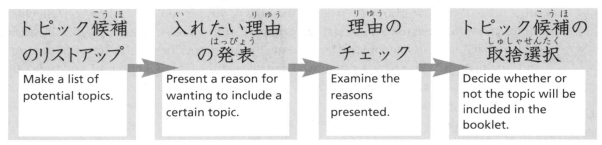

トピック候補のリストアップ	入れたい理由の発表	理由のチェック	トピック候補の取捨選択
Make a list of potential topics.	Present a reason for wanting to include a certain topic.	Examine the reasons presented.	Decide whether or not the topic will be included in the booklet.

C. Make a list of potential topics.

トピック候補をリストアップしてください。

D. Go over the sample meeting conversation below and conduct your own meeting to finalize your topics. Make sure to examine the reasons for all the proposed topics.

下の例に習って編集会議をしてトピックを決めてください。その際、理由のチェックを必ずしてください。

会話の例 (Sample Dialogue)

編集長： 学校のパンフレットはどんなトピックがいいですか。10個のトピックを選びたいと思います。

メンバーA： 学校行事がいいです。

編集長： Bさんは？

メンバーB： 施設がいいです。

(C raises a hand)

編集長： Cさん。

メンバーC： 私は、科目がいいです。

編集長： Dさんは。

メンバーD： あのう、教員がいいです。

編集長： じゃ、Aさん、学校行事の何がいいですか。

---

continued to the next page

メンバーA: 卒業式がいいです。

編集長: どうして卒業式がいいですか。

メンバーA: 卒業式は一番感動的な行事なので、いいと思います。

編集長: Eさんは卒業式をどう思いますか。

メンバーE: 私も卒業式は重要だと思います。だから、いいトピック
だと思います。

編集長: 他の皆さんもいいと思いますか。

メンバーB, C, D: はい、いいです。

編集長: じゃ、Aさん、卒業式について調べて書いてください。

メンバーA: わかりました。

編集長: Bさん、どの施設について調べたいですか。

メンバーB: まず、施設全体の紹介をしたいです。それから、講堂に
ついて調べたいです。

編集長: どうして講堂がいいですか。continued.

E. Make a list of 10 topics based on the outcome of your meeting.

ミーティングの結果に基づいて、10個のトピック
のリストを作りましょう。

6 **Set the basic structure of the booklet** 基本構成を決める

*A. Decide in what order to present your topics in the booklet and how many pages you may
need for each of them. Prepare a planning chart like the following.*

パンフレットの各項目の順番やページ数を決め、次のような
予定表を作りましょう。

ページ	項目	スタイル		ビジュアル
	前書きと目次 Preface and Table of Contents	You will create them later in section 4.9.		
1-5	基礎情報	基礎情報型	Polite	写真、表、地図
6	施設：講堂			写真
7	施設：日本語の教室	感想文型	Plain and Polite	写真
8	行事：プロム			写真、イラスト
9	行事：卒業式			写真、イラスト
10-11	規則：服装、持ち物 Dress code, Belongings	説明文型	Plain	表、
12	活動：生徒会 Student Council			写真、イラスト
13	活動：サッカー部			写真、表
14	活動：ボランティア活動	感想文型	Plain and Polite	写真、リスト
15	人物：校長先生 Principal			写真
16	人物：生徒会長			イラスト
17	授業：演技 Classes: Acting			写真
	後書き Afterword	You will create this later in section 4.9.		

8 Create main texts and visuals　本文とビジュアルを作る

A. Create main texts and visuals for your assigned topics based on the your planning chart.

予定表に従って、担当するトピックの本文とビジュアルを作成してください。

New Kanji 6: 新出漢字 6

心
ON: シン   KUN: こころ
心: こころ heart   中心: ちゅうしん center   心配: しんぱい worry
`ノ 心 心 心`

思
ON: シ   KUN: おも(う)
思う: おもう think   思想: しそう thought
`一 口 田 田 田 思 思 思`

好
ON: コウ   KUN: す(き)
好き: すき like   好意: こうい favor
`く タ 女 女 好 好`

知
ON: チ   KUN: し(る)
知る: しる know   知人: ちじん acquaintance
`ノ ト ヒ チ 矢 矢 知 知 知`

毎
ON: マイ   KUN:
毎日: まいにち every day   毎朝: まいあさ every morning
`ノ ト 仁 匂 匂 毎`

同
ON: ドウ   KUN: おな(じ)
同じ: おなじ same   同意: どうい agreement   共同: きょうどう cooperation
`一 冂 冂 冋 同 同`

意
ON: イ   KUN: ─
同意: どうい agreement   意見: いけん opinion   意思: いし will
`一 亠 立 立 产 音 音 音 音 意 意`

味
ON: ミ   KUN: あじ
味: あじ taste   意味: いみ meaning
`一 口 口 吁 吽 味 味`

Additional Kanji 10: 追加漢字 10

磨く	みがく、brush　　　　　磨：ON:マ　　　　KUN: みが(く) 歯を磨く。　I brush my teeth.
起きる	おきる、wake　　　　　起：ON:キ　　　　KUN:おき(る) 6時に起きる。　I wake at 6 o'clock.
歯	は、teeth　　　　　　歯：ON:シ　　　　KUN: は 歯を磨く。　I brush my teeth.
洗う	あらう、wash　　　　　洗：ON:セン　　　KUN: あら(う) 顔を洗う。　I wash my face.
顔	かお、face　　　　　　顔：ON:ガン　　　KUN: かお 顔を洗う。　I wash my face.
自転車	じてんしゃ、bike　　　自：ON:ジ、シ　　KUN:みずか(ら) 　　　　　　　　　　転：ON:テン　　　KUN:ころ(ぶ) 　　　　　　　　　　車：ON:シャ　　　KUN:くるま 自転車に乗る。　I ride my bike.
他に	ほかに、besides/others　他：ON:タ　　　　KUN:ほか この他にもたくさんあります。　There are more besides this.
主食	しゅしょく、main dish　主：ON:シュ　　　KUN:おも(な) 　　　　　　　　　　食：ON:ショク　　KUN:た(べる) 主食は米です。　Main dish is rice.
室内	しつない、indoor　　　室：ON:シツ　　　KUN:むろ 　　　　　　　　　　内：ON:ナイ、ダイ　KUN:うち 室内で遊ぶ。　We play indoors.

FORM

1. Verb classification

ます form and the dictionary form

Japanese verbs conjugate according to style (plain/polite), tense (nonpast/past), and affirmativeness/negativeness. So far, you have learned some useful verbs in a form that ends with ます, such as 食べます, 行きます, and します. The so-called ます form is a polite non-past and affirmative form. Its plain counterpart is called the dictionary form, as it is by this form that all the verbs are listed in dictionaries. Even though the dictionary form is a plain style form by itself, it is frequently used in a polite sentence as well. This is due to the fact that this form, along with other plain forms, is used in many idiomatic expressions and patterns. Knowing both the ます form and the dictionary form will enable you to easily classify verbs and make other forms.

日本語の動詞の基礎：Basic Japanese verbs:

五段動詞 (U-verbs)、一段動詞 (RU verbs)、不規則動詞 (Irregular verbs)

The Japanese word for "verb" is どうし. Verbs can be classified into two groups：ごだんどうし (U-verbs) and いちだんどうし (Ru-verbs). There are a few verbs which cannot be classified into either. They are called ふきそくどうし, "irregular verbs."

verb 動詞	Group 1	五段動詞	(U-verbs)	くぐすうつるぶむぬ ending
	Group 2	一段動詞	(RU-verbs)	eru/iru ending
	Group 3	不規則動詞	(Irregular-verbs)	する／来る

五段動詞 (U-verbs)

If the dictionary form of a verb does not end with る, the verb is ごだん. If the verb's dictionary form ends with る, but the characters preceding their ます form and the dictionary form are not identical, then the verb is also ごだん. The majority of Japanese verbs are ごだん. The characters preceding the ない form of ごだん(U-verbs) always are a (あ) lines. The characters preceding the ます form of ごだん (U-verbs) always are i (い) lines. The characters preceding the dictionary form of ごだん (U-verbs) always are u (う) lines.

ます form	dic. form	nai form	ます form	dic. form	nai form
書きます	書く (write)	書かない	聞きます	聞く (listen, ask)	聞かない
kak-i-masu	kak-u	kak-a-nai	kik-i-masu	kik-u	kik-a-nai
飲みます	飲む(drink)	飲まない	話します	話す (speak)	話さない
nom-i-masu	nom-u	nom-a-nai	hanash-i-masu	hanas-u	hanas-a-nai
遊びます	遊ぶ(play)	遊ばない	会います	会う (meet)	会わない
asob-i-masu	asob-u	asob-a-nai	a-i-masu	a-u	aw-a-nai

625

ますform	dic. form	nai form	ます form	dic. form	nai form
終わります	終わる(end)	終らない	帰ります	帰る(go back)	帰らない
owar-i-masu	owar-u	owar-a-nai	kaer-i-masu	kaer-u	kaer-a-nai

一段動詞 (RU- verbs)

The dictionary form of a verb in this group always ends with る (eru or iru). Furthermore, the character preceding る in the dictionary form and preceding ます in the ます form and the ない form are identical. See the following examples.

ますform	dic. form	ない form	ます form	dic. form	ない form
食べます	食べる(eat)	食べない	見ます	見る(look)	見ない
tab-e-masu	tab-e-ru	tab-e-nai	m-i-masu	m-i-ru	m-i-nai
閉めます	閉める(close)	閉めない	起きます	起きる(wake up)	起きない
shim-e-masu	shim-e-ru	shim-e-nai	ok-i-masu	ok-i-ru	ok-i-nai

There are some verbs which are not いちだんどうし, despite the fact that their dictionary form ends with る, because they do not share the same character preceding their ます form and the dictionary forms.

帰ります(return)	kae-r-i-masu	帰る	ka-e-ru	帰らない	kara-nai
減ります(reduce)	he-r-i-masu	減る	h-e-ru	減らない	he-ra-nai
走ります(run)	hashi-r-i-masu	走る	hash-i-ru	走らない	hashi-ra-nai
知ります(know)	shi-r-i-masu	知る	sh-i-ru	知らない	shi-ra-nai
切ります(cut)	ki-r-i-masu	切る	k-i-ru	切らない	ki-ra-nai
入ります(enter)	hai-r-i-masu	入る	ha-i-ru	入らない	hai-ra-nai

不規則動詞 (Irregular-verbs)

There are two irregular verbs in Japanese. They are します/する (do) and 来ます/来る (come). Because of their irregular inflection patterns, you have to learn different forms of these verbs individually.

ます form	dic. form	nai form
します	する (do)	しない
shimasu	suru	shinai
来ます	来る (come)	来ない
kimasu	kuru	konai

2. た form of a verb

た form is similar to て form. You can convert た form to てform easily, by changing て to た or で to だ in the end of verbs. した is the plain and informal form of ました and it is called the "た form." The た form is used in casual conversations and other situations in which politeness and formality are not called for. One such situation is when listing things in the form of a chart or a memo.

3. Topic—comment structure

In Japanese sentences, the so called "topic and comment" structure is so useful. The topic part consists of two elements: the noun and the topic particle "wa." The comment parts contain two basic parts: the subject part and the predicate part. Subject parts consist of two elements: the noun or nominalized word and the subject particle "ga." The predicate parts consist of two elements: the noun or adjective with copula "desu."

リサはたべるのがすきです。たべることがすきです。　　Lisa likes eating.

まさはゲームをするのがすきです。　Masa likes playing a game.

リサは頭がいいです。　　　　　　As for Lisa, her head is good. (lit trans)

Topic —comment　　　　　　　　(Lisa is smart.)

（ subject —predicate)

4. Modifying noun using の or こと

In Japanese a noun can be modified not only by an adjective but also by a plain style verb + "no" or " koto."

たべるのがすきです。たべることがすきです。　　　　I like eating.

ゲームをするのがすきです。ゲームをすることがすきです。

I like playing a game.

Add の, こと after the plain form of the verb to make a noun. の is more personal. こと is more abstract and formal. However, の and こと are interchangeable in many cases.

(1) の is a very appropriate indicator for the reader. When the reader finds "the plain form of the verb + の" in the sentence, the reader will be able to connect with some noun modifying phrases or word in the paragraph.

(2) こと is a very appropriate indicator for the writer. When the writer uses "the plain form of the verb +こと" in the sentence, the writer will be able to show the reader the connection that この is linked with some noun modifying phrases or word.

5. Expressing opinions

～とおもいます can be placed at the end of a statement to indicate that the statement is a view, an opinion, or a belief of the speaker. と is a particle and it is used here as a quotation marker. おもいます is a verb for "think." In addition, だ is necessary when what precedes ～とおもいます is a noun or a な adjective.

～い (plain non-past form of い adj.) + と思います

トムの部屋は暗いと思います。　　　I think Tom's room is dark.

ちょっとわかりにくいと思います。　I think it's a little difficult to understand.

～かった (plain past form of い adj.) + と思います

はっぴょうはよかったと思います。　I think the presentation was good.

NOUN/な adj. + だ (nonpast form) と思います

キャプテンはだれだと思いますか。　Who do you think is the captain?

627

NOUN/な adj. + だった (past form) と思います

スピーチはスムーズだったと思います。 I think the speech was smooth.

6. Reported speech I

(1) The XというY means "so-called." The speaker nominates Y with X to the listener, who does not have enough information for Y.

これはトヨタという車です。 　　　This is a car called a Toyota.

僕のクラブはタカホウというボランティア系のクラブです。

　　　　　　　　　　　　My club called Tokahoo is a volunteer club.

(2) Reported speech XというY is often used, when Y contains a noun pertaining to communication such as 話 hanashi "story," 規則 kisoku "code or rule," 記事 kiji "article," 情報 jouhou "information," 手紙 tegami "letter," and ニュース "news."

この学校には、夏休みは八月のはじめからだという規則があります。
This school has a rule that the summer vacation starts at the beginning of August.

日本の女の子が来るというニュース/ 話 /情報/記事/手紙があります。
I have news/information/an article/a letter that a Japanese girl will visit us.

The XはYという is used when the speaker describes the meaning of X with the content of Y.

(3) The XはYということです expression will also enable you to express the best reported expression about X by using Y, or a possible reported expression about X by using Y, and it will imply order, command, or rational faculty indirectly. The XはYということです expression has at least two different voices or points of view: the speaker's personal voice or someone else's who(m) the speaker is expressing.

「新学期」はなんのことですか。 　　　　　　　　　What is "shingakki"?
「遠足」は英語で "field trip"ということです。

　　　　　　　　　　　　　　"Ensoku" is a so-called "field trip" in English.

卒業式は "commencement" じゃなくて、"graduation" ということでしょう。

　　　　"Sotsugyoshiki" is not "commencement," but so-called "graduation."

「新学期」は新しい学期ということです。だから、日本の新学期は4月ということです。アメリカの新学期は9月です。

　　　　"Shingakki" is (what it is) a new semester. A new semester in Japan starts in April. The new semester in America starts in September.

7. Reported speech II

〜といいます can be placed at the end of a statement to indicate that the statement is a view, an opinion, or a belief of someone. と is a particle and it is used here as a quotation marker. いいます is a verb for "say." In addition, だ is necessary when what precedes 〜といいます is a noun or な-adjective.

Compare the following.

リサはいもうとがかわいいと言います。　　　Lisa says her younger sister is cute.

リサは「いもうとがかわいいです。」と言いました。

Lisa said "My younger sister is cute."

トムはかぞくが５人だと言います。 Tom says his family consists of five members.

ジルは大きい部屋が必要だったと言いました。 Jill said she needed a large room.

アリはニューヨークへ行ったと言いました。　　Ali said she went to New York.

8. Expressing permission statements

The construction 〜てもいいです makes an English equivalent of "one may do such and such."

学校でテニスをしてもいいです。　　　　　You may play tennis at school.

9. Expressing prohibition statements

The construction 〜てはいけません makes an English equivalent of "one cannot do such and such."

学校でテニスをしてはいけません。　　　　You cannot play tennis at school.

10. Linking

(1) The て form of a verb such as よんで (read) and かいて (write) may be used to connect two or more actions to be performed in sequence. For example, にほんへいって、すもうをみます means "I will go to Japan and watch sumo wrestling" and おんがくをきいて、ねました means "I listened to music and then went to bed." You may want to remember the て form of some useful verbs. By the way, you may recall that 〜てください is used to make a sentence asking someone to do something. たってください (Please stand up) and かいてください (Please write) may be some of the more familiar examples.

日本へ行って、すもうを見ます。 I will go to Japan and watch sumo wrestling.

(2) Attaching で to a noun or a な adjective will enable you to continue to add more information without ending your sentence. For な adjectives, make sure to remove な before attaching で

あしたは木曜日で、テニスのしあいがあります。

Tomorrow is Thursday and we will have a tennis match.

(3) Attaching くて to an い adjective root will enable you to continue to add more information without ending your sentence. An "adjective root" is the part preceding い in い adjectives.

このケーキは安くておいしいです。(安い＋おいしい)

This cake is inexpensive and delicious. Note that いい becomes よくて.

(4) In the て form linking there are many different meanings of connections, such as a succession of actions or events, a cause-and-effect relationship, or two simultaneous actions and two different mixed statements within each chunk connected with the て form.

629

フロリダはアメリカの南部にあって、あつい　です。

The state of Florida is located at the south of the United States and (therefore) is hot.

ニューヨークはアメリカの北東部にあって、とてもにぎやかです。

New York City is at the northeastern part of U.S. and (different statement) it is very lively.

右手で茶碗を持って、左手で箸を持つ。

With the right hand you hold your bowl and (simultaneously) with the left hand you hold your chopsticks.

(5) Many learners make a simple mistake when they link two sentences using "と(to)." "と" links only words.

このケーキとパンは安いと（くて）おいしいです

This cake and bread are inexpensive and delicious.

11. Potential verbs

You already know that 書くことができる (able to write) is used to mark a possibility. Another way to express a possibility is through the use of potential verb forms. The endings of potential verbs are formed as shown below.

五段動詞 (U-verbs) <u>Replace the final - u with -eru</u>
書く一書ける、会う一会える、遊ぶ一遊べる

一段動詞 (RU-verbs) <u>Replace the final- ru with -rareru, alternative way is -reru.</u>
食べる一食べられる（食べれる）、寝る一寝られる（寝れる）
教える一教えられる（教えれる）、始める一始められる（始めれる）
不規則動詞（する）一できる、（来る）一来られる（来れる）
土曜日に日本へ行けますか。来週日本へ行けますが、今週は行けません。

Can you go to Japan on Saturday? I can go to Japan next week, but I cannot go this week.

12. Indicating how easy or difficult it is to do something is

<u>Verb Stem+やすい</u>　　<u>Verb Stem+にくい</u>

"Verb stem" is a term used to indicate the part preceding ます. For example, in よみます, みます, and かきます, the stem is よみ, み and かき, respectively. When verb stems like these are immediately followed by やすい or にくい, they become English equivalents of "easy to do -" or "difficult to do-." よみやすい means "easy to read" and よみにくい means "difficult to read." They are a kind of い adjective and conjugate accordingly.

見やすいビジュアルですね。　　　　　It's an easy-to-see visual, isn't it?

A: 漢字は書きにくいですか。　　　　　Is kanji hard to write?

B: いいえ、書きにくくありません。　　No, it is not hard to write.

13. Indicating excess

<u>Adj. Root +すぎます</u>

"Adjective root" is a term used to indicate the part preceding い in い adjectives. For example, in おおきい and やさしい, the roots are おおき and やさしい, respectively. When adjective roots like these are immediately followed by すぎます, meaning "exceed," the combination indicates the state of being in excess. おおきすぎます means "too large" and やさしすぎます means "too easy" or "too kind." Note that いい becomes よすぎます, not いすぎます. すぎます may also be added to な adjectives, but you must take な out before you do that. しずかすぎます means "too quiet."

A: 読みにくい本ですね。	This book is difficult to read, isn't it?
B: ええ、字が小さすぎます。	Yes, the letters are too small.
A: 大きすぎませんか。	Isn't it too big for you?
B: いいえ、だいじょうぶです。	No, it is all right.

14. Connectors

<u>And connectors</u>

(1) そして

そして is a conjunction which means "and then" and "after that." Its function and meaning is similar to those of それから and the two are often interchangeable. However, そして differs from それから in the following points, and you should keep this in mind when making choices. そして is more appropriate when a statement following the conjunction is a wrap-up or a conclusion of a story.

そして is less colloquial and more formal-sounding than それから.

そして andそれから are not interchangeable under certain conditions such as.

この野球チームは１８９０年に優勝しました。それから、今まで、優勝していません。 This baseball team won a victory in 1890, and has since never gained victory.

(2) それに

それに is a conjunction which means "and then" and "too." Its function and meaning is similar to those of それから, and the two are often interchangeable. However, それに differs from それから, そして in the following point, and you should keep this in mind when making choices.

それに is more appropriate when a statement following the conjunction is a parallel story or an additional story.

(3) その上に

その上に is a conjunction which means "and then" and "too." Its function and meaning is similar to those of それに and the two are often interchangeable. However, その上に differs from それに in the following point, and you should keep this in mind when making choices.

その上に is more appropriate when a statement following the conjunction is a parallel story or an additional story.

その上に is less colloquial and more formal-sounding than それに.

(4) し

A conjunction し is very useful when you want to add information, or give further descriptions.

<u>But connectors</u>

(1) けれども

けれども/けれど/けども/けど usually appears following a subordinate clause ending with the informal form.

> フィギュアスケートを見るけれども/けども/けれど/けど、スケートをし
>
> たことがない　　　Although I watch figure skating, I never have skated.

けれども/けれど/けども/けど can be connected with a preceding clause, usually with one starting with a conjunction like しかし, でも.

> フィギアースケートを見ます。けれども/けども/けれど/けど、スケート
>
> をしたことがありません。 I watch figure skating, however, I never have skated.

けれども/けれど/けども/けど can be connected with a subordinate statement while omitting the main statement. The unfinished statement with けれども/けれど/けども/けど expresses a softer explanation about the reason, apology, or indirect request.

> ちょっと宿題を忘れてきた　けれども/けども/けれど/けど。
>
> I forgot my homework, but...
>
> 明日、友達が遊びにくる　けれども/けども/けれど/けど。
>
> Tomorrow my friend will come to my house, but...

(2) 〜ないで、〜なくて

ないで connects two clauses and expresses two simultaneous actions within negative and positive actions.

なくて connects two clauses and implies a certain cause-and-effect relationship. It has a softer emphasis than ないから, ないので connectors.

<u>Cause-and-effect connector</u>

(1) から Expressing a reason

When you end your speech with からです, rather than です, you indicate that what you have said may be reasonable or be the case, but not for certain. テストがあるからです and あしたはさむいからです mean "The reason is that we will have the test" and "It's reasonable that it will be cold tomorrow." からです can also follow a plain form of a verb, such as the dictionary form. For example, サラはダンスにいくからです means "Sara will go to the dance in all likelihood." You may hear this ending often in a weather forecast or in many conversations. It is also convenient to use this ending when you give an uncertain answer or simply want to avoid being too definitive.

Q: テキサスはどうして暑いですか。　　Why is Texas hot?

A: 南にあるから、暑いです。　　Texas is hot because it's in the south.

(2) ので

Both sentences below include the first clause (the first sentence), which describes the cause (a new facility), a particle から/ので, and the second clause (the second sentence), which describes the effect became fun. Thus, particle から/ので linking suggests a cause-and-effect relationship. The particles から and ので can also follow a plain form of a verb, such as the dictionary form for non-past affirmative, and the た form for past affirmative. In から and ので clauses, informal endings are used more often, even though in the main clauses formal endings are used. The particles から/ので are almost interchangeable. The particle から, however, expresses a cause or reason involving a more personal assumption or belief. The particle ので is used to express a cause or reason in more objective situations. Therefore, it is not possible to express certain commands, or request suggestions in the main clause (the second sentence).

私の学校はきれいで新しいメディアルームができました。＋楽しくなりました。

私の学校はきれいで新しいメディアルームができたから、楽しくなりました。

私の学校はきれいで新しいメディアルームができたので、楽しくなりました。

(3) ための

X (Noun 1) のためのY (Noun 2): The formula corresponds to "Y which is designed/meant for X."

「春一番」は中学生と高校生のための教科書です。

Haruichiban is a textbook intended for junior high and high school students.

<u>Rhetorical Connector</u>

(1) たとえば

たとえば is a conjunction which means "for example."

(2) とくに

とくに is a conjunction which means "especially."

15. Language strategies

When you use a term that is unfamiliar to your potential readers, you will need to provide some information or explanation about it to make it easier to understand. Here are some effective ways to do that.

(1) Paraphrasing (言い換え)

- analogical paraphrasing (類似的言い換え)

私は10年生です。高校2年生です。

I am a 10th grader. I am a 2nd year high school student.

明日は創立記念日です。学校の誕生日です。

Tomorrow is sooritsukinenbi. It is the birthday of our school.

- Paraphrasing with certainty (確信的言い換え)

The XはYのことです expression will also enable you to convey the best expression about X by using Y or the best possible expression about X by using Y , and imply order command or rational faculty indirectly.

「遠足」はなんのことですか。　　What is "Ensoku"?

「遠足」は英語で"field trip"のことです。

"Ensoku" is (what it is) a "field trip" in English.

「新学期」はなんのことですか。　What is "Shingakki"?

「新学期」は新しい学期のことです。日本の新学期は4月です。アメリカの新学期は9月です。

"Shingakki" is (what it is) a new semester. The new semester in Japan starts in April. The new semester in America starts in September.

(2) Giving a definition (定義)

9月1日に始業式があります。始業式とは学期の最初の日にある式のことです。

Shigyooshiki occurs on September 1. Shigyooshiki is a ceremony held on the first day of the term.

(3) Indicating resemblance (類似点の指摘)

- Indicating resemblance (類似点の指摘)

シニアトリップは修学旅行のような行事です。

The senior trip is an event like shuugakuryokoo.

シニアトリップは修学旅行に似ています。

The senior trip resembles shuugakuryokoo.

- Simile (直喩)

The expression "XはYのようなものです" will also enable you to express a simile in a sentence.

日本の学校の遠足はアメリカの学校のフィールドトリップのようなものです。

"Ensoku" in a Japanese school is like that of a "field trip" in an American School.

- Resemblance (類似)

The expression "XはYに似ています" will also enable you to express a simile in a sentence.

日本の学校の遠足はピックニックに似ています。

"Ensoku" in a Japanese school looks like a "picnic."

アメリカの学校の夏休みはどんな夏休みですか。

What kind of summer vacation does your school have in the U.S.?

アメリカの学校（がっこう）の夏休み（なつやす）は日本の夏休み（なつやす）と似ています。でも、日本より長いです。

> Summer vacation in the U.S is like summer vacation in Japan. But the vacation is longer than Japan's.

(4) Describing contents (内容の描写（ないようびょうしゃ）)

10月にホームカミングがあります。ホームカミングではパレードやフットボールの試合（しあい）があります。

> Homecoming takes place in October. A parade and a football game is held at Homecoming.

(5) Reported contents (内容の引用（ないよういんよう）)

7月7日はたなばたという日のことです。 July 7th is so-called Tanabata Day.

16. Paragraph development

Primary source

You learned about the "topic sentence and examples." Before you start to write the examples, you want to describe the primary sources for readers. Primary sources include basic information about the topic, but example sentences are focused on more specific and logical support for the topic sentence. The primary sources give a more overall foundation for readers. For example, if your topic sentence deals with the objectives of the school club, your primary sources should include the number, the advisor, the location, the date and time of the school club, and so on.

Expository writing

The expository writing style model is called せつめいぶんがた. You are already familiar with this style as the essay you wrote about winter weather in chapter 3 was based on this model. You may recall that your weather essay consisted of a topic sentence, supporting sentences and their examples, and sum-up sentences. See the next section (Analogy and attribution tactics).

Analogy and attribution tactics

There are two useful paragraph development tactics, and the first one is called the attribution tactic or the "bits and pieces" approach. In the example below, としょかん, びょういん and こうえん are "bits and pieces" of こうきょうしせつ (the topic). The analogy tactic or the "layer" approach is the second paragraph development tactic. In this tactic, supporting sentences not only add details but also connote the same or similar message expressed in the topic sentence. Let's go over a sample paragraph developed by this tactic. All the supporting sentences below the topic sentences not only provide some details about Asahi village but also imply how quiet the village is. Abundant nature, small population, and absence of heavy traffic are easily considered as characteristics of a quiet place, and reference to such features effectively reinforce the claim made in the topic sentence.

	<u>Attribution tactic</u>	<u>Analogy tactic</u>
Topic	谷川市には公共施設がたくさんあります。	朝日村は静かです。
Support 1	図書館は12あります。	自然が多いです。
Support 2	病院も20あります。	人口が少ないです。
Support 3	それから、公園も25あります。	それから、高層ビルもありません。

Subordinate and main clause

The main paragraph should consist of a topic sentence, supporting sentences, and examples. The topic sentence includes a subordinate clause and a main clause. Thurs, there should be two supporting sentences for the subordinate clause and the main clause each. In addition, there should be three examples for each supporting sentences. You need to think more logically to build up this complex paragraph development.

Sum-up paragraph

A sum-up paragraph is a short paragraph consisting of a few "sum-up" statements. It is the last part of the speech. A sum-up paragraph can reinforce the points made in the topic sentence by:
- incorporating a comparative perspective
- reiterating arguments in the supporting sentences (2nd sentence)
- closing with a wrap-up statement that corresponds with the main point in the topic sentence

Kansoubun (Essay) writing development

Kansoubun (Essay) style writing (descriptive sentence and comment sentence)
A kansoubun or essay style paragraph consists of a leading sentence, the descriptive part, and the comment part. In the descriptive part, you may describe and explain about a variety of topics in a flexible, creative, and somewhat casual manner. In the comment part, you may offer your feelings, opinions, and any other comments about the topics.

Descriptive sentences in kansoubun (essay) style writing

The leading sentence in kansoubun style writing is different from the topic sentence in expository style writing. While the topic sentence controls both the supporting sentences and the examples, the leading sentence is more like an introductory sentence that prepares the readers for your descriptions and comments. Your first descriptive sentence is usually based on your observation, while the second descriptive sentence is based on your research. Your third descriptive sentence is usually based on your comparison through your research or observation.

The extended explanation form (direct comment sentences)

The expression of -noda is useful for producing direct comments. It is known as the extended explanation form and it is used to express the following several functions. At this stage we introduce three functions in the written form. Once you master -noda sentence usage in Japanese conversation, you will reach the advanced level.

(1) 理由 (REASON) Elaborating by giving the reason for a given statement
この学校の生徒は皆私服だ。制服がないのだ。(The writer observed one situation or event where all of the students are wearing regular clothes.) It is the case that the school does not have any uniform.

(2) 解釈 (INTERPRETATIVE EMPHASIS)
A writer is talking about something emotively between the writer and the reader concerning their common interest.

皆は反対するが、私の意見は正しいのだ。(The writer told his situation and the writer writes to the reader about the reason for the previous statement.)

Everybody opposed me, but it is really true [that] my opinion was correct.

(3) 言い換え (MILDER EMPHASIS)
A writer is explaining about someone or something that the reader may not be familiar with. When the nonpast, affirmative form of nouns or na-adjectives is used, add なのです, なのだ, なんです, なんだ.

始業式とは学期の最初の日のことなのだ。

By Shigyooshiki it is meant the first day of the term/semester.

<u>Indirect comment sentences (間接コメント文)</u>

Regarding comment sentences, in Japanese we find two different types of comment sentences: the direct comment sentence like a [noda] sentence in the Japanese writing system and the indirect comment sentence containing a variety of writing styles. In Japanese language, the Japanese like to use indirect comment sentences, because they soften expressions.

(1) Expressing the writer's feelings, thoughts, or opinions (書き手の感情、思想、意見を示す文末表現を使う) Opinion adjectival clauses with と思う.
X はYと思う translates to "I think X is Y."

私たちの町の天気は夏暑いので、カジュアルな洋服を着たほうがいいと思う。

I think you should wear a casual outfit, because summer weather in our town is so humid and hot.

(2) Expressing the writer's modest and inferential attitude (書き手の控え目で推量的態度を示す文末表現を使う) Opinion (意見)
X はYではないだろうか corresponds to "would not X be Y" in English

私たちの町の天気は夏暑いので、東京の天気に似ているのではないだろうか。

Wouldn't the weather in our town resemble the weather in Tokyo, because summer is so humid and hot?

私たちの町の自然は森が多いので、ドイツの黒い森の自然のようではないだろうか。

> Wouldn't nature in our town looks like nature in Germany, because of the many forests.

(3) Expressing the writer's guess (書き手の推理・推測を示す文末表現を使う) Guessing (推量)

X はYだろう　X はYかもしれない　corresponds to "I believe that X is Y" or "It may be that X is Y" in English.

私たちの町の天気は夏暑いので、東京の天気に似ているだろう。

> The weather in our town may resemble the weather in Tokyo, because summer is so humid and hot.

私たちの町の自然は森が多いので、ドイツの黒い森の自然のようかもしれない。

> It may be that nature in our town looks like nature in Germany, because of the many forests.

(4) Expressing the writer's suggestions or preferences (書き手の提案や好みを示す文末表現を使う) Suggestion (提案)

X はYたほうがいい　corresponds to " I suggest that X had better Y" in English.

私たちの町の天気は夏暑いので、カジュアルな洋服を着たほうがいい。

> You should wear casual outfits, because summer weather in our town is so humid and hot.

私たちの町の自然は森が多いので、長そでのシャツをもっと着たほうがいい。

> I suggest that you bring long sleeve shirts because nature in our town has many forests.

(5) Kansoubun writing development

Three approaches in kansoubun writing development.

You may follow one of the three approaches shown below when creating kansoubun style writing. Your decision will depend upon how assertive, strong, and/or confident, or how humble, modest, and/or unsure you may want to sound in your writing.

"Direct comment"approach/strong and straight comment

"Direct and indirect comment" approach /strong and humble comment

"Indirect comment" approach/humble comment

VOCABULARY

Functional Vocabulary

	Formal	Informal	English
Expressing opinions	（だ/だった）と おもいます。	（だ/だった）と おもう。	I think
Reported speech	（だ/だった）と いいます。	（だ/だった）と いう。	I say
Designating information	X という Y	X という Y	so-called
Describing content	X という Y	X という Y	represent/describe
Marking information with a communication noun	X という Y	X という Y	communicate/say
Describing a nonpast negative state	い adj.(root) くありません。 な adj.じゃありません。	い adj.(root) くない。 な adj.じゃない。	It isn't
Describing a past state	い adj.(root) かったです。 な adj.でした。	い adj.(root) かった。 な adj.だった。	It was
Asking how things were	X はどうでしたか。	X はどうだった。	How was X?
Asking how things are	X はどうですか。	X はどう（だ）。	How is X?
Expressing permission	verb てもいいです。	verb てもいい。	one may do
Expressing prohibition	verb てはいけません。	verb てはいけない。	one cannot do
Connecting two or more actions	verb て	verb て	(action) and (action)
Linking/connecting two or more simultaneous actions	verb て	verb て	(action) while (action)
linking cause and effect actions	verb て	verb て	(action), so (action)
Connecting two or more actions	noun -na adjective }で	verb -na adjective }で	(action) and (action)
Connecting two or more actions	adjective くて	verb くて	(action) and (action)
Expressing two representative actions	(past impolite) verb たり〜たりします。	verb たり〜たりする。	do such A and B

	Formal	Informal	English
Expressing two or three actions	verb し、〜します。	verb し、〜する。	do such A and B
Disjunctive conjunction	verb (け)れ(ど)も	verb (け)れ(ど)も、	however
Softened explanation	verb (け)れ(ど)も	verb (け)れ(ど)も	I apologize that
Connecting two or more negative actions	ないで	ないで	(action) without (action)
Connecting cause and effect negative actions	なくて	なくて	because -do not do
Expressing cause and effect actions	からです。	からだ。	The reason is that
Expressing a reason	から	から	because, so
Expressing a valid reason	ので	ので	because
Expressing a reason	ための(に)	ための(に)	in order to, for the sake of
Indicating resemblance	ような	ような	looks like
Indicating resemblance	ようなものです。	ようなものだ。	it seems that
Paraphrasing with certainty	は〜のことです。	は〜のことだ。	it means that
Resemblance	は〜に似ています。	は〜に似ている。	looks like
Interpretive emphasis	は〜のです。	は〜のだ。	that is why that
Opinion	は〜ではないでしょうか。	は〜じゃないだろうか。	Is it not that?
Guessing	は〜でしょう。	は〜だろう。	it is probably
Guessing	は〜かもしれません。	は〜かもしれない。	it may be
Suggesting	は〜たほうがいいです。	は〜たほうがいい。	I suggest that - is better
Potential verb	は〜ことができます。	は〜ことができる。	can do
Indicating how easy it is to do something	は〜やすいです。	は〜やすい。	easy to
Indicating how difficult it is to do something	は〜にくいです。	は〜にくい。	difficult to
Indicating excess	は〜すぎます。	は〜すぎる。	too much

VOCABULARY

Notional Vocabulary
Location and surroundings

いち	位置	location
かんきょう	環境	environment
だいとし	大都市	big city
しょうとし	小都市	small city
こうがい	郊外	suburb
のうそん	農村	farming village
くに	国	country
むら	村	village
し	市	city
しゅう	州	state
まち	町	town
ちほう	地方	local
とうぶ	東部	Eastern part
ちゅうせいぶ	中西部	Midwest part
なんぶ	南部	Southern part
ほくせいぶ	北西部	Northwest part
ほくとうぶ	北東部	Northeast part
なんせいぶ	南西部	Southwest part
せいぶ	西部	Western part
なんとうぶ	南東部	Southeast part
ほくぶ	北部	North part
ちゅうぶ	中部	Central part

School settings and types

だいとしがた	大都市型	big city setting
こうがいがた	郊外型	suburban setting
しょうとしがた	小都市型	small city setting
ちほうがた	地方型	local setting
しゅるい	種類	type
こうりつこう	公立校	public school
しりつこう	私立校	private school
じょしこう	女子校	girls school
だんしこう	男子校	boys school
だんじょきょうがく	男女共学	co-education
インターナショナルスクール		international school
マグネット　スクール		magnet school
チャータースクール		charter school
ぜんりょうせい	全寮制	(full) boarding system
りょうせい	寮制	dormitory system
ぶっきょうけい	仏教系	affiliated with Buddhism
しゅうきょうけい	宗教系	affiliated with a religion
イスラムきょうけい	イスラム教系	affiliated with Islam
キリストきょうけい	キリスト教系	affiliated with Christianity
ユダヤきょうけい	ユダヤ教系	affiliated with Judaism

School events

にゅうがくしき	入学式	entrance ceremony
そつぎょうしき	卒業式	graduation
うんどうかい	運動会	field day
ぶんかさい	文化祭	culture day
しんがっき	新学期	new semester
しけんきかん	試験期間	exam term
えんそく	遠足	field trip
ふぼかい	父母会	parent association
ほごしゃかい	保護者会	faculty teacher conference
なつやすみ	夏休み	summer vacation
はるやすみ	春休み	spring vacation
ふゆやすみ	冬休み	winter vacation
かがいかつどう	課外活動	extra curriculum
せいと	生徒	student
えんげき	演劇	drama
しゅうがくりょこう	修学旅行	school excursion
はっぴょうかい	発表会	recital, presentation
てんらんかい	展覧会	exhibition
コミュニティーアウトリーチかつどう コミュニティーアウトリーチ活動		community outreach
ねんじゅうぎょうじ	年中行事	annual events
たいめんしき	対面式	face to face meeting ceremony
ちゅうかんしけん	中間試験	midterm exam
きまつしけん	期末試験	final(term) exam
きゅうぎたいかい	球技大会	ball game competition
しぎょうしき	始業式	opening ceremony
かきこうしゅう	夏期講習	summer institute
ぶかつどうがっしゅく	部活動合宿	club camp
すいえいたいかい	水泳大会	swimming competition
そうりつきねんび	創立記念日	anniversary
げいじゅつかんしょう	芸術鑑賞	art appreciation
がっしょうコンクール	合唱コンクール	chorus competition
えんげきコンクール	演劇コンクール	drama competition
がくねんまつしけん	学年末試験	final exam of the year
しゅうぎょうしき	終業式	term closing ceremony
たいいくさい	体育祭	athletic day
がっしゅく	合宿	camp
ベークセール		bake sale
プロム		prom
ホームカミング		homecoming
オリエンテーション		orientation

641

VOCABULARY (continued)

School organizations, people, and clubs

せいとかい	生徒会	Student Council
せいとかいちょう	生徒会長	Student Council President
いいんかい	委員会	Committee
いいんちょう	委員長	Committee chair
がっきゅうかい	学級会	class meeting
キャプテン		captain
しゅしょう	主将	captain
こうちょう	校長	principal
たんにんのせんせい	担任の先生	homeroom teacher
きょういん	教員	faculty
しょくいん	職員	staff
アドバイザー		advisor
カウンセラー		counselor
だんしせいと	男子生徒	male student
じょしせいと	女子生徒	female student
りゅうがくせい	留学生	student from abroad
ホームカミングキング		homecoming king
ホームカミングクイーン		homecoming queen
かがいかつどう	課外活動	extra curricular activities
ぶかつ	部活	school clubs, activities
ぶちょう	部長	head (of a club, etc.)
ぶいん	部員	member of a club
ぶしつ	部室	room for a club
うんどうけい	運動系	athletic type clubs
ぶんかけい	文化系	culture type clubs
ボランティアけい		volunteer type clubs
やきゅうぶ	野球部	baseball club/team
りくじょうぶ	陸上部	track&field club/team
すいえいぶ	水泳部	swimming club/team
じゅうどうぶ	柔道部	*judo* club/team
たいそうぶ	体操部	gymnastics club/team
たっきゅうぶ	卓球部	table tennis club/team
えんげきぶ	演劇部	drama/acting club
びじゅつぶ	美術部	fine arts club
がっしょうぶ	合唱部	chorus club
しゃしんぶ	写真部	photography club
さどうぶ	茶道部	tea ceremony club
もぎこくれん	模擬国連	Model UN
こうつうあんぜん	交通安全	traffic safety
こくさいしんぜん	国際親善	international exchange
いんしゅうんてん	飲酒運転	drunk driving
ろうじん	老人	elderly, old person
しょうがいしゃ	障害者	people with disability
こども	子供	child, children

ホームレス		homeless person
こくさいアムネスティー		Amnesty International
りょっか	緑化	afforestation
かんきょうほご	環境保護	environmental protection
どうぶつあいご	動物愛護	animal protection

School rules

きそく	規則	rule, code
こうそく	校則	school rules
けいたいでんわ	携帯電話	cellular phone
ふくそう	服装	dress
せいふく	制服	uniform
かみ	髪	hair
そめる	染める	dye
かみをのばす	髪を伸ばす	grow hair long
かみをきる	髪を切る	cut one's hair
ひげ	鬚	beard
ひげをはやす	鬚をはやす	grow a beard
ひげをそる	鬚を剃る	shave off one's beard
もちもの	持ち物	belongings
けんさ	検査	inspection
おかし	お菓子	snacks
おかね	お金	money
ID	アイディー	ID
みぶんしょうめいしょ	身分証明書	ID
ひつよう	必要	necessary
ナイフ		knife
おさけ	お酒	alcohol
まやく	麻薬	drug
たばこ/タバコ	煙草	cigarette, tobacco
だめ		cannot, bad
きんし	禁止	prohibition
うんてん	運転	driving

Connectors

そして		and then, and again
それに		and then, too
そのうえ	その上	and then, in addition
たとえば	例えば	for example
また	又	additionally
さらに	更に	furthermore
さて		well
けれども		although
けれど		although
けど		although
まず		first of all
つまり		in other words, overall

ようするに	要するに	in short
ところで		by the way
まとめると		to sum up
ていぎすると	定義すると	to define
いいかえると	言い換えると	in other words

Adverbial words

とくに	特に	especially
ひじょうに	非常に	very, extremely
はっきり（と）		clearly
じっさい（に）	実際（に）	actually

Subjects

ぶつり	物理	physics
かがく	科学	science
てんもんがく	天文学	astronomy
せいりがく	生理学	physiology
ラテンご	ラテン語	Latin
ギリシャご	ギリシャ語	Greek
だいすう	代数	algebra
きか	幾何	geometry
びせきぶん	微積分	calculus
しょうせつ	小説	novel
し	詩	poem
ライティング		writing
にほんご	日本語	Japanese
ちゅうごくご	中国語	Chinese
かんこくご・ちょうせんご	韓国語・朝鮮語	Korean
スペインご	スペイン語	Spanish
フランスご	フランス語	French
ドイツご	ドイツ語	German
ロシアご	ロシア語	Russian
アラビアご	アラビア語	Arabic
イタリアご	イタリア語	Italian
おんがく	音楽	music
びじゅつ	美術	art
えんぎ	演技	acting
えんげき	演劇	drama
れきし	歴史	history
せかいし	世界史	world history
せいじがく	政治学	politics
けいざいがく	経済学	economics
じんるいがく	人類学	anthropology
しんりがく	心理学	psychology
てつがく	哲学	philosophy
ほけん	保健	health
たいいく	体育	PE
えいようがく	栄養学	nutrition science

Other descriptive words

あたらしい	新しい	new
ふるい	古い	old
おいしい	美味しい	delicious
まずい	不味い	bad-tasting
ふとい	太い	thick, big, bold
ほそい	細い	thin, fine, small
おおい	多い	many, much
すくない	少ない	few, little
ひろい	広い	wide, spacious
せまい	狭い	narrow, not spacious
ながい	長い	long
みじかい	短い	short
たかい	高い	high, expensive
ひくい	低い	low
こい	濃い	dark (color), thick (soup, hair) strong (tea), dense
うすい	薄い	light (color) thin (paper, hair) weak (tea, coffee)
あかるい	明るい	bright, cheerful
くらい	暗い	dark
はやい	速い	fast
はやい	早い	early
おそい	遅い	slow, late
むしあつい	蒸し暑い	hot and humid
じょうず（な）	上手（な）	skillful
へた（な）	下手（な）	unskillful
とくい（な）	得意（な）	be good at
にがて（な）	苦手（な）	be poor at
ゆたか（な）	豊か（な）	abundant, ample rich (voice)
ゆうめい（な）	有名（な）	famous
さかん（な）	盛ん（な）	thriving, prosperous
べんり（な）	便利（な）	convenient
ふべん（な）	不便（な）	inconvenient
たいへん（な）	大変（な）	overwhelming, hard
めんどう（な）	面倒（な）	annoying, troublesome
ふくざつ（な）	複雑（な）	complex
いろいろ（な）	色々（な）	various
てきせつ（な）	適切（な）	appropriate
ロジカル（な）		logical

シンプル（な）		simple	ジャケット			jacket
スムーズ（な）		smooth	ブレザー			blazer
たいくつ（な）	退屈（な）	boring, dull, dry	ブラウス			blouse
しあわせ（な）	幸せ（な）	happy, fortunate	スーツ			suit
にぎやか（な）	賑やか（な）	lively	タキシード			tuxedo
さびしい	寂しい	lonely	ドレス			dress
あんぜん（な）	安全（な）	safe	きる	着る		wear (upper body clothes)
きけん（な）	危険（な）	dangerous	はく	履く		wear (lower body clothes)
あぶない	危ない	dangerous	スカート			skirt
たのしい	楽しい	fun	パンツ			pants
わるい	悪い	bad	ズボン			trouser, pants
いい	良い	good	ジーンズ			jeans
おもしろい	面白い	interesting	くつ	靴		shoes
ユニーク（な）		unique	くつした	靴下		socks
きびしい	厳しい	strict, severe, harsh	サンダル			sandals
くわしい	詳しい	detailed	ストッキング			stockings, panty hose
すてき（な）	素敵な	lovely, nice	スニーカー			sneaker
こせいてき（な）	個性的な	one of a kind, unique	ブーツ			boots
まじめ（な）	真面目な	serious	ショーツ			shorts
クール（な）		cool	ショートパンツ			short pants
がまんづよい	我慢強い	patient	したぎ	下着		underwear
れいせい（な）	冷静（な）	calm, composed	パジャマ			pajama
こころがひろい	心が広い	open-minded	タンクトップ			tank top
たのもしい	頼もしい	reliable	キャミソール			camisole
カジュアルな		casual	ぼうし	帽子		hat, cap
カラフルな		colorful	やきゅうぼう	野球帽		baseball cap
わかりやすい	分り易い	easy to understand	せいぼう	制帽		uniform cap
わかりにくい	分り難い	difficult to understand	かぶる	被る		put on (hat)
みやすい	見易い	easy to see	めがね	眼鏡		eyeglasses
みにくい	見難い	hard to see	かける	掛ける		wear
かわいい	可愛い	cute	ネクタイ			necktie
にんきがある	人気がある	popular	ベルト			belt
やくにたつ	役に立つ	useful, helpful	おび	帯		belt (for kimono)

Outfit

			しめる	締める		fasten, wear
ふく	服	clothes	イヤリング			earring
いふく	衣服	clothes, clothing	アクセサリー			accessories
ようふく	洋服	suit, dress	ブラジャー			bra, brassiere
わふく	和服	traditional Japanese clothes, kimono	かつら	鬘		wig
			つける	付ける		attach
きもの	着物	kimono	うでとけい	腕時計		watch
うわぎ	上着	coat, jacket	ゆびわ	指輪		ring
セーター		sweater	はめる	嵌める		put on
ワイシャツ	Yシャツ	dress shirt	ぬぐ	脱ぐ		take off [clothes, pants]
Tシャツ		T-shirt	とる	取る		take off [hat, tie]
オーバー		overcoat				

Editing

へんしゅう	編集	editing
へんしゅうちょう	編集長	chief editor
ふくへんしゅうちょう	副編集長	assistant chief editor
へんしゅうかいぎ	編集会議	editorial meeting
ないよう	内容	content
わりあて	割り当て	assignment
きほんこうせい	基本構成	basic structure
もくじ	目次	table of contents
ひょうし	表紙	cover
まえがき	前書き	preface
ほんたい	本体	main body
あとがき	後書き	afterword
じゅんばん	順番	order
はなしあう	話し合う	discuss
タイトルをつける		give a title
てがみ	手紙	letter
～さま	～様	Dear ~
たいしょう	対象	object
こうもく	項目	issue
かくにんする	確認する	confirm
しごと	仕事	job
じゅうよう	重要	important
せきにん	責任	responsibility
もくてき	目的	goal, purpose
こうりゅう	交流	exchange
しまいこう	姉妹校	sister school
きょうかしょ	教科書	textbook
ざっし	雑誌	magazine
りゆう	理由	reason
じょうほう	情報	information
きそじょうほう	基礎情報	basic information
がっかそしき	学科組織	department system
くらべる	比べる	compare
ほか	他	other
プロフィール		profile
イラスト		illustration
リスト		list
ちず	地図	map
ひょう	表	table

Presentation terms

はっぴょう	発表	presentation
プレゼンテーション		presentation
はじめ	始め	the beginning
なか	中	the middle part
おわり	終わり	the end
つぎ	次	next
さいご	最後	last, the end
リサーチ		research
くみたて	組み立て	structure
りかい	理解	comprehension
ききて	聞き手	listener
スピーチ		speech
リーディング		reading
しつもん	質問	question
いけん	意見	opinion
～について		about -
きほん	基本	basic
じょうほう	情報	information
ぜんたい	全体	total

School related words

きそく	規則	rule
こうそく	校則	school rules
ちょうれい	朝礼	morning assembly
がっか	学科	department
かもく	科目	subject
じゅぎょう	授業	class, lesson
しけん	試験	examination, test
テスト		test
しょうテスト	小テスト	quiz
キャンパス		campus
カリキュラム		curriculum
ドラマクラブ		drama club
コスチューム		costume
プロダクション		production
ディベート		debate
しあい	試合	match
りゅうがく	留学	studying abroad
せいとすう	生徒数	number of students
きょういんすう	教員数	number of faculty
りょこう	旅行	trip
きょうみ	興味	interest
せいじ	政治	politics
ボランティアかつどう	ボランティア活動	volunteer activity
さんかする	参加する	participate
こうせい	構成	construction
えらぶ	選ぶ	choose
きめる	決める	decide
けんがく	見学	observation
せいふく	制服	academic uniform
がっきせい	学期制	term system
がくねん	学年	grade

645

まつり	祭り	festival
うた	歌	song
たてもの	建物	facility
かがくさい	科学祭	science fair
しんがっき	新学期	new semester
かんきょうもんだい	環境問題	environmental problem
けいざいもんだい	経済問題	economic problem
おうえん	応援	cheering
しゅうかい	集会	assembly
けんどう	剣道	Japanese fencing
とくべつ（な）	特別（な）	special
ふつう	普通	normally
ゆうしょう	優勝	victory
もくてき	目的	objectives
さっきょくか	作曲家	composer
ひつよう	必要	need
ぜんたいしゃしん	全体写真	whole picture
へや	部屋	room
こくさい	国際	international
かいぎ	会議	meeting
ちこく	遅刻	late
けいたい	携帯	cellular phone
びじゅつかん	美術館	fine art museum
はくぶつかん	博物館	museum
こうみんかん	公民館	community center
こうきょうしせつ	公共施設	public facilities
かつどう	活動	activity
いかがですか		What do you think?

Events

ぎょうじ	行事	event
メモリアルデー		Memorial Day
ハロウィーン		Halloween
かんしゃさい	感謝祭	Thanksgiving
パレード		parade
クリスマス		Christmas Day
おおみそか	大晦日	New Year's eve
しょうがつ	正月	New year
ゴールデンウイーク	(May in Japan)	Golden week
まつり	祭り	festival

Abbreviated/Shortened Words

アメフト	American football
デジカメ	digital camera
ファミレス	family restaurant
パソコン	personal computer
エアコン	air conditioner

リモコン	remote control
プロレス	professional wrestling
カラオケ	karaoke (empty orchestra)
コンビニ	convenience store
デパート	department store
アパート	apartment
パンフ	pamphlet, booklet
アイス	ice cream
チョコ	chocolate

Miscellaneous words

しゅるい	種類	type, kind
かくしゅ	各種	assorted, each kind
せいかく	性格	personality
ついか	追加	addition
じょうほう	情報	information
クラシック		classic, classical
じだい	時代	era, age
ボールペン		ball-point pen
おりがみ	折り紙	*origami*
ボート		boat
クローンにんげん	クローン人間	human clone
チワワ		chihuahua
へや	部屋	room
クエーカー		Quaker
パラグラフ		paragraph
ようこそ		welcome
ここまで		up to this point
けっこん	結婚	marriage
あいて	相手	partner
ゆうかん（な）	勇敢	brave
れんしゅうじかん	練習時間	time for practice
てんきよほう	天気予報	weather forecast
きじ	記事	article

Sentence

ぶん	文	sentence
てけい	テ形	*te* form
たんご	単語	word
どうし	動詞	verb
じしょけい	辞書形	dictionary form
めいし	名詞	noun
けいようし	形容詞	adjective
せつぞく	接続	connector
じりつてきせつぞくし	自律的接続詞	autonomous connector
じゅうぞくてきせつぞくし	従属的接続詞	subordinative connector

だんらく	段落	paragraph
ぎゃくせつ	逆接	disjunctive
せつぞくてきしじし	接続的指示詞	
		connective direction
じゅんじょ	順序	order
ようやく	要約	summary
てんかん	転換	conversion
れいじ	例示	sample
ひしゅうしょくめいし	非修飾名詞	modified noun
ふくし	副詞	adverb
じょし	助詞	particle
モダリティ		modality

Strategy

いいかえ	言い換え	paraphrasing
ちょくゆ	直喩	simile
るいじ	類似	resemblance
にている	似ている	look like
いんよう	引用	quotation
げんご	言語	language
ていぎ	定義	definition
るいじてん	類似点	similarities
してき	指摘	indication
ないよう	内容	content
びょうしゃ	描写	description
しかた	仕方	way
きゅうちしき	既有知識	prior knowledge
ごい	語彙	vocabulary
こうぞう	構造	structure
どっかい	読解	reading comprehension
よみ	読み	reading
しっている	知っている	know
ならった	習った	learned
たんぶん	単文	simple sentence
ふくぶん	複文	complex sentence
しゅうしょくぶ	修飾部	modifier
ひしゅうしょくぶ	被修飾部	modified
せつめいぶん	説明文	informational writing
ものがたりぶん	物語文	narrative writing
じゅうような	重要な	important
いちばん	一番	best
つぎに	次に	next
しらない	知らない	not know
わからない	分からない	not understand
わかる	分かる	understand
はんたい	反対	opposite
とくちょう	特徴	characteristics
しつもんぶん	質問文	question sentence

かんたんに	簡単に	simply
ようやくする	要約する	summarize
せつめいする	説明する	explain
つかって	使って	use
かえて	変えて	change
かいけつする	解決する	solve
イメージして		imagine
まとめて		conclude
こたえる	答える	answer
れいぶん	例文	example sentence
かんけい	関係	relationship

Time and Related Expressions

まいしゅう	毎週	every week
さいきん	最近	recently

Question Words

どんな		what kind of
どうやって		in what way
どうして		why

Writing

きほんじょうほう	基本情報	basic information
しゅうしゅう	収集	gathering
せいり	整理	arrangement
じんこう	人口	population
ぶんるい	分類	classification
とくちょう	特徴	characteristics
きろく	記録	record
けっか	結果	result

Verbs

しつもんする	質問する	ask a question
うまれる	生まれる	be born
ならべる	並べる	arrange
くらべる	比べる	compare
チェックする		check
おわる	終わる	end
おくる	送る	send
おどる	踊る	dance
うたう	歌う	sing
かつ	勝つ	win
まける	負ける	lose
けんきゅうする	研究する	research
ならう	習う	learn
かく	描く	draw, paint
はじめる	始める	start
しらせる	知らせる	inform

647

VOCABULARY

しょうかいする	紹介する	introduce
きまる	決まる	be decided
のせる	載せる	put it on
まとめる	纏める	sum up
つなげる	繋げる	link, join
たのしむ	楽しむ	enjoy
しらべる	調べる	research, investigate
うごく	動く	move
いう	言う	speak, say
もってくる	持ってくる	bring (something)
もっていく	持っていく	take (something)
はいる	入る	enter, join
かぞえる	数える	count
かりる	借りる	borrow
かす	貸す	lend
かえす	返す	return, give back
いけない		must not do
ゆうしょうする	優勝する	win a tournament
がまんする	我慢する	put up with, tolerate
よういする	用意する	prepare
リラックスする		relax
おぼえる	覚える	memorize
わすれる	忘れる	forget
わすれてくる	忘れてくる	forget (to bring)
あそびにくる	遊びに来る	come to play
にている	似ている	look like
しっている	知っている	know
しらない	知らない	not know
おわかりいただく	お分かりいただく	
		have (someone) understand
たのまれる	頼まれる	be asked a favor

Potential verbs

みえる	見える	can see, be seen
きこえる	聞こえる	can hear, be heard
かける	書ける	can write
あえる	会える	can meet
あそべる	遊べる	can play
できる	出来る	can do
こられる	来られる	can come
これる	来れる	can come
たべられる	食べられる	can eat, be eaten
たべれる	食べれる	can eat, be eaten
ねられる	寝られる	can sleep, be slept
ねれる	寝れる	can sleep, be slept
おしえられる	教えられる	can teach, be taught
おしえれる	教えれる	can teach, be taught
はじめられる	始められる	can begin, be began

はじめれる	始めれる	can begin, be began

Adjectival words (Descriptive words)

けいざいてきな	経済的な	economic
かっこうわるい	格好悪い	bad looking
オシャレな	お洒落な	fashionable
ダサイ		senseless
きやすい	着やすい	easy to wear
みすばらしい		shabby
かっこ（う）いい	格好いい	good looking
せがたかい	背が高い	tall
せがひくい	背が低い	short
やせている		thin
ふとっている	太っている	fat
あたまがいい	頭がいい	clever, smart
めがねをかけている	眼鏡を掛けている	
		wearing glasses
あそぶのがすきな	遊ぶのが好きな	
		like playing
べんきょうするのがすきな		like studying
	勉強するのが好きな	
ぶかつにねっちゅうしている		devoted to the club
	部活に熱中している	
ぶかつにてきとうである		not involved in the club
	部活に適当である	
ねっちゅうするものがある		have something to devote to
	熱中するものがある	
ねっちゅうするものがない		have nothing to devote to
	熱中するものがない	
しどうりょくがある	指導力がある	have leadership
ようふくのセンスがある		good sense in clothes
	洋服のセンスがある	
ようふくのセンスがない		no sense in clothes
	洋服のセンスがない	
じょうしきがある	常識がある	have common sense
ひじょうしきである	非常識である	no common sense
しょうらいせいがある	将来性がある	have future
へいぼんである	平凡である	ordinary
しんらいできる	信頼できる	reliable
じゅうなんである	柔軟である	flexible
どくそうせいがある	独創性がある	creative
みんなのひょうばんがいい		fame, good reputation
	皆の評判がいい	
みりょくがある	魅力がある	attractive
みりょくがない	魅力がない	not attractive
かいぜんする	改善する	improved a lot
かいあくする	改悪する	change for the worse
くふうする	工夫する	think well

はってんさせる	発展させる	developed
おしえかたがじょうずだ		skillful instruction
	教え方が上手だ	
へただ	下手だ	bad
きょうみがある	興味がある	be interested in
きょうみがない	興味がない	not interested in
しんらいできない	信頼できない	not reliable
きょうざいがゆたかな	教材が豊かな	materials abound
きょうざいがたりない	教材が足りない	not enough materials
せきにんかんがある	責任感がある	responsible
せきにんかんがない	責任感がない	no responsible
かいぜんがみられる	改善が見られる	improved a lot
しけんがユニークだ	試験がユニークだ	unique exam
みんながたのしい	皆が楽しい	everybody has fun
わかりやすい	分かりやすい	easy to understand
くふうがみられる	工夫が見られる	can see improvement
じゅぎょうないようがおもしろい		interesting instruction
	授業内容が面白い	
しりょうがゆたかである		many materials
	資料が豊かである	
ひとがいい	人が良い	good hearted
きょうざいがふそくしている		lacking teaching materials
	教材が不足している	
せいとがおもしろい	生徒が面白い	have fun students
へやがきれいだ	部屋がきれいだ	clean room
せいとがべんきょうずきだ		hard working students
	生徒が勉強好きだ	
こころがひろい	心が広い	generous
おもしろいけいけんができる		interesting experience
	面白い経験ができる	
かんどうてきである	感動的である	impressive
ないようがいい	内容がいい	good content
やるきがでる	やる気が出る	motivating
ユニークだ	ユニークだ	unique
ひはんてきな	批判的な	critical
じゆうな	自由な	free
じゅんのうてきな	順応的な	adaptable
じぶんのいけんをいう	自分の意見を言う	give own opinion
たにんにきびしい	他人に厳しい	strict towards others
たにんをひはんする	他人を批判する	be critical of others
じかんをまもる	時間を守る	punctual
いつもどりょくする	いつも努力する	always make effort
きそくをまもる	規則を守る	observe regulation
ただしくしたい	正しくしたい	righteous
ぎむかんがある	義務感がある	feel obligated
ねばならないをつかう	ねばならないを使う	use "must"
りょうりがすき	料理が好き	like cooking
しゃかいほうしがすき	社会奉仕が好き	like social service

きがつく	気がつく	realize
おもいやりがある	思いやりがある	considerate
いやといえない	嫌と言えない	cannot say no
せわずき	世話好き	willing to help
きょうかんする	共感する	sympathize with
にんじょうがある	人情がある	warmhearted
もんだいかいけつりょくがある		have problem solving skill
	問題解決力がある	
しごとができる	仕事ができる	skillful
たにんのいけんをきく	他人の意見を聞く	listen to others
むりしない	無理をしない	not overwork
すぐはんだんする	すぐ判断する	judge immediately
りろんてきである	理論的である	theoretical
ただしくはんだんする	正しく判断する	judge rightly
かんじょうてきにならない		not emotional
	感情的にならない	
ぶんせきできである	分析的である	analytical
かんがえてこうどうする		think and act
	考えて行動する	
れいせいにこうどうする		act calmly
	冷静に行動する	
わがまま	我がまま	selfish
たべすぎる	食べ過ぎる	eat too much
いいすぎる	言い過ぎる	say too much
ほしがる	欲しがる	greedy
おこりやすい	怒りやすい	get angry easily
さけびやすい	叫びやすい	shout easily
ちょっかんではんだんする		decide intuitively
	直感で判断する	
ちょうしにのりやすい	調子に乗りやすい	elated
こうきしんがつよい	好奇心が強い	curious
なみだもろい	涙もろい	cry easily
なにもいえない	何も言えない	
		not fight back, speechless
きにいられたい	気に入られたい	
		want to be pleased by others
じぶんでおさえる	自分で押さえる	hold myself
ほんとうのじぶんではない		not true self
	本当の自分ではない	
たにんがきにかかる	他人が気にかかる	
		worry about others
がまんする	我慢する	patient
きたいされる	期待される	be expected
だきょうしやすい	妥協しやすい	compromise easily
れっとうかんがつよい	劣等感が強い	
		complex have inferiority
えんりょしやすい	遠慮しやすい	modest

Design and layout

ページスタイル		page style
さゆうぞろえがた	左右揃え型	left and right margins
センターぞろえがた	センター揃え型	center aligned
しぜんがた	自然型	free form
ずはんりつ	図版率	image-text ratio
ず	図	image
ぶぶん	部分	part
ページレイアウト		page layout
ラフレイアウト		layout draft
おおみだし	大見出し	title
なかみだし	中見出し	subtitle
こみだし	小見出し	section title
こうせい	構成	structure, composition
おも(な)	主(な)	main, principal
かみ	紙	paper
レターサイズ		letter size
こうせい	校正	proofreading
フォント		fonts
サイズ		size
ヘッドライン		headline
パワフル		powerful
プラクティカル		practical
エレガント		elegant
カジュアル		casual
カラー		color
しろくろ	白黒	black and white

Other words

しかい	司会	MC/ host
じっけん	実験	experiment
さくら	桜	cherry blossom
かいもの	買い物	shopping
かこんで	囲んで	enclose
マッチさせる		match
まる	○	circle
ばつ	×	cross (no good)
しつもん	質問	question
あいて	相手	partner
ききましょう	聞きましょう	let's listen
しめす	示す	indicate
みなさん	皆さん	everybody
つくって	作って	make
ばしょ	場所	place
れい	例	example
したがって	従って	follow
まわり	回り	around

もの	物	things
はなしあう	話し合う	discuss
けっか	結果	result
けいようし	形容詞	adjective
さがす	探す	find
ことば	言葉	word
あてはまる	当てはまる	fit
がっき	学期	academic term
かず	数	number
しらべて	調べて	research
ひょうげん	表現	expression
れんしゅう	練習	practice
せつめい	説明	explain
きょか	許可	permission
きんし	禁止	prohibition
あらわす	表す	express
おきかえもんだい	置き換え問題	substitutional drill
かせん	下線	underline
ぶぶん	部分	part
え	絵	picture
かいわ	会話	conversation
かんせい	完成	accomplishment
せつぞく	接続	connection
くわしく	詳しく	detailed
たしざん	足し算	addition
かぞく	家族	family
しょうかい	紹介	introduction
せいしつ	性質	character
じょうたい	状態	situation
りゆう	理由	reason
こたえる	答える	answer
つぎ	次ぎ	next
れんぞく	連続	sequence
こうい	行為	action
むすびつける	結び付ける	connect
できごと	出来事	incident
どうじ	同時	simultaneous
いみ	意味	meaning
はんだん	判断	judgment
いんがかんけい	因果関係	cause and effect
そんざい	存在	existence
ふくむ	含む	including
あげる	挙げる	raise
じょうきょう	状況	situation
たいする	対する	face, oppose

4.9 Virtual Reality 実践
<ruby>実践<rt>じっせん</rt></ruby>

Editing and Presentations
パンフレットの<ruby>編集<rt>へんしゅう</rt></ruby>と<ruby>発表<rt>はっぴょう</rt></ruby>

Overview

You have created all the necessary parts in your booklet, such as articles, photos, and charts. We now proceed to designing the booklet. You will first learn a little bit about page layout and then you will create your assigned pages. Once your booklet is produced, you will evaluate it along with booklets made by other groups and share your thoughts. The chapter will end with a set of presentations you will prepare based on the content of your booklet.

9 Edit a booklet パンフレットを<ruby>編集<rt>へんしゅう</rt></ruby>する

10 Conduct presentations <ruby>発表<rt>はっぴょう</rt></ruby>をする

9 Edit a booklet　　　　　パンフレットを編集する

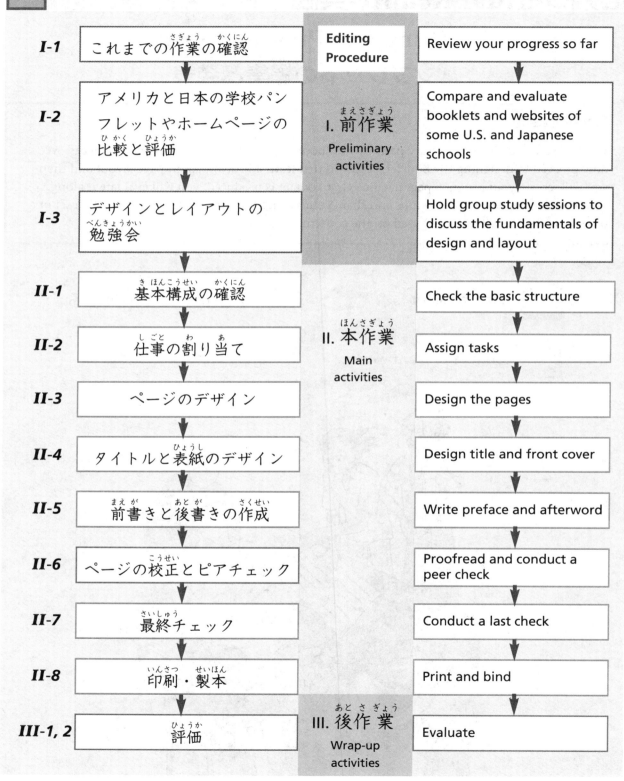

		Editing Procedure	
I-1	これまでの作業の確認		Review your progress so far
I-2	アメリカと日本の学校パンフレットやホームページの比較と評価	I. 前作業 Preliminary activities	Compare and evaluate booklets and websites of some U.S. and Japanese schools
I-3	デザインとレイアウトの勉強会		Hold group study sessions to discuss the fundamentals of design and layout
II-1	基本構成の確認		Check the basic structure
II-2	仕事の割り当て	II. 本作業 Main activities	Assign tasks
II-3	ページのデザイン		Design the pages
II-4	タイトルと表紙のデザイン		Design title and front cover
II-5	前書きと後書きの作成		Write preface and afterword
II-6	ページの校正とピアチェック		Proofread and conduct a peer check
II-7	最終チェック		Conduct a last check
II-8	印刷・製本		Print and bind
III-1, 2	評価	III. 後作業 Wrap-up activities	Evaluate

I. 前作業

1. これまでの作業の確認

4.8で作成した文章と写真や表などのビジュアルが全部あるか確認してください。

2. アメリカと日本の学校のパンフレットやホームページの比較と評価

アメリカと日本の学校のパンフレットかホームページを見てください。それから、比べて評価してください。デザインは同じですか。グループで話しましょう。そして、皆さんのパンフレットのデザインを考えましょう。

3. デザインとレイアウトの勉強会

勉強会を開いてデザインとレイアウトの基礎を勉強してください。次のページからの例も参考にしてください。

I. Preliminary Activities

1. *Review your progress so far*

Check to see if you have all the writings and visuals, such as the photos and charts that you made in section 4.8.

2. *Compare and evaluate booklets and websites of some U.S. and Japanese schools*

Look at several booklets and/or websites of both U.S. and Japanese schools and conduct a comparative evaluation of them. Are they similar in terms of design? Have a group discussion and think about the design of your booklet.

3. *Have a group study session to discuss the design and layout*

Hold a study session and study the fundamentals of design and layout. Use the examples starting on the following pages as your reference.

A. ページスタイル

A. Page Style

ページスタイル

三つのタイプ

Aのイメージ
プラクティカル
Use this style for
the main pages
of the booklet.

Bのイメージ
エレガント

Cのイメージ
カジュアル

メニュー
ハンバーグ　　　　　1200円
エビフライ　　　　　1300円
チキンカツ　　　　　1100円
ビーフシチュー　　　　950円
サーロインステーキ　1800円

メニュー
ハンバーグ
1200円
エビフライ
1300円
チキンカツ
1100円
ビーフシチュー
950円
サーロインステーキ
1800円

メニュー
ハンバーグ　1200円
エビフライ　1300円
チキンカツ　1100円
ビーフシチュー　950円
サーロインステーキ　1800円

A. 左右ぞろえ型

ジョーンズさんは、まいにち6時におきます。6時半にあさごはんをたべます。

B. センターぞろえ型

ジョーンズさんは、まいにち6時におきます。6時半にあさごはんをたべます。

C. 自然型

ジョーンズさんは、まいにち6時におきます。6時半にあさごはんをたべます。

B. 図版率

B. Image-Text Ratio

図 (写真やイラスト) と文の割合

おおきい ↑
図版率
↓ ちいさい

ポスター

しんぶん

じしょ
dictionary

クラブ紹介：科学クラブ
科学クラブの活動は火曜日と木曜日です。メンバーは1年生11人、　　　人、3年　　　　文　Text　　イザーは　　先生と星野先生です。今、秋のサイエンスフェアの準備をしています。サイエンスフェアは11月2日と3日にジムであります。

図版率 **0%**

クラブ紹介：科学クラブ
科学クラブ　　りは火曜　　　ンバー　　　1人、2年生1
4人、3年生9人です。アドバイザーは　木先生と星　です。今、秋のサイエンスフェアの準備をしています。

文　Text

図　Image

20%

クラブ紹介：科学クラブ
科学クラブの活動は火曜日と木曜　　　　ンバーは　　　　生1
4　　生9人です。今、秋のサイエンスフェアの

文　Text

図　Image

45%

C. ページレイアウト　　　C. Page Layout

横書き（よこがき） horizontal writing

縦書き（たてがき） vertical writing

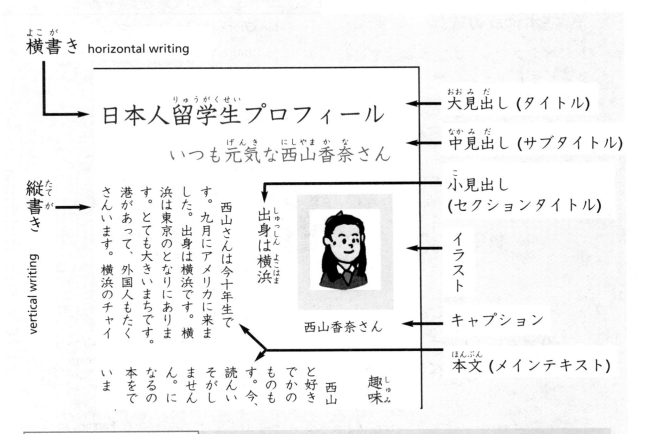

大見出し（おおみだし）(タイトル)

中見出し（なかみだし）(サブタイトル)

小見出し（こみだし）(セクションタイトル)

イラスト

キャプション

本文（ほんぶん）(メインテキスト)

日本人留学生プロフィール
いつも元気な西山香奈さん

出身（しゅっしん）は横浜（よこはま）

西山香奈さん

趣味（しゅみ）

西山さんは今十年生です。九月にアメリカに来ました。出身は横浜です。横浜は東京のとなりにあります。とても大きいまちです。港があって、外国人もたくさんいます。横浜のチャイナタウンはとても大きいまちなのものもでかのでものものもです。今、読んいそがしませんん。に本をでいま

西山と好きでかのものもです。

どれがいいですか。

Which do you think is most suited for promoting the product below as [A] fun and innovative, [B] refined and sophisticated, and [C] useful and practical.

新しい教科書

きせつ『春一番』はクリエイティブな人のための新しい日本語教科書です。学生たちが自分で計画し、作りあげていくアクティビティーがたくさんあり、楽しみながら日本語が勉強できます。

(1)

新しい（あたらしい）教科書（きょうかしょ）

きせつ『春一番』はクリエイティブな人のための新しい日本語教科書です。学生たちが自分で計画し、作りあげていくアクティビティーがたくさんあり、楽しみながら日本語が勉強できます。

(2)

きせつ『春一番』はクリエイティブな人のための新しい日本語教科書です。

学生たちが自分で計画し、作りあげていくアクティビティーがたくさんあります。

新しい教科書

楽しみながら日本語が勉強できます。

(3)

II. 本作業
_{ほん さ ぎょう}

1. 基本構成の確認
_{き ほんこうせい かくにん}

パンフレットの基本構成を確認
_{ほんこうせい かくにん}
しましょう。

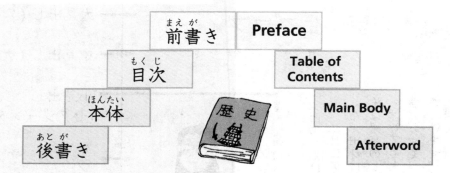

前書き	Preface
目次	Table of Contents
本体	Main Body
後書き	Afterword

2. 仕事の割り当て
_{し ごと わ あ}

仕事をリストしてください。そ
_{し ごと}
れから、割り当ててください。
_{わ あ}

II. Main Activities

1. *Check the basic structure*

Confirm the basic structure of your booklet.

2. *Task assignment*

List all the specific tasks and allocate them among the production team members.

仕事	Tasks	割り当て	Persons in Charge
表紙	Cover	マーク	
前書きと目次	Preface and Table of Contents	サラ	
後書き	Afterword	タイラー	
基礎情報ページ	Basic information pages	リンダ、シャミカ	
規則のページ	"Rules" pages	マーク、サラ	
トピック1	Topic 1 pages	シャミカ	
トピック2	Topic 2 pages	サラ	
トピック3	Topic 3 pages	ホセ、リンダ	
トピック4	Topic 4 pages	タイラー	

Put the names of your topics here.

3. ページのデザイン

レイアウトや見出しも考えながら、割り当てられたページを作りましょう。

3. Page design

Create the pages that have been assigned to you while paying sufficient attention to page layout and captions.

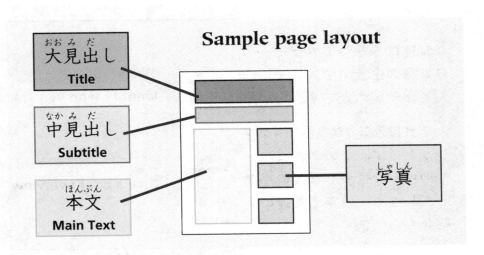

Sample page layout

大見出し Title

中見出し Subtitle

本文 Main Text

写真

4. タイトルと表紙のデザイン

パンフレットにタイトルをつけてください。それから、表紙と目次のデザインも考えましょう。

4. Title and front cover design

Create a title for your booklet. Also, think about the design of the front cover and the table of contents.

きせつアカデミーのすべて

Everything You Want to Know about Kisetsu Academy

きせつアカデミー

私たちの学校

5. 前書きと後書きの作成

下の例のような前書きと後書きを作りましょう。

5. Preface and afterword

Create a preface and an afterword for your booklet like in the example below.

はじめに **Preface**

私達はきせつアカデミーの日本語の生徒です。男子が四人と女子が六人です。

作者の紹介
Identify who you are

これは私達の学校のパンフレットです。この学校についての色々な情報や私達の感想があります。授業や友達の紹介もあります。

パンフレットの紹介
Give a brief overview

きせつアカデミーはすばらしい学校です。ぜひ来てください。早く皆さんに会いたいです。

短いメッセージ
Give a brief message to the readers

短いコメント
Give brief post-production thoughts

おわりに **Afterword**

町のパンフレットのプロジェクトは忙しいプロジェクトです。でも、とても面白いです。

これからのこと
Comment on your future plan

これからもがんばって日本語を勉強します。

協力者へのお礼
Acknowledge those who helped you

ジョアン・タグチ先生、マーク・ジョンソン先生、石井あや子さん、リンダ・キャンベルさんありがとうございました。

20XY年5月1日

6. ページの校正とピアチェック

まず、自分が作ったページの校正をしてください。つぎに、他のメンバーのページも校正してください。それから、編集会議をして、話し合ってください。

6. Proofreading and checking by peers

First, proofread your own pages. Next, proofread the pages created by others. After that, talk about your findings in an editorial meeting. Make any necessary corrections if needed.

7. 最終チェック

必要なものは全部ありますか。正しい順番に並べて、確認しましょう。ページ番号もまだだったら入れてください。

7. Final check of the contents

Are all the pages of your booklet ready for printing/copying and binding? Put them in order and insert page numbers if you have yet to do so.

8. 印刷・製本

これでパンフレットは完成です。おめでとうございます。

8. Printing and binding

Your booklet is now ready for distribution. Congratulations!

III. 後作業

1. 自分達のパンフレットの評価

自分達のパンフレットをもう一度読んでください。そして、例のような評価シートを使って評価し、いい点や改善点を話し合いましょう。

III. Wrap-up Activities

1. Evaluation

Read your school booklet again and evaluate it using an evaluation form like the following example. Then meet with your group and share your thoughts about the booklet.

パンフレット作りの評価
づく　ひょうか
Booklet-Making
Self or Team Evaluation

		もっと がんばって ください	もうすこし がんばって ください	まあまあ です	よく できました	たいへん よく できました
		poor	<---------	fair	--------->	excellent

内容とデザイン　Content & Design
ないよう

ほんぶん 本文 Main texts	こうぞう 構造 Structure	1	2	3	4	5
	ないよう 内容 Content	1	2	3	4	5
	かた 型　grammar/ Form　spelling	1	2	3	4	5
ひょう 表、 Charts, graphs	Clear and effective	1	2	3	4	5
しゃしん 写真、イラスト Photos, illustrations	Attractive and blends well with the rest	1	2	3	4	5
レイアウト Page layout	All the components well coordinated	1	2	3	4	5
けいかく 計画 Planning	Product reflects advanced thinking and planning	1	2	3	4	5
ひょうし 表紙 Cover	Well-designed and attractive	1	2	3	4	5
ぜんたい 全体 As a whole	Overall quality	1	2	3	4	5

プロセス　Production Process

きょうりょく 協力 Cooperation	Teamwork and team communication	1	2	3	4	5
こうけん 貢献 Contribution	Quality of individual contribution	1	2	3	4	5
日本語 Japanese	Always communicated in Japanese	1	2	3	4	5

コメント

2. 他のパンフレットの評価

今度は他のグループのパンフレットを読んでください。そして、同じような評価シートを使って評価してください。さらに、いい点と問題点を3〜5つずつリストし、それをもとにコメントを述べてください。

2. Proofreading and checking by peers

This time, read the booklets made by other groups and evaluate them using the same evaluation form as before. After that, list 3-5 things that you liked about the booklet and 3-5 things that may need some improvement. Then prepare brief comments based on the list and share them in class.

リストの例 (Sample List)

基礎情報がとても役に立つ。
Basic information is useful.

プロムについての感想文が面白い。
The *kansoubun* about the prom is interesting.

イラストが上手。
Illustrations are skillfully made.

表紙のデザインが個性的。
The cover design is unique.

字が小さすぎる。
The letters are too small.

写真が少ない。
There aren't enough photos.

校則の説明文が分かりにくい。
The expository writing about the school rules is a bit hard to follow.

コメントの例 (Sample Comments)

ええと、基礎情報がとても役に立つと思います。プロムについての感想文も面白いです。それに、イラストが上手だし、表紙のデザインも個性的です。でも、字が小さすぎるから、大きくした方がいいと思います。写真も多い方がいいでしょう。それから、校則の説明文がちょっと分かりにくいです。

10 Conduct presentations

発表する
<ruby>発<rt>はっ</rt></ruby><ruby>表<rt>ぴょう</rt></ruby>する

Since the main goal of this chapter is the production of a school booklet, we have spent a good deal of time working on our writing skills. So it will be fitting if we end this chapter with a set of presentations. You may recall that in chapter 2 you were shown four different styles of activities and you made the activities in your review session accordingly. We will follow the same model at this time as well.

ワークシート/デジタル型 **Worksheet/Digital style**	Create a digital version of your booklet and make a presentation about it in Japanese in class (or in front of a Japanese audience if possible).
音読型 **Read Aloud style**	Read aloud some of the kansoubun you have created for the booklet. Remember you are reading for the audience and not to yourself. Practice your reading with this in mind.
スキット型 **Skit style**	Create a set of skits that can highlight some of the topics covered in your booklet. You will perform some of them by yourself and ask your classmates to perform others.
ロールプレイ型 **Role Play style**	Create a set of school role plays that can highlight some of the topics covered in your booklet. You will perform some of them by yourself and ask your classmates to perform others.

Mini Conversation 4:
ミニ会話 4

Travel to Japan: 日本へ旅行

会話 1

マイク:　あ、ノートを忘れた。どうしよう。

秋子:　　大丈夫ですよ。学校の中にお店がありますから、そこで買うことが
　　　　　できますよ。

マイク:　そうですか。行ってみます。

秋子:　　でも、よかったら(1) この紙を使ってください。

マイク:　いいんですか。

秋子:　　どうぞ。たくさんありますから大丈夫ですよ。

マイク:　ありがとう

会話 2

マイク:　あの、ちょっと頭が痛いんですけど(2)…。

秋子:　　緊張しましたか。

マイク:　いいえ、まだ時差ぼけなんです。

秋子:　　外に出て、いい空気を吸ったらどうですか(3)。それとも保健室に行
　　　　　きますか。

マイク:　うーん、まずちょっと外に出てみます。

会話3（学級会の最後に）

先生：　　　　皆さんにお知らせがあります。明日の3時間目はマイク君の歓迎会を
　　　　　　します。数学の授業はありません。

生徒たち：　わー。やったー。

先生：　　　静かに！マイク君、歓迎会の時、日本語で自己紹介してくださいね。
　　　　　　他の皆は英語で自己紹介してください。

生徒たち：　えー。

先生：　　　じゃあ、マイク君、明日お願いね。

マイク：　　あのー、「歓迎会」って何ですか。

生徒：　　　（笑う）

先生：　　　誰か、英語で言うことができますか。

秋子：　　　「歓迎会」は英語で「Welcome party」です。

マイク：　　あー。わかりました。

Dialogue 1

Mike:　I forgot my notebook. What should I do?
Akiko:　Don't worry. There is a store in the school, so you can buy a notebook there.
Mike:　Oh, is that so? I will try to go.
Akiko:　If you'd like, please use this paper.
Mike:　Is it all right?
Akiko:　Sure. I have many, so please use it.
Mike:　Thank you.

Dialogue 2

Mike:　Umm... I got a headache, but...
Akiko:　Do you feel nervous?
Mike:　No. I still have jet lag.
Akiko:　Why don't you go out and get some fresh air? Or, do you want to go to the nurse's office?
Mike:　Hmm, at first, I will try to go out.

Dialogue 3 (at the end of the class meeting)

Teacher:　I have an announcement. We will have a welcome party for Mike during third period tomorrow. Therfore, we will not have mathematics class.
Students:　Yay!
Teacher:　Please be quiet. Mike, at the welcome party, please introduce yourself in Japanese. The rest of the class must introduce themselves in English.
Students:　Oh no.
Teacher:　Then, Mike, tomorrow could you do it?
Mike:　Umm, what is "kangei kai"?
Students:　(laugh)
Teacher:　Can anyone explain it in English?
Akiko:　"Kangei-kai" means "welcome party" in English.
Mike:　Oh, I got it.

Dialogue 1 Notes

・忘れた：forgot　・どうしよう：What should I do?
・大丈夫です：I'm fine.　・お店：shop　・そこで：there
・行ってみます：I will try to go
・よかったら：If you'd like　・この紙：this paper
・使ってください：please use it
・いいんですか：Is it OK?

Dialogue 2 Notes

・頭が痛いんですけど：I got a headache, but
・緊張しましたか：Do you feel nervous?
・まだ時差ぼけなんです：I still have jet lag.
・外に出て：going out
・いい空気を吸ったらどうですか：How about getting some fresh air?
・保健室：nurse's office
・まず：at first

Dialogue 3 Notes

・学級会 ：class meeting ・皆さんに ：for everybody ・お知らせ ：announcement ・歓迎会 ：welcome party
・授業 ：class ・わー。やったー。：Yay! ・静かに ：be quiet ・の時 ：when... ・自己紹介 ：self-introduction
・他の皆 ：the rest of the class ・お願い ：a request ・英語で言うことができますか ：Can you say it in English?

Grammar Keys and Practice

(1) よかったら

よかったら means "If it is OK..." たら has two different functions: condition and completion.

Speak following sentences in Japanese. 日本語で言いましょう。

1. If it is OK with you, I will go to the movie theater with you. ⇒
2. If it is a fine day, we will have barbecue outside ⇒
3. After watching TV, I will do my homework. ⇒

(2) 頭が痛いんですけど

頭が痛いんですけど is equivalent to "I got headache, but..."

Make a single sentence using the following example. 例にならって、一つの文にしましょう。

EX. あたまがいたいです。(学校に行きます。) ⇒

あたまがいたいんですけど… (学校に行きます。)

1. おなかが痛いです。(学校に行きます。) ⇒
2. 歯が痛いです。(学校に行きます。) ⇒
3. 足が痛いです。(学校に行きます。) ⇒

(3) ～たらどうですか

～たらどうですか means "Why don't you do...?" It is a way of making a suggestion.

Make a single sentence using the following example. 例にならって、一つの文にしましょう。.

EX. シャワーをあびます。⇒ シャワーをあびたらどうですか。

1. メールをチェックします。⇒
2. 歯をみがきます。⇒
3. くつをぬぎます。⇒

Travel Practice 1
When you are with your host family, you will ask your host mother if you can do certain things, using ～たら.

Travel Practice 2
When you are a host, you will give your exchange student some suggestions, using ～たらどうですか.

Travel Practice 3
Make pairs. One person will be a host mother in Japan. The other is an exchange student from outside of Japan. The exchange student will try to communicate with his host mother in Japanese and ask what to do with medical problems using いたいんですけど. The host mother will give suggestions using ～たらどうですか.

Travel Practice 4
Visiting a school will be fun for your group. At least you should prepare your self-introduction and explain your town and school.

Travel Practice 5
Create another activity utilizing what you have learned in the process of describing host family life situations. Be sure to make the activity interesting and to integrate cultural issues.

665

SUM-UP

1. *What differences did you find between your (English) writing customs and the Japanese writing customs during your first encounter?*

2. *Reading kanji in Japanese is: (circle one)*

   a. easy

   b. somewhat easy

   c. somewhat difficult

   d. difficult

3. *What do you think about the Japanese custom of kansoubun style writing?*

4. *Besides the difference, what is the similarity between English writing and Japanese writing ?*

5. *Did you make any progress in your writing ability? Please rate your progress on a scale of 0 to 5. (0 = no progress, 5 = excellent progress)*

0	1	2	3	4	5

6. *Have you been able to use some writing strategies whenever you did not understand what you heard? Please rate your progress on a scale of 0 to 5. (0 = no progress, 5 = excellent progress)*

0	1	2	3	4	5

7. *Were you able to use some reading strategies, including some writing strategies when you want to read another phrase? Please rate your progress on a scale of 0 to 5. (0 = no progress, 5 = excellent progress)*

0	1	2	3	4	5

ADDITIONAL VOCABULARY

Functional Vocabulary

Taking leave

さようなら	sayoonara	バイバイ	baibai	Goodbye
では	Dewa	じゃ	Ja	Bye
いってらっしゃい	itterasshai	to someone who is leaving		

On returning

おかえりなさい	Okaerinasai	おかえり	Okaerinasai	Welcome back to a person who returned
ただいま	Tadaima	I'm home.		

School subjects

ついている	付いている	dispatched
もっとも	最も	most
きもちがいい	気持ちが良い	comfortable
しゅしょく	主食	main dish
きかい	機械	machine
げきじょう	劇場	theater
ギリシャ		Greek
ような		like
えんけい	円形	circle
げき	劇	drama
シェークスピア		Shakespeare
ほっと		be relieved
きゅうしゅう	九州	name of place
かよう	通う	commute
ぼく	僕	I (for boy)
じぶん	自分	self
しょうらい	将来	future
ためになる		concern for
ぐたいてき	具体的	specific, concrete
なにか	何か	something
たいせつ	大切	important
さっか	作家	author
いちぶ	一部	a part
いっさつ	一冊	one book
ぜんぶ	全部	all
ほんとう	本当	truth
とくい	得意	be good at
もんだいかいけつ	問題解決	problem solving
ベクトル		vector
ぎょうれつ	行列	matrix
かいせき	解析	analysis
かんけい	関係	relationship
さいきんまで	最近まで	until recently
べつべつのもの	別々のもの	different things
しゃかいか	社会科	social studies
じゅぎょう	授業	class
もんだい	問題	problem
げんいん	原因	cause

けっか	結果	effect
あまりない	余りない	there is not so much
じじつ	事実	fact
あんき	暗記	memorization
なる	成る	become
おおい	多い	many
じぶんで	自分で	by myself
〜たり、〜たり		represent action and action
しらべ	調べ	research
わかってくる	分かってくる	come to understand

Teachers in the school

ひとり	一人	one person
ふたり	二人	two persons
おしえる	教える	teach
しごと	仕事	job, task
たんとうする	担当する	be in charge of
おしえかた	教え方	how to teach
たとえば	例えば	for example
つくる	作る	make
ごとに		every
よみかき	読み書き	reading and writing
できる	出来る	be able
バイリンガル		bilingual
きみたち	君達	you (plural)
いつも		always
べんきょうしなおす	勉強し直す	relearn, restudy
かわかみ	川上	name
じんかく	人格	personality
ようです		it seems
ほう		more than
からだ	体	body
ひょうげん	表現	expression
ようになります		become such that
みたい		look like

Past student memory

ほった	堀田	name
だいすけ	大介	name
かれ	彼	he

667

にゅうがくご	入学後	after entering
やきゅうぶ	野球部	baseball club
かわる	変わる	change
かぶそしき	下部組織	sub-organization
かつやく	活躍	actively
みやざわけんじ	宮沢賢治	name of author
きょうみ	興味	interest
もつ	持つ	hold
じょうきょう	状況	situation
しなくてはならない		must do
じだい	時代	era
きょういくがくぶ	教育学部	Department of Education
にんげん	人間	human being
いっぽう	一方	on the other hand
ぶ	部	club
ランニングバック		running back
ゆうめい	有名	famous
そつぎょう	卒業	graduation
あと	後	after
かいしゃ	会社	company
つとめる	勤める	work for
やめる	辞める	quit
だいがくいん	大学院	graduate school
どうしよう		what do
せんこう	専攻	major
いきる	生きる	live
しょうせつ	小説	novel
ざんねんながら	残念ながら	unfortunately
ほんかくてき	本格的	seriously
ついきゅう	追究	pursuit
じたく	自宅	home
きょうと	京都	Kyoto
とちゅう	途中	on the way
とうめいこうそくどうろ	東名高速道路	Tomei highway
かべ	壁	wall
し	死	death

Trip In Japan

さがす	探す	search
いってみます	行ってみます	try to go
よかったら		If you'd like
かみ	紙	paper
いいんですか		Is it all right?
あたまがいたいんですけど	頭が痛いんですけど	I got a headache, but
きんちょうする	緊張する	be nervous
まだじさぼけなんです	未だ時差ぼけなんです	still got jet lag

いいくうきをすったら 良い空気を吸ったら
how about do you inhale fresh air

ほけんしつ	保健室	nurse's office
がっきゅうかい	学級会	class meeting
おしらせ	お知らせ	notice
かんげいかい	歓迎会	welcome party
わーやーた		yay
じこしょうかい	自己紹介	self-introduction
ほかのみんな	他の皆	others
おねがい	お願い	request

えいごでいうことができますか 英語で言うことが出来ますか can you say it in English?

Writing words

かんそうぶん	感想文	response essay
せつめいぶんけいしき	説明文形式	form of expository writing
はんだんぶん	判断文	judgment sentence
コメントぶん	コメント文	comment sentence
リードぶん	リード文	lead sentence
びょうしゃぶん	描写文	descriptive sentence
コメントぶん	コメント部分	comment part
なりたつ	成り立つ	consist
じゆうなはっそう	自由な発想	flexible idea
いけん	意見	opinions
かんそう	感想	feelings
のべる	述べる	judgment sentence
かきことば	書き言葉	written words
ちょくせつてき	直接的	direct
かんせつてき	間接的	indirect
やわらかい	柔らかい	soft
たいけつする	対決する	confront
このまれる	好まれる	be favored
すなわち		that is to say
どくしゃ	読者	audience, reader
たいして	対して	at, toward
いんしょうにのこる	印象に残る	leave an impression
てつだってもらう	手伝ってもらう	help
かきかたきょういく	書き方教育	education for writing
ぶんしょうこうぞう	文章構造	structure of writing
いっかんせい	一貫性	coherence
にほんごかんきょう	日本語環境	Japanese language environment
じゅうようなぶんしょうひょうげん	重要な文章表現	important writing expression
しゅかんひょうげん	主観表現	subjective expression
こうか	効果	effective

Other words

9.11じけん	9.11事件	9.11 incident
イラクせんそう	イラク戦争	Iraq war

Additional Kanji 11: 追加漢字 11

変わる	かわる、change　　　　　　変：**ON:**ヘン　　　**KUN:**かわ(る) 時代が変わります。　Times are changing.
活躍	かつやく、actively　　　　活：**ON:**カツ　　　**KUN:**い(かす) 　　　　　　　　　　　　躍：**ON:**ヤク　　　**KUN:**おど(る) 活躍をしていました。　He was quite active.
興味	きょうみ、interest　　　　興：**ON:**キョウ　　**KUN:**おこ(る) 　　　　　　　　　　　　味：**ON:**ミ　　　　**KUN:**あじ 教育に興味を持ちます。　I am interesting in education.
持つ	もつ、hold　　　　　　　持：**ON:**ジ　　　　**KUN:**も(つ) 教育に興味を持ちます。　I am interesting in education.
覚える	おぼえる、memorize　　　覚：**ON:**カク　　　**KUN:** おぼ(える) 新しい言葉を覚えます。　I memorize new word.
機械	きかい、machine　　　　　機：**ON:**キ　　　　**KUN:**はた 　　　　　　　　　　　　械：**ON:**カイ　　　**KUN:**一 機械工学専攻です。　My major is mechanical science.
専攻	せんこう、major　　　　　専：**ON:**セン　　　**KUN:**もっぱ(ら) 　　　　　　　　　　　　攻：**ON:**コウ　　　**KUN:**せめ(る) 機械工学専攻です。　My major is mechanical science.
交通	こうつう、traffic　　　　交：**ON:**コウ **KUN:**まじ(わる)、ま(じる) 　　　　　　　　　　　　　　　　　　　　か(う)、か(わす) 　　　　　　　　　　　　通：**ON:**ツウ **KUN:**とお(る) 交通事故でけがをした。　He was injured in traffic accident.
事故	じこ、accident　　　　　事：**ON:**ジ、ズ　　**KUN:**こと 　　　　　　　　　　　　故：**ON:**コ　　　　**KUN:**ゆえ 交通事故でけがをした。　He was injured in traffic accident.

UNIT 4 REVIEW THROUGH GAMES

ゲームで復習

I. Kanji Memory Game　漢字の神経衰弱
かんじ　しんけいすいじゃく

Playing the memory game (also known as the game of concentration) is a fun and effective way of reviewing words, short expressions, and kanji with your classmates. In an ordinary game a deck of cards is placed face-down in rows, and players try to find two identical cards. Here we will attempt a modified version in which players will try to collect three different forms (kanji expression, hiragana expression, and English expression) whoever gets the same word scores a point. Only Japanese will be used throughout the game.

1. Break up into groups of five　五人のグループに分かれる
わ

The number of players per game is five, though it may change according to the size of your class. Listen to your teacher's instructions and break up into groups.

2. Make the cards　カードを作る

Things needed 　　　ひつようもの　　　(必要な物)	1. Blank index cards (インデックスカード) 2. Markers 　　　　　(マーカー)

You will use a set of 45 cards representing the kanji, the hiragana, and English of the 15 words shown below in sets of three. Everyone in your group should be in charge of one of the sets (A-E) and make 9 cards each.

高い 立つ 海	食べる 日曜日 書き手	答えます 言います 読みます	終わります 行きます 来ます	します 作ります 話します
A.	**B.**	**C.**	**D.**	**E.**

（よう on 日曜日, こた on 答えます, お on 終わります）

670 **Environment**

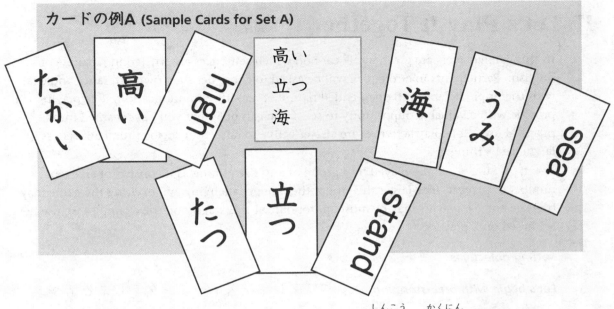

カードの例A (Sample Cards for Set A)

3. Check rules and procedure　ルールと進行の確認をする

> **Rules and Procedure**
>
> 1. Shuffle the cards and place them face-down in rows
> 2. Take turns and try to collect a set of three cards indicating kanji, hiragana, and English of the same word by turning over such cards in succession. You will lose your turn when you turn over a wrong card.
> 3. Read what is written on a card right after you turn it over.
> 4. Place the cards you have collected face up right in front of you.
> 5. The game ends when all the cards have been collected and a player with the most cards is declared a winner.

4. Decide who will play first　順番を決める

Decide upon who will turn over a card first in the game by *janken*. The remaining order may also be determined by *janken* and the players should be seated accordingly.

II. Let's Play It Together　一緒にしょう

In this game players are given a role card on which sentences are written in Japanese or English. Participants in a role play will be asked to construct their own utterance and deal with the unpredictable and open-ended nature of real-life communication. Role playing will provide with a valuable opportunity to see if you can put what you have learned into practical use. Role play activities are also effective to raise your sociocultural awareness in language learning.

いっしょにしょう can be played by a group of any size as long as it consists of an even number of players. The larger the group, the more challenging and exciting the game may become but 2-6 players may be most appropriate at this stage, and the examples we use here are based on 2 players.

A. Setting objectives　目的を決める

Let's begin with brainstorming.　最初にブレインストーミングをしましょう

〜の練習のため

町のセッションの練習のため

会話の練習のため

問題解決の練習のため

文表現の練習のため

ロールプレイの目的

〜の復習のため

ミーティングの表現の復習のため

学校案内の復習のため

形容詞の復習のため

自己紹介の復習のため
self introduction

Make a list of possible objectives.　目的のリストを作ってください

Setting a role play　ロールプレイを決める

Think about what kind of role plays will be most suitable to meet your objectives. The description below is about a role play that will be used as an example for the rest of this section.

B. Sample role making (4 roles)
役作りの例 (役の数: 4)

ロールプレイの目的

自己紹介の復習

学校案内の復習

ミーティングの表現の復習

動詞と形容詞の復習

町の紹介の復習

ロールプレイ

日本語クラスと日本人留学生のロールプレイ
(日本人留学生が日本語クラスに行く)

1. Make cards カードを作る

Things needed ひつよう もの (必要な物)	1. Blank index cards (インデックスカード) 2. Markers (マーカー)

Create 5 sets of role cards using the constructions you have learned so far. Write the role and its description on an index card. Each set needs 2 to 4 role cards. You need to make 10 to 20 role cards all together.

A. *Make a role card* ロールカードを作る

Meet with your group and make role cards based on the chart you have made. Use the cards shown earlier as a model.

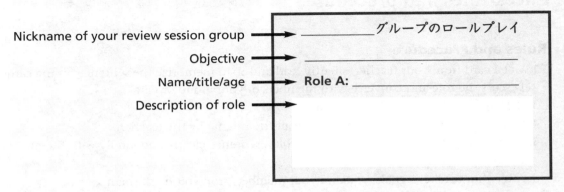

Nickname of your review session group ⟶ _____グループのロールプレイ

Objective ⟶ _____

Name/title/age ⟶ **Role A:** _____

Description of role ⟶

B. *Role cards for the sample role play* ロールカードの例れい

Role play among your group members.

Role A : Party for exchange students
An American High School Student

It's 8:30 in the evening and you are at a nearby park for an event sponsored by a local Japanese youth organization. It is very hot and humid. Go around the area and introduce yourself to some Japanese participants. Exchange the following information with them: birthplace, school, age, grade level, favorite sport, favorite music, and favorite movie.

Role B : Party for exchange students
A Japanese High School Student

You are a Japanese high school student who has been in the U.S. on a short exchange program. It's 8:30 in the evening and you are at a nearby park for an event sponsored by a local Japanese youth organization. It is very hot and humid. Go around the area and introduce yourself to some American participants. Exchange the following information with them: birthplace, school, age, grade level, favorite sport, favorite music, and favorite movie.

673

2. Rehearsal for your role play　ロールプレイのリハーサルをする

A. Set rehearsal　リハーサルをセットする

This is a rehearsal for your role play. You will not only perform the role play to make sure that it is "playable," but also practice giving all the instructions.

B. Practice conversation　会話の練習をしましょう

Practice the conversations for your role play. This assumes that all the members will perform the role play and that your group consists of five members. Also, in order to save time, the leader will assign roles rather than have members choose their role.

3. Check rules and procedure　ルールと進行の確認をする

Rules and Procedure
1. Get a card from your teacher, silently read and then memorize the sentence on the card.
2. Discuss the role and converse with members of your group or pair.
3. Rehearsal with members of the group.
4. Stand in front of your classmates and wait for a signal by the teacher.
5. As soon as you get the signal, say your role's sentence clearly and loudly with the members of your group or pair.
6. After your teacher signals, you and your members stop your performance.
7. Your audience or teacher will ask your group questions based on your performance.
8. You or your members should answer the questions.
9. If you have judges, they will give some comment and points.

4. Play the Role play　ロールプレイをする

A. Assign roles among your group members.
グループで役の割り当てをしてください。

B. Conduct the role play among your group members. Correct any problems you may find so that you use your role play successfully in your final review session.
グループでリーダーと演技者になって、ロールプレイをしてください。そして、問題をチェックしてください。

Appendix

Appendix A: Advanced Study

Samurai Melodrama

季節版：侍 メロドラマ

Originated by Brian Kahn

配役	CAST
邪悪な将軍	W (Wicked general)
変な忍者	N (Weird ninja)
美しい姫	L (Beautiful princess)
殿様	P (Prince)
双子の兄弟	S (Twins)
お祖母さん	O (Old lady)
コーラス	C (Cheruse)
百人の 侍	H (100 samurais)

W: 私は邪悪な将軍。美しい姫をさらった。
強くて恐ろしい百人の侍に姫を見張らせた。

（太鼓の音）X　　XX　　　XXX

強くて、気の荒い、千人の兵隊も姫を囲んでいる。

（太鼓の音）X　　XX　　　XXX

恐ろしい侍や、気の荒い兵隊を全部合わせたよりももっと恐ろしいのが、悪い奇妙な忍者。

（太鼓の音）X　　XX　　　XXX

N: 私は悪い、変な忍者。きれいな姫を助けようとして悪い変な忍者を誤魔化そうとする殿様は誰だ。誰もできない、みんなできない。みんな死ぬ。

（シンバルの音）X　　XX　　　　XXX

L: 私は姫、悪い変な忍者より強い侍やすごく怖い兵隊が私の前にいます。
この私を助けようとしている勇敢な殿様を待っています。でも、いやな将軍は忍者や侍や兵隊を置いています。

（フルート／笛の音）X　　XX　　　XXX

C: 待ちながら、涙が出ます。涙が待っています。
でも、いやな将軍に従わない。

W: 姫が従わない。

N: 将軍、それが姫が従わないのです。

W: なぜ、姫が従わない。

N: 姫は誇りが高い。

W: 私はこの世の中で一番邪悪な将軍だ。

N: 将軍、姫は美しい、長い髪がある。

W: 姫の髪を切れ。姫の誇りを捨てろ。そして私に従わせる

C: お姫様、いやな将軍の怒りが怖い。きれいな姫を助ける殿様は誰だ。

ＰＡＲＴＩ：シーン１［城の中］

P: まて、僕はいやな将軍から姫を助けにきた殿様だ

W: 何者だ、

N: これは弱い殿様。難しくない。

W: 美しい姫を助けに来たのか。

P: 勿論。

W: 命を失ってもいいのか

P: 勿論。

N: ハハハハハハ

W: 百人の恐ろしい侍と千人の気の荒い兵隊とこの悪い忍者が見えるか。

P: 勿論

W: それでは約束しよう。百人の強い兵隊を負かした時、十人の強い侍と戦うことを認める。十人の強い侍を負かした時、悪い忍者と戦うことを認める。

L: 全部いっしょかそれとも一人ずつ？

W: いっておこう。DEMOCRATICにやろう。

L: ちょっと待ってください。百人に一人、不公平だわ。

W: もしそなたが従うなら、やめておこう。それなら殿は死なない。

C: きれいな姫が部屋の中でさびしそう。いやな将軍に従うか。

L: 忘れて！

P: ハッ！

L: どうしたのですか。

P: ちょっとしたトリック

N: 待て、次は十人の強い侍と戦うか。

C: ハンサムな殿様は強い侍に勝てるか。城の中でないて待っているきれいな姫は助かるか。

P: ハッ

S: ヤッ

N: もうだめだ。いやな将軍に従いなさい。

C: 変な人はだれですか。城の中でないて待っている姫を誰かが助けに来る。

W: なにものだ。

S: 私達は双子です。おばあさんが私達を見つけた。湖のそばで本当の親を探している。あなたは私達のお父さんでしょう。

W: 私は悪魔に別れ別れにされた双子の子供がいた。そなたたちは私の子供か。

N: 太鼓を打て、もし将軍の子供なら、この音が聞こえる。山の奥からでも、

L: 私を忘れないで

N: 太鼓を打て

C: 子供たちはこの太鼓の音が聞こえるか。城の中で泣いている姫は忘れられてしまうのか。

O: 待て、わたしは子供を見つけたおばあさん、私の鳥が歌うのは一度だけ。そしてずーと歌わない。

L: たすかるわ。

O: 待て、このこおろぎが歌うのは一度だけ。

N: もうみんな聞いた。

O: 待て。

C: おばあさんが勝つか。きれいな姫は助かるか。子供たちがお父さんが見つかるか。

O: マスクを取れ。

W: 何者だ、この私の仮面を取れというのは

N: 将軍、あのおばあさんを殺しましょう。

W: 一緒にやろう

WN: ハッ！

O: このマスクは悪魔のものだ。城の姫はたすかり。兵隊や侍は全部坊さんになる。嫌な将軍は鳥やこうろぎの王様になる。忍者は金の鳥かごになる。この子供はこの城の王様になる。

C: 姫は助かり、いやな将軍は鳥やこおろぎの王様になった。

L: 殿様は助からないの

O: 悲しそうに見えないが、お望みとあらば殿様も助けよう。

C: マスクは取られた。悪魔はマスクを取られ。よくなった。これでおしまい。

X　　XX　　　XXX

Samurai Melodrama

W: I am a wicked general and I kidnapped the beautiful princess. I made 100 strong, frightening samurais keep watch of the princess. 1000 soldiers that are strong, and rough are also surrounding the princess. What's more frightening than the scary samurai or rough soldiers is the evil and weird ninja.

N: I am the evil and weird ninja. Who is the lord that is trying to trick me to save the princess? No one can do it. Everyone will die.

L: I am the princess, and in front of me there are frightening soldiers, the samurais who are stronger than the evil, weird ninjas. I am waiting for the brave prince to save me, but the wicked general placed the ninjas, samurais, and soldiers in front of me.

C: While waiting the princess cries. Her tears are waiting. But, the wicked general will not budge.

W: The princess won't listen.

N: General, the princess will not listen to you.

W: Why won't she listen?

N: The princess has a high pride.

W: I am the most evil general in this world.

N: General, the princess is beautiful and has long hair.

W: Cut the princess' hair, and throw away her pride. Then I will make her listen to me.

C: Princess, the wicked general's anger is scary. Who is the prince that is going to save you?

Part I Scene 1: Inside the Castle

P: Wait, I am the prince that has come to save the beautiful princess from the wicked general.

W: Who are you?

N: This is a weak samurai. It will be easy to beat him.

W: Have you come to save the beautiful princess?

P: Of course.

W: Even if you risk your life?

P: Of course.

N: Hahahahaha.

W: Can you see that I have 100 scary samurais and 1,000 dangerous soldiers, and this evil ninja?

P: Of course .

W: Then let's make this promise: If you kill my100 soldiers, I will let you fight my 10 strongest samurais. When you kill the10 samurais, I will let you challenge the evil ninja.

L: All at once or one at a time?

W: Let me say this. We will make it democratic.

L: Please wait, 100 against one isn't fair!

W: If you listen to what I say, I won't kill him.

C: The princess looks sad in her room. Will she do as the general says?

L: Forget about me!

P: Ha!

L: What happened?

P: Just a small trick.

N: Wait! Now are you going to battle with the 10 strong samurais?

C: Will the handsome prince will beat the strong samurais? Will the pretty princess who is crying and waiting in the castle be saved?

P: Ha!

S: Ya!

N: It's over. Listen to the general .

C: Who is the wried guy? Someone is coming to save the princess who is crying and waiting in the castle.

W: Who is that?

S: We are twins. An old lady found us. We are trying to find our real parents near them lake. You are our father, right?

W: I had twins who were separated by a devil from me. Are you my kids?

N: Play the drums if you guys are the general's sons, you should be able to hear the drums, even from beyond the mountains.

L: Don't forget me!

N: Play the drums!

C; Can the kids hear the drums? Will the princess who is crying in the castle be forgotten?

O: Wait, I am the old lady who found the kids! My bird will sing only once! And never sing again!

L: That will help!

O: Wait this cricket will sing only once!

N: We already heard that.

O: Wait!

C: Will the old lady win? Will the beautiful princess be saved? Will the kinds find their father?

O: Take off your mask.

W: Who is telling me to take off the mask?

N: General, let's kill that old lady.

W: Let's do it together?

W&N: HHHHHAAAAAAA

O: This mask belongs to the devil. The princess in the castle was saved. The soldiers and samurai became monks. The hateful general became the king of crickets and birds. The ninja became a golden birdcage. The children became the king of the castle.

L: What about the prince? Won't he be saved?

O: You don't look so sad. But if you want me to, I will save him.

C: The devil's mask was taken off. And it is now a happy ending. Done!

The End!!!!!!!!!!!!!!!!!!!!!!!!!!

語彙	Vocabulary
邪悪な	wicked
将軍	general
美しい	beautiful
姫	princess
さらった	kidnapped
強くて	strong
恐ろしい	frightening
百人の	100
侍	samurais
見張らせた	made to watch
気の荒い	rough
千人の	1000
兵隊	soldiers
囲んでいる	surrounding
太鼓の音	sound of drums
恐ろしい	frightening
全部	all
合わせる	add
悪い	bad, evil
奇妙な	strange
忍者	ninja
変な	weird
きれいな	beautiful
助け	save
誤魔化す	trick
殿様	prince
誰だ	who?
誰も	no one
死ぬ	die
シンバル	cymbal
すごく怖い	frightening
前	in front of
勇敢な	brave
待っています	waiting
置いています	placed
フルート	flute
笛の音	sound of flute

待ちながら	while I am waiting
涙	tears
出ます	come out
いやな将軍に	wicked general
従わない	not listen to you
誇りが高い	has a lot of pride
この世の中で	in this world
一番邪悪な将軍	the most evil general
長い髪がある	has long hair
髪を切れ	cut the princess' hair
捨てろ。	throw away
従わせる	make her listen
怒りが	anger
怖い	scary
まて	wait
何者だ	who are you?
弱い	weak
難しくない	not difficult
勿論	of course
命	your life
失う	risk
見える	can you see
約束しよう	let's make a promise
負かした時	when you kill/defeat
戦うこと	fight
認める	acknowledge, allow
全部いっしょ	all at once
それとも	or
一人ずつ	one at a time
いっておこう	let me say this.
DEMOCRATICにやろう	make it democratic
不公平	unfair
もしそなたが従うなら	If you listen to what I say
やめておこう	I won't (kill him)
死なない	no die
さびしそう	sadly
忘れて	Forget about me
ハッ	ha
どうしたのですか	what happened ?
ちょっとしたトリック	Just a small trick
勝てるか	can win?
城	castle

ヤッ	ya!
もうだめだ	no good
変な人はだれですか	who is that weird person?
誰か	anyone
私達は	we
双子	twins
見つけた	found
湖のそばで	near the lake
本当の親	our real parents
探していろ	trying to find
悪魔	devil
別れ別れにされた	were separated by
子供がいた	had kids
太鼓を打て	Play the drums
この音が聞こえる	can hear the drums
山の奥からでも	beyond the mountains
私を忘れないで	don't forget me
忘れられてしまうのか	will be forgotten
鳥が歌うのは一度だけ	My bird will sing only once!
ずーと歌わない	never sing again
たすかるわ	that will help
このこおろぎが	this cricket
歌う	sing
一度だけ	only once
もうみんな聞いた	we heard everything already
見つかるか	can find?
マスクを取れ	take off the mask
仮面を取れ	take off the mask
というのは	is telling me to do
殺しましょう	let's kill
一緒にやろう	do it together
たすかり	saved
坊さんになる	became monks
王様になる	became the king
金の鳥かごになる	became the golden birdcage
殿様は助からないの	what about the prince?
悲しそうに	look so sad
見えないが	you don't look
お望みとあらば	if you want me to
マスクはとられた	mask was taken off
これでおしまい	done/end

Appendix B: Great East Japan Earthquake:

"his face was colder than water…"

Diary of 12-year-old Tsunami Victim   **Mainich Daily News April 25th, 2011**

東日本大震災：「顔が水より冷たく…」　被災児童が日記

　「お父さんが軽トラでもどっていった姿を見ました。津波にのみ込まれませんように。そう祈っていました」。巨大地震と大津波が東日本を襲ったあの日、子供たちは何を見、その後をどう生きたのか。岩手県山田町の町立大沢小学校を３月に卒業した箱石佑太君（１２）が毎日小学生新聞に寄せた体験日記には震災と向き合う姿が率直につづられていた。

Yuta Hakoishi, foreground, replies to letters of encouragement he received from across Japan, at Osawa Elementary School in Yamada, Iwate Prefecture, on April 4 (Mainichi)

◇３月１１日
　卒業式の歌の練習をしていました。とてもゆれの大きい地震が来ました。最初は単なる地震だと思っていました。大津波警報が出ても、どうせこないと思っていました。来たとしても１０センチメートル程度の津波だと思っていました。全然違いました。ぼくが見たのは、国道４５号線を水とがれきが流れているところです。お母さんとお父さんが津波が来る前に大沢小に来ているところは見ました。だけどその後、お父さんが軽トラでもどっていった姿を見ました。お父さんのことが不安でした。車を運転しながら津波にのみ込まれませんように。そう祈っていました。

◇３月１８日
　津波から１週間。お母さんは、もうこんなに日がたっているのに、まだお父さんが見えないとあきらめていました。じいやんは泣いて「家も頑張って建てるし、おまえたちだってしっかり学校にいかせられるように頑張るから、お父さんがもしだめだとしても頑張るからな」と言っていました。

◇３月２３日
　卒業式でした。「ありがとう」の歌を歌っている時、お父さんに「お父さん、お父さんのおかげで卒業できたよ。ありがとう」と頭の中で言いました。そしたらなぜか、声がふるえて涙が少し出てきました。その夜、こんな夢を見ました。お母さんとお父さんが宮古のスーパーマーケットから帰ってきた夢でした。

◇３月２５日
　親せきの人の携帯に電話がかかってきました。内容は、お父さんらしき人が消防署の方で見つかったということでした。急いで行ってみると、口を開けて横たわっていたお父さんの姿でした。ねえちゃんは泣き叫び、お母さんは声も出ず、弟は親せきの人にくっついていました。顔をさわってみると、水より冷たくなっていました。
　ぼくは「何でもどったんだよ」と何度も何度も頭の中で言いました。「おれがくよく

よしてどうすんだ」と自分に言いました。でも、言えば言うほど目がうるんでくるばかりです。お父さんの身に付けていたチタン、東京で買った足のお守りや結婚指輪、携帯。そして驚いたのが時計が動いていたことです。お父さんの息が絶えた時も、津波に飲み込まれている時も、ずっと。お父さんの時計は今はぼくのものになっている。ぼくがその時計をなくしたりすることは一生ないだろう。

◇３月２６〜２７日
　見つかった時のお父さんの顔。まだ頭のどこかで見なきゃよかったと。でも見つかったおかげで火葬もできるし、お父さんをさわることができた。お父さんの体は水を飲んだのか胸がふくらんでいるだけだ。やっぱり見つかってよかった。

◇３月２８日
　きょうは火葬の日。ぼくとねえちゃんとお母さんとけいじろうは、手紙を書いて、お父さんと一緒に入れてやりました。拝んでいる時ぼくは「箱石家は頑張って継ぐからまかせて」と言いました。お墓に骨を埋めるまで、ぼくに骨を持たせてくれました。骨をうめてホッとしました。

◇４月７日
　きょうは、ありがたいと心から言える日でした。お父さんとぼくたちの記事を見て、

お父さんが東京マラソンを走った時の写真とお手紙を新聞の人が持ってきてくれました。ぼくたち家族に贈る言葉や、さらにはぼくに贈る言葉の手紙もありました。やっぱりお父さんはすごい。今日は本当にありがたい日だ。

　　　　＊　　　　＊

　箱石君は２５日、１５５人の仲間と一緒に町立山田中学校に入学した。日記は、大沢小の子供たちが復興に立ち向かう様子を紹介する「大沢からの報告」として毎日小学生新聞に１１日に掲載。「何回も読み、涙が止まりません。皆様が少しずつでも前に進める日がくることを願っております」（２人の子を持つ東京都北区の女性）とのメールが届くなど大きな反響を呼んだ。「大沢からの報告」は同紙で随時掲載され、次回は５月１１日の予定。

毎日新聞　2011年4月25日

軽トラ：light truck　　姿：figure　　津波：tsunami　　祈る：pray　　巨大地震：enormous earthquake
襲った：attacked　　卒業：graduation　　体験：experience　　震災：tragedy　　向き合う：face
率直に：frankly　　つづられている：be described　　卒業式：commencement　　歌：song　　練習：practice
単なる：mere　　警報：warning　　程度：about　　違う：different　　国道：National Highway
不安：anxiety　　運転：drive　　１週間：a week　　あきらめる：give up　　しっかり：for sure
頑張る：work hard　　建てる：build　　頭：head　　なぜか：for some reason　　声：voice　　涙：tear
親せき：relatives　　携帯：cell phone　　内容：what they said　　らしき：look like　　消防署：fire station
急いで：rushed　　横たわっていた：lying down　　泣き叫ぶ：cry loudly　　くっつく：cling　　さわる：touch
何度も：many times　　くよくよする：worry　　自分：myself　　目がうるむ：welled up in my eyes
身につけてた：worn　　チタン：Titanium (accessory)　　お守り：amulet　　驚いた：be surprised
動いていた：was working　　息が絶えた：died　　ずっと：all the time　　なくす：lose
一生：in my whole life　　見なきゃよかった：wished I'd never seen　　おかげ：because
火葬：cremation　　胸：chest　　ふくらんでいる：swollen　　やっぱり：after all　　入れてやる：put it in
拝む：pray　　継ぐ：carry on after　　お墓：grave　　骨：bone　　埋める：bury
ホッとしました：feel relieved　　ありがたい：thankful　　心から：from the bottom of my heart
記事：article　　マラソン：marathon　　走った：ran　　写真：photo　　新聞：newspaper　　家族：family
贈る言葉：message　　仲間：friends　　一緒に：together　　町立：municipal　　入学：entering school
日記：diary　　復興：recovery　　立ち向かう：fight against　　様子：situation　　紹介：introduce
報告：reports　　掲載：publication　　止らない：can't stop　　前に進める：can move forward　　届く：reach
反響：response　　同紙：this newspaper　　随時：at anytime　　予定：plan

A. Read the first paragraph of the account using the choosing strategies and answer the following questions.

1. Find the same category of Kanji

    a. 地震：卒業、小学校、運転、震災　　　　b. 津波：電話、冷たい、国道、流れ

2. Write the first sentence: _____

3. Choose the appropriate word in the parenthesis and complete the sentence below.
    佑太君は（西日本、東日本、北日本）の（小学校、中学校、高校）で（津波、火事、戦争）にあった。

B. Read the March 11th diary using the choosing strategies and answer the following questions.

1. Write the first sentence: _____

2. Read happenings and complete Yuta's feelings.

出来事：Happenings	佑太の気持ち：Yuta's feelings
とてもゆれの大きい地震が来た。	最初は＿＿＿＿＿＿＿だと思っていた。
大津波警報が出た。	どうせ津波は＿＿＿＿＿＿と思っていた。 来ても（小さい、大きい）津波だと思っていた。
お父さんが軽トラでもどっていった姿を見た。	＿＿＿＿＿＿＿が不安だった。そして、津波に＿＿＿＿＿＿＿と祈っていた。

C. Read the March 18th diary using the choosing strategies and answer the following questions.

1. Find the similar meaning of Kanji

    a. 頑張る：勉強、日本語、立ち向かう　　　　b. 夢：興味、意味、思う、卒業

2. Write the first sentence: _____

3. Choose the appropriate word in the parenthesis and complete the sentence below.

    （お母さん、お父さん、おじいさん）が佑太君に（お母さん、お父さん、おじいさん）がもしだめでも（頑張ろう、勉強しよう、食べよう）といった。

D. Read the March 23rd diary using the choosing strategies and answer the following questions.

1. Write the first sentence: _____

2. Choose the appropriate word in the parenthesis and complete the sentence below.

    （お母さん、お父さん、おじいさん）の夢を見ました。それは、（お母さん、お父さん、おじいさん）と（お母さん、お父さん、おじいさん）がスーパーマッケットから（頑張って、勉強して、帰って）くるものでした。

E. Read the March 25th diary using the choosing strategies and answer the following questions.

　1. Find the same radical of Kanji and the similar meaning of Kanji

　　a. 顔：親、横、冷、願　　　　　　　　b. 携帯：電話、冷たい、持ち、火葬

　2. Write the first sentence: _____

　3. Read happenings and complete Yuta's feelings.

出来事：Happenings	佑太の気持ち：Yuta's feelings
「おれがくよくよしてどうすんだ」と自分に言った。	言えば言うほど_____ばかりだった。
お父さんの身に付けていた時計を見た。	時計がうごいていたことに（息が絶えた、おどろいた、飲み込まれた）。
お父さんの時計がぼくのものになった。	その時計を_____ことは一生ないだろうと思った。

F. Read the March 26th to 27th diary using the choosing strategies and answer the following questions.

　1. Write the first sentence: _____

　2. Choose the appropriate word in the parenthesis and complete the sentence below.

　　（津波、地震、原発事故）で死んだお父さんを見なきゃよかったと思ったけれど、やっぱり見つかって（よかった、よくなかった、わるかった。）

G. Read the March 28th diary using the choosing strategies and answer the following questions.

　1. Write the first sentence: _____

　2. Choose the appropriate word in the parenthesis and complete the sentence below.

　　（お母さん、お父さん、おじいさん）の火葬の日に、ほくは（漢字、写真、手紙）に、頑張って家を（拝む、埋める、継ぐ）とを書いて入れました。

H. Read the April 7th diary using the choosing strategies and answer the following questions.

　1. Find the same category of Kanji.

　　a. 記事：新聞、日記、生活　　　　　　b. 復興：電話、冷たい、頑張る、火葬

　2. Write the first sentence: _____

　3. Choose the appropriate word in the parenthesis and complete the sentence below.

　　お父さんが（マラソン、新聞、写真）した時の写真と（漢字、手紙、プレゼント）を（新聞、テレビ、ウェブ）の人が持ってきてくれて、うれしかった。

685

I. Read the last paragraph of the article using the choosing strategies and answer the following questions.

1. Write the first sentence: _____

2. Choose the appropriate word in the parenthesis and complete the sentence below.

佑太君が書いた（新聞、テレビ、ウェブ）の記事は、復興についてかかれてあり、読んだ人は（かなしかった、すばらしかった、たのしかった）と思ったでしょう。

Schoolboy's diary reveals struggle of losing father in tsunami

Yuta Hakoishi, foreground, replies to letters of encouragement he received from across Japan, at Osawa Elementary School in Yamada, Iwate Prefecture, on April 4. (Mainichi)
On March 11, the day northeastern Japan was ravaged by a magnitude 9.0 earthquake and tsunami, 12-year-old Yuta Hakoishi saw his father driving back home in his truck, and prayed that he wouldn't be swallowed by the tsunami. It was the last time that the 12-year-old, a student at Osawa Elementary School in the town of Yamada, Iwate Prefecture, saw him alive. The following account that Yuta wrote and submitted to the Mainichi Shogakusei newspaper sheds light on his feelings after the tragedy.

***

March 11: We were practicing a song for our school graduation ceremony, when a huge earthquake hit. At first I thought it was just another earthquake. And even after an alert was issued for a major tsunami, I didn't think there would be one. I thought that if a tsunami did arrive it would only be about 10 centimeters high. But I was completely wrong. What I saw was water and rubble being washed along National Route 45. I saw my mom and dad arrive at Osawa Elementary School before the tsunami arrived. But then I saw my dad going back out in his truck. I was worried about him. "Please don't let him get swallowed by the tsunami while he's driving," I prayed.

March 18: Mom lost hope, saying dad still hadn't been found after all this time. Granddad cried and said, "We'll do our best and build a new home, and make sure that you can all go to school. Even if your dad doesn't make it, we'll do our best."

March 23: The day of our graduation. As we sang the song "Arigato" (Thank you), I was thinking: "Dad, it's because of you that I've been able to graduate. Thank you." Then for some reason, my voice went shaky and I started crying. That night I had a dream. It was a dream about my mom and dad coming back from a supermarket in Miyako.

March 25: One of my relatives got a call on their mobile phone. They said a firefighter had found somebody who looked like my father. We rushed there, and I saw my father lying down, with his mouth open. My older sister started crying. My mom didn't say anything and my younger brother stayed close to our relatives. When I touched my father's face it was colder than water. In my mind I kept thinking, "Why did you go back?" Then I kept telling myself, "What good is it for me to worry?" but the more I said it, the more tears welled up in my eyes. I saw the titanium accessory that my father had worn, a good-luck ankle charm that he bought in Tokyo, and his wedding ring and mobile phone. What surprised me was that his watch was still working. When my father died and even when he was swallowed by the tsunami, it kept ticking. My dad's watch is now mine. I don't think I'll ever lose it my whole life.

March 26-27: Somewhere in my mind I wished I'd never seen the face of my father the way he was when they found him. But because they found him we can cremate his body and I could touch him. Perhaps because he had swallowed water his chest was swollen. It's good that they found him.

March 28: The day of the cremation. My sister, my mom, Keijiro and I wrote letters, and we put them next to my father. While we were bending down to pray I said, "The Hakoishi family will do our best to carry on after you." They let me hold onto the bones until we put them into the grave. I felt relieved when we buried them.

April 7: Today was the day that I could say thank you from the bottom of my heart. A person from the newspaper saw an article about my dad and us, and brought a photo of when my father ran in the Tokyo Marathon and some letters. There was a letter with a message to our family and a message for me. My dad was amazing. Today I'm really thankful.

(Mainichi Japan) April 25, 2011

Appendix C: Verb, Adjective, and Copula Conjugation

plain positive nonpast dictionary form	plain negative nonpast	polite positive nonpast	conditional	volitional	potential	te form	plain positive past	plain negative past
会う au	会わない awanai	会います aimasu	会えば aeba	会おう aoo	会える aeru	会って atte	会った atta	会わなかった awanakatta
書く kaku	書かない kakanai	書きます kakimasu	書けば kakeba	書こう kakoo	書ける kakeru	書いて kaite	書いた kaita	書かなかった kakanakatta
泳ぐ oyogu	泳がない oyoganai	泳ぎます oyogimasu	泳げば oyogeba	泳ごう oyogoo	泳げる oyogeru	泳いで oyoide	泳いだ oyoida	泳がなかった oyoganakatta
話す hanasu	話さない hanasanai	話します hanashimasu	話せば hanaseba	話そう hanasoo	話せる hanaseru	話して hanashite	話した hanashita	話さなかった hanasanakatta
立つ tatsu	立たない tatanai	立ちます tachimasu	立てば tateba	立とう tatoo	立てる tateru	立って tatte	立った tatta	立たなかった tatanakatta
死ぬ shinu	死なない shinanai	死にます shinimasu	死ねば shineba	死のう shinoo	死ねる shineru	死んで shinde	死んだ shinda	死ななかった shinanakatta
飲む nomu	飲まない nomanai	飲みます nomimasu	飲めば nomeba	飲もう nomoo	飲める nomeru	飲んで nonde	飲んだ nonda	飲まなかった nomanakatta
呼ぶ yobu	呼ばない yobanai	呼びます yobimasu	呼べば yobeba	呼ぼう yoboo	呼べる yoberu	呼んで yonde	呼んだ yonda	呼ばなかった yobanakatta
行く iku	行かない ikanai	行きます ikimasu	行けば ikeba	行こう ikoo	行ける ikeru	行って iite	行った iita	行かなかった ikanakatta
ある aru	ない nai	あります arimasu	あれば areba	あろう aroo		あって atte	あった atta	なかった nakatta
帰る kaeru	帰らない kaeranai	帰ります kaerimasu	帰えれば kaereba	帰ろう kaeroo	帰れる kaereba	帰って kaette	帰った kaetta	帰らなかった kaeranakatta
入る hairu	入らない hairanai	入ります hairimasu	入れば haireba	入ろう hairoo	入れる haireru	入って haitte	入った haitta	入らなかった hairanakatta
知る shiru	知らない shiranai	知ります shirimasu	知れば shireba	知ろう shiroo	知れる shireru	知って shitte	知った shitta	知らなかった shiranakatta
走る hashiru	走らない hashiranai	走ります hashirimasu	走えれば hashireba	走ろう hashiroo	走れる hashireru	走って hashitte	走った hashitta	走らなかった hashiranakatta
見る miru	見ない minai	見ます mimasu	見れば mireba	見よう miyoo	見れる mireru	見て mite	見た mita	見なかった minakatta
起きる okiru	起きない okinai	起きます okimasu	起きれば okireba	起きよう okiyoo	起きられる okirareru	起きて okite	起きた okita	起きなかった okinakatta
食べる taberu	食べない tabenai	食べます tabemasu	食べれば tabereba	食べよう tabeyoo	食べられる taberareru	食べて tabete	食べた tabeta	食べなかった tabenakatta
教える oshieru	教えない oshienai	教えます oshiemasu	教えれば oshiereba	教えよう oshieyoo	教えられる oshierareru	教えて oshiete	教えた oshieta	教えなかった oshienakatta
する suru	しない shinai	します shimasu	すれば sureba	しよう shiyoo	できる dekiru	して shite	した shita	しなかった shinakatta
来る kuru	来ない konai	来ます kimasu	来れば kureba	来よう koyoo	来れる koreru	来て kite	来た kita	来なかった konakatta

い Adjective conjugation

plain positive nonpast dictionary form	polite positive nonpast	plain negative nonpast	plain positive past	plain negative past	te form	adverbial	polite negative nonpast	polite negative past	pre-nominal
大きい おお	大きい です	大きく ない	大き かった	大きく なかった	大きくて	大きく	大きく ありません 大きくない です	大きくありま せんでした 大きく なかったです	大きい
ookii	ookiidesu	ookikunai	ookikatta	ookiku nakatta	ookikute	ookiku	ookikuarimasen ookikunaidesu	ookikuarimasendeshita ookikunakattadesu	ookii
美しい うつく	美しい です	美しく ない	美し かった	美しく なかった	美しくて	美しく	美しく ありません 美しくない です	美しくあり ませんでした 美しくな かったです	美しい
utsu kushii	utsukushii desu	utsukushiku nai	utsukushi katta	utsukushiku nakatta	utsukushikute	utsukushiku	utsukushiku arimasen utsukunaidesu	utsukushikuarimasen deshita utsukushiku nakattadesu	utsukushii
いい	いいです	よくない	よかった	よく なかった	よくて	よく	よく ありません よくない です	よくありま せんでした よくなかった です	いい
ii	iidesu	yokunai	yokatta	yoku nakatta	yokute	yoku	yokuarimasen yokunaidesu	yokuarimasen deshita yokunakattadesu	ii
食べたい た	食べたい です	食べたく ない	食べた かった	食べたく なかった	食べたくて	食べたく	食べたく ありません 食べたく ないです	食べたくあり ませんでした 食べたく なかったです	食べたい
tabetai	tabetaidesu	tabetakunai	tabetakatta	tabetaku nakatta	tabetakute	tabetaku	tabetaku arimasen tabetaku naidesu	tabetaku arimasendeshita tabetaku nakattadesu	tabetai

な Adjective conjugation

polite positive nonpast	plain negative nonpast	plain positive nonpast dictionary form	plain positive past	plain negative past	te form	adverbial	polite negative nonpast	polite negative past	pre-nomi-nal
静か しず	静かです	静かじゃ ない	静かだ	静か だった	静かじゃ なかった	静かで	静かに	静かじゃ ありません 静かじゃ ないです	静かじゃあり ませんでした 静かじゃ なかったです	静かな
shizu	shizukadesu	shizukajanai	shizukada	shizuka datta	shizukaja nakatta	shizukade	shizukani	shizuka ja arimasen shizukaja naidesu	shizukaja arimasen shizukaja nakattadesu	shizukana

Noun + Copula

本だ ほん	本です	本じゃ ない 本では ない	本だ	本だった なかった 本では ありませんでした	本じゃ なかった 本じゃない 本じゃない	本で		本じゃ ありません	本じゃありま せんでした 本じゃ なかったです	本の 本で ある
honda	hondesu	honjanai hondewa nai	honda	hondatta hondewa arimasendeshita	hon ja nakatta honjanai	honde		honja arimasen	honja arimasen deshhon dewa honja nakattadesu	hon no hon dearu

689

Appendix D: Kanji List

Chapter 1

新出漢字1
書く
話す
読む
聞く
見る
来る
言う
行く

新出漢字2
飲む
食べる
休む
作る
使う
帰る
会う
立つ

新出漢字3
春
秋
冬
夏
次ぎ
始め
今
住んでいる

新出漢字4
私
母
父
妹
弟
兄
姉
友

認識漢字1
夏休み
名前
学校
好き
才
中学
高校
〜年生
一日
二日
三日

認識漢字2
四日
五日
六日
七日
八日
九日
十日
二十日
〜曜日

認識漢字3
何人何人
何年何年
何語何分
何時
父
母
兄
姉
妹
弟
私

認識漢字4
正しい
答える
今週
先週
来週
来月
今月
先月

追加漢字1
冬休み
野球
折り紙
出身
趣味
最高
若者
刀
紹介

追加漢字2
売る
買う
誕生日
例えば
計画
環境
考える
発表
成果

追加漢字3
全部
終わり
英語
勉強
東京
泳ぐ
旅行
仕事
週末

Chapter 2

新出漢字 1
回
間
上
下
左
右
前
後

新出漢字 2
体
手
足
目
耳
口
頭
名

新出漢字 3
気
何
出
入
元
音
電
国

新出漢字 4
大
小
男
女
子
文
中
車

認識漢字 1
回
復習
今日
昨日
明日
去年
今年
来年

認識漢字 2
毎日
毎週
毎年
毎月
午前
午後
早い
説明
漢字

認識漢字 3
会話
季節
一番
問題
名詞
動詞
形容詞
助詞

認識漢字 4
決める
記号
言葉
例
絵
単語
選ぶ
質問
番号

追加漢字 4
深まる
新入生
増える
交流
講堂
始まる
全員
参加
健康

追加漢字 5
色色
次
写真部
面白い
国際
教育
別に
特に
撮る

Chapter 3

新出漢字１
田
森
川
山
町
林
海
店

新出漢字２
雨
天
化
度
暑
寒
雪
晴

新出漢字３
校
島
石
平
野
道
市
村

新出漢字４
花
魚
屋
肉
東
西
北
南

新出漢字５
場
公
交
所
通
週
寺
州

新出漢字６
社
夜
買
家
京
駅
園
地

認識漢字１
自然
人口
交通
家
会社
工場
店
東西南北
東京

認識漢字２
池
空
湖
海岸
砂漠
空港
駅
公園
京都

認識漢字３
電気
電話
静かな
軽い
重い
強い
弱い
遠い
便利な
不便な
厳しい

認識漢字４
時間
場所
昼休み
食べ物
飲み物
入る
寝る
起きる
大阪

認識漢字５
八百屋
市役所
案内所
火山
交番
銀行
寺
神社

認識漢字６
平野
土地
都市
教会
港
橋
住宅
サッカー場

追加漢字６
出会い
風景
日本的
観光客
音読型
道路
劇場
見学
遊ぶ

追加漢字７
野外
動物園
有名
習う
盆踊り
未来
地区
辺り
時代

追加漢字８
明治
昭和
建物
現代的
国連
関係
博物館
中華街

Chapter 4

新出漢字 1
楽
新
古
多
少
広
安
高

新出漢字 2
数
科
外
英
親
半
朝
昼

新出漢字 3
教
育
門
物
理
歴
史
問

新出漢字 4
長
明
近
低
暗
早
正
短

新出漢字 5
速
美
青
赤
白
黒
遠
静

新出漢字 6
心
思
好
知
毎
同
意
味

認識漢字 1
教室
宿題
行事
卒業生
生徒数
科目
教員数
活動

認識漢字 2
部屋
部長
活動
目的
地図
図
写真
教材
品詞

認識漢字 3
練習
3回
最初
最後
家族
曲げる
紹介

認識漢字 4
新学期
卒業式
運動会
文化祭
試験期間
運動系
文化系
制服
規則

認識漢字 5
上着
下着
靴下
洋服
靴
着る
脱ぐ
着物
和服

認識漢字 6
風が強い
雷雨
気温
台風
涼しい
暖かい
気持ちがいい
方角

追加漢字 9
料理店
中心
感じ
地下鉄
郵便局
果物
授業
忙しい

追加漢字 10
磨く
起きる
歯
洗う
頭
自転車
他に
主食
室内

追加漢字 11
変わる
活動
興味
持つ
覚える
機械
専攻
交通
事故

Glossary
English–Japanese

English	かな	漢字	参照
1000 people	せんにん	千人	4.3
100mm	ひゃくミリ	百ミリ	3.7
10th grade	じゅうがくねんせい	十年生	4.2
10 yd	じゅうヤード	十ヤード	3.7
15th	じゅうごにち	十五日	1.2, 1.2.1
16 year	じゅうろくねん	十六年	1.2
18 years old	18さい	十八才	1.3, 2.4
1cm	いちセンチ	一センチ	3.7
1ft	いちフィート	一フィート	3.7
1in	いちインチ	一インチ	3.7
1m	いちメートル	一メートル	3.7
20 people	にじゅうにん	人二十人	4.2
20C	せっしにじゅうど	摂氏二十度	3.1
250 people	にひゃくごじゅうにん	二百五十人	4.2
300 yen	さんびゃくえん	三百円	1.2, 1.1.9
30000 people	さんまんにん	三万人	4.3
35 degrees Celsius	せっしさんじゅうごど	摂氏三十五度	3.4, 3.5, 3.6
35 people	さんじゅうごにん	三十五人	3.7
7 people	しちにん	七人	4.2
8 o'clock	はちじ	八時	1.2 1.2.1
85F (85 degrees Fahr)	かしはちじゅうごど	華氏八十五度	3.1
9.11 incident	9.11じけん	9.11事件	4.9
a great amount	ただい	多大	3.6,4.3
a housing (an apartment) complex	だんち	団地	3.3, 3.8
a little	すこし	少し	1.4, 3.4, 3.6, 4.4, 4.9
a little	ちょっと		1.4, 2.4, 4.4, 1.2.2
a part	いちぶ	一部	4.9
a street stall	やたい	屋台	3.3, 3.8
ability, talent, age	さい	オ	1,2
about	について		2.1, 3.1, 4.9
about 1 meter 50 centimeters	いちメートルごじゅっセンチぐらい	一メートル五十センチぐらい	3.1
about 20 days	にじゅうにちぐらい	二十日ぐらい	3.1
about zero degrees centigrade	ぜろどぐらい	0度ぐらい	3.1
about, approximately	ぐらい		3.7
above	うえの	上の	4.3
academic subjects	きょうかめい	教科名	4.3
academy	アカデミー		1.1
accessory	アクセサリー		4.5
accident	じこ	事故	4.6
accomplishment	せいか	成果	1.6, 2.4
according to~	～によると		1.5
accurately	せいかく(な)	正確(な)	1.6, 3.1, 3.7
acquaintance	ちじん	知人	4.8
acre	エーカー		3.8
act	えんぎする	演技する	2.5. 3.8
acting	えんぎ	演技	2.5, 4.3
action movie	アクションえいが	アクション映画	1.5
active	かつどうてき (な)	活動的な	3.8
active, thriving	さかん	さかん	4.5
actively	かつやく	活躍	4.6, 4.7
activity	かつどう	活動	1.4, 2.3, 2.4,4.2, 4.6, 1.3.11
actually	じっさい	実際	2.4, 4.7
add	くわえる	加える	3.3
add	たしてください	足してください	4.4
address	じゅうしょ	住所	3.8
additional	ついか	追加	2.5
additions	たしざん	足し算	4.2, 4.8
adequately, properly	てきとうである	適当である	4.7
adjective	けいようし	形容詞	2.1, 3.1, 3.2,3.7, 4.2
adjustment	ちょうせい	調整	3.7
administration	ぎょうせい	行政	3.8
adults	おとな	大人	3.6, 4.7
adverb	ふくし	副詞	3.4
advisor	アドバイザー		1.3, 4.8
afforestation	りょっか	緑化	4.3
African-American	アフリカけいアメリカじん	アフリカ系アメリカ人	3.8
African-literature	アフリカぶんがく	アフリカ文学	4.7
after	あと	後	4.9
after entering	にゅうがくご	入学後	4.9
after school	ほうかご	放課後	2.5
after studying	べんきょうしたあと	勉強した後	2.7
afternoon	ひる	昼	3.5, 4.6
afternoon	ごご	午後	2.3
afterward	そのあと	その後	1.4, 2.4
afterword	あとがき	後書き	4.8, 4.9
again	もういちど	もう一度	1.7
age	とし	年	1.3, 1.3.6
ages	ねんれい	年齢	1.3
age, ability, talent	さい	オ	1,2
agreement	どうい	同意	4.7
agriculture	のうぎょう	農業	3.8
agriculture fields	はたけ	畑	3.1, 4.2
ahead	さきに	先に	2.5
aim	あて	当て	2.2
air conditioner	エアコン(エアーコンディショナー)		3.6, 3.9, 4.4, 4.9
airplane	ひこうき	飛行機	1.3, 1.3.1
air pollution	たいきおせん	大気汚染	3.8
airport	くうこう	空港	1.7, 3.1
Akihabara (place name)	あきはばら	秋葉原	1.4
alcohol	おさけ	お酒	4.8
algebra	だいすう	代数	4.3
all	ぜんぶ	全部	1.5, 1.6, 2.4, 4.9
all day long	いちにちじゅう	一日中	3.4, 3.9
all directions	とうざいなんぼく	東西南北	3.2
all members	ぜんいん	全員	2.4
all right	だいじょうぶ	大丈夫	3.8, 3.9
almost	だいたい	大体	1.6, 3.7
along	そう	沿う	3.4, 3.8, 3.9
also/then/in addition/ moreover	それから		1.1, 3.1, 3.3,3.5, 3.7, 4.2, 4.5, 1.2.2
although	けど		3.8, 3.9, 4.8
alumni/alumnae	そつぎょうせい	卒業生	4.4, 4.9
always	いつも		1.1 2.4, 4.5, 4.7, 4.9, 1.3.5
America	アメリカ	亜米利加	1.1, 3.6, 1.0.2
American	アメリカじん	アメリカ人	1.3, 1.3.1
American football	アメフト		2.4
American football	アメフト(アメリカンフットボール)		4.4, 4.7
Amnesty International	アムネスティ インターナショナル		4.3
amount of precipitation	こうすいりょう	降水量	3.7
amount of rain	うりょう	雨量	3.7
amount of snowfall	せきせつりょう	積雪量	3.7

English	Kana	Kanji	References
amusement park	ゆうえんち	遊園地	3.1, 3.2, 3.3, 3.7
analytical	ぶんせきてきである	分析的である	4.8
and	し		2.7
and	で〜で		4.2
and	くて		4.1, 4.2
and	て		4.1, 4.2
and	で		4.1, 4.2
and then, and finally	そして		1.5, 3.7, 4.3, 4.5, 4.8
and, then	それで		3.3
Andy	アンディ		1.3
angers easily	おこりやすい	怒りやすい	4.8
animal	どうぶつ	動物	2.6, 3.7
animation	アニメ		1.1, 3.5, 4.6, 1.3.2
announcement	おしらせ	お知らせ	4.9
announcement	アナウンス		3.8
annual event	ねんじゅうぎょうじ	年間行事	4.5
annual school festival	ぶんかさい	文化祭	2.7, 4.3
answer	こたえ	答え	2.3, 4.7
answer	こたえる／こたえます	答える／答えます	1.1, 2.3, 4.9, 1.3.11
anthropology	じんるいがく	人類学	4.8
Anything else?	ほかにありますか	他にありますか	3.2, 4.9
anyone else	ほかにいますか	他にいますか	2.2
apartment	アパート		3.8
apartment house	アパート		4.4, 4.9
appealing, charming	みりょくてき（な）	魅力的な	3.8
apple	りんご	林檎	2.5, 3.1, 1.0.2
appropriate	てきせつ（な）	適切な	3.3, 3.8
approximately-	やく	約	3.8
April	しがつ	四月	3.6
aquarium	すいぞくかん	水族館	3.8
Arabic	アラビアご	アラビア語	4.3
Are there any who are still writing?	まだかいているひと、いますか。	まだ書いている人、いますか。	3.2
Are you ready?	いいですか。		3.2
Are you done?	できましたか。		2.2
area	めんせき	面積	3.8
Aria (name of girl)	アリア		3.2
Arizona	アリゾナ		4.3
arm	うで	腕	2.1
around	ごろ	頃	2.7
around	まわり	回り	3.1, 3.3. 3.8, 3.9, 4.2
arrive	つく	着く	2.4, 2.5
art	げいじゅつ	芸術	2.5, 4.3, 4.4
art	びじゅつ	美術	4.3
article	きじ	記事	4.8
art appreciation	げいじゅつかんしょう	芸術観賞	4.4
Asahi mura (village of Asahi)	あさひむら	朝日村	3.5
Asakusa (place name)	あさくさ	浅草	1.4
Asian	アジアけい	アジア系	3.8
Asian	アジアじん	アジア人	3.8, 4.9
Asian restaurant	アジアりょうりてん	アジア料理店	3.8
as much as possible	できるだけ		3.4, 3.9
assemble, collect	あつめる	集める	3.8
assembly hall	ぎじどう	議事堂	3.8
assistant, vice	ふく	副	4.8
assign tasks	わりあて	割り当て	2.5, 4.9
astronomy	てんもんがく	天文学	3.5, 4.3
at	で		1.1, 1.0.2
at that time	そのころ	その頃	1.7
at (ni particle)	に		1.1, 1.4.7
stand in line	ならぶ	並ぶ	3.8, 3.9
athletic tournament	スポーツたいかい	スポーツ大会	3.8
Atlanta	アトランタ		4.3
ATM	エーティーエム		3.5
attach	つける	付ける	2.2
attractive, fabulous	すてき（な）	素敵な	1.4,1.5, 3.7, 4.2, 1.0.2
auction	オークション		3.8
audio equipment store	オーディオショップ		3.8
auditorium	こうどう	講堂	2.4,3.7, 4.6, 4.7, 1.2.1
August	はちがつ	8月	3.5, 1.2.1
author	さっか	作家	4.5, 4.9
auto repair shop	じどうしゃしゅうりこうじょう	自動車修理工場	3.8
automobile dealer	じどうしゃはんばいてん	自動車販売店	3.8
autumn foliage	こうよう	紅葉	3.8
autumn/fall	あき	秋	1.3, 2.7, 4.2,4.5, 1.1.4
avalanche	なだれ	雪崩	3.8
average highest temperature	へいきんさいこうおんど	平均最高温度	3.6
awkward	てきせつじゃない	適切じゃない	4.2
back	うしろ	後ろ	2.3, 3.1
back	うら	裏	3.8, 3.9
bad	わるい	悪い	3.1, 3.7
bad instruction	おしえかたがへtだ	教え方が下手だ	4.8
badminton	バドミントン		4.3
bag	かばん	鞄	2.4, 1.0.16
bagel	ベーグル		3.4, 3.9
bake sale	ベークセール		3.8, 4.8, 1.4.9
bakery	パンや	パン屋	3.1, 1.3.11
ball	ボール		3.3, 1.4.9
ball sports day	きゅうぎたいかい	球技大会	4.4
banana	バナナ		2.3, 3.4, 4.3, 1.1.1
band	バンド		4.4,4.5
bank	ぎんこう	銀行	3.4
bank, embankment	どて	土手	3.6
bank, embankment	ていぼう	堤防	3.8
barbershop	とこや	床屋	3.8
base	きち	基地	3.8
baseball	やきゅう	野球	1.4, 4.2, 4.3, 1.1.6
baseball cap	やきゅうぼう	野球帽	4.5
baseball club	やきゅうぶ	野球部	4.7, 4.9, 1.1.9
baseball field	やきゅうじょう	野球場	3.8
baseball stadium	きゅうじょう	球場	1.4
based on	にもとづいて	に基づいて	3.6
basic	きほん	基本	3.4
basic information	きほんじょうほう	基本情報	4.3
basin	ぼんち	盆地	3.8
basketball	バスケットボール		4.3
bay, gulf	わん	湾	3.8
Bay bridge	ベイブリッジ		3.5, 3.8
bazaar	バザー		3.8
[be〜]?	か		1.1, 1.1.6
be (existence)	います(いる)、あります(ある)	居る、有る	3.3, 3.7, 1.0.28
be able to	できる／できます	出来る／出来ます	1.6, 4.9
be able to	ことができます	ことが出来ます	3.1
be awakened/ realize	きがつく	気がつく	4.8
be born	うまれる	生まれる	2.4, 1.4.9
be called	いわれる	言われる	3.8, 3.9
be favored	このまれている	好まれている	4.7
be frozen over	こおりがはる	氷が張る	3.8
be good at	とくい	得意	4.2, 4.6, 1.3.5
be in charge of	たんとうする	担当する	4.8, 4.9
be pleased by you	きにいられたい	気に入られたい	4.8
be popularized/prevailing	ふきゅうしている	普及している	4.9
be relieved	ほっと		4.4
beach volleyball	ビーチバレー		1.4

beach, seashore	かいがん	海岸	3.1, 4.3
beauty shop	びよういん	美容院	3.8
become	なる／なります	成る／成ります	2.1, 4.8
because of explaining	せつめいするから	説明するから	3.8, 3.9
because, so	から		2.7, 4.7
because, so	ので		2.4, 4.6
become clear/sunny	はれる	晴れる	3.5
become cloudy	くもる	曇る	3.8
become such that	ようになります		4.6, 4.8
before going	いくまえ	行く前	3.8, 3.9
before studying	べんきょうするまえ	勉強する前	2.7
began/start	はじめる／はじめる	始める／始めます	2.3, 3.7, 1.0.9
beginning	はじめ	始め	2.1.1, 1.3.0
behind	おくれている		4.9
belongings	もちもの	持ち物	4.5, 4.9
bench	ベンチ		3.3
bend	まげる／まげます	曲げる／曲げます	2.1, 2.4, 4.4
Berlin	ベルリン		3.6
besides, else	ほかに	他に	2.2, 4.5
best, superb	さいこう	最高	1.1, 1.4, 3.3,3.5, 4.3
best, superb	いちばん	一番	4.8
between	あいだ	間	3.1, 3.3
bicycle	じてんしゃ	自転車	1.3, 4.4, 4.5 1.3.9
bicycle parking lot	じてんしゃおきば	自転車置き場	3.3, 3.8
bicycle parking lot	ちゅうりんじょう	駐輪場	3.8
bicycle shop	じてんしゃや	自転車屋	3.8
big	おおきい	大きい	1.3. 3.2, 4.2, 1.3.7
big city	だいとし	大都市	4.3
big hotel	おおきいホテル	大きいホテル	3.7
biggest	さいだい	最大	2.4
bilingual	バイリンガル		4.6, 4.9
Bill	ビル		2.5
billion	じゅうおく	十億	3.4
Bince (boy's name)	ビンス		2.3
bingo game	ビンゴゲーム		3.1
bingo sheet	ビンゴシート		3.7
biology	せいぶつ	生物	4.1, 4.3, 1.3.11
birth place	しゅっしん	出身	1.1, 1.3, 4.2, 1.3.6
bitter cold wind	こがらし	木枯らし	3.8
black	くろい、くろ	黒い、黒	2.3, 3.3, 1.1.9
black people	こくじん	黒人	3.8, 4.7
blank spaces	くうらん	空欄	4.4, 4.5
blazer	ブレザー		4.5
bloom	さく	咲く	1.5, 3.6, 3.9
blossom	さきます	咲きます	1.5, 1.7
blouse	ブラウス		4.8
blue	あおい	青い	2.5, 3.4, 1.0.2
blue sky	あおぞら	青空	3.8
board	ボード		3.2, 1.0.1
boarding school	ボーディングスクール		4.3
boat	ボート		1.3, 4.3
Bob	ボブ		2.5
body	からだ	体	2.1, 4.9, 1.4.6
bon dance	ぼんおどり	盆踊り	3.4, 3.5
book	ほん	本	1.5, 1.1, 3.7, 1.0.2
book club	どくしょクラブ	読書クラブ	3.8
booklet	しょうさっし	小冊子	3.8
boots	ブーツ		4.8
bookstore	ほんや	本屋	3.1, 3.2
boring, not interesting	つまらない		1.4, 3.5, 3.7,4.2, 1.3.5
borrow, rent	かりる	借りる	3.5

borrow, accept	とりいれる	取り入れる	2.7
Boston	ボストン		1.3, 1.6, 3.6, 1.3.6
botanical garden	しょくぶつえん	植物園	3.8
both sides	りょうがわ	両側	3.8
boutique	ブティック		3.8
bowling	ボーリング		4.3
bowling alley	ボーリングじょう	ボーリング場	3.7
box	はこ	箱	3.3
boy	おとこのこ	男の子	3.1
boyfriend	ボーイフレンド		4.2
boys and girls	だんじょ	男女	4.3
boy's school	だんしこう	男子高	4.3
bra	ブラジャー		4.5
brainstorming	ブレインストーミング		2.2,4.9
brave	ゆうかん	勇敢	4.8, 1.3.11
breaking game for watermelon	すいかわり	西瓜割り	1.4
bread	パン		2.3, 1.1.7
break up into small groups	しょうグループになってください		3.2
		小グループになってください	
breakfast	あさごはん	朝ご飯	1.4, 4.4, 1.4.1
bridge	はし	橋	3.7, 3.8
bring	もってくる	持ってくる	2.5, 4.5
brush	みがく	磨く	2.4, 4.5
buckwheat noodle	そば	蕎麦	2.5,4.4, 1.2.4
Buddhism	ぶっきょうけい	仏教系	4.3
build	なりたっています	成り立っています	4.6
build,construct	けんせつする	建設する	3.8
building	たてもの	建物	3.5, 3.9
building	ビル		3.5, 3.9
bus	バス		1.3, 1.3.1
bus going to peace hospital	へいわびょういんいき	平和病院行き	3.8, 3.9
bush, thicket	やぶ	薮	3.8
busy	いそがしい	忙しい	1.3, 1.4, 3.6,4.4, 1.3.5
but, however	けれど、けれども、けど		4.2
but, however	でも		1.1, 3.1, 3.7, 1.3.5
butcher	にくや	肉屋	3.1, 3.2, 3.7
buy	かう／かいます	買う／買います	1.4, 3.5, 3.7,4.7, 4.9
by	で		1.1, 1.3.1
by all means	ぜひ	是非	3.4, 3.8, 3.9
by numbers	すうじで	数字で	3.4
by self	じぶんで	自分で	4.9
by the way	ところで		4.8
by what means	なんで	何で	1.3, 1.4, 1.3.4
bye (to person leaving)	いってらっしゃい	行ってらっしゃい	3.8, 3.9
cafeteria	カフェテリア		1.2, 3.3, 4.2, 1.2.1
cake	ケーキ		1.5, 4.2, 4.4, 1.0.12
cake store (patisserie store)	ケーキや	ケーキ屋	3.1, 3.7
calamity, disaster	さいがい	災害	3.8
calculus	びせきぶん	微積分	4.3
California	カリフォルニア		3.6
called	よんでいる	呼んでいる	1.5
calm and cool	れいせいな	冷静な	4.2
calorie	カロリー		4.6
calm, mild, tranquil	おだやか（な）	穏やかな	3.8
camera	カメラ		1.4, 3.5, 1.4.10
camera shop	カメラや	カメラ屋	3.8
camisole	キャミソール		4.5
camp	がっしゅく	合宿	4.4
camp	キャンプ		1.4, 3.5
campground	キャンプじょう	キャンプ場	3.8
campus	キャンパス		4.3

can eat	たべることができる	食べることができる 2.5	
can have an interesting experience	おもしろいけいけんができる	おもしろい経験ができる 4.7	
can listen	きける	聞ける	3.4, 3.9
can read	よめる	読める	2.7, 4.8
can see, be visible	みえる	見える	3.8,
Can you repeat it again?	もういちどおねがいします	もういちどお願いします	3.2, 1.1.6
can you say it in English?	えいごでいうことができますか		4.9
		英語で言うことが出来ますか	
Canada	カナダ		1.1, 1.3, 3.7, 1.3.2
Canadian	カナダ人	カナダ人	1.3, 4.2
capital city	しゅと	首都	3.8
captain	キャプテン		1.3, 4.6.4.9, 1.3.11
caption	キャプション		4.9
car	くるま	車	1.1, 1.3, 3.3, 1.3.1
card	カード		2.1, 2.5, 3.2
Caribbean Sea	カリブかい	カリブ海	3.3
Casablanca	カサブランカ		3.5
casual	カジュアル		4.8
cat	ねこ	猫	2.1, 3.3, 3.7, 1.0.1
celebrate	おいわい	お祝い	4.7
cell phone	けいたいでんわ	携帯電話	4.5
cellular phone	けいたい	携帯	2.6
Celsius	せっし	摂氏	3.1, 3.5
center	まんなか	真ん中	3.1, 3.3
centered	ちゅうしん	中心	3.5, 3.9, 4.4
centimeters	センチメートル		3.7
Central High School	セントラル・こうこう	セントラル高校	1.3
Central Park	セントラル・パーク		3.4, 1.3.11
ceremonial meeting between old and new students	たいめんしき	対面式	4.4
ceremonies	しき	式	4.4
chairperson	ぎちょう	議長	2.1, 1.2.4
change	かわる	変わる	4.6
change	かえる／かえます	変える／変えます	1.4
chapter	チャプター		4.6
characteristics	とくちょう	特徴	4.8, 1.3.1
chart	ひょう	表	2.3, 3.4
charter school	チャータースクール		4.3
charter school	とくべつきょかこう	特別認可校	4.3
chat	おしゃべり	お喋り	2.4, 2.6, 2.7
check	チェック		2.2, 4.9
check	チェックする		1.1, 3.3
cheer leader	チア・リーダー		2.4, 4.7
cheer, support	おうえんする	応援する	1.1, 1.5, 4.4
cheering	おうえん	応援	1.5
cheese cake	チーズケーキ		4.4　1.2.6
chemistry	かがく	化学	3.4, 3.6, 4.1,4.3, 1.3.1
cherry blossom	さくら	桜	1,5, 1.7, 3.6,3.9, 4.8
chew	かむ／かみます	噛む／噛みます	2.6
Chicago	シカゴ		3.6, 4.3
child(ren)	こども	子供	2.6
chilly	はだざむい	肌寒い	3.8
Chinatown	ちゅうかがい	中華街	3.5, 3.9
Chinese	ちゅうごくご	中国語	1.3, 3.4, 3.5,4.3, 1.3.1
Chinese food	ちゅうごくりょうり	中国料理	1.5, 3.5, 3.9
Chinese restaurant	ちゅうかりょうりてん	中華料理店	3.8
chocolate	チョコ（チョコレート）		4.4, 4.9
choose	えらぶ／えらびます	選ぶ／選びます	2.1, 2.5, 3.5, 4.9
chorus competition	がっしょうコンクール	合唱コンクール	4.4

Christian	キリストきょうけい	キリスト教系	4.3
Christmas	クリスマス		4.8
church	きょうかい	教会	3.7, 3.8
cigarette	たばこ	煙草	4.8
circle	えんけい	円形	4.4
circle	まる	円	1.3
circle	まるでかこんでください	まるで囲んでください	3.3 4.3
circle with red	あかマル	赤マル	3.3
cities of Japan	にほんのとし	日本の都市	3.3
city	し	市	3.7, 4.3
city hall	しやくしょ	市役所	3.8
city, urban area	とし	都市	3.8, 4.2
class	クラス		4.2
class	じゅぎょう	授業	2.5, 2.7,4.4, 4.7
class meeting	がっきゅうかい	学級会	4.9
classic	クラシック		1.5, 4.4, 1.3.8
classics	こてん	古典	4.3
classify	ぶんるいする	分類する	3.5, 4.4, 4.6
classmate	クラスメート		3.4, 4.3, 4.4, 4.5
classroom	きょうしつ	教室	1.3, 2.4, 2.7,3.7, 4.2, 4.4, 1.2.1
clean (adj)	きれいです	綺麗です	1.3, 3.5, 3.7
clean up (n)	そうじ	掃除	1.3, 1.4.10
clean, beautiful	きれい(な)	綺麗	1.1, 3.1, 4.2 1.3.1
clear air	たんたかく	天高く	3.8, 3.9
clearly	はっきり		1.6, 1.1.9
cliff	がけ	崖	3.8
climate	きこう	気候	3.8
climate	てんこう	天候	3.8, 3.9
clinic	いいん	医院	3.8
clinic	しんりょうしょ	診療所	3.8
clothes	ようふく	洋服	4.5
clothing store	ようひんてん	洋品店	3.8
cloud	くも	雲	3.8
cloudy	くもり	曇り	3.1, 3.6
club	クラブ		1.3, 3.5, 4.2, 1.3.2
club	ぶ	部	3.3, 4.9
club activities	クラブかつどう	クラブ活動	4.4, 4.7
club/team camps	ぶかつどうがっしゅく	部活動合宿	4.4
coach	コーチ		1.3, 3.7, 4.7, 1.0.14
coat	コート		3.7, 4.5
coeducation	きょうがっこう	共学校	4.3
coffee shop	コーヒーショップ		3.1, 3.2, 3.7
coffee	コーヒー		1.2, 1.5, 3.7,4.2, 1.0.16
coffee shop, cafe	カフェ		3.8
coffee shop	きっさてん	喫茶店	3.8
cola	コーラ		2.5, 3.2, 4.2, 1.0.21
cold (weather)	さむい	寒い	1.1, 1.4, 3.6,4.2, 1.0.2
cold day	さむいひ	寒い日	3.1
college, university	だいがく	大学	2.5, 3.6, 4.4,4.6, 1.1.9
colorful	カラフルで		4.5
column	らん	欄	4.3, 4.4
combine	つなげる	繋げる	4.2
come	くる／きます	来る／来ます	1.3, 4.7　1.4.7
come (polite)	まいります	参ります	3.8, 3.9
comedy	コメディー		1.5
come to understand	わかってくる	分かってくる	4.5, 4.9
comfortable, pleasant	かいてき(な)	快適な	3.8
comment	コメント		1.4, 1.6, 4.6,4.9, 1.2.6
commerce	しょうぎょう	商業	3.8

committees	いいんかい	委員会	4.6, 4.8
common	きょうどう	共同	4.8
community center	こうみんかん	公民館	3.1, 4.2
commute	かよう	通う	3.8, 4.9
commuter partner	いっしょにくるひと	一緒に来る人	1.3
company	かいしゃ	会社	3.1,3.2, 3.5, 3.7, 4.3, 1.4.10
comparative statement	ひかくのぶん	比較の文	3.6
comparatively	ひかくてき	比較的	3.6, 3.8, 3.9
compare	くらべる	比べる	4.8
compare	ひかくする	比較する	3.6, 3.8
compare	ひかくをする	比較をする	3.1, 3.6
comparison	ひかく	比較	3.1, 3.6
competitions	コンクール		4.4
competitions, contest	こんてすと		4.4, 1.4.9
competitions	たいかい	大会	4.4
complete it, please	かんせいさせてください	完成させてください	3.7
complete	かんせいする	完成する	2.2, 3.7, 4.4
complex	ふくざつ	複雑	4.8
complex sentence	ふくざつぶん	複雑文	4.8
composite gymnasium	そうごうたいいくかん	総合体育館	3.8
composition	さくぶん	作文	2.6
composition paper	げんこうようし	原稿用紙	1.1, 3.1, 3.7, 3.8
computer	コンピューター		3.3, 1.0.27
computer store	パソコンショップ		3.8
concentration	しゅうちゅうりょく	集中力	2.2
concern for	ためになる		4.9
concert	コンサート		1.4, 1.3.5
concert hall	コンサートホール		3.7, 1.2.1
Concord	コンコード		1.3, 4.3
concreate	ぐたいてき	具体的	4.5, 4.9
condominium, apartment	マンション		3.8
conduct exercises	れんしゅうもんだいをする	練習問題をする	3.2
conducting, implementation	じっせん	実践	4.9
confectionary store	おかしや	お菓子屋	3.8
cornfield	とうもろこしばたけ	玉蜀黍畑	3.8
confirm	かくにんする	確認する	1.1, 1.3, 3.1, 4.8
congratulations	おめでとう	御目出度う	2.7, 3.7
connect	つなげて		4.5
connector	せつぞくご	接続語	1.1, 1.6
consciousness	いしき	意識	2.2
conservative	ほしゅてき（な）	保守的な	3.8
consider, think	かんがえる	考える	1.4, 2.5, 3.8
considerably	かなり	可成り	3.1, 3.7
considerate	おもいやりがある	思いやりがある	4.6
consideration	はいりょ	配慮	4.9
construct, build up	こうちくする	構築する	3.1, 3.2
consulate	りょうじかん	領事館	3.8
contemporary	げんだいてき	現代的	3.8, 3.9
content	ないよう	内容	1.6
continue	つづき	続き	2.6
contrasting	たいしょうてき（な）	対照的（な）	3.7
contribution	こうけん	貢献	4.9
convenience store	コンビニ		2.7, 3.1, 3.4,4.2, 4.4
convenient	べんり（な）	便利（な）	3.1,4.2
convention center	コンベンションセンター		3.8
conversation	かいわ	会話	1.1, 3.4, 4.4
cook	りょうりする	料理する	4.6, 1.3.1
cookie	クッキー		4.4, 1.2.1
cool	すずしい	涼しい	3.1, 3.7, 4.2
cooperate	きょうりょくする	協力する	1.1
cooperative	きょうどう	共同	1.6
corner	かど	角	3.8, 3.9
correct	ただしい	正しい	2.2, 2.3 , 3.7,4.7
costume	コスチューム		4.5
Could you do that?	できましたか	出来ましたか	3.2

council person, congressman	ぎいん	議員	3.8
council, assembly	ぎかい	議会	3.8
counselor	カウンセラー		1.4, 4.7, 1.3.11
counter for any solid objects esp. small and solid ones	こ	個	3.1, 3.4, 4.9
counter for big animals (horses, tigers, etc.)	とう	頭	3.1, 3.4
counter for bound objects (books, notebooks, magazines etc.)	さつ	冊	3.1, 3.4
counter for cars, trucks, buses, machines, appliance	だい	台	3.1, 3.4
counter for long/slender object, video/audio tapes, trees	ほん、ぼん、ぽん	本	3.1, 3.4
counter for small animals (dogs, cats, mice etc.)	ひき、びき、ぴき	～匹	3.1, 3.7
counter for thin/flat objects (CDs, paper, T-shirts etc.)	まい	～枚	3.1, 3.7
counter of temperature	ど	～度	3.7
counter of week	しゅうかん	週間	3.7, 3.8
counters	じょすうし	助数詞	3.1
county	ぐん	群	3.8
Courtney (name of girl)	コートニー		1.4
courthouse	さいばんしょ	裁判所	3.8
cover	ひょうし	表紙	4.9
cram school	じゅく	塾	2.7
creative	クリエイティブ		4.2
criterion	きじゅん	基準	3.7
critical	たにんをひはんする	他人を批判する	4.8
critical	ひはんてきな	批判的な	4.8
cross country	クロスカントリー		4.3
cross out, erase	けす	消す	3.7
cry easily	なみだもろい	涙もろい	4.8
cultural festival	ぶんかさい	文化祭	2.7, 4.1
cultural field	ぶんかけい	文化系	4.1, 4.3, 4.6
culture	ぶんか	文化	2.3, 4.9, 1.4.10
curious	こうきしんがつよい	好奇心が強い	4.8
curriculum	カリキュラム		4.3
cut	きる	切る	4.5, 4.7
cute, pretty	かわいい	可愛い	1.3, 4.2, 4.5, 1.3.0
Daisuke Hotta (name)	ほった　だいすけ	堀田大介	4.7
dam	ダム		3.8
dance	ダンス		1.3, 3.5,4.2,4.3, 4.7, 1.1.7
dance contest	ダンスコンテスト		4.4
dance party	ダンスパーティ		4.2, 1.2.2
dangerous	きけん（な）	危険な	3.8 , 4.6, 4.8
dark	くらい	暗い	3.1, 3.7, 4.2
data	データ		3.3
date	ひにち	日にち	2.2, 1.2.3
day after tomorrow	あさって	明後日	1.4, 1.4.1
day before yesterday	おととい	一昨日	1.4
day care center	デイケアセンター		3.3
day of week	ようび	曜日	1.3, 1.2.1
days	にち、か	日	3.7, 1.0.24
deal	たいしょする	対処する	2.6
deal with	あいてになる	相手になる	4.7
death	し	死	4.9
December	じゅうにがつ	十二月	1.2, 1.2.1
debate	ディベート		4.6
decide	きめる／きめます	決める／決めます	2.1, 2.5, 3.1, 4.9
decide	しましょう		2.2
decided to take	とることにしました	撮ることにしました	1.5
decision making	いしけってい	意志決定	2.7, 4.9
decision sentence	はんだんぶん	判断文	4.6
decline	すいたいする	衰退する	3.8
decrease(intransitive)	へる	減る	3.8, 4.7
deepen	ふかまる	深まる	2.4
definition	ていぎ	定義	4.4, 4.8

English			
degree	ど	度	3.7
delicious, tasty	おいしい	美味しい	1.1, 1.4, 3.2,3.7, 4.2
deliver	でまえする	出前する	3.8
department store	デパート		1.3, 1.6, 3.1,4.2, 1.4.11
department of education	きょういくがくぶ	教育学部	4.7
depth	ふかさ	深さ	3.8
describe weather conditions	てんきのびょうしゃをする	天気の描写をする	3.6
description	きじゅつ	記述	4.5
description	びょうしゃ	描写	1.4, 3.6, 4.4
desert	さばく	砂漠	2.3, 3.1
design	デザイン		2.4, 4.5, 4.9
designer	デザイナー		4.5
desk	つくえ	机	3.1, 3.3, 1.0.2
dessert	デザート		1.5, 4.6, 1.2.4
detailed, be versed	くわしい	詳しい	3.5, 3.7
develop	はってんさせる	発展させる	3.5, 4.8
development	はってん	発展	3.8, 3.9
diary	にっき	日記	1.4, 1.7
diagram	ず	図	4.3
dictionary	じしょ	辞書	1.7
dictionary form	じしょけい	辞書形	2.3
did	しました		4.2
dietetics	えいようがく	栄養学	4.3
different	ちがう	違う	3.8, 3.9
different things	べつべつのもの	別々のもの	4.9
difficult	むずかしい	難しい	1.3, 2.7,4.2, 1.3.5
difficult/serious	たいへん(な)	大変な	1.3, 3.7,4.5, 4.9, 1.3.5
digital camera	デジカメ(デジタルカメラ)		4.4,4.9
dining room, cafeteria	しょくどう	食堂	3.8
direct	ちょくせつ	直接	2.3, 2.6, 4.7
direction	ほうがく	方角	3.1, 3.3, 3.7, 4.7
direction	ほうこう	方向	2.5
directions	しじ	指示	1.1
dirty	きたない	汚い	3.1, 3.3, 3.5, 3.7
dirty	よごれている	汚れている	4.6
disco tech,disco club	ディスコ		3.5,4.6, 4.8
discount shop	ディスカウントショップ		3.8
discuss	はなしあう	話し合う	4.8
discussion	ディスカッション		4.6
disguise	ばける	化ける	3.4
dish	さら	皿	2.7
dislike	きらい	嫌い	1.3, 3.2, 1.3.1
Disney World	ディズニーワールド		3.7
distance	きょり	距離	3.8
distribute	くばる／くばります	配る／配ります	2.1, 2.5, 3.2, 1.0.09
distribute the cards	カードをくばる	カードを配る	3.1
distributor	くばるひと	くばる人	3.2
district	ちく	地区	3.5
do	おこなう	行う	2.7
do	する／します		1.1, 3.5, 4.7, 1.0.2
do	やる／やります		1.6, 2.3
do not do that	ないでください		2.1
Do you have Y?	Yがありますか。		3.2
dog	いぬ	犬	1.3, 3.3, 3.7, 1.0.2
dollar	ドル		3.6, 1.1.1
dollar store	ひゃくえんショップ	百円ショップ	3.8
door	ドア		3.7
dormitory	りょう	寮	1.3, 3.5, 4.6, 4.7
down	した	下	2.1, 3.1
down coat	ダウンコート		3.1, 3.7
draft	ドラフト		1.4, 4.9, 1.4.10
drama competition	えんげきコンクール	演劇コンクール	4.4
drama club	えんげきぶ	演劇部	4.3
draw	えがく	描く	4.6
drama contest	ドラマコンテスト		4.4
dress	ドレス		4.5
dress shirt	わいしゃつ		4.5
dress up	オシャレな		4.5
drink (n)	のみもの	飲み物	2.1, 4.2, 4.4, 1.2.1
drink (v)	のむ／のみます	飲む／飲みます	2.3, 3.5, 3.7,4.2, 1.4.1
drive	うんてんする	運転する	4.6
drought	かんばつ	早魃	3.8
drugstore	ドラッグストア		3.2, 3.7
drunk drive	いんしゅうんてん	飲酒運転	4.8
(dry) cleaner	クリーニングや	クリーニング屋	3.8
during that time	そのあいだ	その間	2.7
dye one's hair	かみをそめている	髪を染めている	4.5
each academic division	かくがっか	各学科	4.3
early	はやい	早い	1.1
early part of the Showa era (1926-1989)	しょうわのはじめころ	昭和の始め頃	3.5, 3.9
earrings	イヤリング, ピアス		4.5
earthquake	じしん	地震	3.6, 3.8
earth science	ちがく	地学	4.7
east	ひがし	東	3.7, 4.2
East Park	ひがしこうえん	東公園	3.6
East River	イーストかわ	イースト川	3.6
east side	とうぶ	東部	4.3
eastern part	とうぶ	東部	3.8
eastern side/end	ひがしがわ	東側	3.8
easy	かんたんな	簡単な	1.2, 3.5, 4.6
easy	やさしい	易しい	3.7
easy to	やすい		4.7
easy to understand	わかりやすくする		4.4
easy to wear	きやすい	気やすい	4.5
eat	たべる／たべます	食べる／食べます	1.1, 3.5, 4.7, 1.4.1
eat too much	たべすぎる	食べ過ぎる	4.8
eating out	がいしょく	外食	3.8
economical	けいざいてきで	経済的で	4.5
economics	けいざいがく	経済学	4.3
edit	へんしゅう	編集	1.1, 1.5, 4.8
editor in chief	へんしゅうちょう	編集長	4.8
editorial timetable	しんこうひょう	進行表	4.9
education	きょういく	教育	4.5
educational facility	きょういくしせつ	教育施設	3.8
effect	こうか	効果	4.5, 4.9
Egypt	エジプト		3.7, 1.3.9
eight (quantity)	はっこ	八個	3.4
eight big animals (horses, tigers, etc.)	はっとう	八頭	3.4
eight bound objects (books, notebooks, magazines etc.)	はっさつ	八冊	3.4
eight cars and other rides, machines, appliances	はちだい	八台	3.4
eight houses, eight stores	はっけん	八軒	3.4
eight long/slender objects	はっぽん	八本	3.4
eight small animals (dogs, cats, mice etc.)	はっぴき	八匹	3.4
eight thin/flat objects (CDs, paper, etc.)	はちまい	八枚	3.4
eighth day	ようか	八日	1.2, 1.2.1
elbow	ひじ	肘	2.1
elder brother	おにいさん	お兄さん	1.3, 1.0.2
elder sister	おねえさん	お姉さん	1.3, 1.0.2

English	Hiragana	Kanji	Sections
elderly	ろうじん	老人	4.8
election	せんきょ	選挙	3.8
electricity	でんき	電気	2.5, 3.4, 1.4.9
electronic shop	でんきや	電気屋	1.4
elementary school	しょうがっこう	小学校	3.4, 1.1.1
elementary student	しょうがくせい	小学生	1.4, 3.6, 4.3
elevated railway	こうかてつどう	高架鉄道	3.8, 3.9
email	eメール		2.3
embassy	たいしかん	大使館	3.8
enclose	かこむ	囲む	1.3
encounter	であいます	出会います	1.5, 1.7
end	おわり	終わり	1.1, 1.5, 1.3.1
end, edge	はし	端	3.8
England	イギリス		3.7, 1.3.9
English Japanese dictionary	えいわじてん	英和辞典	2.3
English language	えいご	英語	1.1, 1.6, 2.7, 3.4, 4.3, 1.0.2
enhance	たかめる	高める	2.2
enjoy, get pleasure	たのしむ	楽しむ	3.8
enjoyable, fun	たのしい	楽しい	1.1, 1.4, 3.3, 3.8, 4.3, 4.7, 1.3.5
Enoshima (place name)	えのしま	江ノ島	1.4
enter	はいる	入る	3.5
entertainment facility	ごらくしせつ	娯楽施設	3.3
entrance ceremony	にゅうがくしき	入学式	4.4
entry	でている	出ている	2.4
environment	かんきょう	環境	1.4, 3.1, 3.6, 4.2, 4.3,
environmental issues	かんきょうもんだい	環境問題	4.7
equality	びょうどう	平等	3.5
era	じだい	時代	3.5, 4.9
especially	とくに	特に	1.5, 1.7, 2.5, 4.3, 4.5
etc.	など	等	3.8, 3.9
ethics	りんりがく	倫理学	4.3
Evaluation	ひょうか	評価	1.1, 1.4, 3.1, 3.8, 4.9, 1.4.1
evening dinner	ばんごはん	晩ご飯	1.4, 1.4.1
event	ぎょうじ、イベント	行事	1.4, 2.7, 3.7, 3.8, 4.3, 1.2.1
every month	まいつき	毎月	2.3, 3.6, 3.9, 4.5
every morning	まいあさ	毎朝	1.1
every week	まいしゅう	毎週	2.3, 3.5, 4.2
every year	まいとし／まいねん	毎年	2.3
everybody	みなさん	皆さん	1.1, 3.2, 4.3, 4.8
everybody	みんな	皆	2.1, 1.1.9
everyday	まいにち	毎日	1.1, 1.3, 3.5, 1.4.1
everyone	みな	皆	1.5, 4.7
examination	しけん	試験	1.7, 4.2, 4.4
example	れい	例	1.2
example sentence	れいぶん	例文	4.3
exception	いがい	以外	4.6
exchange	こうりゅう	交流	2.4
Exchange it.	いれかえてください。	入れ替えてください	3.3
excuse me, I am sorry	すみません	済みません	2.5, 3.2, 1.0.1
exercises	れんしゅうもんだい	練習問題	2.6
exhibit	てんらんかい	展覧会	3.8
exist (inanimate)	ある／あります	有る／有ります	2.1, 3.1, 4.7, 1.4.1
exist (animate)	いる／います	居る／居ます	2.3, 4.9, 1.0.2
existence	そんざい	存在	3.3
expand	かくだいする	拡大する	3.5
expensive	たかい	高い	1.4, 1.3.7
experiment	じっけん	実験	4.6, 4.8
explanation	せつめい	説明	2.6, 3.4, 4.9
expository writing	せつめいぶんけいしき	説明文形式	4.5, 4.9

English	Hiragana	Kanji	Sections
express	あらわす	表す	3.3, 4.8
expressing summarization for preceding statement	まとめると		4.9
expression	ひょうげん	表現	1.2, 4.9
expressway	こうそくどうろ	高速道路	3.3
extra curricular activities	かがいかつどう	課外活動	4.7, 1.1.9
eyes	め	目	2.4, 1.0.27
fabulous, cool	クール		4.4
face	かお	顔	1.6, 2.4, 3.5, 1.0.2
facility	しせつ	施設	3.7, 4.2
fact	じじつ	事実	2.4, 4.9
factory	こうじょう	工場	3.1, 3.5, 3.7, 4.2
Fahrenheit	かし	華氏	3.5, 3.6
fair	フェア		3.8
fairly, pretty much	けっこう	結構	3.1, 3.7, 4.3
fall down	ふります	降ります	3.1
false	うそ	嘘	1.4, 2.4, 3.4, 4.4, 1.1.1
family	かぞく	家族	1.3, 3.5, 4.4, 4.9, 1.3.4
Family Day	ファミリーデー		4.4
family restaurant	ファミレス(ファミリーレストラン)		4.4, 4.9
famous	ゆうめい（な）	有名な	2.4, 2.7, 3.3, 3.5, 3.7, 4.2, 4.4
far, far away	とおい	遠い	3.1, 3.4, 3.5, 3.7, 1.4.5
farm	のうじょう	農場	3.8
farm village	のうそん	農村	4.3
fashion	ファッション		4.5
fashion show	ファッションショー		3.5, 4.2
fast food	ファーストフード		3.8
father	おとうさん	お父さん	1.3, 1.0.2.
favor	このみ	好み	1.5
favor, request	おねがい	お願い	1.1, 4.9, 1.1.2
favorite	すきな	好きな	4.2
February	にがつ	二月	3.1, 3.5, 3.6, 1.2.1
feedback	フィードバック		1.6, 3.7
feel refreshed	さっぱりした		2.7
feeling	かんじがする	感じがする	3.5, 3.9, 4.4
feel obligation	ぎむかんがある	義務感がある	4.8
fencing	フェンシング		4.4
Ferris (last name)	フェリス		1.6
festivals	まつり	祭り	4.4
few, little	すくない	少ない	3.1, 3.6, 3.7
field day	たいいくさい(うんどうかい)	体育祭(運動会)	3.8, 3.9, 4.3
field hockey	フィールドホッケー		4.4
fifth day	いつか	五日	1.2, 1.2.1
field day	うんどうかい	運動会	2.7
final exams	きまつしけん	期末試験	4.4
final exams for the year	がくねんまつしけん	学年末試験	4.4
finally	さいごに、おわりに	最後に、終わりに	2.4
finance	ざいせい	財政	3.8
financial industry	きんゆうぎょう	金融業	3.8
finish, end	おわる／おわります	終わる／終わります	1.2, 2.3, 4.7, 1.2.1
fire department	しょうぼうしょ	消防署	3.1, 3.2
fireworks	はなび	花火	2.3, 3.6
first (of all)	はじめに	始めに	2.4
first day	ついたち	一日	1.2, 1.2.1
first day of school	はつとうこうび	初登校日	3.8, 3.9
first of all	てはじめ	手始めに	1.5
first period	いちじかんめ	一時間目	2.5
first semester	いちがっき	一学期	4.4
first spring storm/wind	はるいちばん	春一番	3.8
first year middle school student	ちゅうがくいちねんせい	中学一年生	4.2

English	Japanese (kana)	Japanese (kanji)	Reference
firstly	さいしょに	最初に	4.3
fish	さかな	魚	3.4, 1.0.25
fish market	さかなや	魚屋	3.1
fishery	ぎょぎょう	漁業	3.8
five (DVDs)	ごまい	五枚	3.4
five (quantity)	ごこ	五個	3.4
five big animals (horses, tigers, etc.)	ごとう	五頭	3.4
five bound objects (books, notebooks, magazines etc.)	ごさつ	五冊	3.4
five cars and other rides, machines, appliances	ごだい	五台	3.4
five houses, five stores	ごけん	五軒	3.4
five long/slender objects	ごほん	五本	3.4
five o'clock	ごじ	五時	1.1, 1.2.1
five small animals (dogs, cats, mice etc.)	ごひき	五匹	3.4
five thin/flat objects (CDs, paper, etc.)	ごまい	五枚	3.4
five units	いつつ	五つ	2.5, 1.2.9
flat	たいら	平ら	3.5
flea market	フリーマーケット		3.8
flexible	じゅんのうてきな	順応的な	4.7
flood	こうずい	洪水	3.8
(floor) size	ひろさ	広さ	3.8
Florida	フロリダ		3.6, 3.7, 4.9
flowchart	フローチャート		1.1, 2.5, 3.1, 4.9
flower	はな	花	3.4, 1.0.2
flower shop	はなや	花屋	3.1, 3.2, 3.4, 4.2
folder	フォルダ		2.6
follow	したがう	従う／従います	1.2, 2.1
follow up	フォローアップ		2.6
food	たべもの	食べ物	1.1, 1.4, 4.2, 1.2.1
food court	フードコート		3.8
food, cooking	りょうり	料理	1.6, 3.7, 4.4, 1.4.11
foot/feet (ft)	フィート		3.7
for	よう	用	2.7
for example	たとえば	例えば	1.4, 3.5, 3.7, 4.2
for	のための		3.5, 4.9
foreign country	がいこく	外国	2.5, 3.4
foreign languages	がいこくご	外国語	3.4, 4.3, 1.3.1
foreigner	がいこくじん	外国人	3.7
forest	もり	森	3.2, 4.2
forest fire	やまかじ	山火事	3.8
forestry	りんぎょう	林業	3.8
forget	わすれる	忘れる	2.7
form	かた	型	3.4
former	まえの	前の	4.2
fortunate, happy	しあわせな	幸せな	4.6
funding anniversary	そうりつきねんび	創立記念日	4.4, 4.9
fountain	ふんすい	噴水	3.3
four (quantity)	よんこ	四個	3.4
four big animals (horses, tigers, etc.)	よんとう	四頭	3.1, 3.4
four bound objects (books, notebooks, magazines etc.)	よんさつ	四冊	3.4
four cars and other rides, machines, appliances	よんだい	四台	3.4
four houses, four stores	よんけん	四軒	3.4
four long/slender objects	よんほん	四本	3.4
four small animals (dogs, cats, mice, etc.)	よんひき	四匹	3.4
four thin/flat objects (CDs, paper, etc.)	よんまい	四枚	3.4
fourth day	よっか	四日	1.2, 1.2.1
fourth station	よっつめのえき	四つ目の駅	3.8, 3.9
France	フランス		3.4, 4.3
Francis (name)	フランシス		4.6
free	じゆう（な）	自由な	3.8
free form	じゆうがた	自由型	4.8, 4.9
free time	じゆうじかん	自由時間	4.7
freedom	じゆう	自由	2.3
Freedom City College	じゆうとしだいがく	自由都市大学	3.8, 3.9
freely	じゆうに	自由に	4.5
freeze	こおる／おります	凍る凍ります	3.1, 3.6
French language	フランスご	フランス語	1.1, 1.6, 3.4, 4.3, 1.3.1
Friday	きんようび	金曜日	1.2, 3.4, 4.2, 1.2.1
friend	ともだち	友達	1.1, 1.4, 3.4, 1.3.4
from now on	これから	これから	1.1, 1.7
front	まえ	前	2.1, 2.3, 3.1
frost	しも	霜	3.8
fruit	フルーツ	果物（くだもの）	4.3, 4.4, 1.2.1
fruits market	くだものや	果物屋	3.1, 3.7, 1.3.2
fundraising	ファンドレイジング		4.4
furniture store	かぐや	家具屋	3.8
funny, interesting	おもしろい	面白い	1.1, 2.5, 2.6, 3.7, 4.2, 1.0.2
furthermore	それに		3.1, 3.7, 4.5
futon	ふとん	布団	1.7
future	しょうらい	将来	3.5, 4.5, 4.9
gathering, event	もよおし	催し	3.5, 3.7, 4.2
game	ゲーム		2.2, 4.6, 4.8, 1.2.9
game	しあい	試合	1.5, 4.2, 1.4.6
garage sale	ガレージセール		3.8
gas station	ガソリンスタンド		3.8
gas station	サービスステーション		3.8
general housecleaning	おおそうじ		4.9
general restaurant	いっぱんしょくどう	一般食堂	3.8
geographical knowledge	ちりのちしき	地理の知識	4.3
geometry	きか	幾何	4.7, 1.3.9
German	ドイツ		4.7, 1.3.9
Germany	ドイツご	ドイツ語	3.4, 4.3, 1.3.5
get excited	こうふんする	興奮する	2.7
get expected	きたいされたい	期待されたい	4.8
get help	てつだってもらう	手伝ってもらう	4.9
get off	おりる	降りる	3.8, 3.9
get mad	おこる	怒る	3.6
game center	ゲームセンター		3.3
Ginga High School	ぎんがこうこう	銀河高校	3.8, 3.9
girl	おんなのこ	女の子	3.3
girlfriend	ガールフレンド		1.4, 4.2, 4.6
girls	じょし	女子	4.5
girl's school	じょしこう	女子高	4.3
Give a short vocabulary test to one another.	みじかいごいのテストをしましょう	短い語彙のテストをしましょう	3.2
give examples	あげてください	挙げてください	4.3
give examples	れいをあげる	例を挙げる	4.5
give own opinion	じぶんのいけんをいう	自分の意見を言う	4.8
glasses	めがね	眼鏡	4.5
gloves	てぶくろ		4.5
glue	のり		2.5
go	いく／いきます	行く／行きます	1.1, 3.1, 3.5, 3.7, 1.0.2
go	いって	行って	4.2
go ahead	どうぞ		1.7
go break up into groups of three	さんにんのグループになってください。	3人のグループになってください。	3.7
Godzilla	ゴジラ		3.5, 4.2, 4.4
going out	でかける	出かける	1.5, 3.6
going to cultural park	ぶんかこうえんいき	文化公園行き	3.8, 3.9
golf	ゴルフ		3.4, 4.4, 1.1.6
golf course	ゴルフじょう	ゴルフ場	3.8
good	いい	良い	3.1, 3.7, 4.2, 1.1.1

English	Kana	Kanji	Reference
good	よい	良い	3.7
good afternoon, hi	こんにちは	今日は	1.2 1.0.13
good evening	こんばんは	今晩は	1.2 1.0.13
good morning	おはようございます	お早うございます	1.2 1.0.13
good night	おやすみなさい	お休みなさい	2.3 1.0.12
good-looking, cool	かっこ(う)いい	格好いい	4.7
Gordon (name of boy)	ゴードン		1.3
government	せいふ	政府	4.7
government office	やくしょ	役所	3.8
governor	ちじ	知事	3.8
gown	ガウン		4.5
grade level	がくねん	学年	1.2, 1.5, 4.3, 1.1.1
graduate (n)	そつぎょうせい	卒業生	4.2
graduate (v)	そつぎょうする	卒業する	4.7
graduate school	だいがくいん	大学院	4.9
graduation	そつぎょう	卒業	4.9
graduation ceremony	そつぎょうしき	卒業式	4.3, 4.4
grandfather	おじいさん	お祖父さん	1.3, 1.3.11
grandmother	おばあさん	お祖母さん	1.3, 1.3.11
grassland	そうげん	草原	3.8
greasy	あぶらっこい	油っこい	4.2
greedy	ほしがる	欲しがる	4.8
Greece	ギリシャ		4.9
Greek	ギリシャご	ギリシャ語	4.3
green	みどり	緑	2.5, 3.3, 1.1.9
green market	グリーンマーケット		3.8, 3.9
Greenwich Village	グリニッチ・ビッレジ		3.8, 3.9
greeting	あいさつ		1.3, 4.9, 1.3.6
ground, playground	うんどうじょう	運動場	3.8
group	ぐるーぷ		4.3, 4.9
group competition	グループたいこうきょうそう	グループ対抗競争	3.7
group work	グループワーク		1.3, 3.4
grow, develop	はってんする	発展する	3.8
gym clothes	たいそうふく	体操服	4.5
gymnasium	たいいくかん	体育館	3.1, 3.2, 4.7, 1.4.9
gymnastics	たいそう	体操	2.6, 4.3
hail	ひょう	雹	3.8
Hakone (name of place)	はこね	箱根	3.6
half past 6 (am/pm)	ろくじはん	六時半	4.2
Halloween	ハローウィーン		4.8, 1.0.24
hamburger	ハンバーガー		1.4.4.2, 1.2.1
hand	て	手	1.5, 2.6, 1.0.24
handkerchief	ハンカチ		2.7
handout	プリント		2.1
hang	かける		4.5
Hang on/ do one's best	がんばって		4.7, 4.9
hard rock	ハードロック		3.5
hardware store	かなものや	金物屋	3.8
hat	ぼうし	帽子	4.5
have a sense of responsibility	せきにんかんがある	責任感がある	4.6
have frost	しもがおりる	霜が降りる	3.8
Hawaii	ハワイ		1.1, 1.3, 3.5, 1.4.6
he	かれ	彼	4.9
head	あたま	頭	1.7, 2.4
headache	あたまがいたい	頭がいたい	4.9
health	けんこう	健康	2.4
health	ほけん	保健	4.3
health and physical education	ほけんたいいく	保健体育	4.3
health club	ヘルスクラブ		3.7
health, energetic	げんき	元気	1.3, 2.3, 4.2, 1.0.2
healthy	ヘルシー		4.2, 4.7
heat wave	もうしょ	猛暑	3.6
heater	だんぼう	暖房	3.6, 3.9
heavy	おもい	重い	1.7, 3.1, 3.4
heavy rain	おおあめ	大雨	3.8
heavy snow	おおゆき	大雪	3.5, 3.8
height	たかさ	高さ	3.8
help	てつだう	手伝う	1.7
High Line	ハイライン		3.8, 3.9
high school	こうこう	高校	1.1, 3.4, 1.0.2
high school student	こうこうせい	高校生	3.7, 1.4.4
high/expensive	たかい	高い	1.1, 3.1, 1.3.7
highest temperature	さいこうきおん	最高気温	3.6
highly	たかく	高く	4.5
high-rise building	こうそうビル	高層ビル	3.5
hill	おか	丘	3.8
hiragana	ひらがな		1.2, 1.0.2
Hiroshima (name of prefecture)	ひろしま	広島	3.6, 3.7, 1.3.2
history	れきし	歴史	1.3, 2.4, 3.4,3.7, 4.2, 4.3, 1.0.2
hobby	しゅみ	趣味	2.1, 4.2, 1.3.6
Hokkaido (name of prefecture)	ほっかいどう	北海道	3.5, 4.3
hold	もつ	持つ	1.7, 4.9
holiday	きゅうじつ	休日	1.4
home coming	ホームカミング		4.8
home decor store	ホームセンター		3.8
home electric appliances store	かでんりょうはんてん	家電量販店	3.8
homeless	ホームレス		4.8
homework	しゅくだい	宿題	1.3, 1.4, 2.5,3.2, 4.2, 4 3, 4.7, 1.0.2
homeroom teacher	たんにんのせんせい	担任の先生	1.3, 3.6 1.3.1
Honolulu	ホノルル		3.6
horizontal writing	よこがき	横書き	4.9
horror	ホーラー		1.5
horse	うま	馬	3.4, 1.0.2
horse gets fat	うまこゆる	馬肥ゆる	3.8, 3.9
hospital	びょういん	病院	3.1, 3.3, 3.4,3.7, 1.4.11
hot (weather)	あつい	暑い	1.1, 1.3, 3.5, 1.1.6
hot (teste)	からい	辛い	1.4
hotel	ホテル		3.5, 3.6
hours	じかん	時間	3.7
house	いえ	家	3.2, 3.7
house	うち	家	1.3, 1.3.5
houses, stores, restaurants etc.	けん、げん	軒	3.1, 3.7
how	どうやって		2.7
how about you get fresh air?	いいくうきをすったら	良い空気を吸ったら	4.9
how about?	どうですか		2.5, 3.2
how do you do	はじめまして	初めまして	2.1.1, 1.0.1
how many (cars, trucks, buses, machines, appliances)	なんだい	何台	3.4
how many (long/slender object)	なんぼん	何本	3.4
how many (quantity)	なんこ	何個	3.4
how many big animals (horses, tigers, etc.)	なんとう	何頭	3.4
how many bound objects (book, notebook, magazine etc.)	なんさつ	何冊	3.4
how many houses, stores	なんげん	何軒	3.4
how many minutes	なんぷん	何分	3.8, 3.9
how many people	なんにん	何人	3.4, 1.2.1
how many sets (of cards)	なんくみ	何組	2.7
how many small animals (dogs, cats, mice, etc.)	なんびき	何匹	3.4
how many thin/flat objects (CDs, paper, T-shirts etc.)	なんまい	何枚	3.4
how much	いくら	幾ら	2.5, 4.5, 1.1.3
how old	なんさい	何才	2.5, 1.1.1
how to teach	おしえかた	教え方	4.9
how to?~	しかた	仕方	2.3, 2.6, 4.4
how was	どうでしたか		1.1

English	Japanese (kana)	Japanese (kanji)	Ref
How was ~?	はどうだった		1.4, 4.9
How was ~?	はどうでしたか		1.4, 4.9
however	けれども		4.1, 4.2
Hudson River Park	ハドソンリバー　パーク		3.4, 3.9
human being	にんげん	人間	4.9
human clone	クローンにんげん	クローン人間	4.8
humid	むしあつい	蒸し暑い	1.6,.8, 3.9 ,4.4, 1.1.6
humidity	しつど	湿度	3.6
hurricane	ハリケーン		3.8
hurt	いたい	痛い	2.6
hybrid	ハイブリッド		3.5, 4.9
I am going to distribute X.	Xをくばります。		3.2
I for boy	ぼく	僕	4.9
I got headache, but	あたまがいたいんですけど	頭が痛いんですけど	4.9
I hear that	そうです		1.4
I heard it's different	ちがういみだそうです	違う意味だそうです	3.6, 3.9
I'm leaving	いってきます	行って来ます	3.8, 3.9
I rely on your suggestion	おまかせします		2.2, 1.2.4
I say	といいます		4.9
I think it is better to	たほうがいいとおもう	たほうがいいと思う	4.7
I think	とおもいます/とおもう	と思います/と思う	4.6, 4.8. 4.9
I would appreciate	よろしく		1.1, 1.1.1
I would like to	どうしても~たい		4.9
I(for girls and adults)	わたし	私	1.1, 1.2.4
ice	こおり	氷	3.8
ice coffee	アイスコーヒー		4.2, 1.1.9
ice cream	アイスクリーム		1.2, 1.5, 4.4,4.9, 1.0.1
ice hockey	アイスホッケー		4.3, 1.1.6
Ichiro (name of boy)	いちろう	一郎	4.6
if necessary	ひつようなら	必要なら	3.7, 4.4
if you would like	よかったら		4.9
image text ratio	テキストのわりあいをイメージして	テキストの割合をイメージして	4.8
imagine	イメージして		4.8
introduction	じょろん	序論	1.1, 3.1
illustration	イラスト		2.2, 4.8
immigrant	いみん	移民	3.8
important	じゅうよう(な)	重要(な)	1.3, 3.7, 4.2,4.9, 1.8.5
important	たいせつ	大切	4.5, 4.9
important writing expression	じゅうようなぶんしょうひょうげん 重要な文章表現		4.9
impossible	むり	無理	4.9
impression	かんそう	感想	1.4
impress	いんしょうにのこる	印象に残る	4.9
impressive	かんどうてきである	感動的である	4.7
improvement, reform	かいぜん	改善	2.7, 4.9
improve	かいぜんする	改善する	4.8
inappropriate	てきせつでない	適切でない	3.5
in an interesting manner	おもしろく	面白く	3.1, 3.7
in charge	たんにん	担任	1.3
in contract to	それにたいして	それに対して	2.7
in detail	くわしく	詳しく	3.1, 3.5, 3.7
include	ふくむ	含む	4.8
in many places	あちこちら		3.8, 3.9
in-low	ぎりの	義理の	1.6
in short	ようするに	要するに	4.8
in this way	こうやって		2.7
in the class	クラスない	クラス内	2.7
in total	ぜんぶで	全部で	3.1, 3.7
inch	インチ		3.7
inconvenient	ふべん(な)	不便(な)	3.1, 3.4
incorrect	ちがいます	違います	1.1.1.2　1.1.4
increase(intransitive)	ふえる	増える	2.4, 3.8

English	Japanese (kana)	Japanese (kanji)	Ref
Indian dish	インドりょうり	インド料理	1.6
Indian food, cuisine	インディアンりょうり	インディアン料理	3.7
indicate existence of something そんざいをあらわすみじかいぶん			
		存在を表す短い文	3.3
indication	してき	指摘	4.4
indirect	かんせつてき	間接的	4.7
individual	こじんてき	個人的	2.4
India	インド		4.3, 1.3.9
indoor gym	しつないきょうぎじょう	室内競技場	4.4
indoor swimming pool	おくないプール	屋内プール	3.8
industry	さんぎょう	産業	3.8
inexpensive	やすい	安い	1.1, 1.4, 3.2, 4.2
inform	しらせる	知らせる	4.8
information	じょうほう	情報	3.3, 4.4, 4.9
information center	あんないしょ	案内所	3.6
information gathering/sorting	じょうほうしゅうしゅう	情報収集	4.3
ingredients	ざいりょう	材料	3.5, 3.9, 4.6
inside	なか	中	3.1, 3.3, 1.3.1
inspection	けんさ	検査	4.8
instructions, direct	しじ	指示	1.1, 2.5, 4.9
intercity rapid train	かいそくでんしゃ	快速電車	3.8, 3.9
interest	きょうみ	興味	4.6
international education	こくさいきょういく	国際教育	2.5,2.6,3.5
international exchange	こくさいこうりゅう	国際交流	3.8
international hall	こくさいかいかん	国際会館	3.8, 3.9
international	こくさい	国際	1.7
international	こくさいてき	国際的	3.5, 3.9
international school	インターナショナルスクール		4.3, 4.9
international school	こくさいがっこう	国際学校	3.5, 3.9
introduce	しょうかい	紹介	1.4. 1.6, 3.4, 4.4
introductory sentences	しょうかいぶん	紹介文	4.6
Inuit	エスキモー		3.8
investigate, search	しらべる	調べる	3.8
Iowa	アイオワ		3.6
is	です		1.1, 1.0.1
is (explanation)	とは		4.4
is doing	ている／ています		2.1
Is it OK?	いいんですか		4.9
Is it right?	いいですか		1.2, 2.5
Is it right?	そうですか		1.2
Is it so?	そうですか		3.8, 3.9, 1.2.2
is like	のような		4.4, 4.8
is something like	のようなものです		4.4, 4.8
Ishida	いしだ	石田	1.3
island	しま	島	3.5
IT industry	じょうほうぎじゅつさんぎょう 情報技術産業		3.8
it is about ~	ことです	ことです	2.3, 1.4.3
it is good	いいです	良いです	1.3, 1.4.3
It is necessary	ひつようです	必要です	3.1, 3.7, 4.5, 1.4.1
It is OK.	だいじょうぶです。	大丈夫です。	3.8
It is probably	だろう		3.7, 4.7
It is reason that	からです		4.8
it is said that	という	と言う	1.4
It is so.	そうですねえ		3.8, 3.9, 1.2.2
It isn't	くありません、じゃありません		4.9
It isn't	くない、じゃない		4.9
it means that	は~のことだ		4.4
it means that	は~のことです		4.8
it seems	ようです		4.4
it seems that	ようなものだ		4.4
it seems that	ようなものです		4.4
it will probably be~.	でしょう		3.1
Italian dish	イタリアりょうり	イタリア料理	1.5
Italian food, cuisine	イタリアンりょうり	イタリアン料理	3.7
jacket	ジャケット		4.5
Jacky Sands (name of girl)	ジャッキー・サンズ		3.7

English	Japanese	Kanji	Reference
Jakarta	ジャカルタ		3.6
January	いちがつ	一月	3.1, 3.5, 3.6, 1.1.7
Japan	にほん	日本	1.1, 3.6, 4.2, 1.3.2
Japan day	ジャパンディ		3.4
Japanese	にほんご	日本語	1.1, 3.2, 3.4, 3.5, 1.3.1
Japanese archery	きゅうどう	弓道	2.4
Japanese belt for kimono	おび	帯	4.5
Japanese culture	にほんぶんか	日本文化	4.6, 4.7
Japanese dish	にほんりょうり	日本料理	1.5, 1.4.9
Japanese inn	りょかん	旅館	3.3, 3.8
Japanese language environment	にほんごかんきょう	日本語環境	4.9
Japanese pampas grass	すすき	薄	3.4
Japanese restaurant	にほんりょうりてん	日本料理店	3.8
Japanese style	にほんてきな	日本的な	1.4
Japanese style food	わしょく	和食	2.7, 1.2.9
Japanese style outfit	わふく	和服	4.5, 4.6
Japanese traditional clothes	きもの	着物	4.5, 4.6
Japanese-English dictionary	わえいじてん	和英辞典	2.3
jazz	ジャズ		1.1, 1.6, 4.3, 1.2.1
jeans (name)	ジーンズ		4.5
Jenny (name)	ジェニー		1.3, 2.5, 2.6, 3.7, 4.7, 1.1.2
Jessica (name)	ジェシカ		2.1, 2.3, 2.5, 2.6 2.7, 4.9
Jet lag	じさぼけ	時差ぼけ	4.3
Jewish	ゆだやきょうけい	ユダヤ教系	4.2, 4.6, 4.7
Jill (name)	ジル		2.3, 3.2, 4.9, 1.4.10
job, task	しごと	仕事	4.2
jogging	ジョギング		3.3
jogging course	ジョギングコース		1.3, 3.4, 1.4.3
John (name)	ジョン		3.4
join	さんかする	参加する	1.2, 1.2.10
Jones (name)	ジョーンズ		2.1, 2.5, 2.6, 4.9, 1.1.2
Jose (name)	ホセ		1.4
Josh (name)	ジョッシュ		3.1, 3.7
Joytown (name of town)	ジョイタウン		4.7
Journalism	ジャーナリズム		3.1, 3.2
judge	ジャッジをする		4.7
judgment sentence	はんだんぶん	判断文	1.1, 4.2, 1.1.6
judo	じゅうどう	柔道	1.5, 1.1.9
juice	ジュース		3.5, 1.2.1
July	しちがつ	7月	3.5, 1.2.1
June	ろくがつ	6月	1.6
just about	ちょうど	丁度	3.7
just about	ほぼ		1.1, 1.4.9
Kabuki	かぶき	歌舞伎	3.7, 1.3.2
Kagoshima (name of prefecture)	かごしま	鹿児島	4.3
Kamishibai (paper play)	えぞうし	絵草子	4.6
Kana	かな		1.2
kana (writing character)	かな		4.3
Kanagawa prefecture	かながわけん	神奈川県	1.2, 1.5, 3.5, 4.2, 4.8, 1.3.8
kanji	かんじ	漢字	3.2
kanji list	かんじのリスト	漢字のリスト	1.1, 2.1, 1.0.28
karaoke	からおけ		2.4
karate	からて	空手	1.2, 1.0.1
katakana	カタカナ		4.9
Kawakami (name)	かわかみ	川上	4.7
keep to a rule	きそくをまもる	規則を守る	1.4, 1.5, 1.7
Kei (name)	けい	恵	4.4, 1.4.8
Kendo (Japanese martial arts)	けんどう	剣道	1.1
Kent (name)	ケント		

English	Japanese	Kanji	Reference
Kevin (name)	ケビン		1.6
kilometer	キロ（メートル）		3.8
Kim (name)	キム		1.5, 1.6, 4.7
kimono for summer	ゆかた	浴衣	3.6, 3.9
kind	やさしい	優しい	1.1, 1.3, 3.5, 4.2, 4.7, 1.0.2
kind help	おせわに	お世話に	1.7
kindergarten	よちえん	幼稚園	3.7, 1.1.9
king (name)	キング		1.2
knee	ひざ	膝	2.1
know	しる	知る	3.5, 3.9, 4.7
Korean	かんこくご	韓国語	4.8, 1.3.1
Kouchi (name of prefecture)	こうち	高知	3.7
Kyoto (name of prefecture)	きょうと	京都	2.5, 3.2, 3.7, 4.9, 1.3.8
Kyushu (name of Japanese region)	きゅうしゅう	九州	3.7, 4.5, 4.9
lacrosse	ラクロス		4.3
lake	みずうみ	湖	3.1, 4.2, 4.4
Lake Biwa	びわこ	琵琶湖	4.4
Lake High School	レイクこうこう	レイク高校	3.6
lamp	ランプ	ランプ	3.3
language arts	こくご	国語	2.7, 4.5
large, big, spacious	ひろい	広い	3.1, 3.7, 4.2
last	さいご	最後	1.1, 1.4
last month	せんげつ	先月	1.5, 2.1, 4.2
last week	せんしゅう	先週	1.4, 1.5
last year	きょねん	去年	1.1, 1.3, 2.1, 3.1, 3.5
late	ちこく	遅刻	3.6, 3.9, 4.8
Latin	ラテンご	ラテン語	4.3
Latino	ラテンけい	ラテン系	3.8
laundromat	コインランドリー		3.8
layout	レイアウト		3.8
leader	リーダー		2.2, 3.2, 4.2, 4.9
league	リーグ		4.7
leadership	しどうりょく	指導力	4.6, 4.7
learn	ならう	習う	3.4, 4.6
learn	まなぶ	学ぶ	3.1, 3.4, 3.7, 4.1
leave	のこる	残る	3.5, 3.9
left	ひだり	左	2.1, 3.1, 3.3, 4.2, 4.6
leg	あし	足	2.1
lend	かす	貸す	4.8
length	ながさ	長さ	3.8
lesson	レッスン		2.1
lesson plan	きょうあん	教案	2.1, 2.6
let me know	しらせてください	知らせてください	2.3
let's decide on the theme	テーマをきめましょう。	テーマを決めましょう	3.2
Let's make any corrections	しゅうせいしましょう	修正しましょう	4.4
Let's role play according to the example	れいをみながらロールプレイをしましょう	例を見ながらロールプレイをしましょう	
Let's think	かんがえましょう	考えましょう	4.7
let's write	かきましょう。	書きましょう	3.1
letter	てがみ	手紙	4.8, 4.9
library	としょかん	図書館	1.2, 3.1, 3.2, 3.5, 3.7, 4.2, 4.9, 1.2.2
lie, false	うそ	嘘	1.4, 2.4, 3.4, 4.4
left side	ひだりがわ	左側	3.8, 3.9
life	じんせい	人生	4.9
life style	せいかつ	生活	4.9
light	かるい	軽い	3.1, 3.4
light rain, shower	こさめ	小雨	3.8
light snow	こゆき	小雪	3.8
light, bright	あかるい	明るい	3.1, 3.7, 4.2
like	すき	好き	1.1, 1.4, 3.2, 1.0.2

like	すきな	好きな	1.1, 1.0.2
like, similar	ような		4.4, 4.9
like	のように		4.9
like caring for others	せわずき	世話好き	4.8
like much	だいすきです	大好きです	4.6
like social service	しゃかいほうしがすき	社会奉仕が好き	4.8
like very much	だいすき	大好き	1.5, 3.5
Linda (name)	リンダ		1.3, 2.5, 2.7,3.6, 4.7, 1.4.1
link	つなげる	繋げる	4.8
linking expression	せつぞくひょうげん	接続表現	4.1
lion	ライオン		3.4, 1.0.2
liquor store	さかや	酒屋	3.8
Lisa (name)	リサ		1.4, 4.6, 4.7, 1.1.6
list	リスト		2.2, 3.7, 4.2,4.3, 4.9
list up	リストアップ		4.3
listen, ask	きく／ききます	聞く／聞きます	1.3, 3.5 4.2, 4.7 1.4.1
listening comprehension	ちょうかい	聴解	2.5
literature	ぶんがく	文学	2.6
live	いきる	生きる	4.9
lively, bustling	にぎやか（な）	賑やかな	3.8 , 4.9
lobby	ろびー		4.4
lobster	ロブスター		1.4
local train	かくえき	各駅	3.8, 3.9
location	いち	位置	3.6, 4.3, 4.8
locational information	ばしょのじょうほう	場所の情報	3.3
logically	ろんりてきに	論理的に	3.1, 3.7
lonely	さびしい	寂しい	4.8
long	ながい	長い	1.1, 1.4, 3.7, 4.2
long and narrow	ほそながい	細長い	3.4, 3.8
Look at the map.	ちずをみてください。	地図を見てください 3.3
looks like	は〜ににている	は〜に似ている	4.4
look like	みたい		4.4
look like	ような		4.4
look like	みたいです		4.5
look over	みなおす	見直す	2.7, 4.9
loss	まけ	負け	3.8
lose	まける／まけます	負ける／負けます	1.5
low	ひくい	低い	3.1
luggage	にもつ	荷物	1.7
lunch	ひるごはん	昼ご飯	1.2, 2.7, 1.4.1
lunch	ランチ		4.2
lunch break	ひるやすみ	昼休み	3.5, 1.3.11
machines	きかい	機械	4.6
mad	おこる	怒る	3.8, 3.9
magazine	ざっし	雑誌	2.4, 3.5, 4.9
magnet school	マグネットスクール		4.3, 4.4
mail	メール		2.3
main activity	ほんさぎょう	本作業	2.6, 3.7, 4.9
main dish	しゅしょく	主食	4.5
Maine State	メーンしゅう	メーン州	3.3
main store, headquarter	ほんてん	本店	3.3
major	せんこう	専攻	4.5, 4.7, 4.9
make	つくる／つくります	作る／作ります	1.1, 3.1, 3.5,3.7, 4.9, 1.4.6
make effort	どりょくする	努力する	4.8
make examples	れいをつくる	例を作る	3.7
make it for me	つくってくれます	作ってくれます	2.4
make mistakes	まちがえる	間違える	1.6, 2.6, 3.8, 3.9
make up	けしょう	化粧	4.5
make use of	りようする	利用する	3.8
management	うんえい	運営	2.6
man, male	おとこのひと	男の人	2.5, 3.4
man, male	だんせい	男性	3.8
manage	けいえい	経営	3.5, 3.9
manager	ぶちょう	部長	4.3
Manchester	マンチェスター		1.6
manufacturing industry	せいぞうぎょう	製造業	3.8
many times	なんども	何度も	2.4
many, a lot, much	たくさん	沢山	1.1, 1.4, 3.1, 3.4
many, much	おおい	多い	1.5, 3.7, 3.1, 4.9
many, much	たくさん		4.2
map	ちず	地図	2.1, 3.3, 3.4,4.3, 1.3.11
marathon	マラソン		4.7
March	さんがつ	三月	3.6, 1.2.1
Marin Day	うみのひ	海の日	1.4
Mark (name)	マーク		1.4 ,4.9, 1.1.4
markers	マーカー		2.5
market	いちば	市場	3.5
marriage	けっこん	結婚	4.8
marriage partner	けっこんのあいて	結婚の相手	4.2
Masa (name)	まさ		4.8
Masako (name)	まさこ	雅子	2.4, 2.7
match	あてはまる	当てはまる	4.3
match	マッチさせてください		4.3, 4.4, 4.5
matching	マッチング		2.6
mathematic	すうがく	数学	1.4, 2.4, 2.7,3.4, 3.6, 3.7, 4.2,4.3, 1.0.2
matrix	ぎょうれつ	行列	4.5
may be	かもしれない/いいかもしれない		2.4, 4.7
may be severe	きびしいでしょう	厳しいでしょう	3.1
May I.. ?	をしてもいいですか。		4.5
mayor of city	しちょう	市長	3.5
MC, host	しかいしゃ	司会者	1.1, 1.6
mean	いじわるな		4.2
meaning	いみ	意味	2.6, 4.7, 1.3.3
meat	にく	肉	3.4, 1.0.25
media room	メディアルーム		4.2,4.9
meet	あう／あいます	会う／会います	1.4, 2.3, 4.6,4.7, 1.4.11
meeting	かいぎ	会議	2.7, 4.8, 4.9, 1.0.27
meeting	ミーティング		1.2, 2.2, 3.7, 1.0.1
Meiji era (1868-1912)	めいじだい	明治時代	3.5, 3.9, 1.1.3
melon	メロン		4.3, 1.1.9
member	メンバー		2.2
member of a club	ぶいん	部員	4.8
memorandum	メモ		1.1, 1.1.3
memory game	しんけいすいじゃく	神経衰弱	4.6
memorization	あんき	暗記	4.5
memorize	おぼえる	覚える	3.8, 3.9
menu	メニュー		4.7, 1.2.6
message	でんごん	伝言	2.6
message	メッセージ		4.9
meters	メートル		3.6, 3.7
method	ほうほう	方法	2.7
Mexican dish	メキシコりょうり	メキシコ料理	1.5
Mexican food, cuisine	メキシカンりょうり	メキシカン料理	3.7
Mexico	メキシコ		1.1, 1.4, 1.3.2
Michael (name)	マイケル		4.6
middle	なか	中	1.1, 3.1, 1.3.1
middle school	ちゅうがく	中学	1.2, 3.4, 1.1.1
middle area	ちゅうぶ	中部	4.3
middle west side	ちゅうせいぶ	中西部	4.3
Midori Memorial Station	みどりきねんえき	みどり記念駅	3.8, 3.9
midterm	ちゅうかんしけん	中間試験	4.4
Mike (name)	マイク		1.4, 1.7, 2.5,3.4, 4.6, 1.0.17

English	Reading	Kanji	Reference
mild	おんだん（な）	温暖な	3.8
mile	マイル		3.8
militaristic	ぐんたいのような	軍隊のような	4.5
millimeters	ミリメートル	▢	3.7
million	ひゃくまん	100万	3.4
Minato Mirai 21 district	みなとみらい２１ちく	港未来２１地区	3.5, 3.9
mind	き	気	2.0
mind map	マインドマップ		2.2, 3.4, 4.8, 4.9
minutes	ふん、ぶん、ぷん	分	3.7, 1.4.1
miso soup	みそしる	味噌汁	2.7
mistakes	まちがえ	間違え	1.6
Miyazawa Kenji (name of author)	みやざわけんじ	宮沢賢治	4.9
modality	モダリティ		4.8
model UN	もぎこくれん	模擬国連	4.3
modern	きんだいてき（な）	近代的な	3.8
moisture, humidity	しっけ	湿気	3.8
Monday	げつようび	月曜日	1.2, 2.2, 3.4, 1.2.1
months (duration)	かげつ	ヵ月	3.8, 4.9
monthly temperature	つきべつきおん	月別気温	3.7
Montreal	モントリオール		1.1
mood, feeling	きぶん	気分	3.4
more	もっと		1.1, 1.6
more details	よりくわしく	より詳しく	3.1
morning	あさ	朝	4.6
morning	ごぜん	午前	2.3
morning assembly	ちょうれい	朝礼	4.7
Moscow	モスクワ		3.6
mosque	モスク		3.8
most likely, maybe	たぶん	多分	3.1, 3.6
mother	おかあさん	お母さん	1.2, 1.3, 1.0.2
mother (my)	はは	母	1.3
mountain	やま	山	1.3, 2.1, 3.1,4.2, 1.3.9
mountain chain	さんみゃく	山脈	3.8
mouse	ねずみ	鼠	3.2,3.3, 1.1.4
mouth	くち	口	2.4 1.0.24
move	いどうする	移動する	2.5
move	うごく	動く	4.8
movement, action	どうさ	動作	2.4, 4.1
movie	えいが	映画	1.1, 1.4, 4.2, 1.2.1
movie club	えいがぶ	映画部	4.2
movie theater	えいがかん	映画館	1.6, 3.1, 3.3,3.7, 4.2, 1.4.11
Mr. Ms.Mrs.	さん		1.3, 1.1.2
Mr. Ms.Mrs.	さま	様	4.7
Ms/Mr. Ishikawa (teacher)	いしかわせんせい	石川先生	3.7
Mt. Fuji (the highest mountain in Japan)	ふじさん	富士山	3.3
multiple	ふくすう	複数	4.6
museum	びじゅつかん	美術館	3.1
museum	はくぶつかん	博物館	3.5, 3.9, 4.3
music	おんがく	音楽	1.1, 1.5, 2.7,4.2, 4.3, 1.3.1
musician	おんがくか	音楽家	3.4, 1.3.11
museum for material	しりょうかん	資料館	3.5, 3.9
Muslim	イスラムきょうけい	イスラム教系	4.3
must	ねばならない		4.8
must do	しなくてはならない		4.9
must do	しなければなりません		2.5
must understand	りかいしなくてはなりません		
		理解しなくてはなりません	2.7
my elder brother	あに	兄	1.3
my elder sister	あね	姉	1.1, 1.3, 1.3.1
my father	ちち	父	1.3
my grand father	そふ	祖父	1.3
my grand mother	そぼ	祖母	1.3
Nagano(name of prefecture)	ながの	長野	3.1, 3.7
Nagahama (place name)	ながはま	長浜	2.4
Naha (name of city)	なは	那覇	3.7
Nairobi	ナイロビ		3.6
Nakata (name)	なかた	中田	2.4
Nakano (name)	なかの	中野	1.3, 1.3.2
name	なまえ	名前	1.2 , 3.2, 4.9, 1.1.2
narrative writing	ものがたりぶん	物語文	4.8
narrow, small	せまい	狭い	3.1, 3.7
national competition	ぜんこくたいかい	全国大会	2.4
national park	こくりつこうえん	国立公園	3.8
nation	くに	国	4.3,4.4
nationality	こくせき	国籍	1.3 1.3.6
national-language dictionary	こくごじてん	国語辞典	2.3
Native American	ネイティブアメリカン		3.8
Natural Environment Hospital	しぜんかんきょうびょういん	自然環境病院	3.8, 3.9
natural feature, landscape	ふうけい	風景	1.5, 4.3
nature	しぜん	自然	3.2, 3.4, 3.7,4.2, 4.7, 1.3.11
near	ちかい	近い	2.4, 3.1, 3.5, 3.7
nearby	すぐそば		3.8, 3.9
nearby	ちかくに	近くに	4.2
necessary	ひつよう(な)	必要(な)	1.3, 2.3, 3.6,4.5, 1.4.1
neck	くび	首	2.1, 2.2
necklace	ネックレス		4.5
necktie	ねくたい		4.5
need	ひつようだ	必要だ	4.7
neighborhoods	うちのちかく	うちの近く	3.5
neighborhoods	きんじょ	近所	4.6
new	あたらしい	新しい	3.3, 3.7, 4.2
new car	あたらしくるま	新しい車	3.7
New England	ニューイングランド		4.3
new Kanji	しんしゅつかんじ	新出漢字	3.4
new semester	しんがっき	新学期	1.1, 4.8
new year	しょうがつ	正月	3.8, 3.9, 1.1.2
new year	しんねん	新年	3.6, 4.3
New York	ニューヨーク		3.6, 3.7,4.9, 1.3.3
next time	こんど	今度	4.2
NY Mets	ニューヨーク・メッツ		4.7
newspaper	しんぶん	新聞	3.5, 3.6, 4.3
next	つぎ	次	1.1, 1.5, 4.3
next	つぎに	次に	2.4, 2.5, 2.6, 3.7
next	となり	隣	2.7, 3.1
next month	らいげつ	来月	1.3, 1.5, 2.1
next student	しんにゅうせい	新入生	2.4
next time	こんど	今度	1.5
next week	らいしゅう	来週	1.5, 2.1, 3.4,4.2, 1.4.10
next year	らいねん	来年	1.3
night	ばん	晩	2.3
night	よる	夜	3.7, 1.3.9
night shift	よるのシフト	夜のシフト	3.5
Niigata (name of prefecture)	にいがた	新潟	3.7
Nina (name)	ニーナ		2.5, 1.0.1
nine (quantity)	きゅうこ	九個	3.4
nine big animals (horses, tigers, etc.)	きゅうとう	九頭	3.4
nine bound objects (books, notebooks, magazines etc.)	きゅうさつ	九冊	3.4
nine cars and other rides, machines, appliances	きゅうだい	九台	3.4
nine houses, nine stores	きゅうけん	九軒	3.4
nine long/slender objects	きゅうほん	九本	3.4
nine small animals (dogs, cats, mice etc.)	きゅうひき	九匹	3.4
nine thin/flat objects (CDs, paper, etc.)	きゅうまい	九枚	3.4

English	Japanese (kana)	Japanese (kanji)	Ref
ninth day	ここのか	九日	1.2, 1.2.1
Nishiyama city	にしやまち	西山町	3.4
no	いいえ		1.1, 1.1.2
noon	ひる	昼	1.2, 1.2.1
no one	だれも	誰も	2.4
noisy	うるさい		1.3, 3.2, 3.5,3.7, 4.2, 4.5, 1.3.5
north	きた	北	3.1, 3.3, 3.7
north west side	ほくせいぶ	北西部	4.3
northeast	ほくとう	北東	3.1, 3.3
northern part	ほくぶ	北部	3.8, 4.3
northern side/end	きたがわ	北側	3.8
northwest	ほくせい	北西	3.1, 3.2
not as much as	あまり〜じゃない		3.1
not at all	ぜんぜん	全然	1.3, 1.4, 3.4, 1.3.5
not busy	いそがしくないです	忙しくないです	3.7
not buy	かいません	買いません	4.2
not cool	かっこうわるい	格好わるい	4.5, 4.8
not difficult	むずかしくありません	難しく	3.7
not know	しらない	知らない	4.8
not long	ながくありません	長くありません	3.7
not OK	だめです	駄目です	3.1
not overwork	むりをしない	無理をしない	4.8
not quiet	しずかじゃありません	静かじゃありません	3.7
not really	べつに	別に	2.5, 2.6
not so much	あまり		1.1, 1.6, 3.7,4.2, 1.3.5
not understand	わからない	分らない	4.8
Not yet.	まだです	未だです	3.2
notebook	ノート		3.2, 4.2, 1.0.1
noteworthy	とくちょうてきな	特徴的な	4.3
No thank you	けっこうです	結構です	1.7, 1.1.1
nothing	ない	無い	2.1
notify	しらせる／しらせます	知らせる／知らせます	2.3
noun	めいし	名詞	2.1, 3.2
novel	しょうせつ	小説	4.3,4.9
now	いま	今	2.3, 2.7 1.2.2
Now, we are going to distribute X.	これから、Xをくばります		3.2
nuclear power plant	げんしりょくはつでんしょ	原子力発電所	3.8
number	かず、ばんごう	数、番号	4.2, 4.3, 4.5
number	ばんごう	番号	2.5
number of academic terms	がっきすう	学期数	4.2
number of students	せいとすう	生徒数	4.2
number of teachers	きょういんすう	教員数	4.3
number one	いちばん	一番	1.2
number three	さんばん	三番	1.1
number two	にばん	二番	1.2
nursing care facility	かいごしせつ	介護施設	3.8
nursing home	ようろういん	養老院	3.8
obliging, like caring others	せわずき	世話好き	4.7
object particle	を		1.1, 1.4.7
o'clock	じ	時	1.1, 1.2.1
October	じゅうがつ	十月	3.6, 1.2.1
often	よく		1.1, 1.6, 3.1,4.2, 1.0.3
of course	もちろん	勿論	1.7
office	オフィス		2.4
oh	あ		2.5, 1.3.0
oh my god	あ		2.5, 1.3.0
oil, petroleum	せきゆ	石油	3.5
old	ふるい	古い	3.1, 3.3, 3.7,4.2
old, long ago	むかし	昔	3.4, 3.9
on foot	あるいて	歩いて	1.6, 1.3.9
concerned about others	たにんがきになる	他人が気にかかる	4.7
on the way	とちゅう	途中	4.7, 4.9
once again	もういちど	もう一度	2.6, 3.7, 1.1.3

English	Japanese (kana)	Japanese (kanji)	Ref
one (quantity)	いっこ	一個	3.4
one big animal (horse, tiger, etc.)	いっとう	一頭	3.4
one book	いっさつ	一冊	4.9
one bound object (book, notebook, magazine etc.)	いっさつ	一冊	3.4
one cannot do	てはいけない		4.5
one may not do	てはいけません		4.5
one car and other ride, machine, appliance	いちだい	一台	3.4
one house, one store	いっけん	一軒	3.4
one long/slender object	いっぽん	一本	3.4
one may do	てもいい		4.5
one may do	てもいいです		4.5
one more, another	もうひとつ	もう一つ	4.5
one person	ひとり	一人	4.9
one small animal (dog, cat, mouse etc.)	いっぴき	一匹	3.4
one thin/flat object (CDs, paper, etc.)	いちまい	一枚	3.4
one unit	ひとつ	一つ	2.5,, 1.2.9
one's term of office	にんき	任期	3.8
only	だけ		3.6, 3.9
open	あける	開ける	2.5
open minded	こころがひろい	心が広い	4.6
opinion, thought, belief	いけん	意見	2.7, 4.7, 4.8, 4.9
opposite	はんたい(な)	反対(な)	3.6, 1.2.9
optician	めがねや	眼鏡屋	3.8
orange	オレンジ		3.3, 1.1.9
orchard	かじゅえん	果樹園	3.8
orchestra	オーケストラ		2.3
order	じゅんじょ	順序	2.3
order (v)	ちゅうもんする	注文する	3.8
Oregon	オレゴン		3.6, 1.4.1
organic	オーガニック／ゆうきてき	有機的	4.6
organization, mechanics	くみたて	組み立て	1.1, 3.2
organize	せいり	整理	4.3
origin of fire	ひもと	火元	2.5
orientation	オリエンテーション		4.4
origami	おりがみ	折り紙	1.4, 3.7, 4.2, 4.9
original words	もとのことば	元の言葉	4.4
other	ほか	他	2.7
on the other hand	いっぽう	一方	4.9
our town	わたしたちのまち	私達の町	3.3
go out	でかける	出かける	3.8, 3.9
outlet store	アウトレットストア		3.8
outside	やがい	野外	3.5, 3.8, 3.9
outside	そと	外	3.1, 3.3
outwear	うわぎ	上着	4.6
over coat	オーバー		4.5
over there	あそこ	彼所	3.7
over, too	すぎる	過ぎる	2.7, 4.9
packed lunch	べんとう	弁当	2.4
rice paddy	た	田	3.1, 4.3
rice paddy	たんぼ	田んぼ	3.1
paddy field	すいでん	水田	3.8
page style	ページ・スタイル		4.9
pairs	ペア		2.4, 4.4
pair with	ペアで		4.4
pair work	ペアワーク		1.6, 3.4
pajama	パジャマ		4.7
pamphlet	パンフ(パンフレット)		4.4, 4.8, 4.9
panda	パンダ		3.4
pants	パンツ		4.5
paper	かみ	紙	2.5, 4.9
parade	パレード		4.4
paradoxical	ぎゃくせつ	逆接	4.1, 4.2
paragraph	パラグラフ		3.1, 3.4, 3.5,3.7, 4.6
paraphrasing strategy	いいかえるのストラテジー	言い換えるのストラテジー	4.4
parent meeting	ほごしゃかい	保護者会	4.4

parents/guardian teacher meeting	ほごしゃかい	保護者会	4.4
park	こうえん	公園	2.3, 3.1, 3.4, 1.3.4
parking lot	ちゅうしゃじょう	駐車場	3.8
part	ぶぶん	部分	1.3, 4.6
part of speech	ひんし	品詞	2.6, 4.3
part 1	そのいち	其の一	3.1
part time job	アルバイト		1.4, 3.4, 1.4.11
participate	さんかする	参加する	4.8
particle	じょし	助詞	2.1
particle ga	が		1.1, 1.4.7
partner	あいて	相手	1.6, 4.7
party	パーティー		1.4, 2.5, 3.5, 1.0.2
pass	とおる	通る	3.8, 3.9
pass, crosss	わたる	渡る	3.8, 3.9
past	かこ	過去	1.4
pasta	パスタ		3.2, 3.7, 4.2, 1.2.4
be patient	がまんする	我慢する	4.7
patient	がまんづよい		4.2, 4.6
pay attention	ごちゅうい	御注意	3.8, 3.9
PE (Physical Education)	たいいく	体育	4.3
peach	もも	桃	3.6, 3.9
peace	へいわ	平和	3.5
peace of mind	あんしん	安心	4.3
Pedro (name)	ペドロ		1.4, 4.9
peer evaluation	ピアひょうか	ピア評価	3.7
pen	ペン		2.5, 3.1, 4.4
peninsula	はんとう	半島	3.5
perform	えんそうする	演奏する	3.8
performance	えんそう	演奏	3.4, 3.9
permission	きょか	許可	4.8
person	ひと	人	1.3, 3.2, 3.7, 4.2, 1.0.2
person with disability	しょうがいしゃ	障害者	4.3
personal	こじんてきな	個人的な	2.4
personal computer	パソコン (パーソナルコンピューター)		3.5, 4.4, 4.9, 1.0.2
personality	じんかく	人格	1.6, 4.6, 4.9
pet shop	ペットショップ		3.8
pharmacy	くすりや	薬屋	3.8
Phoenix	フェニックス		4.3
philosophy	てつがく	哲学	4.3, 4.6
phone number	でんわばんごう	電話番号	2.2, 1.1.6
photo	しゃしん	写真	1.5, 2.1, 4.4, 1.1.9
photo club	しゃしんぶ	写真部	1.5, 1.7, 2.6, 3.5
physics	ぶつり	物理	4.3
physiology	せいりがく	生理学	4.3
picnic	ピクニック		3.1
picture	え	絵	2.1, 2.5, 3.4, 4.7, 1.0.2
pie	パイ		1.5
piece / work	さくひん	作品	3.1
pimple	にきび	面皰	2.4
pink	ピンク		3.3, 1.1.9
pitcher	ピッチャー	投手	2.3
Peter	ピーター		1.4
Pittsburg	ピッツバーグ		1.4, 1.3.11
pizza	ピザ		1.4, 3.2, 3.5, 3.9, 4.2, 1.2.1
pizza shop	ピザや	ピザ屋	3.8
place	ところ	所	1.7
place	ばしょ	場所	1.4, 3.7, 3.8, 3.9, 4.2, 1.0.2
Place a checkmark	しるしをつけてください	印をつけてください	4.4

place of interest	めいしょ	名所	3.8
plain	へいや	平野	3.5, 3.7
plum	うめ	梅	3.8, 3.9
plans, goals	ほうふ	抱負	1.5
planetarium	プラネタリウム		3.8
planning	けいかくせい	計画性	1.4, 4.7
plant	しょくぶつ	植物	3.8
play	あそぶ／あそびます	遊ぶ／遊びます	2.3, 3.4, 3.9, 4.6
play a match	しあいする	試合する	3.8
play bingo games	ビンゴゲームをする		3.2
play,drama	げき	劇	2.3, 3.4, 4.4
player	せんしゅ	選手	1.4, 2.4
pleasant	きもちがいい	気持ちがいい	3.1, 3.7, 4.2, 4.4
Please circle Z.	Ｚをまるでかこんでください	Ｚを○で囲んでください	3.2
Please describe	びょうしゃしてください	描写してください	4.5
Please discuss	はなしあってください	話し合ってください	4.3
Please do	てください		4.2
Please do so.	おねがいします。	お願いします。	2.4, 3.2, 1.1.2
please give me	ください		1.1, 1.0.1
Please make any corrections	しゅうせいしてください	修正してください	3.7
Please wait for a moment.	ちょっとまってください	ちょっと待ってください	3.2, 3.8
Please write (something) on/in Y.	Ｙにかいてください	Ｙに書いてください	3.2
plum tree	うめ	梅	3.6
police	けいさつ	警察	3.1
police booth/box	こうばん	交番	3.3, 3.6
political rally	せいじしゅうかい	政治集会	3.8
political science	せいじがく	政治学	1.4, 4.3
pond	いけ	池	3.1
pool	プール		1.6, 3.3, 3.6, 4.2, 4.8, 1.1.7
popular	にんき	人気	2.4, 4.6
popular, prevail, spread	はやる	流行る	4.8
population	じんこう	人口	3.2, 3.7, 4.3
Portland	ポートランド		1.3
possession	の		1.1, 1.1.4
positional information	いちのじょうほう	位置の情報	3.3
positional words	いちのたんご	位置の単語	3.1
post office	ゆうびんきょく	郵便局	1.6, 3.1, 3.2, 3.5, 4.4, 4.6, 1.4.11
poster	ポスター		1.4, 1.3.11
posture	しせい	姿勢	1.6
potential	こうほ	候補	4.8
potential verb	かのうどうし	可能動詞	4.7
power plant	はつでんしょ	発電所	3.8
practice, exercise	れんしゅう	練習	2.7, 3.4, 4.6, 4.8, 1.3.9
prairie, plan	へいげん	平原	3.8
praise	ほめる	誉める	4.7
practice	れんしゅうする	練習する	1.1, 2.1, 4.4
preface	まえがき	前書き	4.9
prefecture	けん	県	3.8
preliminary activities	まえさぎょう	前作業	2.6, 4.9
preparation	じゅんび	準備	1.3, 2.7, 4.2
presentation	はっぴょう	発表	1.1, 1.4
presentation	プレゼンテーション		1.5, 1.4.11
preview, preparation	よしゅう	予習	2.7, 4.9
price	ねだん	値段	3.7, 1.2.2
primary industry	だいいちじさんぎょう	第一次産業	3.8
prison, jail	けいむしょ	刑務所	3.8
private clothes	しふく	私服	4.5, 4.7
private school	しりつこう	私立校	4.3
Priya (name)	プリヤ		1.4
problem	もんだい	問題	1.2, 2.4, 2.7, 4.9, 1.0.2
problem solving	もんだいかいけつ	問題解決	4.5
profile	プロフィール		1.1, 4.8

English	Japanese (kana)	Japanese (kanji)	Lesson
progress	しんこう	進行	1.6, 2.3
program	プログラム		4.8
progressive	しんぽてき（な）	進歩的な	3.8
prohibition	きんし	禁止	4.8
proofreading	こうせい	校正	4.8, 4.9
property	とち	土地	3.7
protect	まもる	守る	4.7
prior knowledge	きぞんのちしき	既存の知識	4.8, 4.9
project	プロジェクト		1.2, 4.6, 1.0.1
project partner	プロジェクトのあいて	プロジェクトの相手 4.2	
prom	プロム		4.4, 4.8
pronunciation	はつおん	発音	1.1, 1.5, 3.4
prosper, thrive	はんえいする	繁栄する	3.8
prosperous	さかんです	盛んです	4.3, 4.4
psychology	しんりがく	心理学	4.8
public	こうりつの	公立の	3.7
public facilities	こうきょうしせつ	公共施設	3.1, 3.2, 4.3
public school	こうりつこう	公立校	4.3
punctual	じかんをまもる	時間を守る	4.7
Pumpkin Fest	パンプキンフェスト		4.4
pumpkin pie	パンプキンパイ		4.4
purpose	もくてき	目的	2.3, 4.3
pursuit	ついきゅう	追究	4.7, 4.9
put a circle	えんでかこむ	円で囲む	3.7
put in	いれる	入れる	1.3, 2.7
pyramid	ピラミッド		3.7
qualities	せいしつ	性質	4.2
quantity	りょう	量	3.4
Queens street (name of street)	クイーンズストリート		3.3
question	しつもん	質問	1.2, 2.5, 2.7,3.5, 4.5, 1.0.2
questionnaire	アンケート		1.5
quick, fast	はやい	速い	1.6, 3.6
quiet	しずか（な）	静か（な）	1.3, 3.1, 3.4,3.7, 4.2, 1.3.7
quiet	しずかに	静かに	2.5, 1.1.9
quit	やめる	辞める	4.9
Rachel (name)	レーチェル		1.1, 1.1.4
racket ball	ラケットボール		4.3
radio station	ラジオきょく	ラジオ局	3.8
Rafutee (Okinawan cuisine)	ラフテー	(沖縄の食べ物)	4.4
rejoice	よろこぶ	喜ぶ	1.7
rain	あめ	雨	3.1, 3.5, 4.2
rainbow	にじ	虹	3.8
rainbow appears	にじがでる	虹が出る	3.8
rainy day (s)	あめのひ	雨の日	3.5
rainy season	つゆ	梅雨	3.6, 4.4
raise, lift	あげる	上げる	1.6
raise a hand	てをあげる	手を上げる	2.2, 3.2, 3.7
Raise your hands.	てをあげてください。	手をあげてください 3.2	
ramen noodle	ラーメン		1.1 , 4.4, 1.0.1
ramen noodle shop	ラーメンや	ラーメン屋	3.8
ranch	ぼくじょう	牧場	3.8
rate of speed	そくど	速度	4.7
reach	リーチ	リーチ	3.7
read	よむ／よみます	読む／読みます	1.1, 1.3, 2.3, 3.1 1.4.1
read aloud	おんどくがた	音読型	2.5, 4.9
readers, audience	どくしゃ	読者	4.7
reading	どくしょ	読書	1.3
reading and writing	よみかき	読み書き	4.6, 4.9
reading comprehension	どっかい	読解	4.8
ready to study	べんきょうしておく	勉強しておく	2.7
really	ほんとうに	本当に	4.2
reason	りゆう	理由	4.2, 4.9
rebuild, reconstruct, renovate	かいちくする	改築する	3.8
recently, lately	さいきん	最近	1.4, 3.5, 4.5
recognize, understand	にんしき	認識	4.2
recommendation	おすすめ	お勧め	3.4, 3.9
recording	きろく	記録	4.3
red	あかい	赤い	2.5, 3.7, 1.1.9
Reed (name)	リード		1.1
reference	さんこう	参考	4.8
reflection meeting	はんせいかい	反省会	2.7
reflection	ふりかえり	振り返り	1.6, 2.1,3.1,3.8, 4.9
refreshing, delightful	さわやか（な）	爽やかな	3.8
region	ちほう	地方	4.3
regrettable	ざんねん	残念	1.5, 4.7
regular, common	ふつうの	普通の	4.8
rehearsal	リハーサル		2.6
relationship	かんけい	関係	2.7, 4.5, 4.9
relative	しんせき	親戚	2.6
relax	リラックス		1.6, 4.7
reliable	しんらいできる	信頼できる	4.6, 4.8
religious	しゅうきょうけい	宗教系	4.3
religious	しゅうきょうてき（な）	宗教的な	3.8
remedy, relearn	べんきょうしなおす	勉強し直す	4.9
remember	おもいだす	思い出す	1.6
remote controller	リモコン(リモートコントロール)		4.4, 4.9
report	レポート		2.2, 3.6
reply	へんしん	返信	2.6
represent action and action	たり、たり		4.5, 4.9
request	おねがい	お願い	4.9
resemblance	るいじてん	類似点	4.4
resemble	ににています	に似ています	4.4
research	しらべ	調べ	3.6, 4.9
research institution	けんきゅうしょ	研究所	3.8
reside, live	すむ	住む	1.5, 3.5
residence	じたく	自宅	4.7, 4.9
residence area	じゅうたくち	住宅地	3.8
residence, housing	じゅうたく	住宅	3.7, 3.8
resort	ひしょち	避暑地	3.6
response essay	かんそうぶん	感想文	4.9
rest	やすむ	休む	1.4
restaurant	レストラン	料理店／りょうりてん	1.4, 3.1, 3.7, 1.2.6
result	けっか	結果	3.8, 4.3, 4.4
return	かえる／かえります	帰る／帰ります	1.4, 4.7 1.4.1
return	もどす／もどします	戻す／戻します	2.4
return	かえす	返します	4.8
review	ふくしゅうする	復習する	1.1, 1.3.9
review	ふくしゅう	復習	3.4, 3.6, 4.9
revise	すいこう	推敲	1.1, 1.5
rewrite	かきかえてください	書き換えてください 3.6	
rewrite	かきなおす	書き直す	4.2, 4.9
ribbon	リボン		4.5
ride (n)	のりもの	乗り物	3.3
ride (v)	のる	乗る	1.6, 2.4
right	みぎ	右	2.1, 3.1, 3.3,4.2, 4.6
righteous	ただしくしたい	正しくしたい	4.8
ring	ゆびわ	指輪	4.5
river	かわ	川	3.2, 3.5
riverbank	どて	土手	3.8, 3.9
River High School	リバーこうこう	リバー高校	3.6
road	どうろ	道路	3.8
robot club	ロボットクラブ		4.3
rock	いわ	岩	3.8
rock	ロック		1.5,4.4, 1.2.1
rock concert	ロックコンサート		3.5
role	やくわり	役割	2.5, 3.1, 3.2
role play	ロールプレイ		1.6, 2.1, 3.3, 4.9
romance	ロマンス		1.5

English	かな	漢字	Ref
room	へや	部屋	3.3, 3.7, 4.3
roommate	ルームメイト		4.2
Rose Middle School	ローズちゅうがっこう	ローズ中学校	1.3
rotate	まわす／まわします	回す／回します	2.1, 2.3
rugby	ラグビー		4.3
rule	ルール		1.1
runningback	ラニングバック		4.7, 4.9
Russian	ろしあご	ロシア語	4.3
safe	あんぜん（な）	安全な	3.8
sell	うる	売る	1.7
Sally (name of girl)	サリー		3.3
same as	とおなじ	と同じ	3.1
small	ちいさい	小さい	1.4, 3.1, 1.0.2
sample conversation	かいわのれい	会話の例	3.2
samurai	さむらい	侍	1.4, 4.2
sand beach	すなはま	砂浜	3.8
sandals	サンダル		4.6
sandwich	サンドイッチ		4.4
Sapporo (name of city)	さっぽろ	札幌	3.1, 3.7
Sara (girl's name)	サラ		4.9
Sarah (girls name)	サラ		1.3,2.5, 4.4, 4.7
Saturday	どようび	土曜日	1.2, 4.2, 1.2.1
say	いう／いいます	言う／言います	1.3, 2.3
scalpel	メス		2.3
scary	こわい	こわい	4.2
scenery	けしき	景色	3.8
schedule	スケジュール		1.2 , 2.2, 4.8, 1.0.1
school	がっこう	学校	1.1, 3.2, 3.5,4.2, 1.0.1
school code	きそく	規則	4.5
school excursion	えんそく	遠足	4.4
school gate	こうもん	校門	3.5
I school (school name)	Iこう	I校	1.7
school principal	こうちょうせんせい	校長先生	4.4, 4.7
school reunion	どうそうかい	同窓会	3.8
school rule	こうそく	校則	4.3
school trip	しゅうがくりょこう	修学旅行	4.4
school yard	こうてい	校庭	4.7
science	かがく	科学	1.3, 3.4, 4.2, 1.0.2
science	りか	理科	2.7,4.3
science fair	かがくさい	科学祭	4.8
science fiction	エスエフ		1.5
scissors	はさみ	鋏み	2.5
Sea Side Academy	シーサイドがくえん	シーサイド学園	1.6
sea, ocean	うみ	海	1.1, 1.4, 3.1, 4.8
seaport, harbor	みなと	港	3.2, 3.8
seafood	シーフード		1.4
seal	はん	判	2.3
sea port	みなと	港	3.1
search	さがう	探す	4.9
seashore	かいがん	海岸	3.1
seasonal theater	きせつげきじょう	季節劇場	3.1
seasons	きせつ	季節	2.4, 3.8, 3.9
second day	ふつか	二日	1.2, 1.2.1
second semester	にがっき	二学期	4.4
secondary industry	だいにじさんぎょう	第二次産業	3.8
section	セクション		3.5
see again	じゃ、また		2.3, 1.0.1
see,watch	みる／みます	見る／見ます	1.1 , 3.5,4.7, 1.4.1
Seinan line	せいなんせん	西南線	3.8, 3.9
self	じぶん	自分	4.7, 4.9
self evaluation	じこひょうか	自己	3.7
self introduction	じこしょうかい	自己紹介	4.9
selfish	かって	勝手	2.3
selfish	わがまま		4.8
sell	うります	売ります	1.4, 4.6
semester	がっき	学期	4.2, 4.3
second year student	にねんせい	二年生	1.3
send	おくる	送る	4.8
Sendai (name of city)	せんだい	仙台	3.7
senior trip	シニアトリップ		4.4
sense of responsibility	せきにんかん	責任感	4.6
senseless	ださい		4.5
sentence	ぶん	文	1.3, 2.6, 3.1
sentence construction	ぶんをつくる	文を作る	1.3, 3.3
September	くがつ	九月	3.6
September 8th	くがつようか	九月八日	1.2, 1.2.1
serious	まじめ	真面目	4.2, 1.3.5
seriously	ほんかくてき	本格的	4.7, 4.9
service	サービス		3.8
service industry	サービスぎょう	サービス業	3.8
session	セッション		2.2
set topic appropriately	テーマをかんがえてぶんをつくる	テーマを考えて文を作る	3.3
seven (quantity)	ななこ	七個	3.4
seven big animals (horses, tigers, etc.)	ななとう	七頭	3.4
seven bound objects (books, notebooks, magazines, etc.)	ななさつ	七冊	3.4
seven cars and other rides, machines, appliances	ななだい	七台	3.4
seven houses, stores	ななけん	七軒	3.4
seven long/slender objects	ななほん	七本	3.4
seven o'clock	しちじ	七時	4.2
seven persons	しちにん	七人	1.4, 1.2.3
seven Samurai	しちにんのさむらい	七人の侍	4.2
seven small animals (dogs, cats, mice, etc.)	ななひき	七匹	3.4
seven thin/flat objects (CDs, paper, etc.)	ななまい	七枚	3.4
seventh day	なのか	七日	1.2, 1.2.1
several	いくつか	幾つか	3.4
severe	きびしいです	厳しいです	3.1
severe than	よりきびしい	より厳しい	3.1
severe, strict	きびしい	厳しい	1.3, 3.1, 3.7,4.2. 4.5, 1.3.5
shabby	みすぼらしい		4.5
Shakespeare	シェイクスピアー		4.4
Shamika (name)	シャミカ		4.9
shape	かたち	形	3.4
Shantal (name)	シャンタル		2.1, 2.2, 2.3, 2.6
shave	そる	剃る	4.5, 4.8
sheep	ひつじ	羊	2.2.5, 1.1.4
sheet	シート		3.2
sheriff	ほあんかん	保安官	3.8
Shiga prefecture	しがけん	滋賀県	2.7
Shinano River (the longest river in Japan)	しなのがわ	信濃川	3.3
ship	ふね	船	1.3, 3.5, 1.3.1
Shiroyama machi	しろやままち	城山町	3.3
Shizuka mura	しずかむら	静か村	3.3
shoe store	くつや	靴屋	3.8
shoes	くつ	靴	2.4, 4.5, 4.6
shoes for floor	うわばき	上履き	2.4
Shonan beach (place name)	しょうなんかいがん	湘南海岸	1.4, 3.6, 4.7
shop,store	みせ	店	1.4, 3.1, 3.5,4.2, 1.2.6
shopping	かいもの	買い物	1.4, 3.5, 1.4.11
shopping arcade,mall	しょうてんがい	商店街	1.4, 3.1,3.8, 3.9
shopping center	ショッピングセンター		3.8, 4.2
shopping mall	ショッピングモール		1.4, 3.3
short	みじかい	短い	1.4, 2.1, 3.7,4.6
short	せがひくい	背が低い	4.6
short sentence	みじかいぶん	短い文	3.3
shorts	ショーツ		4.5

English	Kana	Kanji	Ref
shout easily	さけびやすい	叫びやすい	4.7
shoveling of snow	ゆきかき	雪掻き	3.8
Showa Era	しょわじだい	昭和時代	3.5
shrine	じんじゃ	神社	3.6
side	よこ	横	2.5, 3.1, 3.3
sight seeing	かんこう	観光	3.4
sight seeing guide	かんこうあんない	観光案内	3.4, 3.8, 3.9
sign	きごう	記号	1.3, 2.2, 2.5
signal	しんごう	信号	3.8, 3.9
similarity statement	そうじのぶん	相似の文	3.6
simile	ちょくゆ	直喩	4.4
simple	かんたん (な)	簡単 (な)	1.1, 3.4
simple sentence	たんぶん	単文	4.8
simultaneous	どうじに	同時に	4.8
sing	うたう	歌う	4.6
Singapore	シンガポール		3.7
sister city	しまいとし	姉妹都市	3.8
sister schools	しまいこう	姉妹校	4.8
sit	すわる/すわります	座る/座ります	2.4, 2.6
situation	じょうきょう	状況	4.9
situation	ばあい	場合	3.7
six (pens)	ろっぽん	六本	3.4
six (quantity)	ろっこ	六個	3.4
six big animals (horses, tigers, etc.) ろくとう		六頭	3.4
six bound objects (books, notebooks, magazines etc.)	ろくさつ	六冊	3.4
six cars and other rides, machines, appliances ろくだい		六台	3.4
six houses, six stores	ろっけん	六軒	3.4
six long/slender objects	ろっぽん	六本	3.4
six small animals (dogs, cats, mice etc.) ろっぴき		六匹	3.4
six thin/flat objects (CDs, paper, etc.) ろくまい		六枚	3.4
six units	むっつ	六つ	2.5, 1.2.9
sixteen years old	じゅうろくさい	十六才	1.1, 4.2, 1.1.2
sixth day	むいか	六日	1.2, 1.2.1
size	おおきさ	大きさ	3.8
skating rink	スケートリンク		2.5, 4.6, 4.9
ski	スキー		3.7, 4.4
ski slope/resort	スキーじょう	スキー場	3.8
skillful	じょうず	上手	1.1, 1.4
skillful instruction	おしえかたがじょうずだ	教え方が上手だ	4.8
skinny	やせている	やせている	4.6
skirt	スカート		4.5
skit	スキット		4.9
sky	そら	空	3.3, 3.8
sleep	ねる/ねます	寝る/寝ます	1.5, 2.3, 3.2,3.5, 3.7, 4.7, 1.4.1
sleeping	ねている	寝ている	2.7
sleepy	ねむい	眠い	2.7
sleet	みぞれ	霙	3.8
slide	スライド		2.5
slope	さか	坂	3.8
slow	おそい	遅い	1.1, 1.0.1
slowly	ゆっくり		1.6, 1.1.9
small	ちいさい	小さい	1.4, 3.7
small island	こじま	小島	3.6
small group	しょうグループ	小グループ	2.4
small city	しょうとし	小都市	4.3
smart	あたまがいい	頭がいい	3.2
smith	スミス		1.2, 3.5, 4.6
smooth	スムーズ		1.6, 4.9
snake	へび	蛇	3.3, 3.7
snow	ゆき	雪	3.1, 3.5
snow day	ゆきのひ	雪の日	3.6
snow festival	スノーフェスティバル		3.7
snowstorm	ふぶき	吹雪	3.1
so	そこで		1.4
soba noodle shop	そばや	蕎麦屋	3.8
so-called, represent, describe, XというY, XというY inferms of y, say			4.4
soccer	サッカー		1.3, 3.6, 4.2,4.3, 1.1.4
soccer field	サッカーじょう	サッカー場	3.7, 3.8
social studies, society	しゃかい	社会	2.7, 3.8, 4.3
social studies	しゃかいか	社会科	4.9
socks	くつした	靴下	4.5
softball	ソフトボール		4.2, 4.3, 4.8
Soho (name of place)	ソーホー		3.3
solution	かいけつ	解決	2.7
someday	いつか		2.5
sometimes	ときどき	時々	1.4, 1.6, 2.7, 1.4.1
something	なにか		4.9
something you forget	わすれもの	忘れ物	2.7
soon	まもなく		3.8, 3.9
so-so, fair, moderately ~	まあまあ		1.1, 1.4, 3.7, 4.9
south	みなみ	南	3.1, 3.3, 3.7
south east side	なんとうぶ	南東部	4.3
south entrance	みなみぐち	南口	3.8, 3.9
South Park	サウスこうえん	サウス公園	3.6
south side	なんぶ	南部	4.3
south west side	なんせいぶ	南西部	4.3
southeast	なんとう	南東	3.1, 3.3
southern side/end	みなみがわ	南側	3.8
southern part	なんぶ	南部	3.8
southwest	なんせい	南西	3.1, 3.3
souvenir	おみやげ	お土産	1.7
souvenir shop	おみやげや	お土産屋	3.8
soy source	しょうゆ	醤油	2.7
spacious	ひろい	広い	3.2
spaghetti	スパゲティー		4.4
Spanish	スペインご	スペイン語	3.9, 4.3
speak	はなす/はなします	話す/話します	1.1, 3.5, 4.7, 1.3.2
speaker	スピーカー		1.1, 1.6, 1.4.6
special curriculum school	とくしゅカリキュラムのがっこう 特別カリキュラムの学校		4.3
speciality (product)	めいさん	名産	3.8
speech	スピーチ		1.1, 1.4, 4.9
speech contest	スピーチコンテスト		4.4
spoon	スプーン		2.7
sporting goods store	スポーツショップ		3.8
sports	スポーツ		1.3, 3.5, 4.2
sports center	スポーツセンター		3.3
sports fan	ファン		2.3
sports team	スポーツチーム		4.4, 4.7, 4.8
spread	しく	敷く	1.7
spread	ひらく/ひらきます	開く/開きます	2.1
spring	はる	春	1.5, 2.7, 3.6,4.2, 4.5, 1.1.6
spring break	はるやすみ	春休み	1.5, 3.7, 4.4
Spring Fling	スプリングフリング		4.4
spring rain	はるさめ	春雨	3.8
square dance	スクエアダンス		3.8
square (area)	へいほう	平方	3.6, 3.8
squash	スカッシュ		4.3
squished	はさまれる	挟まれる	4.7
stadium	スタジアム		3.8
stand in line	ならぶ	並ぶ	3.5
stand	たつ/たちます	立つ/立ちます	1.4, 2.6, 4.7
start	はじめる	始める	1.5
state	しゅう	州	3.8
state office building	しゅうちょうしゃ	州庁舎	3.8
states	じょうたい	状態	4.2
stationary	ぶんぼうぐや	文房具屋	3.8

712 *Appendix E*

English	Hiragana	Kanji	Section
Thanksgiving	かんしゃさい	感謝祭	4.8
that	その	其の	2.5, 1.4.7
that is to say	すなわち	即ち	4.7
that one	それ	其れ	2.5
that one over there	あの		2.5
that over there	あれ		2.5
that time	そのとき/そのころ	その時/その頃	2.7
that's correct	そうです		1.1, 1.0.1
the galaxy	ぎんが	銀河	3.8
the Great Wall	ばんりのちょうじょう	万里の長城	1.4
Marine holiday	うみのひ	海の日	1.7
the opposite side/end	はんたいがわ	反対側	3.8
the other side	むこうがわ	向こう側	3.8
The person slated to distribute X.	Xをくばるひと	Xをくばる人	3.2
the rest of class	ほかのみんな	他の皆	4.9
the track	りくじょうきょうぎ	陸上競技	4.4
theater	げきじょう	劇場	3.4, 3.8, 4.9
then	じゃあ		3.8, 3.9
Then, let's start.	じゃ、はじめましょう。	じゃ、始めましょう	3.2
there are many~	たくさんあります		4.4
there is no...	ありません		1.1, 1.4.5
there is not so much	あまりない	余りない	4.5, 4.9
therefore, thus	だから		1.1, 1.6, 3.3,3.5, 3.7, 1.3.5
things	もの	物	1.4,4.3
things such as the following	つぎのようなもの	次のようなもの	4.3
think	おもう	思う	1.4, 3.8
think over	はんせい	反省	2.7, 4.9
think well, devise	くふうする	工夫する	4.8
third day	みっか	三日	1.2, 1.2.1
third semester	さんがっき	3学期	4.4
third year student	さんねんせい	三年生	1.3, 1.1.6
this	この	此の	2.5, 1.3.1
this month	こんげつ	今月	1.5, 2.1, 4.2
this one	これ	此れ	2.5, 1.1.1
this week	こんしゅう	今週	1.5, 2.1
this year	ことし	今年	1.3, 1.4, 1.1.7
Those who don't have Z, please raise your hand.	Zがないひと、てをあげてください	Zがない人、手を上げてください 3.2	
Those who have Y, please raise your hand.	Yがあるひと、てをあげてください	Yがある人、手を上げてください 3.2	
thousand	まん	万	3.4
three (quantity)	さんこ	三個	3.4
three big animals (horses, tigers, etc.)	さんとう	三頭	3.4
three bound objects (books, notebooks, magazines etc.)	さんさつ	三冊	3.4
three cars and other rides, machines, appliances	さんだい	三台	3.4
three houses, stores	さんげん	三軒	3.4
three long/slender objects	さんぼん	三本	3.4
three persons	さんにん	三人	1.3, 3.4, 1.2.1
three small animals (dogs, cats, mice etc.)	さんびき	三匹	3.4
three thin/flat objects (CDs, paper, etc.)	さんまい	三枚	3.4
three times	さんかい	三回	2.1
thunderstorm	らいう	雷雨	3.1, 3.6, 4.7
Thursday	もくようび	木曜日	1.2, 3.5,4.2, 1.2.1
tie	しめる	締める	4.5
tie, put on	つける	着ける	4.5
tiger	とら	虎	2.5, 3.1, 3.7 1.0.2,
time	じかん	時間	2.2, 3.5, 1.2.1
time	じき	時期	3.6, 3.9
time	とき	時	2.7
tired	つかれる	疲れる	1.7
title	おおみだし	大見出し	4.8
to	へ		1.1, 1.0.2
to my regret, unfortunate	ざんねんながら	残念ながら	4.9
to rain	あめがふる	雨がふる	3.5
to(ni) particle	に		1.1, 2.2, 1.1.1
today	きょう	今日	1.3, 1.4, 3.2,4.2, 1.3.5
today's homework	きょうのしゅくだい	今日の宿題	3.2
together	いっしょに	一緒に	1.3, 2.7, 1.4.2
toilet	トイレ		3.7
Tokyo	とうきょう	東京	1.6, 2.1, 3.2,3.4, 3.7, 1.3.2
Tokyo	とうきょうと	東京都	4.3
tolerate	がまんする	我慢する	4.8
Tom (name)	トム		1.3, 2.2, 2.5,2.6, 3.7, 4.2
Tomei high way	とうめいこうそくどうろ	東名高速道路	4.7, 4.9
tomorrow	あした	明日	1.3, 4.6, 1.2.2
tomorrow's weather	あしたのてんき	明日の天気	1.3, 3.1
Tony (name of boy)	トニー		3.3
too much say	いいすぎる	言い過ぎる	4.8
tooth	は	歯	2.4, 4.5
top three	トップスリー		4.2
topic	トピック		2.2, 3.1, ,4.9
topic	わだい	話題	2.4
topic particle	は		1.1, 3.3, 1.4.7
topic sentence	トピックセンテンス		3.4, 3.7
topics	こうもく	項目	4.9
tornado	たつまき	竜巻	3.8
Toronto	トロント		3.6
tourism, sightseeing	かんこう	観光	3.8
towel	タオル		4.2
town	まち	町	3.1, 3.2, 4.2, 4.3, 4.4
town hall	まちやくば	町役場	3.8
town manager, mayor	ちょうちょう	町長	3.8
toy store	おもちゃや	おもちゃ屋	3.1, 3.4
track and field	りくじょう	陸上	4.3
trade	ぼうえき	貿易	3.8
traditional	でんとうてき（な）	伝統的な	2.4, 3.8
train	でんしゃ	電車	1.3, 1.3.1
train going to central station	のぼりでんしゃ	上り電車	3.8, 3.9
train station	えき	駅	3.1,3.7, 4.2,1.4.11
transportation, traffic	こうつう	交通	1.3, 3.2, 3.7, 1.3.6
travel	りょこう	旅行	4.6
travel agency	りょこうだいりてん	旅行代理店	3.8
tree	き	木	3.1, 3.3, 1.0.2
trip	りょこう	旅行	1.5, 1.6
troublesome	めんどうな	面倒な	4.8
truck	トラック		3.5, 4.7
trustworthy	しんらいができる	信頼ができる	4.6
truth	ほんとう	本当	4.8
try to go	いってみます	行ってみます	4.9
try to think	かんがえてみる	考えてみる	2.7
T-shirt	T-しゃつ		4.5
tsunami	つなみ	津波	3.6
Tuesday	かようび	火曜日	1.2, 1.2.1
tulip	チューリップ		3.6, 3.9
turn, order	じゅんばん	順番	3.8, 4.9
Tucson (name of city)	ツーソン		3.6
Tuvalu (name of country)	ツバル		4.4
tuxedo	タキシード		4.5
TV station	テレビきょく	テレビ局	3.8
twelfth grade	こうこう3ねんせい	高校3年生	2.7
two (quantity)	にこ	二個	3.4
two big animals (horses, tigers, etc.)	にとう	二頭	3.4
two bound objects (books, notebooks, magazines etc.)	にさつ	二冊	3.4
two cars and other rides, machines, appliances	にだい	二台	3.4

two houses, two stores	にけん	二軒	3.7
two long/slender objects	にほん	二本	3.7
two persons	ふたり	二人	3.3 4.9, 1.2.1
two small animals (dogs, cats, mice etc.)	にひき	二匹	3.4
two thin/flat objects (CDs, paper, etc.)	にまい	二枚	3.4
type	タイプ		4.3, 4.7
type, kind	しゅるい	種類	2.4, 4.3
typhoon	たいふう	台風	3.1, 3.6, 4.7
udon noodle shop	うどんや	うどん屋	3.8
Ukiyoe(Japanese woodblock prints)	うきよえ	浮世絵	4.3
Umino (name)	うみの	海野	1.7
umm,well then	あのう、それから		1.6, 1.3.6
umm,well, let's see	あのう		1.6, 4.2, 1.1.1
umm,well, let's see…	ええと		1.6, 4.2, 1.2.2
unbelievable	しんじられない	信じられない	2.7
under	した	下	3.3
underline	かせんをひいてください	下線を引いてください	3.3
understand	わかる	分かる	1.6, 1.0.1
underwear	したぎ	下着	4.5, 4.6
uniform	せいふく	制服	2.4,4.5
uniform hat	せいぼう	制帽	4.5
Union	ユニオン		1.6
Union Square Park	ユニオンスクウェアーパーク		3.4, 3.9
unique	こせいてきな	個性的な	4.2
unique	ユニーク（な）		3.8
unit of measurement	どりょうこう	度量衡	3.8
United Nations related	こくれんかんけい	国連関係	3.5, 3.9
unpalatable, bad-tasting	まずい	不味い	1.1, 1.4, 3.7
until recently	さいきんまで	最近まで	4.9
up, top	うえ	上	2.1, 3.1, 1.0.2
up to now	これまで		2.2
use	つかう	使う	1.4, 1.6, 3.5, 4.7
use often	よくつかう	よく使う	4.5
used car dealer	ちゅうこしゃはんばいてん	中古車販売店	3.8
useful, helpful	やくにたつ	役に立つ	2.5
US history	アメリカし	アメリカ史	4.7
valley	たに	谷	3.8
variety	かくしゅ	各種	4.6
various	いろいろ（な）	色々な	1.5, 3.3, 3.7,4.3, 4.6
vase	かき	花器	3.6
vector	ベクトル	ベクトル	4.9
vegetable store	やおや	八百屋	3.1, 3.2, 3.4
verb	どうし	動詞	2.1, 2.3, 3.2, 4.2, 4.6
very hard	いっしょうけんめい	一生懸命	2.5, 4.6
very much	どうも		2.3, 1.0.1
very much	とても		1.1, 1.6, 3.7, 4.2, 4.9
vertical writing	たてがき	縦書き	4.9
vicinity, nearby	ちかく	近く	3.1, 3.5
video	ビデオ		2.6
video shop	ビデオや	ビデオ屋	3.7
village	むら	村	3.5,4.3
village chief, mayor	そんちょう	村長	3.5
vicinity	あたり	辺り	3.5, 3.9
violation of rules	はんそく	反則	3.8
visiting	けんがく	見学	3.4, 3.9
visual aid	ビジュアルエイド		2.5
vocabulary	ごい	語彙	3.1, 4.8, 4.9
vocabulary building	ごいのこうちく	語彙の構築	3.2
voice	こえ	声	1.6, 2.6
volcano	かざん	火山	3.6
volleyball	バレーボール		4.3
volunteer	ボランティア		3.7, 4.1
vote	とうひょう	投票	3.8
waist	こし	腰	2.1

wait please	おまちください	お待ち下さい	3.8, 3.9
wake up	おきる／おきます	起きる／起きます	1.1, 3.6, 4.2, 4.6 4.7, 1.3.5
Wakkanai (name of place)	わっかない	稚内	3.1, 3.7
wall	かべ	壁	4.6, 4.9
want to	〜たい		1.1
ward, district	く	区	3.3, 3.8
warm	あたたかい	暖かい	3.1, 3.6, 3.7, 4.7, 1.3.11
warmhearted	にんじょうがる	人情がある	4.8
warm up	ウォームアップ		2.3
was	でした		1.1
was built	つくられた	作られた	3.4
was made	つくられた	作られた	3.8, 3.9
wash	あらう	洗う	2.4, 2.7, 4.5
wash	あらう／あらいます	洗う／洗います	2.3, 1.4.6
Washington	ワシントン		1.6, 1.3.11
Washington Square Park	ワシントン　スクウェアー　パーク		3.4, 3.9
washroom, toilet	おてあらい	お手洗い	3.8
watch	みます	見ます	1.3, 2.3, 3.2, 4.2
watch	うでとけい	腕時計	4.8
water	みず	水	1.2, 1.6, 1.0.2
water polo	すいきゅう	水球	4.3
waterfall	たき	滝	3.7
we	わたしたち	私達	2.6, 2.7,4.3
we have a variety of ~	いろいろあります		4.4
weak	よわい	弱い	3.1, 3.4, 3.7
weak of	にがて	苦手	1.4, 4.2, 1.3.5
weak point	たんしょ	短所	4.6
weak subjects	にがてなかもく	苦手な科目	4.2
wear	かぶる		4.5
wear	きる	着る	2.4, 3.6, 4.5
wear	する		4.5
wear	はく	履く	4.5
wear	はめる	はめる	4.5
weather	てんき	天気	2.5, 3.4, 3.5,3.7, 4.2, 1.1.1
weather forecast	てんきよほう	天気予報	3.6, 4.8
Wednesday	すいよう(び)	水曜(日)	1.2, 3.4, 1.2.1
weekend	しゅうまつ	週末	1.1, 1.4, 3.7, 4.5
weight, heaviness	おもさ	重さ	3.8
welcome	ようこそ		4.8
welcome party	かんげいかい	歓迎会	4.9
welfare	ふくし	福祉	3.5
welfare facility	ふくししせつ	福祉施設	3.5
well	よく	良く	1.6, 1.3.5
well then	じゃ		1.5 , 3.2, 1.1.4
went	いきました	行きました	4.2
west	にし	西	3.1, 3.7, 4.2
West High School	ウエストこうこう	ウエスト高校	4.3
West Park	にしこうえん	西公園	3.6
West River	ウエストかわ	ウエスト川	3.6
western side/end	にしがわ	西側	3.8
western part	せいぶ	西部	4.3
Western restaurant	せいようりょうりてん	西洋料理店	3.8
western style food	ようしょく	洋食	2.7
wetland	しっちたい	湿地帯	3.8
what	なに	何	1.4, 1.0.2
what color	なにいろ	何色	2.5
what day?	なんようび	何曜日	3.4
what does it mean ?	どういういみ	どう言う意味	2.1, 1.3.1
what grade	なんねんせい	何年生	1.3, 2.5, 1.1.5
what kind of	どんな	どんな	1.5, 4.5,1.3.11
what language	なにご	何語	1.4
what nationality?	なんじん	何人	1.4
what one can do	かのうなこと	可能なこと	3.5
what time?	なんじ	何時	2.5

What will you do now?	これからなにをしますか		4.2
what year?	なんねん	何年	1.4
what;s the temperature?	きおんはなんど?	気温は何度?	3.1
when	いつ	何時	1.4, 1.3.1
where	どこの	何所の	1.4, 1.0.2
which	どれ	何れ	2.5, 1.2.1
which one is	どちらが		2.3, 3.6
which	どの		2.5, 4.9
white	しろい	白い	3.1, 4.5
white people	はくじん	白人	3.8, 4.7
whiteboard	ホワイトボード		3.2, 1.3.11
who	だれ	誰	2.2, 3.7
Why~?	どうして		4.5
wig	かつら		4.5
willing to help	せわずき	世話好き	4.8
win a victory	ゆうしょう	優勝	4.6
win(noun)	かち	勝ち	2.7, 3.8
wind	かぜ	風	3.6
wind blows	かぜがふく	風が吹く	3.6
windowshoping	ウィンドー・ショッピング		3.4, 3.9
windy	かぜがつよい	風が強い	3.1
winter	ふゆ	冬	1.3, 2.7,4.5, 1.1.6
winter break	ふゆやすみ	冬休み	3.7, 4.4
wish	がんぼう	願望	1.5
wishes	ねがいごと	願いごと	1.1, 1.3, 4.9
with/and	と		1.1, 1.0.3
with whom	だれと	誰と	1.3, 1.0.2
woman	じょせい	女性	3.8, 3.9
woman, female	おんなのひと	女の人	2.5, 3.4, 1.3.7
wonderful	すばらしい	素晴らしい	1.4, 3.7, 4.3
woods	はやし	林	3.1
woods and forest	しんりん	森林	3.8
word	ことば	言葉	1.3, 2.5, 4.3
word	たんご	単語	2.5, 3.1,3.7, 4.3, 4.6, 4.8
work	はたらく	働く	3.8
work hard,do one's best	がんばる／がんばります	頑張る／頑張ります	2.3, 2.7
motivating	やるきがでる	やる気がでる	4.8
workshop	ワークショップ		3.8
world drama	せかいのドラマ	世界のドラマ	4.7
world history	せかいのれきし	世界の歴史	4.7
world weather	せかいのてんき	世界の天気	3.6
worry about	しんぱい	心配	2.4, 3.8, 3.9
worst, awful	さいてい	最低	1.1, 1.4, 3.5
worksheet	ワークシート		2.5, 3.2
wrap-up	まとめ	纏め	2.3
wrap-up activity	あとさぎょう	後作業	2.6, 3.8, 4.9
wrestling	レスリング		4.3
write	かく／かきます	書く／書きます	1.3, 3.2,4.7, 1.4.1
writing	ライティング		4.3,4.6
Wyoming	ワイオミング		3.7
X is (just about) the same as Y in terms of Z.		XはYとZが(ほぼ)同じです	
	XはYとZが(ほぼ)おなじです		3.1
X is (just about) the same as Y.	XはYとほぼおなじです	XはYとほぼ同じくらいです	3.1
X is ... than (Y).	Xのほうが～です		3.1
X is just about as ... as Y.	XはYとおなじくらい～です	XはYと同じくらい～です	3.1
X is more (less) ... than Y.	XはYより～です		3.1
X is not as much ... as Y.	XはYほど～じゃ／くありません		3.1
Yamaguchi prefecture	やまぐちけん	山口県	4.3
yard	ヤード		3.7
Yamashiota Park	やましたこうえん	山下公園	3.5, 3.8, 3.9
yawn	あくびする	欠伸する	2.7
yay	わーやーた		4.9
year	とし	年	1.3, 1.1.5

years old	さい	オ	1.1, 1.1.1
yellow	きいろ	黄色	3.3, 1.1.9
yellow line	きいろいせん	黄色い線	3.3, 3.8, 3.9
Yellowstone National Park	イエローストーンこくりつこうえん		2.3, 3.7
		イエローストーン国立公園	
yes	うーん		3.8, 3.9, 1.1.4
yes	ええ		3.7, 4.4
yes	はい		1.1, 3.2, 1.1.2
yesterday	きのう	昨日	1.4, 2.1 ,4.2
yoga	ヨガ		3.5, 4.2
Yokohama (place name)	よこはま	横浜	1.5, 3.8,3.9,4.7
Yokohama city	よこはまし	横浜市	2.5, 4.3
Yoon (name)	ユーン		1.4
you	きみたち	君達	4.9
you may~	をしてもいいです		4.5
you must not~	をしてはいけません		4.5
you must~	なければなりません		4.5
young people	わかもの	若者	1.4, 3.5,4.2,4.8
younger brother	おとうと	弟	1.3 ,4.2,4.6, 1.3.1
younger sister	いもうと	妹	1.3, 4.2,4.6
your residence	おたく	お宅	2.3
zone	ゾーン		1.4
zoo	どうぶつえん	動物園	3.1, 3.4,3.5,3.8

Glossary
Japanese – English

じかん	時間	hours	3.7
そうです		I hear that	1.4
たい		want to	1.1
たり、〜たり		represent action and action	4.5, 4.9
ている／ています		is doing	2.1
です		is	1.1, 1.0.1
ど	度	degree	3.7
という	と言う	it is said that	1.4
とおなじ	と同じ	same as	3.1
ないでください		do not do that	2.1
について		about	2.1, 3.1, 4.9
によると		according to	1.5
よりきびしい	より厳しい	severe than	3.1
てください		Please do	4.2
18さい	十八才	18 years old	1.3, 2.4
9.11じけん	9.11事件	9.11 incident	4.9
eメール		email	2.3
Iこう	I校	school name	1.7
T-シャツ		T-shirt	4.5
XというY/XというY		so-called, represent, describe, interms of y, say	4.4
Xのほうが〜です		X is ... than (Y).	3.1
XはYほど〜じゃ/くありません		X is not as much... as Y	3.1
XはYとZが(ほぼ)おなじです	XはYとZが(ほぼ)同じです	X is (just about) the same as Y in terms of Z.	3.1
XはYとおなじくらい〜です	XはYとおなじくらい〜です	X is just about as... as Y.	3.1
XはYとほぼおなじぐらいです	XはYとほぼ同じくらいです	X is (just about) the same as Y.	3.1
XはYより〜です	XはYとほぼ同じくらいです	X is more (less)... than Y.	3.1
Xをくばります	Xを配ります	I am going to distribute X.	3.2
Xをくばるひと	Xを配る人	The person slated to distribute X	3.2
Yがありますか。		Do you have Y?	3.2
Yがあるひと、てをあげてください	Yがある人、手を挙げてください	Those who have Y, please raise your hand.	3.2
Yにかいてください	Yに書いてください	Please write (something) on/in Y.	3.2
Zがないひと、てをあげてください	Zがない人、手を挙げてください	Those who don't have Z, please raise your hand	3.2
Zをまるでかこんでください		Please circle Z.	3.2
	Zを○で囲んでください		
あ		oh	2.5, 1.3.0
アイオワ		Iowa	3.6
あいさつ	挨拶	greeting	1.3, 4.9, 1.3.6
アイスクリーム		ice cream	1.2, 1.5, 4.4, 4.9, 1.0.1
アイスコーヒー		ice coffee	4.2, 1.1.9
アイスホッケー		ice hockey	4.3, 1.1.6
あいだ	間	between	3.1, 3.3
あいて	相手	partner	1.6, 4.7
あいてになる	相手になる	deal with	4.7
あう／あいます	会う／会います	meet	1.4, 2.3, 4.6,
アウトレットストア		outlet store	3.8
あおい	青い	blue	2.5, 3.4, 1.0.2
あおぞら	青空	blue sky	3.8
あかい	赤い	red	2.5, 3.7, 1.1.9
アカデミー		academy	1.1
あかマル	赤マル	circle with red	3.3
あかるい	明るい	light, bright	3.1, 3.7, 4.2
あき	秋	autumn, fall	1.3, 2.7, 4.2, 4.5, 1.1.4
あきはばら	秋葉原	Akihabara (place name)	1.4
アクションえいが	アクション映画	action movie	1.5
アクセサリー		accessory	4.5
あくびする	欠伸する	yawn	2.7
あげてください	挙げてください	give examples	4.3
あける	開ける	open	2.5
あげる	上げる	raise, lift	1.6
あさ	朝	morning	4.6
あさくさ	浅草	Asakusa (place name)	1.4
あさごはん	朝ご飯	breakfast	1.4, 4.4, 1.4.1
あさって	明後日	day after tomorrow	1.4, 1.4.1
あさひむら	朝日村	Asahi mura (village of Asahi)	3.5
あし	足	leg	2.1
アジアけい	アジア系	Asian	3.8
アジアじん	アジア人	Asian	3.8, 4.9
アジアりょうりてん	アジア料理店	Asian restaurant	3.8
あした	明日	tomorrow	1.3, 4.6, 1.2.2
あしたのてんき	明日の天気	tomorrow's weather	1.3, 3.1
あそこ	彼所	over there	3.7
あそぶ／あそびます	遊ぶ／遊びます	play	2.3, 3.4, 3.9, 4.6
あたたかい	暖かい	warm	3.1, 3.6, 3.7, 4.7, 1.3.11
あたま	頭	head	1.7, 2.4
あたまがいい	頭がいい	smart	3.2
あたまがいたい	頭が痛い	headache	4.9
あたまがいたいんですけど	頭が痛いんですけど	I got headache, but	4.9
あたらしい	新しい	new	3.3, 3.7, 4.2
あたらしくるま	新しい車	new car	3.7
あたり	辺り	vicinity	3.5, 3.9
あちこちら		in many places	3.8, 3.9
あつい	暑い	hot (weather)	1.1, 1.3, 3.5, 1.1.6
あつめる	集める	assemble, collect	3.8
あて	当て	aim	2.2
あてはまる	当てはまる	match	4.3
あと	後	after	4.9
あとがき	後書き	afterword	4.8, 4.9
あとぎょう	後作業	wrap-up activity	2.6, 3.8, 4.9
アドバイザー		advisor	1.3, 4.8
アトランタ		Atlanta	4.3
アナウンス		announcement	3.8
あに	兄	my elder brother	1.3
アニメ		animation	1.1, 3.5, 4.6, 1.3.2
あね	姉	my elder sister	1.1, 1.3, 1.3.1
あの		that one, over there	2.5
あのう		umm, well, let's see	1.6, 4.2, 1.1.1
あのう、それから		umm, well then	1.6, 1.3.6
アパート		apartment	3.8
アパート(アパートメント)		apartment house	4.4, 4.9
あぶらっこい	油っこい	greasy	4.2
アフリカけいアメリカじん	アフリカ系アメリカ人	African-American	3.8
アフリカぶんがく	アフリカ文学	African-literature	4.7
あまり〜じゃない		not as much as	3.1
あまり		not so much	1.1, 1.6, 3.7, 4.2, 1.3.5
あまりない		there is not so much	4.5, 4.9
アムネスティ インターナショナル		Amnesty International	4.3
あめ	雨	rain	3.1, 3.5, 4.2
あめがふる	雨がふる	to rain	3.5
あめのひ	雨の日	rainy day (s)	3.5
アメフト	アメフト	American football	2.4
アメフト(アメリカンフットボール)		American football	4.4, 4.7
アメリカ	亜米利加	America	1.1, 3.6, 1.0.2
アメリカし	アメリカ史	US history	4.7
アメリカじん	アメリカ人	American	1.3, 1.3.1
あらう	洗う	wash	2.4, 2.7, 4.5
あらう／あらいます	洗う／洗います	wash	2.3, 1.4.6
アラビアご	アラビア語	Arabic	4.3
あらわす	表す	express	3.3, 4.8
アリア		Aria (name of girl)	3.2
ありがとう		thank you	2.3, 1.0.1
ありがとうございました	有り難うございます	thank you	1.6, 2.6, 1.0.1
アリゾナ		Arizona	4.3

ありません		there is no...	1.1, 1.4.5
ある／あります	有る／有ります	exist (inanimate)	2.1, 3.1, 4.7, 1.4.1
あるいて	歩いて	on foot	1.6, 1.3.9
アルバイト		part time job	1.4, 3.4, 1.4.11
あれ		that over there	2.5
あんき	暗記	memorization	4.5
アンケート		questionnaire, survey	1.5
あんしん	安心	peace of mind	4.3
あんぜん（な）	安全な	safe	3.8
アンディ		Andy	1.3
あんないしょ	案内所	information center	3.6
いい	良い	good	3.1,3.7,4.2, 1.1.1
いいえ		no	1.1, 1.1.2
いいかえのストラテジー	言い換えのストラテジー	paraphrasing strategy	4.4
いいかもしれない		may be OK	2.4
いいくうきをすったら	良い空気を吸ったら	how about you get fresh air?	4.9
いいすぎる	言い過ぎる	too much say	4.8
イーストかわ	イースト川	East River	3.6
いいです	良いです	it is good	1.3, 1.4.3
いいですか		Are you ready?	3.2
いいですか		Is it right?	1.2, 2.5
いいん	医院	clinic	3.8
いいんかい	委員会	committees	4.6, 4.8
いいんですか		Is it OK?	4.9
いう／いいます	言う／言います	say	1.3, 1.4,2.3
いえ	家	house	3.2, 3.7
イエローストーンこくりつこうえん イエローストーン国立公園		Yellowstone National Park	2.3, 3.7
いがい	以外	exception	4.6
いきました	行きました	went	4.2
イギリス		England	3.7, 1.3.9
いきる	生きる	live	4.9
いく／いきます	行く／行きます	go	1.1, 3.1, 3.5, 3.7 1.0.2
いくありません、じゃありません		It isn't	4.9
いくつか	幾つか	several	3.4
いくない、なじゃない		It isn't	4.9
いくまえ	行く前	before going	3.8, 3.9
いくら		how much	2.5, 4.5, 1.1.3
いけ	池	pond	3.1
いけん	意見	opinion, thought, belief	2.7, 4.7, 4.8, 4.9
いし	石	stone	3.5
いしかわせんせい	石川先生	Ms/Mr. Ishikawa (teacher)	3.7
いしき	意識	consciousness	2.2
いしけってい	意志決定	decision making	2.7, 4.9
いしだ	石田	Ishida	1.3
いじわるな		mean	4.2
イスラムきょうけい	イスラム教系	Muslim	4.3
いそがしい	忙しい	busy	1.3, 1.4, 3.6,4.4, 1.3.5
いそがしくないです	忙しくないです	not busy	3.7
いたい	痛い	hurt	2.6
イタリアりょうり	イタリア料理	Italian dish	1.5
イタリアンりょうり	イタリアン料理	Italian food, cuisine	3.7
いち	位置	location	3.6, 4.3, 4.8
いちインチ	一インチ	1in	3.7
いちがつ	一月	January	3.1,3.5,3.6, 1.1.7
いちがっき	一学期	first semester	4.4
いちじかんめ	一時間目	first period	2.5
いちしているばめん	位置している場面	the setting of being located	4.9
いちセンチ	一センチ	1cm	3.7
いちだい	一台	one car and other ride, machine, appliance	3.4
いちにちじゅう	一日中	all day long	3.4, 3.9
いちのじょうほう	位置の情報	positional information	3.3
いちのたんご	位置の単語	positional words	3.1
いちば	市場	market	3.5
いちばん	一番	best, superb	4.8
いちばん	一番	number one	1.2
いちぶ	一部	a part	4.9
いちフィート	一フィート	1ft	3.7
いちまい	一枚	one thin/flat object (CDs, paper, etc.)	3.4
いちメートル	一メートル	1m	3.7
いちメートルごじゅっセンチぐらい 一メートル五十センチぐらい		about 1 meter 50 centimeters	3.1
いちろう	一郎	Ichiro (name of boy)	4.6
いつ	何時	when	1.4, 1.3.1
いつか	五日	fifth day	1.2, 1.2.1
いつか		someday	2.5
いっかんせい	一貫性	coherence	4.9
いっけん	一軒	one house, one store	3.4
いっこ	一個	one (quantity)	3.4
いっさつ	一冊	one bound object (book, notebook, magazine etc.)	3.4
いっしょうけんめい	一生懸命	very hard	2.5, 4.6
いっしょに	一緒に	together	1.3, 2.7, 1.4.2
いっしょにくるひと	一緒に来る人	commuter partner	1.3
いつつ	五つ	five units	2.5,1.2.9
いって	行って	go	4.2
いってきます	行って来ます	I'm leaving	3.8, 3.9
いってみます	行ってみます	try to go	4.9
いってらっしゃい	行ってらっしゃい	bye (to person leaving)	3.8, 3.9
いっとう	一頭	one big animal (horse, tiger, etc.)	3.4
いっぱんしょくどう	一般食堂	general restaurant	3.8
いっぴき	一匹	one small animal (dog, cat, mouse etc.)	3.4
いっぽう	一方	on the other hand	4.9
いっぽん	一本	one long/slender object	1.1, 2.4, 4.5,4.7,
いつも		always	4.9.1.3.5
いどうする	移動する	move	2.5, 4.4
いぬ	犬	dog	1.3,3.3,3.7, 1.0.2
いま	今	now	2.3, 2.7, 1.2.2
います(いる)、あります(ある)	居る、有る	be (existence)	3.3 3.7, 1.0.28
いみ	意味	meaning	2.6, 4.7, 1.3.3
いみん	移民	immigrant	3.8
イメージして		imagine	4.8
いもうと	妹	younger sister	1.3, 4.2,4.6
イヤリング、ピアス		earrings	4.5
イラクせんそう	イラク戦争	Iraq War	4.9
イラスト		illustration	2.2, 4.8
いる／います	居る／居ます	exist (animate)	2.3, 4.9, 1.0.2
いれかえてください	入れ替えてください	Exchange it.	3.3
いれる	入れる	put in	1.3, 2.7
いろいろ（な）	色々な	various	1.5, 3.3, 3.7,4.3, 4.6
いろいろあります		we have a variety of	4.4
いわ	岩	rock	3.8
いわれる	言われる	be called	3.8, 3.9
いんがかんけい	因果関係	cause & effect	4.8
いんさつ	印刷	print	4.9
いんしゅうんてん	飲酒運転	drunk drive	4.8
インターナショナルスクール		international school	4.3, 4.9
インチ	インチ	inch	3.7
インディアンりょうり	インディアン料理	Indian food, cuisine	3.7
インド	インド	India	4.3, 1.3.9
インドりょうり	インド料理	Indian dish	1.6
ウィンドーショピング	window-shopping		3.4, 3.9
うーん		yes	3.8, 3.9, 1.1.4
うえ	上	up, top	2.1, 3.1, 1.0.2
ウエストかわ	ウエスト川	West River	3.6
ウエストこうこう	ウエスト高校	West High School	4.3
うえの	上の	above	4.3
ウォームアップ		warm up	2.3
うきよえ	浮世絵	Ukiyoe (Japanese woodblock prints)	4.3
うごく	動く	move	4.8
うしろ	後ろ	back	2.3, 3.1
うそ	嘘	false	1.4, 2.4, 3.4,4.4, 1.1.1
うそ	嘘	lie, false	1.4, 2.4, 3.4, 4.4
うたう	歌う	sing	4.6
うち	家	house	1.3, 1.3.5
うちのちかく	うちの近く	neighborhoods	3.5
うで	腕	arm	2.1
うでとけい	腕時計	watch	4.8
うどんや	うどん屋	udon noodle shop	3.8
うま	馬	horse	3.4, 1.0.2
うまこゆる	馬肥ゆる	horse gets fat	3.8, 3.9
うまれる	生まれる	be born	2.4, 1.4.9
うみ	海	sea, ocean	1.1, 1.4, 3.1, 4.8
うみの	海野	Umino (name)	1.7
うみのひ	海の日	Marin Day	1.4
うみのひ	海の日	Marine holiday	1.7

仮名	漢字	English	Ref
うめ	梅	plum	3.8, 3.9
うめ	梅	plum tree	3.6
うら	裏	back	3.8, 3.9
うります	売ります	sell	1.4, 4.6
うりょう	雨量	amount of rain	3.7
うる	売る	sell	1.7
うるさい	煩い	noisy	1.3, 3.2, 3.5,3.7, 4.2, 4.5, 1.3.5
うわぎ	上着	outwear	4.6
うわばき	上履き	shoes for floor	2.4
うんえい	運営	management	2.6
うんてんする	運転する	drive	4.6
うんどうかい	運動会	field day	2.7
うんどうじょう	運動場	ground, playground	3.8
え	絵	picture	2.1, 2.5, 3.4,4.7, 1.0.2
エアコン(エアーコンディショナー)		air conditioner	3.6, 3.9, 4.4, 4.9
えいが	映画	movie	1.1,1.4,4.2, 1.2.1
えいがかん	映画館	movie theater	1.6, 3.1, 3.3,3.7, 4.2, 1.4.11
えいがぶ	映画部	movie club	4.2
えいご	英語	English language	1.1, 1.4, 2.7,3.4, 4.3, 1.0.2
えいごでいうことができますか	英語で言うことが出来ますか	can you say it in English?	4.9
えいようがく	栄養学	dietetics	4.3
えいわじてん	英和辞典	English Japanese dictionary	2.3
ええ		yes	3.7, 4.4
エーカー		acre	3.8
エーティーエム (ATM)		ATM	3.5
ええと		umm,well, let's see…	1.6, 4.2, 1.2.2
えがく	描く	draw	4.6
えき	駅	train station	3.1, 3.7, 4.2 1.4.11
エジプト		Egypt	3.7, 1.3.9
エスエフ		science fiction	1.5
エスキモー		Inuit	3.8
えぞうし	絵草子	Kamishibai(paper play)	4.3
えのしま	江ノ島	Enoshima (place name)	1.4
えらぶ/えらびます	選ぶ/選びます	choose	2.1, 2.5, 3.5, 4.9
えんぎ	演技	acting	2.5, 4.3
えんぎする	演技する	act	2.5. 3.8
えんけい	円形	circle	4.4
えんげきコンクール	演劇コンクール	drama competition	4.4
えんげきぶ	演劇部	drama club	4.3
えんそう	演奏	performance	3.4, 3.9
えんそうする	演奏する	perform	3.8
えんそく	遠足	school excursion	4.4
えんでかこむ	円で囲む	put a cirdle	3.7
おいしい	美味しい	delicious, tasty	1.1, 1.4, 3.2,3.7, 4.2
おいわい	お祝い	celebrate	4.7
おうえん	応援	cheering	1.5
おうえんする	応援する	cheer, support	1.1, 1.5, 4.4
おおあめ	大雨	heavy rain	3.8
おおい	多い	many, much	1.5, 3.7, 3.1, 4.9
オーガニック/ゆうきてき	有機的	organic	4.6
おおきい	大きい	big	1.3.3.2,4.2, 1.3.7
おおきいホテル	大きいホテル	big hotel	3.7
おおきさ	大きさ	size	3.8
オークション		auction	3.8
オーケストラ		orchestra	4.3
おおそうじ	大掃除	general housecleaning	4.9
オーディオショップ		audio equipment store	3.8
オーバー		over coat	4.5
おおみだし	大見出し	title	4.8
おおゆき	大雪	heavy snow	3.5, 3.8
おオリエンテーション		orientation	4.4
おか	丘	hill	3.8
おかあさん	お母さん	mother	1.2, 1.3, 1.0.2
おかしや	お菓子屋	confectionary store	3.8
おきる/おきます	起きる/起きます	wake up	1.1, 3.6, 4.2,4.5, 4.7
おくないプール	屋内プール	indoor swimming pool	3.8
おくる	送る	send	4.8
おくれている		behind	4.9
おこなう	行う	do	2.7
おこりやすい	怒りやすい	angers easily	4.8
おこる	怒る	get mad	3.6
おこる	怒る	mad	3.8, 3.9
おさけ	お酒	alcohol	4.8
おじいさん	お祖父さん	grandfather	1.3, 1.3.11
おしえかた	教え方	how to teach	4.9
おしえかたがじょうずだ	教え方が上手だ	skillful instruction	4.8
おしえかたがへただ	教え方が下手だ	bad instruction	4.8
おしえる	教える	teach	3.7, 4.6, 4.9
おしゃべり	お喋り	chat	2.4, 2.6, 2.7
おしゃれな		dress up	4.5
おしらせ	お知らせ	announcement	4.9
おすすめ	お勧め	recommendation	3.4, 3.9
おせわに	お世話に	kind help	1.7
おそい	遅い	slow	1.1, 1.0.1
おたく	お宅	your residence	2.3
おだやか (な)	穏やかな	calm, mild, tranquil	3.8
おちゃ	お茶	tea	1.7, 2.5
おてあらい	お手洗い	washroom, toilet	3.8
おとうさん	お父さん	father	1.3, 1.0.2.
おとうと	弟	younger brother	1.3,4.2, 4.6,1.3.1
おとこのこ	男の子	boy	3.1
おとこのひと	男の人	man, male	2.5, 3.4
おとい	一昨日	day before yesterday	1.4
おとな	大人	adults	3.6, 4.7
おにいさん	お兄さん	elder brother	1.3, 1.0.2
おねえさん	お姉さん	elder sister	1.3, 1.0.2
おねがい	お願い	favor, request	1.1, 4.9,1.1.2
おねがい	お願い	request	4.9
おねがいします。	お願いします。	Please do so.	2.4, 3.2, 1.1.2
おばあさん	お祖母さん	grandmother	1.3, 1.3.11
おはようございます	お早うございます	good morning	1.2, 1.0.13
おび	帯	Japanese belt for kimono	4.5
オフィス		office	2.4
おぼえる	覚える	memorize	3.8, 3.9, 4.6
おまかせします		I rely on your suggestion	2.2 1.2.4
おまちください	お待ち下さい	wait please	3.8, 3.9
おみやげ	お土産	souvenir	1.7
おみやげや	お土産屋	souvenir shop	3.8
おめでとう	御目出度う	congratulations	2.7, 3.7
おもい	重い	heavy	1.7, 3.1, 3.4
おもいだす	思い出す	remember	1.6
おもいやりがある	思いやりがある	considerate	4.6
おもう	思う	think	1.4, 3.8
おもさ	重さ	weight, heaviness	3.8
おもしろい	面白い	funny, interesting	1.1,3.7,4.2, 1.0.2
おもしろいけいけんができる	面白い経験ができる	can have an interesting experience	4.7
おもしろく	面白く	in an interesting manner	3.1, 3.7
おもちゃや	おもちゃ屋	toy store	3.1, 3.4
おやすみなさい	お休みなさい	good night	2.3, 1.0.12
およぐ/およぎます	泳ぐ/泳ぎます	swim	1.1, 1.4, 1.5,3.5, 3.7
おりがみ	折り紙	origami	1.4, 3.7, 4.2, 4.9
おりる	降りる	get off	3.8, 3.9
オレゴン	オレゴン	Oregon	3.6, 1.4.1
オレンジ	オレンジ	orange	3.3, 1.1.9
おわり	終わり	end	1.1, 1.5, 1.3.1
おわる/おわります	終わる/終わります	finish, end	1.2,2.3,4.7, 1.2.1
おんがく	音楽	music	1.1, 1.5, 2.7,4.2, 4.3, 1.3.1
おんがくか	音楽家	musician	3.4, 1.3.11
おんだん (な)	温暖な	mild	3.8
おんど	温度	(general) temperature	3.6
おんどくがた	音読型	read aloud	2.5, 3.4, 4.9
おんなのこ	女の子	girl	3.3
おんなのひと	女の人	woman, female	2.5, 3.4, 1.3.7
か		[be~]~?	1.1, 1.1.6
が		particle ga	1.1, 1.4
カード		card	2.1, 2.5, 3.2
カードをくばる	カードを配る	distribute the cards	3.1
ガールフレンド		girlfriend	1.4, 4.2, 4.6
かいがん	海岸	beach, seashore	3.1, 4.3
かいがん	海岸	seashore	3.1

Reading	Kanji	English	References
かいぎ	会議	meeting	2.7, 4.8, 4.9, 1.0.27
かいきょう	海峡	strait	3.8
かいけつ	解決	solution	2.7
がいこく	外国	foreign country	2.5, 3.4
がいこくご	外国語	foreign languages	3.4, 4.3, 1.3.1
がいこくじん	外国人	foreigner	3.7
かいごしせつ	介護施設	nursing care facility	3.8
かいしゃ	会社	company	3.1,3.2, 3.5, 3.7, 4.3, 1.4.10
がいしょく	外食	eating out	3.8
かいせき	解析	analysis	4.5, 4.9
かいぜん	改善	improvement, reform	2.7, 4.9
かいぜんする	改善する	improve	4.8
かいそくでんしゃ	快速電車	intercity rapid train	3.8, 3.9
かいちくする	改築する	rebuild, reconstruct, renovate	3.8
かいてき（な）	快適な	comfortable, pleasant	3.8
かいます	買います	buy	1.4
かいません	買いません	not buy	4.2
かいもの	買い物	shopping	1.4, 3.5, 1.4.11
かいわ	会話	conversation	1.1, 3.4, 4.4
かいわのれい	会話の例	sample conversation	3.2
かう／かいます	買う／買います	buy	1.4, 3.5, 3.7,4.7, 4.9
ガウン		gown	4.5
カウンセラー		counselor	1.4, 4.7, 1.3.11
かえす	返します	return	4.8
かえる／かえます	変える／変えます	change	1.4
かえる／かえります	帰る／帰ります	return	1.4, 4.5, 4.7, 1.4.1
かお	顔	face	1.6, 2.4, 1.0.2
かがいかつどう	課外活動	extra curricular activities	4.7, 1.1.9
かがく	化学	chemistry	3.4, 3.6, 4.1,4.3, 1.3.1
かがく	科学	science	1.3, 3.4, 4.2, 1.0.2
かがくさい	科学祭	science fair	4.8
かかる	かかる	take (time)	3.8, 3.9
かき	花器	vase	3.6
かきかえてください	書き換えてください	rewrite	3.6
かきかたきょういく	書き方教育	education for writing	4.9
かきこうしゅう	夏期講習	summer sessions	4.4
かきなおす	書き直す	rewrite	4.2, 4.9
かきましょう。	書きましょう	let's write	3.1
かく／かきます	書く／書きます	write	1.3,3.2,4.7, 1.4.1
かくえき	各駅	local train	3.8, 3.9
かくがっか	各学科	each academic division	4.3
かくしゅ	各種	variety	4.6
かくだいする	拡大する	expand	3.5
かくにんする	確認する	confirm	1.1, 1.3, 3.1, 4.8
がくねん	学年	grade level	1.2,1.5,4.3, 1.1.1
がくねんまつしけん	学年末試験	final exams for the year	4.4
かぐや	家具屋	furniture store	3.8
がけ	崖	cliff	3.8
かげつ	ヵ月	months (duration)	3.8, 4.9
かける	掛ける	hang	4.5
かこ	過去	past	1.4
かごしま	鹿児島	Kagoshima (name of prefecture)	3.7, 1.3.2
かこむ	囲む	enclose	1.3
カサブランカ		Casablanca	3.5
かざん	火山	volcano	3.6
かし	華氏	Fahrenheit	3.5, 3.6
かしはちじゅうごど	華氏85度	85F (85 degrees Fahr)	3.1
カジュアル		casual	4.8
かじゅえん	果樹園	orchard	3.8
かす	貸す	lend	4.8
かず、ばんごう	数、番号	number	4.2, 4.3, 4.5
かぜ	風	wind	3.6
かぜがつよい	風邪が強い	windy	3.1
かぜがふく	風が吹く	wind blows	3.6
かせんをひいてください	下線を引いてください	underline	3.3
かぞく	家族	family	1.3, 3.5, 4.4,4.9, 1.3.4
ガソリンスタンド		gas station	3.8
カタカナ		katakana	1.2, 1.0.1
かた	型	form	3.4
かたち	形	shape	3.4
かたな	刀	sword	1.4
かち	勝ち	win(noun)	2.7, 3.8
がっき	学期	semester	4.2, 4.3
がっきすう	学期数	number of academic terms	4.2
がっきゅうかい	学級会	class meeting	4.9
かっこ(う)いい	格好いい	good-looking, cool	4.7
がっこう	学校	school	1.1, 3.2, 3.5,4.2, 1.0.1
かっこうわるい	格好悪い	not cool	4.5, 4.8
がっしゅく	合宿	camp	4.4
がっしょうコンクール	合唱コンクール	chorus competition	4.4
かって	勝手	selfish	2.3
かつどう	活動	activity	1.4, 2.3, 2.4,4.2, 4.6, 1.3.11
かつどうてき（な）	活動的な	active	3.8
かつやく	活躍	actively	4.6, 4.7, 4.9
かつら	かつら	wig	4.5
かでんりょうはんてん	家電量販店	home electric appliances store	3.8
かど	角	corner	3.8, 3.9
かな		Kana	4.6
かな	かな	kana (writing character)	1.2
かながわけん	神奈川県		
かながわけん	神奈川県	Kanagawa prefecture	4.3
カナダ	カナダ	Canada	1.1,1.3,3.7, 1.3.2
カナダじん	カナダ人	Canadian	1.3, 4.2
かなものや	金物屋	hardware store	3.8
かなり	可成り	considerably	3.1, 3.7
かのうどうし	可能動詞	potential verb	4.7
かのうなこと	可能なこと	what one can do	3.5
かばん	鞄	bag	2.4, 1.0.16
カフェ		coffee shop, cafe	3.8
カフェテリア		cafeteria	1.2,3.3,4.2, 1.2.1
かぶき	歌舞伎	Kabuki	1.1, 1.4.9
かぶそしき	下部組織	sub organization	4.7, 4.9
かぶる	被る	wear	4.5
かべ	壁	wall	4.6, 4.9
がまんする	我慢する	be patient	4.7
がまんする	我慢する	tolerate	4.8
がまんづよい	我慢強い	patient	4.2, 4.6
かみ	紙	paper	2.5, 4.9
かみをそめている	髪を染めている	dye one's hair	4.5
かむ／かみます	噛む／噛みます	chew	2.6
カメラ		camera	1.4, 3.5, 1.4.10
カメラや	カメラ屋	camera shop	3.8
かもく	科目	subjects	3.2, 4.2
かもしれない		may be	4.7
かよう	通う	commute	3.8, 4.9
かようび	火曜日	Tuesday	1.2, 1.2.1
から		because, so	2.7, 4.7
からい	辛い	hot	1.4
カラオケ		karaoke	1.1, 2, 1.0.28
からだ	体	body	2.1, 4.9, 1.4.6
からて	空手	karate	2.4
からです		It is reason that	4.8
カラフルで		colorful	4.5
カリキュラム		curriculum	4.3
カリフォルニア		California	3.6
カリブかい	カリブ海	Caribbean Sea	3.3
かりる	借りる	borrow, rent	3.5
かるい	軽い	light	3.1, 3.4
かれ	彼	he	4.9
ガレージセール		garage sale	3.8
カロリー		calorie	4.6
かわ	川	river	3.2, 3.5
かわいい	可愛い	cute, pretty	1.3,4.2,4.5, 1.3.0
かわかみ	川上	Kawakami (name)	4.9
かわる	変わる	change	4.6
かんがえてみる	考えてみる	try to think	2.7
かんがえましょう	考えましょう	Let's think	4.7
かんがえる	考える	consider, think	1.4, 2.5, 3.8
かんきょう	環境	environment	1.4, 3.1,3.6, 4.2, 4.3, 4.7
かんきょうもんだい	環境問題	environmental issues	4.7
かんけい	関係	relationship	2.7, 4.5, 4.9
かんげいかい	歓迎会	welcome party	4.9

かんこう	観光	sight seeing	3.4
かんこう	観光	tourism, sightseeing	3.8
かんこうあんない	観光案内	sight seeing guide	3.4, 3.8, 3.9
かんこうきゃく	観光客	tourist	3.4
かんこくご	韓国語	Korean	4.8 1.3.1
がんこな	頑固な	stubborn	4.2
かんさつ	観察	observation	4.9
かんじ	漢字	kanji	1.2, 1.5, 3.5,4.2, 4.8, 1.3.8
かんじがする	感じがする	feeling	3.5, 3.9, 4.4
かんじのリスト	漢字のリスト	kanji list	3.2
かんしゃさい	感謝祭	Thanksgiving	4.8
かんどうてき	感動的	moving, touching	4.9
かんせいさせてください	完成させてください	complete it, please	3.7
かんせいさせる	完成させる	complete	4.9
かんせいする	完成する	complete	2.2, 3.7, 4.4
かんせつてき	間接的	indirect	4.7
かんそう	感想	impression	1.4
かんそうぶん	感想文	response essay	4.9
かんたん（な）	簡単（な）	simple	1.1, 3.4
かんたんな	簡単な	easy	1.2, 3.5, 4.6
かんどうてきである	感動的である	impressive	4.7
かんばつ	旱魃	drought	3.8
がんばって	頑張って	Hang on/ do one's best	4.7, 4.9
がんばる／がんばります	頑張る／頑張ります	work hard,do one's best	2.3, 2.7
がんぼう	願望	wish	1.5
き	気	mind	2
き	木	tree	3.1, 3.3, 1.0.2
きいろ	黄色	yellow	3.3, 1.1.9
きいろいせん	黄色い線	yellow line	3.3, 3.8, 3.9
ぎいん	議員	council person, congressman	3.8
きおん	気温	temperature	3.1, 3.5, 4.7
きおんはなんど	気温は何度？	what's the temperature?	3.1
きか	幾何	geometry	4.3
きかい	機械	mechine	4.6
ぎかい	議会	council, assembly	3.8
きがつく	気がつく	be awakened/ realize	4.8
きく／ききます	聞く／聞きます	listen, ask	1.3, 3.5 4.2, 4.7 1.4.1
きける	聞ける	can listen	3.4, 3.9
きけん（な）	危険な	dangerous	3.8, 4.6 4.8
きこう	気候	climate	3.8
きごう	記号	sign	1.3, 2.2, 2.5
きじ	記事	article	4.8
きじどう	議事堂	assembly hall	3.8
きじゅつ	記述	description	4.5
きじゅん	基準	criterion	3.7
きせつ	季節	seasons	2.4, 3.8, 3.9
きせつげきじょう	季節劇場	seasonal theater	3.1
きそく	規則	school code	4.5
きそくをまもる	規則を守る	keep to a rule	4.7
きた	北	north	3.1, 3.3, 3.7
きたいされたい	期待されたい	get expected	4.8
きたがわ	北側	northern side/end	3.8
きたない	汚い	dirty	3.1, 3.3, 3.5, 3.7
きち	基地	base	3.8
ぎちょう	議長	chairperson	2.1, 1.2.4
きっさてん	喫茶店	coffee shop	3.8
きにいられたい	気に入られたい	be pleased by you	4.8
きのう	昨日	yesterday	1.4, 2.1, 4.2
きびしい	厳しい	severe, strict	1.3, 3.1, 3.7,4.2. 4.5, 1.3.5
きびしい	厳しい	strict	1.4, 3.4
きびしいでしょう	厳しいでしょう	may be severe	3.1
きびしいです	厳しいです	severe	3.1
きぶん	気分	mood, feeling	3.4
きほん	基本	basic	3.4
きほんじょうほう	基本情報	basic information	4.3
きまつしけん	期末試験	final exams	4.4
きみたち	君達	you	4.9
キム		Kim (name)	1.5, 1.6, 4.7
ぎむかんがある	義務感がある	feel obligation	4.8
きめる／きめます	決める／決めます	decide	2.1, 2.5, 3.1, 4.9
きもちがいい	気持ちがいい	pleasant	3.1, 3.7, 4.2, 4.4
きもの	着物	Japanese traditional clothes	4.5, 4.6
ぎゃくせつ	逆接	paradoxical	4.1, 4.2
きやすい	気やすい	easy to wear	4.5
キャプション		caption	4.9

キャプテン		captain	1.3, 4.6, 4.9, 1.3.11
キャミソール		camisole	4.5
キャンパス		campus	4.3
キャンプ		camp	1.4, 3.5
キャンプじょう	キャンプ場	campground	3.8
きゅうぎたいかい	球技大会	ball sports day	4.4
きゅうけん	九軒	nine houses, nine stores	3.4
きゅうこ	九個	nine (quantity)	3.4
きゅうさつ	九冊	nine bound objects (books, notebooks, magazines etc.)	3.4
きゅうじつ	休日	holiday	1.4
きゅうしゅう	九州	Kyushu (name of Japanese region)	3.7, 4.5, 4.9
きゅうじょう	球場	baseball studium	1.4,
きゅうだい	九台	nine cars and other rides, machines, appliances	2.4
きゅうとう	九頭	nine big animals (horses, tigers, etc.)	3.4
きゅうどう	弓道	Japanese archery	3.4
きゅうひき	九匹	nine small animals (dogs, cats, mice etc.)	3.4
きゅうほん	九本	nine long/slender objects	3.4
きゅうまい	九枚	nine thin/flat objects (CDs, paper, etc.)	3.4
きょう	京	capital city	3.8
きょう	今日	today	1.3, 1.4, 3.2,4.2, 1.3.5
きょうあん	教案	lesson plan	2.1, 2.6
きょういく	教育	education	4.5
きょういくがくぶ	教育学部	department of education	4.7
きょういくしせつ	教育施設	educational facility	3.8
きょういん	教員	teacher	4.2, 4.3
きょういんすう	教員数	number of teachers	4.3
きょうかい	教会	church	3.7 3.8
きょうかしょ	教科書	textbook	1.6, 2.7, 4.3, 4.5
きょうがっこう	共学校	coeducation	4.3
きょうかめい	教科名	academic subjects	4.3
きょうざい	教材	study material	2.1, 2.5, 3.4
ぎょうじ、イベント	行事	event	1.4, 2.4, 2.7,3.7, 3.8, 4.3, 1.2.1
きょうしつ	教室	classroom	1.3, 2.4, 2.7,3.7, 4.2, 4.4, 1.2.1
ぎょうせい	行政	administration	3.8
きょうと	京都	Kyoto (name of prefecture)	2.5, 3.2, 3.7, 4.9, 1.3.8
きょうどう	共同	common	4.8
きょうどう	共同	cooperative	1.6
きょうのしゅくだい	今日の宿題	today's homework	3.2
きょうみ	興味	interest	4.6
きょうりょくする	協力する	cooperate	1.1
ぎょうれつ	行列	matrix	4.5
きょか	許可	permission	4.8
ぎょぎょう	漁業	fishery	3.8
きょねん	去年	last year	1.1, 1.3, 2.1,3.1, 3.5
きょり	距離	distance	3.8
きらい	嫌い	dislike	1.3, 3.2 1.3.1
ギリシャご	ギリシャ語	Greece	4.9
ギリシャご	ギリシャ語	Greek	4.3
キリストきょうけい	キリスト教系	Christian	4.3
ぎりの	義理の	in-low	1.6
きる	切る	cut	4.5, 4.7
きる	着る	wear	2.4, 3.6, 4.5
きれい（な）	綺麗な	clean, beautiful	1.1,3.1,4.2, 1.3.1
きれいです	綺麗です	clean (adj)	1.3, 3.5, 3.7
キロ（メートル）		kilometer	3.8
きろく	記録	recording	4.3
きをつける	気を付ける	take care	2.4, 3.6, 3.9
ぎんが	銀河	the galaxy	3.8
ぎんがこうこう	銀河高校	Ginga High School	3.8, 3.9
キング		king (name)	1.2
ぎんこう	銀行	bank	3.4
きんし	禁止	prohibition	4.8
きんじょ	近所	neighborhoods	4.6
きんだいてき（な）	近代的な	modern	3.8
きんちょうする	緊張する	feel nervous	4.9
きんゆうぎょう	金融業	financial industry	3.8
きんようび	金曜日	Friday	1.2,3.4,4.2,

Kana	Kanji	English	Reference
			1.2.1
く	区	ward, district	3.3, 3.8
クイーンズストリート		Queens street (name of street)	3.3
くうこう	空港	airport	1.7, 3.1
くうらん	空欄	blank spaces	4.4, 4.5
クール		fabulous, cool	4.4
くがつ	九月	September	3.6
くがつようか	九月八日	September 8th	1.2, 1.2.1
くすりや	薬屋	pharmacy	3.8
ぐたいてき	具体的	concreate	4.5, 4.9
ください		please give me	1.1, 1.0.1
くだもの	果物	fruits	4.4, 1.3.2
くだものや	果物屋	fruits market	3.1, 3.7, 1.3.2
くち	口	mouth	2.4, 1.0.24
くつ	靴	shoes	2.4, 4.5, 4.6
クッキー		cookie	4.4, 1.2.1
くつした	靴下	socks	4.5
くつや	靴屋	shoe store	3.8
くて		and	4.1, 4.2
くに	国	nation	4.3, 4.4
くばる／くばります	配る／配ります	distribute	2.1,2.5,3.2, 1.0.9
くばるひと	くばる人	distributor	3.2
くび	首	neck	2.1, 2.2
くふう	工夫	strategies, invention	4.4, 4.8
くふうする	工夫する	think well, devise	4.8
くみたて	組み立て	organization, mechanics	1.1, 3.2
くも	雲	cloud	3.8
くもり	曇り	cloudy	3.1, 3.6
くもる	曇る	become cloudy	3.8
くらい	暗い	dark	3.1, 3.7, 4.2
ぐらい		about, approximately	3.7
クラシック		classic	1.5, 4.4 1.3.8
クラス		class	4.2
クラスない	クラス内	in the class	2.7
クラスメート		classmate	3.4, 4.3, 4.4, 4.5
クラブ		club	1.3,3.5,4.2, 1.3.2
クラブかつどう	クラブ活動	club activities	4.4, 4.7
くらべる	比べる	compare	4.8
クリーニングや	クリーニング屋	(dry) cleaner	3.8
クリエイティブ		creative	4.2
クリスマス		Christmas	4.8
グリニッチ・ビレッジ		Greenwich Village	3.8, 3.9
くる／きます	来る／来ます	come	1.3, 4.7, 1.4.7
ぐるーぷ		group	4.3, 4.9
グループたいこうきょうそう	グループ対抗競争	group competition	3.7
グループワーク		group work	1.3, 3.4
グルーンマーケット		green market	3.8, 3.9
くるま	車	car	1.1,1.3,3.3, 1.3.1
くろい	黒い、黒	black	2.3, 3.3, 1.1.9
クローンにんげん	クローン人間	human clone	4.8
クロスカントリー		cross country	4.3
くわえる	加える	add	3.3
くわしい	詳しい	detailed, be versed	3.5, 3.7
くわしく	詳しく	in detail	3.1, 3.5, 3.7
ぐん	群	county	3.8
ぐんたいのような	軍隊のような	militaristic	4.5
けい	恵	Kei (name)	1.4, 1.5, 1.7
けいえい	経営	manage	3.5, 3.9
けいかくせい	計画性	planning	1.4, 4.7
けいけん	経験	experience	4.9
けいざいがく	経済学	economics	4.3
けいざいてきで	経済的で	economical	4.5
けいさつ	警察	police	3.1
げいじゅつ	芸術	art	2.5, 4.3, 4.5
げいじゅつかんしょう	芸術観賞	art appreciation	4.4
けいたい	携帯	cellular phone	2.6
けいたいでんわ	携帯電話	cell phone	4.5
けいむしょ	刑務所	prison, jail	3.8
けいようし	形容詞	adjective	2.1, 3.1, 3.2,3.7, 4.2
ケーキ		cake	1.5, 4.2, 4.4, 1.0.12
ケーキや	ケーキ屋	cake store (patisserie store)	3.1, 3.7
ゲーム		game	2.2,4.6,4.8, 1.2.9
ゲームセンター		game center	3.3
げき	劇	play,drama	2.3, 3.4, 4.4
げきじょう	劇場	theater	3.4, 3.8, 4.9
けしき	景色	scenery	3.8
けしょう	化粧	make up	4.5
けす	消す	cross out, erase	3.7
けっか	結果	result	3.8, 4.3, 4.9
けっこう	結構	fairly, pretty much	3.1, 3.7, 4.3
けっこうです	結構です	No thank you	1.7, 1.1.1
けっこん	結婚	marriage	4.8
けっこんのあいて	結婚の相手	marriage partner	4.2
げつようび	月曜日	Monday	1.2,2.2,3.4, 1.2.1
けど		although	3.8, 3.9, 4.8
ケビン		Kevin (name)	1.6
けれど、けれども、けど		but, however	4.2
けれども		however	4.1, 4.2
けん	県	prefecture	3.8
けん、げん	軒	houses, stores, restaurants etc.	3.1, 3.7
げんいん	原因	cause	4.5, 4.9
けんがく	見学	visiting	3.4, 3.9
げんき	元気	health, energetic	1.3,2.3,4.2, 1.0.2
けんきゅうしょ	研究所	research institution	3.8
げんこう	健康	health	2.4,
げんこうようし	原稿用紙	composition paper	1.1, 3.1, 3.7, 3.8
けんさ	検査	inspection	4.8
げんしりょくはつでんしょ	原子力発電所	nuclear power plant	3.8
けんせつする	建設する	build,construct	3.8
げんだいてき	現代的	contemporary	3.6, 3.8, 3.9
ケント	ケント	Kent (name)	1.1
けんどう	剣道	Kendo (Japanese martial arts)	2.4,4.4, 1.4.8
こ	個	counter for any solid objects esp. small and solid ones	3.1, 3.4, 4.9
ごい	語彙	vocabulary	3.1, 4.8, 4.9
ごいのこうちく	語彙の構築	vocabulary building	3.2
コインランドリー		laundromat	3.8
こうえん	公園	park	2.3,3.1,3.4, 1.3.4
こうか	効果	effect	4.5, 4.9
こうがい	郊外	suburbs	4.3
こうかてつどう	高架鉄道	elevated railway	3.8, 3.9
こうきしんがつよい	好奇心が強い	curious	4.8
こうきょうしせつ	公共施設	public facilities	3.1, 3.2, 4.3
こうこう	高校	high school	1.1, 3.4, 1.0.2
こうこう3ねんせい	高校三年生	twelfth grade	2.7
こうこういちねんせい	高校一年生	tenth grade	1.1
こうこうせい	高校生	high school student	3.7, 1.4.4
こうじょう	工場	factory	3.1, 3.5, 3.7, 4.2
こうずい	洪水	flood	3.8
こうすいりょう	降水量	amount of precipitation	3.7
こうせい	校正	proofreading	4.8, 4.9
こうぞう	構造	structure	3.1, 3.4, 4.9
こうぞうビル	高層ビル	high-rise building	3.5
こうそく	校則	school rule	4.3
こうそくどうろ	高速道路	expressway	3.3
こうち	高知	Kouchi (name of prefecture)	3.7
こうちくする	構築する	construct, build up	3.1, 3.2
こうちょうせんせい	校長先生	school principal	4.4, 4.7
こうつう	交通	transportation, traffic	1.3,3.2,3.7, 1.3.6
こうてい	校庭	school yard	4.7
こうどう	講堂	auditorium	2.6, 3.7, 4.6,4.7, 1.2.1
こうばん	交番	police booth/box	3.3, 3.6
こうふんする	興奮する	get excited	2.7
こうほ	候補	potential	4.8
こうみんかん	公民館	community center	3.1, 4.2
こうもく	項目	topics	4.9
こうもん	校門	school gate	3.5
こうやって		in this way	2.7
こうよう	紅葉	autumn foliage	3.8
こうりつこう	公立校	public school	4.3
こうりつの	公立の	public	3.7
こうりゅう	交流	exchange	2.4
こえ	声	voice	1.6, 2.6
コーチ		coach	1.3,3.7,4.7,

721

Japanese	Kanji	English	Reference
コート		coat	1.0.14
コートニー		Courtney (name of girl)	3.7, 4.5
ゴードン		Gordon (name of boy)	1.4
コーヒー		coffee	1.3
			1.2, 1.5, 3.7,4.2, 1.0.16
コーヒーショップ		coffee shop	3.1, 3.2, 3.7
コーラ		cola	2.5, 3.2, 4.2, 1.0.21
こおり	氷	ice	3.8
こおりがはる	氷が張る	be frozen over	3.8
こおる／こおります	凍る／凍ります	freeze	3.1, 3.6
こがらし	木枯らし	bitter cold wind	3.8
こくご	国語	language arts	2.7, 4.5
こくごじてん	国語辞典	national-language dictionary	2.3
こくさい	国際	international	1.7
こくさいかいかん	国際会館	international hall	3.8, 3.9
こくさいがっこう	国際学校	international school	3.5, 3.9
こくさいきょういく	国際教育	international education	3.5
こくさいこうりゅう	国際交流	international exchange	3.8
こくさいてき	国際的	international	3.5, 3.9
こくじん	黒人	black people	3.8, 4.7
こくせき	国籍	nationality	1.3, 1.3.6
こくりつこうえん	国立公園	national park	3.8
こくれんかんけい	国連関係	United Nations related	3.5, 3.6, 3.9
ごけん	五軒	five houses, five stores	3.4
ごこ	五個	five (quantity)	3.4
ごご	午後	afternoon	2.3
ここのか	九日	ninth day	1.2, 1.2.1
こころがひろい	心が広い	open minded	4.6
ごさつ	五冊	five bound objects (books, notebooks, magazines etc.)	3.4
こさめ	小雨	light rain, shower	3.8
こし	腰	waist	2.1
ごじ	五時	five o'clock	1.1, 1.2.1
こじま	小島	small island	3.6
ゴジラ	ゴジラ	Godzilla	3.5, 4.2, 4.4
こじんてき	個人的	individual	2.4
こじんてきな	個人的な	personal	2.4
コスチューム		costume	4.5
こせいてきな	個性的な	unique	4.2
ごぜん	午前	morning	2.3
ごだい	五台	five cars and other rides, machines, appliances	3.4
こたえ	答え	answer	2.3, 4.7
こたえる／こたえます	答える／答えます	answer	1.1,2.3,4.9, 1.3.11
ごちゅうい	御注意	pay attention	3.8, 3.9
こてん	古典	classics	4.3
ごとう	五頭	five big animals (horses, tigers, etc.)	3.4
ことができます		be able to	3.1
ことし	今年	this year	1.3, 1.4, 1.1.7
ことです		it is about	2.3, 1.4.3
ことば	言葉	word	1.3, 2.5, 4.3
こども	子供	child(ren)	2.6
この	此の	this	2.5, 1.3.1
このまれている	好まれている	be favored	4.7
このみ	好み	favor	1.5
ごひき	五匹	five small animals (dogs, cats, mice etc.)	3.4
ごほん	五本	five long/slender objects	3.4
ごまい	五枚	five (DVDs)	3.4
ごまい	五枚	five thin/flat objects (CDs, paper, etc.)	3.4
コメディー		comedy	1.5
コメント		comment	1.4, 1.6, 4.6,4.9, 1.2.6
こゆき	小雪	light snow	3.8
ごらくしせつ	娯楽施設	entertainment facility	3.3
ゴルフ	ゴルフ	golf	3.4, 4.4, 1.1.6
ゴルフじょう	ゴルフ場	golf course	3.8
これ	此れ	this one	2.5, 1.1.1
これから		from now on	1.1, 1.7
これから、Xをくばります	これから、Xを配ります	Now, we are going to distribute X.	3.2
これからなにをしますか	これから何をしますか	What will you do now?	4.2
これまで		up to now	2.2
ごろ	頃	around	2.7
こわい	恐い	scary	4.2

Japanese	Kanji	English	Reference
コンクール		competitions	4.4
こんげつ	今月	this month	1.5, 2.1, 4.2
コンコード		Concord	1.3, 4.3
コンサート		concert	1.4, 1.3.5
コンサートホール		concert hall	3.7, 1.2.1
こんしゅう	今週	this week	1.5, 2.1
こんてすと		competitions, contest	4.4, 1.4.9
こんど	今度	next time	4.2
こんど	今度	next time	1.5
こんにちは	今日は	good afternoon, hi	1.2, 1.0.13
こんばんは	今晩は	good evening	1.2, 1.0.13
コンビニ		convenience store	2.7, 3.1, 3.4,4.2, 4.4
コンピューター		computer	3.3, 1.0.27
コンベンションセンター		convention center	3.8
サービス		service	3.8
サービスぎょう	サービス業	service industry	3.8
サービスステーション		gas station	3.8
サーフィン		surfing	1.4
さい	オ	ability, talent, age	1.2
さい	オ	age, ability, talent	1.2
さい	オ	years old	1.1, 1.1.1
さいがい	災害	calamity, disaster	3.8
さいきん	最近	recently, lately	1.4, 3.5, 4.5
さいきんまで	最近まで	until recently	4.9
さいご	最後	last	1.1, 1.4
さいこう	最高	best, superb	1.1, 1.4, 3.3,3.5, 4.3
さいこうきおん	最高気温	highest temperature	3.6
さいごに、おわりに	最後に、終わりに	finally	2.4
さいしょに	最初に	firstly	4.3
ざいせい	財政	finance	3.8
さいだい	最大	biggest	2.4
さいてい	最低	worst, awful	1.1, 1.4, 3.5
さいばんしょ	裁判所	courthouse	3.8
ざいりょう	材料	ingredients	3.5, 3.9,4.6
サウスこうえん	サウス公園	South Park	3.6
さか	坂	slope	3.8
さがう	探す	search	4.9
さかな	魚	fish	3.4, 1.0.25
さかなや	魚屋	fish market	3.1
さかや	酒屋	liquor store	3.8
さがる	下がる	step back	3.8, 3.9
さかん	盛ん	active, thriving	4.5
さかんです	さかんです	prosperous	4.3, 4.4
さきに	先に	ahead	2.5
さきます	咲きます	blossom	1.5, 1.7
さく	咲く	bloom	1.5, 3.6, 3.9
さくひん	作品	piece / work	3.1
さくぶん	作文	composition	2.6
さくら	桜	cherry blossom	1.5, 1.7, 3.6,3.9, 4.8
さけびやすい	叫びやすい	shout easily	4.7
サジェスチョン／ていあん	サジェスチョン／提案	suggestion	1.6, 4.8
さつ	冊	counter for bound objects (books, notebooks, magazines etc.)	3.1, 3.4
さっか	作家	author	4.5, 4.9
サッカー	サッカー	soccer	1.3, 3.6, 4.2,4.3, 1.1.4
サッカーじょう	サッカー場	soccer field	3.7, 3.8
ざっし	雑誌	magazine	2.4, 3.5, 4.9
さっぱりした	さっぱりした	feel refreshed	2.7
さっぽろ	札幌	Sapporo (name of city)	3.1, 3.7
さどうぶ	茶道部	tea ceremony club	4.3
さばく	砂漠	desert	2.3, 3.1
さびしい	寂しい	lonely	4.8
サポートセンテンス		supporting sentence	3.4, 3.7
さま	様	Mr. Ms.Mrs.	4.7
さむい	寒い	cold (weather)	1.1, 1.4,3.6, 4.2, 1.0.2
さむいひ	寒い日	cold day	3.1
さむらい	侍	samurai	1.4, 4.2
さら	皿	dish	2.7
さら		Sara (name)	4.9
サラ		Sarah (name)	1.3,2.5, 4.4, 4.7
サリー		Sally (name of girl)	3.3
さわやか（な）	爽やかな	refreshing, delightful	3.8
さん		Mr. Ms.Mrs.	1.3, 1.1.2

さんかい	三回	three times	2.1
さんかする	参加する	join	3.4
さんかする	参加する	participate	4.8
さんがつ	三月	March	3.6, 1.2.1
さんがっき	三学期	third semester	4.4
さんぎょう	産業	industry	3.8
サングラス		sunglasses	4.5
さんげん	三軒	three houses, stores	3.4
さんこ	三個	three (quantity)	3.4
さんこう	参考	reference	4.8
さんさつ	三冊	three bound objects (books, notebooks, magazines etc.) 3.4	
さんじゅうごにん	三十五人	35 people	3.7
さんだい	三台	three cars and other rides, machines, appliances	3.4
サンダル		sandals	4.6
サンドイッチ		sandwich	4.4
さんとう	三頭	three big animals (horses, tigers, etc.) 3.4	
さんにん	三人	three persons	1.3, 3.4 1.2.1
さんにんのグループになってください	三人のグループになってください		
		go break up into groups of three 3.7	
ざんねん	残念	regrettable	1.5, 4.7
さんねんせい	三年生	third year student	1.3, 1.1.6
ざんねんながら	残念ながら	to my regret, unfortunate	4.9
さんばん	三番	number three	1.1
さんびき	三匹	three small animals (dogs, cats, mice etc.)	
			3.4
さんびゃくえん	三百円	300 yen	1.2, 1.1.9
さんぼん	三本	three long/slender objects	3.4
さんまい	三枚	three thin/flat objects (CDs, paper, etc.) 3.4	
さんまんにん	三万人	30000 people	4.3
さんみゃく	山脈	mountain chain	3.8
し		and	2.7
し	市	city	3.7, 4.3
し	死	death	4.9
じ	時	o'clock	1.1, 1.2.1
しあい	試合	game	1.5, 4.2, 1.4.6
しあいする	試合する	play a match	3.8
しあわせな	幸せな	fortunate, happy	4.6
シーサイドがくえん	シーサイド学園	Sea Side Academy	1.6
シート		sheet	3.2
シーフード		seafood	1.4
ジーンズ		jeans (name)	4.5
シェイクピア		Shakespeare	4.4
ジェシカ		Jessica (name)	2.1, 2.3, 2.5, 2.6
ジェニー		Jenny (name)	1.3, 2.5, 2.6, 3.7, 4.7, 1.1.2
しかいしゃ	司会者	MC, host	1.1, 1.6
しがけん	滋賀県	Shiga prefecture	2.7
シカゴ		Chicago	3.6, 4.3
しかた	仕方	how to	2.3, 2.6, 4.4
しがつ	四月	April	3.6
じかん	時間	time	2.2, 3.5, 1.2.1
じかんをまもる	時間を守る	punctual	4.7
しき	式	ceremonies	4.4
じき	時期	time	3.6, 3.9
しぎょうしき	始業式	term opening ceremony	4.4
しく	敷く	spread	1.7
しけん	試験	examination	1.7, 4.2, 4.4
しけんきかん	試験期間	testing period	4.5
じこ	事故	accident	4.6
じこしょうかい	自己紹介	self introduction	4.9
しごと	仕事	job, task	2.3, 3.2, 4.9, 1.4.10
じこひょうか	自己	self evaluation	3.7
じさばけ	時差ぼけ	Jet lag	2.7, 4.9
しじ	指示	directions	1.1
しじ	指示	instructions, direct	1.1, 2.5, 4.9
じじつ	事実	fact	2.4, 4.9
じしょ	辞書	dictionary	1.7
じしょけい	辞書形	dictionary form	2.3
じしん	地震	earthquake	3.6, 3.8
しずか (な)	静かな	quiet	1.3, 3.1, 3.4, 3.7, 4.2, 1.3.7
しずかじゃありません	静かじゃありません	not quiet	3.7
しずかに	静かに	quiet	2.5 1.1.9
しずかむら	静か村	Shizuka mura	3.3

しせい	姿勢	posture	1.6
しせつ	施設	facility	3.7, 4.2
しぜん	自然	nature	3.2, 3.4, 3.7, 4.2, 4.7, 1.3.11
しぜんかんきょうびょういん	自然環境病院	Natural Environment Hospital 3.8, 3.9	
した	下	down	2.1, 3.1
した	下	under	3.3
じだい	時代	era	3.6
したがう	従う／従います	follow	1.2, 2.1
したぎ	下着	underwear	4.5, 4.6
じたく	自宅	residence	4.7, 4.9
しちがつ	七月	July	3.5, 1.2.1
しちじ	七時	seven o'clock	4.2
しちにん	七人	seven persons	1.4, 1.2.3
しちにんのさむらい	七人の侍	Seven Samurai	4.2
しちょう	市長	mayor of city	3.5
しっけ	湿気	moisture, humidity	3.8
じっけん	実験	experiment	4.6, 4.8
じっさい	実際	actually	2.4, 4.7
じっせん	実践	conducting, implementation 4.9	
しっちたい	湿地帯	wetland	3.8
しつど	湿度	humidity	3.6
しつないきょうぎじょう	室内競技場	indoor gym	4.4
しつもん	質問	question	1.2, 2.5, 2.7, 3.5, 4.5, 1.0.2
してき	指摘	indication	4.4
じてんしゃ	自転車	bicycle	1.3, 4.4, 4.5, 1.3.9
じてんしゃおきば	自転車置き場	bicycle parking lot	3.3, 3.8
じてんしゃや	自転車屋	bicycle shop	3.8
じどうしゃしゅうりこうじょう	自動車修理工場 auto repair shop		3.8
じどうしゃはんばいてん	自動車販売店	automobile dealer	3.8
しどうりょく	指導力	leadership	4.6, 4.7
シドニー		Sydney	3.6
しなくてはならない		must do	4.9
しなければなりません		must do	2.5
シナゴーグ		synagogue	3.8
しなのがわ	信濃川	Shinano River (the longest river in Japan)	
			3.3
シニアトリップ		senior trip	4.4
しふく	私服	private clothes	4.5, 4.7
じぶん	自分	self	4.7, 4.9
じぶんで	自分で	by self	4.9
じぶんのいけんをいう	自分の意見を言う	give own opinion	4.8
しま	島	island	3.5
しまいこう	姉妹校	sister schools	4.8
しまいとし	姉妹都市	sister city	3.8
しました		did	4.2
しましょう		decide	2.2
しめる	締める	tie	4.5
しも	霜	frost	3.8
しもがおりる	霜が降りる	have frost	3.8
じゃ		well then	1.5, 3.2, 1.1.4
じゃ、はじめましょう。じゃ、始めましょう		Then, let's start.	3.2
じゃ、また		see again	2.3, 1.0.1
じゃあ		then	3.8, 3.9
ジャーナリズム		Journalism	4.7
しゃかい	社会	social studies, society	2.7, 3.8, 4.3
しゃかいか	社会科	social studies	4.9
しゃかいほうしがすき	社会奉仕が好き	like social service	4.8
ジャカルタ		Jakarta	3.6
しゃくしょ	市役所	city hall	3.8
ジャケット		jacket	4.5
しゃしん	写真	photo	1.5, 2.1, 4.4, 1.1.9
しゃしんぶ	写真部	photo club	1.5, 1.7, 2.5, 2.6, 3.5
しゃしんをとる	写真を撮る	take pictures	3.5
ジャズ		jazz	1.1, 1.6, 4.3, 1.2.1
ジャッキー・サンズ		Jacky Sands (name of girl) 3.7	
ジャッジをする		judge	3.1, 3.2
ジャパンデイ		Japan day	3.4
シャミカ		Shamika (name)	4.9
シャワーをあびる	シャワーを浴びる	take (a shower)	2.7
シャンタル		Shantal (name)	2.1, 2.2, 2.3, 2.6
しゅう	州	state	3.8
じゆう	自由	freedom	2.3

じゆう（な）	自由な	free	3.8
じゅうおく	十億	billion	3.4
じゅうがくねんせい	十年生	10th grade	4.2
しゅうがくりょこう	修学旅行	school trip	4.4
じゅうがた	自由型	free form	4.8, 4.9
じゅうがつ	十月	October	3.6, 1.2.1
しゅうかん	週間	counter of week	3.7, 3.8
しゅうきょうけい	宗教系	religious	4.3
しゅうぎょうしき	終業式	term closing ceremony	4.4
しゅうきょうてき（な）	宗教的な	religious	3.8
じゅうごにち	十五日	15th	1.2, 1.2.1
じゆうじかん	自由時間	free time	4.7
じゅうしょ	住所	address	3.8
ジュース		juice	1.5, 1.1.9
しゅうせいしてください	修正してください	Please make any corrections	3.7
しゅうせいしましょう	修正しましょう	Let's make any corrections	4.4
じゅうだい	十台	ten cars and other rides, machines, appliances	3.4
じゅうたく	住宅	residence, housing	3.7, 3.8
じゅうたくち	住宅地	residence area	3.8
しゅうちゅうりょく	集中力	concentration	2.2
しゅうちょうしゃ	州庁舎	state office building	3.8
じゅうどう	柔道	judo	1.1, 2.4, 4.2, 1.1.6
じゆうとしだいがく	自由都市大学	Freedom City College	3.8, 3.9
じゆうに	自由に	freely	4.5
じゅうにがつ	十二月	December	1.2 1.2.1
じゅうまい	十枚	ten thin/flat objects (CDs, paper, etc.)	3.4
しゅうまつ	週末	weekend	1.1, 1.7, 1.4, 3.7, 4.5
じゅうヤード	十ヤード	10 yd	3.7
じゅうよう（な）	重要な	important	1.3, 3.7, 4.2, 4.9, 1.8.5
じゅうろくさい	十六才	sixteen years old	1.1, 4.2, 1.1.2
じゅうろくねん	十六年	16 years	1.2
しゅかんひょうげん	主観表現	subjective expression	4.9
じゅぎょう	授業	class	2.5, 2.7, 4.4, 4.7, 4.9
じゅく	塾	cram school	2.7
しゅくだい	宿題	homework	4.5
しゅしょく	主食	main dish	1.3, 1.4, 2.5,
じゅっけん	十軒	ten houses, ten stores	3.4
じゅっこ	十個	ten (quantity)	3.4
じゅっさつ	十冊	ten bound objects (books, notebooks, magazines etc.)	3.4
しゅっしん	出身	birth place	1.1, 1.3, 4.2, 1.3.6
じゅっとう	十頭	ten big animals (horses, tigers, etc.)	3.4
じゅっぴき	十匹	ten small animals (dogs, cats, mice etc.)	3.4
じゅっぽん	十本	ten long/slender objects	3.4
しゅみ	趣味	hobby	1.4, 2.1, 4.2, 1.3.6
しゅるい	種類	type, kind	2.4, 4.3
じゅんじょ	順序	order	2.3
じゅんのうてきな	順応的な	flexible	4.7
じゅんばん	順番	turn, order	3.8, 4.9
じゅんび	準備	preparation	1.3, 2.7, 4.2
ジョイタウン		Joytown (name of town)	3.1, 3.7
しょうかい	紹介	introduce	1.4. 1.6, 3.4, 4.4
しょうがいしゃ	障害者	person with disability	4.3
しょうかいぶん	紹介文	introductory sentences	4.6
しょうがくせい	小学生	elementary student	1.4, 3.6, 4.3
しょうがつ	正月	new year	3.8, 3.9, 1.1.2
しょうがっこう	小学校	elementary school	3.4, 1.1.1
しょうぎょう	商業	commerce	3.8
じょうきょう	状況	situation	4.9
しょうグループ	小グループ	small group	2.4
しょうグループになってください	小グループになってください	break up into small groups.	3.2
しょうさっし	小冊子	booklet	3.8
じょうず	上手	skillful	1.1, 1.4
しょうせつ	小説	novel	4.3, 4.9
じょうたい	状態	states	4.2
しょうてんがい	商店街	shopping arcade, mall	1.4, 3.1, 3.8, 3.9
しょうとし	小都市	small city	4.3
しょうなんかいがん	湘南海岸	Shonan beach (place name)	1.4, 3.6, 4.7
じょうほう	情報	information	3.3, 4.4, 4.9
じょうほうぎじゅつさんぎょう	情報技術産業	IT industry	3.8
じょうほうしゅうしゅう	情報収集	information gathering/sorting	4.3
しょうぼうしょ	消防署	fire department	3.1, 3.2
しょうゆ	醤油	soy source	2.7
しょうらい	将来	future	4.5, 4.9
しょうわじだい	昭和時代	Showa Era	2.6, 3.5
しょうわのはじめころ	昭和の始め頃	early part of the Showa era (1926-1989)	3.5, 3.9
ショーツ		shorts	4.5
ジョーンズ		Jones (name)	1.2, 1.2.10
ジョギング		jogging	4.2
ジョギングコース		jogging course	3.3
しょくどう	食堂	dining room, cafeteria	3.8
しょくぶつ	植物	plant	3.8
しょくぶつえん	植物園	botanical garden	3.8
じょし	女子	girls	4.5
じょし	助詞	particle	2.1
じょしこう	女子高	girl's school	4.3
じょすうし	助数詞	counters	3.1
じょせい	女性	woman	3.8, 3.9
ジョッシュ		Josh (name)	1.4
ショッピングセンター		shopping center	3.8, 4.2
ショッピングモール		shopping mall	1.4, 3.3
じょろん	序論	introduction	1.1, 3.1
ジョン		John (name)	1.3, 3.4, 1.4.3
しらせてください	知らせてください	let me know	2.3
しらせる	知らせる	inform	4.8
しらせる／しらせます	知らせる／しらせます	notify	2.3
しらない	知らない	not know	4.8
しらべ	調べ	research	3.6, 4.9
しらべる	調べる	investigate, search	3.8
しりつこう	私立校	private school	4.3
しりょうかん	資料館	museum for material	3.5, 3.9
しる	知る	know	3.5, 3.9, 4.7
ジル	ジル	Jill (name)	4.2, 4.6, 4.7
しるしをつけてください	印をつけてください	Place a checkmark	4.4
しろい	白い	white	3.1, 4.5
しろやままち	城山町	Shiroyama machi	3.3
じんかく	人格	personality	1.6, 4.6, 4.9
しんがっき	新学期	new semester	1.1, 4.8
シンガポール		Singapore	3.7
しんけいすいじゃく	神経衰弱	memory game	4.6
しんこう	進行	progress	1.6, 2.3
しんごう	信号	signal	3.8, 3.9
じんこう	人口	population	3.2, 3.7, 4.3
しんこうひょう	進行表	editorial timetable	4.9
じんじゃ	神社	shrine	3.6
しんしゅつかんじ	新出漢字	new Kanji	3.4
しんじられない	信じられない	unbelievable	2.7
じんせい	人生	life	4.9
しんせき	親戚	relative	2.6
しんにゅうせい	新入生	new student	2.4
しんねん	新年	new year	3.6, 4.3
しんぱい	心配	worry about	2.4, 3.8, 3.9
しんぶん	新聞	newspaper	3.5, 3.6, 4.3
しんぽてき（な）	進歩的な	progressive	3.8
しんらいができる	信頼ができる	trustworthy	4.6
しんらいできる	信頼できる	reliable	4.6, 4.8
しんりがく	心理学	psychology	4.8
しんりょうしょ	診療所	clinic	3.8
しんりん	森林	woods and forest	3.8
じんるいがく	人類学	anthropology	4.8
ず	図	diagram	4.3
すいえい	水泳	swimming	4.4
すいえいたいかい	水泳大会	swimming competition	4.4
すいかわり	西瓜割り	breaking game for watermelon	1.4
すいきゅう	水球	water polo	4.3
すいこう	推敲	revise	1.1, 1.5
すいぞくかん	水族館	aquarium	3.8
すいたいする	衰退する	decline	3.8
すいでん	水田	paddy field	3.8
すいよう(び)	水曜(日)	Wednesday	1.2, 3.4, 1.2.1
すうがく	数学	mathematic	1.4, 2.4, 2.7, 3.4, 3.6, 3.7
すうじで	数字で	by numbers	3.4
スーツ		suits	4.5
スーパー		supermarket	3.2, 3.4
スカート		skirt	4.5

スカッシュ		squash	4.3
すき	好き	like	1.1,1.4,3.2, 1.0.2
スキー		ski	3.7, 4.4
スキーじょう	スキー場	ski slope/resort	3.8
スキット		skit	4.9
すきな	好きな	favorite	4.2
すきな	好きな	like	1.1, 1.0.2
すぎる	過ぎる	over, too	2.7, 4.9
スクエアダンス		square dance	3.8
すぐそば	すぐ側	nearby	3.8, 3.9
すくない	少ない	few, little	3.1, 3.6, 3.7
スケートリンク		skating rink	2.5, 4.6, 4.9
スケジュール		schedule	1.2,2.2,4.8, 1.0.1
すこし	少し	a little	1.4, 3.4, 3.6,4.4, 4.9
すし	寿司	sushi	1.4, 3.2, 4.4, 1.0.2
すしや	寿司屋	sushi restaurant	3.8
すすき	薄	Japanese pampas grass	3.4
すずしい	涼しい	cool	3.1, 3.7, 4.2
スタイル		style	4.6, 4.9
スタジアム		stadium	3.8
ステージ		stage	4.6
すてき (な)	素敵 (な)	attractive, fabulous	1.4,1.5, 3.7, 4.2, 1.0.2
ステファニー		Stephanie (name of girl)	3.2
ステレオ		stereo	3.5, 4.6, 4.8
ストッキング		stocking	4.5
ストラテジー		strategy	4.4
すなはま	砂浜	sand beach	3.8
すなわち	即ち	that is to say	4.7
スノーフェスティバル		snow festival	3.7
スパゲティー		spaghetti	4.4
すばらしい	素晴らしい	wonderful	1.4, 3.7, 4.3
スピーカー		speaker	1.1, 1.6, 1.4.6
スピーチ		speech	1.1, 1.4, 4.9
スピーチコンテスト		speech contest	4.4
スプーン		spoon	2.7
スプリングフリング		Spring Fling	4.4
スペインご	スペイン語	Spanish	3.9, 4.3
スポーツ		sports	1.3, 3.5, 4.2
スポーツショップ		sporting goods store	3.8
スポーツセンター		sports center	3.3
スポーツたいかい	スポーツ大会	athletic tournament	3.8
スポーツチーム		sports team	4.4, 4.7, 4.8
スミス		Smith	1.2, 3.5, 4.6
すみい	住まい	rediednce	2.4
すみません	済みません	excuse me, I am sorry	2.5, 3.2, 1.0.1
すむ	住む	reside, live	1.5, 3.5
すもう	相撲	sumo wrestling	1.5, 3.5
スムーズ		smooth	1.6, 4.9
スライド		slide	2.5
する		wear	4.5
する／します		do	1.1,3.5,4.7, 1.0.2
すわる／すわります	座る／座ります	sit	2.4, 2.6
せいか	成果	accomplishment	1.6, 3.1, 3.7
せいかく(な)	正確(な)	accurately	1.6, 3.1, 3.7
せいかつ	生活	life style	4.9
せいじがく	政治学	political science	4.3
せいじしゅうかい	政治集会	political rally	3.8
せいしつ	性質	qualities	4.2
せいぞうぎょう	製造業	manufacturing industry	3.8
せいと	生徒	student	2.7, 3.5, 4.2, 4.8
せいとかい	生徒会	student council	4.3, 4.6, 4.7
せいとかいちょう	生徒会長	student president	4.6, 4.7
せいとすう	生徒数	number of students	4.2
せいなんせん	西南線	Seinan line	3.8, 3.9
せいふ	政府	government	4.7
せいぶ	西部	western part	4.3
せいふく	制服	uniform	2.4,4.5
せいぶつ	生物	biology	4.1, 4.3, 1.3.11
せいぼう	制帽	uniform hat	4.5
せいようりょうりてん	西洋料理店	Western restaurant	3.8
せいり	整理	organize	4.3
せいりがく	生理学	physiology	4.3

セーター		sweater	4.5
せかいのてんき	世界の天気	world weather	3.6
せかいのドラマ	世界のドラマ	world drama	4.7
せかいのれきし	世界の歴史	world history	4.7
せがたかい	背が高い	tall	4.6
せがひくい	背が低い	short (in short)	4.6
せきせつりょう	積雪量	amount of snowfall	3.7
せきにんかん	責任感	sense of responsibility	4.6
せきにんかんがある	責任感がある	have a sense of responsibility	4.6
せきにんかんがある	責任感がある	take responsibility	4.6, 4.7
せきゆ	石油	oil, petroleum	3.5
セクション		section	3.5
せっし	摂氏	Celsius	3.1, 3.5
せっしさんじゅうごど	摂氏三十五度	35 degrees Celsius	3.4, 3.5, 3.6
せっしにじゅうど	摂氏二十度	20C	3.1
セッション		session	2.2
せつぞくご	接続語	connector	1.1, 1.6
せつぞくひょうげん	接続表現	linking expression	4.1
せつめい	説明	explanation	2.6, 3.4, 4.9
せつめいするから	説明するから	because of explaining	3.8, 3.9
せつめいぶんけいしき	説明文形式	expository writing	4.5, 4.9
ぜひ	是非	by all means	3.4, 3.8, 3.9
せまい	狭い	narrow, small	3.1, 3.7
ぜろどぐらい	0度ぐらい	about zero degrees centigrade	3.1
せわずき	世話好き	like caring for others	4.8
せわずき	世話好き	willing to help	4.8
ぜんいん	ぜんいん	all members	2.4
せんきょ	選挙	election	3.8
せんげつ	先月	last month	1.5, 2.1, 2.4, 4.2
せんこう	専攻	major	4.7, 4.9
ぜんこくたいかい	全国大会	national competition	2.4
せんしゅ	選手	player	1.4, 2.4
せんしゅう	先週	last week	1.4, 1.5
せんせい	先生	teacher	1.2,3.4,4.2, 1.0.2
ぜんぜん	全然	not at all	1.3,1.4,3.4, 1.3.5
せんだい	仙台	Sendai (name of city)	3.7
センチメートル		centimeters	3.7
セントラル・こうこう	セントラル高校	Central High School	1.3
セントラル・パーク		Central Park	3.4, 1.3.11
せんにん	千人	1000 people	4.3
ぜんぶ	全部	all	1.6, 2.4, 4.9
ぜんぶで	全部で	in total	3.1, 3.7
そう	沿う	along	3.4, 3.8, 3.9
そうげん	草原	grassland	3.8
そうごうたいいくかん	総合体育館	composite gymnasium	3.8
そうじ	掃除	clean up (n)	1.3, 1.4.10
そうじのぶん	相似の文	similarity statement	3.6
そうですか		that's correct	1.1, 1.0.1
そうですか		Is it right?	1.2
そうですか		Is it so?	3.8, 3.9, 1.2.2
そうですねえ		It is so.	3.8, 3.9, 1.2.2
そうりつきねんび	創立記念日	funding anniversary	4.4, 4.9
ソーホー		Soho (name of place)	3.3
ゾーン		zone	1.4
そくど	速度	rate of speed	4.7
そこで		so	1.4
そして		and then, and finally	1.5, 3.7, 4.3,4.5, 4.8
そつぎょう	卒業	graduation	4.9
そつぎょうしき	卒業式	graduation ceremony	4.3, 4.4
そつぎょうする	卒業する	graduate (v)	4.7
そつぎょうせい	卒業生	alumni/alumnae	4.4, 4.9
そつぎょうせい	卒業生	graduate (n)	4.2
そと	外	outside	3.1, 3.3
その	其の	that	2.5, 1.4.7
そのあいだ	その間	during that time	2.7
そのあと	その後	afterward	1.4, 2.4
そのいち	其の一	part 1	3.1
そのころ	その頃	at that time	1.7
そのとき／そのころ	その時／その頃	that time	2.7
そば	蕎麦	buckwheat noodle	2.5,4.4, 1.2.4
そばや	蕎麦屋	soba noodle shop	3.8
そふ	祖父	my grand father	1.3
ソフトボール		softball	4.2, 4.3, 4.8
そぼ	祖母	my grandmother	1.3
そら	空	sky	3.3, 3.8

そる	剃る	shave	4.5, 4.8
それ	其れ	that one	2.5
それから		also/then, in addition, moreover	1.1, 3.1, 3.3, 3.5, 3.7, 4.2, 4.5, 1.2.2
それで		and, then	3.3
それに		furthermore	3.1, 3.7, 4.5
それにたいして	それに対して	in contract to	2.7
そんざい	存在	existence	3.3
そんざいをあらわすみじかいぶん	存在を表す短い文	indicate existence of something	3.3
そんちょう	村長	village chief, mayor	3.5
た	田	rice paddy	3.1, 4.3
ターミナル		terminal	3.8
だい	台	counter for cars, trucks, buses, machines, appliance	3.1, 3.4
たいいく	体育	PE (Physical Education)	4.3
たいいくかん	体育館	gymnasium	3.1, 3.2, 4.7, 1.4.9
たいいくさい(うんどうかい)	体育祭(運動会)	sports festival/field day	3.8, 3.9, 4.3
だいいちじさんぎょう	第一次産業	primary industry	3.8
たいかい	大会	competitions	4.4
だいがく	大学	college, university	2.5, 3.6, 4.4, 4.6, 1.1.9
だいがくいん	大学院	graduate school	4.9
たいきおせん	大気汚染	air pollution	3.8
だいさんじさんぎょう	第三次産業	tertiary industry	3.8
たいしかん	大使館	embassy	3.8
たいしょうてき(な)	対照的(な)	contrasting	3.7
だいじょうぶ	大丈夫	all right	3.8, 3.9
だいじょうぶです。	大丈夫です	It is OK.	3.8
たいしょする	対処する	deal	2.6
だいすう	代数	algebra	4.3
だいすき	大好き	like very much	1.5, 3.5
だいすきです	大好きです	like much	4.6
たいせつ	大切	important	4.5, 4.9
たいそう	体操	gymnastics	2.6, 4.3
たいそうふく	体操服	gym clothes	4.5
だいたい	大体	almost	1.6, 3.7
だいとし	大都市	big city	4.3
だいにじさんぎょう	第二次産業	secondary industry	3.8
タイプ	タイプ	type	4.3, 4.7
たいふう	台風	typhoon	3.1, 3.6, 4.7
たいへん(な)	大変な	difficult/serious	1.3, 3.7, 4.5, 4.9, 1.3.5
たいめんしき	対面式	ceremonial meeting between old and new students	4.4
たいら	平ら	flat	3.5
タイりょうりてん	タイ料理店	Thai restaurant	1.6, 3.8
ダウンコート		down coat	3.1, 3.7
タオル		towel	4.2
たかい	高い	expensive, high	1.1, 1.4, 3.1, 1.3.7
たかく	高く	highly	4.5
たかさ	高さ	height	3.8
たかめる	高める	enhance	2.2
だから		therefore, thus	1.1, 1.6, 3.3, 3.5, 3.7, 1.3.5
たき	滝	waterfall	3.7
タキシード		tuxedo	4.5
だきょうしやすい	妥協しやすい	compromise easily	4.8
たくさん	沢山	many, a lot, much	1.1, 1.4, 3.1, 3.4, 4.2
たくさんあります	沢山あります	there are many	4.4
タクシー		taxi	1.3, 1.3.1
タクティック		tactic	3.5
だけ		only	3.6, 3.9
ださい		senseless	4.5
たしざん	足し算	additions	4.2, 4.8
たしてください	足してください	add	4.4
たじま	田島	Tajima (name of the place)	3.4
ただい	多大	a great amount	3.6, 4.3
ただしい	正しい	correct	2.2, 2.3, 3.7, 4.7
ただしくしたい	正しくしたい	righteous	4.8
たつ/たちます	立つ/立ちます	stand	1.4, 2.6, 4.7
たっきゅうぶ	卓球部	table tennis	4.8
たつまき	竜巻	tornado	3.8

たてがき	縦書き	vertical writing	4.9
たてもの	建物	building	3.5, 3.9
たとえば	例えば	for example	1.4, 3.5, 3.7, 4.2, 4.9
たなか	田中	Tanaka (name)	4.7
たに	谷	valley	3.8
たにがわし	谷川市	Tanigawa shi (city of Tanigawa)	3.4
たにんがきになる	他人が気にかかる	concerned about others	4.7
たにんにきびしくする	他人に厳しくする	strict (to others)	4.7
たにんをひはんする	他人を批判する	critical	4.8
たのしい	楽しい	enjoyable, fun	1.1, 1.4, 3.3, 3.8, 4.3, 4.7, 1.3.5
たのしむ	楽しむ	enjoy, get pleasure	3.8
たばこ	煙草	cigarette	4.8
たぶん	多分	most likely, maybe	3.1, 3.6
たべすぎる	食べ過ぎる	eat too much	4.8
たべもの	食べ物	food	1.1, 1.4, 4.2, 1.2.1
たべる/たべます	食べる/食べます	eat	1.1, 3.5, 4.7, 1.4.1
たべることができる	食べることができる	can eat	2.5
たほうがいいとおもう	た方がいいと思う	I think it is better to	4.7
ダム		dam	3.8
だめです	駄目です	not OK	3.1
ためになる	駄目になる	concern for	4.9
だれ	誰	who	2.2, 3.7
だれと	誰と	with whom	1.3, 1.0.2
だれも	誰も	no one	2.4
たろう	太郎	Taro (name)	4.6
だろう		It is probably ~.	3.7, 4.7
たんぶん	単文	simple sentence	4.8
タンクトップ		tank top	4.5
たんご	単語	word	2.5, 3.1, 3.7, 4.3, 4.6, 4.8
だんしこう	男子高	boy's school	4.3
たんしょ	短所	weak point	4.6
だんじょ	男女	boys and girls	4.3
たんじょうび	誕生日	birthday	1.6
ダンス		dance	1.3, 3.5, 4.2, 4.3, 4.7, 1.1.7
ダンスコンテスト		dance contest	4.4
ダンスパーティ		dance party	4.2, 1.2.2
だんせい	男性	man, male	3.8
だんち	団地	a housing (an apartment) complex	3.3, 3.8
たんとうする	担当する	be in charge of	4.8, 4.9
たんにん	担任	in charge	1.3
たんにんのせんせい	担任の先生	homeroom teacher	1.3, 3.6, 1.3.1
たんぼ	田んぼ	rice paddy	3.1
だんぼう	暖房	heater	3.6, 3.9
チアー・リーダー		cheer leader	2.4, 4.7
ちいさい	小さい	small	1.4, 3.1, 1.0.2
ちいさい	小さい	small	1.4, 3.7
チーズケーキ		cheese cake	4.4, 1.2.6
チームメイト		teammate	4.2
チェック		check	2.2, 4.9
チェックする		check	1.1, 3.3
ちかい	近い	near	2.4, 3.1, 3.5, 3.7
ちがいます	違います	incorrect	1.1.1.2, 1.1.4
ちがう	違う	different	3.8, 3.9
ちがういみだそうです	違う意味だそうです	I heard it's different	3.6, 3.9
ちかく	近く	vicinity, nearby	3.1, 3.5
ちがく	地学	earth science	4.7
ちかくに	近くに	nearby	4.2
ちかてつ	地下鉄	subway	3.5, 4.4, 1.3.1
ちく	地区	district	3.5
ちこく	遅刻	late	3.6, 3.9, 4.8
ちじ	知事	governor	3.8
ちじん	知人	acquaintance	4.8
ちず	地図	map	1.22.1, 3.3, 3.4, 4.3, 1.3.11
ちずをみてください。	地図を見てください	Look at the map.	3.3
ちち	父	my father	1.3
ちほう	地方	region	4.3
チャータースクール		charter school	4.3
チャプター		chapter	4.6
ちゅうかがい	中華街	Chinatown	3.5, 3.6, 3.9
ちゅうがく	中学	middle school	1.2, 3.4, 1.1.1

ちゅうがくいちねんせい	中学一年生	first year middle school student	4.2
ちゅうかりょうりてん	中国料理店	Chinese restaurant	3.8
ちゅうかんしけん	中間試験	midterm	4.4
ちゅうごくご	中国語	Chinese	1.3, 3.4, 3.5, 4.3, 1.3.1
ちゅうごくりょうり	中国料理	Chinese food	1.5, 3.5, 3.9
ちゅうこしゃはんばいてん	中古車販売店	used car dealer	3.8
ちゅうしゃじょう	駐車場	parking lot	3.8
ちゅうしん	中心	centered	3.5, 3.9, 4.5
ちゅうせいぶ	中西部	middle west side	4.3
ちゅうぶ	中部	middle area	4.3
ちゅうもんする	注文する	order (v)	3.8
チュウリップ		tulip	3.6, 3.9
ちゅうりんじょう	駐輪場	bicycle parking lot	3.8
ちょうかい	聴解	listening comprehension	2.5
ちょうせい	調整	adjustment	3.7
ちょうちょう	町長	town manager, mayor	3.8
ちょうど	丁度	just about	1.6
ちょうれい	朝礼	morning assembly	4.7
ちよがみ	千代紙	Japanese paper with colored pattern 1.4	
ちょくせつ	直接	direct	2.3, 2.6, 4.7
ちょくゆ	直喩	simile	4.4
チョコ(チョコレート)		chocolate	4.4, 4.9
ちょっと		a little	1.4.2, 2.4, 4.4, 1.2.2
ちょっとまってください	ちょっと待ってください	Please wait for a moment. 3.2, 3.8	
ちりのちしき	地理の知識	geographical knowledge	4.3
ついか	追加	additional	2.5
ついきゅう	追究	pursuit	4.7, 4.9
ついたち	一日	first day	1.2, 1.2.1
ツーソン		Tuson (name of city)	3.6
つかう	使う	use	1.4, 1.6, 3.5, 4.7
つかれる	疲れる	tired	1.7
つぎ	次	next	1.1, 1.4, 1.5, 2.5, 2.6, 4.3
つぎに	次に	next	2.4, 3.7
つぎのようなもの	次のようなもの	things such as the following 4.3	
つきべつきおん	月別気温	monthly temperature	3.7
つく	着く	arrive	2.4, 2.5
つくえ	机	desk	3.1, 3.3, 1.0.2
つくってくれます	作ってくれます	make it for me	2.4
つくられた	作られた	was built	3.4
つくられた	作られた	was made	3.8, 3.9
つくる／つくります	作る／作ります	make	1.1, 3.1, 3.5,
つける	付ける	attach	2.2
つける	付ける	tie, put on	4.5
つづき	続き	continue	2.6
つなげて	繋げて	connect	4.5
つなげる	繋げる	combine	4.2
つなげる	繋げる	link	4.8
つなみ	津波	tsunami	3.6
ツバル		Tuvalu (name of country)	4.4
つまらない	詰らない	boring, not interesting	1.4, 3.5, 3.7, 4.2, 1.3.5
つゆ	梅雨	rainy season	3.6, 4.4
つよい	強い	strong	2.4, 3.4, 3.7, 4.3
つよいチーム	強いチーム	strong teams	4.4
て		and	4.1, 4.2
て	手	hand	1.5, 2.6, 1.0.24
で		and	4.1, 4.2
で		at	1.1, 1.0.2
で		by	1.1, 1.3.1
で～で		and	4.2
であいます	出会います	encounter	1.5, 1.7
ていぎ	定義	definition	4.4, 4.8
ディケアセンター		day care center	3.3
ディスカウントショップ discount shop		3.8	
ディスカッション		discussion	4.6
ディスコ		disco tech, disco club	3.5, 4.6, 4.8
ディズニーワールド		Disney World	3.7
ディベート		debate	4.6
ていぼう	堤防	bank, embankment	3.8
データ		data	3.3
テーブル		table	3.3, 1.3.11
テーマをかんがえてぶんをつくる			
テーマを考えて文を作る set topic appropriately 3.3			
テーマをきめましょう	テーマを決めましょう	let's decide on the theme 3.2	
でかける	出かける	going out	1.5, 3.6

でかける	出かける	go out	3.8, 3.9
てがみ	手紙	letter	4.8, 4.9
テキサス		Texas	3.6 , 4.9, 1.0.1
テキストのわりあいをイメージして			
テキストの割合をイメージして image text ratio 4.8			
てきせつ(な)	適切	appropriate	3.3, 3.8
てきせつじゃない	適切じゃない	awkward	4.2
てきせつでない	適切でない	inappropriate	3.5
てきとうである	適当である	adequately, properly	4.7
できましたか	できましたか	Are you done?	2.2
できましたか	出来ましたか	Could you do that?	3.2
できる／できます	出来る／出来ます	be able to	1.6, 4.9
できるだけ	出来るだけ	as much as possible	3.4, 3.9
デザート		dessert	1.5, 4.6, 1.2.4
デザイナー		designer	4.5
デザイン		design	2.4, 4.5, 4.9
デジカメ(デジタルカメラ)		digital camera	4.4, 4.9
でした		was	1.1
でしょう		it will probably be	3.1
テスト		test, examination	1.1, 1.4, 3.4
てつがく	哲学	philosophy	4.3, 4.6
てつだう	手伝う	help	1.7
でている	出ている	entry	2.4
テニス		tennis	1.3, 1.4, 3.5, 4.3, 4.8, 1.1.6
デパート		department store	1.3, 1.6, 3.1, 4.2, 1.4.11
てはいけない		one cannot do	4.5
てはいけません		one may not do	4.5
てはじめ	手始めに	first of all	1.5
てぶくろ	手袋	gloves	4.5
でまえする	出前する	deliver	3.8
でも		but, however	1.1, 3.1, 3.7, 1.3.5
てもいい		one may do~	4.5
てもいいです		one may do~	4.5
てら	寺	temple	3.6
テレビ		television	1.4, 3.2, 3.7, 1.3.9
テレビきょく	テレビ局	TV station	3.8
てをあげてください。	手をあげてください	Raise your hands.	3.2
てをあげる	手を上げる	raise a hand	2.2, 3.2, 3.7
てんき	天気	weather	2.5, 3.4, 3.5, 3.7, 4.2, 1.4.9
でんき	電気	electricity	2.5, 3.4, 1.4.9
てんきのびょうしゃをする 天気の描写をする describe weather conditions 3.6			
でんきや	電気屋	electronic shop	1.4
てんきよほう	天気予報	weather forecast	3.6, 4.8
てんこう	天候	climate	3.8, 3.9
でんごん	伝言	message	2.6
でんしゃ	電車	train	1.3, 1.3.1
てんたかく	天高く	clear air	3.8, 3.9
でんとうてき（な）	伝統的な	traditional	2.4, 3.8
てんぷら	天婦羅	Tempura	1.5, 1.2.4
てんもんがく	天文学	astronomy	3.5, 4.3
てんらんかい	展覧会	exhibit	3.8
でんわ	電話	telephone	1.6, 2.2, 3.4, 1.0.2
でんわばんごう	電話番号	phone number	2.2, 1.1.6
と		with/and	1.1, 1.0.3
ど	度	counter of temperature	3.7
ドア		door	3.7
といいます	と言います	I say	4.9
ドイツ		German	4.7, 1.3.9
ドイツご	ドイツ語	Germany	3.4, 4.3, 1.3.5
トイレ		toilet	3.7
とう	頭	counter for big animals (horses, tigers, etc.) 3.1, 3.4	
どうい	同意	agreement	4.7
どういういみ	どう言う意味	what does it mean ?	2.1, 1.3.1
とうきょう	東京	Tokyo	1.6, 2.1, 3.2, 3.4, 3.7, 1.3.2
とうきょうと	東京都	Tokyo	4.3
どうさ	動作	movement, action	2.4, 4.1
とうざいなんぼく	東西南北	all directions	3.2
どうし	動詞	verb	2.1, 2.3, 3.2, 4.2, 4.6
どうして		Why?	4.5

どうしても〜たい		I would like to	4.9
どうじに	同時に	simultaneous	4.8
どうぞ		go ahead	1.7
どうそうかい	同窓会	school reunion	3.8
どうでしたか		how was	1.1
どうですか		how about?	2.5, 3.2
とうひょう	投票	vote	3.8
とうぶ	東部	east side	4.3
とうぶ	東部	eastern part	3.8
どうぶつ	動物	animal	2.6, 3.7
どうぶつえん	動物園	zoo	3.1, 3.4, 3.5, 3.8
とうめいこうそくどうろ	東名高速道路	Tomei high way	4.7, 4.9
どうも		very much	2.3, 1.0.1
とうもろこしばたけ	トウモロコシ畑	cornfield	3.8
どうやって		how	2.7
どうろ	道路	road	3.4, 3.8
とお	十	ten unit	2.5, 1.2.9
とおい	遠い	far, far away	3.1, 3.4, 3.5, 3.7, 1.4.5
とおか	十日	tenth day	1.2, 1.2.1
とおもいます/〜とおもうと思います/と思う		I think	4.6, 4.8. 4.9
とおる	通る	pass	3.8, 3.9
とき	時	time	2.7
ときどき	時々	sometimes	1.4, 1.6, 2.7, 1.4.1
とくい	得意	be good at	4.2, 4.6, 1.3.5
とくいなかもく	得意科目	strong subject	1.2, 4.2, 1.3.5
どくしゃ	読者	readers, audience	4.7
どくしょ	読書	reading	1.3
どくしょクラブ	読書クラブ	book club	3.8
とくちょう	特徴	characteristics	4.8, 1.3.1
とくちょうてきな	特徴的な	noteworthy	4.3
とくに	特に	especially	1.5, 1.7, 2.5, 2.6, 4.3, 4.5
とくべつカリキュラムのがっこう	特別カリキュラムの学校	special curriculum school	4.3
とくべつきょかこう	特別認可校	charter school	4.3
どこの	何所の	where	1.4, 1.0.2
とこや	床屋	barbershop	3.8
ところ	所	place	1.7
ところで		by the way	4.8
とし	年	age	1.3, 1.3.6
とし	都市	city, urban area	3.8, 4.2
とし	年	year	1.3, 1.1.5
としょかん	図書館	library	1.2, 3.1, 3.2,3.5, 3.7,4.2,4.9, 1.2.2
とち	土地	property	3.7
とちゅう	途中	on the way	4.7, 4.9
どちらが		which one is ~	2.3, 3.6
どっかい	読解	reading comprehension	4.8
トップスリー		top three	4.2
どて	土手	bank, embankment	3.6
どて	土手	riverbank	3.8, 3.9
とても		very much	1.1, 1.6, 3.7,4.2, 4.9
となり	隣	next	2.7, 3.1
トニー		Tony (name of boy)	3.3
どの		which	2.5, 4.9
とは		is (explanation)	4.4
トピック		topic	2.2, 3.1, ,4.9
トピックセンテンス		topic sentence	3.4, 3.7
とまる	止まる	stop	3.6, 3.9
トム		Tom	1.3, 2.2, 2.5,2.6, 3.7, 4.2
ともだち	友達	friend	1.1,1.4,3.4, 1.3.4
どようび	土曜日	Saturday	1.2, 4.2, 1.2.1
とら	虎	tiger	2.5,3.1,3.7, 1.0.2
トラック		truck	3.5, 4.7
ドラッグストア		drugstore	3.2, 3.7
ドラフト		draft	1.4, 4.9, 1.4.10
ドラマコンテスト		drama contest	4.4
とりいれる	取り入れる	borrow, accept	2.7
どりょうこう	度量衡	unit of measurement	3.8
どりょくする	努力する	make effort	4.8
とる	撮る	take (a picture)	1.5, 1.7, 2.5, 2.6
とる	取る	take off	4.5
ドル		dollar	3.6, 1.1.1
とる／とります	取る／取ります	take	2.5
とることにしました	撮ることにしました	decided to take	1.5
どれ		which	2.5, 1.2.1
ドレス		dress	4.5
トロント		Toronto	3.6
どんな		what kind of	1.5, 4.5, 1.3.11
ない	無い	nothing	2.1
ないよう	内容	content	1.6
ナイロビ		Nairobi	3.6
なか	中	inside	3.1, 3.3, 1.3.1
なか	中	middle	1.1, 3.1, 1.3.1
ながい	長い	long	1.1, 1.4, 3.7, 4.2
ながくありません	長くありません	not long	3.7
ながさ	長さ	length	3.8
なかた	中田	Nakata (name)	2.4
なかの	中野	Nakano (name)	1.3, 1.3.2
ながの	長野	Nagano (name of prefecture)	3.1, 3.7
ながはま	長浜	Nagahama (place name)	2.4
なかみだし	中見出し	subtitle	4.8
なければなりません		you must~	4.5
なだれ	雪崩	avalanche	3.8
なつ	夏	summer	1.5, 2.5, 2.7,3.6, 4.5, 1.1.6
なつやすみ	夏休み	summer vacation	1.1, 1.5, 3.4,4.4, 1.3.9
など	等	etc.	3.8, 3.9
ななけん	七軒	seven houses, stores	3.4
ななこ	七個	seven (quantity)	3.4
ななさつ	七冊	seven bound objects (books, notebooks, magazines, etc.)	3.4
ななだい	七台	seven cars and other rides, machines, appliances	3.4
ななとう	七頭	seven big animals (horses, tigers, etc.)	3.4
ななにん	七人	7 people	4.2
ななひき	七匹	seven small animals (dogs, cats, mice, etc.)	3.4
ななほん	七本	seven long/slender objects	3.4
ななまい	七枚	seven thin/flat objects (CDs, paper, etc.)	3.4
なに	何	what	1.4, 1.0.2
なにいろ	何色	what color	2.5
なにか	何か	something	4.9
なにご	何語	what language?	1.4
なにじん	何人	what nationality?	1.4
なのか	七日	seventh day	1.2, 1.2.1
なは	那覇	Naha (name of city)	3.7
なまえ	名前	name	1.2,3.2,4.9, 1.1.2
なみだもろい	涙もろい	cry easily	4.8
ならう	習う	learn	3.4, 4.6
ならぶ	並ぶ	stand in line	3.8, 3.9
ならぶ	並ぶ	stand in line	3.5
なりたっています	成り立っています	build	4.6
なる／なります	成る／なります	become	2.1, 3.5, 4.8
なんくみ	何組	how many sets (of cards)	2.7
なんげん	何軒	how many houses, stores	3.4
なんこ	何個	how many (quantity)	3.4
なんさい	何才	how old	2.5, 1.1.1
なんさつ	何冊	how many bound objects (book, notebook, magazine etc.)	3.4
なんじ	何時	what time	2.5
なんせい	南西	southwest	3.1, 3.3
なんせいぶ	南西部	south west side	4.3
なんだい	何台	how many (cars, trucks, buses, machines, appliances)	3.4
なんで	何で	by what means	1.3, 1.4, 1.3.4
なんとう	何頭	how many big animals (horses, tigers, etc.)	3.4
なんとう	南東	southeast	3.1, 3.3
なんとうぶ	南東部	south east side	4.3
なんども	何度も	many times	2.4
なんにん	何人	how many people	3.4, 1.2.1
なんねん	何年	what year?	1.4
なんねんせい	何年生	what grade	1.3, 2.5, 1.1.5
なんびき	何匹	how many small animals (dogs, cats, mice, etc.)	3.4

Kana	Kanji	English	Ref
なんぶ	南部	south side	4.3
なんぶ	南部	southern part	3.8
なんぷん	何分	how many minutes	3.8, 3.9
なんぼん	何本	how many (long/slender object)	3.4
なんまい	何枚	how many thin/flat objects (CDs, paper, T-shirts etc.)	3.4
なんようび	何曜日	what day?	3.4
に		at (ni particle)	1.1, 1.4.7
に		to(ni) particle	1.1, 2.2, 1.1.1
にいがた	新潟	Niigata (name of prefecture)	3.7
ニーナ		Nina (name)	2.5　1.0.1
にがつ	二月	February	3.1,3.5,3., 1.2.1
にがっき	2学期	second semester	4.4
にがて	苦手	weak of	1.4, 4.2, 1.3.5
にがてなかもく	苦手な科目	weak subjects	4.2
にきび	面皰	pimple	2.4
にぎやか（な）	賑やかな	lively, bustling	3.8, 4.9
にく	肉	meat	3.4　1.0.25
にくや	肉屋	butcher	3.1, 3.2, 3.7
にけん	二軒	two houses, two stores	3.7
にこ	二個	two (quantity)	3.4
にさつ	二冊	two bound objects (books, notebooks, magazines etc.)	3.4
にし	西	west	3.1, 3.7, 4.2
にじ	虹	rainbow	3.8
にじがでる	虹が出る	rainbow appears	3.8
にしがわ	西側	western side/end	3.8
にしこうえん	西公園	West Park	3.6
にしやまち	西山町	Nishiyama city	3.4
にじゅうにちぐらい	二十日ぐらい	about 20 days	3.1
にじゅうにん	二十人	20 people	4.2
にだい	二台	two cars and other rides, machines, appliances	3.4
にち、か	日	days	3.7, 1.0.24
にちようび	日曜日	Sunday	1.2, 4.2, 1.2.1
にっき	日記	diary	1.4, 1.7
にとう	二頭	two big animals (horses, tigers, etc.)	3.4
ににています	に似ています	resemble	4.4
にねんせい	二年生	second year student	1.3
にばん	二番	number two	1.2
にひき	二匹	two small animals (dogs, cats, mice etc.)	3.4
にひゃくごじゅうにん	二百五十人	250 people	4.2
にほん	日本	Japan	1.1,3.6,4.2, 1.3.2
にほん	二本	two long/slender objects	3.7
にほんご	日本語	Japanese	1.1, 3.2, 3.4,3.5, 1.3.1
にほんてきな	日本的な	Japanese style	1.4
にほんのとし	日本の都市	cities of Japan	3.3
にほんぶんか	日本文化	Japanese culture	4.6, 4.7
にほんりょうり	日本料理	Japanese dish	1.5, 1.4.9
にほんりょうりてん	日本料理店	Japanese restaurant	3.8
にまい	二枚	two thin/flat objects (CDs, paper, etc.)	3.4
にもつ	荷物	luggage	1.7
にもとづいて	に基づいて	based on	3.6
ニューイングランド		New England	4.3
にゅうがくご	入学後	after entering	4.9
にゅうがくしき	入学式	entrance ceremony	4.4
ニューヨーク		New York	3.6,3.7,4.9, 1.3.3
ニューヨーク・メッツ		NY Mets	4.7
にんき	任期	one's term of office	3.8
にんき	人気	popular	2.4, 4.6
にんげん	人間	human being	4.9
にんしき	認識	recognize, understand	4.2
にんじょうがる	人情がある	warmhearted	4.8
ぬぐ	脱ぐ	take off	2.4, 2.7, 4.5
ぬま	沼	swamp. marsh	3.8
ネイティブアメリカン		Native American	3.8
ねがいごと	願いごと	wishes	1.1, 1.3, 4.9
ねくたい		necktie	4.5
ねこ	猫	cat	2.1,3.3,3.7, 1.0.1
ねずみ	鼠	mouse	3.2,3.3, 1.1.4
ねだん	値段	price	3.7, 1.2.2
ネックレス		necklace	4.5
ねている	寝ている	sleeping	2.7
ねばならない		must	4.8
ねむい	眠い	sleepy	2.7
ねる／ねます	寝る／寝ます	sleep	1.5, 2.3, 3.2, 3.5
ねんじゅうぎょうじ	年間行事	annual event	4.5
ねんれい	年齢	ages	1.3
の		possession	1.1, 1.1.4
のうぎょう	農業	agriculture	3.8
のうじょう	農場	farm	3.8
のうそん	農村	farm village	4.3
ノート		notebook	3.2, 4.2, 1.0.1
のこる	残る	leave	3.5, 3.9
のための		for	3.5, 4.9
ので~		because, so	2.4, 4.6
のばす／のばします	伸ばす／伸ばします	stretch	2.3
のぼりでんしゃ	上り電車	train going to central station	3.8, 3.9
のみもの	飲み物	drink (n)	2.1,4.2,4.4, 1.2.1
のむ／のみます	飲む／飲みます	drink (v)	2.3, 3.5, 3.7,4.2, 1.4.1
のような		is like	4.4, 4.8
のようなものです		is something like	4.4, 4.8
のように		like	4.9
のり		glue	2.5
のりもの	乗り物	ride (n)	3.3
のる	乗る	ride (v)	1.6, 2.4
は	歯	tooth	2.4, 4.5
は		topic particle	1.1, 3.3, 1.4.7
は～ににている	は～に似ている	looks like	4.4
は～のことだ		it means that	4.4
は～のことです		it means that	4.8
ばあい	場合	situation	3.7
パーティー		party	1.4,2.5,3.5, 1.0.2
ハードロック		hard rock	3.5
はい		yes	1.1, 3.2, 1.1.2
パイ		pie	1.5
ハイブリッド		hybrid	3.5, 4.9
ハイライン		High Line	3.8, 3.9
バイリンガル		bilingual	4.6, 4.9
はいる	入る	enter	3.5
はく	履く	wear	4.5
はくじん	白人	white people	3.8, 4.7
はくぶつかん	博物館	museum	3.5, 3.9,4.3
ばける	化ける	disguise	3.4
はこ	箱	box	3.3
はこね	箱根	Hakone (name of place)	3.6
バザー		bazaar	3.8
はさまれる	挟まれる	squished	4.7
はさみ	鋏み	scissors	2.5
はし	橋	bridge	3.7, 3.8
はし	端	end, edge	3.8
はじめ	始め	beginning	2.1.1, 1.3.0
はじめに	始めに	first (of all)	2.4
はじめまして	初めまして	how do you do	2.1.1, 1.0.1
はじめる	始める	start	1.5
はじめる／はじめる	始める／始めます	began/start	2.3, 3.7, 1.0.9
パジャマ		pajama	4.7
ばしょ	場所	place	1.4, 3.7,3.8, 3.9, 4.2, 1.0.2
ばしょのじょうほう	場所の情報	locational information	3.3
バス		bus	1.3, 1.3.1
バスケットボール		basketball	4.3
パスタ		pasta	3.2,3.7,4.2, 1.2.4
パソコン		personal computer	3.5,4.4,4.9, 1.0.2
パソコンショップ		computer store	3.8
はたけ	畑	agriculture fields	3.1, 4.2
はださむい	肌寒い	chilly	3.8
はたらく	働く	work	3.8
はちがつ	八月	August	3.5, 1.2.1
はちじ	八時	8 o'clock	1.2, 1.2.1
はちだい	八台	eight cars and other rides, machines, appliances	3.4
はちまい	八枚	eight thin/flat objects (CDs, paper, etc.)	3.4
はつおん	発音	pronunciation	1.1, 1.5, 3.4
はっきり		clearly	1.6, 1.1.9
はっけん	八軒	eight houses, eight stores	3.4

Japanese	Kanji	English	Reference
ぶ	部	club	3.3, 4.9
ファーストフード		fast food	3.8
ファッション		fashion	4.5
ファッションショー		fashion show	3.5, 4.2
ファミリーデー		Family Day	4.4
ファミレス(ファミリーレストラン)		family restaurant	4.4, 4.9
ファン		sports fan	2.3
ファンドレイジング		fundraising	4.4
フィート		foot/feet (ft)	3.7
フィードバック		feedback	1.6, 3.7
フィールドホッケー		field hockey	4.4
ぶいん	部員	member of a club	4.8
ふうけい	風景	natural feature, landscape	1.5, 4.3
ブーツ		boots	4.8
フードコート		food court	3.8
プール		pool	1.6, 3.3, 3.6, 4.2, 4.8, 1.1.7
フェア		fair	3.8
フェニックス		Phoenix	4.3
フェリス		Ferris (last name)	1.6
ふえる	増える	increase(intransitive)	2.4, 3.8
フェンシング		fencing	4.4
フォルダ		folder	2.6
フォローアップ		follow up	2.6
ふかさ	深さ	depth	3.8
ぶかつどうがっしゅく	部活動合宿	club/team camps	4.4
ふかまる	ふかまる	deepen	2.4
ふきゅうしている	普及している	be popularized/prevailing	4.9
ふく	副	assistant, vice	4.8
ふくざつ	複雑	complex	4.8
ふくざつぶん	複雑文	complex sentence	4.8
ふくし	副詞	adverb	3.4
ふくし	福祉	welfare	3.5
ふくししせつ	福祉施設	welfare facility	3.5
ふくしゅう	復習	review	3.4, 3.6, 4.9
ふくしゅうする	復習する	review	1.1, 1.3.9
ふくすう	複数	multiple	4.6
ふくむ	含む	include	4.8
ふじさん	富士山	Mt. Fuji (the highest mountain in Japan)	3.3
ふたり	二人	two persons	3.3, 4.9, 1.2.1
ぶちょう	部長	manager	4.3
ふつうの	普通の	regular, common	4.8
ふつか	二日	second day	1.2, 1.2.1
ぶっきょうけい	仏教系	Buddhism	4.3
ぶつり	物理	physics	4.3
ブティック		boutique	3.8
ふとん	布団	futon	1.7
ふね	船	ship	1.3,3.5,3.6, 1.3.1
ふぶき	吹雪	snowstorm	3.1
ぶぶん	部分	part	1.3, 4.6
ふべん(な)	不便(な)	inconvenient	3.1, 3.4
ふゆ	冬	winter	1.3,2.7,4.5, 1.1.6
ふゆやすみ	冬休み	winter break	3.7, 4.4
ブラウス		blouse	4.8
ブラジャー		bra	4.5
プラネタリウム		planetarium	3.8
フランシス		Francis (name)	4.6
フランス		France	3.4, 4.3
フランスご	フランス語	French language	1.1, 1.6, 3.4 ,4.3 1.3.1
フリーマーケット		flea market	3.8
ふりかえり	振り返り	reflection	1.6, 2.1,3.1, 3.8, 4.9
ふります	降ります	fall down	3.1
プリヤ		Priya (name)	1.4
プリント		handout	2.1
ふるい	古い	old	3.1, 3.3, 3.7,4.2
フルーツ		fruit	4.3 1.2.1
ブレインストーミング		brainstorming	2.2,4.9
ブレザー		blazer	4.5
プレゼンテーション		presentation	1.5, 1.4.11
フローチャート		flowchart	1.1, 2.5, 3.1, 4.9
プログラム		program	4.8
プロジェクト		project	1.2, 4.6, 1.0.1
プロジェクトのあいて	プロジェクトの相手	project partner	4.2
プロフィール		profile	1.1, 4.8
プロム		prom	4.4, 4.8
フロリダ		Florida	3.6, 3.7, 4.9
ぶん	文	sentence	1.3, 2.6, 3.1
ぶん、ぶん、ぶん	分	minutes	3.7, 1.4.1
ぶんか	文化	culture	2.3, 4.9, 1.4.10
ぶんがく	文学	literature	2.6
ぶんかけい	文化系	cultural field	4.1, 4.3, 4.6
ぶんかこうえんいき	文化公園行き	going to cultural park	3.8, 3.9
ぶんかさい	文化祭	annual school festival	2.7, 4.3
ぶんかさい	文化祭	cultural festival	2.7, 4.1
ふんすい	噴水	fountain	3.3
ぶんせきてきである	分析的である	analytical	4.8
ぶんぼうぐや	文房具屋	stationary	3.8
ぶんるいする	分類する	classify	3.5, 4.4, 4.6
ぶんをつくる	文を作る	sentence construction	1.3, 3.3
へ		to	1.1, 1.0.2
ペア		pairs	2.4, 4.4
ペアで		pair with	4.4
ペアワーク		pair work	1.6, 3.4
へいきんさいこうおんど	平均最高温度	average highest temperature	3.6
へいげん	平原	prairie, plan	3.8
ベイブリッジ		Bay bridge	3.5, 3.8
へいほう	平方	square (area)	3.6, 3.8
へいや	平野	plain	3.5, 3.7
へいわ	平和	peace	3.5
へいわびょういんいき	平和病院行き	bus going to peace hospital	3.8, 3.9
ベークセール		bake sale	3.8, 4.8, 1.4.9
ベーグル		bagel	3.4, 3.9
ページ・スタイル		page style	4.9
ベクトル		vector	4.9
ペットショップ		pet shop	3.8
べつに	別に	not really	2.5, 2.6
べつべつのもの	別々のもの	different things	4.9
ペドロ		Pedro (name)	1.4, 4.9
へび	蛇	snake	3.3, 3.7
へや	部屋	room	3.3, 3.7, 4.3
へる	減る	decrease(intransitive)	3.8, 4.7
ヘルシー		healthy	4.2, 4.7
ヘルスクラブ		health club	3.7
ベルリン		Berlin	3.6
ペン		pen	2.5, 3.1, 4.4
へん(な)	変な	strange	3.8
べんきょう	勉強	study	1.1,1.6,3.6, 1.3.1
べんきょうかい	勉強会	study group	3.8, 4.9
べんきょうしたあと	勉強した後	after studying	2.7
べんきょうしておく	勉強しておく	ready to study	2.7
べんきょうしなおす	勉強し直す	remedy, relearn	4.9
べんきょうする	勉強する	study	2.7, 3.2
べんきょうするまえ	勉強する前	before studying	2.7
へんしゅう	編集	edit	1.1, 1.5, 4.8
へんしゅうちょう	編集長	editor in chief	4.8
へんしん	返信	reply	2.6
ベンチ		bench	3.3
べんとう	弁当	packed lunch	2.4
べんり(な)	便利な	convenient	3.1,4.2
ほあんかん	保安官	sheriff	3.8
ぼうえき	貿易	trade	3.8
ほうがく	方角	direction	3.1, 3.3, 3.7,4.7
ほうかご	放課後	after school	2.5
ほうこう	方向	direction	2.5
ぼうし	帽子	hat	4.5
ほうふ	抱負	plans, goals	1.5
ほうほう	方法	method	2.7
ボーイフレンド		boyfriend	4.2
ボーディングスクール		boarding school	4.3
ボート		boat	1.3, 4.3
ボード		board	3.2, 1.0.1
ポートランド		Portland	1.3
ホームカミング		home coming	4.8
ホームセンター		homedecor store	3.8
ホームレス		homeless	4.8
ボーリング		bowling	4.3
ボーリングじょう	ボーリング場	bowling alley	3.7
ボール		ball	3.3, 1.4.9
ほか	他	other	2.7
ほかに	他に	besides, else	2.2, 4.5
ほかにありますか	他にありますか	Anything else?	3.2, 4.9

ほかにいますか	他にいますか	anyone else	2.2
ほかのみんな	他の皆	the rest of class	4.9
ぼく	僕	I for boy	4.9
ぼくじょう	牧場	ranch	3.8
ほくせい	北西	northwest	3.1, 3.2
ほくせいぶ	北西部	north west side	4.3
ぼくちくぎょう	牧畜業	stock farming	3.8
ほくとう	北東	northeast	3.1, 3.3
ほくぶ	北部	northern part	3.8, 4.3
ほけん	保健	health	4.3
ほけんしつ	保健室	nurse's office	4.9
ほけんたいいく	保健体育	health and physical education	4.3
ほごしゃかい	保護者会	parents/guardian teacher meeting	4.4
ほしがる	欲しがる	greedy	4.8
ほしゅてき(な)	保守的な	conservative	3.8
ポスター		poster	1.4, 1.3.11
ボストン		Boston	1.3,1.6,3.6, 1.3.6
ホセ		Jose (name)	2.1, 2.5,2.6, 4.9, 1.1.2
ほそながい	細長い	long and narrow	3.4, 3.8
ほっかいどう	北海道	Hokkaido (name of prefecture)	3.5, 4.3
ほっただいすけ	堀田大介	Hotta Daisuke (name)	4.9
ほっと		be relieved	4.4
ホテル		hotel	3.5,3.6
ホノルル		Honolulu	3.6
ボブ		Bob	2.5
ほぼ		just about	3.7
ほめる	誉める	praise	4.7
ホラー		horror	1.5
ボランティア		volunteer	3.7, 4.1
ホワイトボード		whiteboard	3.2, 1.3.11
ほん	本	book	1.5,1.1,3.7, 1.0.2
ほん、ぼん、ぽん	本	counter for long/slender object, video/audio tapes, trees	3.1, 3.4
ぼんおどり	盆踊り	bon dance	3.4, 3.5
ほんかくてき	本格的	seriously	4.7, 4.9
ほんさぎょう	本作業	main activity	2.6, 3.7, 4.9
ぼんち	盆地	basin	3.8
ほんてん	本店	main store, headquarter	3.3
ほんとう	本当	truth	4.8
ほんとうに	本当に	really	4.2
ほんや	本屋	bookstore	3.1, 3.2
マーカー		markers	2.5
マーク		Mark (name)	1.4 ,4.9, 1.1.4
まあまあ		so-so, fair, moderately	1.1, 1.4, 3.7,4.9
まい	枚	counter for thin/flat objects (CDs, paper, T-shirts etc.)	3.1, 3.7
まいあさ	毎朝	every morning	1.1
マイク		Mike (name)	1.4, 1.7, 2.5,3.4, 4.6, 1.0.17
マイケル		Michael (name)	4.6
まいしゅう	毎週	every week	2.3, 3.5,4.2
まいつき	毎月	every month	2.3, 3.6, 3.9,4.5
まいとし／まいねん	毎年	every year	2.3
まいにち	毎日	everyday	1.1,1.3,3.5, 1.4.1
まいります	参ります	come (polite)	3.8, 3.9
マイル		mile	3.8
マインドマップ		mind map	2.2, 3.4, 4.8, 4.9
まえ	前	front	2.1, 2.3, 3.1
まえがき	前書き	preface	4.9
まえさぎょう	前作業	preliminary activities	2.6,4.9
まえの	前の	former	4.2
マグネットスクール		magnet school	4.3, 4.4
まけ	負け	loss	3.8
まける／まけます	負ける／負けます	lose	1.5
まげる／まげます	曲げる／曲げます	bend	2.1, 2.4, 4.4
まさ		Masa (name)	4.8
まさこ	雅子	Masako (name)	2.4, 2.7
まじめ	真面目	serious	4.2, 1.3.5
まずい	不味い	unpalatable, bad-tasting	1.1, 1.4, 3.7
まだ		still	2.3, 3.7, 1.0.1
まだかいているひと、いますか	まだ書いている人、いますか	Are there any who are still writing?	3.2
まだじさぼけなんです	未だ時差ぼけなんです	still got jet lag	4.9
まだです	未だです	Not yet.	3.2

まち	町	town	3.1, 3.2, 4.2,4.3, 4.4
まちがえ	間違え	mistakes	1.6
まちがえる	間違える	make mistakes	1.6, 2.6, 3.8, 3.9
まちやくば	町役場	town hall	3.8
マッチさせてください		match	4.3,4.4, 4.5
マッチング		matching	2.6
まつり	祭り	festivals	4.4
まと	的	target	4.3
まとめ	纏め	sum up	2.1,3.7,4.9, 1.3.6
まとめ	纏め	wrap-up	2.3
まとめる／まとめます	纏める／纏めます	summarize	2.1
まとめると		expressing summarization for preceding statement	4.9
まなぶ	学ぶ	learn	3.1, 3.4, 3.7,4.1
マネージメント		management	2.6
まもなく		soon	3.8, 3.9
まもる	守る	protect	4.7
マラソン		marathon	4.7
まる	円	circle	1.3
まるでかこんでください	まるで囲んでください	circle	3.3 4.3
まわす／まわします	回す／回します	rotate	2.1, 2.3
まわり	回り	around	3.1, 3.3. 3.8,3.9, 4.2
まん	万	thousand	3.4
マンション		condominium, apartment	3.8
マンチェスター		Manchester	1.6
まんなか	真ん中	center	3.1, 3.3
ミーティング		meeting	1.2,2.2,3.7, 1.0.1
みえる	見える	can see, be visible	3.8,
みがく	磨く	brush	2.4, 4.5
みぎ	右	right	2.1, 3.1, 3.3,4.2, 4.6
みじかい	短い	short	1.4, 2.1, 3.7,4.6
みじかいごいのテストをしましょう	短い語彙のテストをしましょう	Give a short vocabulary test to one another.	3.2
みじかいぶん	短い村	short sentence	3.3
みず	水	water	1.2, 1.6, 1.0.2
みずうみ	湖	lake	3.1, 4.2, 4.4
みずぎ	水着	swimming suits, bathing suits	4.5
みすぼらしい		shabby	4.5
みせ	店	shop,store	1.4, 3.1, 3.5,4.2, 1.2.6
みそしる	味噌汁	miso soup	2.7
みぞれ	霙	sleet	3.8
みたい		look like	4.4
みたいです		look like	4.5
みち	道	street	3.5
みっか	三日	third day	1.2, 1.2.1
みどり	緑	green	2.5, 3.3, 1.1.9
みどりきねんえき	みどり記念駅	Midori Memorial Station	3.8, 3.9
みな	皆	everyone	1.5, 4.7
みなおす	見直す	look over	2.7, 4.9
みなさん	皆さん	everybody	1.1, 3.2, 4.3,4.8
みなと	港	seaport, harbor	3.2, 3.8
みなと	港	sea port	3.1
みなとみらい２１ちく	港未来２１地区	Minato Mirai 21 district	3.5, 3.9
みなみ	南	south	3.1, 3.3, 3.7
みなみがわ	南側	southern side/end	3.8
みなみぐち	南口	south entrance	3.8, 3.9
みます	見ます	watch	1.3, 2.3, 3.2, 4.2
みやざわけんじ	宮沢賢治	Miyazawa Kenji (name of author)	4.9
みらい	未来	future	2.5,
ミリメートル		millimeters	3.7
みりょくてき（な）	魅力的な	appealing, charming	3.8
みる／みます	見る／見ます	see,watch	1.1,3.5,4.7, 1.4.1
みんな	皆	everybody	2.1, 1.1.9
むいか	六日	sixth day	1.2, 1.2.1
むかし	昔	old, long ago	3.4, 3.9
むこうがわ	向こう側	the other side	3.8
むしあつい	蒸し暑い	humid	1.6, 3.6, 3.7,4.8, 1.1.6
むずかしい	難しい	difficult	1.3,2.7,4.2,

			1.3.5
むずかしくありません	難しく	not difficult	3.7
むっつ	六つ	six units	2.5, 1.2.9
むら	村	village	3.5, 4.3
むり	無理	impossible	4.9
むりをしない	無理をしない	not overwork	4.8
め	目	eyes	2.4, 1.0.27
めいさん	名産	speciality (product)	3.8
めいし	名詞	noun	2.1, 3.2
めいじじだい	明治時代	Meiji era (1868-1912)	3.5,3.6,3.9, 1.1.3
めいしょ	名所	place of interest	3.8
メートル		meters	3.6, 3.7
メール		mail	2.3
メーンしゅう	メーン州	Maine State	3.3
めがね	眼鏡	glasses	4.5
めがねや	眼鏡屋	optician	3.8
メキシカンりょうり	メキシカン料理	Mexican food, cuisine	3.7
メキシコ	メキシコ	Mexico	1.1, 1.4, 1.3.2
メキシコりょうり	メキシコ料理	Mexican dish	1.5
メス		scalpel	2.3
メッセージ		message	4.9
メディアルーム		media room	4.2, 4.9
メニュー		menu	4.7, 1.2.6
メモ		memorandum	1.1, 1.1.3
メロン		melon	4.3, 1.1.9
めんせき	面積	area	3.8
めんどうな	面倒な	troublesome	4.8
メンバー		member	2.2
もういちど	もう一度	again	1.7
もういちど	もう一度	once again	2.6, 3.7, 1.1.3
もういちどおねがいします	もういちどお願いします	Can you repeat it again?	3.2, 1.1.6
もうしょ	猛暑	heat wave	3.6
もうひとつ	もう一つ	one more, another	4.5
もぎこくれん	模擬国連	model UN	4.3
もくじ	目次	table of contents	4.8
もくてき	目的	purpose	2.3, 4.3
もくようび	木曜日	Thursday	1.2, 1.6, 4.7, 4.8, 4.9, 1.2.1
モスク		mosque	3.8
モスクワ		Moscow	3.6
モダリティ		modality	4.8
もちもの	持ち物	belongings	4.5, 4.9
もちろん	勿論	of course	1.7
もつ	持つ	hold	1.7,4.9
もってくる	持ってくる	bring	2.5, 4.5
もっと		more	1.1, 1.6
もどす／もどします	戻す/戻します	return	2.4
もとのことば	元の言葉	original words	4.4
もの	物	things	1.4, 4.3
ものがたりぶん	物語文	narrative writing	4.8
もも	桃	peach	3.6, 3.9
もよおし	催し	gathering, event	3.5, 3.7, 4.2
もり	森	forest	3.2,4.2
もんだい	問題	problem	1.2, 2.4,2.7, 4.9, 1.0.2
もんだいかいけつ	問題解決	problem solving	4.5
モントリオール		Montreal	1.1
ヤード		yard	3.7
やおや	八百屋	vegetable store	3.1, 3.2, 3.4
やがい	野外	outside	3.5, 3.8, 3.9
やきゅう	野球	baseball	1.4, 4.2,4.3, 1.1.6
やきゅうじょう	野球場	baseball field	3.8
やきゅうぶ	野球部	baseball club	4.7,4.9, 1.1.9
やきゅうぼう	野球帽	baseball cap	4.5
やく	約	approximately	3.8
やくしょ	役所	government office	3.8
やくにたつ	役に立つ	useful, helpful	2.5
やくわり	役割	role	2.5, 3.1, 3.2
やさしい	易しい	easy	3.7
やさしい	優しい	kind	1.1,1.3,3.5,4.2, 4.7, 1.0.2
やすい		easy to	4.7
やすい	安い	inexpensive	1.1, 1.4,3.2,4.2
やすむ	休む	rest	1.4
やせている		skinny	4.6

やたい	屋台	a street stall	3.3, 3.8
やぶ	薮	bush, thicket	3.8
やま	山	mountain	1.3, 2.1, 3.1,4.2, 1.3.9
やまかじ	山火事	forest fire	3.8
やまぐちけん	山口県	Yamaguchi prefecture	4.3
やましたこうえん	山下公園	Yamashita Park	3.5, 3.8, 3.9
やむ	止む	stop, cease	3.6
やめる	辞める	quit	4.9
やる／やります		do	1.6, 2.3
やるきがでる	やる気がでる	motivating	4.8
ゆうえんち	遊園地	amusement park	3.1, 3.2,3.3, 3.7
ゆうかん	勇敢	brave	4.8, 1.3.11
ゆうしょう	優勝	win a victory	4.6
ゆうびんきょく	郵便局	post office	1.6, 3.1,3.2, 3.5, 4.6, 1.4.11
ゆうめい(な)	有名な	famous	2.4, 2.7,3.3,3.5, 3.7, 4.2, 4.4
ユーン		Yoon (name)	1.4
ゆかた	浴衣	kimono for summer	3.6, 3.9
ゆき	雪	snow	3.1, 3.5
ゆきかき	雪掻き	shoveling of snow	3.8
ゆきのひ	雪の日	snow day	3.6
ゆだやきょうけい	ユダヤ教系	Jewish	4.3
ゆっくり		slowly	1.6, 1.1.9
ユニーク(な)		unique	3.8
ユニオン		Union	1.6
ユニオンスクウェアーパーク		Union Square Park	3.4, 3.9
ゆびわ	指輪	ring	4.5
よい	良い	good	3.7
よう	用	for	2.7
ようか	八日	eighth day	1.2, 1.2.1
ようこそ		welcome	4.8
ようしょく	洋食	western style food	2.7
ようするに	要するに	in short	4.8
ようです		it seems	4.8
ような		like, similar	4.4, 4.9
ような		look like	4.4
ようなものだ		it seems that	4.4
ようなものです		it seems that	4.4
ようになります		become such that	4.6, 4.8
ようび	曜日	day of week	1.3, 1.2.1
ようひんてん	洋品店	clothing store	3.8
ようふく	洋服	clothes	4.5
ようふくや	洋服屋	tailor shop	3.8
ようろういん	養老院	nursing home	3.8
ヨガ		yoga	3.5, 4.2
よかったら		if you would like	4.9
よく		often	1.1, 1.6, 3.1,4.2, 1.0.3
よく	良く	well	1.6, 1.3.5
よくつかう	よく使う	use often	4.5
よこ	横	side	2.5, 3.1, 3.3
よこがき	横書き	horizontal writing	4.9
よこはま	横浜	Yokohama (place name)	1.5, 3.8,3.9, 4.7
よこはまし	横浜市	Yokohama city	2.5, 4.3
よごれている	汚れている	dirty	4.6
よしゅう	予習	preview, preparation	2.7, 4.9
よちえん	幼稚園	kindergarten	3.7, 1.1.9
よっか	四日	fourth day	1.2, 1.2.1
よっつめのえき	四つ目の駅	fourth station	3.8, 3.9
よみかき	読み書き	reading and writing	4.6, 4.9
よむ／よみます	読む/読みます	read	1.1, 1.3,2.3, 3.1, 1.4.1
よめる	読める	can read	2.7, 4.8
よりくわしく	より詳しく	more details	3.1
よる	夜	night	3.7, 1.3.9
よるのシフト	夜のシフト	night shift	3.5
よろこぶ	喜ぶ	rejoice	1.7
よろしく	宜しく	I would appreciate	1.1, 1.1.1
よわい	弱い	weak	3.1, 3.4, 3.7
よんけん	四件	four houses, four stores	3.4
よんこ	四個	four (quantity)	3.4
よんさつ	四冊	four bound objects (books, notebooks, magazines etc.)	3.4
よんだい	四台	four cars and other rides, machines, appliances	3.4

Kana	Kanji	English	References
よんでいる	呼んでいる	called	1.5
よんとう	四頭	four big animals (horses, tigers, etc.)	3.1, 3.4
よんひき	四匹	four small animals (dogs, cats, mice, etc.)	3.4
よんほん	四本	four long/slender objects	3.4
よんまい	四枚	four thin/flat objects (CDs, paper, etc.)	3.4
ラーメン		ramen noodle	1.1, 4.4, 1.0.1
ラーメンや	ラーメン屋	ramen noodle shop	3.8
らいう	雷雨	thunderstorm	3.1, 3.6, 4.7
ライオン		lion	3.4, 1.0.2
らいげつ	来月	next month	1.3, 1.5, 2.1
らいしゅう	来週	next week	1.5, 2.1,3.4, 4.2, 1.4.10
ライティング		writing	4.3,4.6
らいねん	来年	next year	1.3
ラグビー		rugby	4.3
ラクロス		lacrosse	4.3
ラケットボール		racket ball	4.3
ラジオきょく	ラジオ局	radio station	3.8
ラテンけい	ラテン系	Latino	3.8
ラテンご	ラテン語	Latin	4.3
ラニングバック		runningback	4.7, 4.9
ラフテー	(沖縄の食べ物)	Rafutee (Okinawan cuisine)	4.4
らん	欄	column	4.3, 4.4
ランチ		lunch	4.2
ランプ		lamp	3.3
リーグ		league	4.7
リーダー		leader	2.2, 3.2,4.2, 4.9
リーチ		reach	3.7
リード		Reed (name)	1.1
りか	理科	science	2.7,4.3
りかいしなくてはなりません	理解しなくてはなりません	must understand	2.7
りくじょう	陸上	track and field	4.3
りくじょうきょうぎ	陸上競技	the track	4.4
リサ		Lisa (name)	1.4,4.6,4.7, 1.1.6
リスト		list	2.2, 3.7,4.2, 4.3, 4.9
リストアップ		list up	4.3
リバーこうこう	リバー高校	River High School	3.6
リハーサル		rehearsal	2.6
リボン		ribbon	4.5
リモコン(リモートコントロール)		remote controller	4.4, 4.9
りゆう	理由	reason	4.2, 4.9
りゅうがくせい	留学生	student from abroad	4.8
りょう	寮	dormitory	1.3, 3.5, 4.6, 4.7
りょう	量	quantity	3.4
りょうがわ	両側	both sides	3.8
りょうじかん	領事館	consulate	3.8
りょうする	利用する	make use of	3.8
りょうり	料理	food, cooking	1.6, 3.7, 4.4, 1.4.11
りょうりてん	料理店	restaurant	1.6
りょうり	料理	food, cooking	1.6, 3.7, 4.4, 1.4.11
りょかん	旅館	Japanese inn	3.3 3.8
りょこう	旅行	travel	4.6
りょこう	旅行	trip	1.5
りょこうだいりてん	旅行代理店	travel agency	3.8
りょっか	緑化	afforestation	4.3
リラックス		relax	1.6, 4.7
りんぎょう	林業	forestry	3.8
りんご	林檎	apple	2.5, 3.1, 1.0.2
リンダ		Linda (name)	1.3, 2.5, 2.7,3.6, 4.7, 1.4.1
りんりがく	倫理学	ethics	4.3
るいじてん	類似点	resemblance	4.4
ルームメイト		roommate	4.2
ルール		rule	1.1
れい	例	example	1.2
レイアウト		layout	3.8
レイクこうこう	レイク高校	Lake High School	3.6
れいせいな	冷静な	calm and cool	4.2
レイチェル		Rachel (name)	1.1, 1.1.4
れいぶん	例文	example sentence	4.3
れいをあげる	例を挙げる	give examples	4.5
れいをつくる	例を作る	make examples	3.7
れいをみながらロールプレイをしましょう	例を見ながらロールプレイをしましょう	Let's role play according to	3.3
れきし	歴史	history	1.3, 2.4, 3.4,3.7, 4.2, 4.3, 1.0.2
レストラン		restaurant	1.4,3.1,3.7, 1.2.6
レスリング		wrestling	4.3
レッスン		lesson	2.1
レポート		report	2.2, 3.6
れんしゅう	練習	practice, exercise	2.7, 3.4, 4.6,4.8, 1.3.9
れんしゅうする	練習する	practice	1.1, 2.1, 2.4, 4.4
れんしゅうもんだい	練習問題	exercises	2.6
れんしゅうもんだいをする	練習問題をする	conduct exercises	3.2
ろうじん	老人	elderly	4.8
ローズちゅうがっこう	ローズ中学校	Rose Middle School	1.3
ロールプレイ		role play	1.6, 2.1, 3.3, 4.9
ろくがつ	六月	June	3.5, 1.2.1
ろくさつ	六冊	six bound objects (books, notebooks, magazines etc.)	3.4
ろくじはん	六時半	half past 6 (am/pm)	4.2
ろくだい	六台	six cars and other rides, machines, appliances	3.4
ろくとう	六頭	six big animals (horses, tigers, etc.)	3.4
ろくまい	六枚	six thin/flat objects (CDs, paper, etc.)	3.4
ろしあご	ロシア語	Russian	4.3
ロック		rock	1.5, 4.4, 1.2.1
ロックコンサート		rock concert	3.5
ろっけん	六軒	six houses, six stores	3.4
ろっこ	六個	six (quantity)	3.4
ろっぴき	六匹	six small animals (dogs, cats, mice etc.)	3.4
ろっぽん	六本	six (pens)	3.4
ろっぽん	六本	six long/slender objects	3.4
ろびー		lobby	4.4
ロブスター		lobster	1.4
ロボットクラブ		robot club	4.3
ロマンス		romance	1.5
ろんりてきに	論理的に	logically	3.1, 3.7
ワークシート		worksheet	2.5, 3.2
ワークショップ		workshop	3.8
わーやーた		yay	4.9
ワイオミング		Wyoming	3.7
わいしゃつ		dress shirt	4.5
わえいじてん	和英辞典	Japanese-English dictionary	2.3
わかってくる	分かってくる	come to understand	4.5, 4.9
わがまま		selfish	4.8
わかもの	若者	young people	1.4, 3.5, 4.2, 4.8
わからない	分らない	not understand	4.8
わかりやすくする	分かり易くする	easy to understand	4.4
わかる	分かる	understand	1.6, 1.0.1
わしょく	和食	Japanese style food	2.7, 1.2.9
ワシントン		Washington	1.6, 1.3.11
ワシントン　スクウェアー　パーク		Washington Square Park	3.4, 3.9
わすれもの	忘れ物	something you forget	2.7
わすれる	忘れる	forget	2.7
わだい	話題	topic	2.4
わたし	私	I (for girls and adults)	1.1, 1.2.4
わたしたち	私達	we	2.6, 2.7, 4.3
わたしたちのまち	私達の町	our town	3.3
わたる	渡る	pass, crosss	3.8, 3.9
わっかない	稚内	Wakkanai (name of place)	3.1, 3.7
わふく	和服	Japanese style outfit	4.5, 4.6
わりあて	割り当て	assign tasks	2.5, 4.9
わるい	悪い	bad	3.1, 3.7
わん	湾	bay, gulf	3.8
を		object particle	1.1, 1.4.7
をしてはいけません		you must not	4.5
をしてもいいです		you may	4.5
をしてもいいですか		May I... ?	4.5

Index

Credits

Kisetsu series

The Way to Successful Japanese

Volume 1: Haruichiban

Getting Started
Unit 1: Encounter
Unit 2: Awareness

Haruichiban Workbook Vol. 1
Haruichiban Workbook Vol. 2
Haruichiban Workbook blackmaster

Volume 2: Ginga

Unit 3: Reflection
Unit 4: Environment

Coming soon...

Ginga Workbook
Kisetsu Kanji Book
Volume 3: Akimatsuri

Further information: www.kisetsu.org